Dedication

Here's to the old house.

Thanks To

Everyone involved in creating earlier editions of this book; I hope this one does you proud.

All the good people at Peachpit Press, especially Rebecca Gulick, Tiffany Taylor, Liz Welch, Simmy Cover, Becky Winter, Kelli Kamel, Danielle Foster, George Mattingly, and James Minkin.

The clever folks at Adobe Systems.

Shortstack.

Family and friends who've let me share their beautiful photos and faces (and everyone else to whom I've made some sly reference).

My family, as always.

TABLE OF CONTENTS

TABLE OF CONTENTS

Chapter 9: **Keyframe Interpolation** **283**

Chapter 10: **Mask Essentials** **331**

Chapter 11:   **Effects Fundamentals**   **373**

Chapter 12:   **Creating and Animating Text**   **409**

TABLE OF CONTENTS

After Effects: The Big Picture

"It's the Photoshop of dynamic media."

Summing up After Effects often leads to a comparison to its more famous sibling, Adobe Photoshop. Just as Photoshop lends you precise control over still images, After Effects gives you startling command over moving images. And, like Photoshop, After Effects has established itself as one of the leading programs of its kind. But don't take the comparison too far: Judge After Effects for its unique merits.

After Effects brings together typography and layout, photography and digital imaging, digital video and audio editing, even 3D animation. You can edit, composite, animate, and add effects to each element. And you can output the results for presentation in traditional media, like film and video, or in newer forms, like CD-ROM, DVD, or the Web.

In this sense, a more apt metaphor would be that After Effects is the opera of digital media. Just as Wagner sought to combine disparate forms of performance into a "total work of art"—or *gesamtkunstzwerk*—After Effects allows you to unite various media into a unique, dynamic whole. That may sound a bit grandiose. If it's more convenient, "the Photoshop of dynamic media" works just fine.

Because After Effects draws from so many sources, it also appeals to a wide range of users. You may want to add motion to your typography or design work. Or perhaps your interest in photography and digital imaging brought you to After Effects. Maybe you're a film or video maker who requires visual effects. Or possibly you're an animator who wants to expand your repertoire of tools. Maybe you've heard that After Effects is fun. Whatever your background, whatever your goal, you're ready to get started.

This chapter acquaints you with After Effects. It explains how After Effects works and what you'll need to get started. If you're not already familiar with the QuickStart and QuickPro series, this chapter also introduces you to the book's step-by-step, visual approach to explaining After Effects. Now, let's get to *gesamtkunstzwerk*.

The QuickPro Series

Chances are, you're already familiar with Peachpit Press's QuickStart series of books. They're known for their concise style, step-by-step instructions, and ample illustrations.

As you might guess, the *Pro* appellation implies that the software under discussion appeals to more advanced users. After Effects is such a program. For this reason, this QuickPro guide is designed for intermediate to advanced users and assumes you have significant experience not only with computers, but also with using some form of digital media.

That said, the QuickPro series remains true to the essential QuickStart traditions. The approach still emphasizes step-by-step instructions and concise explanations. If the book looks a little thick for a "concise" guide, consider that literally hundreds of screen shots clearly illustrate every task. You don't have to be a beginning user to find a visual, step-by-step guide appealing.

Occasionally, this guide departs from the standard layout to accommodate larger screen shots, tables, or, most notably, sidebars. Sidebars set aside important background information about the task at hand. If you're already familiar with the concept, feel free to skip ahead. If not, look to the sidebars for some grounding.

Because After Effects combines assets from several disciplines—typography, design, digital imaging, animation, film, and video—it also intersects with the vast bodies of information associated with each of them. Explaining the fundamentals and background of these topics is outside the scope of this book (and even books that don't have the word *quick* in their titles). Nevertheless, this guide tries to provide enough information to keep you moving.

Adobe's Video Bundle

Because After Effects brings together a range of digital media, Adobe hopes you'll use it with Premiere Pro, Audition, Encore DVD, Photoshop, and (with Adobe's acquisition of Macromedia) Flash Professional 8, as a suite of tools. (In fact, Adobe offers these programs as a bundled package called the Adobe Video Bundle—and at a lower price than the sum of the individual programs' cost.) As these software packages have matured, they have also become more integrated. Over time, it has become easier to move files from one program to another without taking intermediate steps or sacrificing elements of your work. Even the programs' interfaces have grown more consistent. However, although the landscapes are similar, the customs aren't always the same: You may find that not all shared features employ exactly the same procedures or keyboard shortcuts.

Minimum Requirements

To use After Effects, your system must meet the following minimum requirements.

Mac OS

◆ PowerPC G4 processor (G5 processor or multiple processors recommended)

◆ Mac OS X 10.3.2 or higher

Windows

◆ Intel Pentium 4 processor (multiple processors recommended)

◆ Microsoft Windows XP Service Pack 2 (SP2) Pro or Home Edition

All systems

◆ At least 256 MB of RAM installed

◆ At least 150 MB of available storage for full installation of the software, plus additional storage for source materials and rendered files

◆ 24-bit color display

◆ CD-ROM drive

Suggested System Features

Although these features aren't required, they can make working with After Effects a lot more satisfying:

Faster/multiple processors. The faster your system can make calculations, the faster it can create the frames of your animation. After Effects has been optimized to take advantage of the Macintosh's G5 processor. The program also makes full use of multiple processors on both Windows and the Mac.

Additional RAM. The number of frames you can preview is directly related to the amount of RAM you give After Effects. The same is true for the size of the images you can work with.

Large hard drives. Ample storage space lets you work with large, high-quality files and output longer animations. Like RAM, it seems you can never have enough drive space. Uncompressed full-screen, full-motion video, for example, consumes nearly 30 MB for every second of footage. DV footage uses a more modest 3.6 MB for every second.

Fast hard drives. Your system's ability to play back footage smoothly relies partly on how quickly information can be read from the drives. Certain high-data-rate codecs and capture devices require speedy hard drives.

Large or multiple displays. After Effects can take up a lot of screen space. A large monitor is appropriate; two monitors are luxurious.

QuickTime 6.5 (or later). QuickTime is Apple's multimedia technology; it's used widely on both the Mac and Windows platforms. The Pro version is well worth the modest investment. QuickTime also permits you to export movies without using After Effects' Render Queue window.

DirectX 9.0b (or later). DirectX is Microsoft's set of application program interfaces (APIs) that facilitates better video and audio performance.

OpenGL card. After Effects can render and display frames much more quickly if you have an After Effects–supported video card that utilizes OpenGL technology.

Professional System Additions

Other additions can elevate your motion graphics system for working on broadcast video or film projects:

After Effects Professional. The Professional version of After Effects includes a number of additional tools geared toward professionals in video and film. See "After Effects Standard and Professional," later in this chapter.

Third-party plug-ins. A multitude of third-party developers offer software plug-in effects. Some are enhanced versions of effects already available in After Effects, whereas others are highly specialized visual or audio effects otherwise unavailable in the program.

Video capture/playback device. To capture or export video footage, you can add a hardware capture card to your system. Of course, you also need a deck to play and record tapes in your format of choice. Capture devices range from consumer-level gear that captures images comparable to VHS to professional cards that capture uncompressed, 10-bit video signals over a serial digital interface (SDI) connection. To use DV footage, your computer needs a FireWire or iLink connection (aka IEEE 1394 controller card) and a similarly equipped camera or deck. Some DV devices use the more common USB 2 (aka Fast USB) interface instead of FireWire/iLink. Many cards come bundled with the software you'll need to capture video, such as Adobe's own Premiere Pro.

Video monitor. *Video monitor* is really just a fancy way of saying a very good television, with professional inputs and excellent color reproduction. Video monitors and computer monitors display images differently, so if your work is destined for video or broadcast, a good video monitor will allow you to judge it more accurately. A video capture device typically supports both your computer and your video monitor. With a DV configuration, you can use a DV camcorder or deck to send video to a video monitor.

Hardware acceleration. For the serious user, add-on cards offer accelerated effect rendering and can markedly decrease turnaround time on projects.

Non-linear editor. A non-linear editing (NLE) program doesn't enhance After Effects so much as complement it. After Effects is optimized for animation, compositing, and effects. But for serious editing, it can't beat a dedicated editing program such as Premiere Pro, Final Cut, or Avid. Recognizing the symbiotic relationship between editing and effects, developers are eager to point out how their NLE works with After Effects. If you're running After Effects on a Windows-based system and haven't already committed to a particular NLE, consider taking advantage of After Effects' sibling Premiere Pro (see the section "Adobe's Video Bundle," earlier in this chapter).

New Features

Some of the more notable features introduced in After Effects 7 include the following:

Enhanced user interface. After Effects 7 incorporates a more efficient, panel-based user interface like that now found in all the programs in Adobe's Video Bundle. The new interface ensures the program always makes the most of your available screen space and optimizes your workflow. Icons have been redesigned for an even more professional look, and functionality has been tweaked for better workflow. And now you can select and modify a number of preset workspace arrangements designed for particular tasks.

Improved animation paradigm. After Effects 7 includes numerous improvements to how you animate layer properties—most notably the new Graph Editor. The Graph Editor redefines how you view and adjust property graphs in the timeline. It provides a more efficient and comprehensible view of a layer's properties, allowing you to adjust the animation more easily.

Product integration. After Effects 7 works with other programs in the Video Bundle more effectively than ever before. Through a feature called Dynamic Link, the changes you make in an After Effects composition are reflected in Premiere Pro, and vice versa—without having to render or re-import footage. You can also copy and paste between After Effects and Premiere Pro and access Premiere Pro through After Effects to capture video footage. In addition, a New > Photoshop File command lets you access Photoshop quickly and then seamlessly utilize the image you create in your After Effects project.

Integrated Adobe Bridge. After Effects 7 ships with Adobe Bridge, a separate but tightly integrated program that not only makes browsing for assets easier but also lets you browse for presets and ready-made project templates. Moreover, Adobe Bridge can act as a gateway to Stock Photo, Adobe's extensive online library of images; you can use and evaluate these images before you buy them and incorporate them into your final project.

Enhanced export. Among other enhancements to export, After Effects for Windows incorporates an export mechanism called the Adobe Media Encoder, which facilitates the export of Windows Media, MPEG2, and MPEG2-DVD files.

Improved handling of projects and footage. After Effects 7 includes numerous enhancements to projects and footage, including an auto-save feature, support for 32 bits-per-channel (bpc) footage and camera raw footage, improved support for High Definition (HD), a freeze-frame command, enhanced frame blending options, and more.

Performance improvements and other enhancements. After Effects 7 improves overall performance, supporting more memory on Mac systems, better adaptive resolution and OpenGL performance, improved mask rendering, and autotracing. It also includes new and enhanced effects, per-character blur for text, a reference axis for viewing 3D, numerous new scripting features, and much more.

NEW FEATURES

After Effects Standard and Professional

You've probably noticed that After Effects comes in two flavors, a Standard version and a Professional version. (If you're a longtime After Effects user, you've noticed that Adobe traded the moniker *Production Bundle* for the more straightforward *Professional*.)

The Professional version, or After Effects Pro, includes all the features of the Standard program, as well as a package of extra tools and effects geared toward the professional user. After Effects Pro includes more sophisticated tools for controlling motion, such as motion tracking, stabilization, and automation. It also includes superior keying effects to composite footage, such as blue-screen footage. In addition, the Professional version contains more advanced warping and distortion effects, particle effects, and better audio processing effects. The Professional version also lets you work with images that contain 16 or 32 bits per channel rather than the more common 8 bits per channel.

By offering Standard and Professional versions of the program, Adobe makes it possible for you to gain admission to the world of After Effects for a relatively modest investment. Then, when your work demands it, you can upgrade to After Effects Pro. (Rest assured, if you're an After Effects professional, sooner or later you'll need After Effects Professional.)

This book covers the features and procedures common to both the Standard and Professional versions—that is, all the essential features—and refers to both simply as "After Effects" (unless pointing out a feature found only in After Effects Pro). Once you've mastered the core skills, you'll be more than ready to explore the specialized features found exclusively in After Effects Pro—such as the motion tracker, particle effects, and the motion math feature—on your own.

Television Standards

People often refer to equipment by the type of video standard it supports. Hence, it's not a *video monitor* but an *NTSC monitor*. NTSC stands for the National Television Standards Committee, the folks who develop the television standards used in North America and Japan, and whose name describes everything that meets those standards. Some have derisively joked that NTSC stands for "never the same color." But to be fair, the standard has served us well for more than 50 years, which you can't say for every technical standard that comes along.

Most of Europe uses a different standard, Phase Alternation Line (PAL). France and some countries that were formerly part of the Soviet Union use a standard called Sequential Couleur avec Memoire (SECAM).

Figure 1.1 An After Effects panel as seen on the Mac...

Figure 1.2 ...looks almost the same on a Windows system.

Mac vs. Windows

After Effects runs on both the Mac and Windows platforms. This book features screen shots from both systems. Similarly, both Mac and Windows keyboard shortcuts and instructions are included in the text. With few exceptions, After Effects works the same on both systems, and apart from mostly cosmetic differences between the operating systems, the windows are also nearly identical (**Figures 1.1** and **1.2**). In the instances where a process or window differs between the two versions of the program, it's clearly noted. Otherwise, you'll find the most significant differences on the operating system level, not in the program itself.

✔ Tip

- One notable difference between After Effects (and other programs) for the Mac and Windows is the location of the Preferences command. On a Mac, choose After Effects > Preferences; on Windows, choose Edit > Preferences.

Workflow Overview

Any project, it can be argued, begins at the same point: the end. Setting your output goal determines the choices you make to achieve it. Whether your animation is destined for film, videotape, DVD, CD-ROM, or the Web, familiarize yourself with the specifications of your output goal, such as frame size, frame rate, and file format. Only when you've determined the output goal can you make intelligent choices about source material and setting up a project.

That established, the typical workflow might resemble the outline that follows. However, every aspect of After Effects is tightly integrated and interdependent. Between import and output, the steps of the project won't necessarily proceed in a simple linear fashion:

Import. After Effects coordinates a wide range of source materials, including digital video, audio, bitmapped still images, path-based graphics and text, and even 3D and film transfer formats. However, it doesn't furnish you with a way to directly acquire these assets—you need a video and audio capture device, a digital still camera, a scanner, or other software packages to do that. This is not to say that After Effects doesn't generate its own graphic and sound elements; it does.

Arranging layers in time. Although it's not designed for long-form nonlinear editing, After Effects ably arranges shorter sequences for compositing and effects work. You can instantly access and rearrange layers, and use the same file repeatedly without copying or altering it.

Arranging layers in space. After Effects' ability to layer, combine, and compos-ite images earned it its reputation as the Photoshop of dynamic media. Moreover, these capabilities extend into the 3D realm.

Adding effects. Or does "the Photoshop of dynamic media" refer to After Effects' ability to add visual effects to motion footage? After Effects offers many effects to combine, enhance, transform, and distort layers of both video and audio. An entire industry has grown up around developing and accelerating effects for After Effects.

Animating attributes. One of After Effects' greatest strengths is its ability to change the attributes of layers over time. You can give layers motion, make layers appear and fade, or intensify and diminish an effect. The timeline's Graph Editor makes it easier than ever to focus on a property and control it with precision.

Previewing. You can play back your anima-tion at any time to evaluate its appearance and timing and then change it accordingly. After Effects maximizes your computer's playback capabilities by utilizing RAM to render frames, dynamically adjusting reso-lution, allowing you to specify a region of interest, and taking advantage of OpenGL.

Adding complexity. Some projects require more complex structures than others. You may need to group layers as a single element or circumvent the program's default render-ing hierarchy to achieve a certain effect. Or, you may need to restructure your project to make it more efficient and allow it to render more quickly. With features like parenting and expressions, you have the power to create complex animations with relatively little effort.

Output. When you're satisfied with your composition, you can output the result in a number of file formats, depending on the presentation media (which, of course, you planned for from the start).

Interface Overview

Before you begin exploring the program's terrain, let's take in a panoramic view.

Primary panels

Most of your work will be concentrated in three panels: the Project panel, the Composition panel, and the Timeline panel (**Figure 1.3**).

The **Project panel** lists references to audio and visual files, or footage, that you plan to use in your animation. It also lists compositions, which describe how you want to use the footage, including its arrangement in time, motion, and effects.

The **Composition panel** represents the layers of a composition spatially. The visible area of the Composition panel corresponds to the frame of the output animation and displays the composition's current frame. You can open more than one Composition panel; doing so is particularly useful when you want to compare the image in a composition to a corresponding frame in a nested composition, or view a 3D composition from different angles. It's common to call compositions *comps* and a Composition panel a *Comp panel*, for short.

Project panel   Composition panel

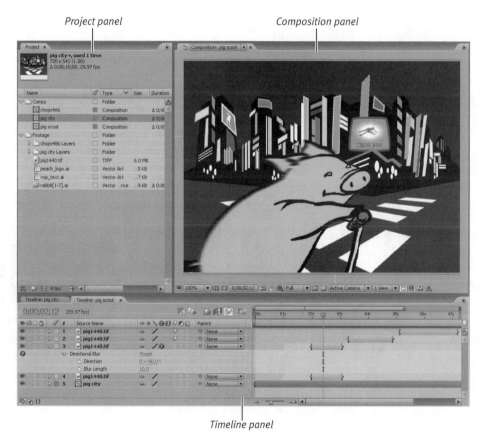

Timeline panel

Figure 1.3 Your work takes place primarily in the Project, Composition, and Timeline panels.

The **Timeline panel** represents the composition as a graph in which time is measured horizontally. When a footage item is added to the composition, it becomes a layer. The horizontal arrangement of layers indicates their place in the time of the composition; their vertical arrangement indicates their stacking order. You access and manipulate layer properties from the Timeline panel.

✔ Tip

- You can control the brightness and color of UI elements by choosing Edit > Preferences > User Interface Colors (Windows) or After Effects > Preferences > User Interface Colors (Mac).

Secondary panels

Although the Windows menu lists them in the same group as the three primary panels, you might consider the Footage, Layer, and Effect Controls panels to be ancillaries (**Figure 1.4**). The Flowchart and Render Queue panels are also among this important ensemble.

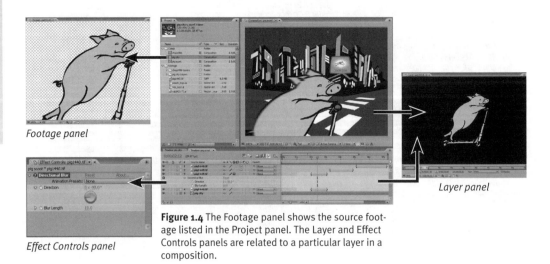

Footage panel

Effect Controls panel

Layer panel

Figure 1.4 The Footage panel shows the source footage listed in the Project panel. The Layer and Effect Controls panels are related to a particular layer in a composition.

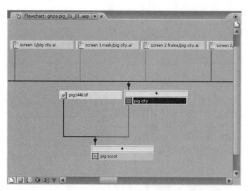

Figure 1.5 The Flowchart window helps you analyze the hierarchical structure of a complex project.

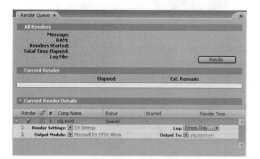

Figure 1.6 The Render Queue window lets you control and monitor the rendering process.

Figure 1.7 The Tools panel contains tools that help you perform special tasks using the mouse, as well as 3D axis buttons and a Workspace pull-down menu. (Typically, it extends horizontally across the workspace; this figure shows a more compact configuration.)

The **Footage panel** allows you to view the source footage listed in the Project panel before it becomes an editable layer in a composition.

The **Layer panel** lets you view each layer in a composition individually, outside the context of the Composition or Timeline panel. For example, it can be the most convenient place to manipulate a layer's mask shape. When you paint on a layer, you do so in the Layer panel.

The **Effect Controls panel** provides separate, roomier, and often more convenient effect controls than those available in the Timeline panel.

The **Flowchart panel** lets you see your project's elements in the form of a flowchart, which can make it easier to understand the structure and hierarchies of your project—particularly a complex one (**Figure 1.5**).

The **Render Queue panel** lets you control and monitor the rendering process (**Figure 1.6**).

Specialized panels

The panels listed so far—the panels you use most often—all appear at the bottom of the list in the Windows menu, below a horizontal line. Above that separator are a host of other, more specialized panels:

The **Tools panel**, as its name implies, contains an assortment of tools that change the function of the mouse pointer. Each tool allows you to perform specialized tasks (**Figure 1.7**). The Tools panel also contains buttons for changing the 3D axis and a pulldown menu for selecting a workspace.

As in other programs, a small triangle in the corner of a tool button indicates that related tools are hidden. Click and hold the button to reveal and select a hidden tool.

INTERFACE OVERVIEW

The **Info panel** displays all kinds of information about the current task, from the cursor's current position in a composition to the In and Out points of a layer (**Figure 1.8**).

The **Time Controls panel** contains controls for playing back and previewing the composition. When you set a composition's current time, the time is also set in all panels related to that composition (**Figure 1.9**).

The **Audio panel** lets you monitor and control audio levels (**Figure 1.10**).

The **Effects & Presets panel** provides a convenient way to view and apply effects. You can reorganize the list, create and view favorites, and find a particular effect in the list or on your hard drive (**Figure 1.11**).

The **Character panel** provides convenient text controls to support After Effects' direct text creation feature. It includes all the controls you'd expect—font, size, fill and stroke, kerning, leading, and the like. It also includes a few you might not expect—baseline shift, vertical and horizontal scaling, superscript and subscript, and a feature to aid in laying out characters in vertically oriented languages like Chinese, Japanese, and Korean (**Figure 1.12**).

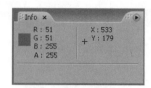

Figure 1.8 The Info panel displays information such as the current position of the cursor in a composition and the In and Out points of a layer.

Figure 1.9 The Time Controls panel contains controls to play back and preview the composition.

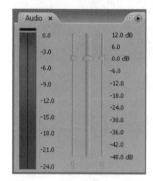

Figure 1.10 The Audio panel lets you monitor and control audio levels.

Figure 1.11 The Effects & Presets panel makes it easy to find effects and save custom presets for animation.

Figure 1.12 The full-featured Character panel lets you control the characteristics of text you create in After Effects.

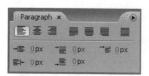

Figure 1.13 You can control blocks of text using the Paragraph panel, which lets you adjust things like alignment, justification, and indentation.

Figure 1.14 The Paint panel gives you control over After Effects' painting and cloning features...

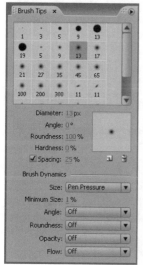

Figure 1.15 ...and its companion, the Brush Tips panel, lets you select the characteristics of the brush you employ.

The **Paragraph panel** lets you control blocks of text as you would in a word-processing or layout program. You can specify justification, alignment, indents, and the spacing before and after paragraphs (**Figure 1.13**).

The **Paint panel** gives you full control over the characteristics of paint, such as color, opacity, and flow. You can also specify which channel you want to paint onto and whether to apply a mode to each stroke (**Figure 1.14**).

The **Brush Tips panel** not only provides a menu of preset brushes but also lets you create brushes and specify their characteristics, such as diameter, angle, roundness, hardness, and so on (**Figure 1.15**).

✔ Tip

- After Effects' flexible interface allows you to substantially alter the appearance of each panel. Don't be distracted if a figure in this book depicts a variant of a panel that differs from the one you're using.

INTERFACE OVERVIEW

Even more specialized panels

You can open the previously listed nine panels by using keyboard shortcuts; but to open the following panels, you'll have to choose them from the Windows pull-down menu:

The **Motion Sketch panel** lets you set motion keyframes by dragging the mouse (or by using a pen stroke on a graphics tablet) (**Figure 1.16**).

The **Smart Mask Interpolation panel** (Professional only) helps you animate mask shapes more precisely (**Figure 1.17**).

The **Smoother panel** helps you smooth changes in keyframe values automatically, to create more gradual changes in an animation (**Figure 1.18**).

The **Wiggler panel** (Professional only) generates random deviations in keyframed values automatically (**Figure 1.19**).

The **Align panel** helps you arrange layers in a comp vis-à-vis one another (**Figure 1.20**).

The **Tracker Controls panel** (Professional only), an advanced feature, helps you generate keyframes by detecting and following a moving object in a shot. You can use this information to make an effect track an object or to stabilize a scene shot with shaky camera work (**Figure 1.21**).

Figure 1.16 The Motion Sketch panel lets you set motion keyframes by dragging your mouse.

Figure 1.17 The Smart Mask Interpolation panel (Professional only) provides a greater degree of control when you're animating mask shapes.

Figure 1.18 The Smoother panel helps you smooth changes in key-frame values.

Figure 1.19 You can generate random deviations in keyframed values automatically using the Wiggler panel (Professional only).

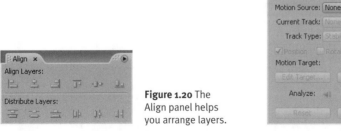

Figure 1.20 The Align panel helps you arrange layers.

Figure 1.21 Using the Tracker Controls panel (Professional only), you can generate keyframes to follow a moving object automatically or, conversely, to stabilize a shaky image.

Figure 1.22 This figure shows the Standard workspace.

Figure 1.23 Selecting the arrangement you want from the Tools panel's Workspace pull-down menu...

Figure 1.24 ...arranges the panels according to the workspace you choose. Here, note how the Effects workspace places the Effect Controls panel where the Project panel is located in the Standard workspace (shown in Figure 1.22).

Setting a Workspace

With so many controls at your disposal, it's clear that you must arrange the panels to suit the task at hand and change the arrangement for each phase of your workflow. Conveniently, After Effects provides several preset arrangements, or *workspaces*, optimized to accomplish particular tasks, such as animation or effects (**Figure 1.22**). Selecting the appropriate workspace from a list (or using a keyboard shortcut) opens and configures the panels you need.

When you modify a preset workspace (using methods explained in the section "Customizing the Workspace," later in this chapter), After Effects maintains the changes until you reset the preset to its defaults. You can even create your own preset workspace.

To specify a preset workspace:

◆ *Do either of the following:*

  ▲ Choose Window > Workspace, and then choose the name of the arrangement that corresponds with the task at hand.

  ▲ In the Tools panel's Workspace pull-down menu, choose the name of the workspace (**Figure 1.23**).

  For example, changing from the preset Standard workspace to the preset Effects workspace opens the Effect Controls panel in place of the Project panel (**Figure 1.24**). The workspace retains any modifications you make to it until you reset the workspace.

To create a new workspace preset:

1. If you want, set the workspace that uses an arrangement on which you want to base a custom workspace.

2. In the Tools panel's Workspace pull-down menu, choose New Workspace (**Figure 1.25**).

   A New Workspace dialog box appears.

3. In the New Workspace dialog box, type a name for the custom workspace, and click OK (**Figure 1.26**).

   The current workspace becomes the newly named workspace preset.

4. Modify the workspace using any of the methods described in the section "Customizing the Workspace," later in this chapter.

To reset a preset workspace:

1. With the workspace set to a modified preset workspace (such as Standard), choose Reset "*workspace name*" (**Figure 1.27**).

2. When prompted, confirm that you want to discard the changes you made to the workspace.

   The workspace reverts to its original preset arrangement.

✔ Tips

- The Workspace pull-down menu also contains commands for deleting a workspace and for assigning a keyboard shortcut to a workspace.

- The Window menu (in After Effects' main menu bar) also contains all the commands pertaining to workspaces.

Figure 1.25 In the Tools panel's Workspace pull-down menu, choose New Workspace.

Figure 1.26 Enter a name for the custom workspace in the New Workspace dialog box.

Figure 1.27 Choosing Reset "workspace name" in the Tools panel's Workspace pull-down menu reverts the workspace to its original state.

SETTING A WORKSPACE

Customizing the Workspace

Using the preset workspaces is convenient, not compulsory. By customizing the size and arrangement of the panels, you can optimize your workspace and your workflow. You just have to know a few things about frames, panels, and tabs.

The After Effects interface consists of an interconnected system of *panels* contained within *frames*. Unlike a collection of free-floating windows that can be arranged like playing cards on a tabletop, frames are joined together in such a way that the interface may remind you of a mosaic or stained glass. Resizing one frame affects the adjacent frames so that, as a whole, the frames always fill the screen (or, more strictly speaking, After Effects' main application window, which most users maximize to fill the screen). With frames and panels, it's easy to change the relative size of each part of the interface without wasting screen space. And you don't have to worry about one window disappearing behind another.

You can also customize a workspace by taking advantage of tabs. The tab that appears at the top of each panel looks a lot like its real-world counterpart in your office filing cabinet. By dragging a panel's tab into the same area as another panel, you *dock* the panels together. When panels are docked, it's as though they are filed one on top of the other. But like physical file-folder tabs, the tabs of the panels in the back are always visible along the top edge of the stack; you click a panel's tab to bring it to the front. (The Footage, Comp, and Layer panel tabs include a lock option and pull-down menu, discussed in the section "Using Viewers," later in this chapter.)

Just as docking reduces the number of spaces in the interface's mosaic of frames, dragging a panel between other panels creates an additional space, or frame.

Finally, you can separate a panel from the system of frames, creating a free-floating window. A floating window may be useful for tasks you don't perform often or when you can move it to a second computer screen.

To resize panels:

◆ Position the mouse pointer on the border between panels, so that the resize icon ⊞ appears (**Figure 1.28**), and then drag.

The size of adjacent panels changes automatically, according to your adjustments (**Figure 1.29**).

Figure 1.28 Position the mouse pointer over the border between panels so that the resize icon appears...

Figure 1.29 ...and drag to resize the panels that share that border. Note how resizing hides the optional areas of the Time Controls panel.

Figure 1.30 Dragging a panel into another panel...

Figure 1.31 ...combines the two panels into a tabbed group.

To dock panels:

1. *Do either of the following:*

   ▲ To dock a panel, drag its tab or the textured area at the top of the panel.

   ▲ To dock a floating window, click and drag the top of the window.

2. Drag the mouse pointer within another panel, so that a highlighted area indicates the panel will appear docked as a tab (**Figure 1.30**), and then release the mouse.

   The panels are docked together, so that they occupy the same area (or frame) in the interface's grid of panels (**Figure 1.31**). If the panel wasn't docked in its previous position, then docking it eliminates the frame.

To view tabbed panels:

◆ To view a panel that's hidden behind another panel, click the tab of the panel you want to view (**Figures 1.32** and **1.33**).

◆ To view tabs that are don't fit within the width of the panel area, drag the thin scroll bar that appears above the tabs (**Figures 1.34** and **1.35**).

Figure 1.32 Clicking the tab of a panel in the back of the stack...

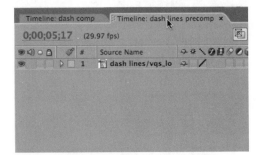

Figure 1.33 ...brings that panel to the front.

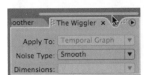

Figure 1.34 When the panel is too narrow to show all tabs, a thin scroll bar appears above the tabs.

Figure 1.35 Drag the scroll bar to bring the hidden tabs into view.

Figure 1.36 Dragging a panel between other panels...

Figure 1.37 ...allows the panel to occupy a new space, or frame, in the grid of panels.

To create a new frame:

1. *Do either of the following:*
   - ▲ To move a panel, drag its tab or the textured area at the top of the panel.
   - ▲ To move a floating window, click and drag the top of the window.

2. Drag the mouse pointer near the side of any other panel, so that a highlighted area indicates where the panel will be inserted in the grid of frames (**Figure 1.36**), and then release the mouse.

   The panel occupies a new space in the grid of frames (**Figure 1.37**).

To convert a panel into a floating window:

◆ *Do either of the following:*

▲ Drag a panel's tab or the textured area at the top of the panel to the empty space above the interface, so that the highlighted area indicates where the floating window will appear, and then release the mouse.

▲ In the tab's pull-down menu, choose Undock Panel (**Figure 1.38**).

The panel becomes a floating window (**Figure 1.39**). If the panel wasn't docked in its previous position, then undocking it eliminates the space it had occupied in the grid of panels.

✔ Tips

■ You can also undock and close panels and frames by using commands in each panel's pull-down menu (accessed by clicking the arrow in the panel's upper-left corner).

■ When you move a panel, After Effects highlights the destination, indicating the new placement. Initially, it can be tricky to distinguish the indicators, but you'll get it with a little practice.

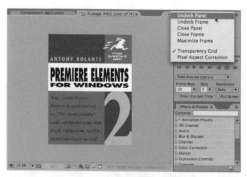

Figure 1.38 Dragging a panel to an empty area or choosing Undock Panel in the panel menu (shown here)...

Figure 1.39 ...separates the panel from the others, converting it into a floating window.

Using Viewers

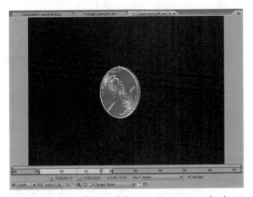

Figure 1.40 By default, all footage items open in the same Footage panel; comps share the same Comp panel; and layers share the same Layer panel.

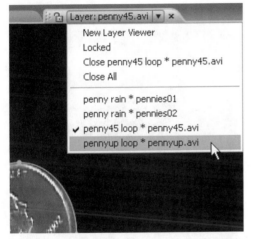

Figure 1.41 You can view another image by selecting it in the panel's viewer pull-down menu. This Layer panel's viewer lets you select another layer in the project.

Figure 1.42 However, selecting the viewer's Lock icon prevents items from opening in the panel; instead, they open in a separate panel. Here, a locked Layer panel forces subsequent layers to open in another Layer panel.

As you work, you'll need to open numerous footage items, compositions, and layers. To prevent a frame from becoming overcrowded with tabs, the Footage, Comp, and Layer panels utilize *viewers*. (And because each layer can contain a set of effects, the Effect Controls panel also employs the viewer system.)

Instead of opening in separate tabbed panels, multiple items of the same type (footage, comps, layers, and a layer's effects) share a single panel of that type (Footage panel, Comp panel, and so on) (**Figure 1.40**).

A pull-down menu in the panel's tab allows you to switch to another image, or *viewer*. For example, you can see any layer in the project by selecting it in a Layer panel's viewer menu (**Figure 1.41**).

However, you can prevent new items from opening in a viewer by *locking* the viewer. When locked, the viewer pull-down menu still works, but the panel doesn't accept new viewers. Instead, the item opens as a separate tabbed panel (**Figure 1.42**). (If another compatible panel is visible and unlocked, then new items open in it.)

Naturally, the viewer feature doesn't prevent you from using any of the methods described in the section "Customizing the Workspace"). Viewers are just another feature to help you manage your workspace and your workflow effectively.

To select a viewer:

◆ In a Footage, Layer, Comp, or Effect
Controls panel, select the name of the
item you want to see in the tab's viewer
pull-down menu (**Figure 1.43**).

The image in the panel changes accordingly (**Figure 1.44**).

To lock or unlock a view:

◆ In a Footage, Layer, Comp, or Effect
Controls panel's tab, select the Lock
icon to toggle it on and off (**Figures 1.45**
and **1.46**).

The 🔓 icon indicates the panel's viewer
is unlocked and will let items open in the
panel. The 🔒 icon indicates the panel's
viewer is locked; new items must open
in a separate, unlocked panel.

✔ Tips

■ Comps open as separately tabbed Timeline
panels and don't utilize viewers. Typically,
the frame that contains Timeline panels
is wide and easily accommodates
numerous tabs.

■ The Comp panel also has a View Layout
pull-down menu, which allows the panel
to display multiple images simultaneously. Seeing the adjustments you make
to a comp from several perspectives at
once is particularly useful when you're
working with 3D layers. Using multiple
comp views is discussed in detail in
Chapter 4, "Compositions," and Chapter 15,
"3D Layers."

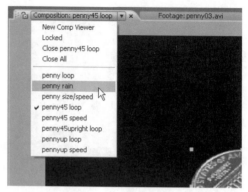

Figure 1.43 The viewer pull-down menu lists other
items (note how layer names are preceded by the
comp that contains them). Select the name of the
item you want to view...

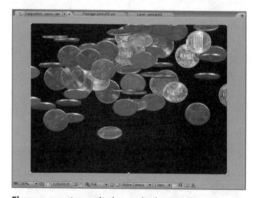

Figure 1.44 ...to see its image in the panel.

Figure 1.45 Click the lock icon in the panel's tab to
toggle it from unlocked...

Figure 1.46 ...to locked.

USING VIEWERS

IMPORTING FOOTAGE INTO A PROJECT

Think of an After Effects project as a musical score. Just as a score refers to instruments and indicates how they should be played, your project lists the files you want to use and how you want to use them. When you've finished creating your project, you can output an animation as a movie file or an image sequence. The important thing to remember is that the project contains only references to the source files, not the files themselves. The project contains neither the sources nor the end result, any more than a sheet of music contains a tuba or a recording of the concert. For this reason, a project file takes up little drive space.

Source files, on the other hand, consume considerably more storage. You need both the project and the source files to preview or output your animation, just as a composer needs the orchestra to hear a work in progress or, ultimately, to perform it in concert. Nonlinear editing systems (such as Adobe Premiere Pro and Apple Final Cut Pro) also work by referring to source files. Thus, if you're familiar with those programs, you have a head start on the concept of using file references in a project.

In this chapter, you'll learn how to create a project and import various types of footage. The chapter covers the specifics of importing still-images, motion footage, audio, and even other projects. In fact, After Effects ships with a number or astonishingly useful preset project templates. And that's not all: After Effects arrives accompanied by a full-fledged asset management program, Adobe Bridge.

Don't be intimidated by the length or depth of the chapter. Importing different types of footage into your project is a simple and straightforward process. As you go through the chapter, take just what you need. As you begin to incorporate a wider range of formats in your work, revisit sections to learn the idiosyncrasies of those particular formats. To revisit the musical metaphor, if a project is like a score, start by composing for an ensemble, and then build up to an orchestra.

Creating and Saving Projects

Creating a project is especially simple in After Effects, which doesn't prompt you to select project settings. Although there are a few project settings, you can change their default values at any time (as explained later in this chapter). As you'll see in the next chapter, most settings you specify are associated with compositions within the project.

To more easily track changes to your work, you can instruct After Effects to save each successive version of a project using an incremental naming scheme.

To create a new project:

Do one of the following:

◆ Launch After Effects.

◆ With After Effects running, choose File > New > New Project (**Figure 2.1**).

If a project is open, After Effects prompts you to save it. Otherwise, a new Project panel appears (**Figure 2.2**).

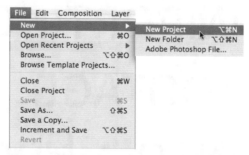

Figure 2.1 Choose File > New > New Project.

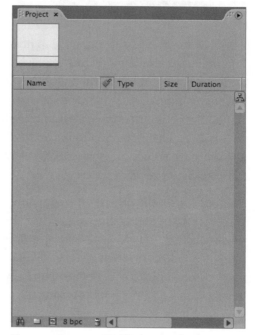

Figure 2.2 A new, untitled Project panel appears.

Figure 2.3 Choose File >
Save As.

Figure 2.4 Specify a name and location for your
project.

To save a project for the first time or using a new name or location:

1. Choose File > Save As (**Figure 2.3**).
   A Save As dialog box appears.

2. Type a name for the project, and choose
   a location (**Figure 2.4**).

3. Click Save.

To save a project using the same name and location:

◆ After the project has been saved the
   first time, choose File > Save, or press
   Command-S (Macintosh) or Ctrl-S
   (Windows).

To save using incremental project names automatically:

◆ After the project has been saved, choose
   File > Increment and Save, or press
   Command-Opt-Shift-S (Mac) or Ctrl-Alt-
   Shift-S (Windows).

   After Effects saves a copy of the project,
   appending a number to the filename that
   increases incrementally with each successive Increment and Save command.

✔ Tips

■ A project's name appears at the top of
   the main application window, not the
   Project panel. When a project has unsaved
   changes, an asterisk (*) appears next to
   the project's name.

■ You can instruct After Effects to save the
   current project at an interval you specify
   by choosing After Effects > Preferences >
   Auto-Save (Mac) or Edit > Preferences >
   Auto-Save (Windows) and specifying
   how frequently After Effects saves.

■ As you might expect, the File menu also
   includes Save, Copy, and Revert to Last
   Saved commands.

CREATING AND SAVING PROJECTS

Opening and Closing Projects

In After Effects, you may have only one project open at a time. Opening another project closes the current project. However, closing the Project panel doesn't close the project; it merely removes the Project panel from the workspace.

As you learned in this chapter's introduction, an After Effects project contains footage items that refer to files on your system. When you reopen a project, After Effects must locate the source files to which each footage item refers. If After Effects can't locate a source file, the project considers it missing (**Figure 2.5**). (In Premiere Pro and other nonlinear editing programs, missing footage is called *offline*.) The names of missing footage items appear in italics in the Project panel (**Figure 2.6**), and a placeholder consisting of colored bars temporarily replaces the source footage. You can continue working with the project, or you can locate the source footage. For more about missing source footage, see Chapter 3, "Managing Footage."

To close a project:

◆ Choose File > Close Project.

The project and the sequences it contains close, and are removed from the workspace. If the current workspace includes a Project panel, then the Project panel becomes empty.

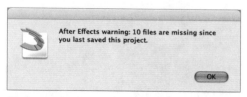

Figure 2.5 After Effects alerts you if it can't locate source files.

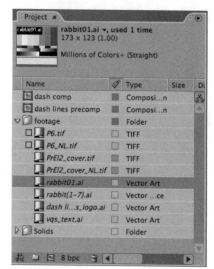

Figure 2.6 The names of missing footage items appear in italics, and the source footage is temporarily replaced by a color bar placeholder.

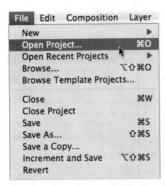

Figure 2.7 Choose File > Open
Project to open an existing project
while After Effects is running.

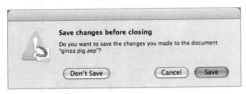

Figure 2.8 Because you may have only one project
open at a time, After Effects prompts you to save an
open project before opening another one.

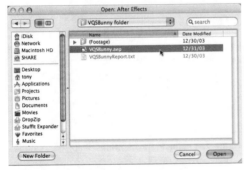

Figure 2.9 In the Open dialog box, locate an After
Effects project and click Open.

To open a project:

1. In After Effects, choose File > Open
   Project, or press Command-O (Mac)
   or Ctrl-O (Windows) (**Figure 2.7**).

   An Open dialog box appears.

   If you already have a project open, After
   Effects prompts you to save the existing
   project (**Figure 2.8**). Click Save to save
   the open project before closing it.

2. In the Open dialog box, locate an After
   Effects project, and click Open (**Figure 2.9**).

✔ Tips

■ To open a project you worked on recently,
   choose File > Open Recent Projects and
   choose the name of the project in the
   submenu.

■ With After Effects running, press Shift-
   Command-Opt-P (Mac) or Shift-Ctrl-Alt-P
   (Windows) to open the most recently
   opened project (think *p* for *previous project*).

■ After Effects ships with a number of
   incredibly useful and inspiring preset
   project templates. See the section
   "Importing with Adobe Bridge," later
   in this chapter, for details.

Choosing a Time Display

When you begin a project, you may want to pay a quick visit to the Project Settings dialog box, which includes options for setting the style in which the time is displayed in your compositions.

The display style doesn't affect the frame rate of your compositions, only the way time is counted and displayed. This means you can change the display style whenever you want without adversely affecting the project (or its compositions).

To set the project display style:

1. *Do either of the following*:

   ▲ In the Project panel's pull-down menu, choose Project Settings (**Figure 2.10**).

   ▲ Choose File > Project Settings.

   The Project Settings dialog box appears (**Figure 2.11**).

2. In the Project Settings dialog box, set the display style by selecting the radio button next to the appropriate option:

   Timecode Base—After Effects uses timecode to number frames (displayed as hours, minutes, seconds, and frames).

   Frames—Frames are numbered sequentially, without regard to time.

   Feet + Frames—Frame numbers are based on 16mm or 35mm motion picture film (both of which are displayed at 24 frames per second, or *fps*).

3. If necessary, choose additional options for the Timecode Base or Feet + Frames display options (explained in the following sections), and then click OK to close the dialog box.

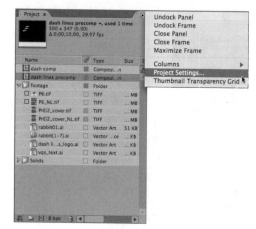

Figure 2.10 Choose Project Settings in the Project panel's menu.

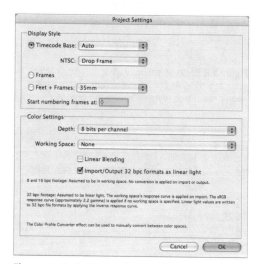

Figure 2.11 In the Project Settings dialog box, set the display style.

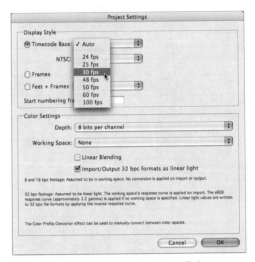

Figure 2.12 Choose an option from the pull-down menu.

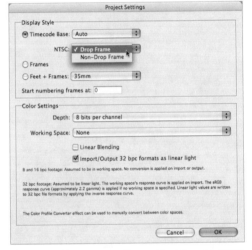

Figure 2.13 Choose a counting method from the NTSC pull-down menu.

To select Timecode Base display options:

1. If you chose Timecode Base as the time display in the Project Settings dialog box, choose an option from the pull-down menu (**Figure 2.12**).

   For standard video projects, choose 30 fps.

2. *Choose one of the following* counting methods from the NTSC pull-down menu (**Figure 2.13**):

   Drop Frame—Uses NTSC drop-frame timecode to count frames. Most master tapes and DV camera–recorded video use drop-frame timecode.

   Non-Drop Frame—Employs NTSC non-drop frame timecode to count frames.

   For a detailed explanation of drop-frame and non-drop frame timecode, see the sidebar "Counting Time," later in this chapter.

3. Click OK to close the Project Settings dialog box.

CHOOSING A TIME DISPLAY

To select Feet + Frames time display options:

1. If you chose Feet + Frames as the display style in the Project Settings dialog box, *choose one* of two film standards from the pull-down menu (**Figure 2.14**):

   16mm—Runs at 24 frames per second and 40 frames per foot

   35mm—Runs at 24 frames per second and 16 frames per foot

2. If you want, in the Start Numbering Frames At field, enter a frame number at which you want the project to begin.

3. Click OK to close the Project Settings dialog box.

✔ Tips

■ The time display you select in the Project Settings dialog box will also be reflected in the settings for compositions you create within the project. See "Choosing Composition Settings," in Chapter 4.

■ You can also change the time display directly from the Composition panel or from the Timeline panel by Command-clicking (Mac) or Ctrl-clicking (Windows) the time display in those windows.

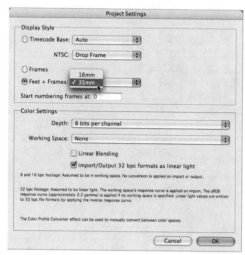

Figure 2.14 Choose a film standard from the pull-down menu.

Counting Time: Non-Drop Frame vs. Drop-Frame Timecode

Timecode refers to a method of counting video frames that was developed by the Society of Motion Picture and Television Engineers (SMPTE). Timecode is counted in hours, minutes, seconds, and frames. It extends to just under 24 hours: 23:59:59:29.

Because the true frame rate of NTSC video is always 29.97 fps, measuring time accurately in hours, minutes, seconds, and frames can get complicated. (In fact, 29.97 is only a commonly used approximation—but that's another story.) To simplify matters, SMPTE timecode rounds off the decimal and counts at an even 30 fps. However, it can use one of two counting schemes: non-drop frame or drop-frame timecode.

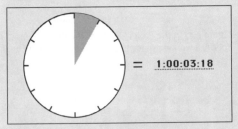

Figure 2.15 For every hour of real time that elapses, non-drop frame timecode counts an additional 3 seconds and 18 frames.

Figure 2.16 To accurately reflect elapsed time, DF timecode skips two frame numbers at the end of every minute except every tenth minute.

Non-Drop Frame Timecode

Even though the true frame rate of NTSC video is 29.97 fps, non-drop frame (NDF) timecode counts 30 fps. Over time, this discrepancy results in a small but significant difference between the duration indicated by the timecode display and the actual elapsed time (**Figure 2.15**). Nevertheless, NDF is easy to understand and calculate, so camera originals and other source tapes usually use this type of timecode. Video equipment typically displays NDF timecode with colons between the hours, minutes, seconds, and frames.

Drop-Frame Timecode

To compensate for the discrepancy caused by the 30-fps counting scheme, SMPTE developed drop-frame (DF) timecode. Drop-frame timecode also counts 30 fps, but it skips two frame numbers—not actual frames—at the end of every minute except every tenth minute (**Figure 2.16**).

If you do the math, you'll find that DF timecode displays durations that closely match the actual elapsed time. For this reason, master tapes usually employ DF timecode. (Of course, the missing numbers also make it difficult to do timecode calculations manually.) After Effects and other video equipment display drop-frame timecode semicolons between hours, minutes, seconds, and frames.

CHOOSING A TIME DISPLAY

Specifying Color Settings

Color space refers to the method a device uses to represent colors. By default, After Effects uses the same color space as the computer's monitor. However, you can set the color space you work in to match your output goal. This way, the colors of previews will most accurately represent the eventual output.

The working color space also determines the way colors are blended (when you composite layers, text, and paint strokes). However, blending high-contrast and saturated colors can result in artifacts, such as an unpleasant fringe or halo. Fortunately, you can instruct After Effects to blend colors using a superior method, by enabling *linear blending*.

On the downside, setting a working color space or using linear blending can slow previews. After Effects Pro also includes a Color Bit Depth option (see the sidebar "Choosing the Color Bit-Depth Mode," later in this chapter).

To specify color settings:

1. *Do either of the following:*
   - ▲ In the Project panel's pull-down menu, choose Project Settings.
   - ▲ Choose File > Project Settings.
   The Project Settings dialog box appears.

2. To specify a working color space, choose an option from the Working Space pull-down menu that matches your output goals (**Figure 2.17**).

   For example, choose SDTV (Rec 601 NTSC) if your output goal is standard definition broadcast video.

3. To enable linear blending, select Linear Blending (**Figure 2.18**).

✔ Tip

■ You can also press Shift-Command-Opt-K (Mac) or Shift-Ctrl-Alt-K (Windows) to open the Project Settings dialog box.

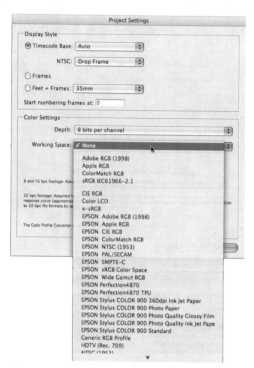

Figure 2.17 In the Project Settings dialog box, you can specify a working space that matches your output goal.

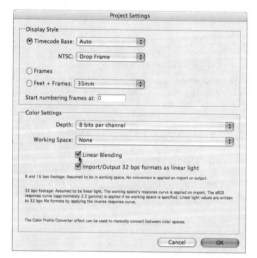

Figure 2.18 You can also enable the Linear Blending option.

Importing Files

After Effects allows you to import a wide variety of still-images, motion footage, and audio, as well as projects from After Effects and Premiere Pro. The procedures for importing footage are essentially variations on a theme, so you should get the hang of them quickly.

Although you may be tempted to speed through some sections in this part of the chapter, make sure you understand how the methods differ for each file type. Depending on the file, you may need to invoke the Interpret Footage command, which contains special handling options such as how to set the duration of stills or the frame rate of motion footage. The Interpret Footage command also lets you properly handle other aspects of footage, such as the alpha channel, field order, and pixel aspect ratio. If you're already familiar with these concepts, go directly to the numbered tasks; if not, check out the sidebars in this chapter for some technical grounding.

You'll find that you can often use several methods to import footage: menu bar, keyboard shortcuts, or context menu. You can even drag and drop from the desktop. Once you know your options, you can choose the method that best fits your needs or preferences.

The maximum resolution for import and export is 30,000 × 30,000 pixels. However, the PICT format is still limited to 4,000 × 4,000 pixels; BMP to 16,000 × 30,000; and PXR to 30,000 × 16,000 pixels.

As you've already learned, After Effects Professional lets you import images with 16 bpc and 32 bpc—an indispensable capability if you're doing high-end work.

Of course, the maximum image size and bit depth are limited by the amount of RAM available to After Effects (see the sidebar "Wham, Bam—Thank You, RAM").

After Effects supports an extensive and growing list of file formats, depending on your platform. Photoshop and other third-party plug-ins can also expand the possibilities.

Choosing the Color Bit-Depth Mode

If you're using After Effects Professional, the Project Settings dialog box also allows you to set the color bit-depth mode. In addition to supporting standard 8 bits-per-channel (bpc) images, After Effects Pro lets you process images using 16 and even 32 bpc.

This means your images not only can have higher color fidelity from the start, but they also retain that quality even after repeated color processing (for example, from transfer modes and effects).

But naturally, greater precision comes at a cost. For example, processing color in 16 bpc is twice as demanding as processing it in 8 bpc—that is, doing so requires twice the RAM and processing time. To save time, you may want to work in 8 bpc initially and then switch to 16 bpc when you're ready for critical color processing.

Although you can set the bit depth from the Project Settings dialog box, it's more convenient to toggle the bit-depth mode by Option-clicking (Mac) or Alt-clicking the bit depth display in the Project panel.

To import a file or files:

1. *Do one of the following:*

▲ Choose File > Import > File to import one item.

▲ Choose File > Import > Multiple Files to import several items (**Figure 2.19**).

The Import File or Import Multiple Files dialog box appears (**Figure 2.20**).

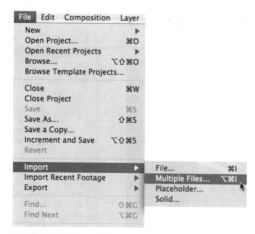

Figure 2.19 Choose File > Import > File or > Multiple Files.

Figure 2.20 The Import File or Import Multiple Files dialog box appears.

Wham, Bam—Thank You, RAM

Here's the formula for calculating how much RAM an image requires:

Width in pixels × height in pixels × 4 bytes = RAM needed to display image

So, the largest file allowed would require 3.35 GB of RAM (30,000 × 30,000 × 4 bytes)—ouch!

A tall image used as an end credit roll for video output provides a less extreme example, as you can see:

720 × 30,000 × 4 bytes = 82.4 MB of RAM

Figure 2.21 To sift the list of files, specify an option in the Enable pull-down menu.

Figure 2.22 Select the file or files you want to import and click Open.

2. To expand or reduce the list of files, choose an option for Enable (**Figure 2.21**):

All Files—Enables all files in the list, including files of an unrecognized file type

All Acceptable Files—Enables only file types supported by After Effects

All Footage Files—Enables only files that can be imported as footage items, and excludes otherwise acceptable file types (such as After Effects or Premiere Pro project files)

AAF, AE Project, and so on—Enables only files of the same file type you select

Enabled files can be selected for import, whereas other files are unavailable and appear grayed-out.

3. In the Import File or Import Multiple Files dialog box, choose Footage from the Import As pull-down menu.

To import files as compositions or to import projects, see the corresponding sections later in this chapter.

4. Select the file you want to import, and then click Open (**Figure 2.22**).

To select a range of files in the same folder, click the file at the beginning of the range to select it, Shift-click the end of the range, and then click Open.

To select multiple noncontiguous files in the same folder, Command-click (Mac) or Ctrl-click (Windows) multiple files, and then click Open.

continues on next page

IMPORTING FILES

5. If prompted, specify other options for each file you import (such as its alpha channel type, or how to import a layered file).

The options for particular file types are discussed later in this chapter.

6. If you chose to import multiple files in step 1, repeat the subsequent steps until you've imported all the files you want to use; then, click Done to close the Import Multiple Files dialog box (**Figure 2.23**).

The file(s) appear as item(s) in the Project panel (**Figure 2.24**).

✔ Tips

■ Double-clicking in an empty area of the Project panel is a great shortcut for opening the Import File dialog box.

■ You can also import files by dragging them directly from the operating system to the Project panel. But because After Effects' interface usually covers the entire screen, it may discourage this technique. The integration of Adobe Bridge (covered later in this chapter) provides yet another convenient way to browse for files to import.

Figure 2.23 If you chose to import multiple files, click Done to close the dialog box.

Figure 2.24 Imported items appear in the Project panel as footage files.

IMPORTING FILES

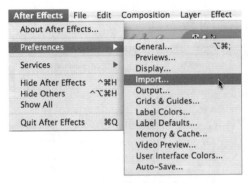

Figure 2.25 Choose After Effects > Preferences > Import (Mac) or Edit > Preferences > Import (Windows).

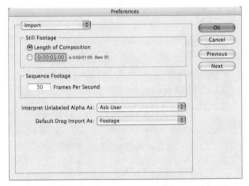

Figure 2.26 The Import panel of the Preferences dialog box appears.

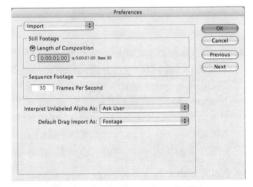

Figure 2.27 Set the default duration of still images to the duration of the composition, or enter a custom duration.

Setting Still-Image Durations

When you import a still-image as a footage file and make it a layer in a composition, you can set its duration to any length. By default, the duration of a still-image matches the duration of the composition. However, you can also manually set the default duration for still-images. Doing so comes in handy when you plan to use several stills for the same duration, such as a series of title cards for a credit sequence. Of course, you can always change the duration (or trim) of the layer later. See Chapter 4, "Compositions," for more about adding footage to a composition as layers; see Chapter 6, "Layer Editing," for more about editing layers.

To change the default duration of still-images:

1. Choose After Effects > Preferences > Import (Mac) or Edit > Preferences > Import (Windows) (**Figure 2.25**).

   The Import panel of the Preferences dialog box appears (**Figure 2.26**).

2. In the Still Footage section, *do one of the following* (**Figure 2.27**):

   ▲ Select Length of Composition to make the still-images' duration the same as that of the composition you're adding them to.

   ▲ Select the radio button next to the Time field, and enter a default duration for imported still-images.

3. Click OK to set the changes and exit the Preferences dialog box.

SETTING STILL-IMAGE DURATIONS

Preparing Still-Images for Import

If you prepare a still-image beforehand, you spare After Effects from having to process every frame in which the image appears in a composition. To avoid adding time to previews and renders, do the following before you import a still-image into After Effects:

◆ Set the pixel dimensions to the size at which the image will be used in After Effects. If you plan to scale up the image (as in a zoom-in effect), you should set its pixel dimensions to be proportionally greater. If you don't do this, the image will appear more and more pixelated as you scale it up.

◆ Set the pixel dimensions of the still-image to even numbers if the composition uses even-numbered pixel dimensions and to odd numbers if the composition uses odd-numbered pixel dimensions. (Most standard screen sizes use even pixel resolutions.) This makes it easier to position the image without causing it to be resampled and appear to soften.

◆ Crop the areas of the image that won't be visible in the After Effects composition.

◆ Create an alpha channel to define transparent areas in the image. (See "Importing Files with Alpha Channels," later in this chapter.)

◆ Make any other image adjustments, such as color corrections or touch-ups.

◆ If you're using a still-image grabbed from interlaced video, deinterlace areas that show field artifacts. Field artifacts often appear in areas of the image where the subject is moving. (See the sidebar "Working the Fields," later in this chapter).

◆ Consider the pixel aspect ratio of your final output. Most images generated on your computer use a square-pixel aspect ratio, whereas some output resolutions (such as D1 or DV) are based on a nonsquare-pixel aspect ratio. (See "Pixel Aspect Ratios," later in this chapter.)

◆ Save the still-image in a format that After Effects supports. Even after you import a still-image, After Effects lets you edit the file using the original application and reflects any changes you make to the original file. (See Chapter 3 for more about the Edit Original command.)

For broadcast video output, you should also consider doing the following:

◆ Make sure color saturation doesn't exceed National Television Standards Committee (NTSC) safe color limitations.

◆ Make sure luminance values don't exceed NTSC limits for "legal" black-and-white levels.

◆ Avoid thin horizontal lines in both images and text (including serifs), because interlaced video makes 1-pixel lines appear to flicker. To get around the problem, increase the thickness of the lines or apply a blur. (See the sidebar "Working the Fields," later in this chapter.)

◆ Take television's 4:3 image aspect ratio into consideration, as well as title and action safe zones. (See the sidebar "Better Safe than Sorry" in Chapter 3.)

Figure 2.28 In After Effects, choose File > Import > File.

Figure 2.29 In the Import dialog box, select the first image in the sequence, and select the Sequence option.

Figure 2.30 The image sequence appears in the Project panel as a single item.

Importing Still-Image Sequences

Many programs (including After Effects) can export motion footage not as a single movie file, but as a series of still-images, or a *still-image sequence*. You can import all or part of a still-image sequence as a single motion footage item.

To import a still-image sequence:

1. Make sure all the still-image files in the sequence follow a consistent numeric or alphabetical filename pattern and are contained in the same folder.

2. In After Effects, choose File > Import > File (**Figure 2.28**).

   The Import File dialog box appears.

3. *Do either of the following*:

   ▲ To import the entire sequence as a single motion footage item, select the first file in the sequence.

   ▲ To import part of the sequence as a single motion footage item, select the first file in the range, and then Shift-click the last file in the range.

4. Select the box for the Sequence option (**Figure 2.29**).

   The Import File dialog box automatically indicates the file format for the Sequence check box (for example, TIFF Sequence). If you specified a limited range of sequence to import, the dialog box also displays the range next to the Sequence check box.

5. Click Open to import the file sequence and close the dialog box.

   The image file sequence appears as a single footage item in the Project panel (**Figure 2.30**).

IMPORTING STILL-IMAGE SEQUENCES

To set the default frame rate for still-image sequences:

1. Choose After Effects > Preferences > Import (Mac) or Edit > Preferences > Import (Windows) (**Figure 2.31**).

   The Import panel of the Preferences dialog box appears.

2. In the Sequence Footage section of the Preferences dialog box, enter a frame rate (**Figure 2.32**). See Chapter 4 for more about frame rates.

3. Click OK to set the default frame rate and close the Preferences dialog box.

✔ Tip

■ Dragging a folder of stills from the operating system is another way to import the folder's contents as an image sequence. (To import separate footage items within a folder, Option-drag (Mac) or Alt-drag (Windows) the folder to the Project panel.)

Figure 2.31 Choose After Effects > Preferences > Import (Mac) or Edit > Preferences > Import (Windows).

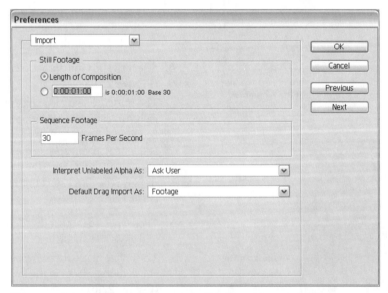

Figure 2.32 Enter a frame rate for imported still-image sequences.

Figure 2.33 Misinterpreting the type of alpha results in an unwanted halo or fringe around objects. Note the dark fringe around the letters and the darkness in the transparency.

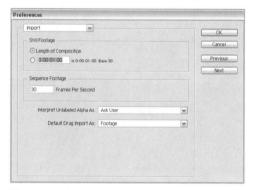

Figure 2.34 The Import panel of the Preferences dialog box appears.

Importing Files with Alpha Channels

A file containing an alpha channel can be saved in two ways: as straight alpha or as premultiplied alpha. When you import a file containing an alpha channel, After Effects tries to detect a label (encoded in the file) that indicates whether the alpha is straight or premultiplied. If the alpha is unlabeled, After Effects prompts you with an Interpret Footage dialog box where you manually select how to interpret the alpha. You may ignore the alpha; interpret it as straight, premultiplied with black, or premultiplied with white; or allow After Effects to guess the type of alpha.

If you know how you want to interpret the alpha of your imported footage, you can select a default interpretation. You can also change the interpretation of a footage file after you import it.

If you interpret the alpha channel incorrectly, footage may appear with an unwanted black or white halo or fringe around the edges of objects (**Figure 2.33**). Incorrect interpretation can also cause color inaccuracies. If you need help interpreting footage containing an alpha channel, see the sidebar "Alpha Bits: Understanding Straight and Premultiplied Alpha," later in this chapter.

To set the default alpha interpretation:

1. Choose After Effects > Preferences > Import (Mac) or Edit > Preferences > Import (Windows).

The Import panel of the Preferences dialog box appears (**Figure 2.34**).

continues on next page

2. *Choose one of the following* default interpretation methods from the Interpret Unlabeled Alpha As pull-down menu (**Figure 2.35**):

Ask User—You're prompted to choose an interpretation method each time you import footage with an unlabeled alpha channel.

Guess—After Effects attempts to automatically detect the file's alpha channel type. If After Effects can't make a confident guess, it beeps at you.

Ignore Alpha—After Effects disregards the alpha channel of imported images.

Straight (Unmatted)—After Effects interprets the alpha channel as straight alpha. Choose this option for a single Photoshop layer with an alpha or layer mask.

Premultiplied (Matted With Black)—After Effects interprets the alpha channel as premultiplied with black.

Premultiplied (Matted With White)—After Effects interprets the alpha channel as premultiplied with white. Choose this option to import merged Photoshop layers that use transparency.

3. Click OK to close the Preferences dialog box.

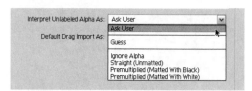

Figure 2.35 Choose a default interpretation method from the pull-down menu.

Figure 2.36 Choose File > Interpret Footage > Main.

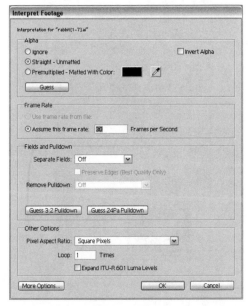

Figure 2.37 The Interpret Footage dialog box appears.

To set the alpha channel interpretation for a file in a project:

1. In the Project panel, select a file containing an alpha channel.

2. Choose File > Interpret Footage > Main (**Figure 2.36**).

   The Interpret Footage dialog box appears (**Figure 2.37**).

3. In the Alpha section of the Interpret Footage dialog box, choose an interpretation method (**Figure 2.38**).

   If the options are grayed out, the footage doesn't contain an alpha channel.

4. Click OK to close the Interpret Footage dialog box.

   continues on next page

Figure 2.38 Choose an alpha channel interpretation method from the Interpret Footage dialog box.

✔ Tips

- If an unexpected fringe or halo appears around the edges of a composited image, you should change the alpha interpretation.

- Internally, After Effects works in 32-bit depth (when a project is set to 8-bpc mode; see "Choosing the Bit-Depth Mode" earlier in this chapter). If a footage item's color space is less than this—as with a grayscale image—After Effects converts it to 32-bit depth when it displays. Similarly, if the footage doesn't contain an alpha channel, After Effects automatically supplies a full white alpha channel (which defines the image as fully opaque and visible).

Alpha Bits: Understanding Straight and Premultiplied Alpha

In 8-bit RGB color images, each channel—red, green, and blue—uses 8 bits (for a total of 24 bits), yielding millions of colors. A 32-bit file contains a fourth 8-bit channel, known as an *alpha channel*. Whereas the RGB channels define the visible color of each pixel in the image, the alpha channel defines the pixels' transparency. The alpha channel is usually depicted as a grayscale matte, where black defines a pixel as transparent, white as opaque, and gray as semitransparent. After Effects and other programs can use the alpha channel to make parts of an image transparent—a familiar concept to users of these programs (**Figure 2.39**).

continues on next page

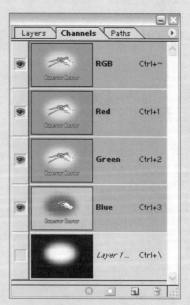

Figure 2.39 The channels of a 32-bit image, as viewed in Photoshop.

Alpha Bits: Understanding Straight and Premultiplied Alpha *(continued)*

Less widely known, however, is the fact that you can save files containing an alpha channel in two ways: as *straight alpha* or as *premultiplied alpha*. The alpha is the same in both types of files; however, the files differ in the way they factor visible channels into the transparency information.

A file saved with a *straight alpha* channel stores transparency information strictly in the alpha channel, not in any of the visible color channels. Ordinarily, you see the RGB channels combined, or multiplied, with the alpha channel. In After Effects, however, you can see the color information without the alpha channel (or an *unmultiplied* RGB image) by Shift-clicking the channel switch. Because the RGB channels don't take into account the transparency information, the color information bleeds across areas that the alpha channel defines as semitransparent. The all-or-nothing RGB channels of a straight alpha image look bad by themselves, but when they're combined with the

alpha channel, transparent areas and soft edges are perfectly represented (**Figures 2.40**, **2.41**, and **2.42**). Incorrectly interpreting a straight alpha as premultiplied causes semitransparent objects to appear more opaque and brighter than they should.

continues on next page

Figure 2.40 The RGB channels of an image with a straight alpha don't factor in transparency. If you Shift-click the alpha switch, you can see how the unmultiplied color information bleeds across transparent areas.

Figure 2.41 An image with a straight alpha stores transparency information strictly in the alpha channel. You can view the alpha channel if you click the alpha switch.

Figure 2.42 In the final composite, the RGB and the alpha channel create smooth edges and transparencies.

Alpha Bits: Understanding Straight and Premultiplied Alpha *(continued)*

A file saved with a *premultiplied alpha* also stores transparency values in the alpha channel. However, the RGB channels take the transparency information into account as well. In semitransparent areas (including antialiased edges), the RGB channels are mixed—or *multiplied*—with the background color (usually black or white). Instead of bleeding across transparent areas, the RGB colors fade to the background color according to the amount of transparency. This is why incorrectly interpreting a premultiplied alpha as straight causes objects to appear with a black or white halo or fringe around them.

After Effects correctly interprets premultiplied alpha by unmultiplying, or removing, the background color before it composites the image (**Figures 2.43**, **2.44**, and **2.45**).

Although it achieves great results from footage using either kind of alpha, After Effects works internally with straight alpha.

Because straight alpha is native to After Effects, many consider it to be more precise—and more desirable—than premultiplied alpha.

Straight alpha is also known as *unmatted alpha*. Premultiplied alpha is also called *matted*, or *preshaped*, alpha.

Figure 2.43 In an image with premultiplied alpha, RGB colors are mixed with a background color according to the amount of transparency. Correctly interpreted, transparent areas composite smoothly.

Figure 2.44 Incorrectly interpreting the alpha as matted with white results in a dark halo, revealing how the colors are matted with black.

Figure 2.45 Incorrectly interpreting the alpha as straight has a similar effect.

Photoshop and Illustrator Files

Not surprisingly, After Effects fully embraces files generated by its Adobe siblings, Photoshop and Illustrator. After Effects not only accepts the standard single-layer file types (PCT, TIF, EPS, Filmstrip, and so on) but also supports layered Photoshop and Illustrator files.

After Effects can import Photoshop and Illustrator files as individual layers, as merged layers, or as a layered composition. After Effects preserves practically every aspect of your Photoshop work, including position, transfer modes, opacity, layer masks, clipping groups, adjustment layers, and layer effects. After Effects even preserves vector masks created in Photoshop. And, as pointed out earlier in this chapter, you can import Photoshop images saved with 16 or 32 bpc when you use the Professional version of After Effects.

When you import an Illustrator or EPS file, After Effects automatically converts text to paths, creates alpha channels from empty areas, and antialiases the edges of the artwork. After Effects also lets you control how it rasterizes your artwork in order to preserve smooth edges at any scale. Just as After Effects has kept pace with the latest innovations in Photoshop, it also supports the transparency settings and transfer modes created for Illustrator.

In addition, After Effects allows you to copy a path from Illustrator or Photoshop and paste it directly as an After Effects mask. (See Chapter 10, "Mask Essentials," for more on copying paths.)

If these features don't mean much to you yet, don't worry. Their advantages will become apparent as you transfer your work seamlessly from one program to the other. The following sections cover the basics of importing Photoshop and Illustrator files. Future chapters show you how to take advantage of that footage once it's in your After Effects composition.

PHOTOSHOP AND ILLUSTRATOR FILES

Importing a Layered File as a Single Footage Item

When you import a layered Photoshop or Illustrator file as a footage item, you can either import all the layers as a single merged item or import layers individually. Naturally, importing the merged file results in a footage item with the same dimensions of the source file (**Figure 2.46**).

However, when you import individual layers, you have a choice. You can import the layer at the document's dimensions so that the layer appears as it did in the context of the other layers (**Figure 2.47**). On the other hand, you can choose to use the layer's dimensions—that is, the size of the layer only, regardless of the document's size (**Figure 2.48**). (Of course, After Effects can also import all the layers assembled just as they were in Photoshop or Illustrator; you'll learn that technique in the following section.)

To import a Photoshop or Illustrator file or layer as a single footage item:

1. Choose File > Import > File.

   The Import File dialog box appears.

2. Locate and select a Photoshop or Illustrator file.

Figure 2.46 You can import a layered file so that the layers are merged into a single footage item that uses the source document's dimensions.

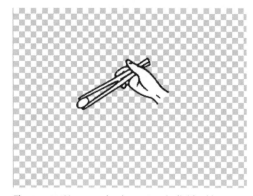

Figure 2.47 You can also import an individual layer using either the dimensions of the document (in this case, 720x486)...

Figure 2.48 ...or the minimum dimensions to contain the layer's image (this layer is 228x142).

Figure 2.49 In the Import File dialog box, locate a Photoshop or Illustrator file and be sure Footage is selected in the Import As pull-down menu.

Figure 2.50 You can choose to import a single layer of a Photoshop or Illustrator file or to import merged layers.

3. Make sure Footage is selected in the Import As pull-down menu, and then click Open (**Figure 2.49**).

The Import Photoshop/Illustrator dialog box appears. The dialog box has the same name as the file you're importing.

4. In the dialog box's Import Kind pull-down menu, make sure Footage is selected.

5. In the Layer Options area, *do either of the following* (**Figure 2.50**):

▲ Choose Merged Layers to import all layers in the file as a single footage item in After Effects.

▲ Select Choose Layer. Then, in the pull-down menu, choose a layer to import.

6. If you chose a single layer in step 5, specify an option in the Footage Dimensions pull-down menu (**Figure 2.51**):

Layer Size—Imports the layer at its native size. Choose this option when you plan to use the layer outside the context of the other layers in the file.

Document Size—Imports the layer using the frame size of the document that contains the layer. Choose this option to maintain the layer's size and position relative to the document as a whole.

7. Click OK to close the dialog box.

A footage item appears in the Project panel. When you import a single layer, the name of the footage item is the name of the layer followed by the name of the Photoshop or Illustrator file. When you import merged layers, the name of the footage item is the name of the Photoshop or Illustrator file (**Figure 2.52**).

continues on next page

✔ Tips

- Dragging a file directly from the Finder or Explorer imports it either as a footage item or as a composition, depending on the option you choose in the Import panel of the Preferences dialog box.

- A single Photoshop layer with a layer mask uses straight alpha.

- When you import a layered Photoshop file as a merged layer, transparent areas of all layers are merged into a single alpha channel premultiplied with white.

- Empty areas of Illustrator artwork are converted into straight alpha.

- Although After Effects can import Illustrator files in the CMYK color space, you should convert them to RGB first.

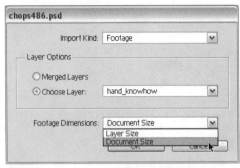

Figure 2.51 If you chose to import a single layer, specify an option in the Footage Dimensions pulldown menu.

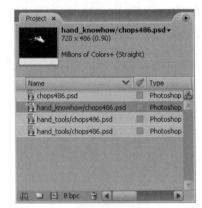

Figure 2.52 In the Project panel, single and merged Photoshop or Illustrator layers are clearly named.

Figure 2.53 After Effects can convert a layered file into a composition containing the same layers. This way, you can manipulate each layer individually in After Effects.

Figure 2.54 When you choose Composition-Cropped Layers, the imported footage includes the image only—in this case, the footage's dimensions are 314 x 125.

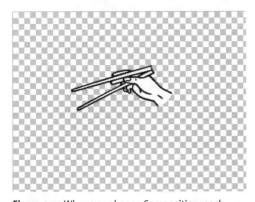

Figure 2.55 When you choose Composition, each layer uses the source document's dimensions—which, of course, match those of the imported composition. In this example, the source file's and comp's dimensions are 720 x 846.

Importing a Layered File as a Composition

One of After Effects' greatest strengths is its ability to import a layered Photoshop or Illustrator file as a ready-made composition—which, as you'll recall from Chapter 1, consists of footage items arranged in time and space. After Effects not only imports all the layers as footage items but also arranges the layers in a composition of the same dimensions. In essence, the composition replicates the layered file—suddenly transported into the world of After Effects (**Figure 2.53**).

As when you import layers separately (see "Importing a Layered File as a Single Footage Item," earlier in this chapter), you can choose whether the imported footage items (conveniently located in their own folder) use their native dimensions or share the new comp's dimensions (**Figures 2.54** and **2.55**).

To import an Adobe Photoshop or Illustrator file as a composition:

1. Choose File > Import > File (**Figure 2.56**). The Import File dialog box appears.

2. Select an Adobe Photoshop or Illustrator file.

3. In the Import As pull-down menu, *choose either of the following* (**Figure 2.57**):

Composition - Cropped Layers— Imports each source layer at its native size

Composition—Imports each source layer at the document's size

4. Click Import.

In the Project panel, the imported Photoshop or Illustrator file appears both as a composition and as a folder containing the individual layers imported as separate footage items (**Figure 2.58**).

✔ Tip

■ After Effects imports Photoshop clipping groups as nested compositions within the main composition of the Photoshop file. After Effects automatically applies the Preserve Underlying Transparency option to each layer in the clipping group.

Figure 2.56 Choose File > Import > File.

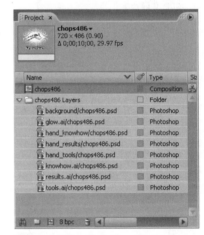

Figure 2.58 The Photoshop file appears both as a composition and as a folder containing individual layers.

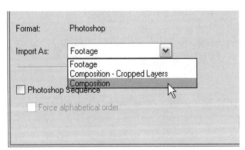

Figure 2.57 In the Import As pull-down menu of the Import File dialog box, choose the appropriate option.

Importing Premiere Pro and After Effects Projects

Because After Effects can import projects from Premiere Pro, it's simple to move work from Adobe's nonlinear editor for treatment in the company's advanced animation/compositing/effects program (and vice versa).

Each sequence in the Premiere Pro project appears in After Effects as a composition (in which each clip is a layer) and a folder of clips. In the composition, After Effects preserves the clip order, duration, and In and Out points, as well as marker and transition locations (**Figures 2.59** and **2.60**). Because Premiere Pro includes many After Effects filters, any effects shared by the two programs will also be transferred from Premiere Pro into After Effects—including their keyframes.

You'll learn more about compositions in Chapter 4, "Compositions"; more about keyframes in Chapter 7, "Properties and Keyframes"; and more about effects in Chapter 11, "Effects Fundamentals." For the moment, suffice it to say that you can easily integrate Premiere Pro's advantages in nonlinear editing with After Effects' superior compositing and effects features.

Similarly, you can import an After Effects project into your current project—a capability that makes it possible to combine work, create complex sequences as different modules, and repeat complex effects. All the elements of an imported After Effects project are contained in a folder in the current project.

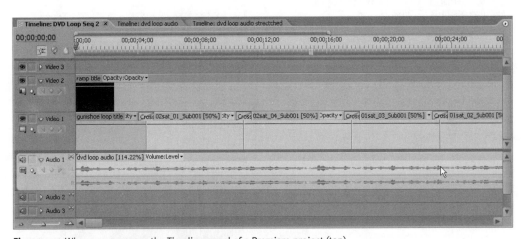

Figure 2.59 When you compare the Timeline panel of a Premiere project (top)...

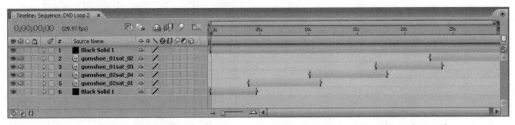

Figure 2.60 ...you can see how clips translate into layers in the Timeline panel of After Effects (bottom).

To import an Adobe Premiere Pro project:

1. Choose File > Import > File.

   The Import File dialog box appears.

2. Select a Premiere Pro project file (**Figure 2.61**).

   After Effects recognizes the file type automatically and selects Composition from the Import As pull-down menu.

3. Click Open.

   An Import Project dialog box appears.

4. Select the Premiere Pro sequences you want to import as compositions (**Figure 2.62**).

5. To import the audio clips in the selected sequences as audio footage items, select Import Audio. Leave the option unselected to omit the audio.

   The Premiere Pro project appears in the Project panel as a composition. Clips appear as footage items, and bins appear as folders (**Figure 2.63**). An After Effects project appears in the Project panel as a folder containing compositions and footage items.

Figure 2.61 In the Import File dialog box, locate a Premiere Pro project and click Open.

Figure 2.62 Specify the Premiere Pro sequences you want to import as compositions in After Effects, and select whether you want to include audio.

Figure 2.63 An imported Premiere Pro sequence appears in the Project panel as a composition. Clips appear as footage items, and bins appear as folders.

✔ Tips

- The dynamic link feature allows After Effects to reflect changes you make in Premiere Pro and vice versa.

- You can embed any movie exported from After Effects with a *program link*—which, as its name implies, is a link to the program that created it. This way, it's easy to reopen the project that created the movie. For more about embedding program links, see Chapter 17, "Output."

- Like After Effects projects, Premiere Pro projects only refer to source files; they don't contain them. These source files must be available on a local storage device in order to be played back. If a file is unavailable, you can use a placeholder or proxy to substitute temporarily for the source file. For more about placeholders and proxies, see Chapter 3, "Managing Footage."

- To use a complex effect from another project, import the project and replace the source footage. Doing so will retain the effect you created before, but with different footage. See Chapter 3 for more about replacing footage.

Importing With Adobe Bridge

Chances are, you've accumulated a seemingly countless number of assets on your hard disks. It can be a chore to find the one you need. Fortunately, After Effects and other Adobe programs ship with a companion program—a research assistant, if you will—called Adobe Bridge.

Bridge facilitates asset management by providing a convenient way to search for, sift, and preview files. Bridge also lets you see information embedded in the file, or *metadata*. You can even apply your own metadata, label, rating, and keywords to a file, adding ways to distinguish the needle from the rest of the haystack (**Figure 2.64**).

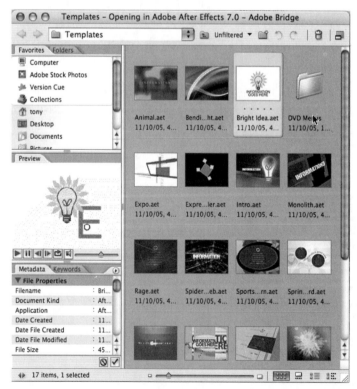

Figure 2.64 Bridge is a companion program that facilitates file management. It can help you locate and preview the file you need, including preset projects (selected here)...

Bridge also provides a great access point to numerous preset project templates. Even if you don't use these ready-made projects as templates per se, they demonstrate useful techniques and provide inspiration for your own work (**Figure 2.65**).

Naturally, this book can't cover all the features of another full-fledged program; this section focuses on browsing and importing using Bridge. Fortunately, you should get the hang of Bridge's familiar and intuitive interface with a little experimentation and a quick visit to its Help system.

Figure 2.65 ...that you can use as a template, or simply as an instructional tool or source of inspiration.

To import a file or project template using Bridge:

1. *Do either of the following:*

▲ To open any file, choose File > Browse.

▲ To navigate to project templates directly, choose File > Browse Template Projects (**Figure 2.66**).

After Effects launches its companion program, Adobe Bridge.

2. To navigate to the file you want to view, *do either of the following:*

▲ Use the navigation tools at upper right of the Bridge window to select a disk volume or folder (**Figure 2.67**).

▲ Select an item in the Favorites or Folders tab (**Figure 2.68**).

The selected item's content appears in Bridge's large main panel. You can also open a folder by double-clicking it in the main panel. (The appearance of items in the main panel depends on the position of the icon size and viewing mode, which you can set using controls at lower right of the window.)

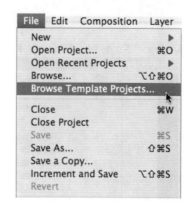

Figure 2.66 To find any file using Bridge, choose File > Browse; to go straight to project templates, choose File > Browse Template Projects (shown here).

Show Previous Folder or Volume   *Show Next Folder or Volume*   *Select item in the pull-down menu*   *Go up one level in the hierarchy*

Figure 2.67 In Bridge, navigate using the browser-style navigation tools at the top of the window...

Figure 2.68 ...or select an item in the Favorites or Folders tab.

Figure 2.69 The selected item appears in the Preview tab; additional information appears in the Metadata and Keywords tabs.

3. To view a preview image and other information about the item, select the item.

   The item's image appears in Bridge's Preview tab. Motion footage and templates include standard playback controls. The item's metadata and keywords appear in the corresponding tabbed areas (**Figure 2.69**).

4. In the Bridge's main panel, double-click the item you want to import (**Figure 2.70**).

   After Effects may prompt you to specify options according to the type of item you import. (Refer to the section in this chapter pertaining to the file type.) The item appears in After Effects' Project panel (**Figure 2.71**).

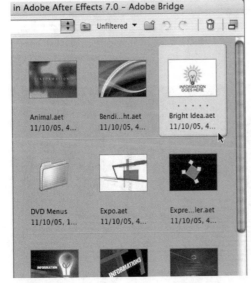

Figure 2.70 Double-clicking the item in Bridge's main panel...

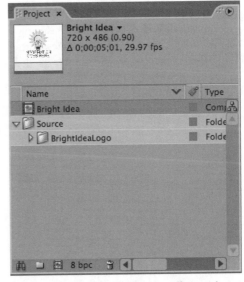

Figure 2.71 ...imports it into the After Effects project.

Working the Fields: Interlaced Video

Video is displayed using either of two different methods: a progressive scan or as interlaced fields.

In a *progressive scan*, the horizontal lines of each frame are displayed (progressively) from the top of the frame to the bottom, in a single pass (**Figure 2.72**).

Interlaced video divides each frame of video into two fields. Each field includes every other horizontal line (*scan line*) in the frame. One field is displayed first, drawn as alternating lines from the top of the image to the bottom (**Figure 2.73**). Starting from the top again, the alternate field is displayed, filling in the gaps to complete the frame (**Figure 2.74**).

The field that contains the topmost scan line is called *field 1*, the *odd field*, or the *upper field*. The other field is known as *field 2*, the *even field*, or the *lower field*. Your video equipment and the settings you choose determine which field is the *dominant field*—that is, the one displayed first.

Computer monitors display images using a progressive scan. Higher-end video monitors also support progressive scan (provided they're connected to video sources that deliver it). But most television is still recorded and presented using interlaced fields.

Figure 2.72 In a progressive scan, the complete image is drawn in a single pass.

Figure 2.73 Interlaced video presents a single field that includes every other line of the image...

Figure 2.74 ...and then interlaces the opposite field to create the full frame.

Figure 2.75 Select a footage item that uses interlaced video fields.

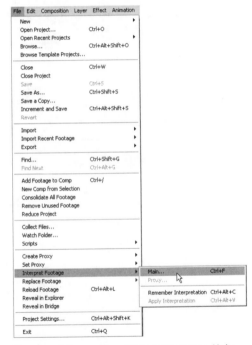

Figure 2.76 Choose File > Interpret Footage > Main.

Interpreting Interlaced Video

When you import interlaced video, After Effects must correctly interpret the field order to play back the video accurately. If the fields are presented in the wrong order, movement appears staggered.

To interpret fields in video footage:

1. In the Project panel, select an interlaced video or field-rendered footage item (**Figure 2.75**).

2. Choose File > Interpret Footage > Main (**Figure 2.76**), or press Command-F (Mac) or Ctrl-F (Windows).

   The Interpret Footage dialog box opens (**Figure 2.77**).

   continues on next page

3. In the Fields and Pull-Down section, *select one of the following* options from the Separate Fields pull-down menu (**Figure 2.78**):

Off—After Effects won't separate fields. Use this option for footage that doesn't contain interlaced video fields.

Upper Field First—The fields of upper-field dominant source files will be separated correctly.

Lower Field First—The fields of lower-field dominant source files will be separated correctly.

4. Click OK to close the Interpret Footage dialog box.

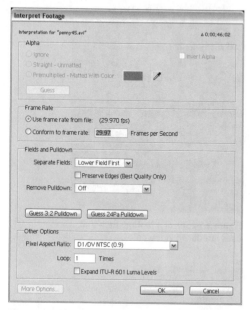

Figure 2.77 The Interpret Footage dialog box opens.

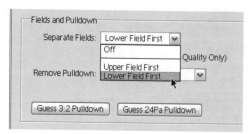

Figure 2.78 Choose the correct field dominance from the pull-down menu.

Motion Footage

Motion footage sources include video digitized from analog video sources (such as Hi8 or Betacam SP), digital video (such as DV transferred via FireWire or USB 2, or Digital Betacam via SDI), and film (scanned as Cineon files or transferred to video using 3:2 pulldown).

The process of importing motion footage varies little from the process of importing other types of files. But, as you've already learned, After Effects must interpret different formats according to their attributes and your requirements. In the following sections, you'll learn about the Interpret Footage command that's used to correctly identify motion footage's frame rate, field order, 3:2 pulldown, and pixel aspect ratio. The Interpret Footage command also enables you to automatically loop footage and set the display quality of EPS footage files. You can even learn to edit After Effects' internal settings.

✔ Tips

- You import audio-only files into an After Effects project just as you would any other file. Video footage that has audio can be imported as a single footage item.

- If your final output is destined for computer display only (not video display), or if it will be displayed at less than full screen size, you should deinterlace the video before you import it. Doing so spares you from separating fields in After Effects and from processing unnecessary information.

- In the sections to follow, you'll use the Interpret Footage dialog box to help After Effects properly interpret a footage item's attributes. You can copy the settings from one item by choosing File > Interpret Footage > Remember Interpolation, and apply it to another item by selecting it and choosing File > Interpret Footage > Apply Interpolation.

- You can customize the rules After Effects uses to interpret footage automatically by modifying the Interpretation Rules.txt file (contained in the After Effects folder) in a text-editing program. This way, you can determine, for example, the default pixel aspect ratio applied to footage items of certain dimensions. For more information, see the Adobe After Effects User Guide and Help System.

MOTION FOOTAGE

Setting the Frame Rate

Generally, you use the footage's native frame rate, which also matches the frame rate of the composition. Sometimes, however, you'll want to specify a frame rate for a footage item manually.

Because features like time stretch (see Chapter 6, "Layer Editing") and time remapping (see Chapter 14, "More Layer Techniques") provide finer control over a layer's playback speed, it's more common to set the frame rate for image sequences than for movie files.

For example, some animations are designed to play back at 10 fps. If you interpreted such a sequence to match a 30-fps composition, 30 frames would play back in one second— three times as fast as they were intended to play. Manually specifying a 10-fps frame rate for a still-image sequence of 30 frames would result in a duration of three seconds when played in a 30-fps composition.

Conversely, many programs can't render interlaced video frames. Sometimes animators choose to render 60 fps, which can be interpreted at a higher frame rate and interlaced at output.

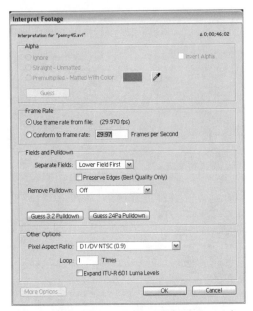

Figure 2.79 The Interpret Footage dialog box contains controls to set the frame rate of footage.

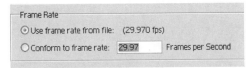

Figure 2.80 You can set movie footage to conform to a different frame rate. Note that the dialog box uses the term conform when referring to motion footage.

Figure 2.81 More often, you use the control to set the frame rate of still-image sequences. Note that the dialog box says "Assume this frame rate" when interpreting still-image sequences.

To set the frame rate for footage:

1. In the Project panel, select a footage item.

2. Choose File > Interpret Footage > Main, or press Command-F (Mac) or Ctrl-F (Windows).

   The Interpret Footage dialog box appears (**Figure 2.79**).

3. For motion footage, *choose one of the following* options in the Frame Rate section (**Figure 2.80**):

   Use frame rate from file—Uses the native frame rate of the footage item

   Conform to frame rate—Lets you enter a custom frame rate for the footage

   Using a frame rate that differs from the original changes the playback speed of the movie.

4. For image sequences, enter a frame rate next to "Assume this frame rate" in the Frame Rate section of the Interpret Footage dialog box (**Figure 2.81**).

5. Click OK to close the Interpret Footage dialog box.

✔ Tip

■ To interpret 60-fps animation sequences for output as interlaced fields, enter 59.94 in the "Assume this frame rate" field and use the footage item in a full-frame, 29.97-fps composition. Be sure to field-render the output. See Chapter 16, "Complex Projects," for more about rendering compositions.

Looping Footage

Often, you need footage to loop continuously. Rather than add a footage item to a composition multiple times, you can set the footage item to loop using the Interpret Footage dialog box.

To loop footage:

1. In the Project panel, select a footage item you want to loop.

2. Choose File > Interpret Footage > Main, or press Command-F (Mac) or Ctrl-F (Windows).

   The Interpret Footage dialog box appears (**Figure 2.82**).

3. In the Other Options section, enter the number of times you want the footage to loop (**Figure 2.83**).

   You may only enter integers for complete cycles, not decimals for partial cycles. When you add the footage item to a composition as a layer, its duration reflects the Loop setting.

✔ Tip

- The Loop setting loops the content of the footage, not the movement of a layer—it's useful for turning an animation of two steps into a long walk, for example. You can't use this setting to repeat animated properties. For that, you'll need to use keyframes (Chapter 7) or expressions (Chapter 16).

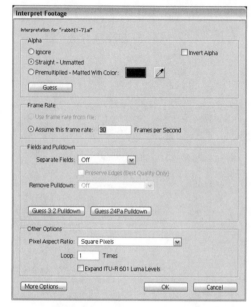

Figure 2.82 The Interpret Footage dialog box contains controls that allow you to loop a footage item (without repeating it in the composition).

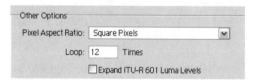

Figure 2.83 Enter the number of times you want the footage item to loop.

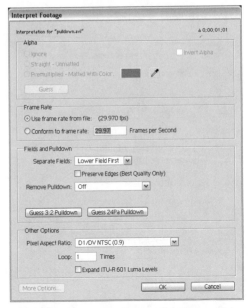

Figure 2.84 The Interpret Footage dialog box contains controls that allow you to remove 3:2 pulldown from a footage item.

Removing Film 3:2 Pulldown and 24Pa Pulldown

Film transferred to video presents special challenges in post-production. One of the most common issues arises from the difference in frame rates: Film plays at 24 fps (full frames); NTSC video plays at about 29.97 fps (interlaced fields). When film is transferred to video, a process called *3:2 pulldown* compensates for the difference in frame rates. In this process, one second of video plays back one second of film footage. (See the sidebar "The Lowdown on Pulldown: 3:2 Pulldown," later in this chapter.)

However, if your final output is destined for film, you should remove 3:2 pulldown from video footage to ensure that your After Effects work will synchronize frames accurately at film's 24 fps. By reducing the number of frames you have to process from 30 fps to 24 fps, you also decrease your work and the time required for rendering.

Similarly, footage shot in the 24P (24 fps progressive scan) format undergoes a pulldown process. As the sidebar "Pulldown for 24P Video" explains in detail, 24P footage is pulled down using either a normal or advanced method. Just as you'd remove 3:2 pulldown from video transferred from film, you should remove 24Pa pulldown in order to restore footage to 24 progressive frames for effects work.

To remove 3:2 or 24Pa pulldown:

1. In the Project panel, select the footage item transferred from film using 3:2 pulldown or from progressive-scan video using 24Pa pulldown.

2. Choose File > Interpret Footage > Main, or press Command-F (Mac) or Ctrl-F (Windows).

   The Interpret Footage dialog box appears (**Figure 2.84**).

3. In the Fields and Pulldown section, select the appropriate field dominance (Upper or Lower), as described previously.

4. In the Fields and Pulldown section, *do one of the following*:

   ▲ Click Guess 3:2 Pulldown if you want After Effects to determine automatically the correct phase in which to remove 3:2 pulldown (**Figure 2.85**).

   ▲ Click Guess 24Pa Pulldown if you want After Effects to determine automatically the correct phase in which to remove 24Pa pulldown.

   ▲ If you know the phase of the pulldown method, choose the correct phase from the Remove Pulldown pull-down menu (**Figure 2.86**).

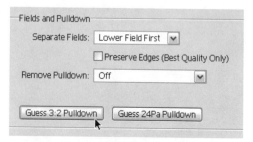

Figure 2.85 Click Guess 3:2 Pulldown to have After Effects determine the pulldown.

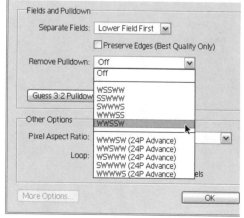

Figure 2.86 If you know the pulldown phase, select it in the Remove Pulldown pull-down menu.

REMOVING FILM PULLDOWN

The Lowdown on Pulldown: 3:2 Pulldown

In 3:2 pulldown, frames of film are transferred to fields of video in a 3:2 pattern—that is, one frame of film is transferred to three fields of video, and the next frame of film is transferred to two fields of video. As this 3:2 pattern repeats, every four frames of film get distributed across five frames of video in a consistent pattern of whole frames and split-field frames. In *whole frames*, both video fields are drawn from the same film frame. In *split-field frames*, each video field is drawn from two different film frames. The pattern of whole frames and split frames in the first five frames of video determines the *phase* (**Figure 2.87**). There are five possible phase

patterns, which are distinguished by the relative position of the two adjacent split-field (S) frames. When you remove pulldown, After Effects can detect the phase, or you can select it manually (**Figure 2.88**).

"Hold on," you say, "this process translates 24 fps to 60 fields per second. That's 30 fps, not 29.97 fps." You're right! Before the frames are distributed using the 3:2 scheme, the film is slowed down by .1 percent to compensate for the difference between 29.97 fps and 30 fps (go ahead and do the math). Remember this when you do your audio post!

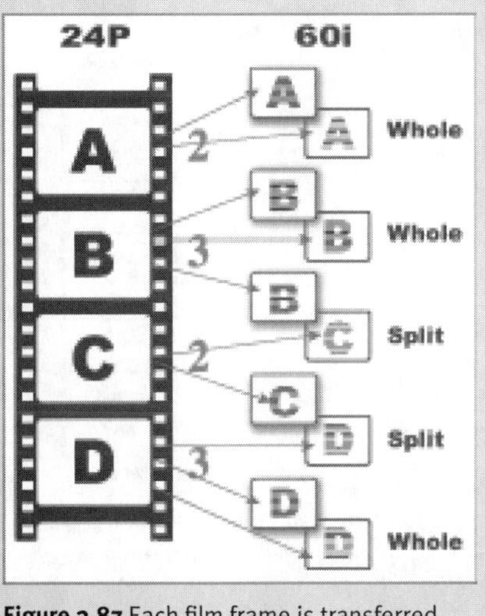

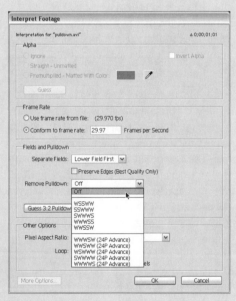

Figure 2.87 Each film frame is transferred to either three or two fields of video. This results in a five-frame pattern, or phase, of whole frames and split-field frames of video. The phase pictured here is described as WWSSW.

Figure 2.88 The Remove Pulldown pull-down menu in the Interpret Footage dialog box lists the possible phases, or patterns, of whole frames (W) and split-field frames (S).

Pulldown for 24P Video

Nowadays, video is no longer restricted to the timeworn NTSC and PAL standards for image size and frame rate. To facilitate video-to-film transfers (or at least to achieve a film look), some video cameras can shoot in 24P—that is, at 24 progressive frames per second. (For more about progressive and interlaced video, see the sidebar "Working the Fields," earlier in this chapter.) Once only available in expensive high-end equipment, 24P has recently found its way into much more affordable "prosumer" level cameras, such as Panasonic's DVX100 (aka DVX100P; the *P* stands for Panasonic, not *progressive* or *PAL*).

But although a camera like the DVX100 can shoot 24P, it stores the video on tape using the familiar 60 interlaced fields per second (60i). It does so using either of two pulldown schemes, known as *standard* and *advanced*.

Standard pulldown uses the same method as film pulldown, distributing 24P to 60i using a 3:2 cadence (explained in the sidebar "The Lowdown on Pulldown," earlier in this chapter). The downside to this method becomes apparent when it's time to convert 60i back to 24P. As you can see in **Figure 2.89**, three out of every four progressive frames—A, B, and D in the diagram—are reconstructed from two fields in the same frame, or whole frames. The C frame, on the other hand, must consist of fields from different frames, or split frames. As a result, these frames must be processed differently

than the others. Unlike the whole frames, the split frames must be decompressed to retrieve the proper fields—which, as you can see, must be reversed to match the field order of the other frames. And because fields extracted from the two split frames differ more than fields taken from whole frames, they're compressed less efficiently when they're combined into a new progressive frame. In short, not all the frames are restored to 24P unscathed.

continues on next page

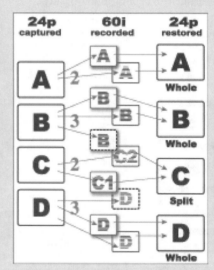

Figure 2.89 Using standard pulldown, certain frames must be reconstructed out of fields from different frames, which requires more processing. In the figure, you can see that the restored frame C must be created from field 2 of one frame and field 1 from the subsequent frame.

Pulldown for 24P Video *(continued)*

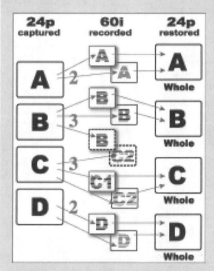

Figure 2.90 With advanced pulldown, all of the frames are restored to 24p using the same clean method.

Advanced pulldown, often referred to as 24Pa, uses a 2:3:3:2 cadence. As you can see in **Figure 2.90**, this pattern permits every 24P frame to be restored from whole 60i frames. This process not only converts all frames using a consistent method but also averts problems associated with processing fields from two split frames.

But you may ask, "Why introduce pulldown at all?" When you use a camera like the DVX100, pulldown permits you to shoot DV at 24P and capture and edit in a DV-native application. You gain this advantage regardless of which pulldown mode you select. Generally speaking, shooting with standard pulldown helps achieve a film look on video. To make the smoothest video-to-film transfer, select advanced pulldown when you shoot. Naturally, you should remove advanced pulldown for effects work (particularly compositing and rotoscoping) in After Effects.

Pixel Aspect Ratios

Generally, computer systems display images using square pixels (a 1:1 pixel aspect ratio, or 1.0 PAR). However, many formats, including common standards like D1 and DV, use nonsquare pixels to represent images. If you display nonsquare pixels on a square-pixel monitor, the image appears distorted. Luckily, After Effects can compensate for the difference between standards so you can use both in the same composition and output them without distortion.

After Effects automatically interprets D1 (720 × 486) and DV (720 × 480) footage to compensate correctly for their pixel aspect ratios. Nevertheless, you should check to see that your footage is interpreted correctly, and you should understand how to set the PAR for other standards. (You can even manually customize how the program automatically interprets footage; see the Help System for more about editing the interpretation rules file.)

To interpret the pixel aspect ratio:

1. In the Project panel, select a footage item.

2. Choose File > Interpret Footage > Main, or press Command-F (Mac) or Ctrl-F (Windows).

The Interpret Footage dialog box appears.

3. In the Other Options section, choose the appropriate Pixel Aspect Ratio setting for your footage (**Figure 2.91**):

Square Pixels—1.0 PAR. Use for footage with a frame size of 640 × 480 or 648 × 486 and a 4:3 image aspect ratio.

D1/DV NTSC—.9 PAR. Use for footage with a frame size o f 720 × 486 (D1) or 720 × 480 (DV) and a 4:3 image aspect ratio.

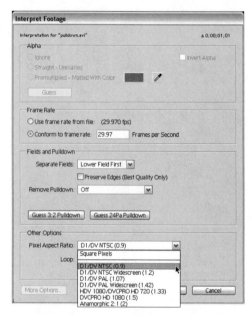

Figure 2.91 In the Interpret Footage dialog box, choose the appropriate pixel aspect ratio. Most computer monitors use square pixels to represent an image with a 4:3 aspect ratio.

D1/DV NTSC Widescreen—1.2 PAR. Use for footage with a frame size of 720 × 486 (D1) or 720 × 480 (DV) to achieve a 16:9 image aspect ratio in standard definition.

D1/DV PAL—1.0666 PAR. Use for footage with a 720 × 576 (PAL) frame size and a 4:3 image aspect ratio.

D1/DV PAL Widescreen—1.422 PAR. Use for footage with a 720 × 576 (PAL) frame size and a 16:9 image aspect ratio in standard definition.

Anamorphic 2:1—2.0 PAR. Use for footage shot with a 2:1 anamorphic film lens.

D4/D16 Standard—.9481481 PAR. Use for footage with a 1440 × 1024 or 2880 × 2048 image size and a 4:3 image aspect ratio.

D4/D16 Anamorphic—1.8962962 PAR. Use for footage with a 1440 × 1024 or 2880 × 2048 image size and an 8:3 image aspect ratio.

✔ Tips

■ If you import a square-pixel image that uses a frame size common to D1 (720 × 486) or DV (720 × 480), After Effects automatically (and incorrectly) interprets that image as using nonsquare pixels. This happens because After Effects' default interpretation rules are set to assume images that use these dimensions use a PAR of .9 . Use the Interpret Footage dialog box to change the pixel aspect ratio setting.

■ To preview compositions that use nonsquare pixel aspect ratios without distortion, you can choose Pixel Aspect Correction from the Composition panel's pull-down menu. See Chapter 4 for more information.

PIXEL ASPECT RATIOS

PAR Excellence: Pixel Aspect Ratios

Image aspect ratio refers to the dimensions of the video frame, expressed as a ratio between the width and the height (horizontal and vertical aspects) of the image. Although most video uses a 4:3 aspect ratio, a more film-like 16:9 aspect ratio is gradually becoming common.

Pixel aspect ratio (PAR) refers to the dimensions of each pixel used to create the image frame. Although some formats share the same image aspect ratio, they use different pixel aspect ratios (**Figures 2.92** and **2.93**). Images appear distorted when the PAR of the footage doesn't match the PAR of the display. Footage in professional video's D1 looks distorted when displayed on a typical computer monitor, which displays square pixels (**Figure 2.94**). Conversely, a 640 × 480 square-pixel image appears distorted when viewed or output at D1 resolution.

By using After Effects' Interpret Footage command, you can compensate for differences among formats, so that they display properly in the composition and in the final output.

When you create square-pixel footage for D1 or DV output, using the following image sizes lets you create the image without distortion:

FORMAT FOR OUTPUT	CREATE IMAGE AT	INTERPRET AS
D1	720 × 540	NTSC D1 720 × 486
DV	720 × 534	NTSC DV 720 × 480

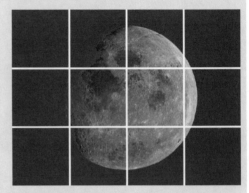

Figure 2.92 Most computer monitors use square pixels to represent an image with a 4:3 aspect ratio.

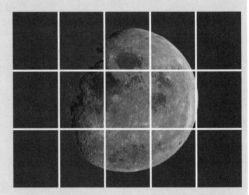

Figure 2.93 Some television standards, such as D1 and DV, use nonsquare pixels to achieve a 4:3 aspect ratio.

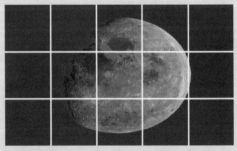

Figure 2.94 If you don't compensate for the difference between the PAR of the image and the PAR of the display, the image will appear distorted.

Figure 2.95 In the Project panel, select an EPS footage item.

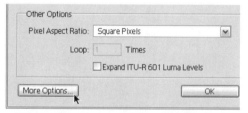

Figure 2.96 In the Interpret Footage dialog box, click More Options to access options for rasterizing EPS files.

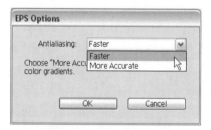

Figure 2.97 In the EPS Options dialog box, choose an option from the pull-down menu.

Setting the EPS Options

As long as you're getting familiar with the Interpret Footage dialog box, there's one more option to explore—and that's, well, Options. The Options button gives you access to an EPS Options dialog box that allows you to control the rasterization method used for EPS images. You can choose between a fast but lower-quality method and a slower but more accurate method. To learn more about rasterization, see the "Rasterization" sidebar in Chapter 5, "Layer Basics."

To set the EPS options:

1. In the Project panel, select an EPS footage item (**Figure 2.95**).

2. Choose File > Interpret Footage > Main, or press Command-F (Mac) or Ctrl-F (Windows).

   The Interpret Footage dialog box appears.

3. Click the More Options button (**Figure 2.96**).

   The EPS Options dialog box appears.

4. *Choose either of the following options* (**Figure 2.97**):

   Faster—After Effects will rasterize the footage more quickly but won't be able to represent smooth edges and color gradients as accurately.

   More Accurate—With this slower method, you're less likely to have rough or hard edges on objects and color banding in gradients.

5. Click OK to close the dialog box.

MANAGING FOOTAGE

As you saw in the previous chapter, the Project panel is basically a list of all your footage and compositions. The more complex the project, the lengthier and more unwieldy this list becomes. As the receptacle of this essential information, the Project panel can resemble either a cluttered junk drawer or a neat filing cabinet, a cardboard box filled with books or the Library of Congress. In this chapter, you'll learn how to use the Project panel to organize and sort the items contained in your project. You'll also learn about other aspects of asset management—such as how to replace missing footage, and how to use placeholders and proxies to temporarily stand in for footage items. As always, taking a little time to prepare will save you a lot of time in the long run.

This chapter also introduces you to the Footage panel, which lets you not only see your footage but really scrutinize it. Most of the controls in the Footage panel are also found in the Composition and Layer panels, which means that learning these controls now will go a long way toward providing the grounding you need later.

The Footage panel also includes editing buttons; however, an in-depth explanation of those features will wait for Chapter 4, "Compositions," where you'll learn how to add footage as layers in a composition.

Displaying Information in the Project Panel

The Project panel (**Figure 3.1**) furnishes you with several ways to manage your footage and compositions. Icons that resemble those used on the desktop (Mac) or Explorer (Windows) provide an easy means of distinguishing between footage types (**Figure 3.2**). You can also view more detailed information about items in the Project panel, organize items into folders, and sort items according to categories. Depending on your needs, you can rearrange, resize, hide, or reveal the categories. You can even create a custom category and custom color labels. And if you still need help locating an item, you can find it using the Project panel's Find button. There's also a button that lets you access a flowchart view of your project—but that explanation will wait for later when it will make more sense (see Chapter 16, "Complex Projects").

Figure 3.1 The Project panel doesn't simply list items; it helps you identify, sort, and organize them.

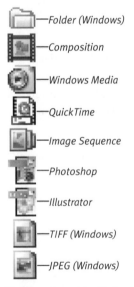

Figure 3.2 Icons identify the types of items in the Project panel. This figure shows an incomplete list.

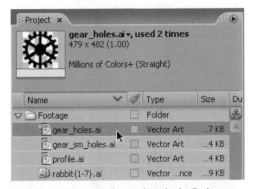

Figure 3.3 When you select an item in the Project panel, information about the selected item appears at the top of the panel.

To display information about a footage item or composition:

◆ In the Project panel, click a footage item to select it.

At the top of the Project panel, a thumbnail image of the footage item appears. Next to the thumbnail image, the name of the footage item appears, as well as information about the footage itself, such as frame size, color depth, codec, and so on (**Figure 3.3**).

✔ Tips

■ By default, the Project panel includes a thumbnail image of the selected item. You can remove the thumbnail by selecting Disable Thumbnails in the Project Panel option in the View panel of the Preferences dialog box.

■ By default, the thumbnail image displays transparency as black. To make transparent areas appear as a checkerboard pattern, choose Thumbnail Transparency Grid in the Project panel's pull-down menu.

■ Option-clicking (Mac) or Alt-clicking (Windows) an item displays its file-type extension in addition to the usual information.

Finding Items in a Project

The Project panel includes a handy Find button to help you unearth items from your project that you've lost track of. Use it, and you'll never need to search through folders again.

To find an item in the Project panel:

1. In the Project panel, click the Find button (**Figure 3.4**).

   A Find dialog box appears.

2. Enter all or part of the name of the item you're looking for in the Find field (**Figure 3.5**).

   You can modify the search parameters by choosing the options described in the next step.

3. In the Find dialog box, select the options you want to use to modify your search:

   Match Whole Word Only—To locate only items that match the entire word you entered in the Find field.

   Match Case—To locate items that include the Find field's content, taking letter case into account. For example, a search for *Background* (with an uppercase *B*) won't locate an item called *background* (with a lowercase *b*).

   Find Missing Footage—To locate missing footage—that is, items that have lost their reference to a source file.

4. Click OK to search for the item.

   The first item that matches the criteria you specified appears selected in the Project panel (**Figure 3.6**).

✔ Tip

- Option-click (Mac) or Alt-click (Windows) the Find button to find the next item that matches the most recent Find criteria.

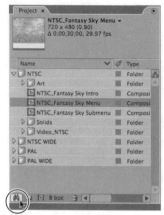

Figure 3.4 In the Project panel, click the Find button.

Figure 3.5 In the Find dialog box, enter all or part of the name of the item you're looking for, and select the options you want.

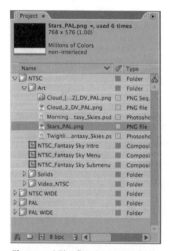

Figure 3.6 The first item matching the criteria you specified appears selected in the Project panel.

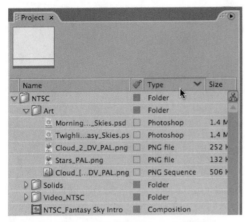

Figure 3.7 Click a heading panel to sort the items according to the information under the heading.

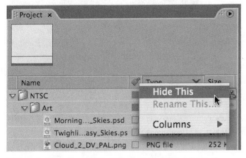

Figure 3.8 Choose Hide This to hide the selected heading panel.

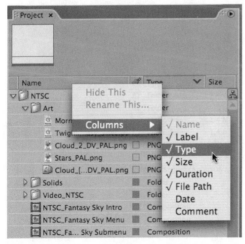

Figure 3.9 Unselect a heading name (in this case, the Type column).

Sorting Footage in the Project Panel

By default, items in the Project panel are sorted by name, but you can sort the list by an assortment of other criteria, such as file type, size, duration, and so on. You can hide the column headings you don't want to use and rearrange their order. You can even assign a custom heading.

To sort footage items in the Project panel:

◆ In the Project panel, click a heading panel to sort the footage items according to the name, label, type, size, duration, file path, date, or comment (**Figure 3.7**).

To hide or display a heading panel in the Project panel:

1. In the Project panel, Ctrl-click (Mac) or right-click (Windows) a heading panel.
   A contextual menu appears.

2. Choose an option:
   ▲ To hide the selected heading panel, choose Hide This (**Figure 3.8**). (This choice isn't available for the Name heading panel.)
   ▲ To hide any heading panel, choose Columns and a heading panel name to unselect it (**Figure 3.9**).
   ▲ To show a hidden heading panel, choose Columns and a heading panel name to select it.

continues on next page

SORTING FOOTAGE IN THE PROJECT PANEL

Depending on your choice, you can hide or display heading panels and the columns beneath them (**Figure 3.10**).

To reorder headings in the Project panel:

1. If necessary, resize the Project panel and make sure it displays the headings you want to rearrange.

2. Drag the heading panel(s) to the right or left to change the relative position of the heading columns (**Figures 3.11** and **3.12**).

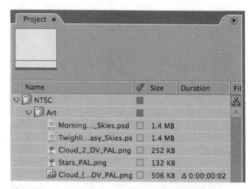

Figure 3.10 The heading and the column beneath it are hidden from view.

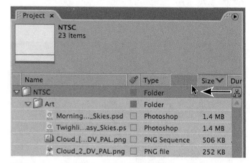

Figure 3.11 Drag the entire heading panel (in this case, the Size column) to the right or left...

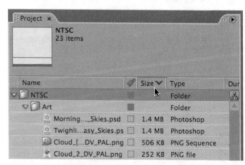

Figure 3.12 ...to change its relative position in the Project panel. Here, the Size column has been moved to the left of the Type column.

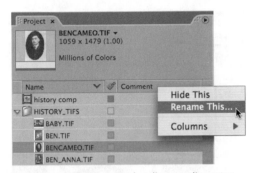

Figure 3.13 In the Comment heading panel's contextual menu, choose Rename This to give the heading a custom name.

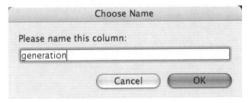

Figure 3.14 In the Choose Name dialog box, enter a custom name.

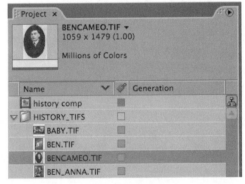

Figure 3.15 The Comment field uses the name you specify.

To give the Comment heading panel a custom name:

1. If the Comment heading panel isn't visible, make it visible using the techniques described earlier.

2. In the Project panel, Ctrl-click (Mac) or right-click (Windows) the Comment heading panel.

   A contextual menu appears.

3. Choose Rename This (**Figure 3.13**).

   The Choose Name dialog box appears.

4. Enter a custom name (**Figure 3.14**).

5. Click OK to close the dialog box.

   The custom heading panel appears with the name you specified (**Figure 3.15**).

SORTING FOOTAGE IN THE PROJECT PANEL

To enter information under the Comment or custom heading:

1. If the Comment or custom heading panel of the Project panel isn't visible, make it visible using the techniques described above.

2. In the same row as an item in the Project panel, click below the Comment or custom heading.

   A text field and cursor appear.

3. Enter a comment for the corresponding footage item, and press Return (Mac) or Enter (Windows) (**Figure 3.16**).

✔ Tip

- By default, each type of footage is associated with a color label. You can sort items by label color, or reassign label colors in the Label Defaults panel of the Preferences dialog box. The timeline also represents layers using the color label.

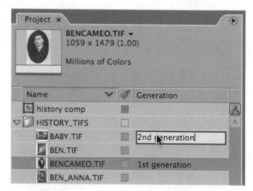

Figure 3.16 Click in the field under the Comment (or custom) heading to enter information.

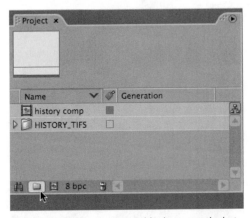

Figure 3.17 Clicking the New Folder button at the bottom of the Project panel is the easiest way to create a new folder.

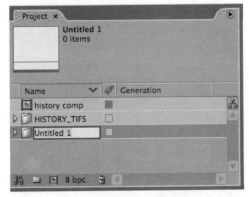

Figure 3.18 Press Return (Mac) or Enter (Windows) to highlight the name of the new folder...

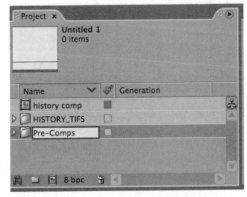

Figure 3.19 ...and type a new name. Press Return (Mac) or Enter (Windows) to apply the name.

Organizing Footage in Folders

As you learned in Chapter 2, "Importing Footage into a Project," footage can be imported into the Project panel as items contained in a folder. Of course, you can also create your own folders to organize items in the project. Folders look and work much like they do on your operating system (particularly on the Mac's desktop). Clicking the triangle next to the folder's icon toggles the folder open and closed. The triangle spins clockwise to reveal the folder's contents in outline fashion; the triangle spins counterclockwise to collapse the outline, hiding the folder's contents. However, the folder can't open in its own window.

To create a folder in the Project panel:

1. In the Project panel, *do one of the following:*
   ▲ Choose File > New > New Folder.
   ▲ Click the folder icon at the bottom (**Figure 3.17**).

   An untitled folder appears in the Project panel.

2. Press Return (Mac) or Enter (Windows) to highlight the name of the folder (**Figure 3.18**).

3. Type a name for the folder (**Figure 3.19**).

4. Press Return (Mac) or Enter (Windows) to apply the name to the folder.

   The folder is sorted with other items according to the currently selected column heading.

To organize footage items in folders:

In the Project panel, *do one of the following*:

◆ To move items into a folder, select and drag items into the folder (**Figure 3.20**).

◆ To move items out of a folder, select and drag items from the folder to the gray area at the top of the Project panel (**Figure 3.21**).

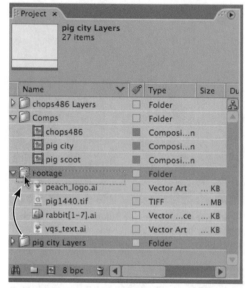

Figure 3.20 You can drag selected items directly into a folder.

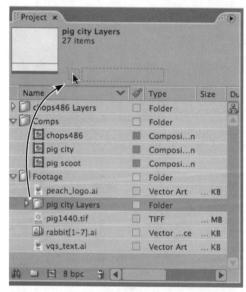

Figure 3.21 To move items out of a folder, drag them from the folder to the top of the Project panel.

Figure 3.22 Select a folder or composition, press Return (Mac) or Enter (Windows) to highlight its name...

Figure 3.23 ...and then type a new name in the text box. Press Return (Mac) or Enter (Windows) again to apply the new name.

Renaming and Removing Items

You can't rename a footage item in the Project panel or even give it a temporary alias. Don't worry: You can rename it when it becomes a layer in a composition. (In later chapters, you'll see how this naming scheme allows you to give unique names to each layer while still tracing their lineage back to a single footage file.) You can, of course, name folders and compositions in the Project panel.

Just as important as organizing the elements you need is disposing of the elements you don't need. You can remove individual items or have After Effects automatically discard the items that haven't been used in a composition.

To rename folders or compositions in the Project panel:

1. In the Project panel, select a folder or composition.

2. Press Return (Mac) or Enter (Windows). The name of the item appears highlighted (**Figure 3.22**).

3. Enter a name for the folder or composition (**Figure 3.23**).

4. Press Return (Mac) or Enter (Windows). The new name of the item is no longer highlighted and becomes the current name.

To remove items from a project:

1. In the Project panel, select one or more items.

2. *Do one of the following:*

   ▲ Press Delete.

   ▲ Click the Delete button  at the bottom of the Project panel (**Figure 3.24**).

   ▲ Drag the items to the Delete button  at the bottom of the Project panel.

   If any of the items are compositions or are being used in a composition, After Effects asks you to confirm that you want to delete the items (**Figure 3.25**).

3. If After Effects prompts you to confirm your choice, click Delete to remove the footage from the project or Cancel to cancel the command and retain the footage in the project.

   The footage is removed from the project and all compositions in the project.

To remove unused footage from a project:

◆ Choose File > Remove Unused Footage (**Figure 3.26**).

   All footage items that aren't currently used in a composition are removed from the project.

Figure 3.24 Click the Delete button at the bottom of the Project panel to delete selected items.

Figure 3.25 After Effects warns you if you attempt to delete an item that is in use.

Figure 3.26 Choose File > Remove Unused Footage to remove items that aren't used in a composition.

Figure 3.27 Choose File > Consolidate All Footage to remove duplicate items from the Project panel.

Figure 3.28 Choose File > Reduce Project to remove unselected comps (except comps nested in selected comps) and unused footage.

To remove duplicate footage from a project:

◆ Choose File > Consolidate All Footage (**Figure 3.27**).

All duplicate footage items are removed from the project. Footage items imported from the same source file that use different Interpret Footage settings are treated as different items.

To remove unselected comps and unused footage from a project:

1. In the Project panel, select the compositions.

2. Choose File > Reduce Project (**Figure 3.28**).

Unselected comps and unused footage are removed. Comps nested in selected comps are preserved.

✔ Tips

■ As you'll see in Chapter 4, you can create layer solids that appear as footage items in the Project panel. In the Project panel, you can rename solids as you would a folder or composition.

■ Although you may not be ready to remove unused and duplicate footage from the Project panel yet, it's a good idea to do some housekeeping as your project nears completion. After all, if the project were a prizewinning recipe, would you list ingredients you never used?

■ After Effects includes a Collect Files command that you can use to copy all of a project's requisite files into a single location, along with a report describing everything you'll need to render the project (such as fonts and effects). The Collect Files command is especially useful when you want to archive a project or move it to a different workstation.

RENAMING AND REMOVING ITEMS

Proxies and Placeholders

Sometimes it's necessary to use stand-in files to take the place of actual footage. For example, you may need to start working even though all your source footage isn't ready. (Your client forgot to send the disk, or another production artist is behind schedule—sound familiar?) For the present, you may have to settle for a temporary placeholder. On the other hand, maybe a high-quality image is slowing down previews. A low-quality version of the footage may work just as well for draft versions and speed up your workflow. In such cases, you may choose to use a proxy instead of the actual footage. When you and your footage are ready, you can easily replace placeholders and proxies with the actual footage.

Placeholders

A *placeholder* is a generic still image that takes the place of missing footage. As pointed out in Chapter 2, After Effects automatically creates placeholders for missing footage. This section shows you how to use After Effects to create a placeholder manually. In the Project panel, the name of the placeholder appears in italic type. Placeholder footage appears in the thumbnail image and in the Composition panel as television color bars (**Figures 3.29** and **3.30**). (Depending on your background, you'll either recognize color bars as one of the standard test patterns used to calibrate video equipment for color and brightness, or as the weird show TV stations broadcast after 2 a.m.) Naturally, the image size and duration of the placeholder should match those of the footage it's temporarily replacing. If you're familiar with nonlinear editing programs, you might equate *placeholders* with *offline files*.

Figure 3.29 Placeholder footage appears in the Project panel...

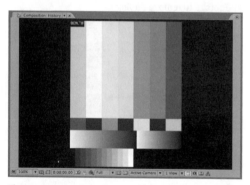

Figure 3.30 ...and the Composition panel as standard color bars.

Figure 3.31 Low-quality proxies (top) don't look as good as the actual footage (bottom), but they also have smaller file sizes and can be processed faster.

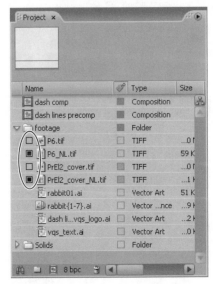

Figure 3.32 Icons indicate whether a proxy is in use or assigned to an item but not in use.

Proxies

A *proxy* is a low-resolution version of the actual footage (**Figure 3.31**). If you're familiar with nonlinear editing applications, you might compare using proxies to using low-quality clips for offline editing (the rough cutting phase, which often utilizes relatively low-quality copies of footage). Low-quality files take less time to process, allowing you to work more quickly. Proxies may also be necessary if you have to work on a less powerful workstation—one with less RAM, for example—than you'll finish on. When you're ready, you can replace the low-quality stand-ins with the high-quality original footage.

Icons next to each item in the Project panel provide an easy way to determine whether source footage or its proxy is currently in use (**Figure 3.32**). A box containing a black square ■ indicates that the proxy is currently in use; the name of the proxy appears in bold text. An empty box □ indicates that a proxy has been assigned but that source footage is currently in use. If there is no icon, this means no proxy has been assigned to the footage item.

Proxies aren't effective for every circumstance, however. Although they can save time when you're animating motion, other effects—such as keying—can only be properly adjusted when using the footage at output quality.

To create a placeholder:

1. Choose File > Import > Placeholder (**Figure 3.33**).

   The New Placeholder dialog box appears.

2. Enter information that matches the missing footage (**Figure 3.34**):

   ▲ For Name, enter the filename for the missing footage.

   ▲ For Size, enter the pixel dimensions of the missing footage.

   ▲ For Duration, enter the duration of the missing footage.

3. Click OK to close the New Placeholder dialog box.

   The Placeholder footage item appears in the Project panel in italics.

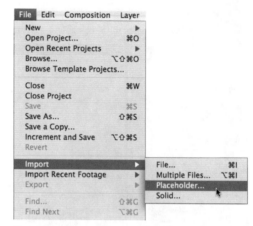

Figure 3.33 Choose File > Import > Placeholder.

Figure 3.34 In the New Placeholder dialog box, enter information that matches the missing footage.

Figure 3.35 Double-click the name or icon of missing footage to open the Replace Footage File dialog box.

To replace a placeholder with source footage:

1. In the Project panel, double-click the placeholder you want to replace with source footage (**Figure 3.35**).

   A Replace Footage File dialog box appears.

2. Locate the source file, and click Open (**Figure 3.36**).

   The footage replaces every instance of the placeholder in the project (**Figure 3.37**).

Figure 3.36 In the Replace Footage File dialog box, locate the missing footage.

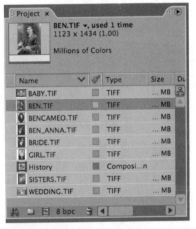

Figure 3.37 The actual footage replaces the placeholder footage wherever it appears in the project.

To assign a proxy to a footage item:

1. In the Project panel, select a footage item to which you want to apply a proxy.

2. *Do either of the following:*

   ▲ Choose File > Set Proxy > File.

   ▲ Ctrl-click (Mac) or right-click (Windows) the item, and choose Set Proxy > File in the contextual menu (**Figure 3.38**).

   The Set Proxy File dialog box appears.

3. Locate the file you want to assign as the proxy (**Figure 3.39**).

4. Click Open to select the file and close the dialog box.

   In the Project panel, a proxy icon ■ appears next to the footage item, indicating that a proxy is currently in use (**Figure 3.40**).

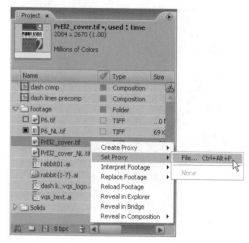

Figure 3.38 Choose File > Set Proxy > File.

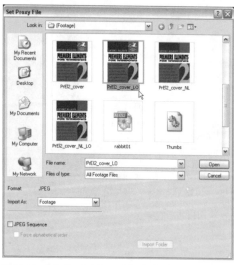

Figure 3.39 In the Set Proxy File dialog box, choose a file to act as a proxy for the actual footage.

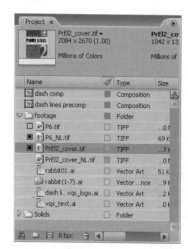

Figure 3.40 A black box appears next to the item, indicating that a proxy is in use.

PROXIES AND PLACEHOLDERS

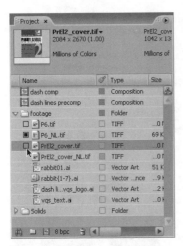

Figure 3.41 Click the proxy icon to toggle between using the proxy and using the actual footage.

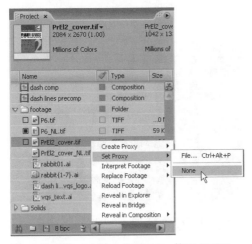

Figure 3.42 Choose File > Set Proxy > None to stop using a proxy.

To toggle between using a proxy and the original footage:

◆ In the Project panel, click the proxy icon to the left of a footage item to toggle between using the assigned proxy and using the original footage (**Figure 3.41**).

To stop using a proxy:

1. In the Project panel, select a footage item that has been assigned a proxy.

2. *Do either of the following:*

   ▲ Choose File > Set Proxy > None

   ▲ Ctrl-click (Mac) or right-click (Windows) the item, and choose Set Proxy > None in the contextual menu (**Figure 3.42**).

   To the left of the footage item's name in the Project panel, the proxy icon disappears.

Viewing Footage

When you open an item in the Project panel, it appears either in an After Effects Footage panel or in the player native to its file type, depending on the file type and your preference.

Still images always open in an After Effects Footage panel. Motion footage and audio items, in contrast, open in the appropriate media player by default. For example, .mov files open in a QuickTime footage window; .avi files open in an Video for Windows footage window. However, you can opt to open them in an After Effects Footage panel instead.

Whereas a media player lets you play back motion and audio footage right away and at the full frame rate, the Footage panel relies on After Effects' frame rendering mechanism (explained fully in Chapter 8, "Playback, Previews, and RAM"). Therefore, the Footage panel won't necessarily play a movie at the full frame rate and won't play audio without rendering a preview. The Footage panel does offer a number of other viewing options (covered in the section "The Footage Panel," later in this chapter) and editing features (covered in Chapter 4, "Compositions").

To view a footage item:

◆ In the Project panel, double-click a footage item.

Still images open in a Footage panel (**Figure 3.43**); movie files open in the appropriate movie player (**Figures 3.44** and **3.45**).

Figure 3.43 Still images always open in an After Effects Footage panel.

Figure 3.44 By default, motion footage opens in a window according to the file type.

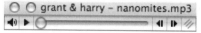

Figure 3.45 Audio files are also easier to preview in their own Footage panel.

VIEWING FOOTAGE

Figure 3.46 However, Alt-clicking motion footage opens it in an After Effects Footage panel.

To open a movie file in an After Effects Footage panel:

◆ In the Project panel, Option-double-click (Mac) or Alt-double-click (Windows) a movie footage item.

The movie file opens in an After Effects Footage panel (**Figure 3.46**).

✔ Tips

■ Some .avi files—including those using Microsoft's DirectX DV codec, and files over 2GB—will open only in an After Effects footage panel.

■ If the footage item opens only in a Footage panel, you can still open it in its native application using the Edit Original command, as explained in the next section.

Opening Footage in the Original Application

As you know, After Effects works with references to source files, not with the files themselves. Sometimes, however, you'll want to make a permanent change to a source file after you've imported it into After Effects. Luckily, you don't have to quit After Effects to do so. After Effects provides an easy way to open the file in the application in which it was created. Of course, the application must be present on your hard drive, and you must have enough available RAM to open both applications simultaneously. After you edit the footage in the original application, every instance of the footage in your After Effects project will reflect your changes.

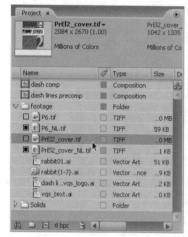

Figure 3.47 Select the footage you want to edit in the Project, Composition, or Timeline panel...

To open a footage item in the original application:

1. In the Project panel, Composition panel, or Timeline panel, select the footage item or layer containing the footage you want to edit (**Figure 3.47**).

   To open an image in a still-image sequence, select the footage in the Composition or Timeline panel, and position the current time indicator at the frame that displays the still image you want to use (**Figure 3.48**).

Figure 3.48 ...or set the current time to the frame of the still image sequence.

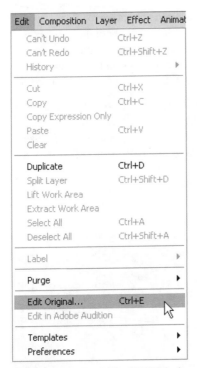

Figure 3.49 Choose Edit > Edit Original, or press Command-E (Mac) or Ctrl-E (Windows) to open the file in its original application.

2. Choose Edit > Edit Original, or press Command-E (Mac) or Ctrl-E (Windows) (**Figure 3.49**).

    After Effects launches the application in which the file was created.

3. Edit the file in the original application, and save the changes. If you don't plan to make further changes, quit the application.

4. Return to After Effects, and continue working on your project.

    Every instance of the footage in your project reflects the changes you saved in the original application.

✔ Tips

■ Make permanent changes to the source file that will reduce your work or processing time in After Effects. For example, add effects and retouching that you don't plan to change or animate over time. For more about prepping still images, see Chapter 2.

■ In the unlikely event that After Effects doesn't update the image you edited in the source application, choose File > Reload Footage.

OPENING FOOTAGE IN THE ORIGINAL APP

The Footage Panel

An After Effects Footage panel has a variety of controls for viewing footage. As you might expect, you can magnify or reduce your view of the image, and you can play back and cue motion footage. In addition, you can view the individual channels: RGB and alpha. The Footage panel also allows you to show rulers, set guides, and superimpose a grid or video-safe zones. There is also a snapshot feature that lets you save and recall a frame of footage that you can use for reference (**Figure 3.50**).

As you'll see in the chapters to follow, you can also find all of these Footage panel controls in the Composition and Layer panels. If some of the controls don't seem useful now, be patient: They'll come in handy later.

The following sections cover these shared controls. Later chapters cover only the features unique to the Composition and Layer panels. Chapter 6, "Layer Editing," discusses in detail the Footage panel's controls for editing motion footage.

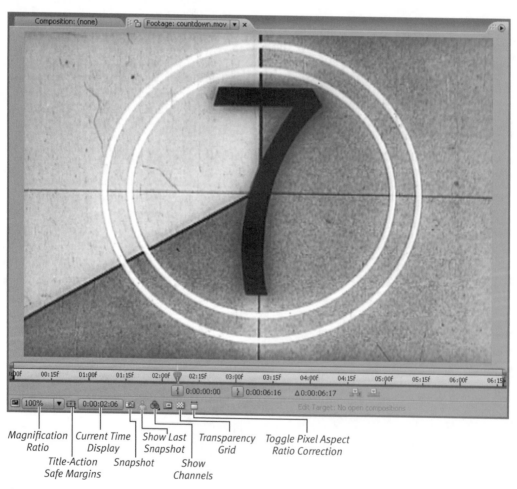

Figure 3.50 The following sections cover several features of the Footage panel that are shared by the Composition and Layer panels.

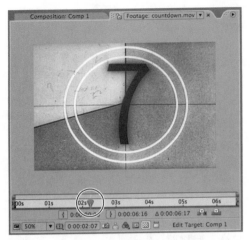

Figure 3.51 Drag the current time indicator to cue the footage to a particular frame.

Figure 3.52 You can click the current time display...

Figure 3.53 ...and enter a frame number in the Go To Time dialog box.

Figure 3.54 The Time Controls panel provides a complete set of playback options.

Cueing Motion Footage

Motion footage appears in the Footage, Composition, and Layer panels with a time ruler, current time indicator, and current time display. You can use the controls to view a specific frame or to play back the footage without sound.

To view a frame of motion footage by dragging:

◆ In the Footage panel, drag the current time indicator to the frame you want to view (**Figure 3.51**).

The Footage panel displays the image at the current frame and the frame number.

To cue a frame of motion footage numerically:

1. In the Footage panel, click the current time display (**Figure 3.52**).

The Go To Time dialog box opens.

2. Enter a time (**Figure 3.53**).

3. Click OK.

The current time display and the image in the Footage panel show the frame you specified.

To play motion footage:

◆ Make sure the Footage, Composition, or Layer panel is active. Press the spacebar to start and stop playback.

✔ Tips

■ The spacebar provides the easiest way to start and stop playback. The Time Controls panel provides more control (**Figure 3.54**).

■ In the Footage panel, the time ruler shows the length of the source file; in the Composition and Layer panels, the time ruler corresponds to the length of the composition.

Magnifying an Image

Sometimes, you'll want to magnify your footage view so that you can closely examine a detail of the image. Other times, you'll want to reduce magnification because viewing footage at 100 percent scale takes up too much screen space. After Effects lets you change the magnification ratio to suit your needs. However, keep in mind that this is for viewing purposes only: The actual scale of the footage doesn't change. You may be surprised to discover that no matter how much you magnify the image in the Footage panel, scroll bars don't appear. To view different parts of a magnified image, use the Hand tool instead.

To change the magnification of the Footage or Composition panel:

◆ In the Footage panel, press and hold the Magnification Ratio pop-up menu to choose a magnification (**Figure 3.55**).

When you release the mouse button, the Footage panel uses the magnification ratio you selected (**Figure 3.56**).

Figure 3.55 Choose a magnification from the pop-up menu.

Figure 3.56 The Footage panel displays the image at the magnification you specified.

Figure 3.57 In the Tools panel, select the Hand tool...

Figure 3.58 ...or position the Selection tool over the image and press the spacebar to toggle it to the Hand tool.

Figure 3.59 Drag the image with the Hand tool to move other areas into view.

To change the visible area of a magnified image in the Footage or Composition panel:

1. Select the Hand tool by doing *either of the following:*
   - ▲ In the Tools panel, click the Hand tool (**Figure 3.57**).
   - ▲ With the Selection tool active (the default tool), position the mouse pointer over the image in the Footage or Composition panel, and press the spacebar.

   The mouse changes to the hand icon (**Figure 3.58**).
2. Drag the hand to change the visible area of the image (**Figure 3.59**).

✔ Tip

- The Display pane of the Preferences dialog box includes the option Auto-zoom When Resolution Changes. Selecting this option makes the image's magnification change when you change the Comp panel's resolution setting. Note that the Footage and Layer panels don't include a resolution option.

Viewing Safe Zones and Grids

You can superimpose a grid or video-safe zones over an image to better judge its placement. Obviously, these simple visual guides aren't included in the final output. In addition, because video-safe zones indicate the viewable area of standard video monitors, you should display safe zones for images that match television's 4:3 aspect ratio. For more about the safe zones, see the sidebar "Better Safe than Sorry: Video Title- and Action-Safe Zones."

To show video-safe zones and grids:

◆ In the Footage panel's Grid and Guides pulldown menu 🖼 choose the options you want (**Figure 3.60**):

Title/Action Safe (**Figure 3.61**)

Proportional Grid (**Figure 3.62**)

Grid (**Figure 3.63**)

You can display any combination of zones and guides at the same time.

✔ Tip

■ You can change the safe zones from the standard setting and change the color, style, and spacing of grid lines in the Grids & Guides pane of the Preferences dialog box.

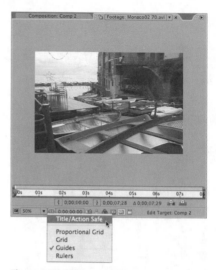

Figure 3.60 Choose whether you want to view safe zones or grids in the Grids and Guides pulldown menu.

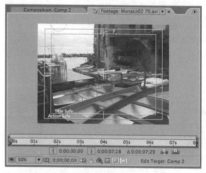

Figure 3.61 You can view Title Safe and Action Safe zones...

Figure 3.62 ...a proportional grid...

Figure 3.63 ...or a standard grid.

Better Safe than Sorry: Video Title- and Action-Safe Zones

Computer monitors display images from edge to edge. Television monitors, on the other hand, *overscan* images, or crop the outer edges. What's more, the amount of overscan differs from one television monitor to another.

Because of overscan, only the inner 90 percent of the full screen is considered *action safe*. That is, you should restrict any important onscreen actions to this area. The inner 80 percent of the image is known as *title safe*. Because you usually can't afford to lose any part of a title, you need a greater margin of error. If you're going to output your project as full-screen video, you'll need to respect the title-safe zone or suffer the consequences (**Figures 3.64** and **3.65**).

Even if you only plan to show your final movie on a computer screen, consider using the title-safe zones anyway. If you, your client, or your boss later decides to repurpose your creation for display on full-screen video, you'll be safe.

Of course, full-screen video also has a 4:3 aspect ratio (typically). In After Effects, safe-zone guides mark the inner 80 and 90 percent of any window, even if the image doesn't match television's 4:3 aspect ratio. Because their only purpose is to indicate the overscanned areas of a standard video monitor, the safe-zone guides are relevant only in windows that correspond with television's 4:3 aspect ratio.

Figure 3.64 Ignoring title safe has little consequence for images displayed less than full screen or on computer monitors.

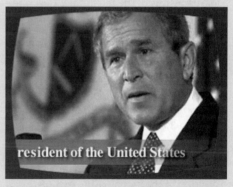

Figure 3.65 However, the same image presented as full-screen video may result in unwanted editing. In this case, the President gets a demotion to a mere "resident," without a proper election.

Rulers and Guides

Like Adobe Photoshop and Illustrator, After Effects lets you view rulers as well as set guides to help you arrange and align images. As usual, you can change the zero point of the rulers and toggle the rulers and guides on and off.

To toggle rulers on and off:

Do either of the following:

◆ In a Footage, Comp, or Layer panel's Grid and Guides pulldown menu ▦, choose Rulers (**Figure 3.66**).

◆ With a Footage, Comp, or Layer panel active, press Command-R (Mac) or Ctrl-R (Windows) to toggle the rulers on and off.

To set the zero point of rulers:

1. If the rulers aren't visible, make them visible using one of the techniques described in the previous task.

2. Position the pointer at the crosshair at the intersection of the rulers in the upper-left corner of the Footage, Composition, or Layer panel.

   The pointer becomes a crosshair (**Figure 3.67**).

3. Drag the crosshair into the image area.

   Horizontal and vertical lines indicate the position of the mouse (**Figure 3.68**).

4. Release the mouse to set the zero point (**Figure 3.69**).

   The rulers use the zero point you selected.

Figure 3.66 After Effects uses the same keyboard shortcut to show and hide rulers—Command-R (Mac) or Ctrl-R (Windows).

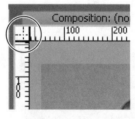

Figure 3.67 When you position the pointer at the intersection of the rulers, it becomes a crosshair icon.

Figure 3.68 Drag the crosshair at the intersection of the rulers into the image area...

RULERS AND GUIDES

Figure 3.69 ...and release to set the zero point of the rulers.

Figure 3.70 Drag from a ruler into the image area to add a guide.

To reset the zero point of the rulers:

◆ Double-click the crosshair at the intersection of the horizontal and vertical rulers.

The rulers' zero point is reset to the upper-left corner of the image.

✔ Tips

■ As you've probably guessed, After Effects includes a Snap to Guides feature. However, it won't do you much good in the Footage panel, so that feature is covered along with the Composition panel in the next chapter.

■ Need to know the exact ruler coordinates of the mouse pointer? Use the Info panel.

To set guides:

1. If the rulers aren't visible, make them visible by pressing Command-R (Mac) or Ctrl-R (Windows).

2. Position the pointer inside the horizontal or vertical ruler.

The pointer changes into a Move Guide icon ←→.

3. Drag into the image area (**Figure 3.70**). A line indicates the position of the new guide.

4. Release the mouse to set the guide.

To reposition or remove a guide:

1. Make sure the guides are visible and unlocked (see the following sections).

You can't move a guide if guides are locked.

2. Position the pointer over a guide.

The pointer changes into a Move Guide icon **↔**.

3. *Do one of the following:*

▲ To reposition the guide, drag it to a new position.

▲ To remove the guide, drag it off the image area.

To show and hide guides:

Do either of the following:

◆ In a Footage, Comp, or Layer panel, select or deselect Guides in the Grid & Guide Options pulldown menu (**Figure 3.71**).

◆ With the panel selected, press Command-; (Mac) or Ctrl-; (Windows).

To lock and unlock guides:

◆ To lock guides, choose View > Lock Guides (**Figure 3.72**).

◆ To unlock guides, choose View > Unlock Guides.

✔ Tip

■ You can customize the default settings for safe zones, grids, and guides in the Grids and Guides pane of the Preferences dialog box.

Figure 3.71 You can toggle guides using the Grid & Guide Options pulldown menu, but it's worth learning the keyboard shortcut: Command-; (Mac) or Ctrl-; (Windows). Photoshop uses the same shortcut.

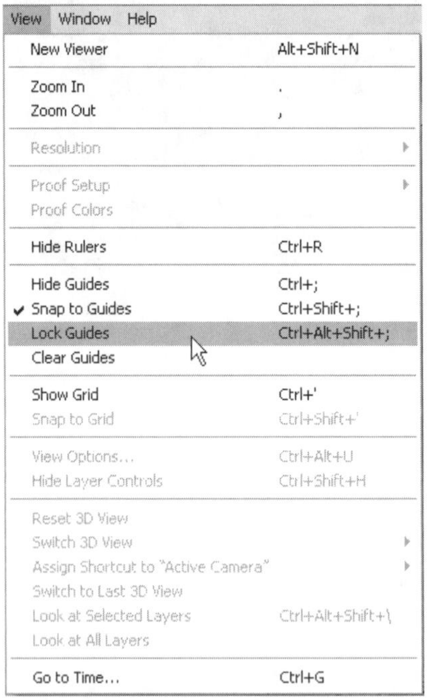

Figure 3.72 Choose View > Lock Guides to prevent guides from being moved unintentionally. To unlock the guides, Choose View > Unlock Guides.

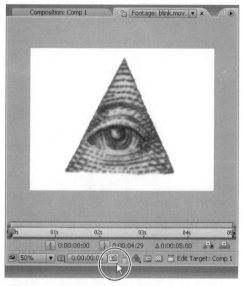

Figure 3.73 Click the Snapshot button to store the current image as a snapshot.

Figure 3.74 The current frame becomes the snapshot, and the Show Last Snapshot button becomes available.

Snapshots

As you work, you'll often need to closely compare different frames. In After Effects, you can take a snapshot of a frame to store for later viewing. Then, with the click of a button, you can temporarily replace the current image in a Footage, Composition, or Layer panel with the snapshot image. The snapshot doesn't really replace anything; it's just used for quick reference—like holding a shirt up to yourself in a mirror to compare it with the one you're wearing. Toggling between the current frame and the snapshot makes it easier to see the differences.

You can take and view as many as four separate snapshots.

To take a snapshot:

1. If necessary, cue the footage to the frame you want to use as a reference snapshot.

2. Click the Snapshot button ▣ (**Figure 3.73**), or press Shift-F5.

   The current frame becomes the snapshot, and the Show Last Snapshot button becomes available ▣ (**Figure 3.74**).

To view the most recent snapshot:

1. If necessary, cue the footage to the frame you want to compare to the snapshot (**Figure 3.75**).

2. Click and hold the Show Last Snapshot button 🔳, or press F5.

   As long as you hold down the mouse, the window displays the snapshot (**Figure 3.76**); when you release the mouse, the window displays the current frame.

To take and view multiple snapshots:

1. In a Footage, Layer, or Composition panel, cue the footage to the frame you want to use as a reference snapshot.

2. To store as many as four separate snapshots, press Shift-F5, Shift-F6, Shift-F7, or Shift-F8—each of which stores a single snapshot.

   The frame is stored as a snapshot.

3. To view a stored snapshot, press F5, F6, F7, or F8.

   The snapshot stored using the corresponding function key is displayed in the window.

To purge a snapshot:

◆ Press Command-Shift (Mac) or Ctrl-Shift (Windows), and press the function key that corresponds to the snapshot you want to erase (F5, F6, F7, or F8).

   The snapshot is purged from memory.

✔ Tips

■ If a window uses a different aspect ratio than that of the snapshot, the snapshot is resized to fit into the window.

■ Snapshots are stored in memory. If After Effects requires the memory that is used by a snapshot, it will discard the snapshot.

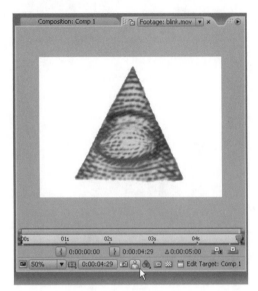

Figure 3.75 Cue to a new frame...

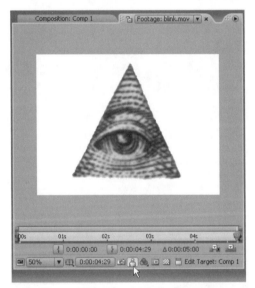

Figure 3.76 ...and then press and hold the Show Last Snapshot button to replace the current image temporarily with the snapshot. Release the Show Last Snapshot button to see the current frame again.

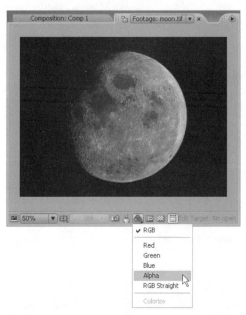

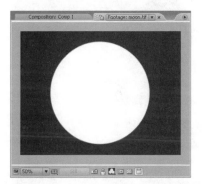

Figure 3.77 Click the Show Channel button, and then select the channel you want to view.

Figure 3.78 Choose Alpha to see the alpha channel.

Figure 3.79 To see the selected channel in color, select Colorize from the pull-down menu.

Channels

The Footage, Composition, and Layer panels allow you to view the individual red, green, blue, and alpha channels of an image. Color channels appear as grayscale images in which the degree of white corresponds to the color value. You can also view the color channel using its own color. The alpha channel appears as a grayscale image as well, where the degree of white corresponds to opacity. As you may recall from Chapter 2, you can even view the unmultiplied color channels—that is, the color channels without the alpha taken into account. For more about alpha channels, see the Chapter 2 sidebar "Alpha Bits: Understanding Straight and Premultiplied Alpha."

To show individual channels:

1. In a Footage, Composition, or Layer panel, click the Show Channel button, and then choose the channel you want to view (**Figure 3.77**):

   RGB—Shows the normal image, with visible channels combined.

   Red, **Green**, or **Blue**—Shows the selected channel as a grayscale.

   Alpha—Shows the alpha channel (transparency information) as a grayscale. If active, the transparency grid is disabled while Alpha is selected (**Figure 3.78**). See the next section, "Viewing Transparency."

   RGB Straight—Shows the unmultiplied RGB channels. If active, the transparency grid is disabled while RGB Straight is selected.

2. To show the selected channel depicted in color, select Colorize (**Figure 3.79**).

   The Channel pulldown menu's icon changes according to the current selection.

Viewing Transparency

In Chapter 2, you learned that the footage items you import can retain almost every aspect of their source files, including transparency. In the Footage panel, transparency always appears as black (**Figure 3.80**). However, if the black background isn't convenient, you can toggle the transparent areas to appear as a checkerboard pattern, or *transparency grid* (**Figure 3.81**).

Like many of the other buttons in the Footage panel, the Toggle Transparency Grid button is also available in the Layer and Composition panels. However, in contrast to the Footage panel, you can set the Composition panel's background to any color. The next chapter revisits viewing transparency and other unique aspects of the Composition panel.

To toggle the transparency grid:

◆ In the Footage, Composition, or Layer panel, click the Toggle Transparency Grid button ▧ (**Figure 3.82**).

When the Toggle Transparency Grid button is selected, transparent areas appear as a checkerboard pattern; when the button isn't selected, transparent areas appear black in a Footage or Layer panel. In a Composition panel, transparent areas appear as the color you set.

✔ Tip

■ The transparency grid is disabled whenever you select the Alpha or RGB Straight viewing option in the Show Channel pull-down menu (covered in the section "Viewing Channels," earlier in this chapter).

Figure 3.80 In the Footage panel, transparent areas of the image appear as black.

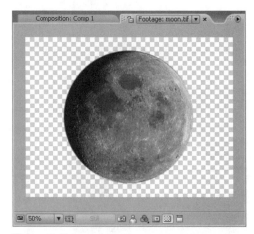

Figure 3.81 You can also make transparent areas appear as a checkerboard pattern, or transparency grid. This also works in the Composition and Layer panels.

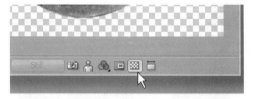

Figure 3.82 Click the Toggle Transparency Grid button to toggle between showing transparent areas as black (in the Footage panel, or as the specified background color in the Composition panel) and showing them as a checkerboard pattern.

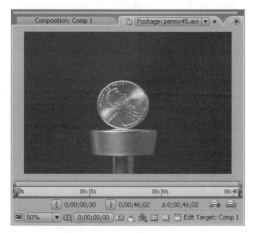

Figure 3.83 This footage uses a PAR of .9, so it appears slightly vertically squashed (or horizontally stretched) when displayed using square pixels.

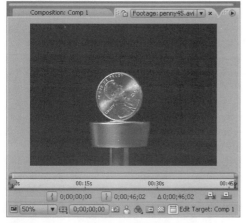

Figure 3.84 You can correct the distortion in the Layer, Composition, and Footage panels.

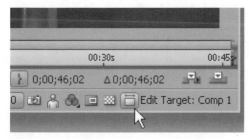

Figure 3.85 Click the Toggle Pixel Aspect Ratio Correction button.

Correcting for Pixel Aspect Ratios

In Chapter 2, you learned the importance of correctly interpreting an image's pixel aspect ratio (PAR) to prevent the image from appearing distorted (if you missed the discussion, turn to the sidebar "PAR Excellence" in Chapter 2). But even properly interpreted footage and comps that use a nonsquare PAR (such as DV or D1, with a PAR of .9) result in an image that looks distorted on a typical computer display (PAR of 1) (**Figure 3.83**). Fortunately, After Effects can compensate for the distortion due to PAR (**Figure 3.84**). As After Effects warns you when you use the Toggle Pixel Aspect Ratio Correction button, correcting the image this way is for viewing purposes only; it doesn't affect the image's actual scale. And because correcting an image requires some processing, it will take slightly longer to render frames.

To toggle pixel aspect correction:

1. In a Footage, Composition, or Layer panel, click the Toggle Pixel Aspect Ratio Correction button 🔲 to select it (**Figure 3.85**).

   If this is the first time you've used the button during this session, After Effects reminds you how PAR correction works and prompts you to specify whether you want to see the warning once per session or never again.

   continues on next page

2. Select an option in the dialog box, and click OK.

If the image's PAR doesn't match your computer monitor's PAR, After Effects scales the image so that it no longer appears distorted.

✔ Tip

■ This chapter hasn't covered a few buttons in the Footage panel. The Region of Interest button will make more sense in the context of playback, covered in Chapter 8, "Playback, Previews, and RAM." The Footage panel for motion footage also contains a number of editing controls, which are fully explained in Chapter 6, "Layer Editing."

CORRECTING FOR PIXEL ASPECT RATIOS

COMPOSITIONS

Without compositions, a project is nothing more than a list of footage items—a grocery list without a recipe; an ensemble without choreography; finely tuned instruments without, well, a composition. This is because compositions perform the essential function of describing how footage items are arranged in space and time. This chapter shows you how to create a composition and define its spatial and temporal boundaries by setting frame size, frame rate, duration, and so on.

This chapter also describes the fundamental process of layering footage in compositions (and in so doing lays the groundwork for the rest of the book, which focuses largely on how to manipulate those layers). The footage items you add to a composition become layers, which are manipulated in the defined space and time of the composition, as represented by Composition and Timeline panels. The following pages will give you an overview of these panels as well as the Time Controls panel. This chapter will also introduce you to the technique of nesting, using comps as layers in other comps—a concept you'll appreciate more fully as your projects grow more complex.

Creating Compositions

A composition contains layers of footage and describes how you arrange those layers in space and time. This section explains how to create a composition; the following section describes how to choose specific settings to define a composition's spatial and temporal attributes.

To create a new composition:

1. *Do one of the following:*

   ▲ Choose Composition > New Composition.

   ▲ Press Command-N (Mac) or Ctrl-N (Windows).

   ▲ At the bottom of the Project panel, click the Create Composition button (**Figure 4.1**).

   A Composition Settings dialog box appears (**Figure 4.2**).

2. Choose a name for the composition, and specify preset or custom composition settings (such as frame size, pixel aspect ratio, frame rate, display resolution, and duration) for the composition. (See "Choosing Composition Settings" later in this chapter for details.)

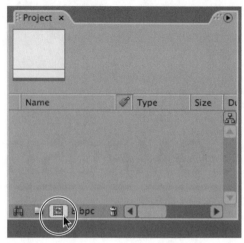

Figure 4.1 Click the Create Composition button at the bottom of the Project panel.

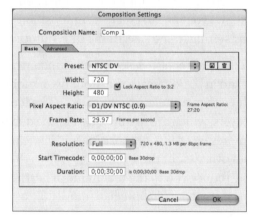

Figure 4.2 In the Composition Settings dialog box, enter the appropriate settings for the composition.

3. Click OK to close the Composition Settings dialog box.

A new composition appears in the Project panel, and related Composition and Timeline panels open (**Figure 4.3**).

✔ Tip

■ You can create a composition that contains a footage item by dragging the item's icon to the Create Composition icon in the Project panel. The new composition will use the same image dimensions as the footage item it contains.

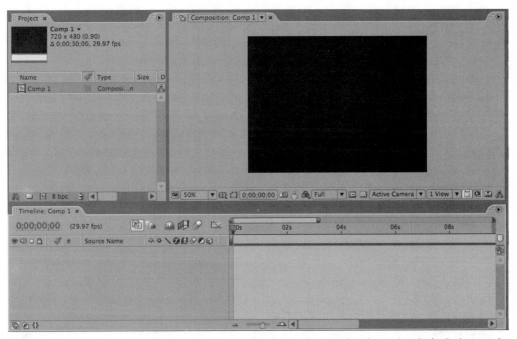

Figure 4.3 A composition appears in a Composition panel and a Timeline panel, and as an icon in the Project panel.

Choosing Composition Settings

Because compositions describe how layers are arranged in space and time, you must define a composition's spatial attributes (such as its frame size and pixel aspect ratio) as well as its temporal aspects (such as its duration and frame rate). Composition settings allow you to specify these characteristics. You can also use the composition settings to specify the resolution or quality of the Composition panel's display. You may change composition settings at any time.

A project usually contains several compositions, most of which are contained as layers (or *nested*) in a final composition. Although you can set the final composition's settings according to your output format (NTSC DV, for example), you may want to employ different settings (particularly for frame size and duration) for intermediate compositions.

✔ Tips

■ It's easy to forget to name your composition or to settle for the default name, *Comp 1*. Do yourself a favor and give the composition a descriptive name. This will help you remain organized as your project becomes more complex.

■ You can open the Composition Settings dialog box for the current composition by pressing Command-K (Mac) or Ctrl-K (Windows).

■ You can also access the Composition Settings dialog box from the Timeline panel's pop-up menu; however, using the keyboard shortcut—Command-K (Mac) or Ctrl-K (Windows)—is the quickest way.

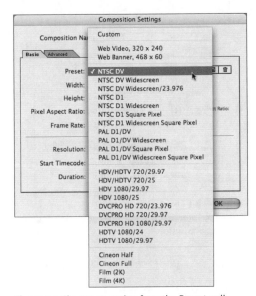

Figure 4.4 Choose an option from the Preset pull-down menu.

Specifying Composition Presets

With After Effects, you don't need to manually enter all the composition settings (frame size, pixel aspect ratio, and so on); instead, you can select the most common ones from a pull-down menu of presets. If the list doesn't include a preset for *your* most commonly used settings, you can save your custom settings to the list. You can even delete the presets you don't want. For a brief explanation of some common presets, see **Table 4.1**.

To select a composition preset:

1. In the Composition Settings dialog box, choose an option from the Preset menu (**Figure 4.4**).

   Choose the preset that matches your needs. Presets include common settings for film, video broadcast, and multimedia projects. Individual settings are set automatically. However, you may want to enter a starting frame number and duration for the comp (see "Setting a comp's start-frame number" and "Setting a comp's duration," later in this chapter).

2. Click OK to close the Composition Settings dialog box.

   The composition appears in the Project panel.

Table 4.1

	Common composition presets			
PRESET	FRAME SIZE	PAR	FRAME RATE	USE
NTSC	640 x 480	1	29.97	Full-screen, full-motion video, used by low-end cards
NTSC DV	720 x 480	.9	29.97	DV standard for North America
NTSC D1	720 x 486	.9	29.97	Broadcast standard for North America
HDTV	1920 x 1080	1	24	High-definition standard using 16:9 image aspect ratio
Film (2k)	2048 x 1536	1	24	Film transfers
Cineon Full	3656 x 2664	1	24	Film transferred using the Cineon file format

To save a composition preset:

1. In the Composition Settings dialog box, enter the settings suitable for the composition.

   See the following sections for instructions on choosing specific settings. You can choose an existing preset to use as a starting point, or you can choose Custom from the Preset pull-down menu.

2. Click the Save button 🖫 (**Figure 4.5**).

   A Choose Name dialog box appears.

3. Enter a name for your preset, and then click OK (**Figure 4.6**).

   The settings you specified are saved as a preset, and the preset's name appears in the Preset pull-down menu of the Composition Settings dialog box.

To delete a composition preset:

1. In the Preset pull-down menu of the Composition Settings dialog box, choose a preset.

2. Click the Delete button 🗑 (**Figure 4.7**).

   A Warning dialog box prompts you to confirm whether you want to delete the preset.

3. In the Warning dialog box, click OK to delete the selected preset (**Figure 4.8**).

   The preset is deleted and no longer appears in the Preset pull-down menu.

✔ Tip

- You can restore the presets that ship with After Effects by Option-clicking (Mac) or Alt-clicking (Windows) the Delete button.

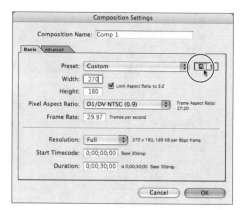

Figure 4.5 Enter the comp settings you want, and click the Save button.

Figure 4.6 In the Choose Name dialog box, enter a name for your preset.

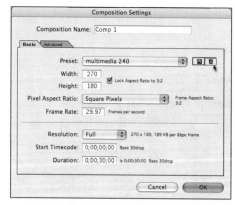

Figure 4.7 Select the preset you want to remove, and click the Delete button.

Figure 4.8 In the Warning dialog box, click OK if you're sure you want to delete the preset.

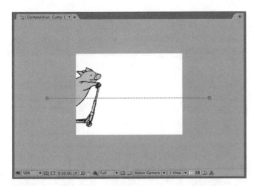

Figure 4.9 The frame size defines the dimensions of the viewable area of the composition. Over time, an element may move from the offscreen work area...

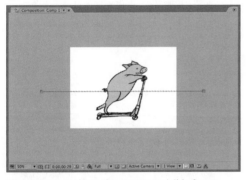

Figure 4.10 ...and into the onscreen visible frame...

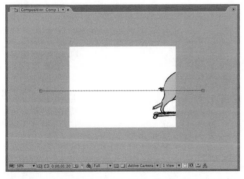

Figure 4.11 ...and vice versa. Only elements within the visible frame appear in the final output.

Setting a comp's frame size

The frame size determines the viewing area of the Composition panel. Although you may position images in the workspace outside of this viewing area (what some call the *pasteboard*), only the elements within the visible frame will be rendered for previews and output (**Figures 4.9**, **4.10**, and **4.11**).

Often, the frame dimensions of the final output determine the frame size of a composition. However, if the composition is to be nested in another composition, the frame size may be larger or smaller than the pixel dimensions of the final output. (See "Nesting Compositions," later in this chapter, or see Chapter 16, "Complex Projects.")

The Composition Settings dialog box provides a list of preset frame sizes, or you may enter a custom frame size. The frame size you choose is centered in a workspace that's limited to the same maximum dimensions as imported image files. As with imported footage files, chances are you'll run out of available RAM before you exceed the maximum image size (up to 30,000 × 30,000 pixels, depending on the output option).

For more about the maximum frame size of images, see the sidebar "Wham, Bam— Thank You, RAM" in Chapter 2, "Importing Footage into a Project." If you change the frame size of an existing composition, the Anchor setting determines where the existing layers are placed in the new comp (see "Setting a comp's anchor," later in this chapter).

SPECIFYING COMPOSITION PRESETS

To set the frame size:

1. In the Composition Settings dialog box, *do one of the following:*
   - ▲ Enter the width and height of the frame in pixels.
   - ▲ Choose a preset frame size from the pull-down menu (**Figure 4.12**).

2. If you're changing the frame size of an existing composition, choose an anchor point from the Anchor section of the Composition Settings dialog box (visible when you select the Advanced tab).

✔ Tips

■ You can enter a custom frame size that uses the same image aspect ratio as a preset frame size. First, choose a preset frame size that uses the image aspect ratio you want to maintain. Then, click the "Lock Aspect Ratio to" check box, and enter a custom frame size. When you enter a value for one dimension, After Effects automatically fills in the other, maintaining the same aspect ratio.

■ When you go back and change a composition's frame size, you should also select an Anchor option in the Advanced tab of the Composition Settings dialog box (see "Setting a comp's anchor," later in this chapter).

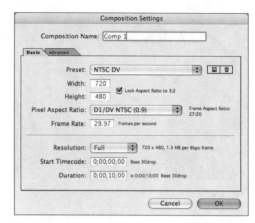

Figure 4.12 Enter the frame dimensions, or choose a preset size from the pull-down menu.

Figure 4.13 Incorrectly interpreted as having non-square pixels, this 640 × 480 square-pixel image seems to lose its 4:3 aspect ratio in this 720 × 486 (D1/nonsquare pixels) composition.

Figure 4.14 Correctly interpreted as having square pixels, the image is automatically resized to compensate for a composition set to the D1 standard.

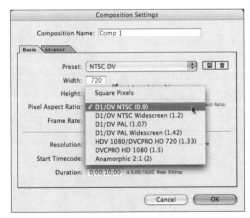

Figure 4.15 In the Pixel Aspect Ratio pull-down menu, choose the PAR that corresponds to your final output.

Setting a comp's pixel aspect ratio

A typical computer monitor uses square pixels to display an image. Professional video, in contrast, uses nonsquare pixels to display images. As a result, an image created on a computer can appear distorted when transferred to video, and vice versa.

One of After Effects' great advantages is that it can compensate for differences in pixel aspect ratios. In fact, when you choose a preset frame size, After Effects automatically selects the corresponding pixel aspect ratio (PAR). If you want to override this setting, or if you enter a custom frame size, you can choose the correct PAR manually.

After Effects compensates for any difference between the PAR of the composition and that of individual footage items. For example, if you add a square-pixel footage item into a D1 composition, After Effects automatically resizes the image to prevent image distortion in the final output (**Figures 4.13** and **4.14**).

For a detailed explanation of PAR, see the sidebar "PAR Excellence" in Chapter 2.

To set the pixel aspect ratio of a composition:

◆ From the Pixel Aspect Ratio pull-down menu in the Composition Settings dialog box, choose a PAR (**Figure 4.15**).

✔ Tip

■ As suggested earlier, the most common PARs are square pixel (with a PAR of 1) and D1/DV NTSC (with a PAR of .9). Square pixels correspond to formats displayed on computer monitors or consumer-level video capture cards. D1/DV NTSC corresponds to the nonsquare pixels used by professional NTSC video formats (D1 or ITU-R 601) and the DV video standards (mini DV, DVCam, and DVCPro).

Frame rate

The *frame rate* is the number of frames per second (fps) used by a composition. Usually, the frame rate you choose matches the frame rate of your output format.

Individual footage items have their own frame rates, which you can interpret. (See "Setting the Frame Rate" in Chapter 2.) Ideally, the footage frame rate and the composition frame rate match. If not, After Effects makes the frame rate of the footage item conform to that of the composition.

To set the frame rate of the composition:

◆ In the Frame Rate field in the Composition Settings dialog box, enter a frame rate (**Figure 4.16**).

Usually, you'll choose a frame rate that matches the frame rate of the output format:

▲ NTSC video: 29.97 fps

▲ PAL video: 25 fps

▲ Film: 24 fps

▲ Computer presentation (often via CD-ROM or Web): 15 fps or 10 fps

Lower frame rates help reduce file size and conform to data-rate limitations.

✔ Tips

■ Film that has been transferred to video often uses video frame rates and has undergone the process of 3:2 pulldown. For more about 3:2 pulldown, see Chapter 2.

■ Use the Interpret Footage command to set the proper frame rate for a footage item; set the composition's frame rate according to your output requirements. If you're interested in changing the speed of a layer, see Chapter 6, "Layer Editing."

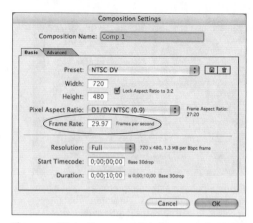

Figure 4.16 Enter the appropriate frame rate for the composition.

Reconciling the Footage's and Comp's Frame Rate

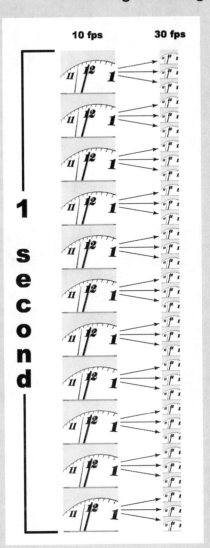

10 fps   **30 fps**

1 second

If both the composition frame rate and the footage frame rate are 30 fps, the footage in a layer advances a frame whenever the composition advances a frame. However, if the footage frame rate is 10 fps and the composition frame rate is 30 fps, After Effects will distribute one second of footage (10 frames) over one second of the composition (30 frames) by displaying each frame of footage three times. In other words, the composition must advance three frames to display a new frame of the footage layer (**Figure 4.17**).

Figure 4.17 The frame rate of a footage item is conformed to the frame rate of the composition. In this case, frames of a 10-fps animation are repeated to play in a 30-fps composition to avoid an apparent change in speed.

Setting a comp's viewing resolution

Frame size sets the actual pixel dimensions of the composition; *resolution* determines the fraction of the pixels that are displayed in the Composition panel.

By lowering the resolution, you reduce not only image quality but also the amount of memory needed to render frames. Rendering speeds increase in proportion to image quality sacrificed. Typically, you work and preview your composition at a lower resolution and then render the final output at full resolution (**Figures 4.18** and **4.19**).

To set a composition's resolution:

1. In the Composition Settings dialog box, choose a setting from the Resolution pull-down menu (**Figure 4.20**):

   Full—After Effects renders and displays every pixel of the composition, resulting in the highest image quality and the longest rendering time.

   Half—After Effects renders every other pixel, or one-quarter of the pixels of the full-resolution image, in one-quarter of the time.

   Third—After Effects renders every third pixel, or one-ninth of the pixels in the full-resolution image, in one-ninth of the time.

   Quarter—After Effects renders every fourth pixel, or one-sixteenth of the pixels in the full-resolution image, in one-sixteenth of the time.

   Custom—After Effects renders whatever fraction of pixels you specify.

Figure 4.18 Typically, you work and preview a composition at a lower resolution (in this case, quarter resolution)...

Figure 4.19 ...and then switch to full resolution when you want to see the image at output quality or render the final version.

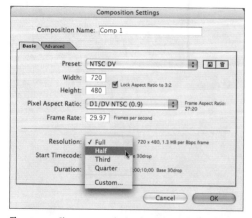

Figure 4.20 Choose a resolution from the pull-down menu.

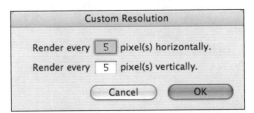

Figure 4.21 If you choose Custom from the pull-down menu, enter values to determine the resolution manually. Rendering every fifth horizontal and vertical pixel would equal one-twenty-fifth of the resolution and rendering time.

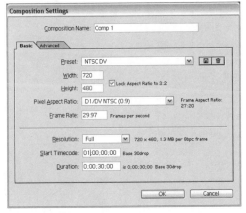

Figure 4.22 You can also change the resolution using the pull-down menu at the bottom of the Composition panel.

Figure 4.23 If you want to, enter a starting frame number.

2. If you choose Custom from the pull-down menu, enter values to determine the horizontal and vertical resolution of the image (**Figure 4.21**).

✔ Tips

■ You can also change the resolution at any time by using the Resolution pull-down menu in the Composition panel (**Figure 4.22**). See "The Composition panel," later in this chapter.

■ You can control the quality setting of individual layers separately from the composition as a whole. See Chapter 5, "Layer Basics," for more details.

Setting a comp's start-frame number

When you began your project, you set its time display—that is, the method used to count your project's frames. As you may recall from Chapter 2, you can set the time display to standard video or film counting schemes (see "Choosing a Time Display" in Chapter 2). You can also set the frame number at which each composition starts. For example, you may want a composition's frame numbers to match the timecode of its source footage.

To set a composition's starting frame number:

1. In the Composition Settings dialog box, enter the starting frame number of the composition (**Figure 4.23**).

The timebase you set for the project determines whether this number is expressed in timecode, feet and frames, or frame numbers.

2. Click OK to close the Composition Settings dialog box.

The composition begins at the frame number you specified.

Setting a comp's duration

Duration—which sets the length of a composition—is expressed in the time display style you set in the Project Settings dialog box (timecode, frames, or feet and frames). See "Choosing Composition Settings" earlier in this chapter for more about time display options. You can change the composition's duration at any time, lengthening it to accommodate more layers or cutting it to the total duration of its layers.

To set the duration of a composition:

◆ In the Duration field in the Composition Settings dialog box, enter the duration of the composition (**Figure 4.24**).

✔ Tip

■ You can also quickly trim the comp's duration to the length of the work area by choosing Composition > Trim Comp to Work Area. For more about the work area, see Chapter 8, "Playback, Previews, and RAM."

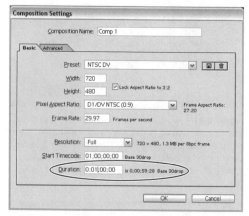

Figure 4.24 Enter the duration for the composition.

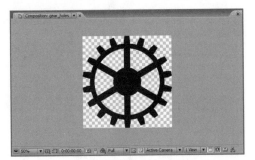

Figure 4.25 Before the composition is resized, it looks like this.

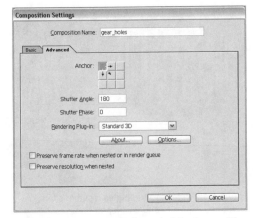

Figure 4.26 In the Advanced panel of the Composition Settings dialog box, click one of the nine anchor positions.

Specifying Advanced Composition Settings

The Composition Settings dialog box is divided into Basic and Advanced panels. The previous sections covered the settings in the Basic panel. Clicking the Advanced tab reveals a number of additional settings, which are discussed here, although many will make more sense to you later as this book delves deeper into the program. You'll be reminded of each setting again when you encounter the task or technique to which it pertains.

Setting a comp's anchor

When you resize a composition, you use the Anchor control to determine how the composition and its layers are placed in the new frame—that is, whether they're anchored in the center, corner, or side of the new frame.

To set the anchor of a resized composition:

1. Select a composition, and press Command-K (Mac) or Ctrl-K (Windows) (**Figure 4.25**).
   The Composition Settings dialog box appears.

2. To change the frame size of the composition, enter new values in the Width and Height fields.

3. Click the Advanced tab.
   The Advanced settings pane of the Composition Settings dialog box appears.

4. In the Anchor control, click one of the nine anchor point positions (**Figure 4.26**).

continues on next page

SPECIFYING ADVANCED COMPOSITION SETTINGS

5. Click OK to close the Composition Settings dialog box.

The layers contained in the composition align to the position you specified (**Figure 4.27**).

✔ Tip

■ Don't confuse the composition's anchor with a layer's anchor point, which is something else altogether. To find out about the layer Anchor Point property, see Chapter 7, "Properties and Keyframes."

Choosing a comp's shutter settings

In many ways, a composition is analogous to a camera. Just as a camera's shutter helps determine how blurry or sharp a moving object appears on film, After Effects compositions include a shutter setting that serves a similar purpose. Layers with motion blur applied to them appear blurred (when motion blur is enabled), according to the shutter settings.

As in a camera, the shutter angle and frame rate work together to simulate an exposure. Wider shutter angles result in a longer simulated exposure and blurrier motion (**Figure 4.28**); narrower shutter angles result in a shorter simulated exposure and sharper moving images (**Figure 4.29**). The optional Shutter Phase setting determines the shutter's starting position at the frame start.

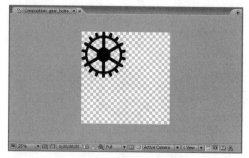

Figure 4.27 The layers are anchored to the position you specified in the resized comp.

Figure 4.28 Wider shutter angles result in a longer simulated exposure and blurrier motion.

Figure 4.29 Narrower shutter angles result in a shorter simulated exposure and sharper motion.

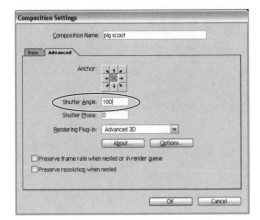

Figure 4.30 In the Advanced panel of the Composition Settings dialog box, enter a value for Shutter Angle.

To set shutter angle and phase:

1. In the Advanced panel of the Composition Settings dialog box, enter a value for Shutter Angle (**Figure 4.30**).

   The default setting is 180 degrees.

2. To set the position of the shutter relative to the start frame, enter a value for Shutter Phase.

   You may enter an angle between 0 and 360 degrees.

3. Click OK to close the Composition Settings dialog box.

✔ Tips

- If you're not sure what shutter angle to use, 180 degrees works fine. You can always change the angle when you start using and previewing motion blur. For more about motion blur, see Chapter 14, "More Layer Techniques."

- You can also set the shutter angle in the Render Queue dialog box. See Chapter 17, "Output," for more information.

Nesting options

As you know by now, compositions can become layers within other compositions, a technique called *nesting*. In the composition's settings, nesting options dictate whether nested compositions retain their own frame-rate and resolution settings or assume those of the composition in which they're nested. For more about nesting compositions, see Chapter 16.

To set nesting options:

1. In the Advanced panel of the Composition Settings dialog box, *select one or both of the following* options (**Figure 4.31**):

   Preserve frame rate when nested or in render queue—Choosing this option allows nested compositions to retain their frame rates, regardless of the frame rate of the composition that contains them.

   Preserve resolution when nested—If this option is selected, nested compositions will retain their resolution settings, regardless of the resolution of the composition that contains them.

   If you select neither option, nested compositions will take on the frame rate and resolution of the composition in which they're nested.

2. Click OK to close the Composition Settings dialog box.

✔ Tips

- By preserving the frame rate of a nested composition, you can achieve results similar to those produced by the Posterize Time effect.

- The Render Queue dialog box allows you to use the current resolution settings or to reset them for all nested comps. See Chapter 17 for more about the render queue.

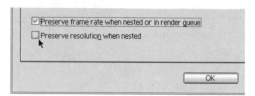

Figure 4.31 Select the nesting option(s) you want.

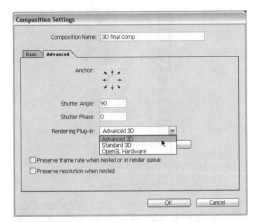

Figure 4.32 Choose a rendering plug-in from the pull-down menu.

Choosing a 3D rendering plug-in

In case you've forgotten, After Effects allows you to composite layers in three-dimensional space. The standard package comes with the standard 3D rendering plug-in; After Effects Pro includes an advanced 3D plug-in, which supports more sophisticated 3D features such as the intersection of 3D layers, diffuse shadows, and the like. If your computer is equipped with an After Effects–compatible OpenGL graphics card, you can designate it for 3D rendering. See Chapter 15, "3D Layers," for more about 3D layers and compositing; see Chapter 8 for more about previewing and OpenGL.

To set the rendering plug-in:

1. In the Advanced panel of the Composition dialog box, *choose one of the following* options in the Rendering Plug-in pull-down menu (**Figure 4.32**):

    Advanced 3D—Select this option to use the advanced 3D plug-in (included with After Effects Pro).

    Standard 3D—Select this option to use the standard 3D plug-in.

    OpenGL Hardware—Select this option to use your After Effects–compatible OpenGL graphics card for 3D rendering.

2. If you chose Advanced 3D in step 1, click Options, and specify the shadow mask resolution in the Advanced 3D Options dialog box.

3. Click OK to close the Composition Settings dialog box.

    If you chose OpenGL Hardware in step 1, the Composition panel displays *OpenGL* in the pasteboard area.

Setting a Comp's Background Color

The default background color of compositions is black; however, you can change the background to any color you choose. Regardless of what color you make it, the background becomes the alpha channel when you output the composition as a still-image sequence or a movie with an alpha channel. Similarly, if you use the composition as a layer in another composition, the background of the nested composition becomes transparent (**Figure 4.33**) (see "Nesting Compositions," later in this chapter). And as with the Footage panel (see Chapter 3, "Managing Footage") and the Layer panel, you can also view the background as a checkerboard pattern, called a *transparency grid*.

To choose a background color for your composition:

1. Select a composition in the Project panel, or activate a composition in a Composition or Timeline panel.

Figure 4.33 The background of the comp (first image) becomes transparent when nested into another comp (second image). The result is the third image.

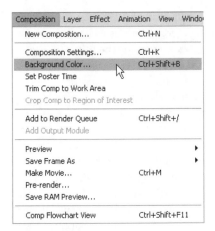

Figure 4.34 Choose Composition > Background Color.

Figure 4.35 Click the eyedropper to pick a screen color, or click the swatch to open a color picker.

2. Choose Composition > Background Color (**Figure 4.34**), or press Shift-Command-B (Mac) or Shift-Ctrl-B (Windows).

   A Background Color dialog box appears.

3. In the Background Color dialog box, *do one of the following* (**Figure 4.35**):

   ▲ Click the color swatch to open the color picker.

   ▲ Click the eyedropper to choose a color from another window.

4. Click OK to close the Background Color dialog box.

   The selected composition uses the background color you specified.

✔ Tip

■ If you need an opaque background—in a nested composition, for example—create a solid layer as described in "To create a solid-color layer," later in this chapter.

The Composition and Timeline Panels

All of your compositions can be represented in the Composition and Timeline panels, which open automatically whenever you create or open a composition. These two panels furnish you with different ways of looking at a composition and manipulating its layers. This section will give you an overview of each panel, emphasizing how they show layers along with their spatial and temporal relationships.

The Composition panel

The Composition—or Comp—panel (**Figure 4.36**) displays the layers of footage visible at the current frame of a composition. You can use the Comp panel to visually preview the way a composition's layers are rendered within the visible frame as well as how those layers are placed outside the frame (in the *pasteboard* area). The Composition panel is where you'll find the controls for viewing composition layers (many of which are shared by the Footage and Layer panels) as well as those for setting a composition's current frame and resolution. You can move and scale layers and masks directly in the Comp panel, and you can also view information such as layer paths, keyframes, and tangents. The Comp panel also includes a few buttons that will be discussed in later chapters. A discussion of the Region of Interest (which is also available in the Footage and Layer panels) and Fast Preview buttons is reserved for Chapter 8. Chapter 15 covers the Camera View pull-down menu along with other features pertaining to 3D compositing.

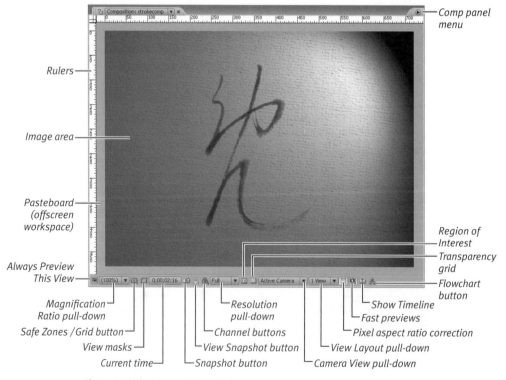

Figure 4.36 The Composition panel.

The Timeline panel

The Timeline panel (**Figure 4.37**) graphically represents a composition as layers in a timeline. A vertical line—called the *time marker*—corresponds to the current frame pictured in the Composition panel. In the Timeline panel, each layer occupies a row, and the rows are stacked vertically. (Unlike the tracks of many nonlinear editing programs, each row contains only one layer.) Layers that are higher in the Timeline panel's stacking order appear in front of lower layers when viewed in the Composition panel. The Timeline panel offers more than just an alternative view of the composition; it gives you precise control over virtually every attribute of each layer in a composition.

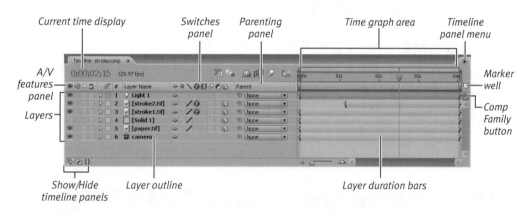

Figure 4.37 The Timeline panel.

Setting the Time

Before you add footage to a composition, you must specify the time at which the layer will begin in the composition. By setting the composition's current time, you can also set the starting point for an added layer. And, of course, setting the time also allows you to view a particular frame of the composition in the Comp panel. You can set the current time via the Time Controls panel, the Composition panel, or the Timeline panel; you can also use keyboard shortcuts to accomplish the task.

Using the Time Controls panel

You can control the playback of the Footage, Composition, Timeline, and Layer panels using the Time Controls panel. **Figure 4.38** describes how the panel's buttons function.

To set the current time in the Timeline panel:

◆ In the Timeline panel, drag the current time indicator to the frame you want (**Figure 4.39**).

Use the current time display to see the current time numerically.

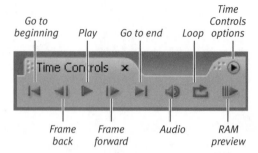

Figure 4.38 The Time Controls panel. (In this figure, the RAM preview options are hidden.)

Figure 4.39 In the Timeline panel, drag the current time indicator to change the current frame (displayed in the Composition panel).

Figure 4.40 Click the time display in the Composition panel...

Figure 4.41 ...or in the Timeline panel...

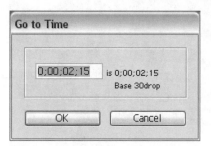

Figure 4.42 ...or use the keyboard shortcut to open the Go to Time dialog box. Enter a specific frame number, or absolute time, to cue the current frame...

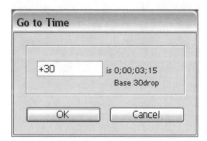

Figure 4.43 ...or enter a time relative to the current frame by entering a plus (+) or minus (-) and the number of frames.

To cue the current time of the composition numerically:

1. *Do any of the following:*
   - ▲ In the Composition panel, click the time display (**Figure 4.40**).
   - ▲ In the Timeline panel, click the time display (**Figure 4.41**).
   - ▲ Press Command-G (Mac) or Ctrl-G (Windows).

   The Go to Time dialog box appears.

2. *Do one of the following:*
   - ▲ Enter an absolute time (a specific frame number) to which you want to cue the current time (**Figure 4.42**).
   - ▲ Enter a plus (+) or minus (-) and a relative time (the number of frames you want to add or subtract from the current frame) (**Figure 4.43**). Numbers greater than 99 are interpreted as seconds and frames.

3. Click OK to close the Go to Time dialog box.

✔ Tips

- ■ By clicking the arrows to the left of the Time Controls panel's name, you can cycle through different views of the window that include fewer or more controls.

- ■ Because you'll frequently need to change the current time in the Composition, Timeline, Footage, and Layer panels, you should familiarize yourself with the keyboard shortcuts that help you get around—for example (on an expanded keyboard), Page Down to advance one frame and Page Up to go back one frame. Consult the Help System for more keyboard shortcuts.

SETTING THE TIME

Adding Footage to a Composition

When you add an item to a composition, you create a layer. A layer can be a footage item in the project, a solid or adjustment layer generated in After Effects, or another composition. You can add an item to a composition more than once to create multiple layers, or you can duplicate existing layers (using the Copy, Paste, and Duplicate commands). In this section, you'll learn to create layers in a composition. Later chapters will show you how to rearrange and modify layers. (Eventually, you'll also learn about specialized layers such as guide layers, and layers used in 3D compositing: 3D layers, lights, cameras, and null objects. But first things first.)

The method you use to add layers depends on how you want to set their initial position, starting point, and layer order in your composition. You can simply drag a layer to the timeline to position it at any time or level in the stacking order.

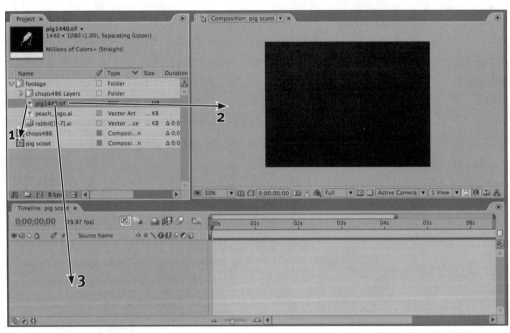

Figure 4.44 You can drag one or more items from the Project panel to a composition in the Project panel (1), its Composition panel (2), or the Timeline panel (3).

To add footage to a composition by dragging:

1. Set the current time of the composition using one of the methods described earlier in this chapter.

2. Drag one or more items from the Project panel to *any of the following* (**Figure 4.44**):

   Composition panel—To place the layers in the desired position, at the current time, and layered in the order in which the files were selected in the Project panel

   Timeline panel—To place the layers at the desired time and layer, and centered in the visible frame of the composition

   Name or icon of a composition in the Project panel—To place the layers at the current time, centered in the visible frame of the composition, and layered in the order in which you selected the items in the Project panel

   Items become layers in the composition whose position, starting time, and layer order all depend on the method you employed to add them to the composition. Layers created from still-image footage use the default duration for stills (see Chapter 2). The duration of other layers is determined by the In and Out points you set in their Footage panel (see "To set source footage edit points" later in this chapter).

✔ Tips

- Another quick way to add footage to the centered composition is to select the footage item in the Project panel and press Command-/ (Mac) or Ctrl-/ (Windows).

- Option-dragging (Mac) or Alt-dragging (Windows) footage to an existing layer in the Timeline replaces the layer with the new footage.

Adding Layers Using Insert and Overlay

You can add motion footage to your composition by using tools and techniques commonly found in non-linear editing (NLE) software. Buttons in the Footage panel, for example, allow you to perform insert and overlay edits—both of which add a layer at the current time, although each affects the timeline's existing layers differently.

When you add a layer using an *overlay* edit, the composition's layers retain their current positions in time. The new layer is added as the topmost layer at the current time (**Figures 4.45** and **4.46**).

In contrast, adding a layer via an *insert* edit causes the composition's existing layers to shift in time to accommodate the new layer. In other words, if the new layer is five seconds long, all layers after the current time move forward five seconds. If the current time occurs midway through a layer, the layer is split into two layers; the portion after the current time shifts forward (**Figure 4.47**).

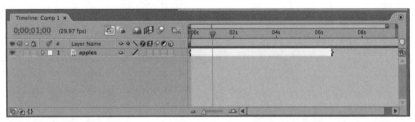

Figure 4.45 Note the arrangement of the layers before an insert or overlay edit, as well as the position of the current time indicator.

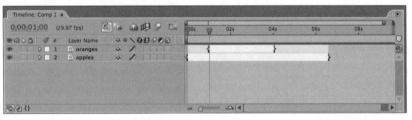

Figure 4.46 After an overlay edit, the new layer is added as the topmost layer at the current time.

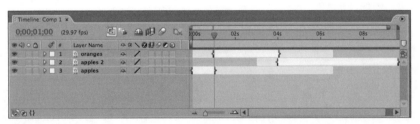

Figure 4.47 After an insert edit, layers after the current time shift forward to accommodate the new layer. One of the layers is split at the edit point, and the portion after the edit point shifts forward.

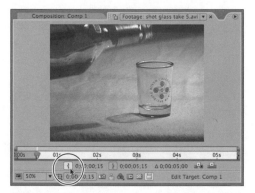

Figure 4.48 Cue the current time to the point at which you want the source footage to start, and click the Set In button to set the source In point.

Figure 4.49 Cue the current time to the point at which you want the source footage to stop, and click the Set Out button to set the source Out point.

To set source footage edit points:

1. Option-double-click (Mac) or Alt-double-click (Windows) a motion footage item in the Project panel.

   The motion footage item opens in an After Effects Footage panel.

2. To set an In point, cue the current time and click the Set In button ⧉.

   The In point display and the duration bar reflect the In point you set (**Figure 4.48**).

3. To set an Out point, cue the current time and click the Set Out button ⧉.

   The Out point display and the duration bar reflect the Out point you set (**Figure 4.49**).

To insert or overlay a layer:

1. Set the current time of the composition to which you want to add the layer.

   You can use the Go To Time command, the Time Controls panel, or the current time indicator in the Timeline panel (as described in the section "Setting the Time," earlier in this chapter).

2. In the Footage panel, set the source footage In and Out points (as described in the previous task).

   Make sure the Edit Target section of the Footage panel displays the name of the composition to which you want to add a layer. If the project contains more than one composition, the window displays the currently selected composition.

continues on next page

3. In the Footage panel, *click either of the following:*

Ripple Insert—If you select this option , all other layers will be shifted forward to accommodate the new layer (**Figure 4.50**).

Overlay—If you select this option , other layers will retain their current positions in time.

The selected footage is added to the composition as the topmost layer at the current time. Other layers' positions in time will depend on whether you selected an insert or overlay edit.

✔ Tips

- To learn about editing in the timeline, see Chapter 6.

- Editors may also be pleased to know that another common video-editing feature, the *slip edit*, has found its way into After Effects. See Chapter 6.

Figure 4.50 Depending on the type of edit you want to perform, click the Ripple Insert or Overlay button.

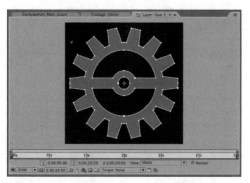

Figure 4.51 You can add text or other effects to a solid; you can mask a solid to create graphical elements (shown here); or you can use it as a solid-color background.

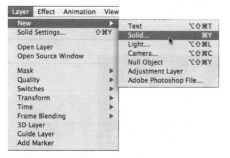

Figure 4.52 Choose Layer > New > Solid, or use the keyboard shortcut.

Figure 4.53 In the Solid Settings dialog box, enter a name for the solid layer. Click the Make Comp Size button to make the solid the same size as the composition, or enter a custom width and height.

Creating Solid Layers

As you might expect, a *solid* layer is a layer in the size and color of your choice. You create a solid layer when you need an opaque background for a nested composition. You can also use solids with masks to create graphic elements (**Figure 4.51**). And you can even use this type of layer to create text effects within After Effects. (For more about text effects, see Chapter 11, "Effects Fundamentals"; for more about masks, see Chapter 10, "Mask Essentials.")

Creating a solid doesn't produce an actual media file on your hard drive. But in other respects, a solid layer works like any other footage item: It has specified dimensions and PAR, as well as a color. (This is notable because older versions of After Effects didn't allow you to set a solid's PAR, forcing you to treat it a little differently than other footage items.) However, this doesn't mean the solid's settings are fixed; you can change its attributes at any time.

To create a solid-color layer:

1. Open the Composition panel or Timeline panel for the composition in which you want to add a solid layer, or make sure one is active.

2. Choose Layer > New > Solid, or press Command-Y (Mac) or Ctrl-Y (Windows) (**Figure 4.52**).

    The Solid Settings dialog box appears (**Figure 4.53**).

3. Enter a name for the new solid.

    After Effects uses the solid's current color as the basis for the default name: for example, Gray Solid 1.

continues on next page

CREATING SOLID LAYERS

4. Set the size by *doing any of the following*:

- ▲ To make the solid the same size as the composition, click the Make Comp Size button.

- ▲ To enter a custom size, choose a unit of measure from the Units pull-down menu, and enter a width and height (**Figure 4.54**).

- ▲ To maintain the aspect ratio of the current width and height, click the Lock Aspect Ratio button before you change the size.

5. Choose an option from the Pixel Aspect Ratio pull-down menu (**Figure 4.55**).

For an explanation of PAR, see the side-bar "PAR Excellence" in Chapter 2.

6. Set the color by *doing one of the following*:

- ▲ Click the color swatch to open the color picker, and choose a color.

- ▲ Click the eyedropper to select a color from the screen.

7. Click OK to close the Solid Settings dialog box.

The solid appears as a layer in the composition. Like any layer, the solid layer starts at the current time and uses the default duration of still images. (See "To change the default duration of still images" in Chapter 2.) In the Project panel, After Effects creates a folder called Solids that contains all the solid footage items you create.

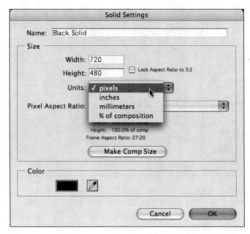

Figure 4.54 Choose a unit of measure from the pull-down menu before you enter a custom size.

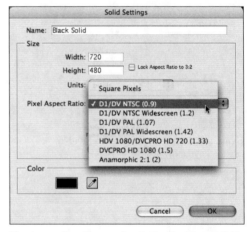

Figure 4.55 Specify an option in the Pixel Aspect Ratio pull-down menu.

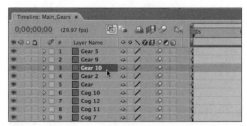

Figure 4.56 Select a solid footage item in the Project panel, or a solid layer in the Comp or Timeline panel (shown here).

Figure 4.57 Choose Layer > Solid Settings.

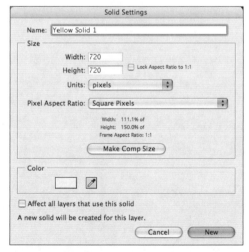

Figure 4.58 Specify new settings, and click New to modify a selected layer only...

To change a solid's settings:

1. *Do either of the following:*

   ▲ In the Project panel, select a solid footage item.

   ▲ In the Composition or Timeline panel, click a solid layer to select it (**Figure 4.56**).

   You may also use a variety of other methods to select a layer; for more information, see "Selecting Layers" in Chapter 5.

2. *Do either of the following:*

   ▲ Choose Layer > Solid Settings (**Figure 4.57**).

   ▲ Press Shift-Command-Y (Mac) or Shift-Ctrl-Y (Windows).

   The Solid Settings dialog box appears.

3. Specify any changes you want to make to the solid footage, such as its name, dimensions, PAR, or color (**Figure 4.58**).

continues on next page

4. If you selected the solid layer from the Timeline or Composition panel in step 1, specify whether you want the changes to affect layers already created from the solid footage item by selecting "Affect all layers that use this solid" (**Figure 4.59**).

Leave this option unselected if you want to change only this layer and not layers already created from it.

5. Click OK.

Depending on your choices, the changes you specified are applied to the selected solid layer, solid footage item, or both.

✔ Tip

■ You can continuously rasterize a solid layer. That way, its edges (particularly when you have a mask applied to it) remain crisp and smooth when you scale it up. See Chapter 5 for more about the Continuously Rasterize switch; see Chapter 10 for more about masks.

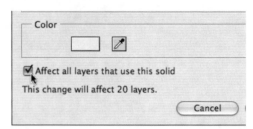

Figure 4.59 ...or select "Affect all layers that use this solid," to modify all layers created from the solid.

Figure 4.60 In this example, part of the composite image is inverted for a "negative" effect. You can do this two ways...

Creating Adjustment Layers

You can also create adjustment layers within After Effects—no surprise, when you consider that After Effects can import adjustment layers from Adobe Photoshop (see Chapter 2). Whether you import them or create them in After Effects, adjustment layers work just as they do in Photoshop.

An *adjustment layer* contains effects, not footage. The effects contained in an adjustment layer are applied to all the layers below it. You save time and effort by applying effects to a single layer rather than multiple layers (**Figures 4.60**, **4.61**, and **4.62**). To cut down rendering time, hide the adjustment layer to temporarily disable its effects. You can even change an existing layer into an adjustment layer.

Figure 4.61 ...either by applying the effect to masked duplicates of each layer...

Figure 4.62 ...or by applying the effect to an adjustment layer, which affects all layers below it in the stacking order. This technique can save time and effort and can even reduce rendering times.

To create an adjustment layer:

1. Open the Composition panel or Timeline panel for the composition in which you want to add an adjustment layer, or make sure one of these windows is active.

2. Choose Layer > New > Adjustment Layer (**Figure 4.63**).

   An adjustment layer appears in the composition. The adjustment layer starts at the current time and uses the default duration for still images.

✔ Tip

■ You can convert an ordinary visible layer to a *guide layer*, an invisible layer you can use to position and align other layers in a composition. See Chapter 16 for more information.

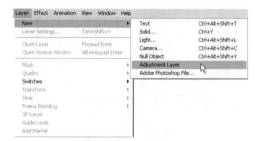

Figure 4.63 Choose Layer > New > Adjustment Layer.

Figure 4.64 Merely rotating each layer in this composition doesn't achieve the desired effect.

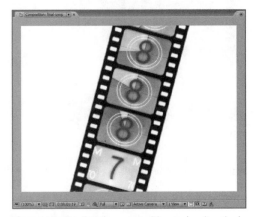

Figure 4.65 Nesting the composition makes it a single layer in another composition. Rotating the nested composition easily achieves the effect.

Nesting Compositions

To achieve many effects, you must make a composition a layer in another composition—a process called *nesting*. For example, rotating each layer in the composition in **Figure 4.64** doesn't achieve the desired effect. Each layer is rotated around its own anchor point and betrays the fact that each layer is a separate element. To make the layers appear unified, it would be extremely inconvenient to adjust each layer individually.

With a nested composition, it's possible to rotate the entire composition as a single layer, as in **Figure 4.65**. As a single layer within another composition, all the elements rotate around a single anchor point. You can use nested compositions to produce complex effects, to control rendering order, or to apply effects to continuously rasterized or collapsed layers. You can always reopen the nested composition. Any changes you make to the original are reflected in the nested layer.

The following tasks show you how to make one composition a layer in another. Chapter 16 revisits nested compositions in more detail.

To make a composition a layer in another composition:

1. Display the Composition panel or Timeline panel of the composition that will contain the nested composition.

2. Drag a composition you want to nest from the Project panel to *any of the following*:

   ▲ Composition panel of the target composition

   ▲ Timeline panel of the target composition

   ▲ Name or icon of the target composition in the Project panel

   The composition becomes a layer in the target composition. The composition layer starts at the current time and has the duration of the original composition (**Figure 4.66**).

To nest one composition in a new one with the same settings:

♦ Drag a composition in the Project panel to the composition icon at the bottom of the Project panel (**Figure 4.67**).

   The composition becomes a layer in a new composition that uses the same composition settings as the nested one.

✔ Tips

■ The default frame rate and resolution of nested compositions depend on the setting you chose in the Advanced panel of the Composition Settings dialog box. You can tell After Effects to preserve the frame rate and resolution of nested comps (see "Nesting Options," earlier in this chapter).

■ After Effects' Parenting feature allows you to create even more complex relationships between layers than nesting allows. Make sure you use the best technique for the job at hand. See Chapter 16 for more about the Parenting feature.

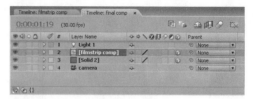

Figure 4.66 The nested composition looks and behaves much like any other layer.

Figure 4.67 Drag a composition to the composition icon at the bottom of the Project panel to nest it in a new composition with the same settings.

LAYER BASICS

Previous chapters laid the groundwork for the central activity of your After Effects work: manipulating a composition's layers. Over the next several chapters, you'll gradually increase your command over layers. This chapter focuses on the bare essentials, describing how to select, name, and label layers. You'll also learn how to control layer quality and how to choose whether to include layers in previews and renders. In addition, you'll see how to simplify working with layers by concealing ones you're not using and by locking ones you don't want to disturb. In the process, you'll become more familiar with your primary workspace, the Timeline panel.

Selecting Layers

Naturally, you must select layers before you can adjust them. In the timeline, selected layers' names appear highlighted, as do their duration bars—the horizontal bar representing the layer under the time ruler. In the Composition panel, selected layers can appear with *handles*—six small boxes that demark each layer's boundaries and that you can use to transform the layer. However, you can specify whether you want these (or other layer controls) to appear in the Comp panel. See the section "Viewing Spatial Controls in the Comp Panel" in Chapter 7, "Properties and Keyframes," for more details.

Figure 5.1 You can select a layer by directly clicking it in the Composition panel. In this figure, the Comp panel is set to show selected layer handles.

To select layers in the Composition panel:

1. If you haven't already done so, cue the current frame of the composition so that the layer you want to select is visible in the Composition panel.

2. In the Composition panel, click the visible layer to select it (**Figure 5.1**).

   The selected layer's handles and anchor point appear, unless these options have been disabled (see "Viewing Spatial Controls in the Comp Panel" in Chapter 7).

3. To select more than one layer, Shift-click other visible layers in the Composition panel (**Figure 5.2**).

Figure 5.2 Shift-click to select additional layers.

To select layers in the Timeline panel:

In the Timeline panel, *do any of the following:*

◆ Click anywhere in the horizontal track containing the layer.

Figure 5.3 You can select layers by clicking them in the Timeline panel—or by entering the layer's number on the numeric keypad.

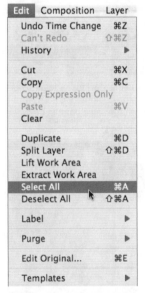

Figure 5.4 You can select all layers in the usual way—by choosing Edit > Select All (or using the keyboard shortcut).

◆ To select a layer by its layer number, type the layer number on the numeric keypad (not the numbers on the main keyboard) (**Figure 5.3**).

◆ To select a range of layers, Shift-click other layers.

◆ To select a range of layers, drag a marquee around several layer names. (Take care not to drag a layer to a new position in the stacking order.)

Selected layers appear highlighted in the Timeline panel. Selected layers are visible in the Comp panel only if the current time is cued to the layer.

To select all layers in a composition:

◆ Choose Edit > Select All, or press Command-A (Mac) or Ctrl-A (Windows) (**Figure 5.4**).

All the layers in the composition are selected.

To deselect all layers in a composition:

Do one of the following:

◆ Click an empty area in the Timeline panel or the Composition panel.

◆ Choose Edit > Deselect All.

✔ Tips

■ Press Command-Up Arrow (Mac) or Ctrl-Up Arrow (Windows) to select the next layer up in the stacking order. See the next section, "Changing the Stacking Order."

■ Press Command-Down Arrow (Mac) or Ctrl-Down Arrow (Windows) to select the next layer down in the stacking order.

Changing the Stacking Order

In the Timeline panel, layers appear, well, *layered*. That is, each layer occupies a horizontal track that is stacked vertically with other layers. The horizontal position of a layer's duration bar determines its place in time; its vertical position shows its place in the *stacking order*. When layers occupy the same point in time, higher layers appear in front of lower layers when viewed in the Composition panel. You can change the relative positions of the layers in the stacking order to determine which elements appear in front and which appear behind (**Figures 5.5** and **5.6**).

A number directly to the left of a layer's name indicates a layer's position in the stacking order. The top layer is always layer 1, and the numbers increase as you go down the stack. Although layer numbers may not seem very informative, they can help you discern when layers are hidden temporarily (see "Making Layers Shy," later in this chapter) as well as provide a way for you to quickly select layers by number (see "Selecting Layers," earlier in this chapter).

✔ Tip

■ In Chapter 3, you learned that the Project panel labels each file type (motion footage, still image, and so on) using a different colored label. In the timeline, each layer's duration bar and label (the color swatch next to the layer's number) reflect the label color scheme. You can assign another color to any selected layer by choosing Edit > Label > and selecting a color.

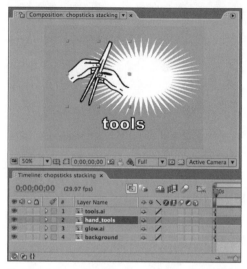

Figure 5.5 Layers higher in the stacking order appear in front of other layers in the Composition panel (provided they're positioned at the same point in time).

Figure 5.6 When a layer is moved to a lower position in the stacking order, it appears behind the higher layers in the Composition panel.

Figure 5.7 As you drag a layer in the stacking order, a line indicates where it will appear if you release the mouse.

Figure 5.8 When you release the mouse, the layer appears in the new position.

Figure 5.9 To move the selected layer using menu commands, choose Layer > and the appropriate command.

To change the stacking order of layers in the Timeline panel:

1. In the Timeline panel, drag a layer name to a new position.

   A horizontal line appears between other layers, indicating where the layer will appear in the stacking order (**Figure 5.7**).

2. Release the mouse to place the layer in the position you want (**Figure 5.8**).

To move layers one level at a time:

1. Select a layer in the Composition or Timeline panel.

2. *Do any of the following* (**Figure 5.9**):

   ▲ Choose Layer > Bring Layer Forward, or press Command-] (Mac) or Ctrl-] (Windows).

   ▲ Choose Layer > Send Layer Backward, or press Command-[(Mac) or Ctrl-[(Windows).

   ▲ Choose Layer > Bring Layer to Front or press Shift-Command-] (Mac) or Shift-Ctrl-] (Windows).

   ▲ Choose Layer > Send Layer to Back or press Shift-Command-[(Mac) or Shift-Ctrl-[(Windows).

   The layer is repositioned in the stacking order according to the command you specified.

✔ Tip

■ Just in case you missed it in the last chapter, you aren't restricted to adding a layer to the top of the stacking order and then moving it down in a separate step (as in older versions of After Effects). After Effects lets you drag footage items directly to any level in the stacking order.

Naming Layers

Although you can rename comps and solids, you can't rename footage items in the Project panel (as explained in Chapter 2, "Importing Footage into a Project"). However, you can change the names of layers in a composition. (Typically, a footage item appears in the Project panel just once; however, it may make numerous appearances as layers in compositions.) In the Timeline panel, you can choose to view either the changeable layer name or the fixed source name.

To change the name of a layer:

1. In the Timeline panel, click a layer to select it.

2. Press Return (Mac) or Enter (Windows).

   The layer name becomes highlighted (**Figure 5.10**).

3. Enter a new name for the layer, and press Return (Mac) or Enter (Windows).

   The layer uses the name you specified; the source name can't be changed (**Figure 5.11**).

Figure 5.10 To change a layer's name, select the layer and press Return (Mac) or Enter (Windows) to edit the name.

Figure 5.11 Enter a name for the layer, and press Return (Mac) or Enter (Windows).

Figure 5.12 In the Timeline panel, click the Name panel heading to toggle between the layer name (which you can change)...

Figure 5.13 ...and the source name (which is fixed).

To toggle between layer name and source name:

◆ In the Timeline panel, click the Layer/ Source Name button to toggle between the layer name and the source name for the layer. When the layer name and source name are the same, the layer name appears in brackets (**Figures 5.12** and **5.13**).

✔ Tips

■ Although you can rename a layer as many times as you like, try to settle on a name and stick with it. Changing a layer's name can affect the expression attached to it, if the expression refers to the layer by name. For more about expressions, see Chapter 16, "Complex Projects."

■ Although footage items typically appear in the Project panel just once, there are exceptions. For example, you may want to import the same file more than once so that you can interpret each footage item differently.

NAMING LAYERS

Switching Video and Audio On and Off

By default, the extreme left side of the Timeline panel displays the A/V Features panel (**Figure 5.14**). The first three columns of the A/V Features panel contain switches that control whether a layer's video and audio are included in previews or renders.

To show or hide the image for layers in the composition:

◆ Next to a layer in the Timeline panel, click the Video switch to toggle the Eye icon 👁 on and off.

When the Eye icon 👁 is visible, the layer appears in the Composition panel (**Figure 5.15**); when the icon is hidden, the layer doesn't appear (**Figure 5.16**).

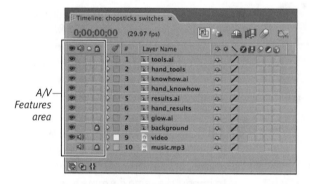

A/V Features area

Figure 5.14 By default, the A/V Features panel appears to the extreme left in the Timeline panel. The panel contains three switches: Video, Audio, and Solo.

Figure 5.15 When the Video switch is on, the layer's image appears in the Composition panel.

Figure 5.16 When the Video switch is off, the layer's image doesn't appear in the Composition panel, previews, or renders.

SWITCHING VIDEO AND AUDIO ON AND OFF

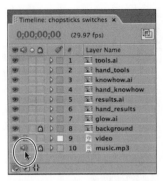

Figure 5.17 When the Audio switch is on, the layer's audio track is included in previews and renders.

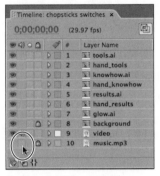

Figure 5.18 When the Audio switch is off, the layer's audio track isn't included in previews and renders.

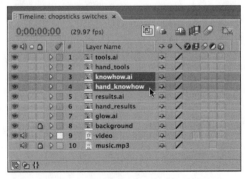

Figure 5.19 Select the layers for which you want to keep the video switched on.

To include a layer's audio track in the composition:

◆ Next to the layer in the Timeline panel, click the Audio switch to toggle the Speaker icon 🔊 on and off.

   When the Speaker icon 🔊 is visible, the audio is included when you preview or render the composition (**Figure 5.17**); when the Speaker icon is hidden, the audio is excluded (**Figure 5.18**).

To hide the video for layers in the composition, except for selected layers:

1. Select one or more layers in the Composition or Timeline panel, and make sure their Video switch is on (**Figure 5.19**).

continues on next page

2. Choose Layer > Switches > Hide Other Video (**Figure 5.20**).

The Video switches for other layers are turned off (**Figure 5.21**).

To show the video for all layers in the composition:

◆ Choose Layer > Switches > Show All Video (**Figure 5.22**).

The Video switches for all layers are turned on.

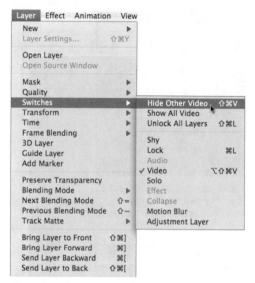

Figure 5.20 Choose Layer > Switches > Hide Other Video...

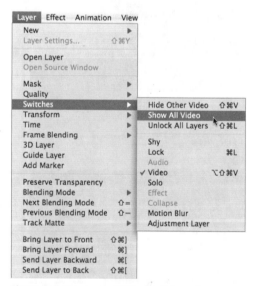

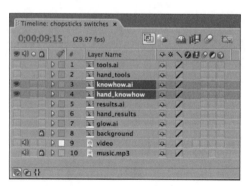

Figure 5.21 ...to turn off the Video switch for the unselected layers.

Figure 5.22 To turn on all Video switches, choose Layer > Switches > Show All Video.

SWITCHING VIDEO AND AUDIO ON AND OFF

Figure 5.23 Make sure the Eye icon is visible to solo video and that the Speaker icon is visible to solo audio, and then click the Solo button.

Figure 5.24 When you solo the layer's video and audio, A/V switches for other layers are deactivated.

To solo a layer:

1. For the layer you want to solo:
   ▲ Make sure the Eye icon 👁 is visible to solo the video.
   ▲ Make sure the Speaker icon 🔊 is visible to solo the audio.

   If the layer contains both video and audio, you can select either or both. If you select neither, the Solo button disappears, and you can't solo the layer.

2. Next to the layer you want to solo, click the Solo button ◉ (**Figure 5.23**).

   If you solo the video, the Video switches for all other layers are deactivated; if you solo the audio, the Audio switches for all other layers are deactivated (**Figure 5.24**).

3. To stop soloing the layer and restore other A/V settings to their original states, click the Solo button again to deactivate it.

✔ Tips

■ When a transfer mode has been applied to a layer, the Eye icon 👁 looks like this: 🔲. For more about transfer modes, see Chapter 14, "More Layer Techniques."

■ When a track matte is applied to a layer, the video for the layer above it is automatically switched off. Switching the video back on eliminates the track matte effect. For more about track mattes, see Chapter 14.

■ Not all layers are visible; adjustment layers, guide layers, lights, cameras, null objects, and, of course, layers created from audio-only footage have no video component.

SWITCHING VIDEO AND AUDIO ON AND OFF

Locking a Layer

The fourth column of the A/V Features panel contains the Lock switch, which you can use to lock layers so that they're protected against accidental changes. When you attempt to select a locked layer, it's highlight blinks on and off to remind you that it's locked and thus can't be selected or altered. You must unlock the layer to make changes.

To lock or unlock a layer:

◆ Next to a layer in the Timeline panel, click the Lock switch to toggle the Lock icon 🔒 on and off.

When the Lock icon 🔒 is visible, the layer can't be selected or modified (**Figure 5.25**); when the Lock icon is hidden, the layer is unlocked (**Figure 5.26**).

To unlock all layers:

◆ Choose Layer > Switches > Unlock All Layers, or press Command-Shift-l (Mac) or Ctrl-Shift-l (Windows) (**Figure 5.27**).

✔ Tip

■ Press Command-L (Mac) or Ctrl-L (Windows) to lock selected layers. You still have to click the Lock switch to unlock layers (you can't select locked layers).

Figure 5.25 Turn on the Lock switch to protect the layer from inadvertent changes.

Figure 5.26 Turn off the Lock switch to unlock a layer.

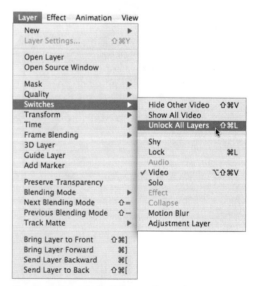

Figure 5.27 To unlock all layers, choose Layer > Switches > Unlock All Layers.

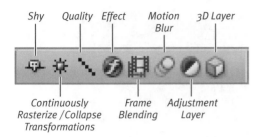

Shy   Quality   Effect   Motion   3D Layer
                            Blur

Continuously   Frame   Adjustment
Rasterize /Collapse Blending   Layer
Transformations

Figure 5.28 The Layer Switches panel contains eight switches.

Basic Layer Switches

By default, the Layer Switches column set appears to the right of the Name column in the Timeline panel.

The Layer Switches column consists of eight switches that control various features for each layer (**Figure 5.28**). This section covers the first three layer switches: Shy, Rasterize, and Quality. Other layer switches are covered later in the book. (The Effect and Adjustment Layer switches are covered in Chapter 11, "Effects Fundamentals"; the Frame Blending and Motion Blur switches are covered in Chapter 14; and the 3D switch is covered in Chapter 15, "3D Layers.")

Although you can control all of the layer switches via menu commands, the switches themselves provide more direct access.

To show or hide the layer switches:

◆ In the Timeline panel, click the Expand / Collapse Layer Switches Pane button 🖼 (**Figure 5.29**).

Clicking the button hides and shows the Switches pane (**Figure 5.30**).

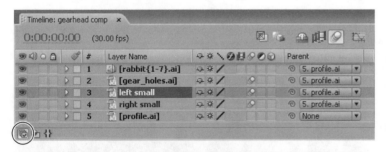

Figure 5.29 Clicking the Expand / Collapse Layer Switches Pane button...

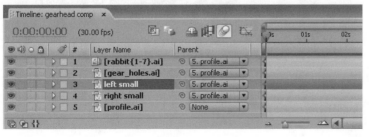

Figure 5.30 ...toggles the switches controls open and closed (shown here).

Making Layers Shy

Because the Timeline panel contains so much information, you'll frequently find yourself scrolling through it or expanding it. Some users even use a secondary monitor just to accommodate a large Timeline panel. If you hate to scroll but are reluctant to buy another monitor, you may want to take advantage of the Shy Layers feature.

Marking layers you're not currently using as *shy* enables you to quickly conceal them in the Timeline panel. This way, you can concentrate on just the layers you're using and conserve precious screen space. Although shy layers may be hidden in the Timeline panel, they always appear in the Composition panel (provided they're visible and their corresponding video switch is on), and layer numbering remains unchanged.

To make a layer shy or not shy:

◆ Click the Shy switch for a layer in the Timeline panel to toggle the icon between Not Shy ▣ and Shy ▬ (**Figures 5.31** and **5.32**).

To hide or show shy layers:

◆ In the Timeline panel, click the Hide Shy Layers button ▣ to select or deselect it.

When the button is deselected, shy layers are visible in the Timeline panel (**Figure 5.33**).

When the button is selected, shy layers are hidden from view (**Figure 5.34**).

Figure 5.31 Click the Shy switch to toggle between Not Shy...

Figure 5.32 ...and Shy.

Figure 5.33 When the Hide Shy Layers button is deselected, shy layers appear in the Timeline panel.

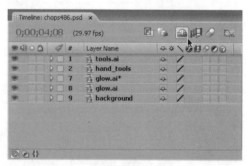

Figure 5.34 When the Hide Shy Layers button is selected, shy layers are concealed in the Timeline panel.

Figure 5.35 By default, After Effects rasterizes the image at its original size.

Figure 5.36 Enlarging an image after it has been rasterized can make the pixels apparent.

Figure 5.37 When the Continuously Rasterize switch is on, the image is scaled before it's rasterized for each frame of the composition.

Continuously Rasterizing a Layer

When you import an Illustrator or EPS file, After Effects rasterizes it, converting it from a vector-based image to a bitmapped image. Depending on how you plan to use the image, you can choose to rasterize the image once or rasterize it continuously.

If you plan to use the image at its original size (After Effects' default setting) or smaller, you only need to rasterize it once (**Figure 5.35**).

If you plan to scale the image more than 100 percent (or plan to change other geometric properties), you should choose to continuously rasterize the layer. Rasterizing the layer for each frame will ensure that image quality is maintained at any scale (**Figures 5.36** and **5.37**). Of course, these recalculations may also increase preview and rendering time. To save time, you may choose to turn off the Continuously Rasterize switch until you want to preview or render the composition at full quality.

When a composition is used as a layer, the Continuously Rasterize switch functions as the Collapse Transformations switch. Having this option selected can increase image quality while decreasing rendering time. You can find out more about the Collapse Transformations option in Chapter 16, "Complex Projects."

To change the rasterization method of a layer:

◆ In the Switches panel of the Timeline panel, click the Continuously Rasterize/Collapse Transformations switch for the layer.

When the switch is set to Off (no icon), the image is rasterized once (**Figure 5.38**); when the switch is set to On ☀, the image is continuously rasterized (**Figure 5.39**).

✔ Tips

■ Regardless of the Continuously Rasterize setting, setting the quality switch to Full smoothes (anti-aliases) the edges of the art.

■ One way to avoid continuous rasterization and its slower rendering times is to steer clear of scaling the image beyond 100 percent. If possible, create the vector graphic at the largest dimensions it appears in the composition.

■ In older versions of After Effects, you couldn't apply an effect to a layer that had the Continuously Rasterize switch on. This is no longer the case; you're free to apply effects to a continuously rasterized layer—and free to forget the workarounds you had to use in the past.

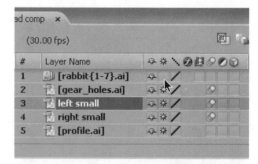

Figure 5.38 When the switch is off, the layer is rasterized once.

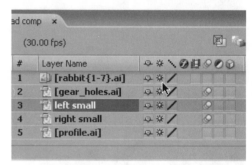

Figure 5.39 When the switch is on, the layer is continuously rasterized.

Rasterization

If you're familiar with Illustrator and Photoshop, rasterization should be a recognizable concept. If not, read on. Illustrator and EPS files are *vector*, or path-based, images. Such images consist of independent objects, which the program describes mathematically. (You may also hear Illustrator referred to as an *object-oriented* program.) Because the objects are essentially mathematical equations, they can be scaled, manipulated, and otherwise transformed and still produce smooth line art. The objects remain independent of resolution until they're printed or presented on a screen.

After Effects *rasterizes* Illustrator files, converting path-based objects into bitmapped, or pixel-based, images. Once rasterized, the image has a fixed number of pixels, or *resolution*. Increasing the size of a bitmapped image also increases the size of its pixels—pixels that can appear blocky when scaled beyond 100 percent.

By default, After Effects rasterizes an image at its size at import (the size it appears in Illustrator). If you intend to scale up the image (or change other geometric properties), you should set After Effects to continuously rasterize the layer. Doing so instructs After Effects to recalculate the image's resolution for every frame. Although this calculation slows previews and renders, it ensures that image quality is maintained at any scale.

CONTINUOUSLY RASTERIZING A LAYER

Quality Setting Switches

As you'll remember from Chapter 4, you can set the resolution of the composition to control its image quality and thereby the speed at which frames are rendered. Just as the resolution setting controls the overall image quality of the composition, a layer's Quality switch controls the quality of an individual layer in the composition.

Figure 5.40 Set the switch to Draft Quality to display the layer at a lower quality in the Composition panel.

To change the Quality setting of a layer:

◆ In the Timeline panel, click the Quality switch to set the quality for the layer:

The Draft Quality icon ◼ indicates that the layer will preview and render at draft quality in the Composition panel (**Figure 5.40**).

The Full Quality icon ◢ indicates that the layer will preview and render at full quality in the Composition panel (**Figure 5.41**).

The Quality switch controls the quality of individual layers. To control your composition's image quality, use the Resolution controls, as described in Chapter 4.

Figure 5.41 Set the switch to Full Quality to display the layer at the highest quality in the Composition panel.

QUALITY SETTING SWITCHES

LAYER EDITING

The term *editing*, in the sense that film and video makers use it, refers to the order and arrangement of images in time. Implicit in this definition, of course, is the term's broader meaning: to include some elements while excluding others to achieve a desired aesthetic effect. This chapter focuses on editing the layers of a composition—defining which segments to include and the order in which to present them.

You'll learn basic editing functions and terms such as *In point, Out point, duration,* and *trimming.* You'll also learn other techniques common to non-linear editing, such as setting markers and controlling the playback speed and direction of layers. In the process, you'll get acquainted with the Layer panel and take a closer look at the time graph of the Timeline panel.

Viewing Layers in the Timeline and Layer Panels

When you arrange layers in time, you work in the Layer panel and the time graph area of the Timeline panel.

As you know, the Timeline panel lets you view all of a composition's elements as vertically stacked layers. On the right side of the Timeline panel, a *time graph* represents the layers in time (**Figure 6.1**). Each layer has a duration bar, and its horizontal position in the time graph indicates when it will start and end as you play back the composition.

Time graph area of the Timeline panel

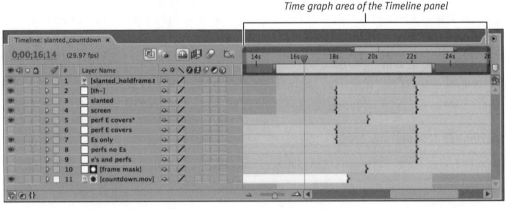

Figure 6.1 At the right side of the Timeline panel, all the layers of a composition are represented as bars in a time graph.

VIEWING LAYERS

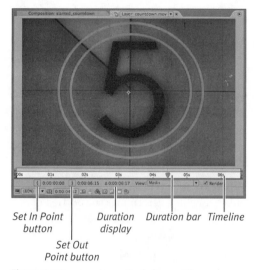

Set In Point button   Duration display   Duration bar   Timeline

Set Out Point button

Figure 6.2 You can view a single layer of the composition in a Layer panel, which includes a timeline and controls for setting the layer's starting and ending points.

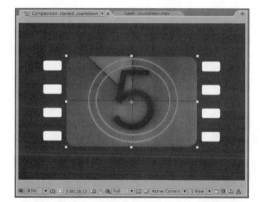

Figure 6.3 Compare the view of the layer in the Layer panel and Timeline panel to the same point in time in the Composition panel. In the Composition panel, you can see how the layer has been manipulated and composited with other layers.

You can view any layer in a composition in a Layer panel. As you'll remember from Chapter 3, "Managing Footage," the Layer panel closely resembles the Footage and Composition panels. Unlike its siblings, however, the Layer panel always includes a timeline and controls for setting the starting and ending points of the layer (**Figure 6.2**).

Both the Layer and Timeline panels depict layers as duration bars. However, each panel displays layers in a different context. In the time graph, the duration bar shows a layer in the context of the entire composition. In the Layer panel, the duration bar shows you the portion of the footage item that you chose to include in the composition.

Compare the Timeline (Figure 6.1), Layer (Figure 6.2), and Composition (**Figure 6.3**) panels to see how the same layer appears in each panel. (Note that the current time always matches in all the open panels of the same composition, as explained in Chapter 4, "Compositions.") The distinctions between the time graph and the Layer panel are explained in greater detail in the sections to follow.

✔ Tip

■ The Layer panel has a few other unique features not covered in detail here: the View pull-down menu and the Render check box. The section "The Layer Panel," later in this chapter, provides a brief explanation, but you'll learn more in later chapters. This chapter focuses on using the Layer panel's unique editing features—that is, on manipulating starting and ending points and on using layer markers.

The Time Graph

Each layer in the composition occupies a separate horizontal track, or cell, in the time graph. The vertical arrangement of layers indicates their position in the stacking order (covered in the previous chapter). Time is displayed horizontally, from left to right, and measured by a time ruler in the increments you selected in the project preferences. Layers appear as color-coded duration bars; their length and position in the time graph indicate when the layers start and end as the composition plays back.

This chapter focuses on how to view and edit layers in the time graph. Later chapters cover how to view and manipulate additional information in the time graph (for example, keyframing attributes). Chapter 9 covers the time graph's other incarnation, the Graph Editor. **Figure 6.4** summarizes the controls covered in the following sections.

Parts of the time graph

Time ruler—Measures time horizontally (according to the time units you selected in the project preferences).

Work area start—Marks the beginning of the work area bar, which determines the portion of the composition that will be rendered during previews (see Chapter 8, "Playback, Previews, and RAM").

Work area end—Marks the end of the work area bar, which determines the portion of the composition that will be rendered during previews (see Chapter 8).

Left Time View bracket—Changes the left edge of the part of the composition visible in the main time graph. (See "The navigator view," later in this chapter.)

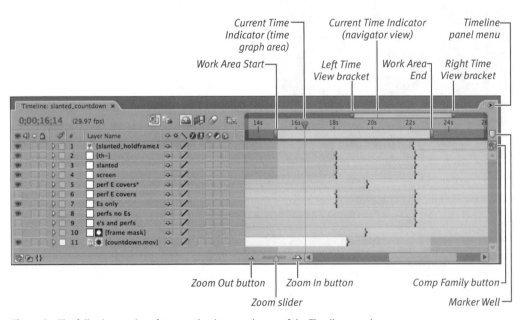

Figure 6.4 The following sections focus on the time graph area of the Timeline panel.

Right Time View bracket—Changes the right edge of the part of the composition visible in the main time graph. (See "The navigator view," later in this chapter.)

Current time indicator (CTI)—Changes the current frame of the composition in the main time graph and in the navigator view. The current time is the same in all the views of the same composition.

Timeline panel menu button—Displays a menu of functions for controlling layers and keyframes as well as accessing the Composition Settings dialog box.

Marker well—Adds markers to the time ruler. Drag a marker out of the well to add a marker or back into the well to remove it.

Comp Family button—Opens the Composition panel associated with the composition displayed in the Timeline panel.

Zoom slider—Displays the time graph in more or less detail.

Zoom In button—Displays a shorter part of the time graph in more detail.

Zoom Out button—Displays a greater part of the time graph in less detail.

THE TIME GRAPH

Navigating the Time Graph

The Timeline panel allows you to view all or part of a composition. As you arrange the layers of a composition in time, you may need to zoom into the time graph for a detailed view or zoom out for a more expansive view.

The navigator view

After Effects' Timeline panel includes a *navigator view,* located at the top of the time graph (**Figure 6.5**). The navigator view looks like a tiny version of the time graph, including a small current time indicator and small work area markers. (See Chapter 11, "Effects Fundamentals," to learn about setting the work area.) The navigator view always represents the entire duration of the composition; the white portion corresponds to the part of the composition you see in the larger main timeline. Thus, dragging the Time View brackets at either end of the white area changes the main view, and vice versa.

The navigator view helps you put the portion of the composition you see in the time graph in the context of its entire duration.

To view part of the time graph in more detail:

In the time graph area of the Timeline panel, *do any of the following* (**Figures 6.6** and **6.7**):

◆ Click the Zoom In button to view an incrementally more detailed area of the time graph.

◆ Drag the Zoom slider to the left.

◆ Drag the Left Time View bracket to the right.

◆ Drag the Right Time View bracket to the left.

◆ Press the equal sign (=) on your keyboard.

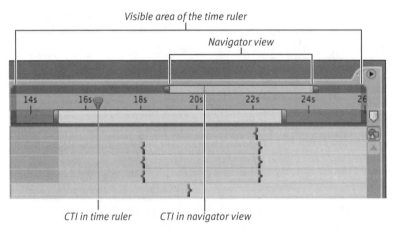

Figure 6.5 The navigator view looks like a miniature version of the time graph. By representing the entire duration of the composition, it helps you put the area visible in the main time graph in context.

To view more of the composition in the time graph:

In the time graph area of the Timeline panel, *do any of the following:*

◆ Click the Zoom Out button to view an incrementally more detailed area of the time graph.

◆ Drag the Zoom slider to the right to view more of the time graph gradually.

◆ Drag the Left Time View bracket to the left.

◆ Drag the Right Time View bracket to the right.

◆ Press the hyphen (-) on your keyboard.

✔ Tip

■ Here's another good keyboard shortcut for zooming in and out of the time graph: Press the semicolon (;) to toggle between the frame view of the time graph and a view of the entire composition.

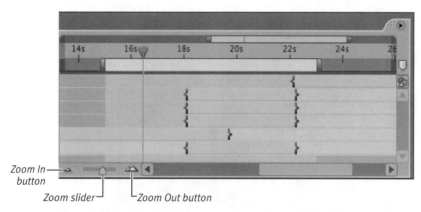

Zoom In button

Zoom slider

Zoom Out button

Figure 6.6 You can use the zoom controls at the bottom of the Timeline panel to control your view of the time graph.

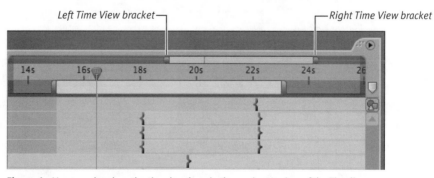

Left Time View bracket

Right Time View bracket

Figure 6.7 You can also drag the time brackets in the navigator view of the Timeline panel to change your view of the time graph.

The Layer Panel

As you learned in Chapter 3, the Layer panel resembles the Composition and Footage panels. The following sections cover the Layer panel's unique editing features, including its timeline and controls for setting In and Out points (**Figure 6.8**). Chapters 7 ("Properties and Keyframes") and 10 ("Mask Essentials") cover the Layer panel's additional features, such as its View pull-down menu and Render check box, which help you to manipulate anchor points and masks.

A Layer panel timeline corresponds to the full, unedited duration of the source footage item. As you recall, the full durations of movie and audio footage are determined by the source; the full durations of still images are determined by the preferences you set (see Chapter 2, "Importing Footage into a Project").

Note that the Layer panel has its own version of the Timeline panel's navigator view, which works in much the same way as that one. See "The navigator view," earlier in this chapter.

Using the Layer panel's controls, you can set the portion of the full duration you want to use in the composition. Time displays show the exact In point, Out point, and duration you set, which are also reflected by a duration bar.

To open a Layer panel:

◆ In the Timeline panel, double-click a layer to open a Layer panel.

Remember: Double-clicking an item in the Project panel opens a Footage panel, not a Layer panel.

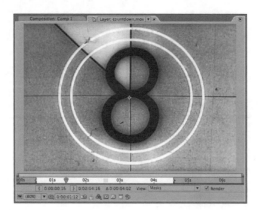

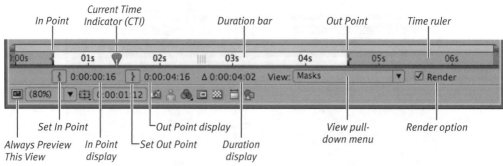

In Point — Current Time Indicator (CTI) — Duration bar — Out Point — Time ruler

Set In Point — Out Point display — View pull-down menu — Render option

Always Preview This View — In Point display — Set Out Point — Duration display

Figure 6.8 The Layer panel includes editing features not found in the Footage and Composition panels.

Parts of the Layer panel

Layer panel time ruler—Matches the full, unedited duration of the source footage.

Current time indicator (CTI)—Corresponds to the current time of the composition and the framcorree of the layer displayed in the Layer panel.

Duration bar—Corresponds to the portion of the source footage included in the composition.

Set In Point button—Marks the current frame of the layer as the first frame in the composition.

Set Out Point button—Marks the current frame of the layer as the last frame included in the composition.

Always Preview This View button—Designates the view as the default for previews (playback at or near the full frame rate), rather than whatever view is frontmost. (See Chapter 8 for more information.)

Region of Interest button—Limits the area of the image in the panel for previewing. (See Chapter 8 for more information.)

Transparency Grid button—Toggles transparent areas between a black background and a checkerboard pattern, or transparency grid. (See Chapter 4 for more information.)

Pixel Aspect Ratio Correction button—Corrects any distortion caused by differences in the layer's pixel aspect ratio (PAR) and the display's PAR. (See Chapter 4 for more information.)

View pull-down menu—Specifies whether to make additional information visible in the Layer panel, including motion-tracking points (Professional only), mask shapes, and anchor point paths. After Effects switches view options according to the task at hand. For example, selecting the Pen tool selects the layer's Mask view option automatically. (See Chapter 10 for more about masks.)

Comp Family button—Makes related composition and Timeline panels appear.

Render option—Specifies whether the window shows the layer's image only or the rendered result of any changes you make to it, such as masks and effects. (See Chapter 8 for more about previews.)

THE LAYER PANEL

Editing Terminology

The most fundamental terms in editing are probably *In point* and *Out point*. *In point* refers to a starting time; *Out point* refers to an ending time. In and Out points are often called *edit marks*, but they shouldn't be confused with *markers*, which are explained in "Using Markers" at the end of this chapter. The difference between the In and Out points defines *duration*. A triangle, or delta symbol Δ, often signifies duration in editing. (Editors borrowed the symbol from mathematicians and scientists, who use it to signify a change in a value.)

Changing the In and Out points is called *trimming*. Trimming a layer changes its duration: Trimming in either edit mark shortens the duration; trimming out an edit mark lengthens the duration.

Editors will tell you that every edit has four edit points: source In, source Out, program In, and program Out. In other words, every edit can be described by the source's start-ing and ending points, and by when it starts and ends in the program (or, in your case, the composition).

In most cases, defining any three of the editing points automatically implies the fourth point—hence the term *three-point editing*. When you change the speed of the source, however, you effectively define all four edit points, forcing the source to fit into the duration defined by the program In and Out points. Many editing programs have a feature called *Fit-to-Fill*, which changes the source's speed to fit into a defined duration. In essence, it's a four-point edit, in which the source duration and program duration are different.

These are just some of the most basic editing terms. Although you may consider yourself to be strictly a designer, animator, or compositor, you should familiarize yourself with basic editing terminology and techniques.

Figure 6.9 Note where the layer begins in the composition before trimming its In point.

Figure 6.10 Trimming the layer's In point by dragging it in the time graph is direct and intuitive; naturally, it also moves the layer's starting point in the composition.

Figure 6.11 Trimming the In point using the Layer panel controls, on the other hand, doesn't affect the layer's starting point in the composition. It does, however, affect its duration.

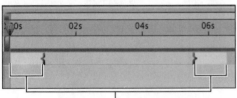

Trimmed frames (excluded
from composition)

Figure 6.12 The trimmed frames of a layer appear as empty outlines extending from the layer's In and Out points. You can restore these frames at any time by extending the In or Out point again.

Trimming Layers

Changing a layer's In or Out point is known as *trimming*. Trimming a layer affects its duration; its timing in the composition depends on the trimming method you choose.

As you trim a layer in the Timeline panel, you also alter the time at which the layer starts or ends in the composition. This means you may have to shift the layer back to its original starting point after you trim it (**Figures 6.9** and **6.10**). Although the Timeline panel provides the most direct method of trimming, it can sometimes be difficult to use with precision.

When you trim a layer using controls in the Layer panel, the layer's duration changes accordingly but its starting point in the composition remains fixed (**Figure 6.11**). Thus, this method works best if you don't want to change the layer's start time in the composition.

Whenever you *trim in* an edit point—making the layer shorter—the unused frames of the layer appear as empty outlines extending from the duration bar's In and Out points (**Figure 6.12**). You can always restore these frames by extending the In and Out points again.

To set the In and Out points in the Layer panel:

1. Set the current time to the frame of the layer you want to trim (**Figure 6.13**).

2. To set the In point, click the Set In Point button ⬇ in the Layer panel (**Figure 6.14**).

   The current frame becomes the layer's In point, but the layer's starting time in the composition remains in place.

3. To set the Out point, click the Set Out Point button ⬇ in the Layer panel (**Figure 6.15**).

   In the Layer panel and Timeline panel, the edit points of the Layer reflect the changes you made.

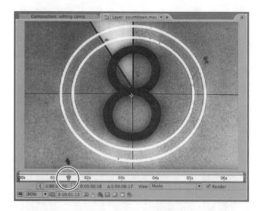

Figure 6.13 Set the current time to a frame of the layer you want to set as an edit point.

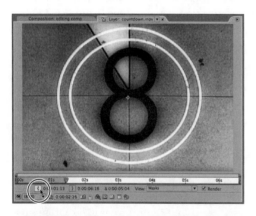

Figure 6.14 Click the Set In Point button in the Layer panel. In the Comp, the layer shifts back so the new In point starts at the same point in the comp time.

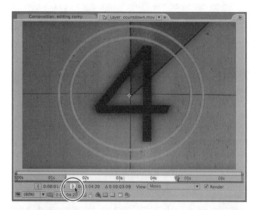

Figure 6.15 Click the Set Out Point button in the Layer panel to set the layer's Out point to the current time.

TRIMMING LAYERS

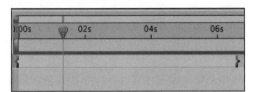

Figure 6.16 Set the current time to the frame of the layer you want to set as an edit point.

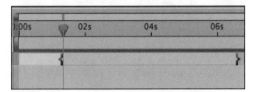

Figure 6.17 Press Option-[(Mac) or Alt-[(Windows) to set the In point of the selected layer to the current time.

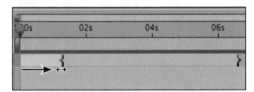

Figure 6.18 Drag the In point handle of a layer's duration bar to change both its In point and where it starts in the composition.

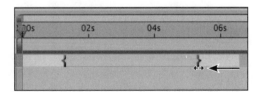

Figure 6.19 Drag the Out point handle of a layer's duration bar to change both its Out point and where it ends in the composition.

- You can see the exact position of an edit point in time by looking at the Info panel's time display as you drag.

- If you reach a point where you're unable to further increase a layer's duration, it means you've run out of source footage.

To set the In and Out points using keyboard shortcuts:

1. In the Layer panel or Timeline panel, set the current frame (**Figure 6.16**).

2. To set the In point of the layer, press Option-[(Mac) or Alt-[(Windows).

   The In point of the layer is set to the current frame in the composition (**Figure 6.17**).

3. To set the Out point of the layer, press Option-] (Mac) or Alt-] (Windows).

   In the Layer panel and Timeline panel, the edit points reflect the changes you made. The layer's frame at the current time becomes both the layer's In point and the layer's starting point in the comp.

To set the In and Out points by dragging:

In the time graph panel of the Timeline panel, *do either of the following*:

- To set the In point, drag the In point of a layer's duration bar (the handle at the left end of the duration bar) (**Figure 6.18**).

- To set the Out point, drag the Out point of a layer's duration bar (the handle at the right end of the duration bar) (**Figure 6.19**).

   Make sure you drag the ends of the layer's duration bar, not the bar itself. Otherwise, you could change the layer's position in time rather than its In or Out point.

✔ Tips

- Pressing Shift after you begin to drag causes the In or Out point to *snap to edges*. That is, the layer's edit point behaves as though it's magnetized and aligns with the edit points of other layers, the current time indicator, and the layer and composition markers.

TRIMMING LAYERS

Moving Layers in Time

When you create a layer, it begins at the current time indicator. After that, you can move its position in time either by dragging the layer's duration bar or by using the controls in the In/Out panel of the Timeline panel.

To move a layer in time by dragging:

◆ In the time graph area of the Timeline panel, drag a layer to a new position in time (**Figures 6.20** and **6.21**).

◆ Dragging a layer to the left causes the layer to begin earlier in the composition.

◆ Dragging a layer to the right causes the layer to begin later in the composition.

 Make sure you drag from the middle section of the layer's duration bar; dragging either end changes the duration of the layer.

✔ Tips

■ A layer's In point can occur before the beginning of the composition, just as its Out point can occur after the end of the composition. Of course, any frames beyond the beginning or end of the comp won't be included in previews or output.

■ As usual, you can press Shift after you begin dragging to cause the layer to snap to edges. When you activate the Snap to Edges feature, the edges of the layer (its In and Out points) align with the edges of other layers as well as with the current time indicator as you drag them near each other. The layer also snaps to layer and composition markers.

Figure 6.20 Drag a layer from the center portion of its duration bar...

Figure 6.21 ...to shift its position in time (without changing its duration). Press Shift after you begin dragging to activate the Snap to Edges feature.

Table 6.1

Layer Editing Shortcuts	
EDIT	SHORTCUT
Move layer's In point to CTI	[(open bracket)
Move layer's Out point to CTI	] (close bracket)
Trim layer's In point to CTI	Opt/Alt-[
Trim layer's Out point to CTI	Opt/Alt-]
Nudge layer one frame forward	Opt/Alt-Page Up
Nudge layer one frame back	Opt/Alt-Page Down

Showing Numerical Editing Controls

You can view and control the timing of each layer in the timeline by revealing four columns of information:

In—The layer's starting time in the comp. Enter a value to change the layer's starting point in the comp (*not* the layer's first frame).

Out—The layer's ending time in the comp. Enter a value to set the layer's ending time in the comp (*not* the layer's last frame).

Duration—The length of the layer, expressed as a corollary of *speed*. Entering a value changes the layer's playback speed and, indirectly, its Out point.

Stretch—The layer's playback frame rate expressed as a percentage of the layer's native playback rate. Entering a value changes the layer's playback rate and, indirectly, its duration and Out point. See the next section, "Changing a Layer's Speed," later in this chapter.

The timeline lets you expand all four columns as a set or each one individually.

Because this book covers several other, more convenient ways to move and trim layers, using the In and Out panels won't be covered in detail. However, turn to the next section to find out how to use the Duration and Stretch columns.

To show and hide the In, Out, Duration, and Stretch columns:

◆ *Do either of the following:*

▲ In the Timeline panel, click the In/Out/Duration/Stretch button ⚏ to reveal the In/Out/Duration/Stretch panel; click the button again to hide the panel (**Figures 6.22** and **6.23**).

▲ Ctrl-click (Mac) or right-click (Windows) any panel of the Timeline panel, and choose the panel you want to view from the contextual menu (**Figure 6.24**).

Figure 6.22 Click the In/Out/Duration/Stretch button to change the In/Out/Duration/Stretch panel from hidden...

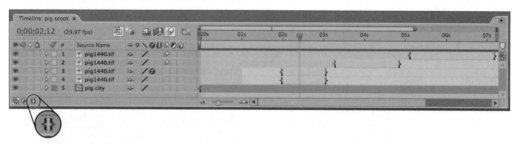

Figure 6.23 ...to visible. Click the button again to hide the panel.

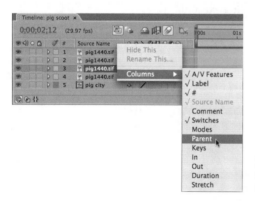

Figure 6.24 You can also Ctrl-click (Mac) or right-click (Windows) any panel to access a contextual menu that allows you to show or hide a panel in the Timeline panel.

Figure 6.25 To change the speed of a layer, click its Duration or Stretch display.

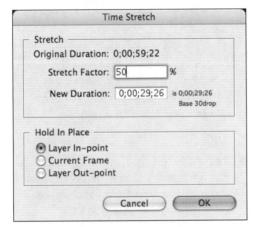

Figure 6.26 In the Time Stretch dialog box, enter a new duration or stretch factor to change the speed of the layer. In the Hold In Place section, choose which frame of the layer will maintain its position in the time graph.

Changing a Layer's Speed

Changing a layer's playback speed is yet another feature After Effects shares with typical non-linear editing programs. However, you should note a crucial difference between how you set the values in those programs and in After Effects. In many non-linear editing programs, you enter a *speed*: A value greater than 100 percent *increases* the speed, and a value less than 100 percent decreases the speed. In After Effects, you can enter a *stretch factor* value: A stretch factor greater than 100 percent *decreases* the speed of a layer (stretching, or increasing, its duration), and a stretch factor less than 100 percent *increases* the speed of a layer.

Entering a negative value reverses the playback direction of the layer—and also reverses the order of its property keyframes. (For more about properties and keyframes, see Chapter 7.) To reverse a layer's speed without also reversing its keyframes, you can use the Time Remapping feature, explained in Chapter 14, "More Layer Techniques." (Time remapping also lets you adjust the playback speed of a layer over time or create a freeze-frame effect.)

To change the playback speed of a layer:

1. *Do one of the following:*
   ▲ In the Timeline panel, click the Duration display or Stretch display for a layer (**Figure 6.25**).
   ▲ In the Timeline panel, select a layer and choose Layer > Time Stretch.
   The Time Stretch dialog box opens (**Figure 6.26**).

continues on next page

CHANGING A LAYER'S SPEED

2. In the Stretch section, *do either of the following:*

▲ For New Duration, enter a new duration for the layer.

▲ For Stretch Factor, enter the percentage change of the layer's duration.

To slow playback speed, enter a duration greater than that of the original or a stretch factor greater than 100 percent. To increase playback speed, enter a duration less than that of the original or a stretch factor less than 100 percent. Enter a negative value to reverse a layer's playback direction.

3. In the Hold In Place section of the Time Stretch dialog box, *select one of the following* options to determine the position of the layer when its speed and duration change:

Layer In-point—Maintains the layer's starting point position in the composition

Current Frame—Moves the layer's In and Out points while maintaining the frame's position at the current time indicator

Layer Out-point—Maintains the layer's ending point position in the composition

4. Click OK to close the Time Stretch dialog box.

The selected layer's speed, duration, and placement in time reflect your changes. However, the range of footage frames you specified to include—the layer's In and Out points—remain the same.

✔ Tips

■ To quickly reverse a layer's playback (a stretch factor of –100 percent), select the layer and press Command-Option-R (Mac) or Ctrl-Alt-R (Windows).

■ You can freeze-frame the current frame of the selected layer by choosing Layer > Time > Freeze Frame. This command automatically applies the appropriate time remapping settings. See Chapter 9 for more about time remapping.

Figure 6.27 Select the Pan Behind tool.

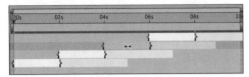

Figure 6.28 When you position the mouse over a layer created from motion footage, the mouse pointer becomes a Slip Edit tool.

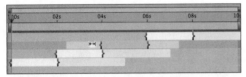

Figure 6.29 Dragging with the Slip Edit tool changes the portion of the motion footage used without changing its duration or position in the time ruler.

✔ Tips

- You can also perform a slip edit by dragging the layer's "hidden" trimmed frames (you can see their outlines extending beyond the layer's In and Out handles).

- To review how to perform insert and overlay edits, see Chapter 4, "Compositions."

- Those who use non-linear editing software know that the counterpart to the slip edit is the *slide edit*. Because each layer in After Effects occupies a separate track, slide editing is an inherent feature: Simply drag the layer to a new position in the time ruler.

Performing a Slip Edit

After Effects includes another editing feature common to non-linear editing programs: *slip edits*.

When you're working with layers created from motion footage, you'll find that you often need to change a portion of video without altering its position or duration in the time ruler. Although you can do this by reopening the Layer panel and setting new In and Out points, you must be careful to set edit points that result in the same duration. By using a slip edit, however, you can achieve the same result in a single step.

To slip a layer:

1. In the Tools panel, select the Pan Behind tool (**Figure 6.27**).

2. Position the mouse over a layer created from motion footage.

   The mouse pointer becomes a Slip Edit icon (**Figure 6.28**).

3. *Do either of the following:*

   Drag left to slip the footage left, using frames that come later in the footage.

   Drag right to slip the footage right, using frames that come earlier in the footage.

   The In and Out points of the source footage change by the same amount, which means the layer maintains its duration and position in the time ruler. As you drag, you can see the "hidden" footage extending from beyond the layer's In and Out points (**Figure 6.29**).

Sequencing and Overlapping Layers

Although you might not choose After Effects for editing, per se, you may find yourself starting many projects by creating a simple sequence. Fortunately, After Effects automates this common request with its Sequence and Overlap features.

The Sequence command quickly places selected layers one after another in the time graph, seamlessly aligning their Out and In points so that the layers play back in an uninterrupted sequence (**Figure 6.30**).

The Overlap command also places the selected layers one after another in the time graph—but in this case, they overlap by a specified amount of time (**Figure 6.31**). The Overlap command prepares layers for transition effects; it can even automatically create cross-fades between layers. (You'll learn more about creating transitions and other keyframed changes in Chapter 9.)

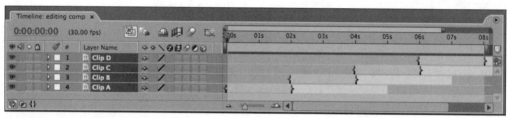

Figure 6.30 The Sequence command places selected layers one after another in the time graph in an uninterrupted sequence.

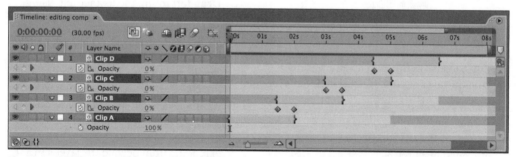

Figure 6.31 The Overlap option places the selected layers in a sequence that overlaps by a specified amount of time. It can automatically set keyframes for simple cross-fades between the layers.

Figure 6.32 Select the layers you want to sequence.

Figure 6.33 Choose Animation > Keyframe Assistant > Sequence Layers.

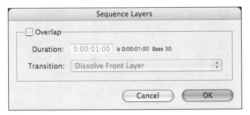

Figure 6.34 In the Sequence Layers dialog box, make sure Overlap is unchecked...

To arrange layers in a sequence:

1. In the Timeline panel, select the layers you want to sequence (**Figure 6.32**).

2. Choose Animation > Keyframe Assistant > Sequence Layers (**Figure 6.33**).

   The Sequence Layers dialog box opens (**Figure 6.34**).

3. Make sure Overlap is unchecked.

4. Click OK to close the dialog box.

   The selected layers are arranged in sequence, top layer first (**Figure 6.35**).

Figure 6.35 ...to arrange the selected layers into a simple sequence.

SEQUENCING AND OVERLAPPING LAYERS

To arrange layers in an overlapping sequence:

1. In the Timeline panel, select the layers you want to arrange in an overlapping sequence.

2. Choose Animation > Keyframe Assistant > Sequence Layers.

   The Sequence Layers dialog box opens.

3. Check Overlap (**Figure 6.36**).

4. In the Duration field, enter the amount of time that the layers should overlap.

5. *Choose one of the following* cross-fade options from the Transition pull-down menu (**Figure 6.37**):

   Off—For no cross-fade

   Dissolve Front Layer—To automatically fade out the end of each preceding layer

   Cross Dissolve Front and Back Layers—To fade out the end of each preceding layer automatically, and to fade up the beginning of each succeeding layer

6. Click OK to close the dialog box.

   The selected layers are arranged in an overlapping sequence (top layer first) and use the cross-fade option you specified (**Figure 6.38**).

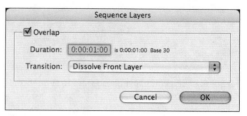

Figure 6.36 To overlap the layers of a sequence, check Overlap in the Sequence Layers dialog box. For Duration, enter the amount of time you want the layers to overlap.

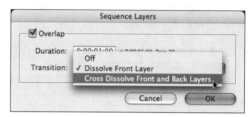

Figure 6.37 In the Transition pull-down menu, choose the appropriate option.

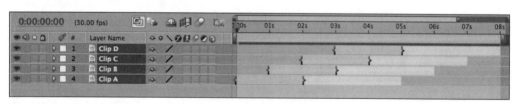

Figure 6.38 The selected layers are arranged in an overlapping sequence.

Removing a Range of Frames

In the previous chapter, you learned to add footage to a composition by using two techniques familiar to non-linear editors: overlay and ripple insert. You can remove a range of frames from a composition using the inverse of those methods: lift and extract.

A *lift edit* removes a defined range from the composition's timeline, leaving an empty gap behind (**Figures 6.39** and **6.40**).

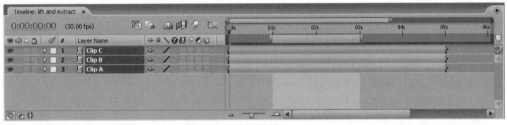

Figure 6.39 Note how the layers in this comp look before the frames under the work area are removed.

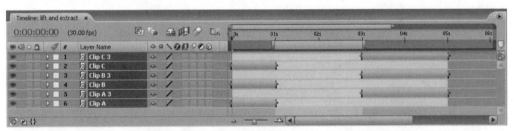

Figure 6.40 Here, the frames under the work area in Figure 6.39 have been lifted from the selected layers, leaving a corresponding gap in the composition. Note how lifting frames splits the affected clips.

An *extract edit* removes the defined range from the composition's timeline and then closes the resulting gap by shifting subsequent layers back in time (**Figure 6.41**). Some editors (and the programs they use) use *extract* synonymously with the term *ripple delete*.

However, whereas the clips in a non-linear editor can occupy a single track, each layer in an After Effects composition must occupy separate tracks. Therefore, any editing method that splits a layer results in two layers: one before and one after the split point.

To perform lift and extract edits, you'll get an early lesson in using the *work area bar*, a bar that resembles a layer's duration bar that's located just above the timeline's time ruler. In this section, you'll use the work area bar to define the range of frames you want to remove from a composition. Other times, however, you'll use the work area bar to define the *work area*, the portion of the composition you want to preview or export. You'll learn these uses for the work area bar in Chapter 8.

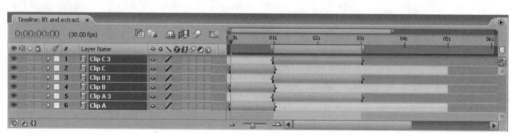

Figure 6.41 An extract edit also splits selected layers at the edit point, but the selected layers after the split are shifted back in time to remove any gap.

Figure 6.42 Set the work area bar over the frames of the comp you want to remove.

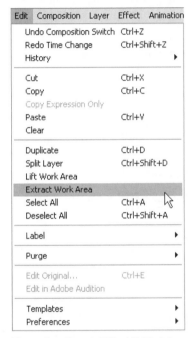

Figure 6.43 Choose Edit > Lift Work Area or Edit > Extract Work Area, depending on the kind of edit you want to perform.

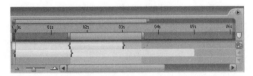

Figure 6.44 The frames you set under the work area are removed according to the type of edit you specified (here, an extract edit).

To lift or extract a range of frames from a composition:

1. Set the current time to the beginning of the range of frames you want to remove from a composition, and press B.

   The beginning of the work area bar is set to the current time.

2. Set the current time to the end of the range of frames you want to remove from a composition, and press N.

   The end of the work area bar is set to the current time (**Figure 6.42**).

3. *Do either of the following:*

   ▲ To lift the range of frames under the work area, choose Edit > Lift Work Area.

   ▲ To extract the range of frames under the work area, choose Edit > Extract Work Area (**Figure 6.43**).

   The range of frames under the work area is removed according to the method you selected. When frames are removed from the middle of a layer, the layer is split (**Figure 6.44**).

REMOVING A RANGE OF FRAMES

Duplicating Layers

As you learned in Chapter 4, you can add a footage item to one or more compositions as many times as you like, creating a new layer each time. However, it's often easier to duplicate a layer that's already in a composition, particularly when you want to use its edit points or other properties (such as masks, transformations, effects, and layer modes). When you create a duplicate, it appears just above the original layer in the stacking order. The duplicate uses the same name as the original, unless you specified a custom name for the original layer. When the original layer uses a custom name, duplicates have a number appended to the name; subsequent duplicates are numbered incrementally.

To duplicate a layer:

1. In the Timeline panel, select a layer.

2. Choose Edit > Duplicate, or press Command-D (Mac) or Ctrl-D (Windows) (**Figure 6.45**).

   A copy of the layer appears above the original layer in the stacking order (**Figure 6.46**). The copy is selected; you may want to rename the new layer (as described in "Naming Layers" in Chapter 5).

✔ Tip

- Older versions of After Effects appended an asterisk after the name of a duplicate layer (or layers resulting from splitting a layer), and subsequent duplicates used additional asterisks. Now After Effects uses a more straightforward incremental numbering system.

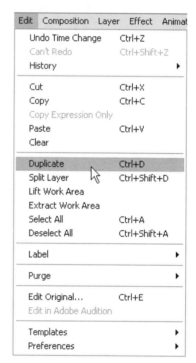

Figure 6.45 To duplicate a layer, select the layer and choose Edit > Duplicate, or press Command-D (Mac) or Ctrl-D (Windows).

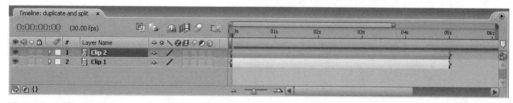

Figure 6.46 A duplicate layer appears in the composition, distinguished by an incrementally higher number (in this case, "2") after its name.

Splitting Layers

You can set a preference to determine which layer—the layer before the split point, or the layer after the split point—is higher in the stacking order.

To split a layer:

1. In the Timeline panel, select a layer.

2. Set the current time to the frame at which you want to split the layer (**Figure 6.47**).

3. Choose Edit > Split Layer, or press Shift-Command-D (Mac) or Shift-Ctrl-D (Windows) (**Figure 6.48**).

The layer splits in two, creating one layer that ends at the current time indicator and another that begins at the current time indicator. The layer that becomes higher in the stacking order depends on the preference you set (**Figure 6.49**).

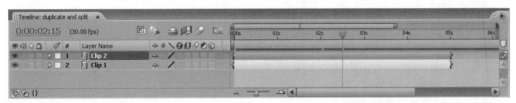

Figure 6.47 Set the current time to the frame at which you want to split the selected layer.

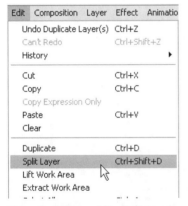

Figure 6.48 Choose Edit > Split Layer.

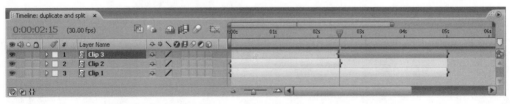

Figure 6.49 The selected layer splits into two layers at the current time.

To set the default stacking order for splitting layers:

1. Choose After Effects > Preferences > General (Mac) or Edit > Preferences > General (Windows) (**Figure 6.50**).

   The General panel of the Preferences dialog box appears.

2. Check Create Split Layer Above Original Layer to make it the default; leave the option unchecked to make the new layer lower in the stacking order (**Figure 6.51**).

3. Click OK to close the Preferences dialog box and set the preference.

✔ Tip

■ As you've seen, other editing functions can result in split layers. Layers split using ripple insert, lift, or extract edits behave like layers split with the Split command, in terms of naming and stacking order. You can also split layers by performing a ripple insert edit. See "Adding Layers Using Insert and Overlay" in Chapter 4 and "Removing a Range of Frames" earlier in this chapter.

Figure 6.50 Choose After Effects > Preferences > General (Mac) or Edit > Preferences > General (Windows).

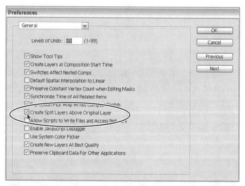

Figure 6.51 Checking Create Split Layer Above Original Layer makes the layer resulting from splitting a layer appear higher in the stacking order.

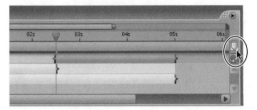

Figure 6.52 To add a composition marker, drag a marker from the marker well...

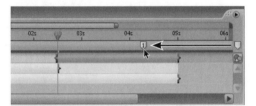

Figure 6.53 ...and drop the marker at the frame you want to mark in the time ruler. Watch the current time display of the Timeline panel to help accurately place the marker.

Using Markers

Like most non-linear editing programs, After Effects enables you to mark important points in time with a visible stamp. *Markers* allow you to identify music beats visually and to synchronize visual effects with sound effects. They can also help you quickly move the current time to particular points in the composition. You can add as many as ten numbered markers to the time graph. And in individual layers, you can add any number of markers, which can include text comments to help you identify them. Because markers are for personal reference, they only appear in the time ruler and layer duration bars; they don't appear in the Composition panel or in previews or renders.

In addition to text comments, layer markers can also contain Web or chapter links. These links are retained when you export to certain Web- or DVD-friendly formats. When a marker containing a link is reached during playback, a Web link automatically opens as a Web page in your browser; a chapter link cues a QuickTime movie or DVD to a specified chapter. Check the After Effects Help System for more detailed information on these specialized features.

To add a composition marker by dragging:

◆   In the Timeline panel, drag a composition time marker from the marker well to the desired point in the time graph (**Figure 6.52**).

A marker appears in the time ruler of the Timeline panel (**Figure 6.53**).

To add a composition marker at the current time indicator:

1. Move the current time indicator to the frame you want to mark in the composition (**Figure 6.54**).

2. Press Shift and a number on the main keyboard (not the numeric keypad).

   A marker with the number you pressed appears in the time ruler of the Timeline panel (**Figure 6.55**).

To move a composition marker:

◆ Drag a composition marker to a new position in the time ruler of the Timeline panel (**Figure 6.56**).

To move the current time indicator to a composition marker:

◆ Press the number of a composition marker on the main keyboard (not the numeric keypad).

   The current time indicator moves to the composition marker with the number you pressed.

To remove a composition marker:

◆ Drag a composition marker to the right until the marker well is highlighted and the marker disappears from the time ruler (**Figure 6.57**).

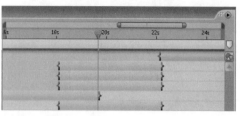

Figure 6.54 You can also place a composition marker by setting the current time...

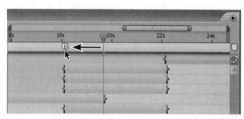

Figure 6.55 ...and then pressing Shift and a number on the main keyboard to place the numbered marker at the current time.

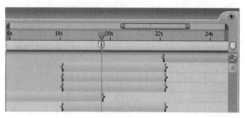

Figure 6.56 You can drag a composition marker to a new position in the time ruler.

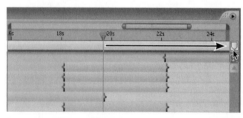

Figure 6.57 To remove a composition marker, drag it to the extreme right, until the marker well is highlighted and the marker disappears.

Figure 6.58 To add a layer marker, select a layer and set the current time to the frame you want to mark.

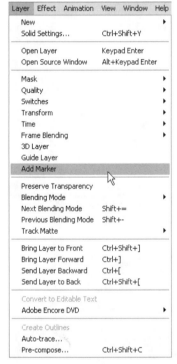

Figure 6.59 Choose Layer > Add Marker, or press the asterisk on the numeric keypad.

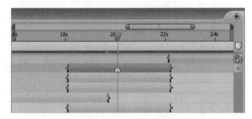

Figure 6.60 The marker appears in the duration bar of the selected layer at the current time indicator.

To add a layer marker:

1. Select the layer to which you want to add a marker.

2. Set the current time to the frame to which you want to add a marker (**Figure 6.58**).

3. *Do one of the following:*

   ▲ Choose Layer > Add Marker (**Figure 6.59**).

   ▲ Press the asterisk (*) on the numeric keypad (not the main keyboard).

   A marker appears on the layer's duration bar at the current time indicator (**Figure 6.60**).

To add a layer marker comment:

1. Double-click a layer marker in a layer's duration bar (**Figure 6.61**).

A Marker dialog box opens. If a Layer panel opens, you must have double-clicked the layer's duration bar or marker name rather than the marker itself.

2. In the Marker dialog box, enter a comment for the marker in the Comment field (**Figure 6.62**).

You can also add chapter links or Web links if your output format supports these features.

3. Click OK to close the dialog box.

The comment you specified appears next to the layer marker (**Figure 6.63**).

To move a layer marker:

◆ Drag a layer marker to a new position in the layer's duration bar (**Figure 6.64**).

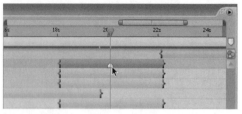

Figure 6.61 Double-click a layer marker to add a name to the marker. Make sure to double-click the marker, not the layer (or the marker name, if it already has one).

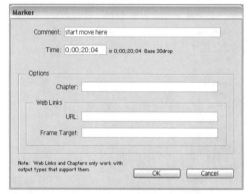

Figure 6.62 In the Marker dialog box, enter a comment for the marker.

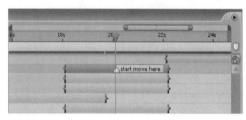

Figure 6.63 The comment you specified appears next to the marker.

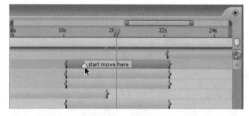

Figure 6.64 Drag a layer marker to a new frame in the layer. Make sure to grab the marker, not its name or the layer's duration bar.

To remove a layer marker:

◆ Command-click (Mac) or Ctrl-click (Windows) a layer marker.

The mouse pointer becomes a Scissors icon ▓ when you position it over the layer marker. The layer marker disappears from the layer's duration bar.

✔ Tips

■ When a composition is nested and becomes a layer, its composition markers appear as layer markers. However, changing its markers as a layer doesn't affect its markers as a comp. In other words, composition markers are converted into layer markers, but they don't retain a relationship thereafter. For example, if you remove a nested comp's layer marker, the corresponding marker in the original comp remains.

■ You can add layer markers on the fly as you preview audio. This makes it especially easy to mark the beats of music or other audio. Press the decimal point (.) on the numeric keypad to preview audio only. As the audio previews, press the asterisk (*) key on the numeric keypad. (Adobe Premiere Pro users should recognize this technique.)

■ As you may remember from Chapter 2, markers from an Adobe Premiere Pro project are retained when you import the project as a composition in After Effects.

PROPERTIES
AND KEYFRAMES

Once they see what After Effects can do, most folks can't wait to take a closer look at the program that produces such artful results. Upon closer inspection, however, it's easy to recoil from the cryptic array of controls that look more like the tools of a scientist than those of an artist.

But don't let a few numbers and graphs intimidate you! This chapter fearlessly unveils layer properties and demystifies animation. Once you understand how to define properties, you can extend a few simple techniques to control practically any property of any layer in a composition. Having conquered that paper tiger, you'll be ready to confront the challenge of animating those properties using something called *keyframes*.

You'll find that the techniques you learn in this chapter are fundamental, and you'll be able to apply them to the features covered in subsequent chapters, from masks to effects to 3D layers. But first, you'll want to see the animation in action, using techniques covered in Chapter 8, "Playback, Previews, and RAM." And then you should build on the core keyframing techniques presented here in Chapter 9, "Keyframe Interpolation." You'll realize that animating in After Effects isn't rocket science, after all. But mastering it is still an art.

Layer Property Types

A *property* refers to any of a layer's visual or audio characteristics to which you can assign different values over time. Properties fall into these main categories: masks, effects, and transform (**Figure 7.1**). In addition, layers that contain audio include an Audio property, and 3D layers include a Material Options property. (For more information on the special characteristics of 3D layers, see Chapter 15, "3D Layers.")

The order in which these categories are listed reflects the order in which After Effects renders each layer's masks, effects, transform, and audio properties. Although you don't need to concern yourself with rendering order now, it does become important as your animations grow in complexity.

Masks

Like the acetate layers used in traditional compositing, masks let you include some portions of an image and conceal others. They also make it possible for you to apply effects to selected portions of layers.

You can apply one or several masks to each layer in a composition and then define the way those masks interact. Not only can you control the shape and feather of a mask, you can also animate these attributes over time. Chapter 10, "Mask Essentials," describes using masks in detail.

Effects

Effects include a wide range of options for modifying sound and images. You can use them to make simple adjustments—such as correcting color or filtering audio—or to make more dramatic changes, such as distorting and stylizing. *Keying effects* help to composite images, and *transition effects* blend one layer into another. You can even use effects to generate visual elements such as text, light, and particles.

Although After Effects includes a variety of built-in effects, you can also add to your effects repertoire by using After Effects Pro or by downloading third-party plug-ins. Chapter 11, "Effects Fundamentals," provides a more detailed introduction about the use of effects.

Transform properties

Although you may not choose to apply any masks or effects to the layers of your compositions, you must still define their basic properties, including position, scale, rotation, and opacity—known as *transform properties*. This chapter focuses on these essential layer properties as they relate to 2D layers. (For a detailed discussion of the transform properties of 3D layers, see Chapter 14, "More Layer Techniques.")

Audio properties

Layers that contain audio display an Audio property in the layer outline. Because only images can have masks or transform properties, audio-only layers contain only the Effects and Audio property categories. The Audio category includes a Levels property to control audio volume as well as a waveform display. Along with transform properties, this chapter explains how to set audio levels.

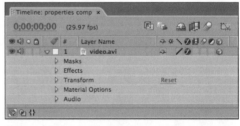

Figure 7.1 There are three major categories of visual properties: masks, effects, and transform. Layers with an audio track contain an Audio property; layers you designate as 3D have a Material Options property.

Viewing Properties

You can view any combination of layer properties in the Timeline panel in what's called a *layer outline* (**Figure 7.2**). That is, each layer works like the heading of an outline: Expanding the layer reveals property headings, which in turn can be expanded to reveal individual properties. (The property headings that are revealed depend on the layer; a layer without masks or audio won't include those headings in the outline.) Using keyboard shortcuts, you can reveal properties selectively and prevent the outline from becoming long and unwieldy.

Revealing a property also displays its current value and its *property track*, an area under the time ruler that shows the property's keyframes. Keyframes, as you'll learn, indicate points at which you define a property's values in order to make them change over time. In other words, the property track is where you can view and control animation.

To fine-tune an animation—particularly between the keyframes—you can go in for an even more detailed view using the Graph Editor (**Figure 7.3**). As its name suggests, the Graph Editor lets you see selected property values as a graph. You can manipulate the graph directly, manually changing not only the keyframes, but also how the values change between keyframes (the interpolated values).

Layer outline   Keyframes   Property track

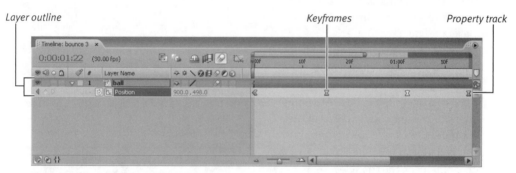

Figure 7.2 Expanding a layer reveals its properties in outline form, or layer outline. Appearing next to the property's name are its current value (under the layer switches) and keyframes (under the time ruler).

Property graph   Keyframe   Graph Editor

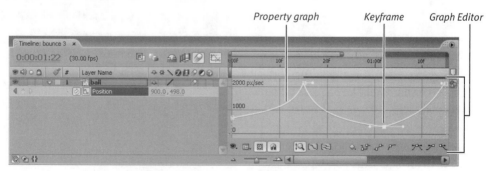

Figure 7.3 You can toggle the area under the time ruler to the Graph Editor. The Graph Editor depicts property values in graph form, allowing you to adjust both keyframed values and the manner in which After Effects calculates values between keyframes.

But don't let yourself get overwhelmed by unfamiliar terminology or seemingly complex choices. For the moment, rest assured that the Timeline panel allows you to reveal the properties you want at the level of detail you need. This chapter covers setting property values and basic keyframing. Chapter 9, "Keyframe Interpolation," covers fine-tuning animation in the Graph Editor.

To expand or collapse a layer outline by clicking:

◆ In the Timeline panel, *do any of the following:*

▲ To expand the first level of property headings, click the triangle to the left of a layer (**Figure 7.4**).

The triangle spins clockwise to point down, revealing the first level of the layer outline.

▲ To further expand the outline, click the triangle to the left of a property heading (**Figure 7.5**).

The triangle spins clockwise to point down, revealing the next level of the outline.

▲ To collapse an expanded layer outline heading, click the triangle again.

The triangle spins counterclockwise, hiding that level of the layer outline.

✔ Tips

■ You can expand the outline for multiple layers simultaneously by selecting more than one layer before expanding the outline. Expanding the outline for one selected layer expands all selected layers (**Figure 7.6**).

■ There are several ways to expand and collapse a layer outline. Although clicking the Timeline panel may be the most intuitive method, doing so often reveals more than you need. Keyboard shortcuts let you expand layer properties selectively.

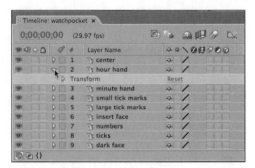

Figure 7.4 Click the triangle to the left of a layer to reveal the first level of properties.

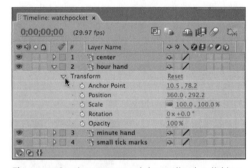

Figure 7.5 Continue to expand the outline by clicking the triangles. Click the triangles again to collapse the outline.

Figure 7.6 Select multiple layers to expand the outline for all of them at once.

Table 7.1

Viewing Layer Properties	
TO EXPAND/COLLAPSE	PRESS THIS SHORTCUT
TRANSFORM	
Anchor Point	A
Position	P
Scale	S
Rotation	R
Opacity	T
Material Options	AA (3D layers)
MASK	
Mask Shape	M
Mask Feather	F
Mask Opacity	TT
Mask Properties	MM
EFFECTS	
Effects	E
Paint Effects	EE
AUDIO	
Audio Levels	L
Audio Waveform	LL
HEADINGS	
Add/remove from outline	Shift-property shortcut
All animated	U (keyframed values)
All modified	UU

To view layer properties using keyboard shortcuts

◆ To expand the layer outline by using keyboard shortcuts, select one or more layers, and use the appropriate keyboard shortcut (see **Table 7.1**).

✔ Tip

■ Some shortcuts work differently for light and camera layers (covered in Chapter 15, "3D Layers"). Because lights aren't visible (only their effects are), pressing T reveals a light layer's Intensity property. For both lights and cameras, A reveals the Point of Interest property, and R reveals the Orientation property.

VIEWING PROPERTIES

Setting Global vs. Animated Property Values

Now that you know how to view layer properties, you can set their values. The following sections describe how to set property values globally—that is, how to set a single value for the duration of the layer. Then, you'll animate properties by setting different values at different points in time. But before we continue, it may be helpful to understand a few basic differences between global and animated properties.

As you proceed, you'll notice that a property that has a *global*, or unchanging, value has an I-beam icon at its current time in the time graph, and the Stopwatch icon next to the property's name appears deselected (**Figure 7.7**).

An animated property, in contrast, displays keyframes, which designate values at specific points in time, and an activated Stopwatch icon (**Figure 7.8**). You can set global properties without regard to the current time, but you must always specify the current frame before setting an animated property. Although global and animated properties look different in the timeline, you always reveal and use property controls the same way.

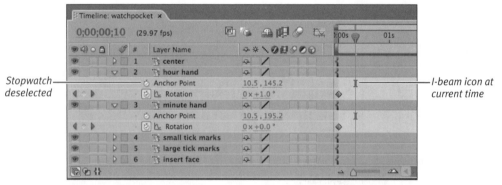

Stopwatch deselected

I-beam icon at current time

Figure 7.7 A deselected Stopwatch icon and an I-beam icon in the selected property track identify a static property.

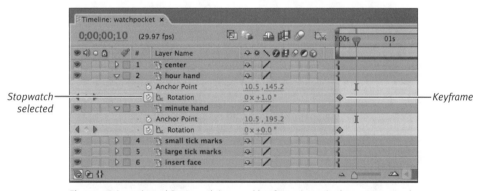

Stopwatch selected

Keyframe

Figure 7.8 An activated Stopwatch icon and keyframe icons in the property track identify an animated property.

Viewing Spatial Controls in the Comp Panel

As you know, the Composition panel lets you view how layers will appear in your final output. It also provides controls for the spatial properties of layers, including the following:

Handles appear at the perimeter of the layer, at each compass point. Dragging them affects the scale of the layer.

Masks appear as editable, color-coded mask paths. You can use them to crop out some parts of the layer while leaving other parts visible.

Effect controls show the spatial controls of many effects, such as the end points of path text.

Keyframes show the position keyframes you set as marks in the motion path. You can move and add keyframes directly in the motion path.

Motion paths show a layer's position as it changes over time as a dotted line. You can't change the path directly, but you can change the keyframes that define the ends of the line segments, as well as the tangents that define the line.

Motion path tangents control the curve of the motion path by affecting how the position values are interpreted between keyframes. They can be extended from keyframes and dragged directly to alter the motion path.

By default, the Composition panel displays this information whenever a layer is selected (**Figure 7.9**). You can also toggle these view options on and off in the View Options dialog box or, in some instances, by using buttons in the Composition panel. You'll appreciate each control more fully as you employ corresponding techniques explained later in this and future chapters.

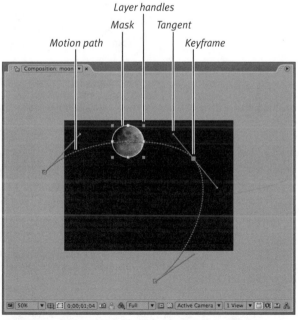

Figure 7.9 By default, the Composition panel displays spatial information and controls for selected layers, such as layer handles, keyframes, and the motion path.

To view layer and effect controls in the Composition panel:

1. In the Composition panel's pull-down menu, choose View Options (**Figure 7.10**).

    The View Options dialog box appears.

2. Select Layer Controls, and then specify the layer controls you want to make visible in the Composition panel.

    A check indicates that the controls are visible in the Composition panel when a layer is selected; no check indicates that the controls are hidden (**Figure 7.11**).

To set motion-path preferences:

1. Choose After Effects > Preferences > Display (Mac) or Edit > Preferences > Display (Windows) (**Figure 7.12**).

    The Display panel of the Preferences dialog box appears (**Figure 7.13**).

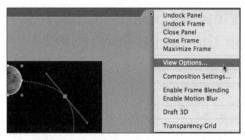

Figure 7.10 In the Composition panel menu, choose View Options.

Figure 7.11 In the View Options dialog box, specify the layer controls you want to be visible in the Composition panel.

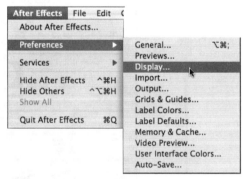

Figure 7.12 Choose After Effects > Preferences > Display (Mac) or Edit > Preferences > Display (Windows).

Figure 7.13 The Display pane of the Preferences dialog box appears.

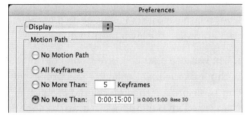

Figure 7.14 In the Motion Path section of the Preferences dialog box, choose an option.

2. In the Motion Path section of the Preferences dialog box, *choose one of the following* options (**Figure 7.14**):

No Motion Path prevents keyframes and motion paths from displaying.

All Keyframes displays all spatial keyframes for the selected layer.

No More Than [ ] Keyframes allows you to enter the maximum number of keyframes displayed, starting from the current time.

No More Than [ ] time allows you to limit the number of keyframes displayed to those within a specified amount of time, beginning at the current time.

3. Click OK to close the Preferences dialog box.

✔ Tips

■ As pointed out in this section, you can view the effect point controls (if present) of a layer's effects in both the Comp and Layer panels. We'll cover the topic in more detail in the section "Setting an Effect Point," in Chapter 11.

■ Instead of selecting Masks in the View Options dialog box, you can use the Toggle View Mask button ▓ at the bottom of the Composition panel.

■ The View Options dialog box also lets you specify whether you want the Comp panel to show icons for cameras and spotlights, which are covered in Chapter 15, "3D Layers."

VIEWING SPATIAL CONTROLS IN THE COMP PANEL

Transform Properties

Although a layer may not use masks or effects, its transform properties—the anchor point, position, scale, rotation, and opacity—are fundamental (**Figure 7.15**). When you create a layer, you actively set its position, either by dragging to the timeline or to the Composition icon to center it, or by dragging to the Composition panel to place it manually. The other transform properties all have default initial values. The following sections describe each transform property and how to change its values.

Keep in mind that even though the following sections focus on transform properties, you employ similar techniques to set values for all types of layer properties.

Anchor point

After Effects calculates the position, scale, and rotation of a layer by its anchor point. The anchor point defines the position of a layer, the point around which a layer is scaled, and the pivot point of the layer's rotation. The placement of the anchor point relative to the layer image can mean the difference between animating, say, a propeller or a pendulum.

By default, a layer's anchor point is positioned in the center of the layer (**Figure 7.16**). You can move the anchor point by using controls in the Layer panel or by using the Pan Behind tool in the Composition panel.

When you change the anchor point in the Layer panel, it may appear that you've also changed the layer's position in the Composition panel. Actually, the layer's Position property remains the same; you simply changed the spot in the layer that determines its position in the composition.

Use the Layer panel to change the anchor point if you haven't already positioned the layer relative to other layers, or if you prefer to manipulate the layer in its own panel.

If you want to change a layer's anchor point without disturbing the layer's position in the composition, use the Pan Behind tool. Using the Pan Behind tool to drag the anchor point in the Composition panel recalculates the layer's position value to compensate for the new anchor point value. This way, the layer maintains its relative position in the composition.

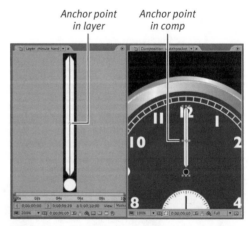

Anchor point in layer   Anchor point in comp

Figure 7.16 Typically, the anchor point is located at the center of a layer. After Effects uses the anchor point to calculate position, rotation, and scale.

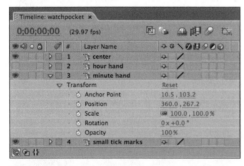

Figure 7.15 Although a layer may not use masks or effects, each of its transform properties has a value—either by default or as you choose to set them.

Figure 7.17 In the Layer panel's View menu, choose Anchor Point Path.

To change the anchor point in the Layer panel:

1. In the Timeline panel or Composition panel, double-click a layer.

   A Layer panel appears.

2. In the Layer panel's View menu, choose Anchor Point Path (**Figure 7.17**).

   The layer's anchor point icon ⊕ appears at its current position. When the anchor point's position is animated, a dotted line represents its motion path.

3. In the image area of the Layer panel, drag the anchor point to the position you want (**Figure 7.18**).

   Because the anchor point maintains its position in the Composition panel, the image in the Comp panel moves relative to the anchor point in the Layer panel (**Figure 7.19**).

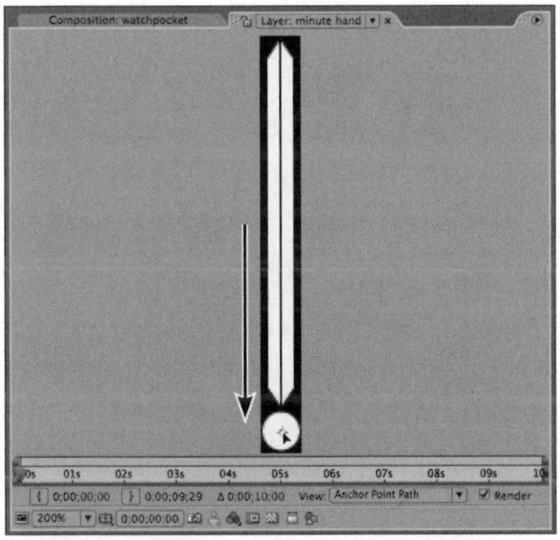

Figure 7.18 When you move an anchor point in a Layer panel...

Figure 7.19 ...the anchor point maintains its position in the comp. Here, the minute hand moves up as the anchor point is moved down to its proper point in the layer.

TRANSFORM PROPERTIES

To change the anchor point without moving the layer in the composition:

1. Select a layer in the composition.

2. If the selected layer's anchor point isn't visible in the Composition panel, choose View Options in the Composition panel menu and select Handles.

3. In the Tools panel, select the Pan Behind tool ▓▓ (**Figure 7.20**).

4. In the Composition panel, drag the anchor point to a new position (**Figure 7.21**). (Make sure to drag the anchor point, not the layer itself.)

   The anchor point and position values for the layer change, so the layer maintains its relative position in the Composition panel.

✔ Tips

- When importing a layered file as a composition, you can opt to import layers at each layer's size or at the document's size. The choice you make helps determine the anchor point's initial position relative to the layer's image. See Chapter 2, "Importing Footage into a Project," for more information.

- You can use the Pan Behind tool to change a layer's position relative to its mask. See Chapter 10 for more information.

Figure 7.20 To move the anchor point without disturbing the arrangement of the layers, select the Pan Behind tool.

Figure 7.21 Using the Pan Behind tool recalculates the layer's position as you move the anchor point in the Composition panel. This moves the anchor point without disturbing the layer's placement.

TRANSFORM PROPERTIES

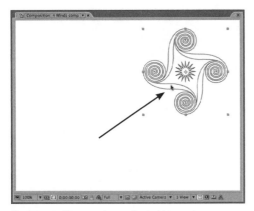

Figure 7.22 You can drag selected layers to new positions.

Position

Setting a layer's position places its anchor point in the two-dimensional space of the composition. The exact position of a layer is expressed in (X, Y) coordinates, where the top-left corner of the composition is (0, 0). (Moving the zero point of the rulers doesn't change the coordinate system.) You can position a layer inside or outside the visible area of the composition. (Position and orientation properties for 3D layers are discussed in Chapter 15.)

To change a layer's position in the Composition panel:

1. Select a layer in the Composition or Timeline panel.

2. In the Composition panel, drag the layer to the position you want (**Figure 7.22**).

   To move a layer offscreen, drag it to the pasteboard, or workspace, outside the visible area of the Composition panel.

   The layer is placed at the position you chose. If the Stopwatch icon hasn't been activated for the layer, the layer will remain at this position for its entire duration. If the Stopwatch is active, a position keyframe is created at this frame.

✔ Tips

- As you'll recall from Chapter 4, "Compositions," dragging a footage item to the Timeline panel or a Composition icon into the Project panel centers the layer automatically.

- Use the Info panel to view the exact X and Y coordinates of the layer as you move it. If you set a custom zero point for the rulers, look at the X1 and Y1 display to see the coordinates in terms of the rulers you set.

Subpixel Positioning

When you set a layer to Draft quality, After Effects calculates the position, rotation, and scale (or any effect that moves the pixels of an image) by using whole pixels. When layers are set to Best quality, however, these values are calculated to the thousandth of a pixel, or on a *subpixel* basis. The more you zoom in to the Composition panel, the greater the precision with which you can move a layer.

Because subpixel positioning allows layers to move with a precision greater than the resolution of the composition, movement appears much smoother than when you're not using subpixel positioning. You can see the difference by contrasting the movement of layers set to Draft quality with the same movement set to Best quality.

Subpixel positioning also requires more precise calculations, which means it takes After Effects longer to render images. Thus, you may want to do much of your work in Draft quality and then switch to Best quality when you're ready to fine-tune.

Scale

TRANSFORM PROPERTIES

By default, a layer is set to 100 percent of its original size, or scale. You scale a layer around its anchor point. In other words, the anchor point serves as the mathematical center of a change in size. When you scale a layer by dragging, you'll notice how the handles of the layer seem to stretch from the anchor point.

Remember that bitmapped images look blocky and pixelated when scaled much beyond 100 percent. When you scale path-based images beyond 100 percent, you can use the Continuously Rasterize switch to help maintain image quality. Review Chapter 2 if you need more information about image size and rasterization; see Chapter 15 for more information about how the Scale property differs for 3D layers.

To scale a layer by dragging:

1. Select a layer, and make sure its layer handles are visible in the Composition panel (see "Viewing Spatial Controls in the Comp Panel," earlier in this chapter) (**Figure 7.23**).

2. In the Composition panel, *do any of the following:*

   ▲ To scale the layer horizontally only, drag the center-left or center-right handle (**Figure 7.24**).

   ▲ To scale the layer vertically only, drag the center-bottom or the center-top handle (**Figure 7.25**).

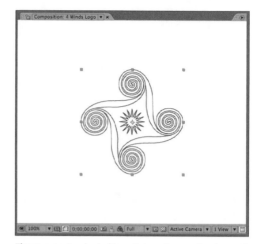

Figure 7.23 A selected layer's handles can be dragged to scale it...

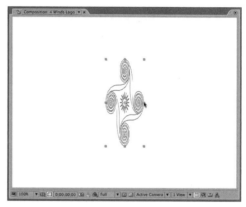

Figure 7.24 ...horizontally...

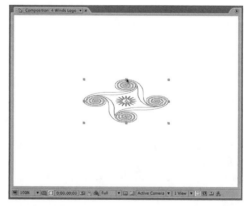

Figure 7.25 ...vertically...

Figure 7.26 ...or by both aspects. Shift-drag a corner handle to scale the layer while maintaining its proportions.

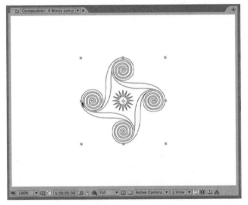

Figure 7.27 You can flip a layer by dragging one side past the other. Note how the spirals in this logo face the opposite direction.

▲ To scale the layer horizontally and vertically, drag a corner handle.

▲ To scale the layer while maintaining its proportions, press Shift as you drag a corner handle (**Figure 7.26**).

▲ To flip a layer, drag one side of the layer's bounding box past the other side (**Figure 7.27**).

3. Release the mouse.

In the Composition panel, the layer appears with the scale you set. If the Stopwatch icon hasn't been activated for the layer, the layer will retain this scale for its duration. If the Stopwatch is active, a scale keyframe is created at this frame.

✔ Tip

■ You can quickly reset the scale of a layer to 100 percent by selecting the layer and double-clicking the Selection tool.

TRANSFORM PROPERTIES

Rotation

When you rotate a 2D layer, it rotates in two-dimensional space, using the anchor point as its pivot point. See Chapter 15 to learn about rotating layers in 3D space.

To rotate a layer by dragging:

1. Select a layer.

2. In the Tools panel, choose the Rotate tool ⟳ (**Figure 7.28**).

3. In the Composition panel, drag a layer to rotate it around its anchor point.

   As you drag, a bounding box represents the layer's new rotation position (**Figure 7.29**).

4. Release the mouse to set the rotation.

   In the Composition panel, the layer appears with the rotation you set. If the Stopwatch icon isn't active for the layer, this is the rotation of the layer for its entire duration. If the Stopwatch icon is active, a rotation keyframe is created at this frame.

✔ Tips

- To quickly reset a selected layer's rotation to 0 degrees, double-click the Rotate tool.

- If you want an object to turn (rotate) in the direction of its motion path (animated position), you can avoid the pain of setting a lot of rotational keyframes by using the Auto-Orient Rotation command instead. See Chapter 9, "Keyframe Interpolation," for details.

Figure 7.28 Choose the Rotate tool.

Figure 7.29 In the Composition panel, drag the layer to rotate it around its pivot point.

Rotational Values

Rotation is expressed as an absolute, not relative, value. You might even think of it as a rotational position. A layer's default rotation is 0 degrees; setting its rotation to 0 degrees always restores it to its original upright angle. This is true when you keyframe rotational values as well (see "To set keyframes for a property" later in this chapter). For example, if you want to rotate a layer 180 degrees clockwise (upside-down) and back again, the rotation values at each keyframe are 0, 180, and 0. Mistakenly setting values of 0, 180, and −180 will cause the layer to turn clockwise 180 degrees and then turn counterclockwise—past its original position—until it's upside down again.

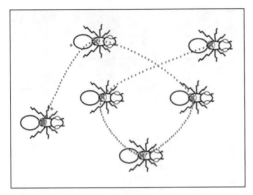

Figure 7.30 Without auto-orient rotation, objects remain upright as they follow the motion path (unless you add rotation). Notice that the ant remains horizontal regardless of the direction of motion.

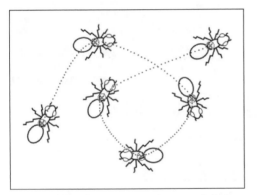

Figure 7.31 Auto-orient rotation automatically keeps a layer perpendicular to the motion path. Here, the ant faces the direction of motion.

Orienting Rotation to a Motion Path Automatically

As a layer follows a motion path, its rotation remains unaffected. The layer maintains its upright position as it follows the path: Picture, for example, someone riding up an escalator, or the cabins on a Ferris wheel; they remain upright although they follow a sloped or curved path (**Figure 7.30**). Frequently, you want the object to orient its rotation to remain perpendicular to the motion path: Now picture a roller coaster climbing a hill (**Figure 7.31**).

Fortunately, you don't have to painstakingly keyframe a layer's Rotation property to ensure that it remains oriented to the motion path; After Effects' Auto-Orient Rotation command does that for you. Technically, auto-orient rotation isn't a type of spatial interpolation; however, like an interpolation method, it dictates the behavior of a layer along a motion path—and in so doing saves you a lot of keyframing work.

To auto-orient rotation to the motion path:

1. Select a layer (**Figure 7.32**).

2. Choose Layer > Transform > Auto-Orient, or press Option-Command-O (Mac) or Alt-Control-O (Windows) (**Figure 7.33**).

   The Auto-Orientation dialog box appears.

3. *Choose either of the following:*

   Off—Controls the layer's rotation manually

   Orient Along Path—Makes the layer automatically orient its *X*-axis tangent to the motion path

4. Click OK to close the Auto-Orientation dialog box.

✔ Tips

■ You can use the Path Text effect to make text follow a path while automatically remaining perpendicular to it. Text you create using the text-creation tools can also follow a path you specify.

■ Chapter 15, "3D Layers," covers 3D compositing, including auto-orient options for 3D layers, cameras, and lights.

Figure 7.32 Select a layer.

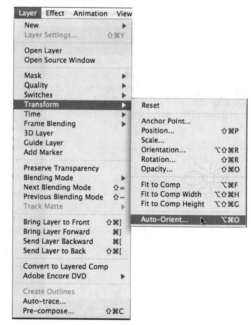

Figure 7.33 Choose Layer > Transform > Auto-Orient.

ORIENTING ROTATION TO A MOTION PATH

Opacity

At any point in time, a layer can be anywhere from 0 percent opaque (completely transparent, and thus invisible) to 100 percent opaque (with absolutely no transparency).

Bear in mind that the Opacity property merely controls the layer's overall opacity. There are plenty of other ways to define areas of transparency and opacity, including transfer modes, track mattes, keying effects, and masking techniques.

Because opacity is the only transform property you can't "grab onto" in the Comp panel, you must alter it by using numerical controls.

To change the opacity of a layer:

1. Select a layer in the Timeline panel or Composition panel.

2. Press T to display the Opacity property for the selected layer.

   The layer's Opacity property appears in the layer outline, and the current value for opacity appears across from the property under the Switches column (**Figure 7.34**).

3. Under the Switches column across from the layer's Opacity property, *do any of the following:*

   ▲ To decrease the current opacity value, drag the opacity value left (**Figure 7.35**).

   ▲ To increase the current opacity value, drag the value right.

   ▲ To set the value in a dialog box, Ctrl-click (Mac) or right-click (Windows) the opacity value, and select Edit Value in the contextual menu.

As you change the opacity value, the layer's opacity changes in the Composition panel. If the Stopwatch icon isn't active for the layer, the layer retains this opacity for its duration. If the Stopwatch icon is active, an opacity keyframe is created at this frame.

✔ Tip

■ The keyboard shortcuts that display most transform properties are often the first letter of the name of the property: P for position, S for scale, and so on. However, you reveal the Opacity property by pressing T.

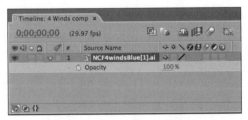

Figure 7.34 Press T to reveal the Opacity property value.

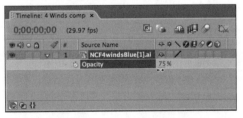

Figure 7.35 To change the value, drag right to increase the value or left to decrease it (as shown here).

ORIENTING ROTATION TO A MOTION PATH

Specifying Property Values

As in most other Adobe programs, numeric values in After Effects appear colored and underlined, indicating that the values are *scrubbable*. This means you can alter a property's current value by dragging, or *scrubbing*, the value display. Clicking the value highlights it so you can enter a numeric value. Pressing Return (Mac) or Enter (Windows) verifies the value; pressing Tab highlights the next value display. Because these controls are familiar to most users, they won't be covered here.

Alternatively, you can open a dialog box to enter property values (**Table 7.2**). Although a dialog box may not offer the convenience of scrubbing or entering the value directly, it does allow you to enter decimal values or to employ different units of measurement for the property value.

To set property values in a dialog box:

1. Select a layer in the Timeline panel or Composition panel.

2. Press the keyboard shortcut to reveal the property you want to adjust, or use the triangles to expand the layer outline to reveal the property.

   The layer property is revealed in the layer outline. The current value of the property is displayed across from the property's name in the Switches/Modes panel of the timeline.

Table 7.2

Property Dialog Box Shortcuts	
TO SHOW THIS DIALOG BOX	PRESS THIS
Anchor Point dialog box	Command-Option-Shift-A (Mac) or Ctrl-Alt-Shift-A (Windows)
Opacity dialog box	Command-Shift-O (Mac) or Ctrl-Shift-O (Windows)
Other dialog boxes (works with P, R, F, and M)	Command-Shift-property shortcut (Mac) or Ctrl-Shift-property shortcut (Windows)

Figure 7.36 You can also Ctrl-click (Mac) or right-click (Windows) the property value to access the Edit Value option.

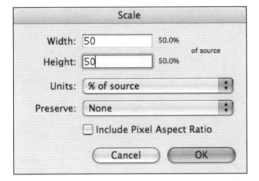

Figure 7.37 In the property value dialog box, enter the new values.

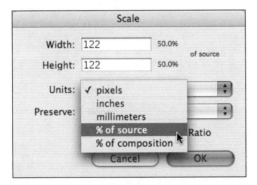

Figure 7.38 Some property value dialog boxes allow you to choose other options, such as a unit of measurement. For example, it may be easier to scale a layer in terms of percentages than in terms of pixels.

3. Ctrl-click (Mac) or right-click (Windows), and select Edit Value from the contextual menu (**Figure 7.36**).

A dialog box that corresponds to the property value appears.

4. In the property value dialog box, enter the new values (**Figure 7.37**).

With some properties, you can choose a unit of measure from a pull-down menu (**Figure 7.38**). Other options (such as maintaining aspect ratio for scale) may also be available. Your options will depend on the property value you're changing.

5. Click OK to close the dialog box.

The value you specified becomes the current value, and the change is reflected in the Comp panel.

✔ Tip

■ When you open a dialog box to change the Scale property, you can select an option for pixel aspect ratio (PAR). If the PAR options leave you scratching your head, see the sidebar "PAR Excellence" in Chapter 2.

Nudging Layer Properties

You can also use keyboard shortcuts to slightly change, or *nudge*, the position, rotation, or scale of a layer. When you nudge a layer, After Effects counts pixels at the current magnification of the Composition panel, not the layer's actual size. Therefore, nudging a layer's position moves it 1 pixel when viewed at 100 percent magnification, 2 pixels when viewed at 50 percent, 4 pixels at 25 percent, and so on. When layer quality is set to Best, you can nudge layers on a subpixel basis (see the sidebar "Subpixel Positioning," earlier in this chapter). Therefore, a layer set to Best quality can be nudged .5 pixel when viewed at 200 percent, .25 pixel when viewed at 400 percent, and so on. **Table 7.3** lists the keyboard shortcuts for nudging properties.

Table 7.3

Nudging Layer Properties	
TO NUDGE THIS VALUE	DO THIS
Nudge position one pixel	Press arrow keys (up, down, right, left)
Nudge rotation 1 degree	Press plus (+) on numeric keypad
Nudge rotation –1 degree	Press minus (-) on numeric keypad
Nudge scale 1%	Press Option-plus (+) (Mac) or Alt-plus (+) (Windows) on numeric keypad
Nudge scale –1%	Press Option-minus (-) (Mac) or Alt-minus (-) (Windows) on numeric keypad
Nudge x10	Press Shift-keyboard shortcut for nudge

Viewing an Audio Waveform

You can expand the outlines of layers containing audio to reveal an audio waveform display that provides a graphical representation of the audio's left and right channels.

The waveform's shape corresponds to characteristics of the audio. For example, you can often identify the beat of the bass drum in a song by finding peaks in the waveform. The size of the waveform corresponds to the level, or volume, of the audio. Increasing the levels (by setting the Levels property or by applying an audio effect) makes the waveform taller; decreasing the levels makes the waveform shorter.

The horizontal detail of the waveform depends on your view of the time ruler. By zooming in to the time ruler to the frame level, you can view the greatest detail in the audio waveform. You can also resize the Waveform property track to increase the vertical detail of the display. Be aware, however, that doing so merely makes the waveform easier to see; it doesn't change the volume levels.

To display a layer's audio waveform:

1. Select a layer containing audio (**Figure 7.39**).

2. Press L to display the layer's Audio Levels and Waveform properties in the layer outline.

3. Click the triangle next to the Waveform property to expand the layer outline further and to reveal the waveform display (**Figure 7.40**).

   Waveforms for the left and right channels appear in the property track. The left channel appears above the right channel.

✔ Tip

■ You can also view audio waveforms in the Graph Editor (see Chapter 9, "Keyframe Interpolation").

Figure 7.39 Select a layer containing audio.

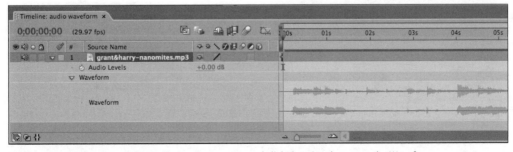

Figure 7.40 Press L to reveal the Audio Levels property, and click the triangle next to the Waveform property to reveal waveform displays for the left and right channels.

VIEWING AN AUDIO WAVEFORM

Using the Audio Panel

You use the Audio panel to monitor and control audio levels much as you would use a traditional audio mixing board (**Figure 7.41**). If it's not included in the current workspace, you can open it and arrange it within the workspace as you would any other panel (see Chapter 1 for detailed instructions).

On the left side of the Audio panel, Volume Units (VU) meters display playback levels. On the right side of the panel, sliders control the levels for the left and right audio channels. You can set the meters to display levels as percentages or on the more traditional decibel (dB) scale. You can also set the lowest value for the slider controls.

To set Audio panel options:

1. Click the arrow in the upper-right corner of the Audio panel, and select Options from the pop-up menu (**Figure 7.42**).

   The Audio Options dialog box appears (**Figure 7.43**).

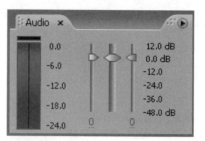

Figure 7.41 The Audio panel is reminiscent of a more traditional audio mixing board.

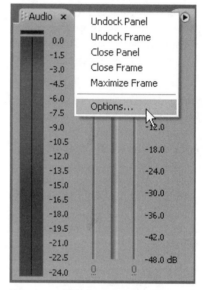

Figure 7.42 Click the arrow in the upper-right corner of the Audio panel, and select Options.

Figure 7.43 The Audio Options dialog box appears. Choose to display the audio in decibels or percentages.

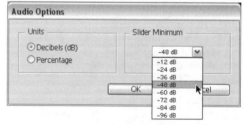

Figure 7.44 In the Audio Options dialog box, set the minimum value of the Levels slider controls.

2. To set the scale of the VU meter, *select one of the following:*

Decibels (dB)—Displays levels in decibels (the standard measure of audio power, or volume)

Percentage—Displays levels in percentages (where 100 percent is equivalent to 0 dB)

Peak audio levels should approach but not exceed 0 dB. Otherwise, audio distortion will occur.

3. To set the minimum value of the Levels slider controls, choose an option from the Slider Minimum pull-down menu (**Figure 7.44**).

To set audio levels using the Audio panel:

1. Select an audio layer (**Figure 7.45**).

2. To reveal the Audio Levels property, press L.

The layer outline expands to reveal the Audio Levels property.

3. To view the audio waveform, click the triangle next to the Waveform property.

The layer outline expands to reveal the audio waveform display (**Figure 7.46**).

continues on next page

Figure 7.45 Select a layer containing audio.

Figure 7.46 If you want, reveal the Audio Levels property and waveform.

4. In the Audio panel, *do any of the following*:

▲ Drag the left slider to change the left channel level, or enter a value below the left slider (**Figure 7.47**).

The center slider adjusts accordingly.

▲ Drag the right slider to change the level for the right channel, or enter a value below the right slider.

The center slider adjusts accordingly.

▲ Drag the center slider to change the level for both the left and right channels.

The left and right sliders adjust accordingly.

In the Timeline panel, the layer's audio waveform reflects the changes in levels (**Figure 7.48**). If the Stopwatch icon isn't active for the layer, the audio levels are set globally. If the Stopwatch icon is active, an audio-level keyframe is created.

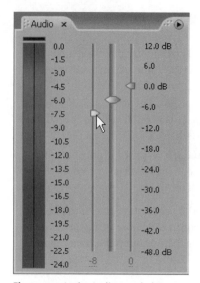

Figure 7.47 In the Audio panel, drag the left or right slider to adjust the corresponding audio channel, or drag the center slider to adjust the overall level.

✔ Tips

■ Increasing the height of the Audio panel makes its meter and controls more precise.

■ Although you can also set audio levels using a value graph, a more detailed discussion of that control is reserved for Chapter 14.

■ The Stereo Mixer effect is one of several audio effects you can use to process audio. In addition to panning the left and right audio channels, the Stereo Mixer effect provides a useful alternative to the Levels property. See Chapter 11 for more about effects.

Figure 7.48 The audio waveform reflects your changes. In this example, the level of the left channel has been lowered for the entire duration of the layer. Alternatively, you can keyframe level adjustments like any other property.

USING THE AUDIO PANEL

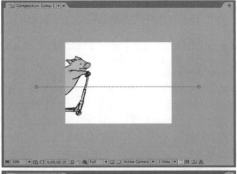

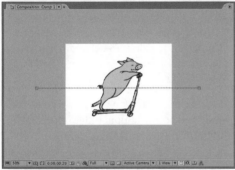

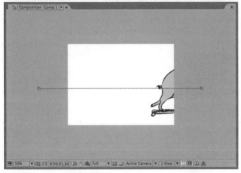

Figure 7.49 You can keyframe any property to animate it over time. In this case, After Effects calculates the position of a layer between two keyframes to create movement.

Animating Layer Properties with Keyframes

To produce animation, you change a layer's properties over time—for example, achieving motion by changing a layer's position over time. In After Effects (as with other programs), you use keyframes to define and control these changes.

A *keyframe* defines a property's value at a specific point in time. When you create at least two keyframes with different values, After Effects interpolates the value for each frame in between. After Effects calculates how to create a smooth transition from one keyframe to another—how to get from point A to point B (**Figure 7.49**).

Basic keyframing

Essentially, keyframing is nothing more than repeating a two-step process: setting the current frame, and setting the property value for that frame. The specific steps are outlined in this section.

If you're new to animating with keyframes, you may want to start with one of the transform properties such as Scale. (Chapter 9 shows how to gain even greater control over your animations by manipulating the spatial and temporal interpolation method used between keyframes.)

To set keyframes for a property:

1. In the Timeline panel, view the property of the layer (or layers) you want to keyframe.

    You may view the same property for more than one layer but not different properties.

2. Set the current time to the frame at which you want to set a keyframe.

    It's possible to set a keyframe beyond the duration of a layer.

continues on next page

ANIMATING PROPERTIES WITH KEYFRAMES

3. Click the Stopwatch icon ⏱ next to the layer property you want to keyframe to activate the icon (and the keyframe process) (**Figure 7.50**).

The Stopwatch icon appears selected 🔘. In the property tracks of the selected layers, an initial keyframe appears; in the keyframe navigator, a check appears.

4. If the property isn't set to the value you want, set the value (as explained in earlier in this chapter).

As long as the current time is set to the keyframe, any new value is applied to the keyframe.

Keyframes

Keyframe is a term borrowed from traditional animation. In a traditional animation studio, a senior animator might draw only the keyframes—what the character looks like at key moments in the animation. The junior animators would then draw the rest of the frames, or *in-betweens* (a process sometimes known as *tweening*). The same principle applies to After Effects animations: If you supply the keyframes for a property, the program calculates the values in between. And you can keyframe any property, not just movement.

With After Effects, you're always the senior animator, so you should only supply the keyframes—just enough to define the animation. Setting too many keyframes defeats the purpose of this division of labor.

Figure 7.50 Activate the Stopwatch icon to set the first keyframe for the property at the current time indicator.

5. Set the current time to another frame.

6. To create additional keyframes, *do one of the following:*

▲ To create a keyframe with a new value, change the value of the property (**Figure 7.51**).

continues on next page

Figure 7.51 To set a keyframe with a new value, set the current time to a new frame, and change the property value.

▲ To create a keyframe without changing the current property value, select the diamond in the keyframe navigator (**Figure 7.52**).

A new keyframe appears at the current time, and the diamond at the center of the keyframe navigator is highlighted.

7. To create additional keyframes, repeat steps 5 and 6.

8. To see your changes play in the Composition panel, use the playback controls or create a preview (see Chapter 8).

✔ Tips

■ The Motion Sketch plug-in panel provides another quick and easy way to create position keyframes: You can draw them in the Composition panel.

■ The Motion Tracker included in After Effects Pro helps you generate keyframes by detecting an object's movement within an image.

■ People often use After Effects to pan and scale large images, emulating the motion-control camera work frequently seen in documentaries. In such cases, you create pans by animating the anchor point, not the position. This technique achieves the panning you want while keeping the anchor point in the viewing area. Because the anchor point is also used to calculate scale, you'll get more predictable results when you zoom in to and out of the image.

ANIMATING PROPERTIES WITH KEYFRAMES

Figure 7.52 To set a keyframe without manually changing the value, select the diamond icon in the keyframe navigator.

Keyframe icons

A property's keyframes appear in its property track of the time graph. When a property heading is collapsed, the keyframes of the properties in that category appear as circles (**Figure 7.53**). When an individual property is visible, its keyframes appear as either icons or indices (**Figures 7.54** and **7.55**).

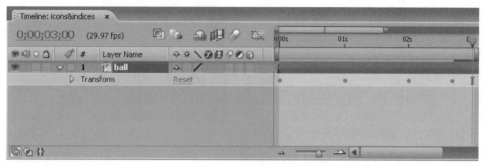

Figure 7.53 When the property heading is collapsed, keyframes appear as small dots.

Figure 7.54 When the property track is visible, keyframes appear either as icons...

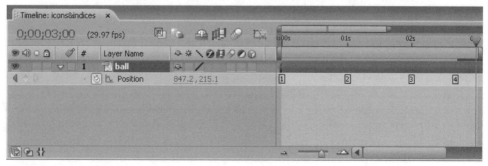

Figure 7.55 ...or as numbered indices.

ANIMATING PROPERTIES WITH KEYFRAMES

237

Keyframe icons vary according to the interpolation method used by the keyframe. Regardless of method, shading indicates that the property value either before or after the keyframe hasn't been interpolated (**Figure 7.56**). This occurs for the first and last keyframes as well as for keyframes that follow hold keyframes, which are used to prevent interpolation. When viewed as indices, keyframes appear as numbered boxes, regardless of their interpolation method. (For more about interpolation, see Chapter 9.)

To toggle between keyframe icons and indices:

◆ In the Timeline panel menu, *choose one of the following* options (**Figure 7.57**):

▲ Use Keyframe Icons

▲ Use Keyframe Indices

The keyframes in the Timeline panel reflect your choice.

✔ Tips

■ Just a reminder: You can quickly view only those properties that have been keyframed by selecting layers and pressing U.

■ Keyframe icons have different shapes, depending on the interpolation type assigned to them. The diamond-shaped icons shown here reflect linear interpolation. See Chapter 9, "Keyframe Interpolation."

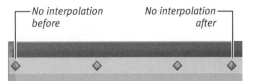

Figure 7.56 Shading indicates that the property value isn't interpolated either before or after the keyframe.

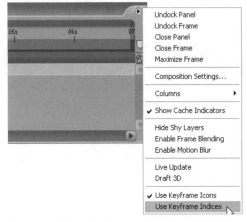

Figure 7.57 In the Timeline panel menu, select whether you want to view keyframe icons or indices.

Setting a New Keyframe with the Keyframe Navigator

As you learned in the section "Basic Keyframing," you can set a new keyframe by selecting the keyframe navigator's Add/Delete Keyframe button—the diamond icon ◈. Instead of using a value you actively specify, a keyframe created this way uses the value already calculated for that frame.

Usually, you use the check box to create keyframes when you want to modify an animation—or, when no animation exists yet, to repeat a value. Initially, the new keyframe doesn't alter the animation; it hasn't changed the property's value at that time. The new keyframe can serve as a good starting point for changing the animation, by changing the keyframe's value or interpolation method (for more about interpolation methods, see Chapter 9).

ANIMATING PROPERTIES WITH KEYFRAMES

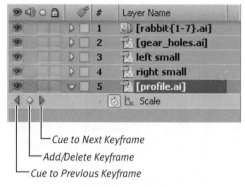

Cue to Next Keyframe
Add/Delete Keyframe
Cue to Previous Keyframe

Figure 7.58 Use the keyframe navigator to cue the current time indicator to the previous or next keyframe. The diamond icon (aka Add/Delete Keyframe button) is highlighted only when the current time is exactly on a keyframe.

Figure 7.59 Clicking an arrow in the keyframe navigator (in this case, the right arrow)...

Figure 7.60 ...cues the current time indicator to the property's adjacent keyframe (here, the next keyframe). (Note that the A/V features panel has been moved closer to the time graph for the purpose of illustration.)

Cueing the Current Time to Keyframes

You can only set or change a keyframe's values at the current time indicator—one reason you need a quick and convenient way to cue the time marker to keyframes. You may also want to jump to keyframes to step through your animation or to create keyframes in other layers or properties that align with existing keyframes. The *keyframe navigator* provides the solution (**Figure 7.58**).

And as you saw in the section, "Basic Keyframing," the diamond at the center of the keyframe navigator serves as the Add/Delete Keyframe button. Because it's highlighted only when the current time is cued to a keyframe, it also provides a visual confirmation, particularly if you want to confirm that keyframes in different properties are perfectly aligned.

To cue the current time to keyframes:

1. Make sure the property with the keyframes you want to see is visible in the layer outline.

2. In the Timeline panel, *do any of the following:*

   ▲ Shift-drag the current time indicator until it snaps to a visible keyframe.

   ▲ In the keyframe navigator for the property, click the left arrow to cue the current time to the previous keyframe.

   ▲ In the keyframe navigator for the property, click the right arrow to cue the current time to the next keyframe (**Figure 7.59**).

   The current time cues to the adjacent keyframe (**Figure 7.60**). If no keyframe exists beyond the current keyframe, the appropriate arrow in the keyframe navigator appears dimmed.

Selecting and Deleting Keyframes

Select keyframes when you want to move them to a different position in time, delete them, or copy and paste them to other properties or layers.

Figure 7.61 Click a keyframe to select it; Shift-click to add to your selection.

To select keyframes:

◆ *Do any of the following:*

▲ To select a keyframe, click it in the property track.

▲ To add keyframes to or subtract them from your selection, press Shift as you click additional keyframes (**Figure 7.61**).

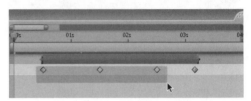

Figure 7.62 You can also select multiple keyframes by dragging a marquee around them.

▲ To select multiple keyframes, drag a marquee around the keyframes in the property track (**Figure 7.62**).

▲ To select all the keyframes for a property, click the name of the property in the layer outline (**Figure 7.63**).

Selected keyframes appear highlighted.

To deselect keyframes:

◆ *Do either of the following:*

▲ To deselect all keyframes, click in an empty area of the Timeline panel.

▲ To deselect certain keyframes, Shift-click an already selected keyframe.

Deselected keyframes no longer appear highlighted.

✔ Tip

■ Selecting a keyframe allows you to move it in time, delete it, or copy it. It doesn't let you edit the values of that keyframe. You can only change the value of a property at the current time.

Figure 7.63 Select all the keyframes for a property by clicking the property's name in the layer outline.

To delete keyframes:

1. Select one or more keyframes, as explained in the previous section.

2. *Do any of the following:*

   ▲ Press Delete.

   ▲ Choose Edit > Clear.

   ▲ With the current time cued to the keyframe, click the keyframe navigator's Add/Delete Keyframe button 🔘.

   The keyframe disappears, and the property's interpolated values are recalculated based on the existing keyframes.

To delete all the keyframes for a property:

◆ Deactivate the Stopwatch icon for the property (**Figure 7.64**).

   All keyframes disappear. You can't restore the keyframes by reactivating the Stopwatch (doing so only starts a new keyframe process).

✔ Tip

■ If you mistakenly remove keyframes by deselecting the Stopwatch icon, choose Edit > Undo to undo previous commands, or choose File > Revert to return to the last saved version of your project.

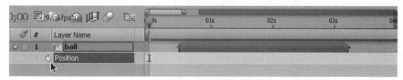

Figure 7.64 Deselecting the property's Stopwatch icon removes all keyframes. The property uses the value at the current time.

Moving Keyframes

You can move one or more keyframes of one or more properties to a different point in time.

To move keyframes:

1. Select one or more keyframes (as explained earlier in this chapter) (**Figure 7.65**).

2. Drag the selected keyframes to a new position in the time graph (**Figure 7.66**). To activate the Snap to Edges feature, press Shift after you begin dragging.

3. Release the mouse when the keyframes are at the position in time you want.

✔ Tip

■ Moving a layer in time also moves its keyframes, which maintain their positions relative to the layer. Trimming a layer, on the other hand, doesn't affect the keyframes. In fact, you can set a keyframe before a layer's In point or after its Out point (**Figure 7.67**).

Figure 7.65 Select the keyframes you want to move...

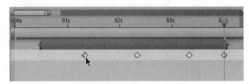

Figure 7.66 ...and drag them to a new position in the timeline. Shift-drag to activate the Snap to Edges feature.

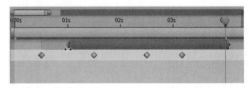

Figure 7.67 Although dragging a layer also moves its keyframes, trimming a layer doesn't trim off its keyframes, which still affect property values.

Copying Values and Keyframes

When you want to reuse values you set for a property, you can copy and paste them to a different point in time or even to different layers. Not only can you paste keyframes to the same property (such as from one position to another), you can also paste them to different properties that use the same kind of values (such as from a position to an anchor point).

Pasted keyframes appear in the property track of the destination in the order and spacing of the original, starting at the current time.

After Effects permits you to copy and paste keyframes one layer at a time. You can copy and paste keyframes of more than one property at a time, as long as you paste them into the same properties. If you want to copy and paste to different properties, however, you must do so one property at a time.

To copy and paste keyframes:

1. Select one or more keyframes (as explained earlier in this chapter) (**Figure 7.68**).

2. Choose Edit > Copy, or press Command-C (Mac) or Ctrl-C (Windows) (**Figure 7.69**).

3. Set the current time to the frame where you want the pasted keyframe(s) to begin.

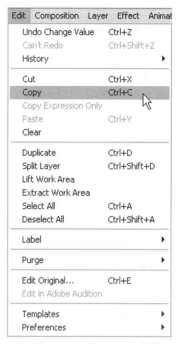

Figure 7.69 Choose Edit > Copy, or press Command-C (Mac) or Ctrl-C (Windows).

COPYING VALUES AND KEYFRAMES

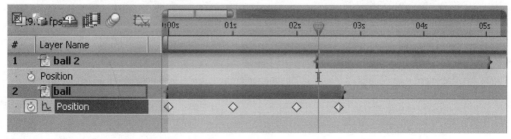

Figure 7.68 Select the keyframes you want to copy.

4. To select the destination, *do one of the following:*

   ▲ To paste keyframes to the same property, select the destination layer.

   ▲ To paste keyframes to a different property, select the destination property by clicking it in the layer outline.

5. Choose Edit > Paste, or press Command-V (Mac) or Ctrl-V (Windows) (**Figure 7.70**). The keyframes are pasted in the appropriate property in the destination layer (**Figure 7.71**).

✔ Tips

■ You can also copy and paste a global (non-keyframed) value using the same process. Selecting the property highlights the I-beam icon in the property track rather than the keyframes.

■ To reuse an animation, you can save it as an animation preset. See the next section, "Using Animation Presets."

■ Certain types of animations are best accomplished by using an expression instead of numerous keyframes. See Chapter 16, "Complex Projects," for more about using expressions.

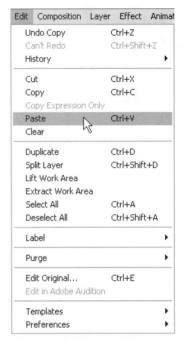

Figure 7.70 Set the current time, select the destination layer or property, and choose Edit > Paste.

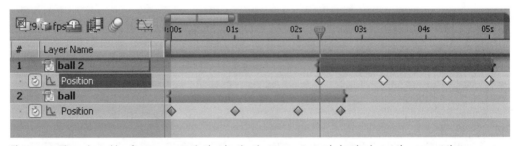

Figure 7.71 The selected keyframes appear in the destination property track, beginning at the current time.

COPYING VALUES AND KEYFRAMES

Figure 7.72 Select one or more keyframes. To select all the keyframes for a property, click the property's name.

Figure 7.73 Choose Animation > Save Animation Preset.

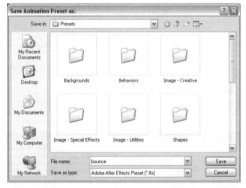

Figure 7.74 In the "Save Animation Preset as" dialog box, specify a name for the preset. You should save the file in the Presets folder (inside the Adobe After Effects folder).

Using Animation Presets

Some animations are worth saving. Fortunately, you can save almost any animation as an *animation preset*. Presets make it easy to apply the same animation to another layer in a project or even in another project.

An animation preset contains a selected set of property keyframes in a file that uses a name you specify (with an .ffx filename extension). By default, it's saved in the Presets folder (inside the Adobe After Effects folder).

This section covers the basics of saving and applying animation presets. Because animation presets can often include effects, Chapter 11, "Effects Fundamentals," revisits the topic. In that chapter, you'll see how to view, organize, and apply animation presets using the Effects & Presets panel. You'll also learn how Adobe Bridge can help you explore After Effects' complimentary collection of presets.

To save an animation preset:

1. Select one or more keyframes (**Figure 7.72**).

   To select all keyframes for a property, click the property's name in the layer outline. You may select keyframes for more than one property in a layer.

2. Choose Animation > Save Animation Preset (**Figure 7.73**).

   A "Save Animation Preset as" dialog box appears.

3. Specify the name and destination for the preset (**Figure 7.74**).

   By default, the preset is saved into the Presets folder in the Adobe After Effects folder. Animation presets use the file extension .ffx.

To apply an animation preset:

1. Select one or more layers in a composition.

2. Set the current time at the point you want the keyframes of the animation preset to begin (**Figure 7.75**).

3. Choose Animation > Apply Animation Preset (**Figure 7.76**).

   An Open dialog box appears, with the After Effects' Presets folder open.

4. Select the preset you want to apply (**Figure 7.77**), and click Open.

   The preset animation is applied to the selected layer(s), beginning at the current time. To view the keyframes, you may need to expand the layer outline to reveal the animated properties. One way to do this is to select the layers and press U (**Figure 7.78**).

✔ Tips

■ You can apply a recently saved animation preset by choosing Animation > Recent Animation Presets and choosing a preset from the list.

■ You can selectively apply certain property keyframes by expanding the preset's name in the Effects & Presets panel and double-clicking the name of the property. (To learn how to manage items in the Effects & Presets panel, see Chapter 11.)

Figure 7.75 Select the layers to which you want to apply the preset animation, and set the current time to the frame at which you want the keyframes to begin.

Figure 7.77 In the Open dialog box, select the preset and click Open.

Figure 7.76 Choose Animation > Apply Preset Animation.

Figure 7.78 The preset animation's keyframes are applied to the selected layers, starting at the current time. To see the keyframes in the time ruler, you can select the layers and press U.

PLAYBACK, PREVIEWS, AND RAM

You've already used some of the standard playback methods for each panel in After Effects. This chapter expands your repertoire and provides a more in-depth explanation of how After Effects renders frames for viewing.

You'll focus on using the Time Controls panel, which can serve as a master playback control for any selected panel. It also includes a button to render a specified range of frames (or *work area*) as a *RAM preview*. And you'll learn about other options, such as viewing your work on a video monitor, how to view changes you make to a layer interactively, and how to preview audio.

Whether you're using standard playback controls, rendering a RAM preview, or adjusting layers, After Effects utilizes RAM to store and more readily display frames. Consequently, the more RAM you have, the more rendered frames you can store (or *cache*) at once. After Effects makes the most of your RAM supply by retaining rendered frames as long as possible, a feature called *intelligent caching*. But you can also control the demand side of the rendering equation. Specifying RAM preview options to skip frames or reduce the resolution can lighten the rendering load—or eliminate the image altogether (along with the associated rendering delays) by previewing a bare-bones *wireframe* version of an animation. In addition, you can limit the area of the image to render by specifying a *region of interest*. After Effects can also reduce processing demands automatically, as needed, by employing *adaptive resolution*. Adaptive resolution reduces image resolution in exchange for increased rendering speed.

But rendering speed isn't necessarily attained at the expense of resolution; you can also utilize a compatible *OpenGL* graphics card. Because software-based processing usually can't match hardware dedicated to the same task, utilizing your OpenGL card's hardware-based graphics processing capabilities renders frames quickly, smoothly, and often without sacrificing resolution.

Rendering and RAM

Before proceeding to the tasks, you should familiarize yourself with how After Effects utilizes RAM. This section contrasts two basic methods used to display frames.

Cache flow

Adobe likes to describe the way After Effects uses RAM as "interactive" and "intelligent." Here's why.

Unless you specify otherwise, After Effects renders frames interactively. Whenever the current time is set to a previously unrendered frame, After Effects renders it and stores, or *caches*, it into RAM—which, as you're probably aware, is the memory your computer can access most quickly. Although it can take time to render a frame, once cached, the frame plays back more readily. The Timeline panel indicates cached frames with a green line at the corresponding point under the time ruler (**Figure 8.1**).

When a change (such as an adjustment to a layer property) makes a rendered frame obsolete, After Effects removes the frame from the cache. However, it intelligently retains the unaffected frames. In other words, After Effects doesn't stupidly discard the entire cache when you make changes that affect only some of the frames. When the cache becomes full, the oldest frames are purged from RAM as new frames are added. You can also purge the cache yourself (as described in the task "To purge the RAM cache," later in this chapter).

Playback and previews

Although the terms *playback* and *preview* are often used interchangeably, this book uses them to refer to two rendering methods that differ in a few important respects. Standard playback caches frames at the current time: sequentially when you click Play, or nonsequentially as you cue the current time. A RAM preview, in contrast, loads a specified range of frames into RAM *before* playing them back.

Green line = Rendered frames

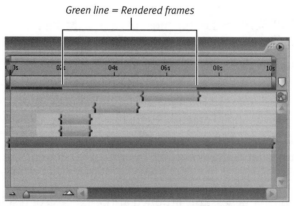

Figure 8.1 Cached frames are signified by a green line in the time ruler.

Both the standard playback mechanism and RAM previews utilize RAM in a similar way, caching frames and retaining them intelligently (see the previous section, "Cache flow"). But whereas standard playback respects the resolution you specified for the panel you're viewing, a RAM preview specifies resolution independent of the panel's current setting. Each method includes different options to help you balance image quality and rendering speed. In addition to the current layer quality and comp resolution settings, standard playback abides by options you set in the Comp panel's Fast Previews button (**Figure 8.2**); you set RAM preview options in the expanded Time Controls panel (**Figure 8.3**). Finally, standard playback options govern how After Effects depicts a frame while you make adjustments—or, in After Effects' parlance, during *interactions*. A RAM preview, on the other hand, only displays a range of frames at or near their full frame rate and doesn't influence the quality or speed of interactions.

No matter what method you use to view frames, processing demands are always related to the footage's native image size (and/or its audio quality) as well as any modifications you make to it as a layer in a composition: masks, transformations, effects, and so on. Note that because the Comp panel's magnification setting (not to be confused with scaling a layer) doesn't change the number or quality of pixels to be rendered, it has little influence on rendering times.

✔ Tips

- After Effects indicates that it's busy rendering a frame (and isn't simply "hanging") by cycling the mouse pointer between black and white. In addition, the lower-right corner of the Comp panel displays a small bar that indicates processing activity (provided the window is wide enough to show it).

- In the Display panel of the Preferences dialog box, you can enable an option to show rendering in progress in the Info panel and the Flowchart panel.

Figure 8.2 Options help you balance quality and rendering speed. The Comp panel's Fast Preview button gives you access to several standard playback options...

Figure 8.3 ...whereas expanding the Time Controls panel allows you to set options for RAM previews.

Previewing to a Video Device

If your system includes a video output device (such as an IEEE-1394/FireWire/iLink connection), you can view your project on a video monitor—which is crucial for evaluating images destined for video output.

Even though you can preview full-screen on your computer monitor (as explained later in this chapter), a computer monitor differs from a television monitor in several important respects. (Refer to this book's sections on interlaced video fields, pixel aspect ratio, safe zones, and NTSC video standards.)

To set video preferences:

1. Choose After Effects > Preferences > Video Preview (Mac) or Edit > Preferences > Video Preview (Windows) (**Figure 8.4**).

   The Video Preview panel of the Preferences dialog box appears (**Figure 8.5**).

2. In the Preferences dialog box, choose an option from the Output Device pull-down menu (**Figure 8.6**).

   Your choices will depend on your particular setup.

Figure 8.4 Choose Edit > Preferences > Video Preview.

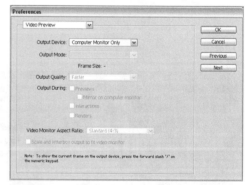

Figure 8.5 The Video Preview panel of the Preferences dialog box appears.

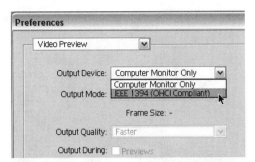

Figure 8.6 Choose an option in the Output Device pull-down menu.

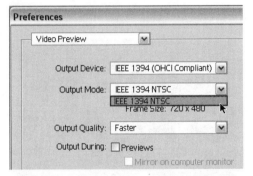

Figure 8.7 Choose an option in the Output Mode pull-down menu.

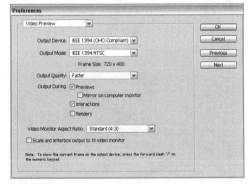

Figure 8.8 Choose an Output Quality, and select other options.

3. Choose an option from the Output Mode pull-down menu (**Figure 8.7**).

Typically, you should choose an option that's equivalent to full-screen video for your output device.

4. For Output Quality, choose whether it's more important to output the video using a Faster or More Accurate method.

5. For Output During, *choose any of the following* (**Figure 8.8**)*:*

Previews—Displays RAM previews on the NTSC monitor

Interactions—Displays all window updates (such as while making adjustments to a layer's properties) on the NTSC monitor

Renders—Displays rendered frames on the NTSC monitor

6. If you selected Previews in step 5, select "Mirror on computer monitor" to display previews on your computer's monitor in addition to the video device.

To output previews to your video device only, leave this option unchecked.

7. For Video Monitor Aspect Ratio, choose the option that matches your video monitor:

Standard (4:3)

Widescreen (16:9)

8. If you wish, select "Scale and letterbox output to fit video monitor."

9. Click OK to close the Preferences dialog box.

Previews appear on the connected NTSC monitor according to the preferences you set.

Setting the Region of Interest

You can limit the portion of an image to be included in playback or previews by setting a *region of interest*. By restricting the image area to render, you decrease each frame's RAM requirements and increase both the rendering speed and the number of frames you can render.

To set the region of interest:

1. In a Comp, Layer, or Footage panel, click the Region of Interest button (**Figure 8.9**).

2. Draw a marquee in the image area to define the region of interest (**Figure 8.10**).

   The area of the image included in playback and previews will be limited to the area within the region of interest (**Figure 8.11**).

3. To resize the region of interest, drag any of its corner handles.

To toggle between the region of interest and the full image:

◆ In the Comp, Layer, or Footage panel, click the Region of Interest button.

   When the button is selected, the window shows the region of interest; when the button is deselected, the window displays the full image.

✔ Tips

■ To redraw the region of interest from the full image, make sure the Region of Interest button is deselected; then, Option-click (Mac) or Alt-click (Windows) the Region of Interest button.

■ As always, you can reduce rendering times by reducing your composition's resolution or by setting layers to Draft quality.

Figure 8.9 Click the Region of Interest button.

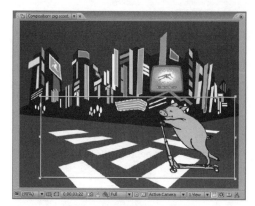

Figure 8.10 Draw a marquee in the image area to define the region of interest.

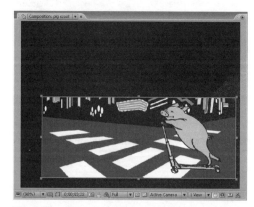

Figure 8.11 The region of interest limits the image included in playback and previews. Click the Region of Interest button to toggle between the region you specified and the full composition image.

Using the Time Controls

Although the Footage, Layer, Composition, and Timeline panels all have their own playback controls, you can use the Time Controls panel to set the current frame in any selected window. With related panels, the current time changes in each panel. For example, changing the current frame in a Layer panel also changes the current time in its related Timeline and Composition panels.

You don't need to be an expert in non-linear editing (NLE) software to recognize most of the following buttons from the Time Controls panel (**Figure 8.12**); however, you may not be able to find a few of these on your home VCR:

First Frame cues the current time to the first frame in the window.

Frame Back cues the current time one frame back.

Play/Pause plays when clicked once and stops when clicked again. Playback performance depends on After Effects' ability to render the frames for viewing. During playback, the Time Controls panel displays two frame rates side by side: the frame rate your system is currently able to achieve and the frame rate you set for the composition, which is the real-time frame rate.

Frame Forward cues the current time one frame forward.

Last Frame cues the current time to the last frame in the window.

Audio lets you hear audio tracks when you preview a composition. Deselect it to suppress audio playback during previews. (Standard playback doesn't include audio.)

Loop comprises three states: Loop, Play Once, and Palindrome (which plays the specified area forward and backward). The frames affected by the loop setting depend on the window selected. In a Footage panel, the entire duration of the footage loops. In a Layer panel, the layer loops from In point to Out point. In a composition—as viewed in the Composition and Timeline panels—frames loop from the beginning to the end of the work area (see "Setting the Work Area," later in this chapter).

RAM Preview creates a RAM preview by rendering a specified range of frames, as defined by the Timeline's work area (explained later in this chapter).

The **Time Controls panel menu** opens a menu to show or hide RAM Preview and Shift-RAM Preview settings in the Time Controls panel (see the sections on RAM previews later in this chapter).

Collapse/Expand collapses the window to hide all controls, or expands it to include RAM Preview Options or show the standard controls.

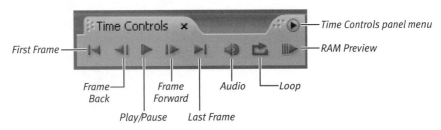

Figure 8.12 The Time Controls panel can control the playback of any selected window.

USING THE TIME CONTROLS

✔ Tips

- By default, the times of related panels are synchronized (for example, changing the current time of a comp is reflected in the open panels related to it, including nested comps). You can change this setting in the General panel of the Preferences dialog box. The implications of synchronizing related items are explained in Chapter 16, "Complex Projects."

- The playback performance of Footage panels doesn't benefit from the same RAM-caching mechanism as the Layer and Composition panels. Until footage becomes a layer in a composition, it depends on the movie-player software installed on your system (QuickTime or Windows Media Player).

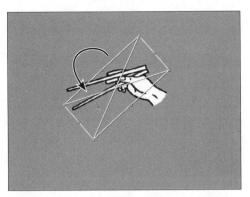

Figure 8.13 With Live Update off, the image doesn't update as you make an adjustment. Here, only the bounding box indicates the layer is being rotated...

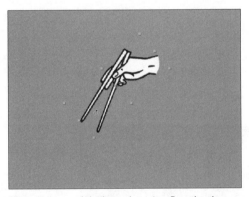

Figure 8.14 ...and the layer doesn't reflect the change until you release the mouse.

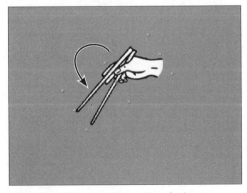

Figure 8.15 With Live Update active, the image updates interactively.

Using the Live Update Option

There are two ways you can view a comp while you make changes to a layer property (during *interactions*). By default, the Comp panel updates *after* you alter the property—after you release the mouse when dragging the layer or property value, or after you press Return (Mac) or Enter (Windows) when changing the value numerically (**Figures 8.13** and **8.14**). Alternatively, you can set the window to update *during* interactions, utilizing a feature called *Live Update*. With Live Update enabled, you can see the layer change as you adjust the property (**Figure 8.15**).

Live Update works with the current Fast Preview setting (explained in "Specifying a Fast Preview Option," later in this chapter). When the Fast Preview option is set to Wireframe, interactions are depicted using layer outlines only. With adaptive resolution enabled (either the standard option, or with OpenGL), After Effects temporarily degrades the image quality during interactions until it can process and display the layer at the specified quality and resolution (see "Using Adaptive Resolution," later in this chapter).

Naturally, you should choose the combination of settings most appropriate to the task at hand, the processing demands of the frame, and your system's processing capability.

USING THE LIVE UPDATE OPTION

To toggle Live Update on and off:

◆ In the Timeline panel, click the Live Update button  (**Figure 8.16**).

When the button is selected, the image updates during interactions (while you change layer properties); when the button is deselected, the image updates after you make an adjustment (when you release the mouse button, for example).

✔ Tips

■ Live Update replaces the Wireframe Interactions feature found in older versions of After Effects. Although the buttons look exactly alike, the features work differently.

■ You specify whether to view interactions on an attached video monitor separately, as explained in the section "Previewing to a Video Device," earlier in this chapter.

Figure 8.16 In the Timeline panel, click the Live Update button.

Specifying a Fast Preview Option

As you learned in earlier chapters, the standard playback method (pressing Play, or cuing the current time) is influenced by a comp's resolution as well as the quality settings of the layers it contains. (Everything else being equal, lowering quality and resolution results in shorter rendering times.) You can specify several other options to view frames as quickly as possible by using the Comp panel's Fast Preview button .

This section covers how to specify the option you want to use, and summarizes each choice. Some choices (Adaptive Resolution and OpenGL options) include additional settings, which are explained fully in later sections.

To enable a Fast Preview option:

1. In a Composition panel, choose an option from the Fast Preview button's pull-down menu  (**Figure 8.17**):

Figure 8.17 Choose an option from the Fast Preview button's pull-down menu.

Off deactivates the Fast Preview option. Standard playback quality is governed by the comp resolution setting and layer quality settings.

Wireframe displays layer outlines only, allowing you to quickly evaluate aspects of an animation such as movement and timing by sacrificing image content.

Adaptive Resolution temporarily reduces the image resolution to a specified minimum setting in order to display changes to layers interactively or to maximize the frame rate.

OpenGL—Interactive utilizes a compatible OpenGL graphics card to process every frame requested, such as when you scrub to preview. When active, the Comp panel's Fast Previews icon appears lit.

OpenGL—Always On utilizes a compatible OpenGL graphics card for all previews. The notice *OpenGL* in the upper-left corner of the Comp panel indicates this mode is active.

OpenGL options are available only if you have a compatible OpenGL graphics card installed in your system and you've enabled OpenGL options in the Previews panel of the Preferences dialog box.

2. To use a compatible OpenGL graphics card to process the image of motion footage layers by using a still frame, choose Freeze Layer Contents in the Fast Previews pull-down menu.

   Using a still image as a proxy for motion footage reduces rendering requirements. This option is available only when you choose an OpenGL option in step 1.

✔ Tip

■ A few more options are available for controlling the rendering quality of 3D layers; these are explained in Chapter 15, "3D Layers."

Using Adaptive Resolution

If your system is slow to update the Comp panel's image, After Effects can reduce the image's resolution automatically—a feature called *adaptive resolution* (**Figures 8.18** and **8.19**). This way, you can get visual feedback even when your system can't keep up at the resolution you previously specified for the window. You set the maximum amount by which adaptive resolution degrades images in the Previews panel of the Preferences dialog box.

Although the adaptive resolution option is separate from the OpenGL options in the Fast Preview pull-down menu, OpenGL can also utilize adaptive resolution. However, you must enable OpenGL and its adaptive resolution setting separately (as described in the next section, "Using OpenGL").

Figure 8.18 With adaptive resolution enabled, the image degrades to keep pace with your adjustments...

Figure 8.19 ...and then assumes the comp's resolution when you stop transforming the layer.

Figure 8.20 Choose Fast Preview Preferences from the Fast Preview button's pulldown menu.

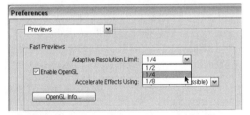

Figure 8.21 Limit the amount of degradation by choosing an option in the Adaptive Resolution Limit pull-down menu.

To set Adaptive Resolution settings:

1. In a Comp panel, click the Fast Preview button, and choose Fast Preview Preferences from the pull-down menu (**Figure 8.20**).

   The Previews panel of the Preferences dialog box appears.

2. *Select one of the following* options from the Adaptive Resolution Limit pull-down menu (**Figure 8.21**):

   1/2—After Effects temporarily displays the image at no less than one-half resolution while updating the comp preview.

   1/4—After Effects temporarily displays the image at one-quarter resolution while updating the comp preview.

   1/8—After Effects temporarily displays the image one-eighth resolution while updating the comp preview.

3. Click OK to close the Preferences dialog box.

Using OpenGL

Generally speaking, software processing can't match hardware dedicated to the same task. After Effects takes advantage of this fact by utilizing the graphics processing power of (After Effects–certified) OpenGL graphics cards.

After Effects detects whether your system has an OpenGL graphics card automatically and, if so, activates it as the default preview option.

When OpenGL is in effect, the Fast Preview button ⚡ turns green. By default, OpenGL kicks in whenever you drag layers in a comp, scrub a motion-related property, or scrub a comp's current time. However, it doesn't provide a rendering boost to non–motion related effect properties. To view effects-intensive frames, you may opt to switch to another Fast Preview method.

Overall, OpenGL provides faster, smoother screen updates than you would get otherwise, and it does so without degrading the image. But as the following task explains, you can set OpenGL to switch to adaptive resolution as you adjust effect property values (see "Using Adaptive Resolution," earlier in this chapter). This way, you can take advantage of OpenGL for most interactions, and adaptive resolution when you're adjusting effects.

You already know how to specify your OpenGL card as the Fast Preview option (see "Specifying a Fast Preview Option" earlier in this chapter). This section explains how to set several options specific to OpenGL.

OpenGL Graphics Cards

OpenGL is a technology utilized by many advanced video graphics cards that helps to enhance graphics processing, particularly for 3D objects and subtleties like shading, lights, and shadows. When a program is designed to recognize OpenGL, the increase in graphics performance can be substantial.

Usually, a high-end graphics card isn't a standard component in an average system configuration; instead, it's an often-expensive option. However, PC gamers and graphics professionals value graphics performance and are eager to upgrade to a more advanced graphics card.

Naturally, features and processing power vary from card to card. Whether your card supports features like lights and shadows in After Effects depends on the particular card.

Before you upgrade your graphics card, check Adobe's Web site to ensure the card has been certified to work with After Effects. This is another quick way to see which features the card supports. And in addition to the card itself, make sure you install the latest software drivers, which should be available for download from the manufacturer's Web site.

Figure 8.22 Choose Fast Preview Preferences from the Fast Preview button's pulldown menu.

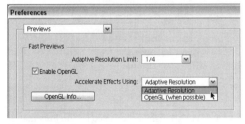

Figure 8.23 Select the OpenGL options you want.

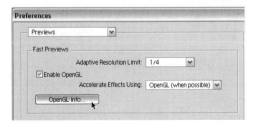

Figure 8.24 Click OpenGL Info to access more options.

To set OpenGL preferences:

1. In a Comp panel, click the Fast Preview button and choose Fast Preview Preferences from the pull-down menu (**Figure 8.22**).

   The Previews panel of the Preferences dialog box appears.

2. Select Enable OpenGL.

3. For Accelerate Effects Using, choose an option (**Figure 8.23**):

   Adaptive Resolution

   OpenGL (when possible)

4. Click OK to close the dialog box.

To specify other OpenGL options:

1. In the Previews pane of the Preferences dialog box, click OpenGL Info (**Figure 8.24**).

   An OpenGL Information dialog box appears.

continues on next page

2. Specify the amount for Texture Memory, in MB (**Figure 8.25**).

Adobe recommends allocating no more than 80% of the video RAM (VRAM) on your display card when using Windows; on a Mac, After Effects determines the ideal value automatically.

3. Specify an option in the Quality pull-down menu (**Figure 8.26**):

Faster—Processes more quickly, at the expense of the quality of lighting, shading, and blending, and by excluding blending modes

More Accurate—Includes blending modes, and improves the quality of lighting, shading, and blending

4. Click OK to close the OpenGL Information dialog box, and click OK to close the Preferences dialog box.

Figure 8.25 In the OpenGL Information dialog box, specify an amount for Texture Memory.

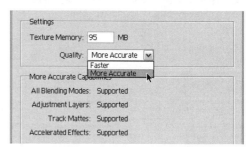

Figure 8.26 If available, choose an option from the Quality pull-down menu.

Suppressing Panel Updates

If frames are difficult to render, it can take time to update an image. You may have already noticed how the Selection tool cycles between black and white as a particularly difficult frame renders (**Figure 8.27**). The lower-right corner of the Composition panel also includes a small activity bar (provided the window is sized wide enough for you to see it). When previewing gets in the way of your progress, you can prevent the Footage, Layer, and Composition panels from updating by activating your keyboard's Caps Lock key.

When you suppress updates, panels continue to display the current frame, even after you make changes. When you alter the image in the current frame or move to a new frame, a red outline appears around the image in the panels that would otherwise be updated (**Figure 8.28**). Although panel controls—anchor points, motion paths, mask outlines, and so on—continue to update, the image doesn't reflect your changes. When you're ready to update, or *refresh*, the affected panels, disengage Caps Lock.

To suppress panel updates:

◆ Press Caps Lock to suppress panel updates; press Caps Lock again to turn suppression off and refresh panels.

✔ Tip

■ If slow updates are a problem, you should consider replacing particularly demanding footage items with lower-quality proxies. See Chapter 3, "Managing Footage," for more information.

Figure 8.27 The Selection tool cycles between black and white as the program pauses to render frames.

Figure 8.28 When Caps Lock is active, a red outline appears around the image in the windows that would otherwise be updated. The window also displays a friendly reminder.

Scrubbing Audio

In After Effects, finding a particular frame based on the image is easy. Finding a particular moment based on the sound is a different matter. An audio preview plays your audio layers, but it doesn't make it easy to cue to a particular sound. When you halt an audio preview (see the next section), the current time indicator goes back to the starting point—the current time indicator doesn't remain at the moment you stop it. Viewing the audio waveform usually doesn't help you pinpoint a sound, either; individual sounds are difficult to discern in a waveform display (**Figure 8.29**). (See Chapter 7, "Properties and Keyframes.")

Fortunately, After Effects allows you to *scrub* the audio—that is, play it back slowly as you drag the current time indicator. The term *scrubbing* refers to the back back-and-forth motion of tape over an audio head. This feature has always been taken for granted in the analog world, but it's long been considered a luxury for digital tools. (High-end equipment is still required to approximate old-fashioned tape scrubbing.)

Remember, you can always see audio levels—even while you scrub—in the Volume Units (VU) meter of the Audio panel (**Figure 8.30**).

To scrub audio:

◆ In the time ruler of the Timeline panel, Command-drag (Mac) or Ctrl-drag (Windows) the current time indicator. The audio plays back as you drag.

✔ Tips

■ To hear every syllable and beat, there's no substitute for scrubbing. Once you find the sound you're looking for, don't forget that you can mark the frame in the layer or the composition (see Chapter 6, "Layer Editing"). You can also set markers on the fly during audio previews by pressing the asterisk (*) key on the numeric keypad.

■ As explained in the sidebar "Ample Samples: Audio Sample Rates," later in this chapter, audio samples occur far more frequently than video frame divisions. For precise audio editing, use a dedicated audio-editing program or NLE that allows for sample-based audio editing (like Adobe Premiere Pro or Apple Final Cut Pro). Remember, you can do all of your straightforward editing tasks in Premiere Pro and then import the entire project (see Chapter 2, "Importing Footage into a Project").

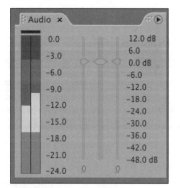

Figure 8.30 As usual, use the VU meter of the Audio panel to see audio levels as they play.

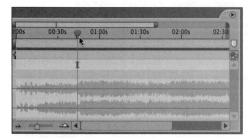

Figure 8.29 Scrubbing the audio provides an alternative (or an enhancement) to expanding the Audio Waveform property to cue the current time to a particular sound.

Comparing Preview Options

Until now, this chapter has focused on playback options and methods you can use to control the way the Composition panel updates when you transform layer properties. The following sections discuss previewing a specified area of the composition.

You can choose from different types of preview methods. Because the complexity of the preview affects the time required to render it, choose the type best suited for your needs:

Video and audio—You can preview any combination of video and audio. Video frames require more memory and processing time than audio. You can control the relative quality of previews and thereby the relative rendering times.

Wireframe—You can preview video as *wireframes*, or outline representations, of layer images. Because they don't render the full image, wireframe previews render quickly, while accurately representing motion (changes in position, scale, and rotation).

COMPARING PREVIEW OPTIONS

Setting the Work Area

To preview part of a composition, you must define a range of frames with the *work area bar*, an adjustable bar located above the time ruler in the Timeline menu (**Figure 8.31**). To make it easier to identify the part of the composition that's included, the entire area under the work area bar is highlighted; it appears a little brighter than the area outside the work area.

As you learned in Chapter 6, the navigator view of the Timeline panel includes a miniature version of the work area bar; however, it's for your reference only.

To set the work area by dragging:

In the Timeline panel, *do any of the following:*

◆ Drag the left handle of the work area bar to the time you want previews to start (**Figure 8.32**).

◆ Drag the right handle of the work area bar to the time you want previews to end (**Figure 8.33**).

◆ Drag the center of the work area bar to move the work area without changing its duration (**Figure 8.34**).

Make sure to grab the center of the bar, where vertical lines imply a textured grip. Otherwise, you'll cue the current time indicator instead.

Press Shift as you drag to snap the edges of the work area bar to the edges of layers, keyframes, markers, or the time indicator.

Work area bar start   Work area bar end

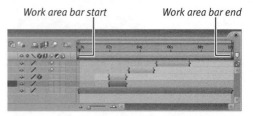

Figure 8.31 The work area bar defines the range of frames in the composition for previews.

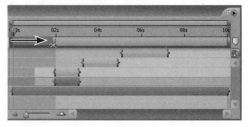

Figure 8.32 Drag the left handle of the work area bar to the time you want previews to start.

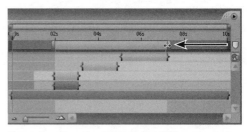

Figure 8.33 Drag the right handle of the work area bar to the time you want previews to end.

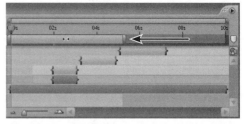

Figure 8.34 Drag the center of the work area bar to move the work area without changing its duration.

To set the work area using keyboard shortcuts:

1. In the Timeline panel, set the current time to the frame at which you want the work area to begin or end.

2. *Do one of the following:*

   ▲ Press B to set the beginning of the work area to the current time.

   ▲ Press N to set the end of the work area to the current time.

✔ Tips

■ You can't set the beginning of the work area bar after the end, or vice versa. If you can't move the end of the work area where you want, you probably have to move the other end first.

■ Using an extended keyboard, you can cue the time to the beginning of the work area by pressing Shift-Home or to the end of the work area by pressing Shift-End.

■ In principle, After Effects' work area bar is equivalent to the one in Premiere Pro. In practice, however, there are a few differences. For example, you can't use the same keyboard shortcuts for setting the work area (unless you create a custom shortcut in Premiere Pro).

SETTING THE WORK AREA

Previewing Audio Only

If you only need to hear the audio tracks of your composition, you don't have to wait for a time-consuming video preview. With After Effects, you can also control the quality of audio previews, which affects rendering times.

To preview audio only from the current time:

1. In the Composition or Timeline panel, cue the current time to the frame at which you want to begin your audio preview (**Figure 8.35**).

2. Choose Composition > Preview > Audio Preview (Here Forward), or press the decimal point (.) on the numeric keypad (**Figure 8.36**).

   The audio starts playing from the current time and plays for the duration you set in the General Preferences (explained in the task "To set preferences for audio previews," on the next page).

3. Press the spacebar to stop the preview.

To preview audio only under the work area:

1. Set the work area over the range of frames you want to preview (**Figure 8.37**).

   See the previous section, "Setting the Work Area."

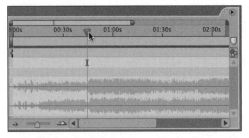

Figure 8.35 Cue the current time to the frame at which you want to begin an audio preview.

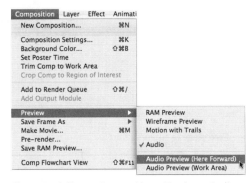

Figure 8.36 Choose Composition > Preview > Audio Preview (Here Forward).

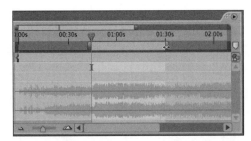

Figure 8.37 Set the work area bar over the range you want to preview.

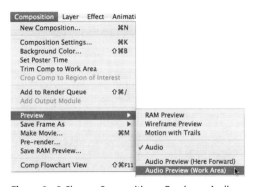

Figure 8.38 Choose Composition > Preview > Audio Preview (Work Area).

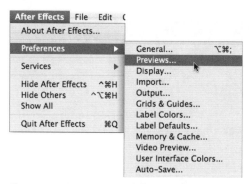

Figure 8.39 Choose After Effects > Preferences > Previews (Mac) or Edit > Preferences > Previews (Windows).

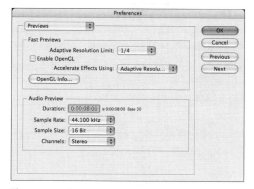

Figure 8.40 The Previews panel of the Preferences dialog box appears.

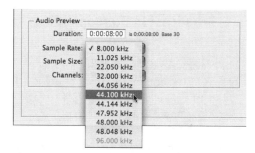

Figure 8.41 Choose an audio sample rate.

2. Choose Composition > Preview > Audio Preview (Work Area) (**Figure 8.38**).

The audio under the work area plays.

To set preferences for audio previews:

1. Choose After Effects > Preferences > Previews (Mac) or Edit > Preferences > Previews (Windows) (**Figure 8.39**).

The Previews panel of the Preferences dialog box appears (**Figure 8.40**).

2. In the Audio Preview section of the dialog box, *specify the following settings:*

▲ For Duration, enter the duration of audio previews.

▲ In the Sample Rate pull-down menu, choose an audio sample rate for previews (**Figure 8.41**). (See **Table 8.1** and the sidebar "Ample Samples: Audio Sample Rates.")

continues on next page

PREVIEWING AUDIO ONLY

Table 8.1

Standard Audio Sample Rates	
SAMPLE RATE	EQUIVALENT/SPECIAL CONSIDERATIONS
48 kHz	DAT or Digital Betacam; not always supported by sound or video cards
44.1 kHz	CD; best for music
32 kHz	Used by some DV cameras
22 kHz	Compromise between size and quality
11 kHz	Adequate for narration
8 kHz	Low data rates and quality; suitable for the Internet

▲ In the Sample Size pull-down menu, choose a bit depth for audio previews (**Figure 8.42**). (See the sidebar "A Bit Deeper into Bit Depth.")

▲ In the Channels pull-down menu, choose to preview the audio in stereo or mono (**Figure 8.43**). (See the sidebar "Broadcast in Stereophonic Sound.")

3. Click OK to close the Preferences dialog box.

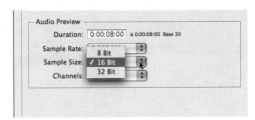

Figure 8.42 Choose an audio bit depth.

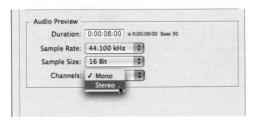

Figure 8.43 Choose Mono or Stereo.

Broadcast in Stereophonic Sound

For previews and renders, you can choose between stereophonic and monophonic audio. In a *stereophonic* (or simply *stereo*) recording, audio is mixed differently in the left and right channels. When the audio is played through stereo speakers (and listened to through two ears), the separate channels give the sound a sense of space. A *monophonic*, or *mono*, recording distributes the audio evenly between the two channels and plays back the same sounds through the left and right speakers.

Ample Samples: Audio Sample Rates

Analog signals are described by a continuous fluctuation of voltage. The analog signal is converted to a digital signal by being measured periodically, or *sampled*. If you think of the original audio as a curve, the digital audio would look like a connect-the-dots version of the curve. The more dots (or samples) you have, the more accurately you can reproduce the curve (**Figures 8.44** and **8.45**). *Sample rate* describes the number of times audio is sampled to approximate the original sound. Sample rates are measured in samples per second, or *hertz* (Hz). One thousand hertz is called a *kilohertz* (kHz). The higher the sample rate, the more accurate the sound and the larger the file (everything else being equal).

The process of converting digital audio from one sample rate to another is called *resampling*. You can reduce the sample rate to decrease file sizes and RAM requirements—and thereby rendering speeds. Although increasing the sample rate also increases file size, it can't restore audio quality where none existed originally.

For audio previews, choose a sample rate that balances the audio quality you desire with the corresponding cost in rendering speed and RAM requirements. For rendered movies, choose the sample rate according to your output goal.

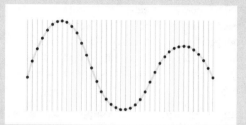

Figure 8.44 You can think of an analog audio signal as being a continuous curve.

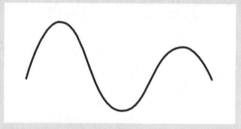

Figure 8.45 The more samples, the more accurately digital audio reproduces the original signal. Because each sample has a defined value, digital audio can be reproduced exactly.

A Bit Deeper into Bit Depth

Audio bit depth means the number of bits used to describe each audio sample. Bit depth affects the range of sound an audio file can reproduce. This range is known as the signal-to-noise (s/n) ratio, which can be measured in decibels (dB).

Audio bit depth is often compared to image bit depth. A gradient with a higher bit depth looks smoother because it uses more steps as it transitions from one value to another (**Figures 8.46** and **8.47**). In much the same way, audio with higher bit depth has a greater range.

In After Effects, as in many other programs, you can choose a bit depth for previews and renders. Higher (or is it deeper?) bit depths produce better sound; however, they also create larger files that require more RAM and render more slowly.

Figure 8.46 Audio bit depth is comparable to image bit depth. This low-bit-depth gradient looks banded...

Figure 8.47 ...whereas this high-bit-depth gradient uses a greater range. Audio bit depth affects the range of sound.

Figure 8.48 A full preview shows everything in detail but requires both more RAM and more processing time.

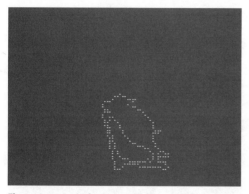

Figure 8.49 A wireframe preview represents the layer as an empty outline. It renders much faster but still shows you the motion of one or more layers.

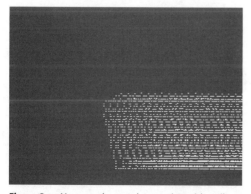

Figure 8.50 You can also preview motion with trails, in which case the wireframes at each frame remain visible as the preview progresses.

Previewing Wireframes

When you want to see just the motion of an animation—changes in position, scale, and rotation—you don't have to waste precious time by rendering a full-fledged preview of the work area. Instead, use a wireframe preview for selected layers.

A *wireframe preview* represents the motion of one or more layers as an empty outline, or wireframe. A wireframe preview gives you a clear sense of motion without consuming much of your RAM or your time (**Figures 8.48** and **8.49**). To get a sense of the sweep of the layer's complete motion, the wireframe can include a trail, which leaves the previous frames visible as the preview progresses (**Figure 8.50**). Because wireframe previews don't render frames fully, no images are stored in the cache, and no green line indicator appears below the work area bar.

To create a wireframe preview:

1. In the Timeline panel, *do one of the following:*

   ▲ Select the layers you want to preview.

   ▲ Deselect all layers to preview all of them.

2. Set the work area over the range of frames you want to preview (as explained in the section "Setting the Work Area") (**Figure 8.51**).

3. *Do one of the following:*

   ▲ Choose Composition > Preview > Wireframe Preview (**Figure 8.52**).

   ▲ Choose Composition > Preview > Motion with Trails.

4. Press the spacebar to stop the preview.

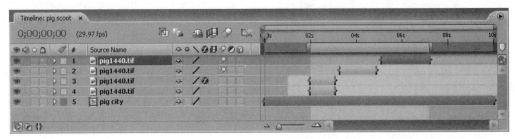

Figure 8.51 Set the work area, and select the layers you want to preview. To preview all the layers, leave them deselected.

Figure 8.52 Select Composition > Preview > Wireframe Preview to view a wireframe preview, or choose Composition > Preview > Motion with Trails to view a wireframe preview with trails.

Table 8.2

Keyboard Shortcuts for Playback and Preview	
TO DO THIS	PRESS THIS
Start/pause	Spacebar
Frame advance	Page Down
Frame reverse	Page Up
First frame	Home
Last frame	End
Scrub video	Option-drag (Mac) or Alt-drag (Windows) the current time indicator
Scrub audio	Command-drag (Mac) or Ctrl-drag (Windows) the current time indicator
Stop window updates	Caps Lock
Preview audio from the current time	Decimal point (.) on the numeric keypad
RAM preview	Zero on the numeric keypad
RAM preview every other frame	Shift-zero on the numeric keypad
Save RAM preview	Command-zero (Mac) or Ctrl-zero (Windows) on the numeric keypad
Wireframe preview	Option-zero (Mac) or Alt-zero (Windows) on the numeric keypad
Wireframe preview using a rectangular layer outline	Command-Option-zero (Mac) or Ctrl-Alt-zero (Windows) on the numeric keypad
Show layers as background during wireframe previews	Add Shift to the wireframe preview shortcut: Shift-Option-zero (Mac) or Shift-Alt-zero (Windows) on the numeric keypad

Rendering RAM Previews

To see a comp at (or near) its full frame rate, you typically render a RAM preview. In contrast to using standard playback controls, a RAM preview renders frames first and then plays them back. By default, a RAM preview renders frames in the work area only; but you can set an option to render frames beginning at the current time (similar to standard playback). RAM previews include several options to balance rendering speed with image quality and frame rate.

You can set separate options for two kinds of RAM previews: a standard RAM preview and a Shift-RAM preview. You can customize each type according to your project's demands, choosing the best RAM preview option for the task at hand. For example, you could set the standard RAM preview to render a relatively smooth, high-resolution image, and set the Shift-RAM preview to render more quickly, at the expense of smooth motion and image quality.

By default, rendering a RAM preview (including a Shift-RAM preview) renders the active panel. But you can specify a particular panel to preview, even if it isn't the currently active panel. Doing so can streamline your workflow by freeing you from finding a particular panel to preview (especially in complex projects). For example, by designating your final comp as the panel to always preview, you can work in other panels and then quickly view your changes in the final comp.

For an overview of keyboard shortcuts for rendering a RAM preview and other playback options, see **Table 8.2**.

RENDERING RAM PREVIEWS

To show and hide RAM preview options:

◆ In the Time Controls panel's menu, *select an option* (**Figure 8.53**):

RAM Preview Options—Expands the panel to reveal the RAM preview options

Shift+RAM Preview Options— Expands the panel to reveal the Shift-RAM preview options

The Time Controls panel expands to reveal the options you selected (**Figure 8.54**). Reselect an option to hide the RAM preview options.

✔ Tip

■ Remember, you can repeatedly click the Time Controls panel to cycle through different views: to show the panel tab only, to add the playback controls, or to add the selected RAM or Shift-RAM preview options.

To set RAM preview options:

1. In the Time Controls panel, reveal either the RAM preview or Shift-RAM preview options, as explained in the previous task.

2. In the RAM Preview Options or Shift+RAM Preview Options area of the Time Controls panel, *enter the following*:

Frame Rate—Enter the frame rate for the preview, or choose one from the pulldown menu (**Figure 8.55**).

Lower frame rates render more quickly but at the expense of smooth motion.

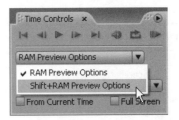

Figure 8.53 In the pull-down menu, choose the RAM preview options you want to show.

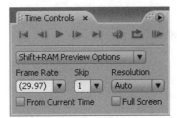

Figure 8.54 The Time Controls panel expands to reveal the options you selected.

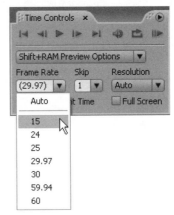

Figure 8.55 Enter a frame rate used by the preview, or choose one from the pull-down menu. Also enter the frequency at which frames are skipped.

Figure 8.56 Choose an option from the Resolution pull-down menu. Select the other options you want.

Skip—Enter the frequency with which frames are skipped and left unrendered. Skipping frames speeds rendering but results in choppier motion.

Resolution—*Choose one of the following* options from the pull-down menu (**Figure 8.56**):

Auto—Previews use the Composition panel's current resolution setting.

Full—After Effects renders and displays every pixel of the composition, resulting in the highest image quality and the longest rendering time.

Half—After Effects renders every other pixel, or one-quarter of the pixels of the full-resolution image in one-quarter of the time.

Third—After Effects renders every third pixel, or one-ninth of the pixels in the full-resolution image in one-ninth of the time.

Quarter—After Effects renders every fourth pixel, or one-sixteenth of the pixels in the full-resolution image in one-sixteenth of the time.

Custom—After Effects renders whatever fraction of pixels you specify.

3. *Select either of the following* options:

From Current Time—After Effects renders previews from the current time (instead of the frames defined by the work area).

Full Screen—After Effects displays previews on a blank screen (with no windows visible).

RENDERING RAM PREVIEWS

To create a RAM preview:

1. In the Timeline panel, set the work area bar to the range of frames you want to preview (**Figure 8.57**).

2. To preview audio as well as video, click the Audio button in the Time Controls panel (**Figure 8.58**).

3. Select an option by clicking the Loop button in the Time Controls panel (**Figure 8.59**).

   Loop —loops playback beginning to end.

   Ping Pong ▬▬—loops playback from beginning to end, then end to beginning.

   Play Once ▬▬—plays once.

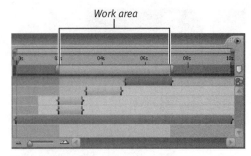

Figure 8.57 Set the work area bar over the range of frames you want to preview.

Figure 8.58 To preview audio in addition to video, click the Audio button in the Time Controls panel.

Loop

Ping Pong

Play Once

Figure 8.59 In the Time Controls panel, click the Loop button repeatedly so the icon corresponds to the option you want.

Figure 8.60 Click the RAM Preview button in the Time Controls panel, or press o in the numeric keypad.

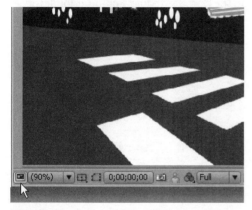

Figure 8.61 In the lower-left corner of the window you want to designate, click the Always Preview This View button.

4. To use the standard RAM preview settings, *do any of the following:*
   ▲ Choose Composition > Preview > RAM Preview.
   ▲ Click the RAM Preview button in the Time Controls panel (**Figure 8.60**).
   ▲ Press 0 on the numeric keypad.

5. To use the Shift-RAM preview settings, *do either of the following:*
   ▲ Shift-click the RAM Preview button in the Time Controls panel.
   ▲ Hold Shift as you press 0 on the numeric keypad.

   In the Timeline panel, a green line appears over the frames that are rendered to RAM. When all the frames in the work area have been rendered, or when the amount of available RAM runs out, the frames play back in the Composition panel.

To specify a panel to always preview:

◆ Click the Always Preview This View button ▣ in the panel you want to designate for previews (**Figure 8.61**).

   RAM previews (including Shift-RAM previews) always render the panel you specified, which becomes active for you to view.

Saving RAM Previews

After Effects not only creates RAM previews relatively quickly, but also lets you retain the ones you like as movie files. You can then use these previews as draft versions for your own reference or for sharing with clients.

Although RAM movies can provide a more convenient way of previewing than rendering a draft movie in the traditional fashion (see Chapter 17, "Output"), they also have limitations. RAM previews saved as movies use the same frame size and resolution as the composition (see Chapter 4, "Compositions"),

but they don't use its current magnification factor. RAM movies can contain alpha channel information only if the composition's background has been set to black. (The RAM movie's alpha is premultiplied with black; see Chapter 2 for more about alpha channels.) Finally, the RAM preview movie can't contain interlaced fields.

Apart from these restrictions, the RAM preview movie settings come from a template in the Output Module. For more about the Output Module and editing templates, see Chapter 17.

RAMming Speed: Getting the Most Out of Your RAM

In addition to using a computer with a fast processor and loads of RAM, here are some other things you can do to use RAM effectively and improve RAM playback.

Optimize Your Display

◆ Use a high-quality display card. Better yet, choose an Adobe-approved OpenGL graphics card, which can take over much of the processing.

◆ Use the latest drivers for your video display. Check with the manufacturer's Web site to make sure you're using the latest and greatest version.

Optimize Your RAM

◆ Reduce the number of undoable actions in General Preferences.

◆ Purge the image cache (as explained in the task "To purge the RAM cache" later in this chapter) to free up RAM.

Reduce Memory Requirements for Compositions

◆ Set the composition to a low resolution (half, third, and so on) to achieve higher frame rates in previews.

◆ Match the composition's resolution and magnification factor. RAM previews work faster this way. For example, preview half-resolution compositions at 50 percent magnification.

◆ Use proxies when possible (see Chapter 3).

◆ Avoid footage items that use temporal compression (MPEG footage, for example). The frame differencing utilized by the compression scheme requires intensive processing.

◆ Prerender nested compositions when possible (see Chapter 16).

◆ Collapse transformations when possible (see Chapter 16).

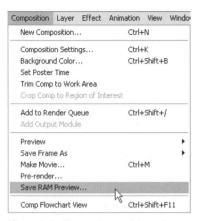

Figure 8.62 Choose Composition > Save RAM Preview.

Figure 8.63 Or, set the work area and Command-click (Mac) or Ctrl-click (Windows) the RAM Preview button.

Figure 8.64 In the Output Movie To dialog box, choose a name and destination for the RAM preview movie, and then click Save.

To save a RAM preview as a movie file:

1. *Do one of the following:*
   - ▲ Choose Composition > Save RAM Preview (**Figure 8.62**).
   - ▲ Set the work area, and Command-click (Mac) or Ctrl-click (Windows) the RAM Preview button (**Figure 8.63**) in the Time Controls panel.

   An Output Movie To dialog box appears.

2. Choose a name and destination for the RAM preview movie.

3. Click Save to close the Output Movie To dialog box (**Figure 8.64**).

   A Render Queue window appears, and After Effects saves the RAM movie to the destination you specified (**Figure 8.65**).

4. Close the Render Queue window to continue working with your project.

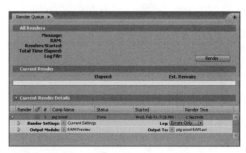

Figure 8.65 A Render Queue window appears briefly as the RAM movie is saved.

Purging the RAM Cache

As you learned earlier, After Effects uses RAM intelligently, discarding cached frames as they become obsolete or as new frames are added to a full cache. Even so, sometimes you want to free up the cache manually.

To purge the RAM cache:

◆ Choose Edit > Purge, and *select any of the following options* (**Figure 8.66**):

All—Clears the Undo, Image, and Snapshot caches

Undo—Clears recent actions from the cache, which prevents you from undoing any recent actions

Image Caches—Clears rendered frames from the cache

Snapshot—Clears the last snapshot from the cache, which means you won't be able to view the last snapshot in any window

Video Memory—Clears the video memory (VRAM) cache

The cached information is purged, freeing up RAM to cache new information.

✔ Tips

■ After Effects calculates the maximum amount of RAM allocated to different uses automatically. However, if you get an "insufficient memory" warning message, you can try increasing the Maximum Memory Usage value in the Memory & Cache pane of the Preferences dialog box. Setting values greater than 200% isn't recommended.

Figure 8.66 Choose Edit > Purge > and select the RAM cache you want to clear.

■ The Memory & Cache pane of the Preferences dialog box also allows you to specify the size and location of a disk cache. When the RAM cache is full, After Effects can move rendered frames to the location you specify. For best performance, the disk that stores source footage and the disk cache disk should use different drive controllers.

KEYFRAME
INTERPOLATION

In Chapter 7, "Properties and Keyframes," you learned to animate layer properties over time by setting keyframes. By defining only the most important, or *key*, frames, you assume the role of head animator. After Effects fills the role of assistant animator, providing all the in-between frames, or *tweens*, using what's known as an *interpolation method* to determine their values.

Fortunately, you can instruct your assistant to use a range of interpolation methods. Some methods create steady changes from one keyframe to the next; others vary the rate of change. Movement can take a direct path or a curved route; an action can glide in for a soft landing or blast off in a burst of speed.

Without a choice of interpolation methods, your loyal assistant's abilities would be severely limited. If animated values always proceeded directly and mechanically from one keyframe to another, all but the most basic animations would seem lifeless and robotic. To create a curved movement would require so many keyframes you'd begin to wonder why you had an assistant at all. Calculating acceleration or deceleration in speed would present an even thornier problem.

This chapter explains how you can assign various interpolation methods to keyframes to impart nuance and variation to your animations using the Timeline panel's Graph Editor. You'll not only learn to decipher how After Effects depicts the ineffable qualities of motion, speed, and acceleration, but you'll also see how it harnesses them. In the process, you'll begin to realize that there's a big difference between animating something and bringing it to life.

Understanding Interpolation

The beauty of keyframes is that they save you work. If you set keyframes, After Effects calculates the values for the frames in between, a process known as *interpolation*. Controlling the interpolation between keyframes allows you to set fewer keyframes than you could otherwise—without sacrificing precise control over your animation. After Effects interpolates values in terms of both space and time: in other words, spatially and temporally.

Spatial interpolation

Spatial interpolation refers to how After Effects calculates changes in position, how a layer or its anchor point moves in the space of the composition. Does it proceed directly from one keyframe to the next, or does it take a curved route (**Figures 9.1** and **9.2**)?

As you've seen, spatial interpolation is represented in the Timeline view as a motion path, a dotted line connecting keyframes. By default, After Effects calculates the values between spatial keyframes—the motion path—using a curved progression called an *auto Bézier* curve. The rate of change through the keyframe is smooth; hence, there are no sharp changes in direction.

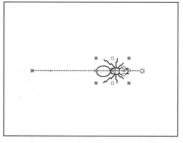

Figure 9.1 Interpolation refers to how After Effects calculates a property's values between keyframed values. Spatial interpolation determines whether movement proceeds directly from one keyframe to the next...

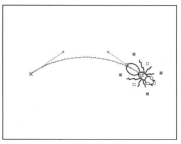

Figure 9.2 ...or takes a more curved, indirect route.

Figure 9.3 Both rabbits have the same keyframes, but they have different interpolation methods.

Temporal interpolation

Temporal interpolation refers to any property value's rate of change between keyframes. Does the value change at a constant rate from one keyframe to the next, or does it accelerate or decelerate?

For example, **Figure 9.3** shows two familiar rabbits (the logo from Peachpit Press's Visual QuickStart series of books). They both travel the same distance in the same amount of time. However, one proceeds from the first keyframe to the last keyframe at a constant rate. The other gradually accelerates, starting slowly and then speeding up. As a result, the second rabbit falls behind at first and then gradually catches up. Both reach their destination simultaneously.

By default, After Effects calculates the values between temporal keyframes using a linear progression, or *linear interpolation* method. This means property values change at a constant rate. However, you can set the rate of change to accelerate or decelerate. You can even specify no interpolation, so that a keyframe value holds until the next keyframe value is reached (in terms of the example, this rabbit would magically appear at the finish line at the moment the others reach it by foot).

Incoming and outgoing interpolation

Although *interpolation* refers to values *between* keyframes, it's important to understand that you assign an interpolation type to keyframes themselves. The interpolation type, in turn, determines how values are calculated before the keyframe and after the keyframe—the *incoming* and *outgoing interpolation*. Therefore, the values between any two keyframes (the interpolated values) are determined by the first keyframe's outgoing interpolation type and the next keyframe's incoming interpolation type.

The concept is most easily understood in spatial terms. Just as a direction handle in a path shape influences the preceding curve, a motion keyframe's tangent affects the path preceding the keyframe. Similarly, the opposite tangent influences the motion path after the keyframe (**Figure 9.4**).

Temporal interpolation also affects a property value's rate of change before and after the keyframe. In a speed or value graph, ease handles work a lot like tangents in a motion path. But because the graph lines don't trace a spatial path, they can be a little more difficult to interpret and adjust (**Figure 9.5**).

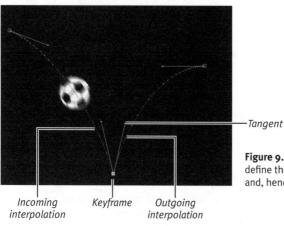

Tangent

Incoming interpolation   *Keyframe*   *Outgoing interpolation*

Figure 9.4 In a motion path, keyframe tangents define the outgoing and incoming interpolation and, hence, the curve of the motion path.

Incoming interpolation   *Keyframe*   *Ease handle*   *Outgoing interpolation*

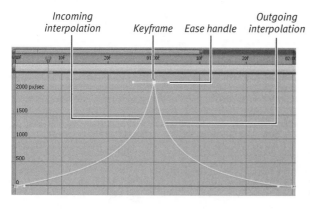

Figure 9.5 A value graph's direction lines and a speed graph's ease handles (shown here) define the incoming and outgoing interpolation. Here, the rate of change gradually accelerates after the first keyframe and then decelerates into the second keyframe.

Viewing spatial interpolation in the motion path

As you learned in Chapter 7, spatial interpolation is represented as a motion path (**Figure 9.6**). Changes in a layer's position value appear as a motion path in the Composition panel; changes in a layer's anchor-point value appear in its Layer panel. Effect point paths can appear in a both panels. So far, you've learned how to set a layer's position at a keyframe by dragging in the appropriate panel; in this chapter, you'll learn how to adjust the path between keyframes, or the interpolated values.

Viewing temporal interpolation in the Graph Editor

As you know, you animate a layer's properties by expanding the layer in the Timeline panel and setting keyframes under the time ruler. The time between keyframed values has a direct effect on the property's rate of change, or speed. But to see and manipulate the values *between* keyframes—the interpolated values—you must toggle the view under the time ruler to the Graph Editor. The *Graph Editor* represents the temporal interpolation as graphs that reflect a property's rate of change and also let you control it (**Figure 9.7**). As you'll see later in this chapter, the Graph Editor provides a spacious and detailed view of any combination of properties.

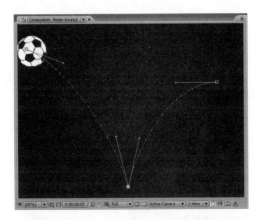

Figure 9.6 Changes in a layer's position are represented by a motion path in the Comp panel (shown here). Changes in an anchor point can be seen as a motion path in a Layer panel.

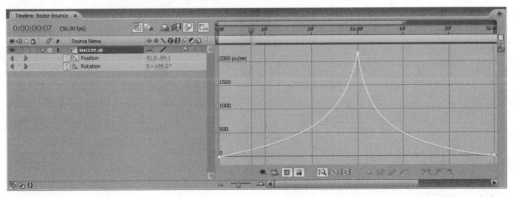

Figure 9.7 You can toggle the area under the time ruler to the Graph Editor, which represents temporal interpolation as value and speed graphs.

Interpolation Types

With the exception of hold interpolation, After Effects uses the same methods to calculate both spatial and temporal interpolation. This section describes how each interpolation type is expressed spatially, in a motion path, and temporally, in a speed graph.

No interpolation

No interpolation is applied to properties that have no keyframes and aren't animated. Static properties display an I-beam icon (rather than keyframes) in the layer outline, and the Stopwatch icon isn't selected.

Linear

Linear interpolation dictates a constant rate of change from one keyframe to the next. Between two keyframes, linear interpolation defines a straight path; temporally, it results in a constant speed. When a keyframe's incoming and outgoing interpolation are linear, a corner is created in the motion path. Temporally, speed changes instantly at the keyframe (**Figures 9.8** and **9.9**).

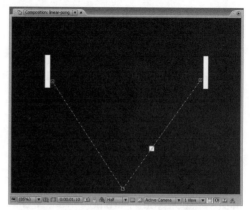

Figure 9.8 Spatially, linear interpolation defines a corner at each keyframe and a straight path between keyframes. The ball in the classic Pong game, for example, moves in perfectly straight lines and ricochets in sharp corners.

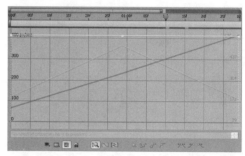

Figure 9.9 Temporally, linear interpolation results in a constant rate of change between keyframes. When speed differs between pairs of keyframes, the change is instantaneous.

Figure 9.10 Auto Bézier interpolation creates a curved path with equal incoming and outgoing interpolation. The keyframes of an orbital path may use perfectly symmetrical curves.

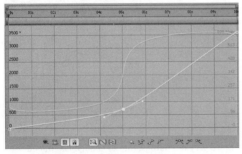

Figure 9.11 Temporally, auto Bézier interpolation yields gradual, even speed changes and a curved graph. For example, the blade of a fan goes from a lower speed to a higher speed gradually (not instantaneously).

Auto Bézier

Auto Bézier interpolation automatically reduces the rate of change equally on both sides of a keyframe.

Spatially, a keyframe set to auto Bézier is comparable to a smooth point, with two equal direction lines extending from it. It results in a smooth, symmetrical curve in a motion path. A satellite in an elliptical orbit, for example, takes even, round turns (**Figure 9.10**). (In addition, the satellite may auto-orient its rotation according to the direction of its movement. See "Orienting Rotation to a Motion Path Automatically," in Chapter 7.)

Temporally, auto Bézier interpolation reduces the rate of change equally before and after a keyframe, creating a gradual deceleration that eases into and out of the keyframe (**Figure 9.11**).

INTERPOLATION TYPES

Continuous Bézier

Like auto Bézier, continuous Bézier interpolation reduces the rate of change on both sides of a keyframe. However, continuous Bézier interpolation is set manually, so it doesn't affect the incoming and outgoing rates of change equally. In the motion path, continuous Bézier interpolation results in a smooth and continuous, but asymmetrical, curve. Typically, the path of a cannonball follows an arc that's continuous but asymmetrical (**Figure 9.12**).

Temporally, continuous Bézier interpolation reduces the rate of change before and after a keyframe unequally (**Figure 9.13**).

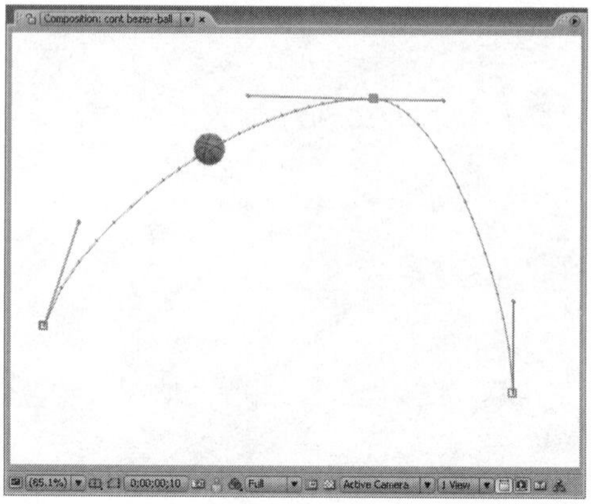

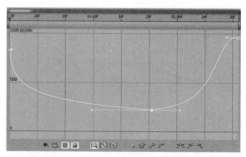

Figure 9.12 You might use continuous Bézier interpolation to trace the asymmetrically arced path of a thrown ball.

Figure 9.13 Temporally, rate of change is reduced smoothly—but unevenly—on either side of a continuous Bézier keyframe. A rolling ball may decelerate gradually as it crests a hill but accelerate more sharply on its descent.

Qu'est-ce Que C'est Bézier? *Qui Est* Bézier?

In case your French is rusty, *Bézier* is pronounced *bay-zee-yay*, after the late Pierre Etienne Bézier, who developed the math behind his namesake curve in the 1970s for use in computer-aided design and manufacture. This same math became the basis for Adobe PostScript fonts, path-based drawing, and—yes—the interpolation methods used in computer animation. Bézier died in 1999. *Merci*, Monsieur Bézier.

Figure 9.14 Bézier interpolation can allow the motion path to follow discontinuous curves, such as the one that describes the path of a ball's bounce.

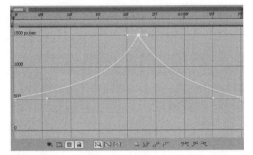

Figure 9.15 Temporally, Bézier interpolation can create sudden acceleration and deceleration. The bouncing ball accelerates until the moment of impact and then suddenly decelerates as it ascends.

Bézier

Like continuous Bézier, you set Bézier interpolation manually, but the change is discontinuous. Bézier interpolation causes an abrupt decrease or increase in the rate of change on either or both sides of a keyframe.

Spatially, Bézier keyframes are comparable to a corner point in a mask path. As in a corner point, the direction lines extending from the keyframe are unequal and discontinuous. In a motion path, Bézier interpolation creates a discontinuous curve, or *cusp*, at the keyframe. Bézier interpolation can achieve the discontinuous curve of a ball's bouncing path (**Figure 9.14**).

In the value graph, Bézier interpolation can reduce or increase the rate of change before and after a keyframe (**Figure 9.15**). For example, you can use Bézier interpolation to create a sharp acceleration at a keyframe (such as when a ball falls and bounces).

Hold

Although you can observe its effects both spatially and temporally, hold interpolation is a strictly temporal type of interpolation, halting changes in a property's value at the keyframe. The value remains fixed until the current frame of the composition reaches the next keyframe, where the property is set to a new value instantly. For example, specifying hold keyframes for a layer's Position property causes the layer to disappear suddenly and then reappear in different places. Instead of a dotted motion path, a thin solid line connects hold keyframes, indicating not the motion path but the order of keyframed positions (**Figure 9.16**). Similarly, non-spatial properties proceed instantly from one held keyframed value to another. Whereas using linearly interpolated keyframes to change a layer's opacity value from 0 to 100 is comparable to using a dimmer light, using hold keyframes is more like using a light switch. In the speed graph, hold keyframes appear as unconnected keyframes with a speed of zero (**Figure 9.17**).

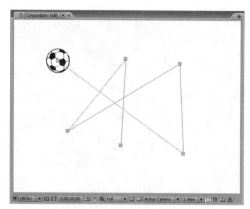

Figure 9.16 In this figure, the layer's position property uses hold keyframes. The layer remains in the position defined by a keyframe until the next keyframe is reached, at which time the layer instantly appears in its new position. A thin solid line between keyframes isn't a motion path; it indicates the order of keyframed positions.

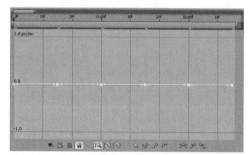

Figure 9.17 Keyframes of other properties that use hold interpolation also retain their current value until the next keyframe. The speed graph of a held property displays as disconnected keyframes at zero.

Bézier Curves and the Motion Path

Motion paths consist of *Bézier curves*: the same kind of curves that define shapes in drawing programs like Photoshop and Illustrator—as well as the masks you create in After Effects. Instead of drawing a shape freehand, you can define a shape using a Bézier curve. In a Bézier curve, you define control points, which are connected by line segments automatically. (It already sounds a lot like keyframes and interpolation, doesn't it?)

The curves of the line segments are defined and controlled by *direction lines*. Two direction lines can extend from each control point. The length and angle of one direction line influences the shape of the curve preceding the control point; the other influences the curve following the control point. (Imagine that the direction lines exert a gravitational pull on the line that enters and exits a control point.) Dragging the end of a direction line alters the line and thus its corresponding curve (**Figure 9.18**).

Just as a Bézier curve consists of control points connected by line segments, a *motion path* consists of position keyframes connected by line segments (albeit dotted lines). The same techniques you use to draw shapes in a drawing program can be applied to creating motion paths in After Effects (**Figure 9.19**). (In fact, you can copy a mask path into a comp as a motion path.)

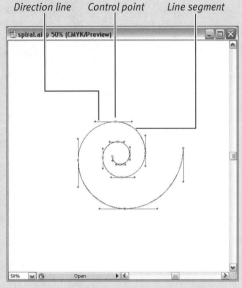

Figure 9.18 The Bézier curves you use to define a shape in a drawing program or a mask in After Effects...

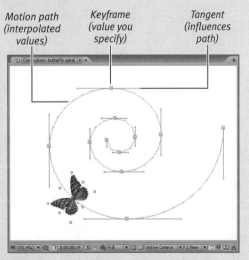

Figure 9.19 ...also define a motion path in After Effects. However, the terms used to describe the curve depend on the context.

Mixed incoming and outgoing interpolation

A keyframe can use different interpolation types for its incoming and outgoing interpolation. A keyframe's incoming and outgoing spatial interpolation can be a mix of linear and Bézier. A keyframe's temporal interpolation may use any combination of linear, Bézier, and hold for its incoming and outgoing interpolation. As usual, the shape of the motion path or graph in the Graph Editor indicates mixed interpolation. In the standard view of the time graph (rather than in the Graph Editor view), keyframe icons also indicate the temporal interpolation type (see the section "Keyframe icons and interpolation," later in this chapter).

✔ Tips

■ The Display pane of the Preferences dialog box lets you specify the maximum number of keyframes visible at once and whether to show the selected layer's motion path. See the section "Viewing Spatial Controls in the Comp Panel" in Chapter 7 for details.

■ This chapter usually illustrates motion paths for a layer's position property, although the techniques discussed also apply to its anchor point and effect point paths. You'll revisit effect point paths in the section "Setting an Effect Point," in Chapter 11.

Motion Paths vs. Mask Path Terminology

In After Effects, Bézier curves define both motion paths and mask paths. Although you adjust both kinds of paths using the same techniques, they're described by different terms. For a quick translation, see **Table 9.1**.

Table 9.1

Comparing Path Terminology

Mask Path	Motion Path
Control point	Keyframe
Line segment	Interpolated values
Direction handle	Motion path tangent
Anchor point	Linear interpolation
Smooth point	Auto Bézier or continuous Bézier interpolation
Corner point	Bézier interpolation

Speed in the Motion Path

In the motion path, the spacing between dots indicates speed. Closely spaced dots indicate slower speeds; more widely spaced dots indicate faster speeds. If the dot spacing changes between keyframes, this means the speed is changing—accelerating or decelerating. When hold temporal interpolation is applied to a spatial property, a thin solid line connects it with the adjacent keyframe (**Figure 9.20**). Although hold interpolation prevents a motion path, the solid line indicates the order of keyframes (see the section "Interpolation Types," earlier in this chapter).

Naturally, changing the distance between keyframes affects the speed and, thereby, the dot spacing in the motion path. But remember that the motion path gives you direct control over the physical distance between keyframes—not their timing or the temporal interpolation. As you use controls in the timeline to alter the speed or temporal interpolation of a spatial property, watch how the motion path also changes.

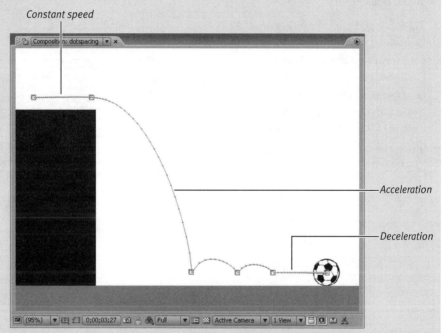

Constant speed

Acceleration

Deceleration

Figure 9.20 The spacing of dots in the motion path indicate speed: the more closely spaced the dots, the slower the motion. A solid line indicates hold interpolation (and no actual motion).

INTERPOLATION TYPES

Specifying the Default Spatial Interpolation

Ordinarily, motion-path keyframes use auto Bézier interpolation. If most of your spatial animation requires linear interpolation (or if you simply prefer it as your initial setting), you can change the default in the Preferences dialog box.

To set the default spatial interpolation:

1. Choose After Effects > Preferences > General (Mac) or Edit > Preferences > General (**Figure 9.21**).

   The General panel of the Preferences dialog box appears.

2. *Do either of the following* (**Figure 9.22**):

   ▲ Select Default Spatial Interpolation to Linear to make new motion paths use linear interpolation.

   ▲ Deselect Default Spatial Interpolation to Linear to make new motion paths use auto Bézier interpolation.

3. Click OK to close the Preferences dialog box.

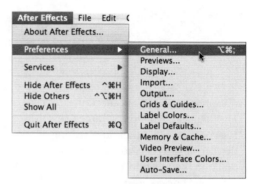

Figure 9.21 Choose After Effects > Preferences > General (Mac) or Edit > Preferences > General (Windows).

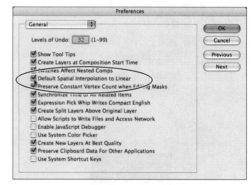

Figure 9.22 In the General panel of the Preferences dialog box, choose whether to use linear interpolation as the default.

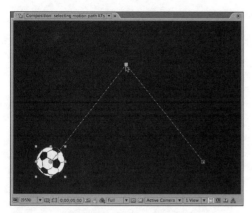

Figure 9.23 To move a position keyframe...

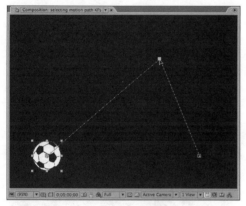

Figure 9.24 ...drag its icon to a new location in the Layer panel (for anchor point or effect point) or Comp panel (for position or effect point).

Specifying Spatial Interpolation in the Motion Path

In Chapter 7, you learned that you can change the spatial positioning of each keyframe by dragging it directly into a Composition or Layer panel. This section focuses on using spatial interpolation to change the course of the motion path from one keyframe to the next.

The following tasks assume you remember how to set a Comp or Layer panel to show motion paths. To refresh your memory, turn to "Parts of the Layer panel" in Chapter 6, and "Viewing Spatial Controls in the Comp Panel" in Chapter 7. And because you can apply your mastery of mask paths to editing motion paths, this section covers just the essentials. (See the sidebar "Bézier Curves and the Motion Path," earlier in this chapter; see Chapter 10, "Mask Essentials," for more about editing mask paths.)

To move a position keyframe:

1. Select a layer with an animated property to reveal its motion path in a Composition or Layer panel.

   Position and effect-point paths appear in the Composition panel (**Figure 9.23**); anchor-point paths appear in the Layer panel.

2. Using the selection tool, drag a keyframe (an x icon in the motion path) to a new position (**Figure 9.24**).

To toggle between auto Bézier and linear interpolation:

1. Select a layer with an animated property to reveal its motion path in a Composition or Layer panel.

   Position and effect-point paths appear in the Composition panel (**Figure 9.25**); anchor-point paths appear in the Layer panel.

2. In the Tools panel, select the Pen tool (**Figure 9.26**).

3. In the motion path, click a keyframe icon to convert it.

   The Pen tool becomes the Convert Vertex tool when you position it over a keyframe (**Figure 9.27**). A keyframe using linear interpolation is converted to auto Bézier, with two equal control handles (motion path tangents) extending from the keyframe. Any Bézier-type keyframe is converted to linear, with no direction handles.

4. In the Tools panel, choose the Selection tool.

   Once you convert a keyframe, adjust it with the Selection tool. Clicking it without changing tools converts it back.

To convert auto Bézier to continuous Bézier:

1. Select a layer with an animated property to reveal its motion path in a Composition or Layer panel.

2. Using the Selection tool, drag one tangent of an auto Bézier keyframe so that it's shorter or longer than the other (**Figure 9.28**).

   Both of the keyframe's tangents form a continuous line, but they influence the path by different amounts.

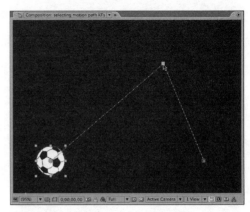

Figure 9.25 Select a layer so that its motion path is visible in the Comp panel.

Figure 9.26 In the Tools panel, select the Pen tool.

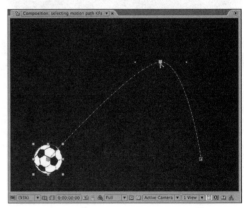

Figure 9.27 Clicking a keyframe with the Convert Vertex tool changes the keyframe from auto Bézier to linear and vice versa.

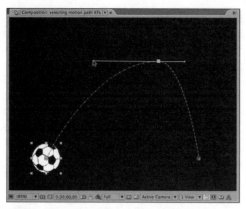

Figure 9.28 Dragging one of an auto Bézier keyframe's tangents makes it a continuous Bézier keyframe. The tangents remain continuous, but they influence the path unequally.

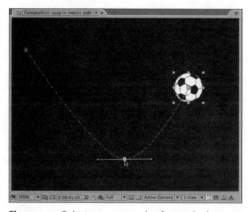

Figure 9.29 Select one or more keyframes in the motion path.

Figure 9.30 Select the Pen tool.

To convert continuous Bézier to Bézier, and vice versa:

1. Select a layer with an animated property to reveal its motion path in a Composition or Layer panel.

2. Select one or more keyframes in the motion path (**Figure 9.29**).

   The selected keyframe's motion path tangents (control handles) become visible.

3. In the Tools panel, select the Pen tool (**Figure 9.30**).

4. In the motion path, drag a direction handle (**Figure 9.31**).

   The Pen tool becomes the Convert Vertex tool ⌐ when you position it over a motion path tangent (direction handle). Dragging a direction handle of a Bézier keyframe converts it to continuous Bézier with two related tangents; dragging a tangent of a continuous Bézier keyframe splits the two tangents, converting it to Bézier.

5. In the Tools panel, choose the Selection tool.

   Once you convert a keyframe, adjust its direction handles with the Selection tool. Otherwise, you'll convert it back.

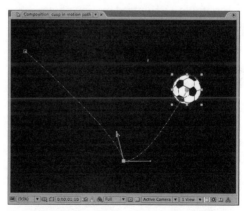

Figure 9.31 When positioned over a path tangent, the Pen becomes the Convert Vertex icon. Drag a tangent to change continuous Bézier to Bézier and vice versa.

To toggle between the Selection tool and a Pen tool:

1. Position the mouse in a Comp or Layer panel, and press and hold the Command (Mac) or Ctrl (Windows) key.

   If the Selection tool is selected, it changes to the Pen tool currently visible in the Tools panel. If one of the Pen tools is selected, it changes to the Selection tool (**Figure 9.32**).

2. Release the key to continue using the currently selected tool.

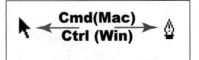

Figure 9.32 Press and hold the Command (Mac) or Ctrl (Windows) key to toggle between the Selection tool and the currently selected Pen tool.

✔ Tips

■ Most of the time, you'll want to use the Selection tool but keep the Pen tool visible in the Tools panel. Use the Selection tool to adjust the motion path; temporarily toggle to the Pen tool to add or convert keyframes.

■ Again, the motion path and the types of spatial interpolation it uses only affect motion. For truly convincing animation, you must also adjust speed (by controlling the time between keyframes) and acceleration (via temporal interpolation). In addition, consider other physical attributes associated with motion—for example, the blurred motion of fast-moving objects, or distortion and elasticity (say, the squashing effect when a ball strikes the ground). (See Chapter 14, "More Layer Techniques," for more about motion blur.)

Using the Graph Editor: An Overview

By taking over the area under the timeline's time ruler, the Graph Editor affords a detailed view of property changes and a spacious area in which to edit them (**Figures 9.33** and **9.34**). The number of options reflects the Graph Editor's flexibility but may also make the process seem more complex than it really is. The following task provides an overview.

Later sections cover each aspect of process in greater detail. First, you'll learn how to adjust the timing and values of keyframes using the Graph Editor instead of the methods you learned in Chapter 7. Then, you'll move on to using the graphs to adjust interpolation (the values between keyframes).

Keyframes

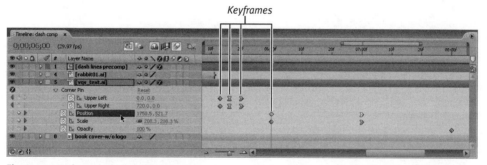

Figure 9.33 In the typical view of the timeline, you can see expanded properties' keyframe icons but no graphical representation of interpolated values.

Keyframes   Value graph (X)   Value graph (Y)   Speed graph   Graph Editor

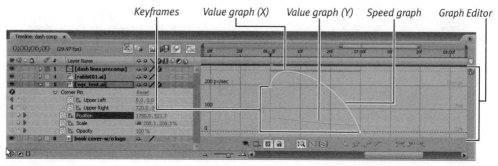

Figure 9.34 The Graph Editor depicts any combination of properties as graphs in a spacious and detailed view under the time ruler.

To adjust properties in the Graph Editor:

1. In the Timeline panel, select the Graph Editor button  (**Figure 9.35**).

2. Specify which properties are visible by choosing an option in the Show Properties pull-down menu (**Figure 9.36**).

3. Specify the graph types you want to edit for the visible properties in the Graph Type and Options pull-down menu.

4. Specify the other information you want to view by selecting the appropriate option in the Graph Type and Options pull-down menu (**Figure 9.37**).

Optional information includes layer In and Out point icons, layer markers, and so on.

5. Edit the visible property graphs using techniques described later in this chapter (**Figure 9.38**).

You can select, move, add, and delete property keyframes; you can adjust their interpolation types using either manual or automatic methods.

✔ Tip

■ Technically, you can use a keyboard shortcut to specify preset interpolation types to a keyframe without switching to the Graph Editor. Both methods are covered in the section "Setting a Keyframe's Temporal Interpolation Type," later in this chapter.

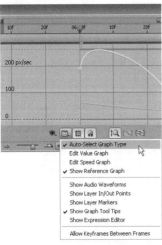

Figure 9.35 Select the Graph Editor button.

Figure 9.37 Specify the graph type you want to edit and other options.

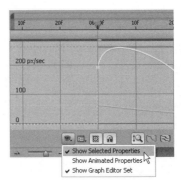

Figure 9.36 Specify the visible properties in the Show Properties pull-down menu.

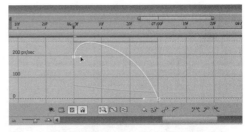

Figure 9.38 Edit a property graph by dragging its keyframe and ease handles or by using an automated method (keyframe assistant).

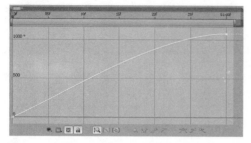

Figure 9.39 The value graph measures value vertically and time horizontally. This is a value graph for rotation (the rate of rotation gradually decelerates as it reaches the second keyframe).

Y coordinate value   *X coordinate value*

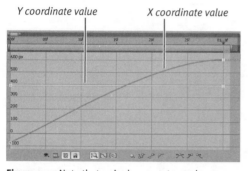

Figure 9.40 Note that a single property can have more than one dimension and thereby more than one graph. This value graph shows the layer is moving left to right (X value increasing) horizontally (Y value constant).

Understanding Value and Speed Graphs

In the following sections, you'll use the Graph Editor to (what else?) edit a graph of a property. But first, let's take a moment to examine the two types of graphs you'll encounter: the value graph and speed graph.

Value graph

A *value graph* measures a property's value vertically and its time horizontally (**Figure 9.39**). The units in which values are expressed depend on the type of property: Rotation is measured in rotations and degrees, Opacity in percentages, and so on. The slope of the line between keyframes represents the rate of change in units/second. Straight lines indicate a constant rate; curved lines indicate a changing rate, or acceleration.

Note that some properties consist of more than one value, or *dimension*. For example, a position property includes values for both an *X* and *Y* coordinate. Hence, a position value graph includes two lines: one representing the *X* coordinate value and the other representing the *y* coordinate value (**Figure 9.40**).

Value graphs tend to be easy to understand: When the increases, the graph goes up; when the value decreases, the graph slopes down. A value graph is particularly well suited to properties such as Opacity and audio Levels, because these properties correspond well with the "up and down" or "high and low" nature of the graph. (You may already know this from your experience with non-linear editing programs, where adjusting value graphs is known as *rubberbanding*.)

Speed graph

A speed graph measures rates of change in a property's values (**Figure 9.41**). The units measured by a speed graph depend on the property type: degrees of rotation/sec, percentage opacity/sec, and so on. Regardless of the specific property, the rate of change (units/sec) is measured vertically, and time (sec) is measured horizontally in both graphs. Therefore, the slope of the graph represents acceleration (units/sec/sec), which is dictated by the temporal interpolation method.

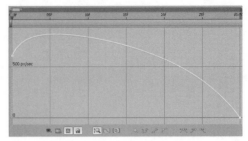

Figure 9.41 A speed graph measure rates of change vertically and time horizontally. Therefore, it represents acceleration in terms of units/sec/sec.

✔ Tips

- You can adjust the curve by dragging the *ease handles*. Ease handles look and work a bit like direction handles or tangents, but they always extend horizontally from a keyframe. As you drag an ease handle, see how it influences curves in both the speed (or velocity) graph and the value graph. (Consult the section "Analyzing Value and Speed Graphs," later in this chapter, to learn more about interpreting the graphs.)

- You can instruct After Effects to show the type of graph most appropriate to the property you're viewing in the Graph Editor. See the section "Specifying the Graph Type," later in this chapter, for details.

Speed and Acceleration

Before you use speed graphs to control temporal interpolation, you may want to take a moment to review the concepts of speed and acceleration.

Speed

Back in physics class, you learned the following:

$$\text{Speed} = \frac{\text{distance}}{\text{time}}$$

If physics class is but a distant memory, imagine a car's speedometer, which expresses speed in miles per hour. In After Effects, the units of measure are smaller—pixels/sec—but the concept is the same: A fast-moving object covers a greater distance in less time; a slow-moving object covers less distance in a greater amount of time.

You can describe other properties in similar terms: a fast fade or quick rotation, for example. In After Effects, the rate of change of a property is also referred to as *velocity*. (In science, both speed and velocity measure a distance in a given amount of time, but velocity also implies direction. For our purposes, the terms can be used interchangeably.)

You can control the speed of an action by changing either the difference in value or the difference in time between keyframes (**Figures 9.42**, **9.43**, and **9.44**).

For example, if an animated gear appears to rotate too slowly, you can increase the number of rotations. Ten rotations in one second spin much faster than one rotation per second. Alternatively, you can decrease the time an action takes to make a corresponding change in value. For example, if a character crosses the screen too slowly, you can have the character traverse the same distance in less time. Crossing the screen in one second is faster than traveling the same distance in five seconds.

continues on next page

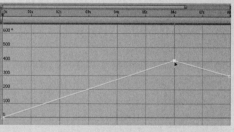

Figure 9.42 Increase the speed between keyframes...

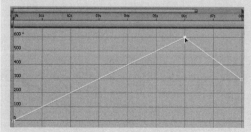

Figure 9.43 ...by increasing the difference in value...

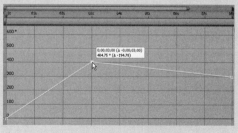

Figure 9.44 ...or decreasing the difference in time.

Speed and Acceleration *(continued)*

Acceleration

Speed and velocity can remain constant, or they can vary from moment to moment. When speed changes over time, it's called *acceleration* or *deceleration*. In After Effects, you can control changes in speed with temporal interpolation (**Figures 9.45** and **9.46**).

It's important to understand that temporal interpolation affects neither the values of the keyframes nor the amount of time between them. If it takes one second for an image to go from point A to point B, no type of temporal interpolation will change that fact. Instead, temporal interpolation determines how the speed changes in that second—at a constant speed (like the hands of a clock); accelerating from its starting point (like a rocket at liftoff); decelerating (like a docking boat); or, in the case of hold interpolation, attaining the next value instantaneously (magically appearing in the next position).

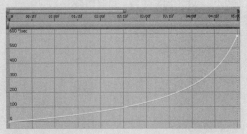

Figure 9.45 Temporal interpolation affects speed changes between keyframes to achieve acceleration...

Figure 9.46 ...and deceleration.

Figure 9.47 In the switches area of the Timeline panel, select the Show Graph Editor button.

Viewing Property Graphs

To view temporal interpolation and control it manually, toggle the area under the time ruler to the Graph Editor.

The Graph Editor's flexible viewing options help you view the combination of properties you want: selected properties, animated properties, or properties you specify by including them in what's known as the *graph editor set*.

To toggle the Graph Editor:

◆ In the Timeline panel, select the Show Graph Editor button ▨ (**Figure 9.47**).

The area under the time ruler changes to the Graph Editor (**Figure 9.48**). The properties visible in the Graph Editor depend on options you specify in the Show Properties pull-down menu; the types of graphs visible depends on the options you specify in the Graph Type and Options pull-down menu. (See the tasks "To specify visible properties in the Graph Editor" and "To specify the graph types displayed in the Graph Editor," later in this chapter.)

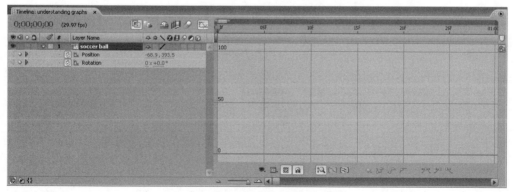

Figure 9.48 The time ruler area toggles to the Graph Editor view.

To specify visible properties in the Graph Editor:

◆ In the Graph Editor, click the Show Properties pull-down menu , and *choose any of the following* (**Figure 9.49**):

Show Selected Properties—Includes the property you select in the layer outline

Show Animated Properties—Includes all of the selected layer's animated properties

Show Graph Editor Set—Includes all properties you specify as part of the graph editor set (see the next task, "To designate a graph editor set")

The properties you specify appear in the Graph Editor.

To designate a graph editor set:

1. In a comp's layer outline, expand layers to reveal the properties you want to add to the graph editor set.

2. For each property you want to add to the graph editor set, select the Include in Graph Editor Set button 🔳 (**Figure 9.50**).

Properties in the set appear in the Graph Editor when the Show Graph Editor Set option is selected (see the previous task, "To specify visible properties in the Graph Editor").

✔ Tips

■ Here's a reminder of something you learned in Chapter 7: Press U to reveal all the animated properties of all the selected layers.

■ Keyboard shortcuts make it easy to reveal just the properties you want. See Chapter 7 for a table of some of the most common keyboard shortcuts.

Figure 9.49 In the Graph Editor's Show Properties pull-down menu, select which properties are visible.

Figure 9.50 Expand the layer outline to reveal the properties you want to add to the graph editor set, and then select their Include in Graph Editor Set button.

Specifying the Graph Type

The Graph Editor can represent any property as a value graph or speed graph. Turn back to the section "Understanding Value and Speed Graphs," earlier in this chapter, to review how the graphs work. Later sections explain how to manipulate the graphs.

To specify the graph types displayed in the Graph Editor:

1. In the Graph Editor, click the Graph Type and Options pull-down menu, and then *choose any of the following options* (**Figure 9.51**):

   Auto-Select Graph Type—After Effects determines the most appropriate type of graph to display for editing.

   Edit Value Graph—Displays the visible properties' value graph for editing.

   Edit Speed Graph—Displays the visible properties' speed graph for editing.

   In the Graph Editor, the type of graph you choose appears for the visible properties (**Figure 9.52**).

2. To display the type of graph you *did not* specify in step 1 for reference, select **Show Reference Graph** (**Figure 9.53**).

   For example, if you chose Edit Speed Graph in step 1, then selecting Show Reference Graph makes the value graph visible. However, you can't edit the reference graph (**Figure 9.54**).

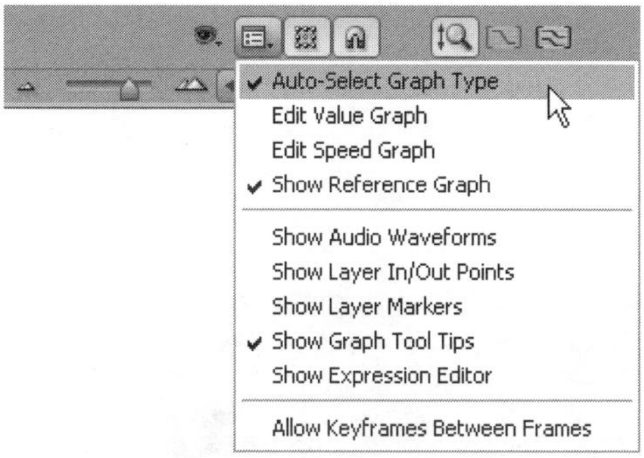

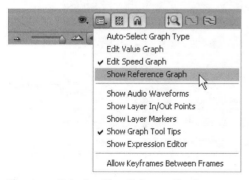

Figure 9.51 Selecting an option in the Graph Editor's Graph Type and Options pull-down menu...

Figure 9.53 Selecting Show Reference Graph...

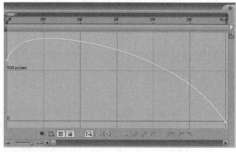

Figure 9.52 ...displays that type of graph for the visible property. Here, the property's speed graph is visible for editing.

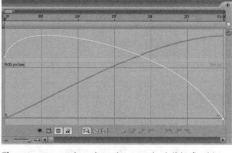

Figure 9.54 ...makes the other graph visible (in this case, the value graph). The reference graph can't be edited, but it reflects the changes you make to the other graph.

Viewing Optional Information in the Graph Editor

The Graph Editor not only lets you select which property and type of graph you want to view but also lets you reveal other helpful information, such as audio waveforms, In point and Out point icons, markers, tool tips, and expressions (**Figure 9.55**). Just as important, you can hide the data you don't need and eliminate unnecessary visual clutter.

To specify Graph Editor options:

◆ In the Graph Editor, click the Graph Type and Options pull-down menu, and then *choose any of the following options* (**Figure 9.56**):

Show Audio Waveforms—When you're viewing an audio layer's Audio Levels property, this option displays a waveform, or graphical representation of audio power.

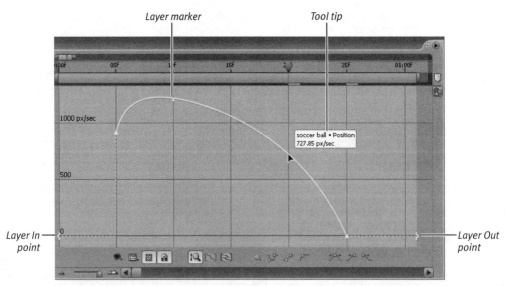

Figure 9.55 The Graph Editor can display optional information. Hovering the mouse over a graph reveals a tool tip, which in this case shows the property value's speed at that point.

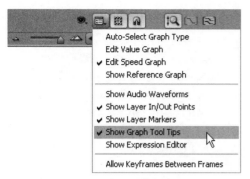

Figure 9.56 Select the options you want in the Graph Editor's Graph Type and Options pull-down menu.

Show Layer In/Out Points—Shows In point and Out point icons for the layer containing properties visible in the Graph Editor.

Show Layer Markers—Shows marker icons for the layer containing properties visible in the Graph Editor.

Show Graph Tool Tips—Displays a tool tip containing the current speed or value at the point where you position the mouse over a graph.

Show Expression Editor—Shows an area to add and edit an *expression*, or script-based formula for determining the property's value (see Chapter 16, "Complex Projects," for more about expressions).

Allow Keyframes Between Frames—Permits you to set keyframes between timebase divisions, which can be especially useful when you're timing keyframes with audio.

The Graph Editor activates the options you specify.

✔ Tips

- You can also view an audio layer's waveform in the normal (not Graph Editor) time ruler area by expanding the layer's Audio Levels property and then expanding Waveform in the layer outline.

- For more about expressions, see Chapter 16, "Complex Projects."

- Typically, keyframes and other edits are based on video frame rates. But because audio is sampled far more frequently than video frame rates, audio can require more precise edits. See the sidebar "Ample Samples" in Chapter 8 for an explanation of audio sample rates, and consult the Help System for more information about the Allow Keyframes Between Frames option.

Resizing Property Graphs Automatically

The Graph Editor helps you home in on the graph you're working with and modify the scale when adjustments make the graph exceed the available space.

To scale the graph automatically:

◆ In the Graph Editor, *select any of the following options* (**Figure 9.57**):

Auto-zoom Graph Height
Fit Selection to View
Fit All Graphs to View

The view adjusts according to your selection (**Figure 9.58**).

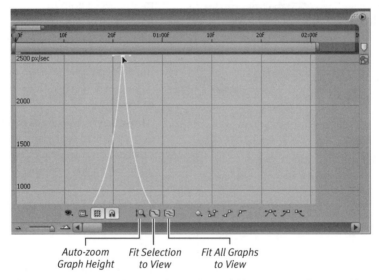

Auto-zoom   Fit Selection   Fit All Graphs
Graph Height   to View   to View

Figure 9.57 Here, the graph doesn't fit into the available space as well as it could. Selecting any of the three options at the bottom of the Graph Editor...

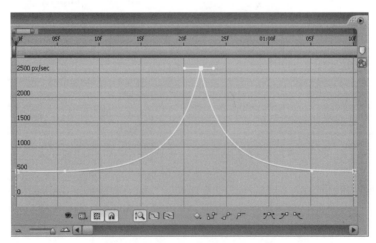

Figure 9.58 ...scales the graph so that it fits better vertically or horizontally.

Analyzing Value and Speed Graphs

As you proceed with the graph-editing tasks in the following sections, note how the shape of a value graph or speed graph corresponds to the animation (**Figures 9.59** and **9.60**, and **Table 9.2**). Remember that a value graph corresponds to a property value directly: The graph goes up as the value increases; it goes down as the value decreases. The steepness, or *slope*, of the graph corresponds with speed: A horizontal line indicates no change; a gradual slope indicates a slow change in the value; a steep slope indicates a faster change.

continues on next page

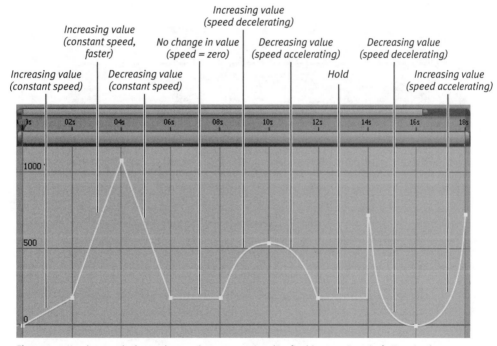

Figure 9.59 A value graph shows changes in a property's value (in this case, Rotation). Examine how each graph shape corresponds with certain types of temporal interpolation.

The speed graph corresponds with the rate of change, not the value itself. A horizontal graph indicates a constant speed; a sloped graph indicates changing speed. Note that the slope and curve of the value graph and the speed graph can differ greatly. For example, an increasing value results in a value graph with a positive, upward slope; however, the rate of change may also be decreasing (even as it approaches a higher value), resulting in a speed graph that slopes down.

Table 9.2

Recognizing Temporal Interpolation		
TEMPORAL INTERPOLATION	**IN THE VALUE GRAPH**	**IN THE SPEED/ VELOCITY GRAPH**
No speed change	Horizontal line	Horizontal line
Constant speed	Straight line with any slope	Horizontal line
Sudden speed change	Sharp corner	Disconnected line/ ease handles
Acceleration	Curve with steep slope	Upward-sloping curve
Deceleration	Curve with shallow slope	Downward-sloping curve
Holding	Horizontal line, unconnected	Horizontal line, where current speed = zero

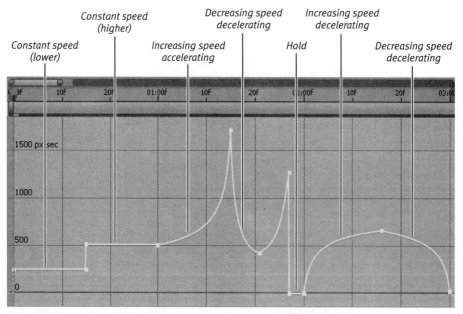

Figure 9.60 A speed graph shows changes in a property's speed (here, Position).

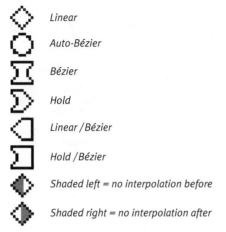

Linear

Auto-Bézier

Bézier

Hold

Linear / Bézier

Hold / Bézier

Shaded left = no interpolation before

Shaded right = no interpolation after

Figure 9.61 Though the standard view of the timeline doesn't graph interpolation, the shape of each keyframe's icons indicates the type of interpolation.

Keyframe icons and interpolation

The Graph Editor shows interpolation explicitly in the form of a value or speed graph. Regardless of the interpolation type, keyframe icons appear as small boxes, or *control points*, on the graph. Roving keyframes always appear as small dots.

But as you saw in Chapter 7, keyframe icons look different when you're not using the Graph Editor. In the standard view of the time ruler, an expanded property's keyframes appear as relatively large icons. Because no graph is visible, each icon's shape helps indicate the incoming and outgoing interpolation (**Figure 9.61**). If you expand a heading only, any individual property's keyframes appear as small dots to indicate their presence and position.

Moving Keyframes in the Graph Editor

You select keyframes in the Graph Editor using the same methods you use to select keyframes in a motion path (covered earlier in this chapter) or, for that matter, to select keyframes in the standard view of the time ruler (covered in Chapter 7). The keyframe icons differ, but the procedures are the same, and we won't review them here. However, the Graph Editor includes a few unique features when it comes to keyframes.

First, the Graph Editor has its own *snap* feature. As you know from other chapters (and other programs), snapping gives objects a magnetic quality, so they tend to align with one another. In the Graph Editor, enabling snapping helps you align keyframes with In points, Out points, markers, the current time indicator (CTI), and other keyframes.

The Graph Editor also includes a more unexpected feature, a *keyframe transform box*. With this option active, selecting multiple keyframes includes them in a transform box—just like the bounding box that lets you scale a layer. Ordinarily, selecting multiple keyframes lets you move all of them by the same amount. In contrast, a transform box lets you adjust keyframes *proportionally*. In other words, keyframes included in the transform box maintain their relative positions on the box.

To enable keyframe snapping in the Graph Editor:

◆ In the Graph Editor, select the Snap button 🔒 (**Figure 9.62**).

When the Snap button is selected, keyframes align with other keyframes, markers, the CTI, and other elements more easily.

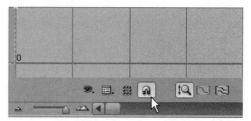

Figure 9.62 Select the Graph Editor's Snap button to assist in aligning keyframes with In points, Out points, the CTI, or other keyframes.

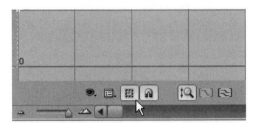

Figure 9.63 Selecting the Graph Editor's Show Bounding Box button...

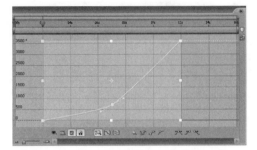

Figure 9.64 ...creates a bounding box around selected keyframes.

To move keyframes using a transform box:

◆ In the Graph Editor, select the Show Bounding Box button ▦ (**Figure 9.63**). When you select multiple keyframes, a bounding box appears around the keyframes (**Figure 9.64**).

To move multiple keyframes using a transform box:

1. With the Show Bounding Box option selected, *do either of the following:*

   ▲ Shift-click multiple keyframes.

   ▲ Drag a marquee around consecutive keyframes.

   A bounding box appears around the selected keyframes.

2. *Do any of the following:*

   ▲ Drag any of the bounding box's handles to scale the box (**Figure 9.65**).

   ▲ Press Option (Mac) or Alt (Windows) to move a handle on the bounding box independently of the other handles (**Figure 9.66**).

   The keyframes contained in the bounding box move according to your adjustments, maintaining their relative positions on the box.

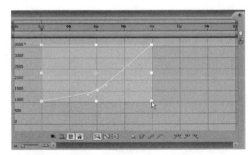

Figure 9.65 Dragging the bounding box scales the box and moves the keyframes accordingly.

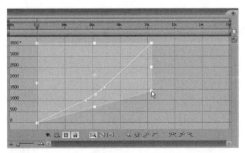

Figure 9.66 Press Option (Mac) or Alt (Windows) to drag a bounding box's handle independently of other handles.

MOVING KEYFRAMES IN THE GRAPH EDITOR

Adding and Removing Keyframes in the Graph Editor

You can add keyframes to and remove keyframes from a property graph as you would a motion or mask path. Even so, it's worth reviewing the techniques in the context of keyframing properties in the Graph Editor. Don't forget that you can still add and remove keyframes using the methods you learned in Chapter 7.

To add keyframes to a graph:

1. *Do either of the following:*

   ▲ In the Tools panel, select the Pen tool ✎ (**Figure 9.67**).

   ▲ With the Selection tool selected, press Command (Mac) or Ctrl (Windows).

2. Position the Pen tool over the line in a graph so that the Pen tool appears as an Add Vertex tool (a Pen tool with a plus sign) ✎₊.

3. Click the graph to create a new keyframe (**Figure 9.68**).

   A keyframe appears as a small solid box in the graph (and as a large keyframe icon when the time ruler isn't set to Graph Editor). Initially, the keyframe uses the default interpolation type.

4. Make sure to choose the Selection tool when you're finished.

Figure 9.67 In the Tools panel, choose the Pen tool (shown here) or press Command (Mac) or Ctrl (Windows) with the Selection tool.

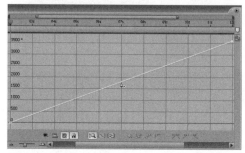

Figure 9.68 The Pen tool becomes the Add Vertex tool. Click the value graph to create a new keyframe.

Figure 9.69 Select the Pen tool...

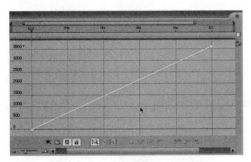

Figure 9.70 ...and position it over a keyframe so that the mouse becomes a Delete Vertex icon, and then click...

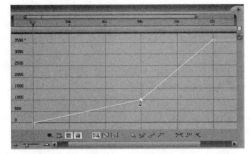

Figure 9.71 ...to remove the keyframe. The graph adjusts accordingly.

To remove keyframes from a graph:

1. *Do either of the following:*
   - ▲ In the Tools panel, select the Pen tool ![pen icon] (**Figure 9.69**).
   - ▲ With the Selection tool selected, press Command (Mac) or Ctrl (Windows).

2. Position the Pen tool over a keyframe so that the Pen tool appears as a Delete Vertex icon ![icon] (**Figure 9.70**).

3. Click the keyframe.

   The keyframe is removed from the graph, and the line (interpolated values) adjusts accordingly (**Figure 9.71**).

4. Make sure to choose the Selection tool when you're finished.

✔ Tip

- ■ If you use the Pen tool to add a keyframe to the graph, dragging extends a direction line, or ease handle.

ADDING AND REMOVING KEYFRAMES

Setting a Keyframe's Temporal Interpolation Type

The Graph Editor includes buttons that apply hold, linear, or auto Bézier interpolation to selected keyframes.

If the automatic method doesn't yield the result you want, you can adjust the interpolation manually or apply a keyframe assistant to achieve other common effects (see the following sections for details).

To set a keyframe's interpolation using a button:

1. In the Graph Editor, select the keyframes you want to adjust.

2. At the bottom of the Graph Editor, click the button that corresponds with the type of temporal interpolation you want the keyframe to use (**Figure 9.72**):

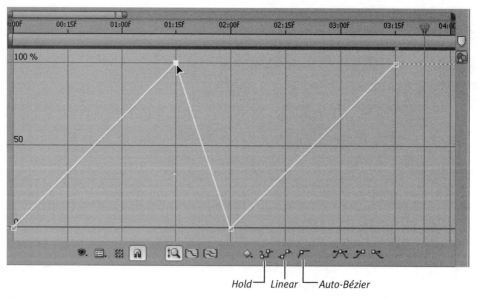

Figure 9.72 Select a keyframe, and select the button that corresponds with the interpolation type you want to use. Here, a keyframe that uses linear interpolation...

Hold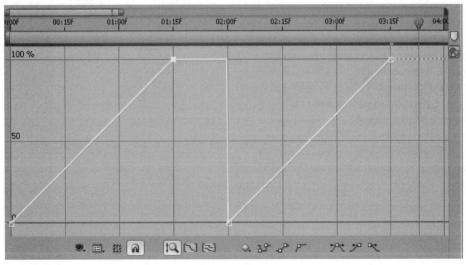

Linear

Auto-Bézier

The selected keyframes use the interpolation method you specify (**Figure 9.73**).

✔ Tips

- You can toggle a keyframe between using linear and auto Bézier interpolation by Command-clicking (Mac) or Ctrl-clicking (Windows) the keyframe.

- You can specify selected keyframes' interpolation by choosing Animation > Keyframe Interpolation in the main menu or Keyframe Interpolation in the Graph Editor's Edit Keyframe pull-down menu. In the dialog box, specify the type of interpolation you want.

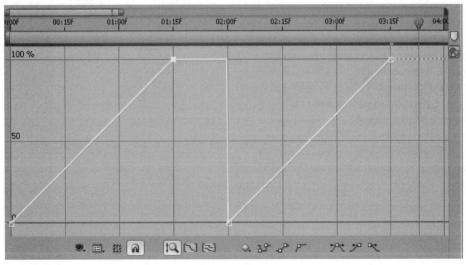

Figure 9.73 ...is converted to one that uses hold interpolation.

SETTING THE TEMPORAL INTERPOLATION TYPE

Adjusting Temporal Interpolation Manually

As you've seen, many of the principles of adjusting a motion path apply to adjusting a property graph. Both are described by Bézier curves, although the terminology can differ. And whereas a motion path traces a literal course through space, the line of a graph corresponds to a property's value or speed. But although the techniques you use to edit Bézier curves resemble one another in principle, they differ in practice. The main difference lies in how you adjust the curves manually: dragging direction lines in a value graph, or ease handles in a speed graph.

In a value graph, you can drag direction lines 180 degrees to influence the graph's curve—and, hence, its incoming and outgoing interpolation. Bézier curves closely resemble their counterparts in a motion path.

In a speed graph, ease handles influence the shape of the curve and, thereby, the interpolation. However, ease handles always extend horizontally from a keyframe; their length but not their angle helps shape the curve. Whereas a sudden change in a value plots a cusp in a value graph, a sudden change in speed splits the keyframe so that it occupies two different vertical positions on the speed graph.

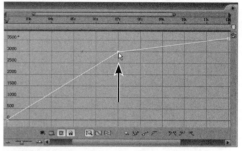

Figure 9.74 Drag a keyframe up to increase...

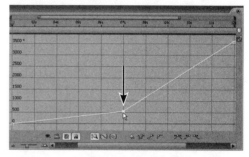

Figure 9.75 ...or down to decrease the value (shown here) or speed.

ADJUSTING MANUALLY

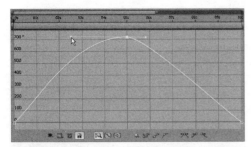

Figure 9.76 In the value graph, extend a direction line manually to use continuous Bézier interpolation.

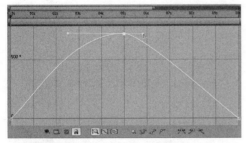

Figure 9.77 In the value graph, Option-drag (Mac) or Alt-drag (Windows) a direction handle.

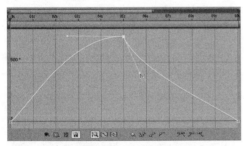

Figure 9.78 Dragging a direction handle of a continuous Bézier keyframe splits the direction handles, converting it to Bézier.

To adjust a value graph manually:

1. Expand the layer outline to view the value graph for an animated layer property.

2. Select the keyframes you want to adjust.

3. *Do any of the following* to the incoming or outgoing direction lines:

   ▲ Drag a keyframe up to increase the value or down to decrease the value (**Figures 9.74** and **9.75**).

   ▲ To convert auto Bézier to continuous Bézier, drag one direction line so that the direction lines are unequal but retain their continuous relationship (**Figure 9.76**).

   ▲ To toggle between continuous Bézier and Bézier, Option-drag (Mac) or Alt-drag (Windows) a direction handle (**Figure 9.77**).

   The Selection tool becomes the Convert Vertex tool when you position it over a direction handle. Dragging a direction handle of a Bézier keyframe converts it to continuous Bézier with two related direction handles; dragging a direction handle of a continuous Bézier keyframe splits the direction handles, converting it to Bézier (**Figure 9.78**).

✔ Tip

■ As usual, avoid converting a keyframe unintentionally: Invoke the Convert Vertex tool only when you want to convert a keyframe; otherwise, use the Selection tool.

ADJUSTING MANUALLY

To adjust a speed graph manually:

1. Expand the layer outline to view the speed graph for an animated layer property.

2. Select the keyframes you want to adjust (**Figure 9.79**).

3. *Do any of the following* to the incoming or outgoing ease handles:

   ▲ Drag an ease handle up to increase the incoming or outgoing speed at a keyframe (**Figure 9.80**).

   ▲ Drag an ease handle down to decrease the incoming or outgoing speed at a keyframe.

   ▲ Drag the left ease handle to change its length and influence on the preceding curve (**Figure 9.81**).

   ▲ Drag the right ease handle to adjust its length and influence on the following curve.

   ▲ Option-click (Mac) or Alt-click (Windows) a keyframe to toggle it between linear and auto Bézier.

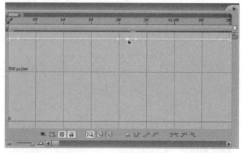

Figure 9.79 Select the keyframes you want to adjust.

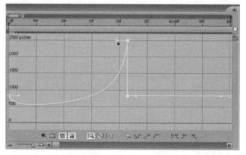

Figure 9.80 Drag an ease handle up to increase the incoming or outgoing speed at a keyframe.

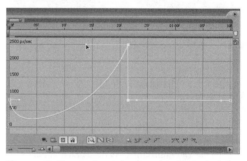

Figure 9.81 Drag an incoming ease handle to the left to increase the influence of the previous keyframe's value.

ADJUSTING MANUALLY

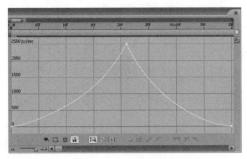

Figure 9.82 An abrupt shift from acceleration to deceleration, or bounce, looks like this in a speed graph.

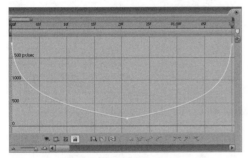

Figure 9.83 A gradual deceleration followed by a gradual acceleration (as when a rising object slows at its apex) looks like this in a speed graph.

The shape of the graph and the corresponding property's speed change according to your adjustments (**Figures 9.82** and **9.83**). When the incoming and outgoing speeds differ, a keyframe's icon splits, occupying two different vertical positions on the graph.

✔ Tip

- As usual, avoid converting a keyframe unintentionally: Invoke the Convert Vertex tool only when you want to convert a keyframe; otherwise, use the Selection tool.

Adjusting Temporal Interpolation Numerically

If neither the speed nor velocity graph provides the precision you need, you can adjust speed and velocity numerically.

To change the speed or velocity numerically:

1. In the Graph Editor, select the keyframe you want to adjust (**Figure 9.84**).

2. Click the Graph Editor's Edit Keyframe button, and choose Keyframe Velocity from the pull-down menu (**Figure 9.85**).

   A Keyframe Velocity dialog box appears, displaying the property type you're adjusting (**Figure 9.86**).

3. In the Keyframe Velocity dialog box, enter values for the incoming velocity and outgoing velocity.

   The unit of measurement used by the velocity value depends on the property.

4. In the Incoming Velocity section of the dialog box, enter a value for Influence.

   This value determines how much influence the previous keyframe's value exerts over the interpolated values. In the graph, it affects the length of the ease handle.

5. In the Outgoing Velocity section of the dialog box, enter a value for Influence.

   This value determines how much influence the next keyframe's value exerts over the interpolated values.

   To automatically maintain equal values for Incoming Velocity and Outgoing Velocity, select Continuous.

6. Click OK to close the Keyframe Velocity dialog box.

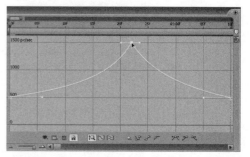

Figure 9.84 Select the keyframe you want to adjust.

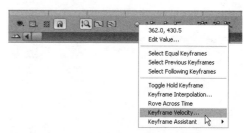

Figure 9.85 Click the Graph Editor's Edit Keyframe button, and choose Keyframe Velocity from the pull-down menu.

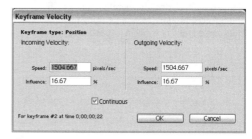

Figure 9.86 A Keyframe Velocity dialog box appears.

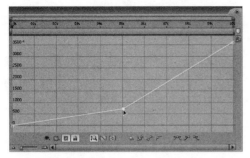

Figure 9.87 Select the keyframes you want to ease with a keyframe assistant. This keyframe uses linear interpolation.

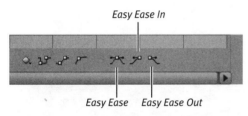

Easy Ease In

Easy Ease   *Easy Ease Out*

Figure 9.88 In the Graph Editor, select the icon that corresponds to the keyframe assistant you want to apply.

Applying Keyframe Assistants

Adding slight deceleration to soften or ease the speed into and out of keyframes is such a commonly used technique that After Effects has provided the following *keyframe assistants* to automate the task:

Easy Ease smoothes both the keyframe's incoming and outgoing interpolation.

Easy Ease In smoothes the keyframe's incoming interpolation.

Easy Ease Out smoothes the keyframe's outgoing interpolation.

Try employing a keyframe assistant and observing its effects on a layer's property graph and animation.

To apply a keyframe assistant in the Graph Editor:

1. In the Graph Editor, select the keyframes to which you want to apply a keyframe assistant (**Figure 9.87**).

2. At the bottom of the Graph Editor, click the icon that corresponds to the keyframe assistant you want to use (**Figure 9.88**):

   Easy Ease 🔧 to ease both incoming and outgoing speed

   Easy Ease In 🔧 to ease incoming speed

   Easy Ease Out 🔧 to ease outgoing speed

continues on next page

APPLYING KEYFRAME ASSISTANTS

The icons and graphs associated with the selected keyframes reflect your choice, and the animation plays accordingly (**Figure 9.89**).

✔ Tip

■ After Effects Pro includes additional keyframe assistants that automate other commonly used and time-consuming keyframing tasks. For example, the Exponential Scale keyframe assistant keyframes a layer's scale property using a method that simulates the layer approaching or receding in three-dimensional space.

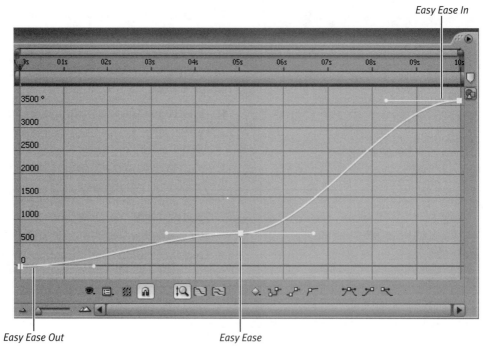

Easy Ease In

Easy Ease Out

Easy Ease

Figure 9.89 The selected keyframe's interpolation is adjusted according to your choice. The linear interpolation pictured in Figure 9.87 looks like this after you apply keyframe assistants.

Smoothing Motion with Roving Keyframes

Frequently, adjusting a motion path causes drastic and unwanted fluctuations in timing. The layer goes where you want in terms of space, but its movement lags and lurches from one keyframe to the next. In the speed graph, these abrupt changes look like steep hills and chasms. You can adjust the speed and timing of the problem keyframes manually, or you can convert them into *roving keyframes*.

Roving keyframes retain their values; but their position in time is adjusted automatically so that the property's speed becomes more consistent, and the property's speed graph flattens out. The adjustments are derived from the values of the standard, time-bound keyframes before and after the roving keyframes. Moving the first or last keyframe automatically readjusts the roving keyframes in between. This way, you can change the duration of the animation without having to carefully adjust the speed between each part.

If you don't want a keyframe to rove, then you can convert it back to a standard keyframe, which is *locked to time*.

To smooth motion with roving keyframes:

1. Reveal a property's speed graph in the Graph Editor.

2. Select a range of keyframes other than the first or last keyframe for the property (**Figure 9.90**).

    The keyframes preceding and after the range must be locked to time. That is, they must be standard, nonroving keyframes.

3. In the Graph Editor, click the Edit Keyframe button, and then choose Rove Across Time from the pull-down menu (**Figure 9.91**).

continues on next page

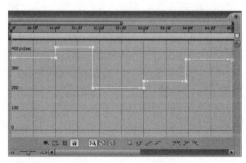

Figure 9.90 Select a range of keyframes between two keyframes. This uneven speed graph indicates sudden changes in speed between keyframed positions.

Figure 9.91 Selecting Rove Across Time in the Graph Editor's Edit Keyframe pull-down menu...

The selected keyframes become roving keyframes, moving in time so that the speed is constant (as evidenced by the speed graph). The roving keyframe icons appear as small dots (**Figure 9.92**).

To convert a roving keyframe to a standard keyframe:

1. Reveal a property's speed graph in the Graph Editor, and select one or more of its roving keyframes (**Figure 9.93**).

2. Click the Graph Editor's Edit Keyframe button, and deselect Rove Across Time in the pull-down menu (**Figure 9.94**).

   The keyframe is converted from a roving keyframe to a standard keyframe that is locked to time. Its keyframe icon changes from a small dot to its standard icon (a small box in the Graph Editor, or a diamond icon in the standard view of the time ruler).

✔ Tip

- You don't have to view Graph Editor to toggle between standard and roving keyframes. After selecting keyframes in the standard view of the time ruler, choose Animation > Keyframe Interpolation, and then specify whether the keyframes Rove Across Time or are Locked to Time.

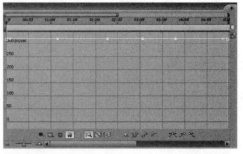

Figure 9.92 ...converts the selected keyframes to roving keyframes, which shift in time to create constant speed between the standard keyframes. Contrast this speed graph with the one in Figure 9.90.

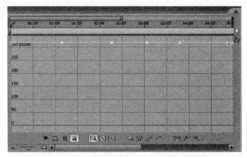

Figure 9.93 Reveal the speed graph of a property, and select one or more of its roving keyframes...

Figure 9.94 ...and deselect Rove Across Time to convert the selection to standard keyframes, which are locked to time.

MASK ESSENTIALS

A *mask* is a shape, or path, that you create in a layer. You can draw a mask manually with a tool, define it numerically using the Mask Shape dialog box, or copy it from Adobe Illustrator or Photoshop. A mask can be a closed shape (such as a circle) or an open path (such as a curved line). Masks are essential to compositing images and to creating a number of other effects. As the name suggests, the most common use for a mask is to mask, or preserve, parts of a layer's image while cropping out the rest. A closed mask modifies a layer's *alpha channel*—which, as you recall, defines the opaque and transparent areas of an image. Even if a footage item lacks an alpha channel of its own, you can define areas of transparency using masks. The image within the masked area remains visible; the area outside the mask reveals the layers below.

Whereas a closed mask defines a shape, an *open* mask creates a curve or path. By itself, an open mask can't modify a layer's transparency. However, you can use it in conjunction with other techniques to achieve a variety of effects. For example, you can use the Stroke effect to trace a mask with a color or to mask the area around the curve. Or, you can paste a mask path into the Comp panel to use it as a motion path. A mask can also define a curved baseline for path text. You can apply these techniques to both open and closed masks, but you can see how an open mask is sometimes the more appropriate choice.

This chapter is devoted to creating and modifying masks; you can apply what you learn in other chapters to animate mask properties, apply effects to masks, and combine masks with other techniques, such as layer modes. As you'll see, you can define masks with Bézier curves, the same type of curve that defines motion paths in After Effects or shapes in other graphics programs; just don't let minor inconsistencies between terms and techniques distract you. If you've already mastered Bézier curves, you can move on to creating masks using the easy-to-use RotoBezier option.

Viewing Masks in the Layer and Comp Panels

Although you mask a layer, you can create and work with masks not only in the Layer panel but in the Composition panel as well. The panel you use will depend on the task at hand as well as your personal preference. A Layer panel shows masks in the context of a single layer, letting you view the image outside the masked areas (**Figure 10.1**). In addition, the Layer panel shows you the layer before any property changes (scale, rotation, and so on) are applied. In contrast, the Composition panel shows only the masked portions of a layer and places them in the context of all the layers that are visible at the current time (**Figure 10.2**). By the time you're able to view a layer in the Comp panel, Mask, Effect, Transform, and 3D properties have all been applied.

When you want to create or modify a mask in the Comp panel, you must select the layer that contains the mask. Tasks throughout this chapter assume you have done so.

Figure 10.1 The Layer panel shows masks in the context of the layer; it also lets you see the image outside the mask.

Figure 10.2 The Comp panel shows the layer after masks and other property changes have taken effect.

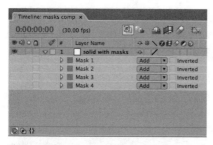

Figure 10.3 Masks appear in the layer outline in the order they were created. Expanding a mask reveals several properties: Shape, Feather, Opacity, and Expansion.

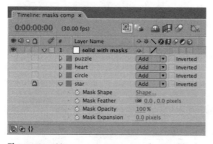

Figure 10.4 You can rename, reorder, and lock masks just like layers. Here, the default names have been replaced with more descriptive names, and the "star" mask has been locked.

Figure 10.5 The Layer > Mask menu contains commands for applying motion blur and for hiding locked masks (shown here).

Viewing Masks in the Layer Outline

Each mask you create appears in the layer outline of the Timeline panel under the Mask property heading. The Target pull-down menu of the Layer panel also lists the layer's masks. The most recent mask appears at the top of the stacking order (**Figure 10.3**).

When you expand the Mask property heading, it reveals four properties: Mask Shape, Mask Feather, Mask Opacity, and Mask Expansion. The following sections deal with these properties as well as other ways to control layer masks.

Because you can rename, reorder, and lock masks just like layers, that information won't be covered here (**Figure 10.4**). (See Chapter 5 to learn the analogous procedures for layers).

You can also hide and apply motion blur to masks much as you can with a layer as a whole. But instead of clicking a button in the Timeline panel, you access these commands in the Layer > Mask menu (**Figure 10.5**). For example, masks don't have a video switch, but you can hide locked masks via the Layer > Mask > Hide Locked Masks command. Again, these commands won't be covered in detail here.

✔ Tip

- Although locked and hidden masks are invisible in the Layer panel, their masking effect can still be seen in the Comp panel's image.

Hiding and Showing Mask Paths

Because the Layer and Comp panels serve several purposes, sometimes you'll want to hide the mask paths from view. When you want to work with the layer masks, you can make them visible again. Creating a new mask reveals the masks for the selected layer automatically.

To view and hide masks in the Layer panel:

1. View a layer in a Layer panel.

2. In the Layer panel's View pull-down menu, select Masks to make mask paths visible (**Figure 10.6**).

   Selecting another option deselects the Masks option.

To view and hide masks in the Composition panel:

◆ In the Comp panel, click the View Masks button (**Figure 10.7**).

   Mask paths for selected layers can be viewed and edited in the Composition panel (**Figure 10.8**). Deselect the View Masks button to hide mask paths.

✔ Tips

■ You can hide locked masks only by choosing Layer > Mask > Hide Locked Masks. Although invisible in the Layer panel, locked and hidden masks still function in the Comp panel.

■ By default, mask paths appear yellow. By double-clicking a mask's color swatch in the timeline, you can assign a unique color to help distinguish one mask from another.

■ You can even have After Effects assign each subsequent mask a different color automatically by selecting the Cycle Mask Colors option in the User Interface Colors pane of the Preferences dialog box.

Figure 10.6 In the Layer panel's View pull-down menu, select Masks to make mask paths visible.

Figure 10.7 In the Comp panel, click the View Masks button...

Figure 10.8 ...to reveal layer masks.

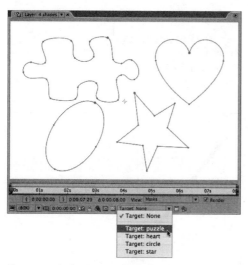

Figure 10.9 In the Target menu, choose a layer you want to select, or target, for changes.

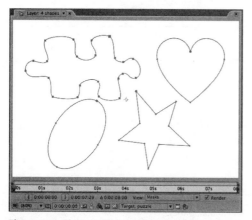

Figure 10.10 The targeted mask appears selected. If you create a new mask shape, it replaces the targeted mask.

Targeting Masks

With After Effects, you can create as many as 127 masks for each layer. The Target pull-down menu at the bottom of the Layer panel provides one way to select the mask you want to use. Note that the Target pull-down menu appears only when the layer contains one or more masks.

To choose the target mask:

1. View a layer containing one or more masks in a Layer panel.

2. At the bottom of the Layer panel, choose a mask from the Target pull-down menu (**Figure 10.9**):

   ▲ Choose None to create a new mask without changing an existing mask.

   ▲ Choose the name of an existing mask to target that mask for changes.

   The mask you choose appears selected (**Figure 10.10**).

✔ Tip

■ Don't forget: To create an additional mask in the same Layer panel, make sure the Target pull-down menu is set to None. Otherwise, the new mask *replaces* the target mask.

Comparing Mask Creation Methods

The Tools panel contains several tools for creating and modifying masks (**Figure 10.11**). (These tools aren't as extensive as those found in Illustrator, but you wouldn't expect them to be—Illustrator is dedicated to such tasks.)

Rectangular Mask ▭—Creates squares and rectangles (**Figure 10.12**)

Elliptical Mask ⬭—Creates closed elliptical and circular shapes (**Figure 10.13**)

Pen ✎—Creates open or closed Bézier curves or RotoBezier curves (**Figure 10.14**)

Shape tools   Pen tools

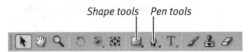

Figure 10.11 The Tools panel contains several tools to create and manipulate mask paths.

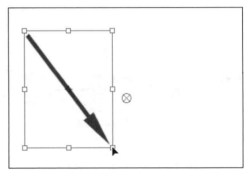

Figure 10.12 The Rectangular Mask tool creates rectangular or square mask paths.

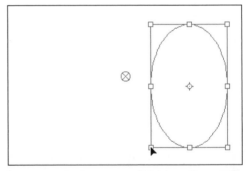

Figure 10.13 The Elliptical Mask tool creates elliptical, or circular, paths.

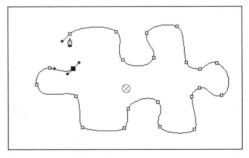

Figure 10.14 The Pen tool creates more complex paths using Bézier curves or RotoBezier curves.

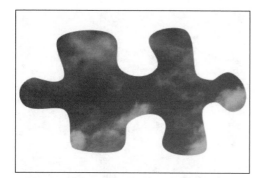

Figure 10.15 A closed path creates a typical mask, which defines the opaque areas of the layer image.

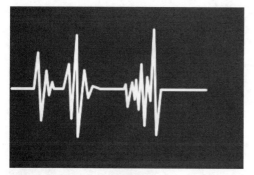

Figure 10.16 An open path doesn't create a mask per se, but it can be used for other effects, such as creating stroked lines. Open paths can also be used to create motion paths.

Comparing Closed and Open Paths

As mentioned in the introduction to this chapter, masks can be closed shapes or open paths:

Closed paths—You can draw closed paths with any of the drawing tools (**Figure 10.15**). By default, the interior of a closed mask shape defines the opaque area of a layer; the exterior defines transparency. However, you can manipulate the transparency in a number of ways (explained in later sections).

Open paths—You can create open paths with the Pen tool 🖊, or you can open a closed path by using a menu command. Open paths aren't useful as masks per se, but they can serve as the basis for path text and path-based effects (**Figure 10.16**). For example, they can be stroked to create graphical objects (such as drawn text) or pasted into a motion path.

✔ Tip

- Path text and the Stroke effect are just a couple of examples of how masks are used as part of more complex techniques. A number of effects utilize masks, including particle, distortion, and morphing effects.

Understanding Mask Anatomy

It can be useful to describe the contour of a mask as a *path*. All mask paths consist of *control points* connected by *segments*. In a straight-sided polygon, control points define the vertices; in a curved shape, however, they determine the curve of adjacent segments. You can control the curve manually by creating a standard mask that uses a *Bézier* curve (**Figure 10.17**). (Many path-based drawing programs, such as Illustrator, also employ Bézier curves.) Alternatively, you can let After Effects calculate curves automatically, creating a *RotoBezier* mask (**Figure 10.18**).

Figure 10.17 A standard mask uses Bézier curves that define curves with direction lines you set manually.

Standard masks and Bézier curves

In a Bézier curve, you can think of a path as a line that exits one control point and enters another; the route the line takes depends on whether either point has a *direction line*. Control points define each end of a segment; direction lines define the curve of the segment.

Direction lines and handles extend from control points to define and control the curve of a path segment. The length and angle of a direction line influence the shape of a curve. (To picture this, imagine that direction lines exert a gravitational pull on the line that enters and exits a control point.) Dragging the dot, or *handle,* at the end of a direction line alters the line and thus its corresponding curve. When a point has two direction lines, the *incoming* direction line influences the preceding curve; the *outgoing* direction line influences the curve that follows.

Figure 10.18 In contrast, a RotoBezier mask lacks direction lines and calculates the curves automatically.

It's helpful to categorize the following control points by how they use, or don't use, direction lines (**Figure 10.19**):

Anchor point—Click with the Pen tool to create an anchor point. Anchor points have no control handles extending from them.

Smooth point—Drag with the Pen tool to create a smooth point. Dragging extends two equal and opposite direction lines from a smooth point. Path segments connected by a smooth point result in a continuous curve.

Corner point—A corner point's direction lines operate independently. You can convert a smooth point into a corner by dragging a direction handle with the Convert Vertex tool ⌐. Path segments connected by a corner point result in a discontinuous curve, or *cusp*.

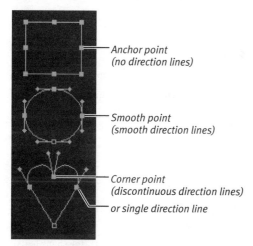

Anchor point
(no direction lines)

Smooth point
(smooth direction lines)

Corner point
(discontinuous direction lines)
or single direction line

Figure 10.19 Mask paths consist of control points connected by segments.

RotoBezier masks

The Pen tool's RotoBezier option lets you define a mask with curved segments without defining direction lines. Instead, you set only the control points; After Effects calculates the curved segments automatically. Without custom direction lines, you can't fully control the character of each curve; however, you can adjust each control point's *tension* to change the relative amount of curve in its adjacent segments.

Choosing a mask type

Although you can create RotoBezier masks more quickly than standard Bézier masks, they tend to require more control points. In addition, it's more difficult to create discontinuous curves (cusps) using a RotoBezier. Fortunately, you don't have to choose one method to the exclusion of the other: You can convert a RotoBezier mask to a standard mask and vice versa.

The following sections cover standard masks and Bézier curves first, then RotoBezier masks. Apart from adjusting their curves, you can edit both standard masks and RotoBezier masks in similar ways. Sections dealing with manipulating control points (such as selecting, moving, adding, and deleting them) and adjusting mask properties (such as inverting, feathering, and using mask modes) apply to both Bézier and RotoBezier masks.

✔ Tip

■ Bézier curves are also used to control the spatial and temporal interpolation of animations; for more on this, see Chapter 9, "Keyframe Interpolation."

Creating Simple Mask Shapes

You can create simple mask shapes quickly with the Rectangle and Ellipse tools. On the other hand, a simple rectangle or ellipse can serve as the starting point of a more complex shape. As you'll see in later sections, you can easily alter any mask's shape. In addition, you can effectively combine masks using mask modes.

To draw a rectangular or elliptical mask:

1. View the layer you want to mask in a Layer panel, or select it in the Composition panel.

2. In the Tools panel, select the Rectangular Mask tool ▣ or Elliptical Mask tool ◉ (**Figure 10.20**).

3. In the Layer or Comp panel, *do any combination of the following*:
   - ▲ Drag from one corner of the mask shape to the opposite corner to create the mask (**Figure 10.21**).

- ▲ Shift-drag to constrain the shape to equal proportions if you want to create a square or circle (**Figure 10.22**).

- ▲ Command-drag (Mac) or Ctrl-drag (Windows) to create a mask shape that extends from the center rather than the corner (**Figure 10.23**).

- ▲ Option-drag (Mac) or Alt-drag (Windows) to view the effects of the mask in the Composition panel as you drag.

4. Release the mouse when you've finished creating the mask.

   In the Layer and Comp panels, the mask appears as a path with selected control points (as long as you set the window to display masks; see "Hiding and Showing Mask Paths," earlier in this chapter). In the Composition panel, the areas of the layer outside the mask are concealed, whereas the areas inside the mask are visible.

✔ Tip

- ■ To create a mask that fills the layer, double-click the Rectangular Mask tool or Elliptical Mask tool.

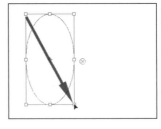

Figure 10.21 In the Layer or Comp panel, drag to define the shape from one corner of the shape to its opposite corner.

Figure 10.20 In the Tools panel, choose the Rectangular Mask or Elliptical Mask tool.

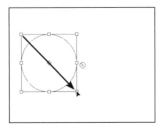

Figure 10.22 Shift-drag to constrain the shape to equal proportions so that you can create a square or circle.

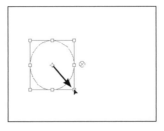

Figure 10.23 Command-drag (Mac) or Ctrl-drag (Windows) to create a mask shape that extends from the center instead of the corner.

Table 10.1

Keyboard Modifiers for Mask Paths	
TO DO THIS	PRESS THIS
Constrain new segment to 45 degrees	Shift
Temporarily switch to the Convert Vertex tool	Option (Mac) or Alt (Windows)
Temporarily switch to the Selection tool	Command (Mac) or Ctrl (Windows)

Figure 10.24 In the Tools panel, select the Pen tool.

Figure 10.25 Click to create an anchor point with no direction lines.

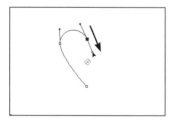

Figure 10.26 Click and drag to create a smooth point with two continuous direction lines.

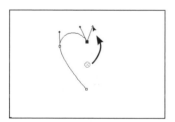

Figure 10.27 Drag a direction handle to break the relationship between the two handles, converting the point into a corner point.

Building a Standard Mask with the Pen

The following steps explain how to create a path using the Pen tool and Bézier curves. You'll probably want to start by creating simple straight segments. Then, as you become comfortable, you can try using smooth points to create curves and then corner points to create even more complex shapes. Once you're fluent in using the keyboard modifiers listed in **Table 10.1**, you've mastered making mask paths.

In later sections, you'll use the RotoBezier option to create curved segments without using direction lines.

To build a path:

1. *Do either of the following:*
   - ▲ Open a Layer panel for the layer for which you want to create a mask.
   - ▲ Select a layer in the Composition panel.

2. In the Tools panel, select the Pen tool 🖊 (**Figure 10.24**).

3. In the Layer or Comp panel, *do one of the following:*
   - ▲ To create an anchor point, click (**Figure 10.25**).
   - ▲ To create a smooth point, drag (**Figure 10.26**).
   - ▲ To create a corner point, drag to create a smooth point, select one of the smooth point's direction handles, and then drag again (**Figure 10.27**).

continues on next page

BUILDING A STANDARD MASK WITH THE PEN

4. Repeat step 3 to create straight and curved segments between points.

Don't click an existing segment unless you want to add a control point to the path. Don't click an existing direction handle unless you want to convert it.

5. To leave the path open, stop clicking in the Layer panel (**Figure 10.28**).

6. To close the path, *do one of the following*:

▲ Double-click in the Layer panel to create the final control point and connect it to the first control point.

▲ Position the Pen tool over the first control point until a circle icon appears, and then click (**Figure 10.29**).

▲ Choose Layer > Mask > Closed.

If the first control point is smooth, the path is closed with a smooth point.

When you are finished, remember to choose the Selection tool, which is required for most other tasks.

✔ Tips

■ In most cases, you'll achieve the smoothest-looking curve if you make each direction line about one-third the length of the curve it influences.

■ Typically, using the minimum possible number of control points results in a curve that's both smoother and easier to control.

■ Combining several simple masks can be faster and more effective than drawing a single complex path. Similarly, you can start with a simple shape and then modify it using techniques explained in the section "Changing the Shape of a Mask," later in this chapter.

■ The Pen tool changes into the Add Vertex tool 🖊₊ when positioned over a path; it changes into the Convert Vertex tool ⌐ when positioned over a direction handle.

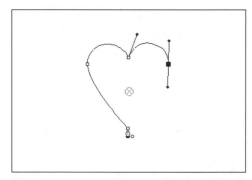

Figure 10.28 Continue clicking to create control points that define straight and curved segments. You can leave the path open, or position the tool over the first point so that a circle icon appears next to the Pen tool...

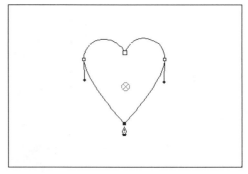

Figure 10.29 ...and click to close the path.

Figure 10.30 Select the Pen tool, and select the RotoBezier option.

Figure 10.31 Click to create control points. After Effects calculates the curved segments automatically.

Creating a RotoBezier Mask

Even if you're a master of Bézier curves, you can often create a mask more quickly and easily using a *RotoBezier mask*. The Pen tool's RotoBezier option lets you define a curved path by clicking to create control points; After Effects calculates curved segments automatically. You avoid using direction lines, which can take time to adjust properly.

To create a RotoBezier mask:

1. In the Tools panel, select the Pen tool.

   The RotoBezier option appears in the Tools panel.

2. In the Tools panel, select the RotoBezier option (**Figure 10.30**).

   Deselect the option to create standard masks with the Pen tool.

3. Cue the current time to the frame you want to use to create the mask, and *do either of the following*:

   ▲ Open the layer to which you want to apply a RotoBezier mask in a Layer panel.

   ▲ Select a layer, and view it in the Composition panel.

4. In the Layer or Composition panel, click with the Pen tool to create the vertices of the mask shape.

   After Effects calculates curved segments between the control points automatically.

5. Repeat step 4 to create additional control points connected by curved segments (**Figure 10.31**).

   Don't click an existing segment unless you want to add a control point to the path.

continues on next page

CREATING A ROTOBEZIER MASK

6. To close the path, *do one of the following*:

▲ Double-click in the Layer panel to create the final control point and connect it to the first control point (**Figure 10.32**).

▲ Position the Pen tool over the first control point until a circle icon appears ✎₀, and then click.

▲ Choose Layer > Mask > Closed.

The mask path closes (**Figure 10.33**).

7. To leave the path open, stop clicking in the Layer panel.

You may want to choose a new tool, such as the Selection tool.

Figure 10.32 Position the Pen tool over the first control point so that a small circle appears next to the tool...

Figure 10.33 ...and click to close the shape. Otherwise, you can leave the mask open and choose another tool.

Figure 10.34 Select the mask you want to convert.

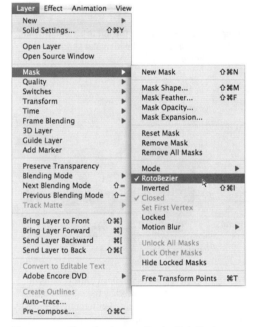

Figure 10.35 Choosing Layer > Mask > RotoBezier converts the selected mask to another type.

Converting Masks

As you've seen, each type of mask has its advantages: A standard mask offers a relatively high degree of control over curved segments, whereas a RotoBezier mask is relatively easy to create. (Or, looking at it another way, creating a Bézier curve can be more time-consuming, and your control over a RotoBezier is more crude.)

You can leverage the advantages of each method—or change your mind about your initial choice—by converting one type of mask into the other. However, the conversion isn't perfect. Converting RotoBezier to Bézier curves can result in changes, because After Effects recalculates curved segments created from manually defined direction lines. And although the reverse process tends to maintain the mask's shape, a slight change may be apparent.

To convert a RotoBezier mask to a standard mask, and vice versa:

1. Select a mask by *doing any of the following*:

   ▲ Select the mask's name in the Layer panel's Target pull-down menu.

   ▲ Click the mask's name in the Timeline panel's layer outline (**Figure 10.34**).

   ▲ Using the Selection tool, select one or more of the mask's control points in the Layer or Comp panel.

   For more details, see the section "Selecting Masks and Points," later in this chapter.

2. Choose Layer > Mask > RotoBezier (**Figure 10.35**).

   Selecting the option converts a standard mask to a RotoBezier mask; deselecting the option converts a RotoBezier to a standard mask. The mask shape may change slightly.

CONVERTING MASKS

345

Changing the Shape of a Mask

You can modify the shape of a mask at any time. The following sections explain how to move, add, and delete control points, as well as how to change the gesture of curves.

The way curves adjust to changes depends on whether you're using a standard mask with Bézier curves or a RotoBezier mask. As you learned in the section "Understanding Mask Anatomy," Bézier curves use direction lines you specify manually, whereas RotoBezier curves are calculated automatically. Each mask type's characteristic behavior continues to operate when you edit it.

For example, when you move or delete a keyframe in a standard mask, other aspects of the control points you specified—the length and angle of their direction lines—remain unchanged. RotoBezier paths, on the other hand, are recalculated when you move the point. Therefore, if you move corresponding points on identical standard and RotoBezier masks the same distance and direction, the new mask shapes will differ slightly (**Figures 10.36** and **10.37**). Bear this difference in mind as you perform the tasks in the following sections.

Later sections cover techniques that affect the entire mask (such as using the Free Transform command), mask properties (mask feather, opacity, and expansion), and mask modes. These tasks don't vary according to the type of mask, and the results are identical.

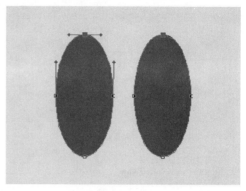

Figure 10.36 The shape on the left is a standard mask that uses Bézier curves; the identical shape on the right is a RotoBezier mask.

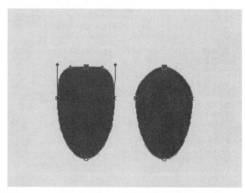

Figure 10.37 Here, corresponding control points in both masks have been moved by the same amount. Because the curves are defined differently, the masks have slightly different shapes.

Selecting Masks and Points

To alter all or part of a mask, you must first select its control points—usually accomplished via (what else?) the Selection tool. (Sorry, Illustrator users; you won't find a Direct Selection tool.) Select one or more control points to change the shape of a mask. Select all the points to move the mask. You can use the same methods to select masks and control points in both standard and RotoBezier masks. As usual, selected control points appear as solid dots; deselected control points appear as hollow dots.

To move, scale, or rotate the entire mask, use the transform technique described in the section "Scaling and Rotating Masks," later in this chapter.

Figure 10.38 In the Tools panel, choose the Selection tool.

Figure 10.39
To select several control points simultaneously, you can drag a marquee around them.

Figure 10.40
Selected points appear as solid squares; deselected points appear as hollow squares.

To select masks or points in a Layer or Comp panel:

1. In the Tools panel, choose the Selection tool (if you haven't done so already) (**Figure 10.38**).

2. Make sure the Layer or Comp panel is set to show masks.

   See the sections on viewing masks, earlier in this chapter.

3. To select mask points in the Comp panel, select the layer containing the mask.

4. To select mask points in either the Layer panel or the Comp panel, *do any of the following*:

   ▲ To select a control point, click the control point on a mask.

   ▲ To add to or subtract from your selection, press Shift as you click or drag a marquee around control points.

   ▲ To select points at both ends of a segment, click the segment.

   ▲ To select an entire mask with the mouse, Option-click (Mac) or Alt-click (Windows) the mask.

5. To select mask points in the Layer panel only, *do any of the following*:

   ▲ To select any or all control points, drag a marquee around the points you want to select (**Figure 10.39**).

   ▲ To select all mask points, press Command-A (Mac) or Ctrl-A (Windows).

   ▲ To select an entire mask by name, choose the mask from the Target pulldown menu in the Layer panel.

   In the Layer or Comp panel, selected control points appear solid; other control points appear as hollow outlines (**Figure 10.40**). Segments associated with the selected points also display direction lines. When no control points of a mask are selected, only the path is visible in the Layer or Comp panel.

To select masks in the Timeline panel:

1. In the Timeline panel, select the layer that includes the mask you want to select.

2. Press M to reveal that layer's masks (**Figure 10.41**).

   The masks and the Mask Shape property appear in the expanded layer outline. If the layer doesn't contain any masks, the outline doesn't expand.

3. To select masks for the layer, *do any of the following*:

   ▲ To select a single mask, click its name in the layer outline (**Figure 10.42**).

   ▲ To select a range of masks, click the name of the first mask in the range and Shift-click the name of the last mask in the range (**Figure 10.43**).

   ▲ To select multiple discontiguous masks, Command-click (Mac) or Ctrl-click (Windows) the names of the masks you want to select (**Figure 10.44**).

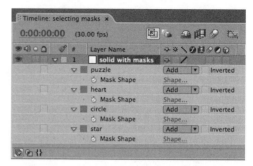

Figure 10.41 In the Timeline panel, select a layer containing a mask, and press M to display its mask property in the layer outline.

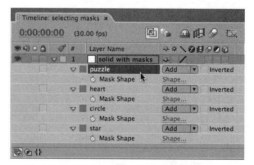

Figure 10.42 Click a mask name to select it.

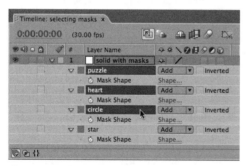

Figure 10.43 Shift-click another mask to select a range of masks...

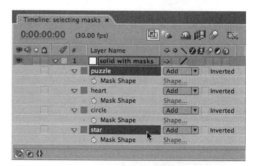

Figure 10.44 ...or Command-click (Mac) or Ctrl-click (Windows) to select several discontiguous masks.

Moving and Deleting Control Points

You can move any combination of a mask's control points by using the mouse or by nudging them with the arrow keys. Just as when you nudge an entire layer, the precision of the arrow keys depends on the window's current magnification setting. For example, the arrow key nudges the selected points 1 pixel when the magnification is set to 100 percent; 2 pixels when set to 50 percent; and .5 pixels when set to 200 percent. (See Chapter 7, "Properties and Keyframes," for more about nudging and subpixel positioning.) You can also remove selected keyframes.

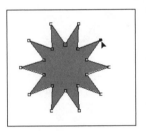

Figure 10.45
Select the points you want to move.

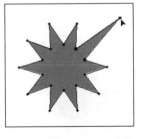

Figure 10.46
Drag the selected points to a new position, or nudge them with the arrow keys.

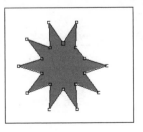

Figure 10.47
Press Delete to remove selected control points; line segments will connect the remaining points.

To move an entire mask (or perform other transformations), you can use the free transform technique described in the next section, "Scaling and Rotating Masks," later in this chapter. You can also delete points using a variation of the Pen tool (see the next section "Adding and Deleting Control Points with the Pen Tool").

To move a mask or its control points:

1. In the Layer panel, select the points of the mask you want to move (**Figure 10.45**).

2. To move the selected points, *do any of the following*:

   ▲ With the Selection tool, drag a selected control point (**Figure 10.46**).

   Don't drag the path segment between control points; doing so will change the curve of the segment.

   ▲ Press the arrow keys to nudge the selected control points at the current magnification of the Layer panel.

   ▲ Hold Shift as you press an arrow key to increase the nudge distance by a factor of 10.

   If all points are selected, the entire mask moves. Otherwise, only selected points move, and line segments reshape to accommodate their new positions.

To delete selected control points:

1. In the Layer or Comp panel, select the mask control points you want to remove.

2. *Do either of the following:*

   ▲ Press Delete.

   ▲ Choose Edit > Clear.

   The selected control points disappear, and the line segments reshape to connect the remaining points (**Figure 10.47**). In a Bézier curve, the direction lines of the remaining points remain unchanged; in a RotoBezier curve, the path is recalculated.

Adding and Deleting Control Points with the Pen Tool

By default, the Tools panel displays the Pen tool. Clicking and holding the tool extends the panel to reveal additional tools: the Add Vertex tool, the Delete Vertex tool, and the Convert Vertex tool. (**Figure 10.48**). Obviously, you can use these tools to add, delete, and convert points on an existing mask path.

Adding and deleting points can yield slightly different results, depending on whether you're editing a Bézier or RotoBezier mask. For a more detailed explanation, turn back to the sections "Understanding Mask Anatomy" and "Changing the Shape of a Mask."

To add a control point:

1. In the Tools panel, choose the Pen tool or the Add Vertex tool.

2. Position the tool on a mask path between existing control points.

   If you're using the Pen tool, it automatically becomes an Add Vertex tool when it's positioned over a segment (**Figure 10.49**). Be careful not to position the Pen tool over a control point inadvertently; if you do, it changes into a Delete Vertex tool.

3. *Do one of the following:*

   ▲ To add a control point without changing the existing path, click the segment.

   A new control point appears in the mask path (**Figure 10.50**). In a standard mask, any direction lines are set to preserve the existing curve; in a RotoBezier mask, the curve is calculated automatically.

Figure 10.48 Clicking the Pen tool in the Tools panel reveals the Add Vertex, Delete Vertex, and Convert Vertex tools.

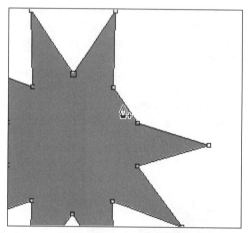

Figure 10.49 Position the Add Vertex tool over a segment...

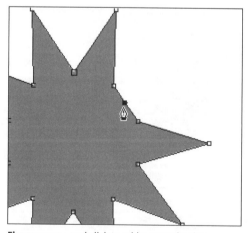

Figure 10.50 ...and click to add a control point.

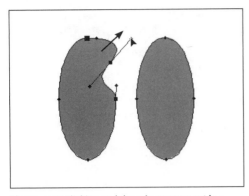

Figure 10.51 Clicking and dragging a segment in a standard path adds a smooth point and extends direction lines.

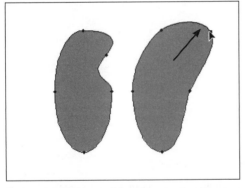

Figure 10.52 Clicking and dragging a segment in a RotoBezier path adds a control point and moves it to where you drag.

▲ To add a control point and change the curve simultaneously, click and drag the segment.

In a standard mask, dragging extends direction lines from the new point (which remains where you clicked), altering the curve of the adjacent segments (**Figure 10.51**). In a RotoBezier mask, dragging moves the new point, and the path is recalculated automatically (**Figure 10.52**).

To remove a control point:

1. In the Tools panel, choose the Delete Vertex tool 🖊.

2. Position the Delete Vertex tool over a control point (**Figure 10.53**).

3. Click the control point to remove it (**Figure 10.54**).

   The selected control points disappear, and the line segments reshape to connect the remaining points. In a Bézier curve, the direction lines of the remaining points remain unchanged; in a Roto-Bezier curve, the path is recalculated.

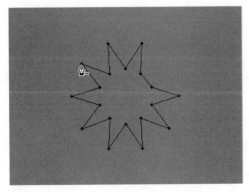

Figure 10.53 Position the Delete Vertex tool over a control point...

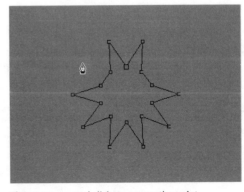

Figure 10.54 ...and click to remove the point.

ADDING AND DELETING CONTROL POINTS

Converting Control Points in a Standard Mask

When you create a standard mask using the Pen tool, you can create any combination of control points: anchor (with no direction lines), smooth (equal and opposite direction lines), or corner (discontinuous direction lines). You can change one type of control point into another using the Convert Vertex tool.

The Convert Vertex tool serves a similar, but more limited, purpose for RotoBezier masks. See the section "Adjusting RotoBezier Mask Tension," later in this chapter.

To convert a smooth point to an anchor point, and vice versa:

1. In the Tools panel, choose the Convert Vertex tool 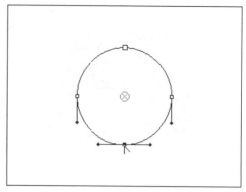.

Figure 10.55 Position the Convert Vertex tool on a control point...

2. Click the control point (**Figure 10.55**).

   A smooth point becomes an anchor point with no direction lines; an anchor point becomes a smooth point with two equal direction lines (**Figure 10.56**).

✔ Tips

■ To convert all points in a path simultaneously, select all the points before you click one with the Convert Vertex tool.

■ When converting to a smooth point, you can click and drag the point to set the length and angle of the direction lines manually in a single step.

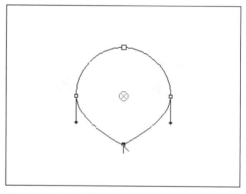

Figure 10.56 ...and click to convert a smooth point into a control point with no direction lines and vice versa.

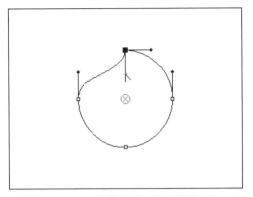

Figure 10.57 Drag a direction handle with the Convert Vertex tool to break the relationship with the opposite handle and create a corner point.

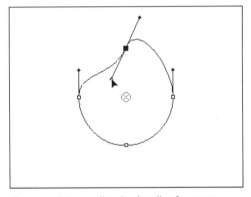

Figure 10.58 Drag a direction handle of a corner point to convert it back into a smooth point with continuous direction handles.

To convert a smooth point to a corner point and vice versa:

1. In the Layer or Comp panel, select one or more smooth points or corner points in a mask path.

   The direction lines of selected points become visible.

2. In the Tools panel, choose the Convert Vertex tool.

3. In the mask path, position the tool on an existing direction handle.

4. Drag the direction line's handle to a new position (**Figure 10.57**).

   A smooth point converts to a corner point, and the direction line moves independently. A corner point converts to a smooth point, and both of its direction lines move together (**Figure 10.58**).

✔ Tips

- You can convert the Pen tool to the Convert Vertex tool by pressing and holding Command (Mac) or Ctrl (Windows); press Command-Opt (Mac) or Ctrl-Alt (Windows) to change the Selection tool to the Convert Vertex tool.

- To remove one direction line from a corner point, drag the direction handle into the point.

- Once you have the kind of control point you want, modify it only with the Selection tool. This way, you can move the point or its direction handle without converting it.

To adjust a Bézier curve:

◆ Using the Selection tool, *do either of the following*:

 ▲ Drag a direction handle for a selected control point (**Figures 10.59** and **10.60**).

 ▲ Drag a curved or straight segment.

 Be aware that this affects the direction lines at both ends of the curve. If you drag a straight segment, direction lines extend from its control points (**Figure 10.61**).

✔ Tips

■ Because it modifies the direction lines at both ends of the segment simultaneously, dragging the path directly often does more harm than good. On the other hand, this technique can serve as a handy way to turn straight segments into curves.

■ Press Command (Mac) or Ctrl (Windows) to switch temporarily from the currently selected Pen tool to the Selection tool and vice versa. Note that when you're editing masks, the Selection tool looks like an arrow ▶, not the typical pointer ▸.

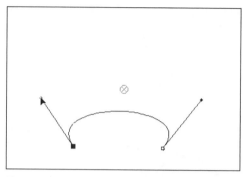

Figure 10.59 Drag a direction handle to adjust the curved segment as it exits a control point...

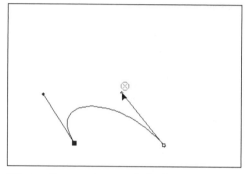

Figure 10.60 ...or enters a control point.

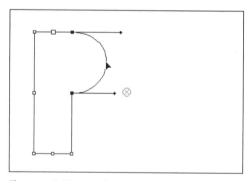

Figure 10.61 You can drag a path segment directly, but doing so always affects the direction lines at both ends of the curve. In this example, dragging a segment turns a rectangle into a *P* shape.

CONVERTING CONTROL POINTS

Adjusting RotoBezier Mask Tension

Naturally, you can't adjust a RotoBezier mask's curves using direction lines; RotoBezier masks don't have them. However, you can adjust the *tension* of any number of its control points to control the relative amount of curve of its adjacent segments. In other words, decreasing a point's tension relaxes the adjacent curves, making them more flat; increasing the tension increases the curve. (You might compare adjusting a RotoBezier mask's tension to adjusting a smooth point in a Bézier curve.)

As you adjust the tension, you can see the current setting in the Info panel. Increasing the tension to 100 percent creates the equivalent of a corner point in a Bézier curve; decreasing the tension makes adjacent segments curved.

Figure 10.62 Select the Convert Vertex tool.

To adjust the tension of RotoBezier mask points:

1. To adjust multiple points at once, select them.

   See the section "Selecting Masks and Points" for more information.

2. In the Tools panel, select the Convert Vertex tool ⌐ (**Figure 10.62**).

3. Drag a control point or one of the control points you selected in step 1.

   The mouse pointer changes into the Adjust Tension icon ⌐. Dragging right decreases tension, relaxing the curve of adjacent segments; dragging left increases tension, contracting the curve (**Figures 10.63** and **10.64**).

✔ Tip

■ Option-clicking (Mac) or Alt-clicking (Windows) a control point in a Bézier curve converts it from a smooth point to a corner point and vice versa; the same shortcut changes the tension of selected RotoBezier control points from an automatically calculated value to 100 percent and vice versa. Although the result is equivalent, this action doesn't convert the mask from one type to another.

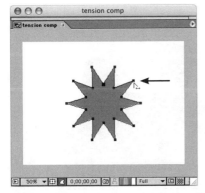

Figure 10.63 Dragging to the left increases tension at the selected points, increasing the curve of adjacent segments. Maximum tension creates a corner.

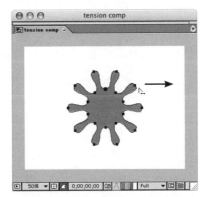

Figure 10.64 Dragging to the right decreases tension at the selected points, flattening the curve of adjacent segments.

Opening and Closing Paths

You can use menu commands to close an open path or open a closed one.

To close an open path:

1. In a Layer panel, choose the control points at each end of an open path (**Figure 10.65**).

2. Choose Layer > Mask > Closed (**Figure 10.66**).

   The control points are connected to close the path (**Figure 10.67**).

To open a closed path:

1. In a Layer panel, choose two adjacent control points in a closed path.

2. Choose Layer > Mask > Closed.

   The Closed option becomes unselected, and the segment between the control points disappears.

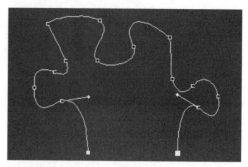

Figure 10.65 Choose the control points at each end of an open path.

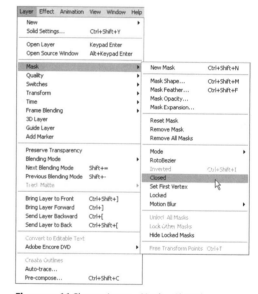

Figure 10.66 Choose Layer > Mask > Closed.

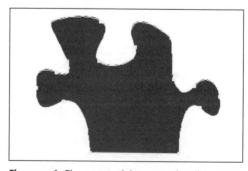

Figure 10.67 The open path becomes closed. You can use the same method to open a closed path.

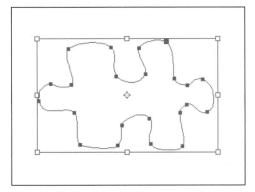

Figure 10.68 A bounding box and mask anchor point appear.

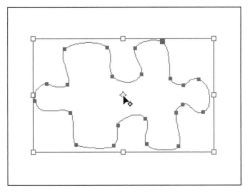

Figure 10.69 If you drag the mask's anchor point, the Selection tool becomes a Move Anchor Point icon.

Scaling and Rotating Masks

Using the Free Transform Points command, you can scale and rotate all or part of one or more masks. Masks are rotated and scaled around their own anchor points, separate from the anchor point of the layer that contains them. As the word *free* suggests, these adjustments are controlled manually, not numerically, and they can't be keyframed to animate over time. Of course, you can still keyframe the rotation and scale of the layer containing the masks.

To move, scale, or rotate all or part of a mask:

1. Open a Layer panel for the layer that contains the mask you want to transform, or select the layer in the Comp panel.

2. *Do one of the following:*

   ▲ Select the mask or mask points you want to transform, and Choose Layer > Mask > Free Transform Points.

   ▲ Double-click a mask to transform it completely.

   A bounding box and mask anchor point appear (**Figure 10.68**).

3. To reposition the anchor point for the mask's bounding box, drag the anchor.

   The selection tool turns into a Move Anchor Point icon when you position it over the anchor point (**Figure 10.69**).

   continues on next page

SCALING AND ROTATING MASKS

4. *Do any of the following*:

▲ To move the mask or selected points, place the cursor inside the bounding box and drag to a new position (**Figure 10.70**).

▲ To scale the mask or selected points, place the cursor on one of the handles of the bounding box until it becomes a Scale icon ⬈, and then drag (**Figure 10.71**).

▲ To rotate the mask or selected points, place the pointer slightly outside the bounding box until it becomes a Rotation icon ↷, and then drag (**Figure 10.72**).

5. To exit Free Transform Points mode, double-click anywhere in the Layer or Comp panel, or press Enter.

✔ Tip

■ As you can see, using the Free Transform Points command to scale and rotate a mask or mask points works much the same way as transforming a layer. You'll be happy to know that all the keyboard modifications—Shift, Command/Ctrl, Option/Alt—also work the same.

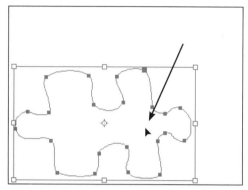

Figure 10.70 To move the mask or selected points, place the cursor inside the bounding box and drag to a new position.

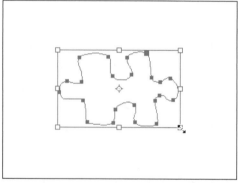

Figure 10.71 To scale the mask or selected points, place the cursor on one of the handles of the bounding box until it becomes a Scale icon, and then drag.

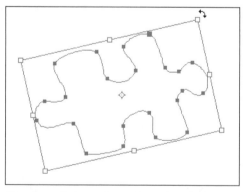

Figure 10.72 To rotate the mask or selected points, place the pointer slightly outside the bounding box until it becomes a Rotation icon, and then drag.

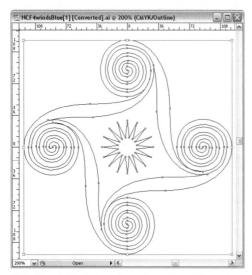

Figure 10.73 Copy a path from Photoshop or Illustrator (shown here)...

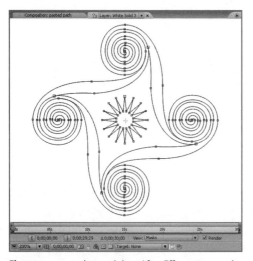

Figure 10.74 ...and paste it into After Effects as a mask.

Using Masks from Photoshop and Illustrator

You can copy paths from Adobe Photoshop or Illustrator and paste them as a layer mask in After Effects. Why not just import the file as a still image? By pasting a path as a layer mask, you can take advantage of After Effects' ability to animate its Shape, Feather, Opacity, and Expansion properties.

To use a mask from Illustrator or Photoshop:

1. In Illustrator or Photoshop, select the paths you want to copy (**Figure 10.73**).

2. Choose Edit > Copy.

3. In After Effects, view a layer in a Layer panel.

4. Choose Edit > Paste.

   The mask is pasted into the Layer panel (**Figure 10.74**).

✔ Tips

- If you try to paste the mask in the Composition panel, it appears as a motion path, not a mask.

- If you don't specify clipboard options in Illustrator's File & Clipboard Preferences, you won't be able to copy from Illustrator into After Effects. Fortunately, After Effects will alert you if this is the case.

Converting Mask Paths into Motion Paths

Not only is an open mask path analogous to a motion path, but it can also be converted into one. Just make sure you paste the path into a compatible layer property, such as its position property. If you paste into a Layer panel, then the path is pasted as a mask (as you saw in the previous section).

To paste a mask path as a motion path:

1. *Do either of the following:*
   - ▲ Select an open mask path in a layer in After Effects.
   - ▲ Select an open mask path in Photoshop or Illustrator.

2. Choose Edit > Copy, or press Command-C (Mac) or Ctrl-C (Windows) (**Figure 10.75**).

3. In the Timeline panel, expand the layer outline to reveal the spatial property you want to paste the path into.

   You can use the Position, Effect Point, or Anchor Point property.

4. Select the property name.

   The property's keyframes are highlighted. If the property has no keyframes, the I-beam icon is highlighted.

5. Set the current time to the frame where you want the pasted keyframes to start (**Figure 10.76**).

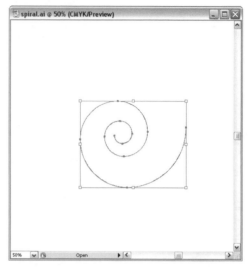

Figure 10.75 Select an open mask path in a layer in After Effects, or in Photoshop or Illustrator (shown here). Press Command-C (Mac) or Ctrl-C (Windows).

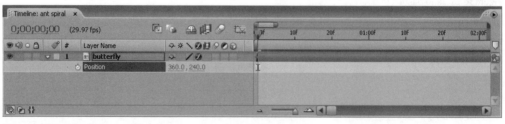

Figure 10.76 In After Effects, select a layer property, and set the current time to the frame you want the pasted motion to start.

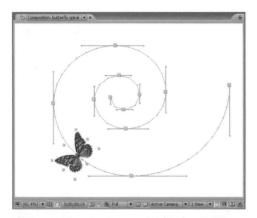

Figure 10.77 Pressing Command-V (Mac) or Ctrl-V (Windows) pastes the path in the composition as a motion path...

6. Choose Edit > Paste, or press Command-V (Mac) or Ctrl-V (Windows).

The path appears in the Comp panel as a motion path (**Figure 10.77**). In the property's track, keyframes begin at the current time and end two seconds later (**Figure 10.78**). The first and last keyframes are standard keyframes; the rest are roving keyframes (see Chapter 7).

7. Edit the motion path as you would any other.

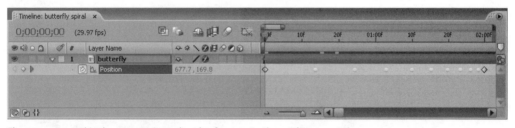

Figure 10.78 ...and in the property's track as keyframes starting at the current time.

Moving Masks Relative to the Layer Image

You can move a mask to reveal a different part of a layer two ways: in a Layer panel or in a Composition panel.

When you move a mask in a Layer panel, its relative position in the Composition panel also changes (**Figures 10.79** and **10.80**).

This approach works well if you want to change both the part of the image revealed by the mask and the mask's position in the composition. The mask moves, but the layer's position remains the same. Think of an iris effect at the end of a cartoon, in which the circular mask closes in on the character for a final good-bye.

Figure 10.79 When you move a mask in a Layer or Comp panel...

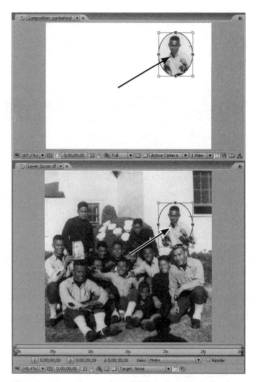

Figure 10.80 ...the mask's position changes in both the layer and the Comp panel. The position value of the layer containing the mask doesn't change.

MOVING MASKS RELATIVE TO THE LAYER IMAGE

Alternatively, you can use the Pan Behind tool in the Composition panel. Panning the layer behind the mask reveals a different part of the image without moving the mask's relative position in the composition. When you look back at the Layer panel, you can see that the mask has moved. However, After Effects recalculates the layer's position to

compensate for this movement, maintaining the layer's position in the composition (**Figures 10.81** and **10.82**). Imagine a scene from a pirate movie, in which a spyglass scans the horizon. The circle doesn't move, but the horizon pans through the viewfinder to reveal an island.

Figure 10.81 When you use the Pan Behind tool in the Composition panel...

Figure 10.82 ...the mask changes its position in the layer while maintaining its position in the composition. After Effects recalculates the layer's position value automatically. You can see the anchor point's new position in the Comp panel.

To move a mask in the Layer panel:

1. Select an entire mask in the Layer panel.

2. Drag one of the control points to move the entire mask to a new position.

   Make sure to drag a control point, not a path segment. The mask changes position in both the Layer panel and the composition.

To pan a layer behind its mask:

1. In the Tools panel, select the Pan Behind tool ▓ (**Figure 10.83**).

2. In the Composition panel, position the Pan Behind tool inside the masked area of the layer, and then drag (**Figure 10.84**).

   In the Composition panel, the mouse pointer becomes the Pan Behind icon ✛, and the layer pans behind the masked area. After Effects calculates the layer's position in the composition and the mask's placement in the Layer panel.

Figure 10.83 In the Tools panel, choose the Pan Behind tool.

Figure 10.84 In the Comp panel, place the Pan Behind tool inside the masked area, and drag.

Figure 10.85 Expand the layer's mask property, and adjust the value for Mask Feather.

Figure 10.86 The edge of the mask feathers, or softens, by the amount you specified.

✔ Tip

- If you set the feather to extend beyond the perimeter of the layer containing the mask, the feather will appear cut off and the edges of the layer will be apparent. Make the mask or feather small enough to fit within the confines of the layer. If the layer is a solid or nested composition, you can also increase the size of the layer.

Adjusting Other Mask Properties

In addition to Mask Shape, mask properties include Feather, Opacity, and Expansion.

Feather controls the softness of a mask's edge; the Mask Feather value determines the width of the edge's transition from opacity to transparency. The feathered width always extends equally from each side of the mask edge—that is, a Feather value of 30 extends 15 pixels both outside and inside the mask edge.

Expansion lets you expand or contract a mask's edges and is particularly useful for fine-tuning the feathered edge of a mask.

Opacity controls the mask's overall opacity—that is, how solid the masked area of the layer appears. Mask opacity works in conjunction with the layer's Opacity setting. If the layer is 100 percent opaque and a mask is 50 percent opaque, the masked area of the layer appears 50 percent opaque. Each mask's opacity also influences the net effect of mask modes, which are explained later in this chapter.

To feather the edges of a mask:

1. In the Timeline panel, select the layer containing the masks you want to adjust, and press MM.

   This shortcut reveals the selected layer's masks and their properties in the layer outline.

2. Adjust the value for Mask Feature (**Figure 10.85**).

   To enter different values for horizontal and vertical feather automatically, click the Link icon so that it appears unlinked.

   The mask edges appear feathered by the value you specified (**Figure 10.86**).

To adjust mask opacity:

1. In the Timeline panel, select the layer containing the masks you want to adjust, and press MM.

   This shortcut reveals the selected layer's masks and their properties in the layer outline.

2. Adjust the Opacity value for the masks you want to adjust (**Figure 10.87**).

   The mask uses the opacity setting you specify. Each mask's opacity setting interacts with the layer's overall Opacity setting as well as its mask mode settings (**Figure 10.88**).

Figure 10.87 Adjust a mask's Opacity value in the layer outline.

Figure 10.88 In this figure, several masks in the same layer use different opacity values.

Figure 10.89 Adjust a mask's Expansion value in the layer outline.

Figure 10.90 This figure shows three masks with identical shapes and feather values. However, each mask's Expansion value is different.

To expand or contract the mask:

1. In the Timeline panel, select the layer containing the masks you want to adjust, and press MM.

   This shortcut reveals the selected layer's masks and their properties in the layer outline.

2. Adjust the Expansion value for the masks you want to adjust (**Figure 10.89**).

   Positive values expand the masked area beyond its defined edges; negative values contract the masked area (**Figure 10.90**).

✔ Tip

■ The Layer Mask properties—Shape, Feather, Opacity, and Expansion—work like other properties. You can adjust their values and animate them as you would other properties. For more about properties and keyframes, see Chapter 7.

Inverting a Mask

Ordinarily, the area within a closed layer mask defines the opaque parts of the layer's image; the area outside the mask is transparent, revealing the layers beneath it. However, just as you can invert a layer's alpha channel, you can invert a layer mask to reverse the opaque and transparent areas.

To invert a mask created in After Effects:

1. In the Layer, Comp, or Timeline panel, select the mask you want to invert.

2. *Do one of the following:*
   ▲ In the Timeline panel, click Inverted for the selected mask (**Figure 10.91**).
   ▲ Choose Layer > Mask > Invert.
   ▲ Press Shift-Command-I (Mac) or Shift-Ctrl-I (Windows).

   Viewed in the Composition panel, the mask is inverted (**Figures 10.92** and **10.93**).

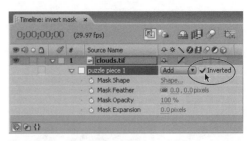

Figure 10.91 Click Inverted for the mask in the layer outline of the Timeline panel, or use the equivalent menu command or keyboard shortcut.

Figure 10.92 Ordinarily, the area within the mask defines the opaque parts of the layer's image.

Figure 10.93 Inverting the mask reverses the opaque and transparent areas of the layer.

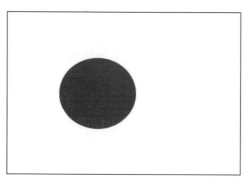

Figure 10.94 Two masks at 75 percent opacity, one with the mask's mode set to None.

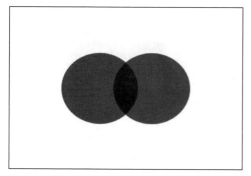

Figure 10.95 Mask mode set to Add.

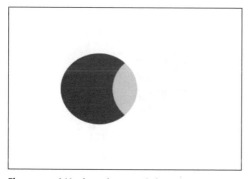

Figure 10.96 Mask mode set to Subtract.

Mask Modes

When you add multiple masks to the same layer, you can determine how the masks interact by selecting a mask *mode*. Although modes don't create compound paths (as do the Boolean functions in Illustrator), you can use them to achieve similar effects in a composition.

In the following examples, the upper mask is set to the default mode: None. See how changing the mode of the lower mask changes the way it interacts with the one above it? Both masks are set to 75 percent opacity so you can see the difference between the Add, Lighten, and Darken modes.

None eliminates the effects of the mask on the layer's alpha channel. However, you can still apply effects (such as strokes or fills) to the mask (**Figure 10.94**).

Add includes the mask with the masks above it to display all masked areas. Areas where the mask overlaps with the masks above it use their combined opacity values (**Figure 10.95**).

Subtract cuts, or subtracts, areas where the mask overlaps with the mask above it (**Figure 10.96**).

MASK MODES

Intersect adds the mask to all the masks above it so that only the areas where the mask overlaps with higher masks display in the composition (**Figure 10.97**).

Lighten adds the mask to the masks above it to display all masked areas. Areas where the mask overlaps with the masks above it use the highest opacity value, not the combined values (**Figure 10.98**).

Darken adds the mask to the masks above it to display only the areas where the masks overlap. Areas where multiple masks overlap use the highest opacity value, not the combined values (**Figure 10.99**).

Difference adds the mask to the masks above it to display only the areas where the masks don't overlap (**Figure 10.100**).

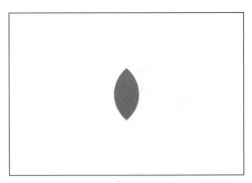

Figure 10.97 Mask mode set to Intersect.

Figure 10.98 Mask mode set to Lighten.

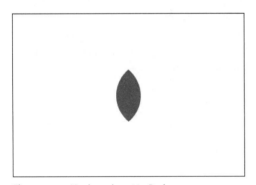

Figure 10.99 Mask mode set to Darken.

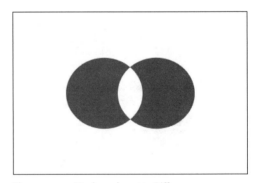

Figure 10.100 Mask mode set to Difference.

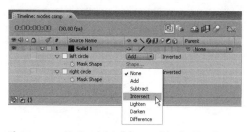

Figure 10.101 To the right of the mask in the Timeline panel, choose a mask mode from the pull-down menu.

To set the mask mode:

1. Select the mask for which you want to set the mode.

2. *Do one of the following:*

   ▲ In the Timeline panel, choose a mode from the pull-down menu across from the mask (in the Switches/Modes panel) (**Figure 10.101**).

   ▲ Choose Layer > Mask > Mode > and select a mode from the submenu.

   The mode you choose affects how the mask interacts with the masks above it in the layer outline (for that layer only).

EFFECTS FUNDAMENTALS

At last, you come to the program's namesake: effects. As if you didn't already know, effects are used to alter the audio and visual characteristics of layers in almost countless ways. You can employ them to enhance, combine, or distort layers. You can simulate audio-visual phenomena from light to lightning. You can make changes that are subtle or spectacular. And, most important, you can animate these effects over time.

Effects are stored in the Plug-Ins folder, which is itself contained in the After Effects folder. The number and type of effects at your disposal will depend on whether you have the standard version of After Effects or After Effects Pro. You can also add to your repertoire by using effects created by third-party developers.

This chapter begins with an overview of effect categories and then goes on to explain the process you use to apply effects to layers. It also describes how to use the Effect Controls panel as a complement or alternative to the property controls in the layer outline.

Effect Categories

By default, the effects in the Effects menu are organized in the following categories according to function. After Effects Pro includes a number of effects and entire effect categories not found in the Standard version. When you add third-party plug-ins, you can often choose whether the added effect appears under an existing category or one that you create specifically for it.

Animation Presets includes any combination of effects or other keyframed properties you save, as well as a number of built-in presets for animating text.

3D Channel (Pro only) includes effects that can use information saved in a number of 3D image file formats, allowing you to incorporate scenes created in 3D applications.

Audio processes audio.

Blur & Sharpen adjusts the focus of a layer's images.

Channel manipulates a layer's individual channels—red, green, blue, or alpha—and the color information derived from them.

Color Correction alters the color and brightness values of a layer's image. This category contains effects formerly found in the now-omitted Adjust and Image Control categories.

Distort deforms or distorts a layer's image.

Expression Controls enables you to more easily manipulate property values contained in expressions—math-like statements you define to create animation (covered in Chapter 16, "Complex Projects").

Generate creates graphical elements. This category replaces the Render category found in previous versions of After Effects.

Keying makes areas of an image transparent, based on color or brightness.

Matte (Pro only) fine-tunes keying effects to create more convincing composites.

Noise & Grain effects either add visual noise or grain—to create a pixilated or film-like texture, for example—or reduce it.

Paint lets you modify a layer using familiar paint and cloning tools, and animate individual paint strokes over time (see Chapter 13, "Painting on a Layer," for a full explanation).

Perspective simulates positioning a layer in three-dimensional space.

Simulation emulates a number of real-world phenomena, such as bubbles, shattering glass, water, and particle effects.

Stylize alters an image's pixels to produce abstract, stylized effects.

Text creates text elements (for other text-creation techniques, see Chapter 12, "Creating and Animating Text").

Time alters the layer image based on its timing.

Transition refers to effects that are designed to gradually replace one image with the one preceding it.

Video prepares images for video output.

Utility (Pro Only) aids in handling issues peculiar to certain footage types or other effects.

✔ Tips

- Effect categories have been reorganized slightly from previous versions of After Effects. If the effect you're looking for has been moved to a different category, just use the Effects & Presets panel's search feature.

- Don't let an effect's name limit how you think of it or prevent you from putting it to imaginative use.

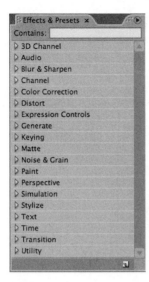

Figure 11.1
The Effects & Presets panel makes it easy to find and apply effects to layers.

Video effect

Audio effect

16 bpc effect

32 bpc effect

Effect preset

Figure 11.2 In the Effects & Presets panel, icons indicate the type of item listed.

Using the Effects & Presets Panel

Although you can find and apply any effect using the Effects menu, it can be more convenient to use the Effects & Presets panel. As its name implies, the Effects & Presets panel lists not only effects, but also animation presets (**Figure 11.1**). In Chapter 7, "Properties and Keyframes," you learned how to save animations as a preset that can be easily applied to other layers. Animation presets also include a number of built-in text animations, as explained in Chapter 12.

The Effects & Presets panel makes it easy to find an effect based on its name. You can sort the list alphabetically or according to category, to help you locate the effect's plug-in file on your system. You can sift the list to show effects or animation presets, and you can specify whether to show the effects contained in a preset.

As usual, you can click the triangle next to the item to expand it, revealing its contents in outline form. By expanding items, you can view effects contained in a category or see the components of a saved preset (when those viewing options are selected).

Icons indicate the type of item listed (**Figure 11.2**):

◆ A standard video effect's icon uses a plug-in symbol, depicting a real-world plug (the two-pronged electrical type).

◆ An audio effect adds a small speaker icon.

◆ 16 bits-per-channel (bpc) effects add the number 16, and 32 bpc effects have the number 32.

◆ Presets use a file icon with the letters *FX*.

◆ Keyframed properties within an animation preset are represented by a Stopwatch icon.

To find an item in the Effects & Presets panel:

◆ In the Effects & Presets panel, type all or part of the name of the item you want in the Contains field (**Figure 11.3**).

As you type, the items on the list that don't match are hidden from view, leaving only matching items (**Figure 11.4**).

To show all the items in the Effects & Presets panel:

◆ Highlight the search criteria in the Effects & Presets panel's Contains field, and press Delete (Mac) or Backspace (Windows).

The panel lists all items (**Figure 11.5**) according to other sorting options you specify (explained in the following tasks).

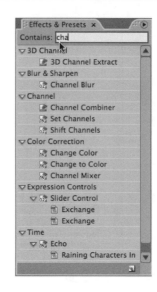

Figure 11.3
As you type the name of the item you want in the Contains field...

Figure 11.4
...the list sifts to show only the matching items.

Figure 11.5
Clear the Contains field to make the panel list all items.

To sort the Effects & Presets panel's list:

◆ In the Effects & Presets panel's menu, *select one of the following* (**Figure 11.6**):

Categories groups items in folders according to categories determined by function (listed earlier in this chapter) (**Figure 11.7**).

Finder Folders (Mac) or **Explorer Folders** (Windows) groups items in pull-down folders according to how their source files are organized on your computer (**Figure 11.8**).

Alphabetical lists all items in alphabetical order (numbered items appear first, then items from A–Z) (**Figure 11.9**).

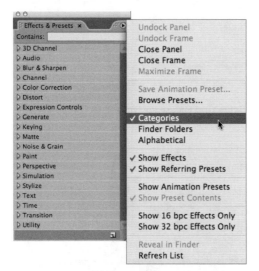

Figure 11.7 Choosing Categories sorts the items according to their general function, such as Adjust and Blur & Sharpen.

Figure 11.6 In the Effects & Presets panel's pull-down menu, choose an option to sort the list by category, finder folders, or alphabetically.

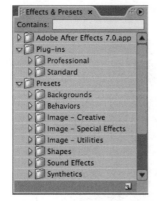

Figure 11.8 Choosing Finder Folders (Mac) or Explorer Folders (Windows) sorts items according to how their plug-in files are organized on your system.

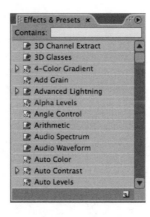

Figure 11.9 Choosing Alphabetical lists all items in alphabetical order.

To include or exclude items in the Effects & Presets panel by type:

◆ In the Effects & Presets panel's pull-down menu, choose the type of items you want the list to include (**Figure 11.10**):

Show Effects shows effects. Deselect this option to exclude effects in order to view presets only.

Show Referring Presets lists effects with the name of any presets that use the effect (**Figure 11.11**).

Show Animation Presets shows animation and effect presets you've saved.

Show Preset Contents shows individual effects included in a preset, in outline form (**Figure 11.12**).

Show 16 bpc Effects Only shows effects that can be applied to 16 bit-per-channel (bpc) images and excludes other effects.

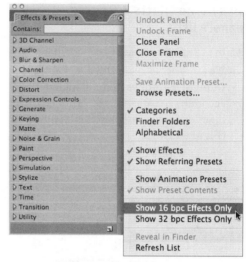

Figure 11.10 Choose the types of items you want to include in the list.

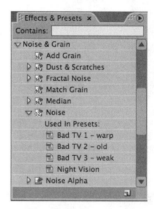

Figure 11.11 Choosing Show Referring Presets lists presets alongside the effects used by the preset.

Figure 11.12 Choosing Show Preset Contents lets you expand a preset to see the individual effects it contains.

USING THE EFFECTS & PRESETS PANEL

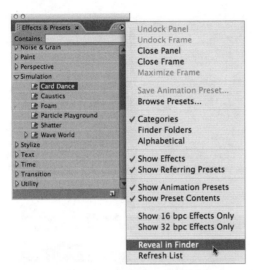

Figure 11.13 Selecting an effect and choosing Reveal in Finder (Mac) or Reveal in Explorer (Windows)...

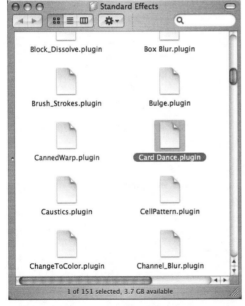

Figure 11.14 ...locates and selects the item's source plug-in file on your system.

To reveal an item in the Finder or Explorer:

1. In the Effects & Presets panel, select an effect.

2. In the Effects & Presets panel's menu, choose Reveal in Finder (Mac) or Reveal in Explorer (Windows) (**Figure 11.13**).

   After Effects locates the item's source file in your system, opens the item's containing folder, and selects the item (**Figure 11.14**).

To refresh the list:

◆ In the Effects & Presets panel's menu, choose Refresh List (**Figure 11.15**).

The list reflects changes caused by adding, deleting, or moving source files on the finder level (the Finder [Mac] or Explorer [Windows]).

✔ Tips

■ After Effects includes a preset workspace for Effects. Where the Standard workspace has a Project panel, the Effects workspace places the Effect Controls panel.

■ If you're using After Effects Pro, the Effects & Presets panel's menu includes an option to show only effects that support 16 and 32 bpc images. For more about using 16 bpc and 32 bpc footage items, see Chapter 4, "Compositions."

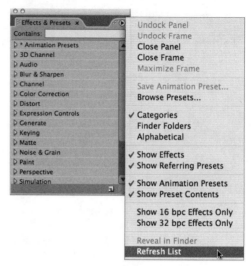

Figure 11.15 To make the Effects & Presets panel reflect any changes you made to the source files, choose Refresh List.

Figure 11.16 Select a layer.

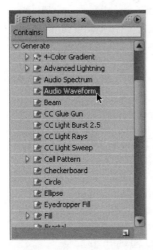

Figure 11.17 In the Effects & Presets panel, double-click the effect or preset you want.

Applying Effects

Although effects are numerous and varied, you apply all of them in essentially the same way.

You can also save any combination of effects (as well as animation keyframes) as a preset. To learn how to save and apply a preset, see the section "Saving and Applying Effect Presets" later in this chapter.

To apply an effect:

1. Select a layer in a composition (**Figure 11.16**).

2. *Do any of the following*:
   - ▲ Double-click the effect or preset you want to apply in the Effects & Presets panel (**Figure 11.17**).
   - ▲ Choose Effect, and then choose an effect category and an individual effect from the submenu.
   - ▲ Ctrl-click (Mac) or right-click (Windows), and hold the mouse button to access an Effects menu.

3. If an options dialog box appears, select options for the effect and then click OK to close the dialog box.

   An Effect Controls panel appears with the effect selected (**Figure 11.18**).

   continues on next page

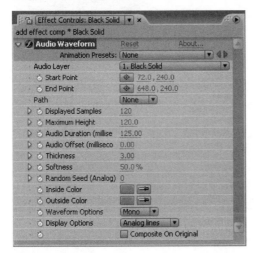

Figure 11.18 The effect appears selected in the Effect Controls panel. You can adjust the settings here...

4. Using controls in the Effect Controls panel or in the expanded layer outline of the Timeline panel, adjust the property values for the effect, and animate them if you want (**Figure 11.19**).

The applied effect appears in the composition (**Figure 11.20**). The quality and aspects (such as shading or shadows) of the effect depend on the preview options you specify; see Chapter 8, "Playback, Previews, and RAM," for more information.

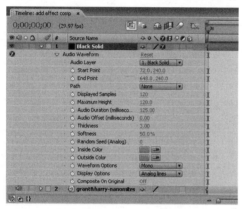

Figure 11.19 ...or in the layer outline of the Timeline panel.

Figure 11.20 You can view and preview the effect in the Composition panel.

To apply the most recent effect:

1. Select a layer in a composition.

2. *Do one of the following:*

   ▲ Choose Effect, and select the most recently used effect from the top of the menu (**Figure 11.21**).

   ▲ Press Shift-Command-Option-E (Mac) or Shift-Ctrl-Alt-E (Windows).

   The effect is applied to the selected layer.

✔ Tip

■ Many effects are best applied to solid-black layers—particularly those that don't rely on a layer's underlying pixels, such as effects in the Generate category. This permits you to manipulate the layer containing the effect independently from other layers, which can give you more flexibility. Other times, you may want to use the effect to interact with a solid color to create graphical elements.

Figure 11.21 Choose Effect, and select the most recently applied effect from the menu.

Viewing Effect Property Controls

Figure 11.22 Pressing E reveals a selected layer's effect properties in the Timeline panel's layer outline...

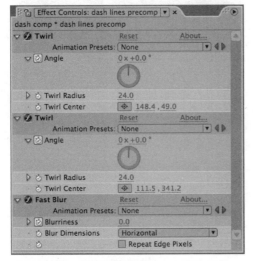

Figure 11.23 ...and selecting a layer containing effects reveals its effect properties in the Effect Controls panel. Typically, you use the two views in tandem to adjust and animate effects.

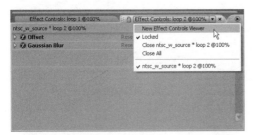

Figure 11.24 Much like the Comp and Layer panels, the Effect Controls panel's tab lets you open a new tabbed viewer; select the tab's lock icon to prevent that viewer from toggling another layer's effects.

Once you add effects to a layer, you can view their property controls in both the Timeline panel and the Effect Controls panel.

As you saw in Chapter 7, you can view any layer property—including effects—by expanding the layer outline. Chances are, you even recall the keyboard shortcut: E for *effects*. However, you'll soon find that many effects include a long list of parameters—often too long to view in the layer outline conveniently (**Figure 11.22**).

For this reason, the Effect Controls panel is indispensable. Selecting a layer makes all of its effects appear in the Effect Controls panel (**Figure 11.23**). Or, if it's not open already, you can invoke the Effect Controls panel by double-clicking the effect in the layer outline. As in the Comp and Layer panels, a viewer pull-down menu in the Effect Controls panel's tab lets you open a new viewer; selecting the tab's lock icon prevents it from toggling to a different layer's effects (**Figure 11.24**).

Generally, you use a Layer or Comp panel to view the result of your adjustments. However, some effects include a spatial property that you can set directly in the Layer or Comp panels by clicking where you want the *effect point* (**Figure 11.25**). See "Setting an Effect Point," later in this chapter.

As you can see, the Timeline panel's property controls are ideally suited for setting viewing the properties in time, whereas the Effect Controls panel provides a dedicated space for viewing and adjusting numerous effect properties at once. Naturally, you'll use both views in tandem. Don't forget that After Effects already includes a preset workspace called Effects that places an emphasis on both areas (see Chapter 1 to review workspaces).

✔ Tip

- As always, you can select the next property in the layer outline by pressing the down arrow and the property higher in the list by pressing the up arrow.

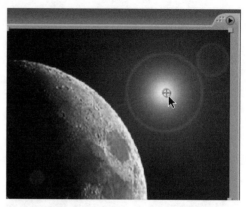

Figure 11.25 Some effects let you set a spatially based property (an effect point) by clicking directly in the Comp panel. Here, the center point of a lens flare effect is being placed using the mouse.

VIEWING EFFECT PROPERTY CONTROLS

Figure 11.26 To remove all of a layer's effects, select the layer...

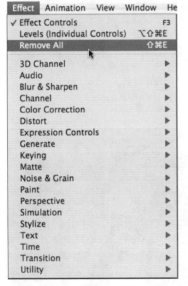

Figure 11.27 ...and choose Effect > Remove All, or use the keyboard shortcut.

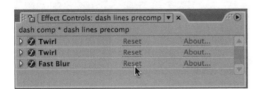

Figure 11.28 In the Effect Controls panel, clicking Reset returns all of the effects' properties to their defaults.

Removing and Resetting Effects

If you don't like an effect, remove it. If you need to restore the default settings, reset them.

To remove an effect:

1. In the Effect Controls panel, select the name of an effect.

2. Press Delete (Mac) or Backspace (Windows).

   The effect is removed.

To remove all effects for a layer:

1. Select a layer containing one or more effects (**Figure 11.26**).

2. Choose Effect > Remove All, or press Shift-Command-E (Mac) or Shift-Ctrl-E (Windows) (**Figure 11.27**).

   All effects are removed from the layer.

To reset an effect to its default settings:

◆ *Do either of the following:*

   ▲ In the Switches panel of the expanded Layer panel, click Reset for the effect.

   ▲ For the effect in the Effect Controls panel, click Reset (**Figure 11.28**).

   All the values for the effect are restored to the defaults.

✔ Tip

■ In addition to a Reset button, each effect includes an About button that displays the name and version number of each effect. A handful of effects also include a button to access additional options not listed in the Effect Controls panel. Depending on the effect, the button is labeled Options, Edit Text, or the like.

Disabling Effects Temporarily

You can turn off effects temporarily without removing them from the layer. Doing so is helpful when you want to see a single effect without other effects obscuring your view. Once you're satisfied with an effect's settings, you may want to disable it to speed up frame rendering.

To disable and enable individual effects:

◆ In the Timeline panel or the Effect Controls panel, click the Effect icon next to the effect's name.

When the icon is visible, the effect is enabled; when the icon is hidden, the effect is disabled (**Figures 11.29** and **11.30**).

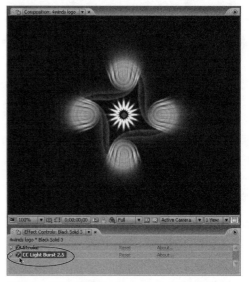

Figure 11.29 In the Effect Controls panel, clicking the Effect icon next to the effect name...

Figure 11.30 ...toggles the icon off and disables the effect.

Figure 11.31 Clicking the Effect switch for a layer in the Switches/Modes panel of the Timeline panel...

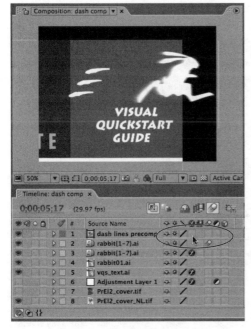

Figure 11.32 ...toggles the icon off and disables all effects contained by the layer.

To disable and enable all effects in a layer:

◆ In the Switches/Modes panel of the Timeline panel, click the Effect icon next to a layer.

When the icon is visible, all effects for the layer are enabled; when the icon is hidden, all effects are disabled (**Figures 11.31** and **11.32**).

Adjusting Effects in the Effect Controls Panel

Although you can adjust effect properties in the layer outline just as you would any other layer property (using techniques covered in Chapter 7), the roomier Effect Controls panel can accommodate larger, more graphical controls for several effect properties. Most are intuitive or should already be familiar to you (**Figure 11.33**), so they won't be covered here. However, this chapter does discuss the slightly less intuitive effect point control (see the following section, "Setting an Effect Point").

Covering every possible graphical control is beyond the scope of this chapter. Other effects may offer a color range control (Hue/Saturation); a grid of control points (Mesh Warp); a histogram (Levels); or other graphs, such as those that represent an image's input/output levels (Curves) or an audio layer's frequency response (Parametric EQ). Some effects include an Options button to open a separate dialog box, and third-party plug-ins

may offer other exotic controls. Consult the documentation for each effect for detailed information on its individual controls.

✔ Tips

- By default, After Effects uses its own color picker for selecting colors. However, you can have After Effects use your system's color picker by selecting the appropriate option in the General panel of the Preferences dialog box.

- Once you start dragging an angle control knob, you may drag the cursor outside the angle controller to move it with greater precision.

- You can set some property values using a slider control. However, the slider's range (say, 0 to 20) doesn't always represent the possible range of values (let's say 0 to 1000). Ctrl-click (Mac) or right-click (Windows) the property name and choose Edit Value to open a dialog box and set the range of the slider.

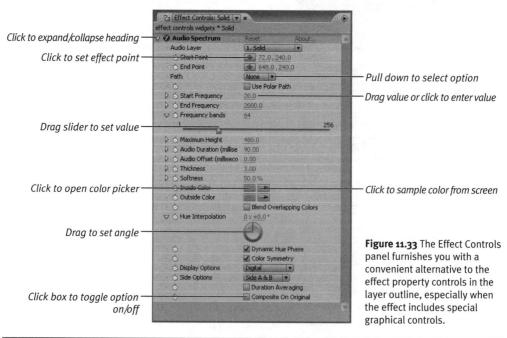

Figure 11.33 The Effect Controls panel furnishes you with a convenient alternative to the effect property controls in the layer outline, especially when the effect includes special graphical controls.

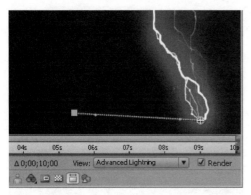

Figure 11.34 You can view and manipulate an effect point and its motion path in the Layer panel. Here, you can see the path of an Advanced Lightning effect's endpoint. See Chapter 9 for more about using motion paths.

Setting an Effect Point

An *effect point* represents the position of an effect on a layer: It can be the focus of a Lens Flare effect, the center point of a Reflection effect, or the starting point for Path Text. Some effects require more than one effect point, such as the start and end of a Stroke effect or the four corners of the Corner Pin effect.

You can set the effect point with the Effect Controls panel's Effect Point button or by manipulating it in the Composition or Layer panel. Because effects are applied to a layer, the coordinates of an effect point refer to the layer, not the composition.

The following tasks explain how to set an effect point; you can animate it as you would any property. When you animate the effect point over time, you can view and manipulate its path in the Layer panel just as you would adjust an anchor point path or motion path in the Composition panel (**Figure 11.34**). In most ways, the effect point path works just like any other kind of motion path. Unlike a layer's position, however, the effect point's coordinates are unaffected by the layer's anchor point. (See "Animating Effects," at the end of this chapter; Chapter 7 about basic animation; and Chapter 9 about adjusting a motion path.)

To set an effect point with the Effect Point button:

1. In the Effect Controls panel, click the Effect Point button for an effect property (**Figure 11.35**).

   Any effect property that uses layer coordinate values has an Effect Point button. When the button is active, the cursor becomes the Effect Point icon ⌖ when positioned in a Composition or Layer panel.

2. Position the cursor in a Composition or Layer panel, and click to set the effect point (**Figure 11.36**).

   The coordinate values reflect the effect point you chose. Even if you clicked the Effect Point icon in the Composition panel, the coordinate values correspond to the coordinate system of the layer that contains the effect.

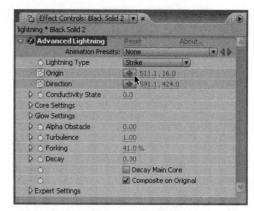

Figure 11.35 Click the Effect Point button for an effect property.

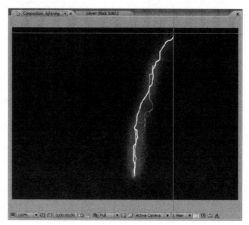

Figure 11.36 Position the cursor in a Layer or Comp panel (shown here), and click to set the effect point.

To set the effect point by dragging in the Composition or Layer panel:

1. To view the effect point in the Composition or Layer panel, *do one of the following:*

   ▲ In the Composition panel's View Options dialog box, make sure Effect Controls is checked (**Figure 11.37**).

   ▲ In the Layer panel menu, make sure the name of the effect is checked (**Figure 11.38**).

2. In the Effect Controls panel, click the name of the effect whose effect point value you want to change.

In the Composition or Layer panel, a crosshairs icon indicates the position of each effect point at the current time (**Figure 11.39**).

3. In the Composition panel or Layer panel, drag the Effect Point icon to a new position (**Figure 11.40**).

   If the property isn't animated, the effect point is set for the duration of the layer; if the property is animated (its Stopwatch icon is selected), then the effect point is set for the current time, and a keyframe is created or updated. An effect point's motion path is visible in the Layer panel only.

Figure 11.37 Make sure Effect Controls is checked in the Composition panel's View Options dialog box...

Figure 11.38 ...or the name of the effect is checked in the Layer panel.

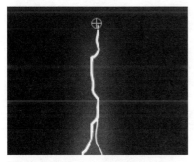

Figure 11.39 When an effect is selected, its position effect points appear in the Composition panel and the Layer panel (shown here). In this example, the effect points correspond to the ends of the lightning effect.

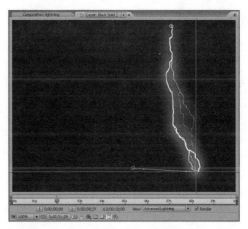

Figure 11.40 In the Comp or Layer panel, drag the Effect Point icon to a new position. (If you are animating the effect point, then a new keyframe is created at the current time, or the current keyframe's value is updated.)

Saving and Applying Effect Presets

Occasionally, you'll create a complex effect that you're particularly proud of or that you need to reuse frequently. You can save a combination of effect settings—including keyframes—as a *preset*.

You save preset effects as independent, cross-platform files, which use an .ffx extension. Because preset effects are independent files, you can store them separately from your project so that you can easily access them for other projects or share them with other After Effects artists. To further facilitate your work, After Effects makes it possible for you to access your saved presets via the Animation > Recent Animation Presets menu command.

To view presets in the Effect Controls panel:

◆ In the Effect Controls panel's menu, select Show Animation Presets (**Figure 11.41**).

When the option is selected, a layer's effects listed in the Effect Controls panel include an Animation Presets pull-down menu (**Figure 11.42**); otherwise the pull-down menu is hidden.

Figure 11.41 In the Effect Controls panel's menu, choose Show Animation Presets.

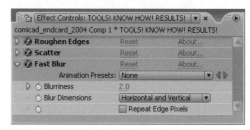

Figure 11.42 An Animation Presets pull-down menu appears.

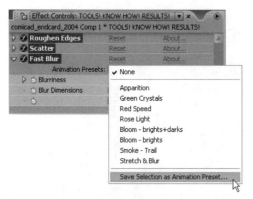

Figure 11.43 In the Effect Controls panel, select one or more of the effects you applied to the layer, and choose Save Selection as Animation Preset in the Animation Presets pull-down menu...

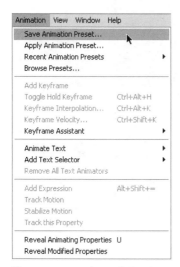

Figure 11.44 ...or choose Animation > Save Animation Preset.

To save effects as a preset:

1. Apply one or more effects to a layer in the composition.

If you want, animate them over time (using techniques explained in Chapter 7).

2. In the Effect Controls panel, select one or more of the effects you applied to the layer.

3. *Do either of the following:*

▲ In any effect's Animation Presets pull-down menu, choose Save Selection as Animation Preset (**Figure 11.43**).

▲ Choose Animation > Save Animation Preset (**Figure 11.44**).

A "Save Animation Preset as" dialog box appears.

4. Specify the name and destination of the preset file (**Figure 11.45**).

The file uses the .ffx extension.

5. Click Save to save the settings and close the dialog box.

The preset is added to the appropriate categories in the Effects & Presets panel.

Figure 11.45 Specify the name and destination of the preset file in the "Save Animation Preset as" dialog box.

To apply a preset effect:

1. Select the layers to which you want to apply a preset, and set the current time to where you want keyframes (if included in the preset) to begin.

2. *Do one of the following:*

    ▲ In the Effects & Presets panel, double-click the name of the preset you want to apply to the selected layers (**Figure 11.46**).

    ▲ Choose Animation > Apply Animation Preset.

    ▲ Choose Animation > Apply Recent Preset, and select the name of a recently used preset.

    The preset is applied to the selected layers. Any animated properties' keyframes begin at the current time.

To apply an effect or preset by dragging:

1. In the Effects & Presets panel, locate and select the effect or preset you want to apply.

2. Drag the selected effect or preset to *any of the following places:*

    ▲ The target layer's name in the Timeline panel

    ▲ The target layer's effect list heading in the Timeline panel

    ▲ Any position in the target layer's list of effects in the Timeline panel (**Figure 11.47**)

Figure 11.46 Select a layer, and apply a preset by using an option in the Animation menu or by double-clicking the preset in the Effects & Presets panel (shown here).

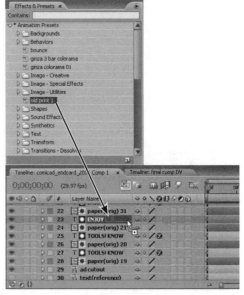

Figure 11.47 You can also drag an effect or preset icon to the target layer in the Timeline, dropping it on the layer's name, on the layer's effect property heading, or at any position in the layer's effect list.

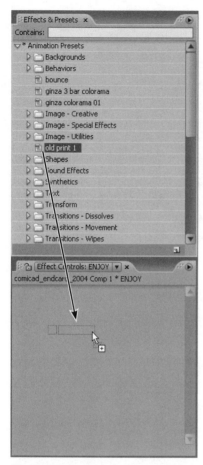

Figure 11.48 Alternatively, you can drag the effect to the layer's effect list in the Effect Controls panel...

Figure 11.49 ...or to the layer in the Comp panel (use the Info panel to verify you have targeted the proper layer).

▲ The target layer's list of effects in the Effect Controls panel (**Figure 11.48**)

▲ The target layer in the Comp panel; the Info panel displays the name of the currently targeted layer as you drag over it (**Figure 11.49**)

When you release the mouse, the effect is added to the layer.

SAVING AND APPLYING EFFECT PRESETS

To apply an animation preset's effect only:

1. In the Effects & Presets panel's menu, make sure Show Preset Contents is checked (**Figure 11.50**).

   In the Effects & Presets panel, each preset lists its constituent effects. Click the triangle next to the preset's name to see the effects it contains.

2. *Do either of the following:*

   ▲ Select the target layer, and double-click the individual effect in the Effects & Presets panel (**Figure 11.51**).

   ▲ Drag the effect from the Effects & Presets panel to the targeted layer (**Figure 11.52**).

   The individual effect is applied to the layer.

Figure 11.50 Make sure Show Preset Contents is checked.

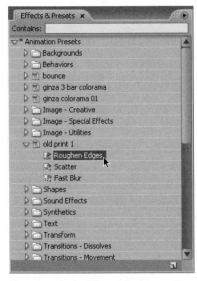

Figure 11.51 In the Effects & Presets panel, double-click an individual effect in a preset...

Figure 11.52 ...or drag an individual effect to the target layer.

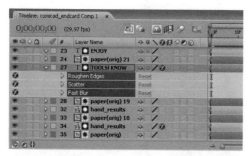

Figure 11.53 In the Effect Controls panel, select one or more effects, and press Command-C (Mac) or Ctrl-C (Windows).

Figure 11.54 Select a target layer, and press Command-V (Mac) or Ctrl-V (Windows).

Figure 11.55 The selected layer contains the pasted effects, but it doesn't contain the same keyframes. (You can press E to view the selected layer's effects in the layer outline.)

Copying and Pasting Effects

To save time and labor, you can copy effects from one layer into another.

To copy a layer's effects into another layer:

1. In the Effect Controls panel, select one or more effects (**Figure 11.53**).

2. Select Edit > Copy, or press Command-C (Mac) or Ctrl-C (Windows).

3. In the Timeline panel, select one or more layers (**Figure 11.54**).

4. Choose Edit > Paste, or press Command-V (Mac) or Ctrl-V (Windows).

   The selected layer contains the pasted effects; however, it doesn't contain the same keyframes (**Figure 11.55**).

✔ Tip

■ You can also copy and paste keyframes from one property to another property that uses compatible values. For example, you can copy position keyframes to an Effect Point property. See Chapter 7 to review this technique.

Applying Multiple Effects

The Effect Controls panel lists effects in the order you add them, from top to bottom. Because each effect is applied to the result of the one above it, changing the order of effects can change the final appearance (or sound) of the layer (**Figures 11.56** and **11.57**). You can reorder effects in the Effect Controls panel as well as directly in the layer outline of the Timeline panel.

To reorder effects:

1. In the Effect Controls panel or in the layer outline of the Timeline panel, drag the name of an effect up or down to a new position in the effect stacking order.

   A dark horizontal line indicates the effect's new position when you release the mouse (**Figure 11.58**).

2. Release the mouse button to place the effect in its new position in the list (**Figure 11.59**).

   Changing the order of effects in the list changes the order in which they're applied to the layer.

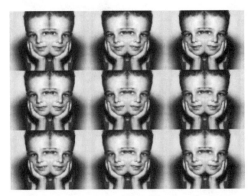

Figure 11.56 The Mirror effect followed by the Motion Tile effect results in this image...

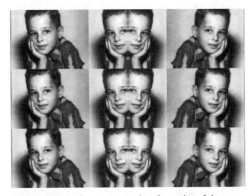

Figure 11.57 ...whereas reversing the order of the effects results in this image.

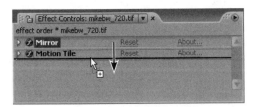

Figure 11.58 Drag the name of an effect up or down to a new position in the stacking order. A dark line indicates the effect's new position.

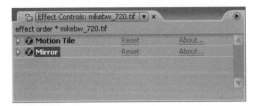

Figure 11.59 Release the mouse to place the effect in its new position in the list.

Figure 11.60 Masking an adjustment layer restricts its effects. Here, the Blur and Brightness & Contrast filters affect only masked areas (defined by an elliptical mask that's inverted).

Applying Effects to an Adjustment Layer

As you'll recall from Chapter 5, "Layer Basics," the effects contained in an adjustment layer are applied to all the layers below it. You save time and effort by applying effects to a single layer rather than multiple layers. You can create an adjustment layer within After Effects; you can also convert a visual layer into an adjustment layer.

Although the concept of adjustment layers is simple enough, it's worth revisiting the topic to examine some of the possibilities it affords. In this section, you'll learn how you can limit the effects of an adjustment layer by using a mask or by employing a layer's existing alpha channel.

Although a mask ordinarily modifies a layer's alpha channel to define opaque and transparent areas of a layer's image, applying a mask to an adjustment layer—which by definition can't contain an image—allows the masked area of the effect to influence the lower layers (the areas outside the mask remain unaffected) (**Figure 11.60**).

You can also use the alpha channel of another layer in a similar manner, by converting the layer to an adjustment layer. As an adjustment layer, its image is ignored. However, any effects you add to the layer are restricted to the areas defined by its alpha channel.

To convert a layer to an adjustment layer, and vice versa:

◆ In the Switches area of the Timeline panel, click the Adjustment Layer switch for the layer you want to convert to make the icon appear or disappear.

When the Adjustment Layer icon is visible, the layer functions as an adjustment layer—its image disappears from the Composition panel, and its effects are applied to lower layers (**Figures 11.61** and **11.62**).

When the Adjustment Layer icon isn't visible, the layer functions as a standard layer, and its image appears in the composition. If the adjustment layer was created in After Effects, it becomes a solid layer. Any effects contained by the layer are applied only to that layer.

Figure 11.61 Clicking the Adjustment Layer switch converts a layer into an adjustment layer.

Figure 11.62 Here a solid containing the Invert effect has been converted into an adjustment layer. The solid isn't visible, but its effect alters the underlying layers, making the left side of the image look like a negative.

Understanding Compound Effects

Effects that require two layers to operate are called *compound effects*. Rather than appear in a separate category, compound effects are distributed among effects in various categories. Although some compound effects use the word *compound* in their names, you can identify others only by knowing their controls.

As with other effects, you apply compound effects to the layers you want to alter. Unlike other effects, however, compound effects rely on a second layer—an effect source or modifying layer—that acts as a kind of map for the effect. Typically, this takes the form of a grayscale image because many compound effects are based on the modifying layer's brightness levels. In a Compound Blur effect, for example, the brightness levels of the modifying layer determine the placement and intensity of the blurry areas of the target layer. The modifying layer can be a still image, movie, or nested composition (**Figure 11.63**).

✔ Tip

- You don't need ready-made footage to serve as an effect source; you can create your own within After Effects. You can use a combination of solids, masks, and effects to create a dynamic effect source. The effect source in Figure 11.63 was created by applying the Fractal Noise effect to a solid.

Figure 11.63 Compound effects rely on a second layer as a kind of map for the effect.

Using Compound Effects

Due to their peculiar nature, compound effects have certain unique features. This section summarizes those attributes. More complex techniques are addressed in Chapter 16.

Specifying an effect source

In compound effects, you must use a pull-down menu to specify the modifying layer (**Figure 11.64**). Although the modifying layer must be included in the composition to appear in the list, you usually switch off its video in the Timeline panel. This is necessary because the modifying layer appears in the composition only as an effect source, not a visible layer.

Resolving size differences between source and target layers

Because compound effects use the pixels of the modifying layer as a map, that layer's dimensions should match those of the layer it affects (**Figure 11.65**). This way, your results will be more predictable and easier to control. If the dimensions of the two layers don't match, compound effects offer several ways to compensate (**Figure 11.66**). Keep in mind that although the following options can work to your advantage, they can also produce unwanted results:

Tile repeats the modifying layer to map the entire target layer. In some cases, the modifying layer won't tile evenly, cutting off some tiles. If images don't tile seamlessly, the edges may be evident in the effect.

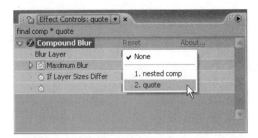

Figure 11.64 Compound effects contain a pull-down menu to specify the modifying layer, or effect source.

Figure 11.65 When the dimensions of the modifying layer match those of the layer it affects, the final result is more predictable. This example shows the effect source, target image, background image, and result of the Gradient Wipe effect.

Figure 11.66 If the dimensions of the two layers don't match, compound effects offer ways to compensate for the difference.

Figure 11.67 Compound effects refer directly to the effect source—before any mask, effect, or transform property changes have occurred. Apply the Displacement Map effect to this layer...

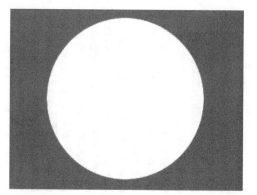

Figure 11.68 ...and use this layer as the effect source (the displacement map)...

Figure 11.69 ...and this is the result.

Center positions the modifying layer in the center of the target layer. If the modifying layer is smaller, the effect may appear to be cut off; if it's larger, the extraneous portions aren't used in the effect.

Stretch to Fit scales the modifying layer to match the dimensions of the target layer. Sometimes, this can distort the modifying layer or make it difficult to position.

Using a nested composition as the effect source

It's important to understand that the three placement options described previously don't alter the modifying layer, only the way its pixels are mapped to the target layer. Conversely, scaling or positioning the modifying layer in the composition doesn't influence the compound effect. This is the case because the compound effect refers directly to the effect source, before any mask, effect, or transform property changes occur (**Figures 11.67**, **11.68**, and **11.69**).

If a layer needs to be scaled (or otherwise treated) before it becomes an effect source, place it into another composition first. The nested composition, in turn, can serve as the modifying layer for the compound effect. This way, you can make any necessary changes to the layer within a composition—before it becomes the effect source. And unlike the layer it contains, the dimensions of the composition can be set to match the compound effect's target layer. As a result, the nested composition—and the layer it contains— maps perfectly to the target layer of the compound effect (**Figures 11.70** and **11.71**).

If all this talk of nesting sounds complicated, don't worry: Chapter 16 explains such topics as nesting and precomposing in greater detail.

Figure 11.70 If a layer requires treatment before becoming an effect source, place it into another comp first. Here, the effect source is scaled and repositioned.

Figure 11.71 You must use the nested comp as the effect source to achieve the desired result.

Animating Effects

Apart from the fact that you can use the Effect Controls panel to adjust values, animating effect properties is no different than animating any other properties. As you learned back in Chapter 7, once you activate the Stopwatch for a property, the procedure for creating keyframes is simple: Set the current time, set a property value, repeat.

Unlike transform and mask properties, however, each effect can contain numerous animated properties—a fact that can lead to an extremely long (and sometimes unwieldy) expanded layer outline or Effect Controls panel. For this reason, you may want to take advantage of property features you overlooked in the past. Remember to use pop-up slider controls to avoid expanding the layer outline ad infinitum. You may also want to reacquaint yourself with the keyboard shortcuts

for hiding properties from the layer outline (showing just the animated properties).

Better yet, learn how you can use the Effect Controls panel to control the keyframing process. Now that the panel includes a Stopwatch icon, you can initiate the keyframing process right from the Effect Controls window. You can also use a contextual menu to set, remove, and navigate property keyframes.

To set keyframes from the Effect Controls panel:

1. Select the layer containing the effect you want to keyframe, and reveal the effect in the Effect Controls panel.

2. Set the current time to the frame at which you want to set an effect property keyframe (**Figure 11.72**).

continues on next page

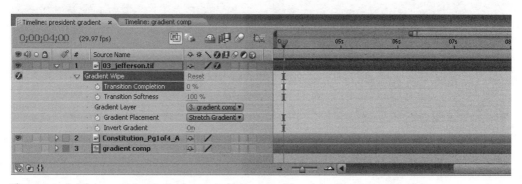

Figure 11.72 Set the current time to the frame at which you want to set an effect property keyframe.

ANIMATING EFFECTS

3. In the Effect Controls panel, select the Stopwatch icon next to the name of the property you want to animate (**Figure 11.73**).

Doing so activates the keyframing process. In the Timeline panel, a keyframe appears at the current time (**Figure 11.74**).

4. Adjust the value of the property in the Effect Controls panel.

5. Set the current time to the point at which you want to set another keyframe.

6. Using the controls in the Effect Controls panel, alter the property's values.

In the Timeline, a new keyframe appears for the property at the current time.

7. Repeat steps 5 and 6 as needed.

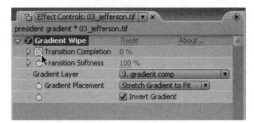

Figure 11.73 In the Effect Controls panel or in the Timeline's layer outline (shown here), select the Stopwatch icon next to the effect property you want to keyframe.

Figure 11.74 A keyframe appears at the current time. The layer outline shown here is expanded for the purpose of illustration; using the Effect Controls panel lets you avoid using the layer outline.

ANIMATING EFFECTS

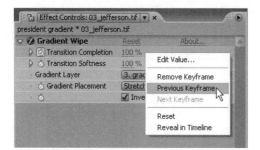

Figure 11.75 Ctrl-click (Mac) or right-click (Windows) the name of an effect property to invoke a contextual menu. In this figure, the current time is cued to a keyframe, so the Remove Keyframe option is present. When the current time isn't cued to a keyframe, the Add Keyframe option is available instead.

To use a contextual menu to set and navigate keyframes:

1. In the Effect Controls panel, Ctrl-click (Mac) or right-click (Windows) the name of an effect property to invoke a contextual menu (**Figure 11.75**).

2. In the contextual menu, *choose one of the following options:*

   Edit Value—Changes the property value at the current time numerically, or changes the range of a value slider.

   Remove Keyframe—Available if the current time is cued to a keyframe. Removes the property's keyframe at the current time.

   Add Keyframe—Available if you *are not* cued to a keyframe. Adds a keyframe for the property at the current time. The keyframe uses interpolated values, unless and until you adjust the values.

   Previous Keyframe—Moves the current time to the previous keyframe (if one exists).

   Next Keyframe—Moves the current time to the next keyframe (if one exists).

   Reset—Resets the property to its default value for the current keyframe.

   Reveal in Timeline—Expands the layer outline to reveal the current keyframe in the Timeline panel.

CREATING AND ANIMATING TEXT

With all its strengths in animation and compositing motion footage, you might expect After Effects to possess more limited text-creation tools, leaving serious typesetting to Photoshop or Illustrator. Not so. After Effects lets you create text with the same ease and flexibility as its software siblings.

True, in older versions of After Effects, creating text meant applying the Basic Text or Path Text effect to a layer. Those effects still exist; but since After Effects 6, you can create a text layer by typing with a type tool directly in a Comp panel. Moreover, you can adjust the text using full-featured Character and Paragraph panels. You can even convert a text layer imported from Photoshop into a text layer you can edit in After Effects. And as in Illustrator, you can convert text into outlines you can manipulate as mask paths.

Naturally, you can animate text layers as you would any other layer in a comp. But you can also animate *the text itself*. Text layers include unique properties that allow you to change the content of the text over time and, yes—like the old Path Text effect—animate the text along a mask path you specify. But more amazing, you can animate individual components of the text—a line, a word, a character—as though it were its own layer. It's like having a text-based animation system within the layer-based animation system. And although the text-animation paradigm employs a unique feature called *animator groups*—each consisting of the properties and parts of the text you want to affect—it also uses the familiar keyframing process you learned about in Chapter 7, "Properties and Keyframes." Animator groups let you create intricate animations using relatively simple controls. Or, if you prefer, you can apply a canned text animation. After Effects includes an astonishingly varied, useful, and generous collection of preset animations you can apply to text with a click of the mouse. OK, *double-click*.

Setting the Workspace for Text

Before you start working with type, familiarize yourself with the relevant tools and specialized panels, and take a moment to optimize your workspace.

Naturally, text creation starts with selecting a type tool. The Tools panel includes both Horizontal and Vertical Type tools, although one is always hidden; press and hold the visible tool to reveal an extended palette (**Figure 12.1**).

To format the text you create, you employ the Character and Paragraph panels. Switching to the Text workspace invokes these panels and rearranges the workspace to accommodate them. When you're using another workspace, you can use the Tools panel's Toggle Panels button to quickly open the panels related to the current tool—in this case, those related to the Text tool.

The tasks in this chapter explain the options in the Character and Paragraph panels but assume you know how to set values: by dragging (or scrubbing) values, clicking and entering new values, or selecting a preset value in a pull-down menu.

Figure 12.1 To create text, select a Type tool.

Figure 12.2 Choosing the Text workspace rearranges the interface so it includes the Character and Paragraph panels.

Figure 12.3 With a Type tool selected, clicking the Toggle Panels button opens and closes the Character and Paragraph panels.

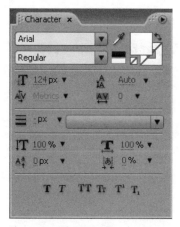

Figure 12.4 The Character panel lets you format text, specifying such attributes as font, font size, and the like.

To specify the Text workspace:

◆ In the Tools panel's Workspace pull-down menu, choose Text (**Figure 12.2**).

 The panels rearrange according to the preset and include the Character and Paragraph panels.

To toggle the Character and Paragraph panels:

1. In the Tools panel, select either the Vertical Type or Horizontal Type tool.

2. In the Tools panel, click the Toggle Panels button ▤ (**Figure 12.3**).

 Clicking the button toggles the Character and Paragraph panels open and closed (**Figures 12.4** and **12.5**).

✔ Tips

■ In previous versions of After Effects, clicking small arrow buttons in the Character and Paragraph panels let you change values incrementally. Because you can change values by scrubbing (dragging a value) just as easily, the arrow buttons have been removed. Similarly, the redesigned interface and preset workspaces have made the Auto Open Palettes option obsolete.

■ Pull-down menus for choosing preset values (such as font size) are represented by a triangle instead of the wide button used in previous versions of the program.

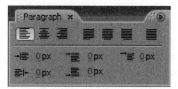

Figure 12.5 The Paragraph panel lets you specify options particular to blocks of text, such as alignment, indents, and so on.

Creating Type

After Effects' Tools panel includes two tools for creating type: the Horizontal Type and Vertical Type tools. Both tools occupy the same location in the panel, but you can access them by clicking and holding one tool to expand the panel and reveal the other (**Figure 12.6**). As you've guessed, the tool you choose depends on whether you want the type to be oriented horizontally or vertically (**Figure 12.7**).

Point text and paragraph text

Both tools let you create two kinds of text objects: *point text* and *paragraph text*. When you create point text, you use a type tool to set the insertion point and start typing. When you create paragraph text, on the other hand, you first define a *text box* that contains the text.

Initially, there seems to be little difference between the two methods (**Figure 12.8**). But a practical distinction emerges when it's time to edit the text. With both kinds of text, changing the size of the text layer's bounding box *transforms* the text (scales or stretches it). That happens because the bounding box consists of layer handles that work like any other layer's handles. But in contrast to point text, paragraph text also lets you resize its *text box*. Paragraph text *reflows* to fit in its text box, creating line breaks if necessary (**Figure 12.9**). This behavior is also known as *word wrap*.

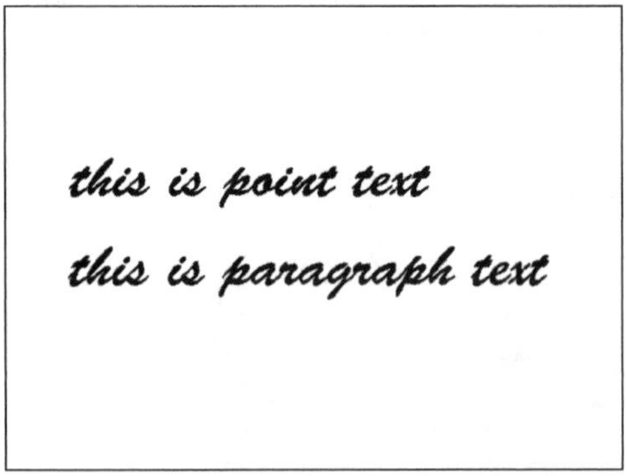

As its name suggests, paragraph text is better suited for lengthier messages that may need to be reflowed to better fit the comp or that require paragraph-style layout adjustments, such as margins.

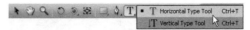

Figure 12.6 Click and hold either type tool to expand the panel and reveal the other.

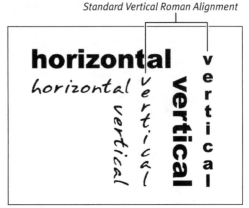

Figure 12.7 The Horizontal Type tool created the horizontal text; the Vertical Type tool created the vertical text. The way characters appear in a vertical line depends on whether you specify Standard Vertical Roman Alignment.

Figure 12.8 Although the point text on top doesn't look any different from the paragraph text on the bottom...

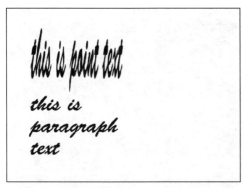

Figure 12.9 ...resizing the point text's bounding box (its normal layer handles) scales the type, whereas resizing the paragraph text's text box reflows the type.

Figure 12.10 Choose the Vertical Type or Horizontal Type tool (shown here).

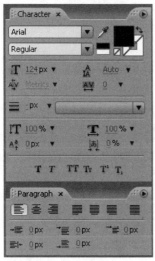

Figure 12.11 Specify how you want the text to look by choosing options in the Character and Paragraph panels.

✔ Tips

■ The four corner handles of a layer's bounding box appear as solid boxes, whereas all the corner handles of a text box appear hollow.

■ The vertical orientation is particularly useful for Chinese, Japanese, and Korean text.

To create point text:

1. In the Tools panel, *choose either of the following tools:*

   ▲ **Horizontal Type** **T**—Creates horizontally oriented text (**Figure 12.10**)

   ▲ **Vertical Type** **T**—Creates vertically oriented text

   Both tools occupy the same location in the panel. To choose the hidden tool, click and hold the tool button to expand the panel, or use the keyboard shortcut Command-T (Mac) or Ctrl-T (Windows).

2. Specify character and paragraph options using controls in the appropriate panel (**Figure 12.11**).

   You can select and modify the text at any time. See sections later in this chapter for more information.

3. In the Composition panel, position the mouse where you want the text to begin.

   As you position the mouse pointer, it appears as an I-beam icon ⏐. The short horizontal line in the I-beam icon indicates the location of the text's baseline.

4. When the I-beam icon is where you want, click the mouse.

   A vertical line appears where you clicked, indicating the text's insertion point.

continues on next page

CREATING TYPE

5. Type the text you want (**Figure 12.12**).

   Text appears at the insertion point, using the current character settings (font, size, fill color, and so on) and paragraph settings. The direction in which characters proceed from the insertion point depends on the current alignment or justification setting (see "Aligning and justifying paragraphs," later in this chapter).

6. When you're finished typing, choose the Selection tool.

   In the Comp panel, bounding box handles indicate that the new text object is selected. In the Timeline panel, a text layer appears, and its name matches what you typed (**Figure 12.13**).

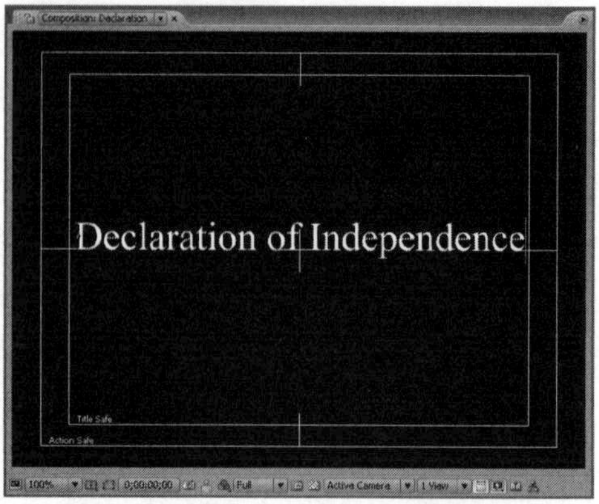

Figure 12.12 Click to set the text's insertion point (indicated by a vertical line), and type the message you want.

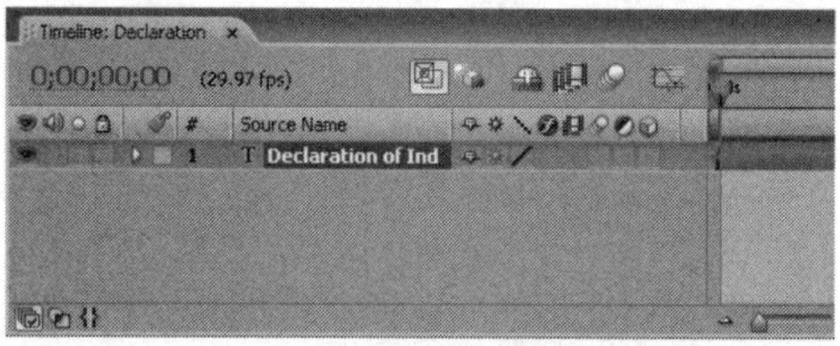

Figure 12.13 When you choose the Selection tool, the new text layer is selected in the Comp panel. In the Timeline panel, its layer name matches what you typed.

To create paragraph text:

1. In the Tools panel, *choose either of the following tools:*
   - ▲ **Horizontal Type**—Creates horizontally oriented text (**Figure 12.14**)
   - ▲ **Vertical Type**—Creates vertically oriented text

   Both tools occupy the same location in the panel. To choose the hidden tool, click and hold the tool button to expand the panel, or use the keyboard shortcut Command-T (Mac) or Ctrl-T (Windows).

Figure 12.14 Choose the Vertical Type or Horizontal Type tool (shown here).

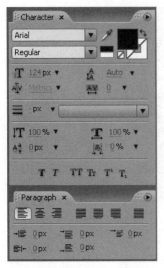

Figure 12.15 Specify character and paragraph options before you enter the text. You can reformat the text later if you want.

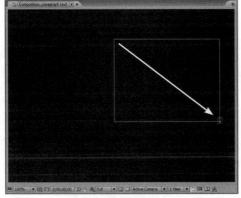

Figure 12.16 In the Comp panel, drag the mouse diagonally to define the size of the text box.

2. Specify character and paragraph options using controls in the appropriate panel (**Figure 12.15**).

You can select and modify the text at any time. See sections later in this chapter for more information.

3. In the Composition panel, drag the mouse diagonally to define a text box (**Figure 12.16**).

When you release the mouse, a text box appears with a vertical insertion point icon in the upper-left corner.

continues on next page

4. Type the text you want.

When the text box you defined can't contain the text horizontally, the text continues on the next line (by means of a *soft return*). Text that exceeds the vertical limit of its text box remains hidden until you resize the text box. When text is hidden this way, the bottom-right handle of the text box includes a plus sign, or crosshairs ⊞ (**Figure 12.17**).

5. To resize the text box to include hidden text or reflow visible text, drag any of its eight handles.

The text reflows to fit within the text box. When the text box is large enough to hold all the text, the bottom-right handle no longer displays a plus sign (**Figure 12.18**).

6. When you're finished creating the message and resizing the text box, click the Selection tool .

In the Timeline panel, a text layer appears; its name matches what you typed (**Figure 12.19**). In the Comp panel, bounding box handles indicate that the new text object is selected. Note that resizing the text layer's bounding box scales the text object. To change the size of the text box and reflow the text, you must enter text-editing mode (as explained in the following task, "To resize a text bounding box").

CREATING TYPE

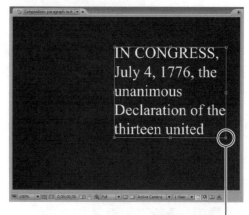

Indicates hidden type

Figure 12.17 When text reaches the side border of the text box, it flows to the next line automatically. If you type more than the text box can contain vertically, the text box's bottom-right handle displays a plus sign (+).

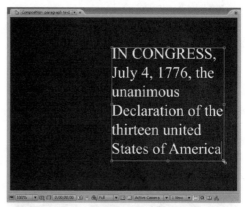

Figure 12.18 While in editing mode, you can drag the text box's handles to resize it and reveal hidden text.

Figure 12.19 Choosing the Selection tool exits editing mode, and the text layer appears selected in the Comp panel. In the Timeline panel, the layer's name matches the text.

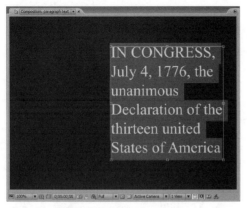

Figure 12.20 Clicking text with a type tool or double-clicking text with the Selection tool (shown here) activates text-editing mode. Layer handles are replaced by text box handles.

Figure 12.21 In text-editing mode, drag any of the text box handles to resize the box...

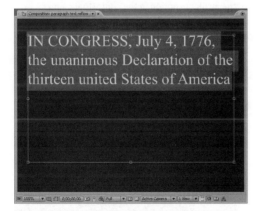

Figure 12.22 ...and reflow the text.

To resize a text bounding box:

1. *Do either of the following:*

▲ Select the Horizontal Type tool or Vertical Type tool , and click paragraph text.

▲ Using the Selection tool , double-click paragraph text (**Figure 12.20**).

An insertion point cursor appears, indicating that you can edit the text. Text box handles also appear. Note that all the handles in a text box are hollow, whereas the four corners of regular layer handles (bounding box handles) are solid (**Figure 12.21**).

2. Drag any of the text box handles to resize the text box.

The text contained in the box reflows to fit in the box horizontally (**Figure 12.22**). Text that doesn't fit in the text box vertically is hidden, and the text box's lower-right handle appears with a crosshair ⊞.

3. When you're finished editing the text box or text, be sure to choose the Selection tool to exit text-editing mode and select the text layer.

To convert point text to paragraph text, and vice versa:

1. Using the Selection tool ▶, select the text layer you want to convert.

2. In the Character panel, select the Horizontal Type tool ▊ or Vertical Type tool ▊.

3. With the type tool, Ctrl-click (Mac) or right-click (Windows) the text layer, and choose the appropriate option (**Figure 12.23**):

   ▲ **Convert to Paragraph Text**

   ▲ **Convert to Point Text**

   The text is converted (**Figure 12.24**). When you're converting paragraph text to point text, soft returns (line breaks caused when text reaches the edge of the text box) are converted into hard returns (line breaks caused by pressing Return [Mac] or Enter [Windows]).

To convert horizontal text to vertical text, and vice versa:

1. Using the Selection tool ▶, select the text layer you want to convert.

2. In the Character panel, select the Horizontal Type tool ▊ or Vertical Type tool ▊.

3. With the type tool, Ctrl-click (Mac) or right-click (Windows) the text layer, and choose the appropriate option (**Figure 12.25**):

   ▲ **Horizontal**

   ▲ **Vertical**

   The text is converted (**Figure 12.26**).

Figure 12.23 With a type tool, Ctrl-click (Mac) or right-click (Windows) the text layer, and choose the available option in the contextual menu.

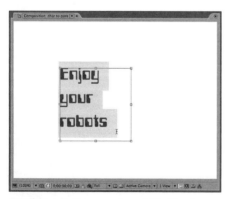

Figure 12.24 In this example, point text has been converted into paragraph text.

Figure 12.25 Ctrl-click (Mac) or right-click (Windows) the text, and choose the available option in the context menu. Here, horizontal text...

Figure 12.26 ...is converted into vertical text.

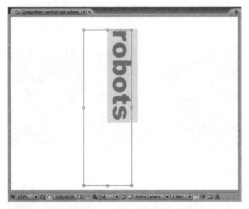

Figure 12.27 Select a range of vertical text. Here, Standard Vertical Roman Alignment is disabled, and characters appear sideways.

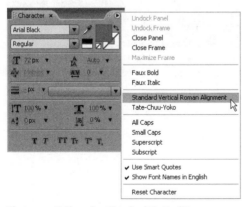

Figure 12.28 Choosing Standard Vertical Roman Alignment in the Character panel's pull-down menu...

To change the alignment of vertically oriented text:

1. Select a range of characters in a vertical text layer (**Figure 12.27**).

2. In the Character panel, choose Standard Vertical Roman Alignment from the pull-down menu (**Figure 12.28**).

   When the option is selected, vertical text characters are upright; when the option is unselected, vertical text is sideways (**Figure 12.29**).

✔ Tip

■ You can't convert a text layer from horizontal to vertical (or vice versa) when it's in text-editing mode.

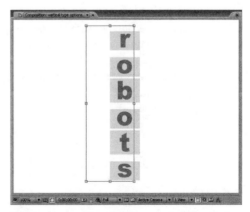

Figure 12.29 ...makes each character in the vertical line appear upright.

Editing Type

Making changes to type in After Effects is as easy and intuitive as in other Adobe applications, such as Illustrator or Photoshop. Just make sure you select the characters you want to modify first, and then use the Character and Paragraph panels to make the adjustments.

It's worth noting that the methods discussed in the following sections change the content and attributes of the selected text. You can also modify the entire text layer, using the same methods you'd use to modify any other layer.

To select characters for editing:

1. To select all the characters in the text layer, double-click the layer in the Comp panel with the Selection tool ▖.

   All characters in the text layer appear highlighted (**Figure 12.30**).

2. With the characters highlighted, *do any of the following*:

   ▲ To set an insertion point between characters, click between the characters (**Figure 12.31**).

   ▲ To highlight a limited range of characters, click and drag to highlight the characters you want to adjust (**Figure 12.32**).

   If you set an insertion point, you can add or delete characters, or adjust the kerning. If you select a range of characters, you can change any of their attributes using controls in the Character and Paragraph panels.

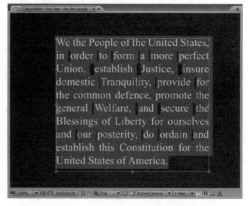

Figure 12.30 Double-clicking the text with the Selection tool activates editing mode. The text is highlighted (and for paragraph text, layer handles are replaced with text box handles).

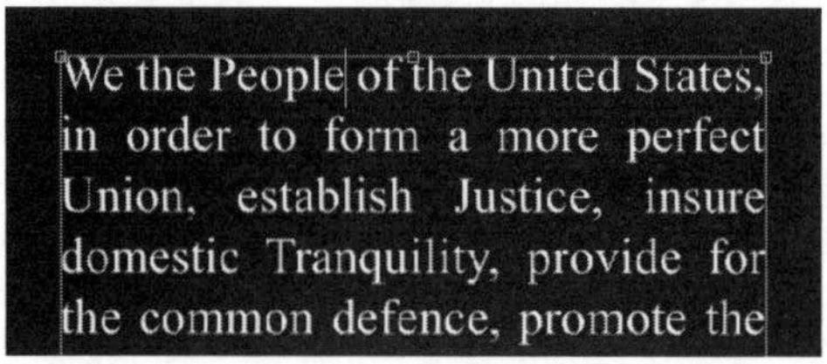

> We the People of the United States, in order to form a more perfect Union, establish Justice, insure domestic Tranquility, provide for the common defence, promote the

Figure 12.31 Click again to set an insertion point (indicated by a vertical line)...

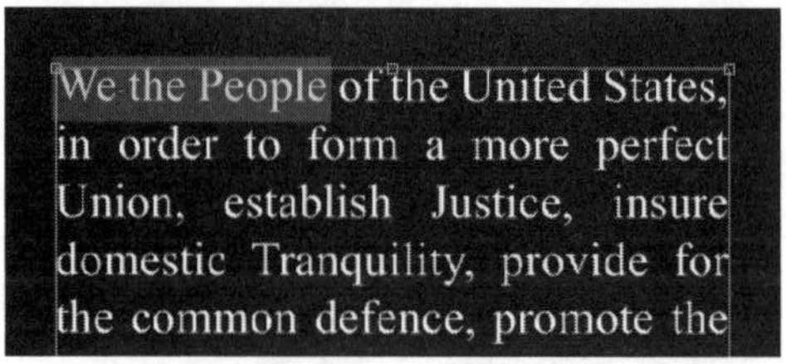

> We the People of the United States, in order to form a more perfect Union, establish Justice, insure domestic Tranquility, provide for the common defence, promote the

Figure 12.32 ...or click and drag to highlight a range of characters. Now you can edit the content or attributes of the selection.

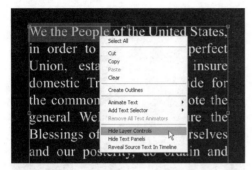

Figure 12.33 With a type tool selected, Option-clicking (Mac) or right-clicking (Windows) text and choosing Hide Layer Controls...

To show and hide layer controls:

◆ With a type tool selected, Option-click (Mac) or right-click (Windows) text, and choose the appropriate option (**Figure 12.33**):

▲ **Hide Layer Controls**

▲ **Show Layer Controls**

The available option depends on the current status of the layer controls. Hiding layer controls prevents highlighted text from obscuring changes such as fill color and the like (**Figure 12.34**).

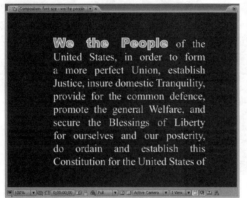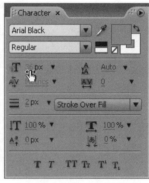

Figure 12.34 ...removes the highlight from the selection. Here, the text is selected, but the usual selection highlight is hidden so it's easier to see adjustments to fill and stroke.

To edit text imported from Photoshop:

1. Import a Photoshop file containing text.

You can import a single layer as a footage item or import a layered file as a comp. See Chapter 2, "Importing Footage into a Project."

2. If necessary, make the imported text a layer in a composition, and select the layer (**Figure 12.35**).

3. Choose Layer > Convert to Editable Text (**Figure 12.36**).

The imported Photoshop text becomes an editable text layer (**Figure 12.37**).

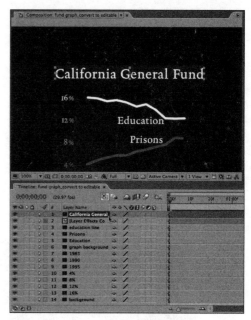

Figure 12.35 Select a layer created from a Photoshop text layer imported as a footage item.

Figure 12.36 Choose Layer > Convert to Editable Text.

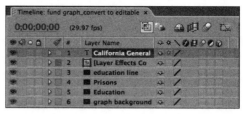

Figure 12.37 The imported Photoshop text becomes a text layer you can edit. Note how layer 1 now bears a T for text icon.

EDITING TYPE

Figure 12.38 Select the characters you want to change to their default settings...

Figure 12.39 ...and choose Reset in the Paragraph panel or Character panel (shown here)...

Figure 12.40 ...to reset the corresponding set of attributes.

✔ Tips

- You can move the layer without deselecting a range of characters by pressing Command (Mac) or Ctrl (Windows) as you drag the text layer.

- Once you set the insertion point cursor, you can use the keyboard to move the cursor and highlight characters. Use the left and right arrow keys to move the cursor; press Shift-arrow to highlight one character at a time; or press Command-Shift-arrow (Mac) or Ctrl-Shift-arrow (Windows) to highlight a word at a time.

- To make changes to a source Photoshop file (or a file created with other Adobe programs), choose Edit > Edit Original.

To reset a character or paragraph to its default settings:

1. In the text layer, select the characters or paragraphs you want to reset to their default formatting settings (**Figure 12.38**).

2. *Do either of the following:*

    ▲ To reset selected characters, choose Reset Character from the Character panel's pull-down menu.

    ▲ To reset selected paragraphs, choose Reset Paragraph from the Paragraph panel's pull-down menu.

    Both panels contain a Reset option (**Figure 12.39**). The selection's formatting settings reset to their defaults (**Figure 12.40**).

EDITING TYPE

Formatting Characters

You can set formatting options before you type, or you can apply formatting options to a range of selected characters. The Character panel includes a number of options found in other Adobe programs: font, style, fill and stroke, size, leading, tracking, kerning, scale, and baseline shift (and its exotic cousin, tsume). You can also apply faux bold, faux italics, small caps, superscript, and subscript to fonts that don't include these forms. You can even use smart quotes in place of standard quotation marks.

Font and style

As you're probably aware, a *font* is a set of *typefaces*, or type designs; it determines the overall look of the text characters. Many fonts include a number of *styles*, or variations on the font: bold, italic, condensed, light, and so on.

Remember: Not all fonts resemble letters. By loading specialized fonts—often called *symbols*, *dingbats*, or *ornaments*—you can easily create useful graphic elements. These fonts are as versatile and scalable as any other elements, and you won't have to draw a thing (**Figure 12.41**).

And don't forget that many foreign-language fonts are also readily available. You can specify whether the font menu lists them in English or in their native language.

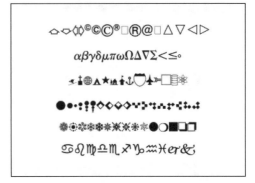

Figure 12.41 Don't forget that a host of specialized fonts—symbols, dingbats, ornaments, and so on—and foreign language fonts are at your disposal.

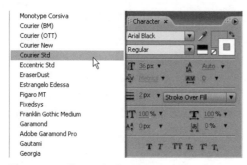

Figure 12.42 Choose the font you want from the Font pull-down menu.

Figure 12.43 Choose a variation in the Style pull-down menu. Style options available in the pull-down menu depend on the font you select.

palatino italic

palatino bold

Figure 12.44 Selected and subsequent characters use the font and style you selected.

To set the font and style:

1. In the Character panel, choose a font from the Font pull-down menu (**Figure 12.42**).

   The font's default style option appears in the Style pull-down menu.

2. In the Style pull-down menu, specify the style you want (**Figure 12.43**).

   The options available in the list depend on the font you selected in step 1. The selected characters use the font you specified (**Figure 12.44**).

✔ Tips

■ You can quickly choose a font name or style by typing the name in the appropriate field. As you type, After Effects specifies the font or style that most closely matches what you enter.

■ If the font you're using doesn't include a bold or italic style option, you can apply a faux bold or faux italic style. See the section "Faux bold and faux italics," later in this chapter.

■ For video output, avoid light text or text with fine features like *serifs* (the little tapering corners of letters in so-called old-style typefaces, like this one). Interlacing causes fine horizontal lines to flicker, making some text difficult to read. See Chapter 2 for more about video interlacing.

Fill and stroke

Each character has two possible color attributes: fill and stroke. Not surprisingly, the *fill color* is the color of the character: the color within its contours. The *stroke color* is the color of the character's contours: its outlines. You can detect the stroke color only if the stroke has a thickness greater than zero. By default, applying a stroke color sets the stroke width to 1 pixel, but you can change the thickness and set whether the stroke is applied over or under the fill (see the task "To set stroke options," later in this chapter).

You can set the fill and stroke color by using controls in the Character panel. If you've used programs like Photoshop and Illustrator, you should already be familiar with these icons. If not, don't confuse the stroke color icon with the drop-shadow color or background color icons sometimes found in other, less-full-featured programs.

To set the fill and stroke color:

1. In the Character panel, click the icon for the color you want to set:

   Fill box—Sets the fill color

   Stroke box—Sets the stroke color

   The selected color's icon appears in front of the other icon.

2. To set the active color, *do any of the following* (**Figure 12.45**):

   ▲ To sample a color from anywhere on the screen, click the Eyedropper icon ⬛, and then click the color.

   ▲ To set the color to black or white, click the appropriate color swatch under the Eyedropper icon.

   ▲ To set the color to transparent, click the No Fill/Stroke color icon ⬚.

   ▲ To set the color using a color picker, click the active color's icon.

   The active color box (fill or stroke) is set to the color you specify; the color is also applied to selected characters and to any subsequent characters you type.

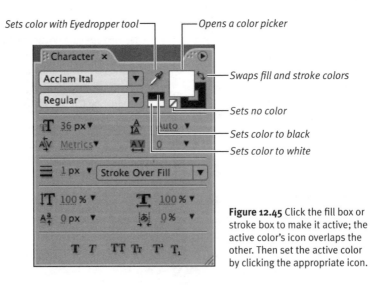

Sets color with Eyedropper tool — — *Opens a color picker*

— *Swaps fill and stroke colors*

— *Sets no color*

— *Sets color to black*

— *Sets color to white*

Figure 12.45 Click the fill box or stroke box to make it active; the active color's icon overlaps the other. Then set the active color by clicking the appropriate icon.

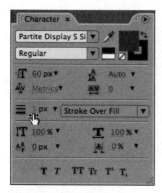

Figure 12.46 Set the Stroke Width, or thickness.

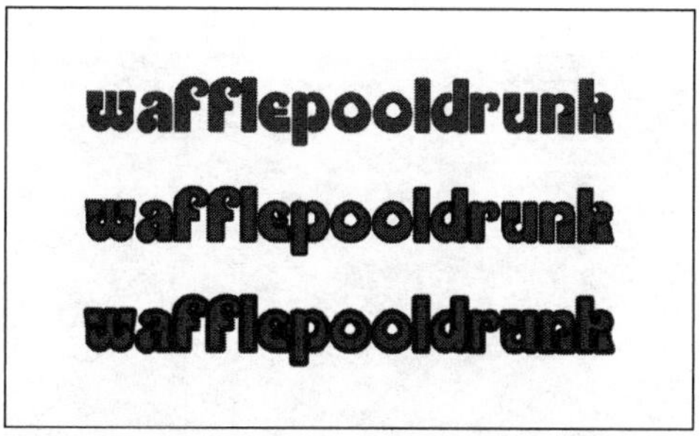

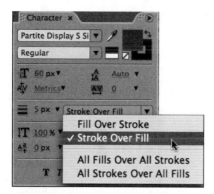

Figure 12.47 Here, words and characters use varying stroke widths.

Figure 12.48 Specify how strokes are applied by choosing an option from the Stroke pull-down menu.

To set the stroke width:

◆ In the Character panel, specify a value for Stroke Width ▬ (**Figure 12.46**).

The stroke width you specify is applied to the selected characters (or to subsequent characters you type) (**Figure 12.47**). You can't set stroke options to characters with stroke color set to No Stroke 🖾.

To set stroke options:

◆ Select the characters you want to modify; and, in the Character panel, *select an option* from the Stroke pull-down menu (**Figure 12.48**):

Fill Over Stroke applies the fill color over the stroke color, so that the fill covers half the thickness of the stroke.

Stroke Over Fill applies the stroke color over the fill color, so that the entire thickness of the stroke is visible and covers part of the interior of the filled character.

All Fills Over All Strokes affects the entire text layer.

All Strokes Over All Fills affects the entire text layer.

Selected and subsequent characters use the stroke options you specify (**Figure 12.49**).

Figure 12.49 In this figure, you can see how applying the stroke over the fill (the upper text) contrasts with applying the fill over the stroke (the lower text).

FORMATTING CHARACTERS

Font size

The size determines—how else can you put it?—the size of a given font. In After Effects, font size is expressed in *pixels* (not points or picas, as in other programs). Note that if you set two different fonts to the same size, one often appears larger than the other.

To set the font size:

◆ In the Character panel, specify a value for the font size  (**Figure 12.50**).

The font size you specified is applied to the selected characters (and to subsequent characters you type) (**Figure 12.51**).

✔ Tip

■ Dragging a text layer's handles scales the entire layer; it won't change the type size, per se, or even affect the horizontal or vertical scaling (explained later in this chapter). But because After Effects continuously rasterizes text layers, the text looks the same whether you resize the font size or the text layer.

Figure 12.50 In After Effects, you specify the font size in pixels (not points or picas).

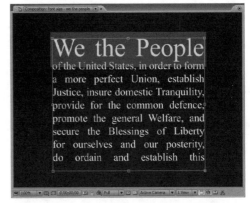

Figure 12.51 This text's font size is so large that the words can only be read once the text layer is animated to move through the screen.

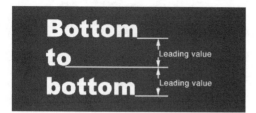

Figure 12.52 Bottom-to-bottom leading is measured from one baseline to the next.

Figure 12.53 Top-to-top leading is measured from the top of one line to the top of the next.

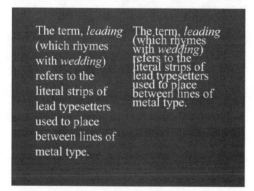

Figure 12.54 Leading can be loose (as in the text on the left) or so tight the text overlaps (as in the text on the right).

Leading

Leading (which rhymes with *wedding*) defines the space between lines of text. The term *leading* refers to the strips of lead that typesetters of old placed between lines of metal type.

In After Effects, leading can be measured either from bottom to bottom or from top to top. The *bottom-to-bottom* method measures from the *baseline* (the invisible floor on which a line of text rests) of one line of text to the baseline of the next line (**Figure 12.52**). The *top-to-top* method, in contrast, measures leading from the top of one line to the top of the next (**Figure 12.53**). Consequently, the first line of text aligns with the top of the text box when you specify top-to-top measurement. (For more about baselines, see "Baseline shift," later in this chapter.)

Whatever method you use, increasing leading expands the space between lines, whereas a negative leading value reduces the space (**Figure 12.54**).

To adjust leading:

1. Select the lines of type you want to adjust.

2. In the Character panel, *do one of the following*:

   ▲ Specify the value for Leading 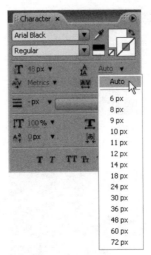 (**Figure 12.55**).

   ▲ To have After Effects calculate the leading, choose Auto from the pull-down menu.

   The leading you specified is applied to the selected characters (or to subsequent characters you type).

To specify how leading is measured:

◆ In the Paragraph panel's pull-down menu, select the leading measurement method you want (**Figure 12.56**):

   Top-to-Top Leading measures between the tops of lines of type; this causes the first line of type to align with the top of the text box.

   Bottom-to-Bottom Leading measures between the baselines of type; space is included between the top of the text box and the first line of type.

   Leading is measured according to the method you specify.

✔ Tip

■ Leading is called Line Spacing in the controls for the Basic Text effect. Because the Path Text effect doesn't accept multiple lines of text, it doesn't include leading controls.

Figure 12.55 Set a value for Leading, or choose Auto from the Leading pull-down menu.

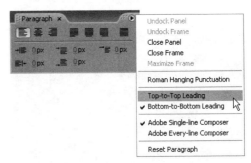

Figure 12.56 Specify how leading is measured in the Paragraph panel's pull-down menu.

Figure 12.57 You can adjust tracking to be tight (so tight that characters overlap) or loose.

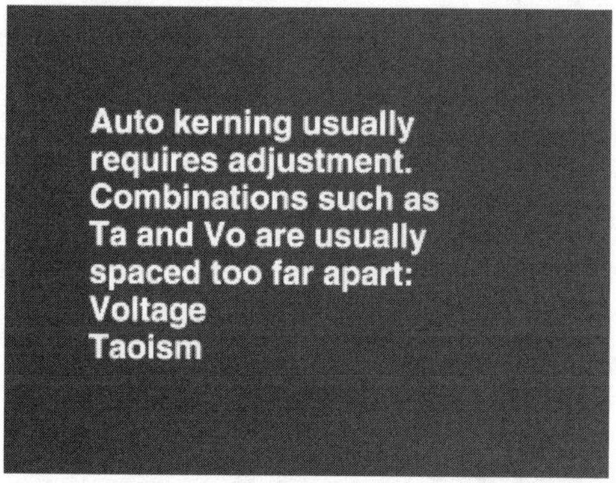

Figure 12.58 Automatic kerning is frequently imperfect, and sometimes it's awful.

Kerning and tracking

When you're working with text, you should understand the subtle but important differences between the typographic terms *tracking* and *kerning*.

Tracking refers to adjusting the overall space between letters in a range of text. High tracking values result in loose, generous letter spacing. Low or negative tracking values result in tight letter spacing or even overlapping letters (**Figure 12.57**).

Kerning describes the process of adjusting the value of *kern pairs*, spacing that the typeface's designer built into particular pairs of characters. This can be an important feature because automatic kerning is rarely perfect; sometimes it can be awful (**Figure 12.58**). As you kern, the space between letters is expressed in *em spaces*, a measurement based on the size of the type.

You can kern between a pair of characters or across a range of characters. The effects of tracking and kerning are cumulative. Typically, you should use tracking to adjust the overall spacing and then use kerning to fine-tune spaces between pairs of characters.

✔ Tips

- The Basic Text effect lets you control tracking but not kerning. The Path Text effect, in contrast, includes kerning controls.

- You can control how overlapping characters interact by setting a blending mode for individual characters. See the section "Blending Characters" later in this chapter. See "Using Blending Modes," in Chapter 14, "More Layer Techniques," for a detailed description of each mode.

FORMATTING CHARACTERS

To adjust kerning:

1. Set the insertion point cursor between two characters, or select a range of characters.

2. In the Character panel, *do one of the following:*

   ▲ Specify the value for Kerning 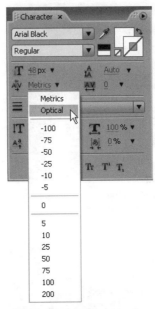 (**Figure 12.59**).

   ▲ To have After Effects calculate the kerning, *choose either of the following options* from the pull-down menu:

   Metrics uses the kern pair values built into the font's design.

   Optical sets the value according to the shape of adjacent characters.

   The kerning you specified is applied to the selected characters (or to subsequent characters you type).

To adjust tracking:

1. Select the range of type you want to adjust.

2. In the Character panel, specify the value for Tracking 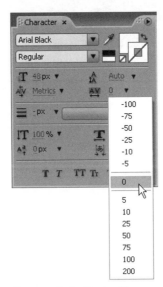 (**Figure 12.60**).

   The tracking value you specified is applied to the selected characters (or to subsequent characters you type).

Figure 12.59 Specify a value for Kerning, or have After Effects calculate it automatically using the Metrics or Optical method.

Figure 12.60 Set the tracking, or overall character spacing.

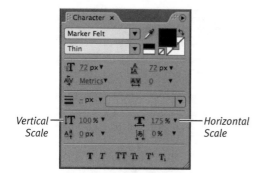

Figure 12.61 You can scale the horizontal and vertical aspects of the text separately.

Figure 12.62 In this example, you can contrast the original unmodified text with the same text scaled horizontally and vertically.

Vertical and horizontal scale

Using controls in the Character panel, you can scale the horizontal or vertical aspect of selected characters, effectively stretching or compressing them. If you scale all the text in the layer, the result is the same as using the text layer's Scale property. But with the Character panel, you don't have to scale *all* the characters; you can scale just the characters you want.

To adjust scale:

1. Select the range of type you want to adjust.

2. In the Character panel, specify the value for Horizontal Scale ■ or Vertical Scale ■ (**Figure 12.61**).

The scale you specified is applied to the selected characters (or to subsequent characters you type) (**Figure 12.62**).

✔ Tip

■ You can skew characters (among other things) using type animation controls, as explained in the sections on animating type later in this chapter.

Baseline shift

Horizontally oriented type sits on an invisible line, or *baseline*. Often, it's useful to shift the baseline up or down so that some characters are higher or lower relative to the other characters in the line. For example, shifting the baseline lets you create the mathematical notation for a fraction with typefaces that don't include fractions (and without resorting to using more than one text layer).

To adjust the baseline shift:

1. Select the range of type you want to adjust.

2. In the Character panel, specify a value for Baseline Shift ᴬ² (**Figure 12.63**).

   The baseline shift you specified is applied to the selected characters (or to subsequent characters you type) (**Figure 12.64**).

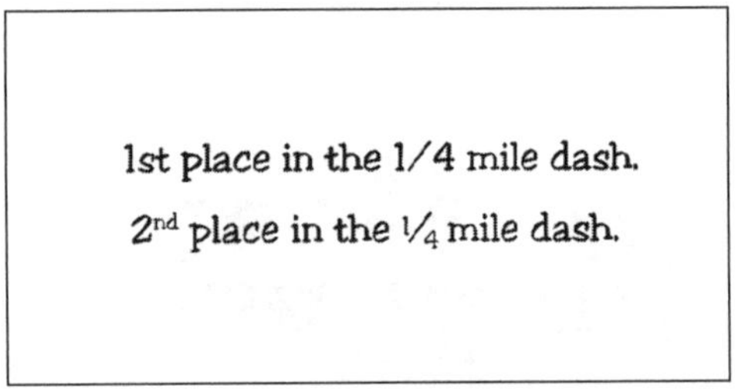

✔ Tips

- Separate controls are available for creating superscript and subscript characters; there's no need to fake these type forms by cleverly shifting the baseline or by inserting a separate text layer.

- Parts of a character that extend below the baseline—such as the bottom of a lowercase *j*—are called *descenders*. Take descenders into account when you're typesetting, especially for text positioned near the bottom of television's title-safe zone.

- The next button in the panel 图 is for adjusting tsume. Because tsume adjusts spacing in Chinese, Japanese, and Korean fonts, it's covered in the section "Setting Options for Chinese, Japanese, and Korean Text," later in this chapter.

Figure 12.63 Specify a value for Baseline Shift.

1st place in the 1/4 mile dash.

2ⁿᵈ place in the ¼ mile dash.

Figure 12.64 Here, the baselines of characters have been shifted to create the fraction within the text. (The font size of the numerals has also been reduced.)

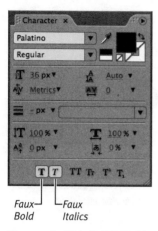

Faux Bold   *Faux Italics*

Figure 12.65 Click the Faux Bold or Faux Italics button to simulate these styles in fonts that don't include them by design.

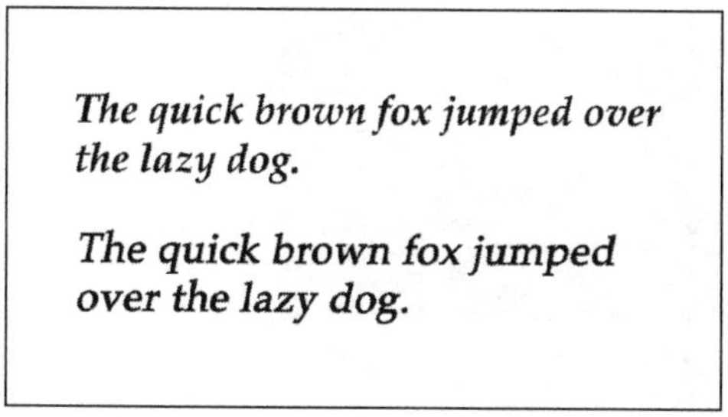

The quick brown fox jumped over the lazy dog.

The quick brown fox jumped over the lazy dog.

Figure 12.66 As you can see, a font that includes a bold and italic typeface (top) looks better than the result of faking those styles (bottom). But if you have no other option, faux bold and faux italics can do the trick.

Faux bold and faux italics

Although many fonts include boldface and italic styles (see "Font and style," earlier in this chapter), others lack these options. In such cases, you can create these typographic effects using the *faux bold* and *faux italic* options. Whereas legitimate bold and italic styles are carefully designed variations of the font, faux bold and faux italics are just that: *faux*, or fake. Using a method more akin to distortion than design, they simulate a bold and italic typeface. Even so, the effect can be convincing, if not ideal.

To specify faux bold and faux italics:

1. Select the range of type you want to adjust.

2. In the character panel, *do any of the following* (**Figure 12.65**):

   ▲ Click the Faux Bold button ▉ to make the selected type bold.

   ▲ Click the Faux Italics button ▉ to make the selected type italic.

   The selected characters (or subsequent characters you type) reflect your choices (**Figure 12.66**).

All caps and small caps

Some fonts include all-caps and small-caps typefaces. All caps is a variation designed to present the font in all capital letters, whereas a small-caps typeface uses a miniature version of capital letters in place of lowercase letters. If the font you're using doesn't include an all-caps or small-caps typeface, you can simulate it in much the same way you simulate a bold or italic font (see the previous section, "Faux bold and faux italics").

To convert lowercase to uppercase:

1. Select the range of type you want to adjust.

2. In the Character panel, click the All Caps button **TT** (**Figures 12.67** and **12.68**).

   The selected lowercase characters (and subsequent lowercase characters you type) are converted to uppercase (**Figure 12.69**).

   You can select characters converted to uppercase and deselect the All Caps option to make the characters lowercase again.

Figure 12.67 Selecting lowercase characters...

Figure 12.68 ...and clicking the All Caps button...

Figure 12.69 ...converts the characters to uppercase.

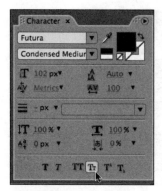

Figure 12.70 Selecting the Small Caps button instead...

Figure 12.71 ...converts the selection to small caps.

To specify small caps:

1. Select the range of type you want to adjust.

2. In the Character panel, select the Small Caps button ▥ (**Figure 12.70**).

   The selected lowercase characters (or subsequent lowercase characters you type) are converted into small caps. Uppercase characters are unaffected (**Figure 12.71**).

   You can select characters converted to small caps and deselect the option to make the characters lowercase again.

Superscript and subscript

The last buttons in the Character panel let you specify characters as superscript and subscript. *Superscript* characters appear higher (and usually smaller) than the rest of a line of text, whereas *subscript* characters appear lower (and usually smaller) than the other characters. These forms are often associated with scientific notation. With proper typesetting, the 2 in the familiar equation $E=Mc^2$, is superscript; the 2 in the chemical notation for water, H_2O, is subscript. As with bold and italics, some characters are already superscripted. In most fonts, for example, the trademark symbol ™ (Option-2 on the Mac or Alt-0153 on Windows) is already superscripted. To superscript or subscript other characters, you can use the buttons in the Character panel.

To make text superscript or subscript:

1. Select the range of type you want to adjust.

2. In the Character panel, do any of the following (**Figure 12.72**):

   ▲ To make the selected type superscript, click the Superscript button .

   ▲ To make the selected type subscript, click the Subscript button .

   The selected characters (and subsequent characters you type) reflect your choices (**Figure 12.73**).

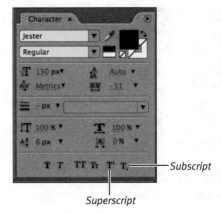

Figure 12.72 In the Character panel, select the Superscript or Subscript button.

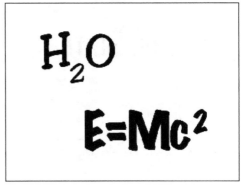

Figure 12.73 Here, the 2 in $E=Mc^2$ is superscripted; the 2 in H_2O is subscripted.

Character
Arial Black
Regular
48 px
Auto
Metrics
0
px
100 %
100 %
0 px
0 %
Undock Panel
Undock Frame
Close Panel
Close Frame
Maximize Frame
Faux Bold
Faux Italic
Standard Vertical Roman Alignment
Tate-Chuu-Yoko
All Caps
Small Caps
Superscript
Subscript
Use Smart Quotes
Show Font Names in English
Reset Character

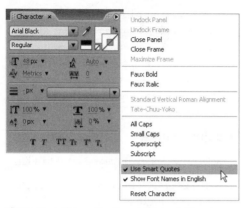

Figure 12.74 Choose Use Smart Quotes in the Character panel's pull-down menu.

"Heavier-than-air flying machines are impossible."
Lord Kelvin, President, Royal Society 1895
“Not everything that counts can be counted, and not everything that can be counted counts.”
sign in Albert Einstein's office at Princeton

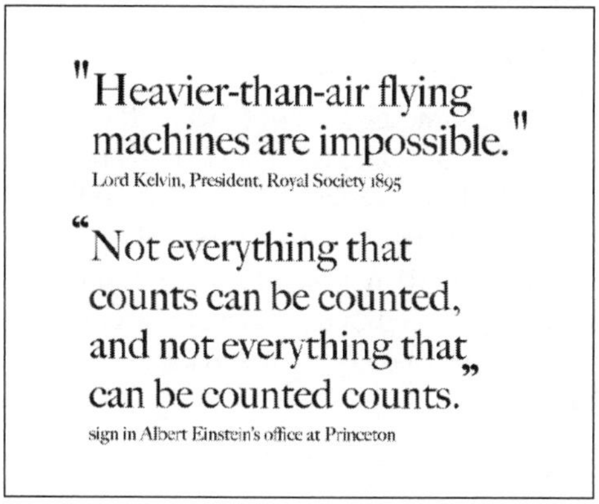

Figure 12.75 Here are a dumb quote using dumb quotation marks and a smart quote using smart quotes.

Smart quotes

Often, quotation marks appear as a pair of short straight lines on each side of a quotation. *Smart quotes*, also called *curly quotes* or *printer's quotation marks*, are a fancier version. Smart quotes look more like a pair of dots, each with a little clockwise-curving tail. The open quote's tails point up; the close quote's tails point down. Because each mark points in the right direction automatically, they're called "smart."

To specify smart quotes:

1. Select the range of type you want to adjust.
2. In the Character panel's pull-down menu, choose Use Smart Quotes (**Figure 12.74**).

   When the option is selected, quotation marks appear curved; when the option is unselected, quotation marks appear straight (**Figure 12.75**).

Setting Options for Chinese, Japanese, and Korean Text

Because they share certain typographic characteristics, Chinese, Japanese, and Korean fonts are referred to collectively as *CJK fonts*. They're also known as *double-byte* fonts, because two bytes of information are required to represent each character instead of the typical one byte.

Tsume

If the term *tsume* sounds exotic, that's because it is (assuming you aren't in China, Japan, or Korea). Tsume determines the amount of space around each character. Adjusting tsume reduces the space on both sides of selected characters by a specified percentage. Zero percent uses the character's default spacing; 100 percent reduces the space by the maximum amount possible.

You might compare tsume to tracking or kerning. However, these methods of adjusting spacing differ significantly. Kerning, you'll remember, adjusts kern pairs—not the space on both sides of a single character. Similarly, tracking only affects the space following a character.

To adjust tsume:

1. Select the range of type you want to adjust.

2. In the Character panel, specify a value for Tsume ▨ (**Figure 12.76**).

   The tsume you specify is applied to the selected characters (or to subsequent characters you type) (**Figure 12.77**).

✔ Tip

■ The character used in the icon for adjusting tsume is the first character in the Japanese syllabary, known as Hiragana (this character あ makes an "ah" sound). A *syllabary* is something like an alphabet, but each symbol can represent both a consonant and a vowel sound.

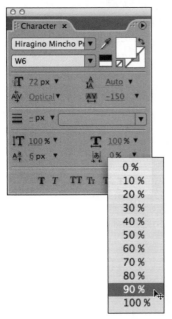

Figure 12.76 Specify a value for Tsume in the Character panel.

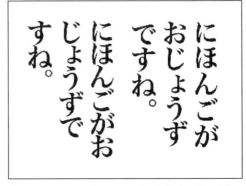

Figure 12.77 Here, the text on the right (reading right to left) uses a tsume value of 0 percent; the text on the left uses a tsume value of 100 percent.

Figure 12.78 Mixing CJK fonts with other character sets can present typesetting problems—specifically, Roman characters and Arabic numerals (shown here) can appear improperly oriented.

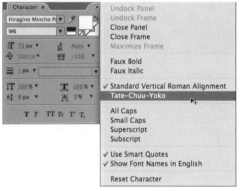

Figure 12.79 Selecting the characters and choosing Tate-Chuu-Yoko in the Character panel...

Figure 12.80 ...reorients the characters and solves the problem.

Tate-chuu-yoko

Another formatting option relevant to CJK fonts is called *tate-chuu-yoko*. If that term doesn't roll off the tongue, you can also refer to it as *kumimoji* or *renmoji*. Tate-chuu-yoko refers to horizontal characters within a vertically oriented line of type.

For example, Japanese writing often includes a combination of *Hiragana* (a syllabary for native Japanese words), *Katakana* (for imported words), *Kanji* (ideographs borrowed from Chinese), *Romanji* (the Roman alphabet), and Arabic numerals. (No wonder you need special options to typeset properly for Japanese readers!) The *kana* (as Hiragana and Katakana are referred to collectively) and Kanji are often laid out as vertical type. But Romanji and numerals must occupy the same vertical line, presenting a unique typesetting problem. You can correct the problem with—you guessed it—tate-chuu-yoko.

To set tate-chuu-yoko:

1. Select the characters you want to adjust (**Figure 12.78**).

2. In the Character panel's pull-down menu, choose Tate-Chuu-Yoko (**Figure 12.79**).

   The selected characters (and subsequent characters you type) are reoriented in the vertical line of text (**Figure 12.80**).

✔ Tip

■ In the Character panel's pull-down menu, select Show Font Names in English to list foreign language fonts in English; deselect the option to list them in their native language.

Blending Characters

As you learned earlier in this chapter, it's possible to make characters in the same text layer overlap (for example, by severely reducing the tracking or leading). If the character's fill or stroke permits it, you'll see that each succeeding character overlaps with the last, a little like the scales of a fish. Each character appears as though it's on a higher layer than the one that precedes it—even though the characters are all on the same layer. (The same is true for each succeeding line of text.)

Nevertheless, you can apply a blending mode to each character in much the same way you'd apply a blending mode to an entire layer. Blending modes for layers aren't covered in detail until Chapter 14, "More Layer Techniques." For now, suffice it to say that blending modes determine how the image in one layer interacts, or combines, with the underlying image. You can choose from the same blending mode options to blend one character with the character it overlaps.

To set a blending mode for overlapping characters:

1. Select the characters to which you want to apply a blending mode (**Figure 12.81**).

2. In the Timeline panel, expand the text layer and the More Options property heading.

3. In the Inter-Character Blending pulldown menu, choose a blending mode (**Figure 12.82**).

   For a detailed explanation of each mode, see Chapter 14.

   The selected characters (and subsequent characters you type) use the blending mode you specified (**Figure 12.83**).

✔ Tip

■ You can apply a blending mode to the text layer, just as you would any other layer.

Figure 12.81 If the fill and stroke options allow, you can see how each succeeding character overlaps with the last. Select the characters to change how they interact.

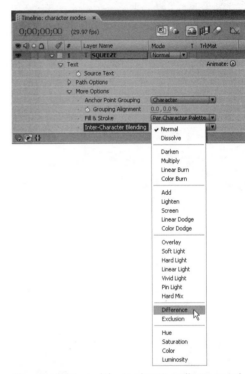

Figure 12.82 Expand the text layer's outline to reveal the Inter-Character Blending property, and choose a mode in the pull-down menu.

Figure 12.83 Here, overlapping characters are set to use the Difference blending mode.

Figure 12.84 Create a text layer, and, with the layer selected, create a mask path.

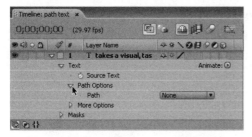

Figure 12.85 In the Timeline panel, expand the text layer's property outline to reveal its Path Options property heading.

Making Text Follow a Path

You can make the type in any text layer follow a path you specify, without sacrificing any of the formatting or text animation options available to the text layer.

To create path text:

1. Create and format a text layer.

   You can use any of the techniques discussed earlier in this chapter.

2. With the text layer selected, create a mask path to serve as the baseline of the text (**Figure 12.84**).

   Use any of the techniques described in Chapter 10, "Mask Essentials." In the Timeline panel, the mask you create appears in the text layer's property outline.

3. In the Timeline panel, expand the text layer's property outline; then, expand its Text property heading and Path Options property heading (**Figure 12.85**).

4. In the Path pull-down menu, choose the path you created in step 2 (**Figure 12.86**).

   The text uses the specified path as its baseline (**Figure 12.87**).

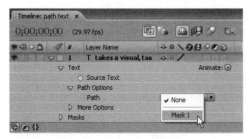

Figure 12.86 Choose the path you want the text to follow in the Path pull-down menu.

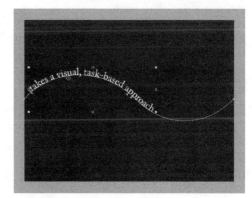

Figure 12.87 The text follows the path.

To animate path text:

1. Create path text as described in the previous task, "To create path text."

2. Set the current time to the frame where you want the animation to begin.

3. In the path text layer's property outline, set the First Margin value to specify the text's starting point on the path, and click the Stopwatch icon to set the initial keyframe (**Figure 12.88**).

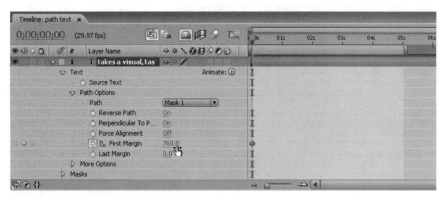

Figure 12.88 Set the current time to the frame where you want the animation to begin, and set a keyframe for the First Margin property value.

Figure 12.89 Set the current time to the frame where you want the animation to end, and change the First Margin property value to its final position along the path.

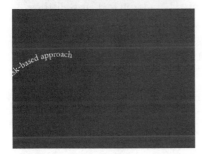

Figure 12.90 Animating the First Margin property moves the text along the path.

4. Set the current time to the frame where you want the animation to end, and set the First Margin value to set the text's starting point on the path when the animation ends (**Figure 12.89**).

When you preview the animation, the text moves along the path (**Figure 12.90**). Use the techniques covered in Chapter 7, "Properties and Keyframes," and Chapter 9, "Keyframe Interpolation," to refine the animation.

Formatting Paragraph Text

Whenever paragraph text reaches the edge of the text box, it flows into another line automatically—something often referred to as a *soft return*. A new *paragraph* occurs when you press Return (Mac) or Enter (Windows), also known as a *hard return*.

You can control each paragraph independently, using a Paragraph panel that's nearly indistinguishable from the one found in Illustrator and Photoshop. An intuitive set of controls lets you set alignment, justification, and indentation. You can also specify hanging punctuation and determine how After Effects creates automatic line breaks within each paragraph.

Aligning and justifying paragraphs

Aligning and justifying paragraph text in After Effects is as easy as in any good word-processing program.

As you probably know, *alignment* determines how the lines in a paragraph are positioned relative to the margins (the left and right sides of the text box). As usual, you can set whether the lines align flush with the left or right or are centered horizontally in the box.

Justification alters the spacing in each line of text so that all the lines are flush with both the right and left margins. (Think of the neat, justified columns you find in a newspaper.) Typically, the last line in a paragraph is shorter than the rest and doesn't easily lend itself to justification. After Effects lets you set whether the last line is aligned with the left side or right side of the text box or is centered horizontally. Or, you can justify all the lines, including the last line of the paragraph.

The following tasks illustrate alignment and justification for horizontal text. You can set alignment and justification options for vertically oriented paragraph text, as well; the icons on the buttons change accordingly. For example, the Align Left button ▦ becomes the Align Top button ▥.

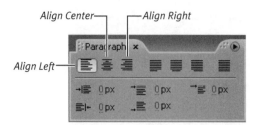

Figure 12.91 Click the button that corresponds with the paragraph alignment you want.

To align paragraph text:

1. Select one or more paragraphs you want to format.

2. In the Paragraph panel, *click one of the following buttons* to set the selected paragraph's alignment (**Figure 12.91**):

   ▲ **Align Left**
   ▲ **Align Center**
   ▲ **Align Right**

   The paragraph aligns according to your choice (**Figure 12.92**).

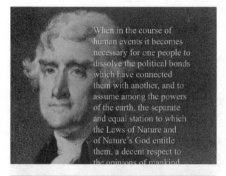

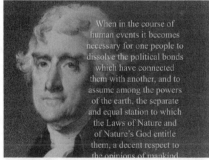

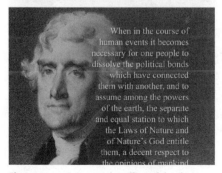

Figure 12.92 Compare the effect of the three alignment options in this composition.

To justify paragraph text:

1. Select one or more paragraphs you want to format.

2. In the Paragraph panel, *click one of the following buttons* to set the selected paragraph's justification (**Figure 12.93**):

   ▲ **Justify Last Left** ▤

   ▲ **Justify Last Center** ▤

   ▲ **Justify Last Right** ▤

   ▲ **Justify All** ▤

   The paragraph is justified, and the last line uses the justification you specified (**Figure 12.94**).

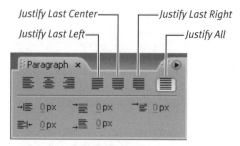

Justify Last Center —   — Justify Last Right

Justify Last Left —   — Justify All

Figure 12.93 Justifying a paragraph eliminates ragged edges, with the possible exception of the last line in a paragraph. The four options format the last line differently.

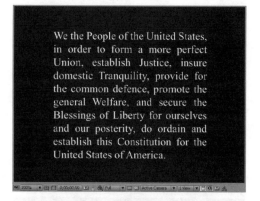

We the People of the United States, in order to form a more perfect Union, establish Justice, insure domestic Tranquility, provide for the common defence, promote the general Welfare, and secure the Blessings of Liberty for ourselves and our posterity, do ordain and establish this Constitution for the United States of America.

We the People of the United States, in order to form a more perfect Union, establish Justice, insure domestic Tranquility, provide for the common defence, promote the general Welfare, and secure the Blessings of Liberty for ourselves and our posterity, do ordain and establish this Constitution for the United States of America.

Figure 12.94 Choosing Justify Last Left (the top paragraph) leaves the last line ragged. However, choosing Justify All (the bottom paragraph) can result in awkward spacing in the last line.

Indenting paragraphs

Indenting a line of text increases one or both of its margins, shifting it away from the margins defined by the sides of the text box. You can indent each paragraph's left and right margins, and indent the left margin of each paragraph's first line separately.

To indent paragraphs:

1. Select one or more paragraphs you want to format.

2. In the Paragraph panel, specify the selected paragraph's Left Indent ⊣≣ or Right Indent ≣⊢ or the indent of the first line ⊤≣ (**Figure 12.95**).

   The indent you specified is applied to the selected paragraph (and subsequent paragraphs you create) (**Figure 12.96**).

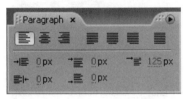

Figure 12.95 Specify a paragraph indent option.

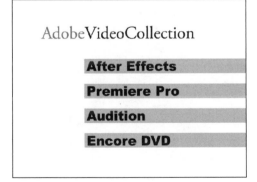

Figure 12.96 The indent is applied to the paragraph. This example shows a single text layer, but the list of software is indented 125 pixels.

Spacing paragraphs

As you know, a hard return—pressing Return (Mac) or Enter (Windows)—creates a new line and paragraph. You can specify the space before or after new paragraphs, independent of the line spacing (or leading) within each paragraph.

To set paragraph spacing:

1. Select one or more paragraphs you want to format.

2. In the Paragraph panel, specify a value for Space Before ⊤≣ or Space After ⊥≣ (**Figure 12.97**).

   The spacing you specify is applied to the selected paragraph and subsequent paragraphs (**Figure 12.98**).

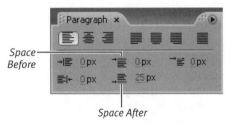

Figure 12.97 In the Paragraph panel, set Space Before and Space After.

Figure 12.98 Here, a single text layer contains several paragraphs. The extra space between paragraphs was created by increasing the default Space After value.

FORMATTING PARAGRAPH TEXT

Hanging punctuation

Generally, the alignment or justification option you apply to a paragraph applies to punctuation marks, as well. However, you can also specify that a paragraph use *hanging punctuation*. Hanging punctuation allows punctuation marks to appear outside the text box. For example, in a quotation with left alignment, the open quote "hangs" outside the left edge of text box, like a gargoyle perched on the side of a building (**Figure 12.99**).

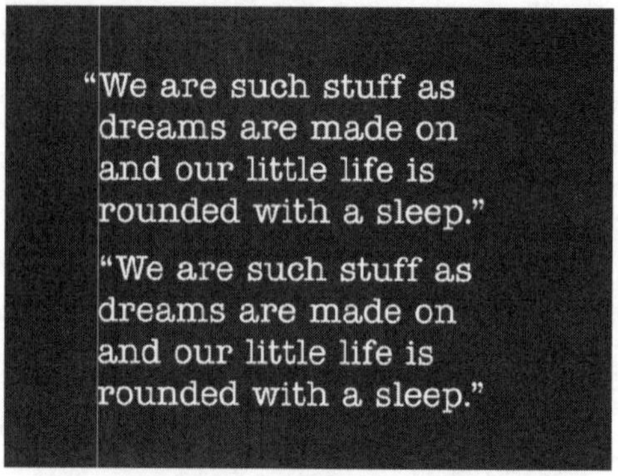

To specify the hanging punctuation option:

1. Select one or more paragraphs you want to format.

2. In the Paragraph panel's pull-down menu, choose Roman Hanging Punctuation (**Figure 12.100**).

   When the option is selected, punctuation at the beginning or end of the paragraph appears outside the paragraph's margins; when the option is unselected, the punctuation marks appear within the margins.

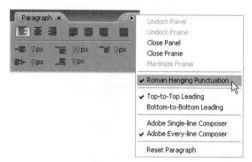

"We are such stuff as dreams are made on and our little life is rounded with a sleep."

"We are such stuff as dreams are made on and our little life is rounded with a sleep."

Figure 12.99 Hanging punctuation places punctuation marks outside the text box. In this example, guides clarify the difference between using and not using hanging punctuation.

Figure 12.100 To enable hanging punctuation, select Roman Hanging Punctuation in the Paragraph panel's pull-down menu.

FORMATTING PARAGRAPH TEXT

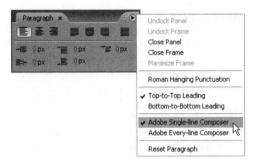

Figure 12.101 In the Paragraph panel's pull-down menu, choose the composer you want to use.

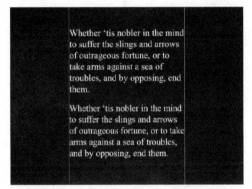

Figure 12.102 Depending on the paragraph, you may see a difference between choosing Single-line Composer (the paragraph on the top) and Every-line Composer (the paragraph on the bottom).

Specifying how After Effects calculates line breaks

To determine how a paragraph flows within its text box, After Effects considers the character and paragraph options you specify and chooses the best possible line breaks—the soft returns that end one line and begin another. After Effects *composes* (as it's called) the text by employing either of two methods:

Adobe Single-line Composer evaluates each line separately to determine where to place line breaks. This relatively simple method works well if you prefer to control line breaks manually.

Adobe Every-line Composer, in contrast, evaluates all the lines in a paragraph to determine the line breaks. By comparing the possible line breaks for a range of lines, After Effects reduces the occurrence of unattractive line breaks and hyphens and achieves more even spacing.

To specify line break options:

1. Select one or more paragraphs you want to format.

2. In the Paragraph panel's pull-down menu, choose the option you want (**Figure 12.101**):

   ▲ **Adobe Single-line Composer**

   ▲ **Adobe Every-line Composer**

   The selected paragraph uses the option you specify (**Figure 12.102**).

Animating Text

In most respects, text layers are just like other layers, and they include the same layer properties you learned about in Chapter 7. But text layers have a number of unique text properties, as well. You can animate the layer and the text within the layer. But, unlike other layers, you can't open a text layer in a Layer panel.

Standard layer properties

Text layers include the same transform properties—Anchor Point, Position, Scale, Rotation, and Opacity—that you find in any layer (and learned about in Chapter 7). Text layers accept masks and effects; and, like other layers, you can make a text layer 3D. But the standard layer property controls affect the *layer as a whole*; they can't alter the content of the text (what it says) or apply to characters individually (not without using masks, anyway).

Text properties

A special set of text properties makes it possible to animate words or individual characters without complex keyframing, elaborate masking techniques, or resorting to using numerous text layers:

Source text lets you change the content of a text message over time. This way, a single text layer can convey a series of messages. Used in combination with animator groups and selectors (described in a moment), you can change the content more gradually. For example, you can make the letters in a word appear to encode themselves, cycling through other letters, and gradually decode themselves into another word.

Path text lets you make a line of text follow a path that you specify. You can animate the border to make the text appear to glide over the path. You can also specify other options, such as whether the type is perpendicular to the path.

Animator groups let you animate properties of any range of characters within the text. Each animator group you create can include any number or combination of properties, including both familiar transform properties and properties unique to text. You can specify the range of text affected by the animator properties with one or more *range selectors*. Numerous other options let you fine-tune the animation.

Figure 12.103 Create a text layer, and format and arrange it into its initial state (before animating it).

Animating Source Text

You can animate a text layer's *source text* (the content of the text message). Source text keyframes always use Hold interpolation. As you'll see in Chapter 16, "Complex Projects," *Hold interpolation* retains a keyframe value until the next keyframe value is reached. The message instantly changes to the text you specify at each keyframe. This way, a single layer can contain multiple text messages; you don't have to create multiple layers.

Note that you can change the source text while animating other properties. For example, by creating an animator group and animating the Character Offset property, you can change the characters in a word—encoding or decoding it. Changing an encoded word's source text during the animation lets you make one word change into another.

To animate source text:

1. Create and format a text layer, and arrange the layer in the comp (**Figure 12.103**).

   To create the text layer, use techniques described earlier in this chapter. To arrange the layer in the comp, use techniques covered in Chapter 5, "Layer Basics," and Chapter 6, "Layer Editing."

2. Set the current time to the frame where you want the message you created in step 1 to begin.

continues on next page

3. In the Timeline panel, expand the text layer's property outline, and click the Stopwatch icon for the layer's Source Text property.

An initial keyframe is created for the Source Text property (**Figure 12.104**). Source text keyframes always use the Hold interpolation method (see Chapter 9, "Keyframe Interpolation").

4. Set the current time to the frame where you want a new message to appear.

5. Select the text, and type a new message (**Figure 12.105**).

A new Hold keyframe appears at the current time for the layer's Source Text property (**Figure 12.106**).

6. Repeat steps 4 and 5 as needed.

When you preview the animation, each message appears until the current time reaches the next source text keyframe.

Figure 12.104 In the text layer's property outline, click the Source Text property's Stopwatch icon to create an initial keyframe.

Figure 12.105 Set the current time to the frame where you want the message to change, and edit the text...

Figure 12.106 ...to create a new Hold keyframe for the Source Text property (seen here in the layer outline).

Figure 12.107 The Effects & Presets panel contains numerous preset text animations.

Figure 12.108 Choose Help > Animation Preset Gallery.

Using Text Animation Presets

As you learned in Chapter 11, "Effects Fundamentals," you can save any combination of effects and animation keyframes as a preset. Because they're listed in the Effects & Presets panel, presets are easy to apply; and because they're saved as separate files, they're easy to share.

After Effects includes a generous and varied collection of text animation presets, conveniently sorted by category in the Effects & Presets panel (**Figure 12.107**). Chances are, you're just as likely to modify one of these excellent presets as you are to build a text animation from scratch.

As you learn about text animation, start by examining some of the presets. Once you see what text animation can do, dig into the sections on animator groups to find out what makes them tick and, ultimately, how to create your own.

To view a gallery of text animation presets:

1. Choose Help > Animation Preset Gallery (**Figure 12.108**).

    The After Effects Help system opens in your browser, set to the page "Gallery of animation presets".

continues on next page

2. To view text animation samples by category, click the appropriate link (**Figure 12.109**).

To apply a text animation preset:

1. Create and format a text layer, and select the layer (**Figure 12.110**).

Make sure to select the entire text layer, not a range of characters. To animate part of a text layer, you can use range selectors (as explained later in this chapter).

2. In the Effects & Presets panel, double-click the text animation preset you want to apply to the selected text (**Figure 12.111**).

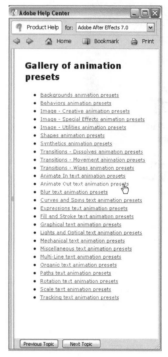

Figure 12.109 Click the category of text animations for which you want to see examples.

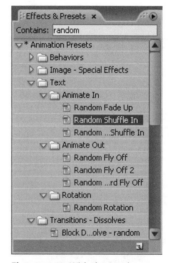

Figure 12.110 Create and format a text layer.

Figure 12.111 With the text layer selected, double-click the text preset you want in the Effects & Presets panel.

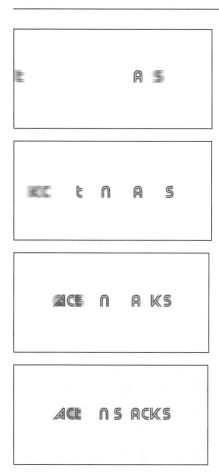

Figure 12.112 The preset is applied to the selected text layer.

The preset you specify is applied to the selected text (**Figure 12.112**). For more about using the Effects & Presets panel, see Chapter 11.

3. If you want, modify the effect by changing the position or value of its keyframed text animation properties (as explained in Chapter 7). You can also add, delete, or modify the preset effect's animator properties or range selector values (as explained later in this chapter).

Understanding Animator Groups

You animate type by adding one or more *animator groups* to a text layer. Animator groups appear in the layer outline under a text layer's Text property heading (**Figure 12.113**). You create an animator group by choosing a property you want to affect in the layer's Animator pull-down menu. You can add as many groups as you need to achieve the animation you want.

Each animator group consists of at least one *animator property* and one *selector*. You can add properties and selectors to a group by using its Add pull-down menu.

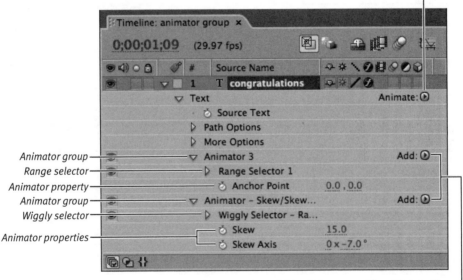

Animator pull-down menu (to add an animator group)

Animator group — Animator 3

Range selector — Range Selector 1

Animator property — Anchor Point

Animator group — Animator – Skew/Skew...

Wiggly selector — Wiggly Selector – Ra...

Animator properties — Skew, Skew Axis

Add pull-down menu (to add properties and selectors to a group)

Figure 12.113 Animator groups appear in the layer outline.

Animator properties

Animator properties include familiar transform properties (such as position, rotation, and so on), properties unique to text (such as fill, stroke, tracking, and so on), and each character's value (the numerical code that determines which character is displayed). Each animator group can have any number and combination of properties, which can be set to any value. But unlike when you're animating layers, you probably won't animate the property values to create the animation. Instead, you'll animate the range of characters affected by the properties by keyframing a selector.

Range selectors

A *selector* lets you specify a *range*, or the part of the type that's affected by an animator group's properties. Most animations are achieved by animating the range, not the properties. Selectors are comparable to layer masks in that they limit the areas affected by your adjustments. Just as you can add multiple masks to a layer, you can add multiple selectors to an animator group. Multiple selectors let you specify ranges that you couldn't define with a single selector (such as a discontinuous range of characters). In addition to a standard range selector, you can apply a *wiggly selector* to vary the selection, giving it a more random or organic feel. You can also specify an *expression selector*, which can link the selection to another property or base it on a mathematical function.

Animating Type with Animator Groups

As you gleaned from the previous section, "Understanding Animator Groups," animator groups grant you a great deal of control over text animation and can include numerous components.

The following task provides an overview of the steps required to create a simple text animation. The basic steps include creating an animator group, specifying its property value and range, and then animating the range. For the sake of clarity, the task doesn't mention particular property and selector options; they're covered in detail in later sections. It also doesn't include steps to add animator groups or to add properties or selectors to existing groups. Follow this task to create a simple animation, and then explore later sections to add complexity to your text animations.

To animate type with animator groups:

1. Create and format a text layer.

   Use the techniques explained earlier in this chapter.

2. In the Timeline panel, expand the text layer to reveal its Text property heading.

3. In the Switches or Modes panel of the Timeline panel, choose the text property you want to animate from the Animate pull-down menu (**Figure 12.114**).

   An Animator property heading appears under the layer's Text property heading. The Animator property contains a Range Selector property heading and the property you specified (**Figure 12.115**).

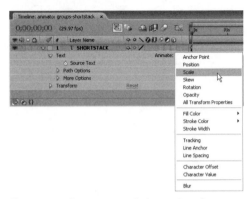

Figure 12.114 To create an animator group, choose a property in the Animate pull-down menu.

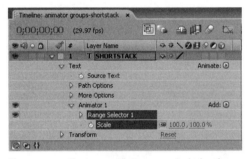

Figure 12.115 The new animator group includes the property you selected and a range selector.

Figure 12.116 Set the property values. Here, the type's vertical scale has been increased. Until you limit the range, the property value affects all of the text.

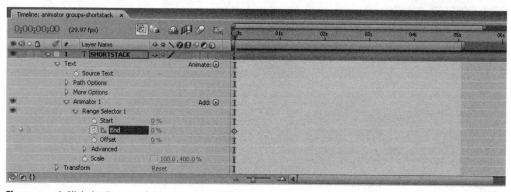

Figure 12.117 Set the current time, and specify values for the range. In this example, the range's end has been moved next to its start, so the property doesn't affect any of the characters at the beginning of the animation.

4. Set the values for the property you specified in step 3.

The values are applied to the entire text (**Figure 12.116**). You can limit the range of affected characters in step 5. Typically, you'll animate the range, not the property values (as explained in the next step).

5. Set the current time, and specify values for the range selector.

You can set the range by dragging the Range Start and Range End icons in the Comp panel (**Figure 12.117**) or by setting Start and End values in the property outline. For details, see "Specifying a Range," later in this chapter.

6. For the range properties you want to animate, click the Stopwatch icon to set the initial keyframe at the current time.

You can set keyframes for any combination of the selector's Start, End, and Offset values (**Figure 12.118**).

continues on next page

Figure 12.118 Click the Stopwatch icon to set the initial keyframe. Here, an initial keyframe is set for the end of the range.

ANIMATING TYPE WITH ANIMATOR GROUPS

7. Set the current time to another frame, and change the animated range property values to set another keyframe (**Figure 12.119**).

For example, you can increase the range over time by animating the range's End property, or make the range travel through the characters by animating the Offset property.

8. If necessary, repeat step 7 to create additional keyframes.

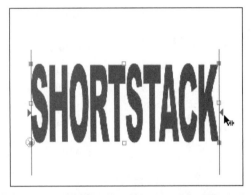

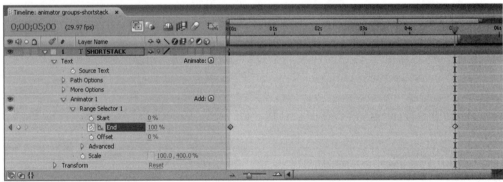

Figure 12.119 Set the current time to another frame, and change the range. Here, the current time is set 5 seconds later, and the end of the range has been moved from its original position (shown in Figure 12.117) so that all the characters are affected.

ANIMATING TYPE WITH ANIMATOR GROUPS

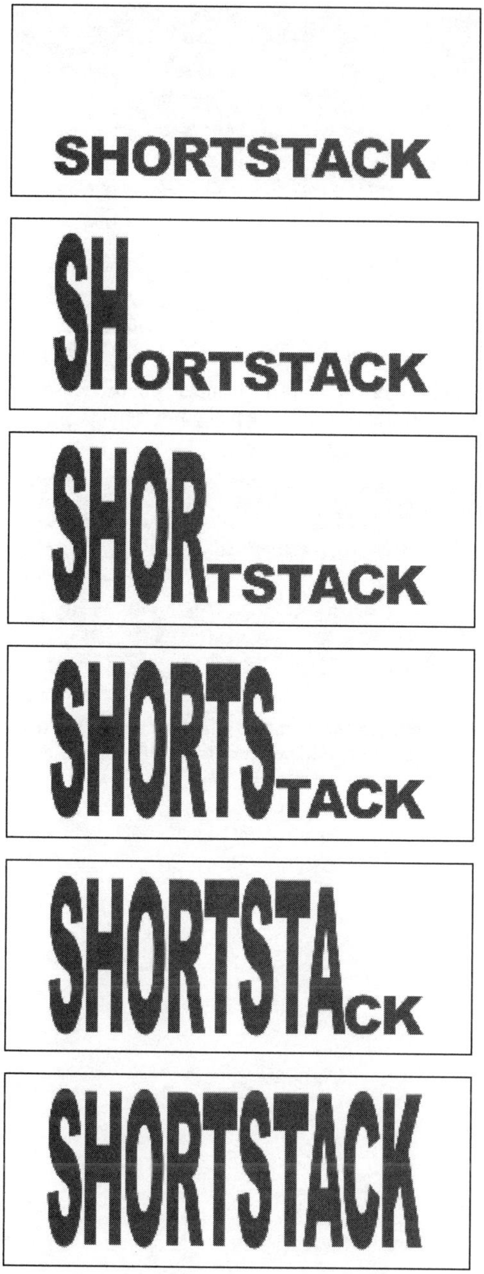

Figure 12.120 Previewing the animation shows how animating the range changes which parts of the text are affected by the animator property you set.

9. Preview the type animation using any of the techniques covered in Chapter 8, "Playback, Previews, and RAM."

As the range animates, different parts of the text are affected by the properties in the animator group (**Figure 12.120**).

✔ Tip

■ As with other elements in a project (comps, duplicate layers, expressions, and so on), it's a good idea to give animator groups and range selectors unique names. Doing so makes it easier to distinguish them and to ascertain their purpose at a glance. Select the animator or range selector, press Return (Mac) or Enter (Windows), edit the name, and press Return (Mac) or Enter (Windows) when you're finished.

Creating Animator Groups

You can add any number of animator groups to a text layer, and each animator group can contain any combination of properties and range selectors. However, each group must contain at least one property and one selector.

To create an animator group:

1. If necessary, expand the text layer's property outline in the Timeline panel.

2. In the Switches/Modes panel of the Timeline, choose a property from the text layer's Animate pull-down menu (across from the layer's Text property) (**Figure 12.121**).

   An Animator property heading appears under the layer's Text property heading. The Animator property (called Animator 1 by default) contains a Range Selector property heading (called Range Selector 1 by default) and the property you specified (**Figure 12.122**).

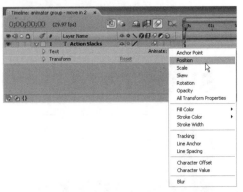

Figure 12.121 To create an animator group, choose a property from the Animate pull-down menu.

Figure 12.122 The animator group appears in the text layer's property outline; it contains the property and a default range selector.

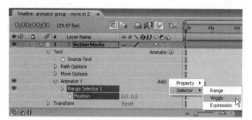

Figure 12.123 To add a property or selector to an existing animator group, select the appropriate option from the group's Add pull-down menu.

Figure 12.124 The group includes the added item. In this example, an additional selector has been added to the group.

To add to an animator group:

1. If necessary, expand the layer outline of a text layer containing at least one animator.

2. In the Switches/Modes panel of the Timeline, choose an option from the *animator's Add pull-down menu* (**Figure 12.123**):

 Property adds a property to the specified animator.

 Selector adds a selector to the specified animator.

 The property or selector is added to the animator (**Figure 12.124**).

To remove a group, property, or selector:

◆ In a text layer's property outline, select an animator group, animator property, or selector, and press Delete.

 The selected item is removed from the layer.

✔ Tips

■ As with other items in a project, it's a good idea to give animator groups unique, descriptive names. You can rename animator groups just like layers and other items: Select the name, press Return (Mac) or Enter (Windows), type the new name, and press Return (Mac) or Enter (Windows) again.

■ Animator properties and selectors include a video switch ☻ just like layers. Turn off a switch to exclude the effects of the item.

Choosing Animator Group Properties

Each animator group can include any combination of animator properties, which you can specify when you create the group or when you add to it using the group's Add pull-down menu. You should already be familiar with transform properties (position, scale, and so on), which work with type much the same way they work with layers. (With type, however, you specify whether each character, word, or line possesses an anchor point.) You can also animate properties unique to text (fill, stroke, tracking, and so on), which you learned about earlier in this chapter. Finally, you can set each character's value—the numerical code that determines which character is displayed. The following list describes your choices of animator properties in detail.

Anchor Point sets the type's *anchor point:* the point at which all other transform properties are calculated. Whether all the text, each line, each word, or each character has an anchor point depends on the option you set for Anchor Point Grouping under the More Options property heading (within the Text property heading).

Position sets the type's placement in the comp, based on its anchor point. You can change the Position values either by using controls in the Timeline panel or by using the Selection tool in the Comp panel; when positioned over type, the Selection tool ⬉ becomes a Move icon ▶.

All Transform adds all the transform properties (Anchor Point, Position, Scale, Rotation, and Opacity) to the animator group at once.

Skew sets the type's skew, or slant, along a skew axis that you specify.

Rotation sets the angle of the type, based on the anchor point you specified.

Opacity sets the opacity of the type. You can control fill and stroke opacity separately using the corresponding option (explained shortly).

Fill Color sets the color values of the fill (the color within the contours of the type) according to your choice in the submenu: RGB, Hue, Saturation, Brightness, or Opacity.

Stroke Color sets the color values of the stroke (the color of the type's outline) according to your choice in the submenu: RGB, Hue, Saturation, Brightness, or Opacity.

Stroke Width sets the thickness of the stroke.

Tracking sets the spacing between characters (see "Kerning and tracking," earlier in this chapter).

Line Anchor sets how tracking is aligned in each line of type—in other words, the point on which tracking calculations are based. To align tracking to the left edge of a line of type, set the value to 0 percent; to align tracking to the right edge, set the value to 100 percent.

Line Spacing sets the spacing between lines of type (see "Leading," earlier in this chapter).

Character Offset adds the value you specify to the characters' Unicode values, thereby replacing the characters with the characters corresponding to the new values. For example, specifying an offset value of 4 shifts the letters in the word *bet* four spaces alphabetically, so that the word becomes *fix*. (Of course, offsetting characters in a word doesn't usually result in another word.)

Character Value sets the characters' Unicode values, thereby replacing the characters with those corresponding to the new values. For example, setting the Character Value property to 63 replaces all characters in the range to question marks (?).

Character Range includes two options that specify whether to restrict the Character Value property. In the Character Range pull-down menu, choose Preserve Case and Digits to restrict characters to their character group—such as Roman, Katakana (a Japanese syllabary), symbols, and so on. Choose Full Unicode to permit unrestricted Character Values.

Unicode

In After Effects, you can change a character from the one you typed initially to any other character by offsetting or specifying its Unicode value.

Developed by a group known as the Unicode Consortium, *Unicode* is a character-encoding scheme designed to supplant its more limited predecessor, ASCII. Whereas ASCII is an 8-bit standard capable of representing only 128 distinct characters, Unicode is a 16-bit scheme capable of representing 65,536 characters. The ambitious Unicode Consortium seeks to unify all character sets into a single table of characters encompassing all major world languages (including so-called dead languages) and symbols (such as signs that denote currency, and mathematical symbols). Unicode even includes space and encoding features to accommodate a language like Chinese—which represents ideas using a literally countless combination of ideographs.

CHOOSING ANIMATOR GROUP PROPERTIES

Choosing a Range Selector

When you create an animator group, it includes the property you specify along with a range selector. You can add three types of selectors to a group: range, wiggly, and expression. Each group can have any number or combination of selectors, but each animator group must have at least one selector.

When you use multiple selectors in a single animator group, you can specify how they interact by stipulating a mode, as explained in "Using Multiple Selectors and Selector Modes," later in this chapter.

Range

You can add range selectors to the same animator group to create more complex selections, in much the same way you can apply multiple masks to a layer to create complex masked areas. A range selector also includes a number of options to control how subsequent characters (or words, or lines of text) are added to the selection, the rate of change in a property value, and other aspects of the range.

Wiggly

A wiggly selector varies the range by the frequency and within limits you specify. Using a wiggly selector can make an animation seem more random or organic. You can use a wiggly selector by itself or to vary part of another selector.

Expression

Whereas the other selectors limit (range) and vary (wiggly) the range of text affected by the properties in the animator group, an expression selector controls the *amount* that properties are applied. It's called an expression selector because its Amount property's value is derived from a JavaScript-based formula known as an *expression*. As you'll learn in Chapter 16, "Complex Projects," an expression can link one property's values to any other value or specify the value using a kind of mathematical formula.

Whereas an expression selector controls only an animator group's Amount property in a text layer, standard expressions can be applied to any property in any layer. Otherwise, expression selectors work just like other expressions. For this reason, expression selectors are covered only briefly here, and a full explanation of expressions is reserved for Chapter 16.

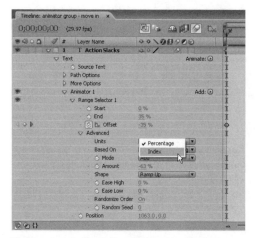

Figure 12.125 In the Units pull-down menu, choose whether range values are expressed as a percentage of the entire type or are expressed by indexing, or numbering, each unit.

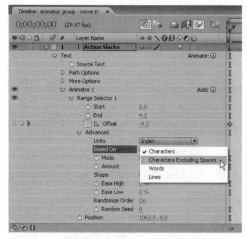

Figure 12.126 For Based On, choose the units on which the range is based.

Specifying a Range

You can set a range either by dragging its left and right borders in the Comp panel or by using controls in the text layer's property outline. A range can be applied to different units of type: each character, word, or line. When you're specifying a range, these units are measured either in terms of a percentage of total units, or by the unit (1, 2, 3, and so on).

To specify how a range is measured:

1. In the layer outline of the Timeline panel, expand the range selector you want to adjust, and expand its Advanced property heading.

2. To specify how start, end, and offset range values are expressed, choose an option in the Units pull-down menu (**Figure 12.125**):

   Percentage expresses values in percentages.

   Index expresses values according to a numerical indexing scheme, in which the first unit of text is assigned a value of 1, the next unit 2, and so on.

3. To specify the units on which a range is based (how the range is counted), choose an option in the Based On pull-down menu (**Figure 12.126**):

   Characters counts each character, including spaces, as a unit in the range.

   Characters Excluding Spaces counts each character as a unit in the range but excludes spaces.

   Words counts each word as a unit in the range.

   Lines counts each line (of a multiline text layer) as a unit in the range.

   The values for Start, End, and Offset are based on the option you specify.

To specify a range:

1. Expand the text layer animator group you want to adjust, and then expand the range selector you want to set.

2. To set the start of the range, *do either of the following:*
   ▲ In the text layer's expanded outline, specify a value for Start.
   ▲ With the text layer's Animator group heading selected in the expanded outline, drag the Range Start icon ⸾ in the Composition panel (**Figure 12.127**).

3. To set the end of the range, *do either of the following:*
   ▲ In the text layer's expanded outline, specify a value for End.
   ▲ With the text layer's Animator property selected, drag the Range End icon ⸾ in the Composition panel (**Figure 12.128**).

4. To change both the Start and End values by the same amount, specify an Offset value in the text layer's expanded outline (**Figure 12.129**).

Figure 12.127 With the range selected in the property outline, you can drag the start of the range in the Comp panel...

Figure 12.128 ...or drag the Range End icon to set the end of the range.

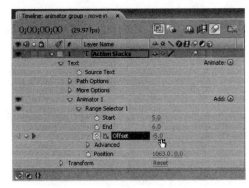

Figure 12.129 To change both the Start and End values by the same amount, change the Offset value in the property outline.

Understanding Range Selector Options

You can fine-tune the rate and manner in which the range includes units by specifying a number of options listed under the Range Selector's Advanced category in the expanded property outline.

Shape

You define a range with distinct borders (for example, between characters in a word). However, you can think of those borders as having a *shape*. The shape you specify determines the rate at which units become included in the range (and, depending on the shape, excluded from the range, as well). In other words, the Shape option controls how soon units added to the range become fully included and achieve the maximum property value.

With some animator properties (such as Position and Scale), the literal shape associated with each option is evident visually. In each of the following examples, the animation is the same except for the selector's Shape option. The range increases character by character, from left to right, until it includes the entire word. Because the animation increases each character's height (the Y aspect of the Scale property), it's easy to see how the Shape option affects the range (**Figure 12.130**):

Square includes and excludes subsequent units (characters, words, and so on) in the range abruptly. You can fine-tune the transition time between units by adjusting the Smoothness value (described in the next section, "Other range options").

Ramp Up includes subsequent units in the range gradually, in a linear progression.

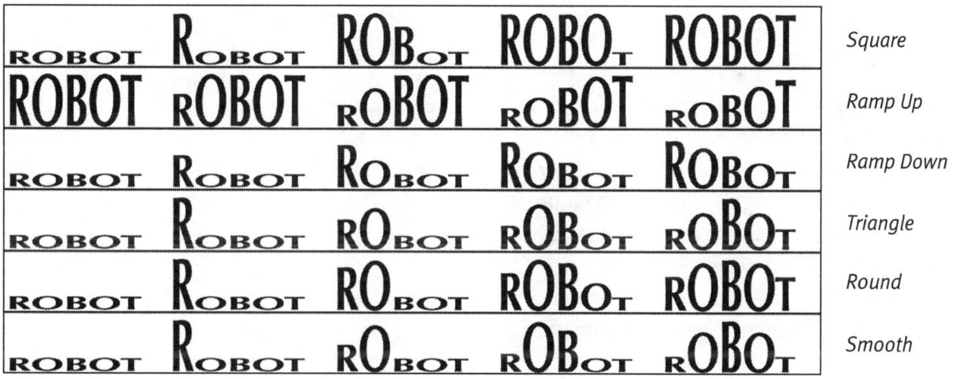

Figure 12.130 You can see how applying different Shape settings to the same animation affects the final result.

Ramp Down excludes subsequent units from the range gradually, in a linear progression.

Triangle includes subsequent units in the range gradually and then excludes preceding units gradually, using a linear progression.

Round includes subsequent units in the range gradually, using a curved, decelerating progression, and then excludes units gradually, using a curved, accelerating progression.

Smooth includes subsequent units in the range gradually, using a curved, accelerating progression, and then excludes units gradually, using a curved, decelerating progression.

Other range options

In the expanded property outline, a range selector's Advanced category includes other options that let you fine-tune the properties' rate of change or randomize the order of the range:

Smoothness adjusts the transition time between units (characters and so on) when you specify the Square shape.

Ease High adjusts the animator property's rate of change as it approaches its maximum value, when the selection is in a fully included state. Setting the Ease High value to 100 percent eases the rate of change as it approaches its maximum, decelerating it; setting Ease High to –100 percent accelerates the rate of change as it approaches the maximum.

Ease Low adjusts the animator property's rate of change as it approaches its minimum value, when the selection is in a fully excluded state. Setting the Ease Low value to 100 percent eases the rate of change as it approaches its minimum, decelerating it; setting Ease Low to –100 percent accelerates the rate of change as it approaches the minimum.

Randomize Order, when turned on, randomizes the order in which the properties in the animator group are applied to the selection you specified with the range selector. For example, you can animate a range selector to gradually include all the letters in a word, from left to right; selecting Randomize Order applies the animator property to the characters in random order instead of sequential order.

Random Seed specifies the basis, or *seed*, on which a random order is generated. Duplicating a text animation also duplicates its selection order, even when the range is set to Randomize Order. To make the duplicate use a unique random order, change the Random Seed value.

UNDERSTANDING RANGE SELECTOR OPTIONS

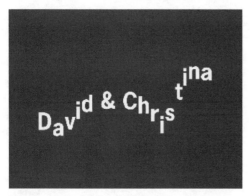

Figure 12.131 In this figure, the Text Bounce animation preset is applied to the text and affects the entire line...

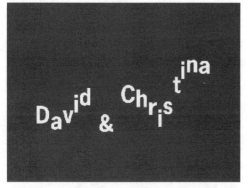

Figure 12.132 ...but adding a selector to single out the ampersand (&) and applying the Subtract mode excludes the character from the animation.

Using Multiple Selectors and Selector Modes

In an animator group's expanded outline, a range selector's Advanced category includes a Mode option. Selector modes are comparable to mask modes (covered in Chapter 10, "Mask Essentials"). Just as mask modes let you combine multiple masks to create shapes you couldn't achieve otherwise, *selector modes* let you combine multiple ranges. Selector modes dictate how one selector interacts with the selectors above it in the animator group's stacking order (**Figures 12.131** and **12.132**). As with layer masks, you don't need to change the mode if you're using only one selector in the group:

Add combines the range with the range defined by selectors higher in the animator group's stacking order. Properties are applied to the sum of the ranges.

Subtract subtracts the range from the range defined by the selectors higher in the animator group's stacking order. Properties are applied to the remaining area of the higher ranges.

Intersect includes only the area shared by the range and those above it in the stacking order. Properties are applied only where the range overlaps with the ranges above it in the stacking order.

Min applies the minimum value of properties where the range *doesn't* intersect with ranges above it.

Max applies the maximum value of properties where the range intersects with those above it.

Difference adds the range to those above it in the animator group's stacking order but excludes the area where the range and those above it in the stacking order overlap.

Specifying Wiggly Selector Options

A wiggly selector includes many of the options found in other selectors, plus a number of unique options to control variations in the selector. When you add a wiggly selector to an animator group, expand the selector's heading to reveal its options:

Min specifies the variation's lowest limit (the minimum value for the wiggler).

Max specifies the variation's highest limit (the maximum value for the wiggler).

Wiggles/Second sets the frequency of variation from the selected range (the number of variations per second).

Correlation sets the extent to which variations in the range match, or correlate, to units (characters, words, lines) in the range. Setting Correlation to 100 percent makes the units wiggle in unison; setting it to 0 percent makes the units wiggle independently.

Temporal Phase sets the starting value, or seed, of the temporal aspect (the timing) of the variations.

Spatial Phase sets the starting value, or seed, of the spatial aspect of the variations.

Lock Dimensions wiggles, or varies, property dimensions—the X and Y dimensions, for example—by the same amount.

About Expression Selector Options

In Chapter 16, you'll learn that instead of keyframing a property, you can specify its values using an *expression*. For now, suffice it to say that an expression can link one property value to any other value. Expressions can also generate values based on a kind of mathematical formula.

An *expression selector* uses the same kind of scripting language to control the amount that animator properties are applied to a given range of text. When the Amount value is 0 percent, the property has no effect on the text within the range; when the value is 100 percent, the property is fully applied. An expression selector can be used by itself or in conjunction with other selectors. This way, an expression selector adds another variable—and another level of control—to an animator group.

As you'll discover in Chapter 16, you can create any sort of expression more quickly and easily using the handy Pickwhip ⊚. Once you become more fluent in expression language (which is based on JavaScript), you can use the expression pull-down menu and even type in your own expressions.

PAINTING ON A LAYER

Although it appears as a single effect in the layer's property outline, the Paint effect feels like an entirely separate set of features meriting a chapter of its own. The Tools panel includes several tools devoted to painting: the Brush tool, Eraser tool, and Clone Stamp tool. And the Paint feature's numerous options require two specialized panels: the Paint panel and Brush Tips panel. With the Brush and Eraser tools, you can simulate handwriting, create hand-drawn graphics, or alter a layer's alpha channel to create (or fix) a track matte. Or you can make more subtle adjustments to an image with each stroke by using blending modes. You can also use a Clone Stamp tool to retouch an image or to aid in tasks like wire removal.

Using your mouse—or, better yet, a tablet and stylus—you can record strokes directly onto a layer in real time, change their characteristics, and play them back in a number of ways. The Brush Tips panel includes a varied set of preset brushes, and allows you to create and save your own variations—small or large, hard or soft-edged, round or elliptical. Because strokes are vector-based, you can scale them without adversely affecting resolution. And like all effects, brush strokes are nondestructive, which means they don't alter your source files. Even strokes you make with the Eraser tool are nondestructive.

Paint also deserves special attention because of its unique animation paradigm. Each stroke appears as its own layer within a layer—that is, each stroke appears as a duration bar within the paint effect. This way, you can toggle strokes on and off, control how they're layered and how they interact with strokes lower in the stacking order, and precisely adjust when and how quickly they appear.

In this chapter, you'll learn this single effect's numerous options so you can explore its unlimited possibilities.

Using the Paint and Brush Tips Panels

After Effects includes two panels for controlling Paint: the Paint panel and Brush Tips panel. Both panels are nearly identical to their counterparts in other Adobe programs.

The panels are part of the Paint preset workspace. You can also summon the panels by clicking the Tools panel's Toggle Panels button whenever the Brush, Clone, or Eraser tool is selected.

To specify the Paint workspace:

◆ In the Tools panel's Workspace pulldown menu, select Paint (**Figure 13.1**).

After Effects arranges the workspace automatically and includes the Paint and Brush Tips panels.

To toggle the Paint and Brush Tips panels:

1. In the Tools panel, *select any paint-related tool*:

   Brush tool
   Clone tool
   Eraser tool

   The Toggle Panels button and the Auto Open Panels option appear in the Tools panel. If Auto Open Panels is already checked, the Paint and Brush Tips panels also open automatically (see the next step).

Figure 13.1 Selecting Paint from the Workspace pulldown menu…

Figure 13.2 ...or clicking the Toggle Panels button when the Brush, Clone, or Eraser tool is selected...

Figure 13.3 ...opens the Paint panel...

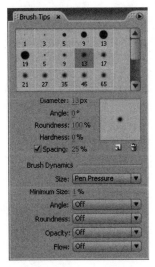

Figure 13.4 ...and the Brush Tips panel.

2. In the Tools panel, click the Toggle Panels button ▤ (**Figure 13.2**).

Clicking toggles the Paint and Brush Tips panels open and closed (**Figures 13.3** and **13.4**).

✔ Tip

■ As always, you can open or close any panel from the menu bar by choosing the name of the panel from the Window menu.

Specifying Paint Stroke Options

Before you start using the Brush and Eraser tools, take a moment to get a more detailed understanding of each option, starting with the options at the top of the Paint panel. These options not only allow you to control the character and color of each stroke, but also let you specify which of the layer's channels are affected by each stroke and how long strokes appear.

Depending on the options you choose, you can make visible strokes, resembling those made by a loaded paintbrush or by an airbrush lightly applying each coat; or you can make strokes that affect the layer's alpha channel, effectively creating or modifying a matte. The strokes can appear for any length of time or reenact the painting process. Later, you'll specify many of the same options to determine the effects of the Clone Stamp tool.

Generally, you set these options before you paint a stroke. However, you can change these and most other options by selecting the stroke under the Paint effect and adjusting its values in the property outline.

Opacity and Flow

Opacity and Flow settings determine the paint's coverage strength and the speed of coverage, respectively. Together, they can make paint seem opaque or semitransparent (**Figure 13.5**). When you're using the Eraser, the same options determine how effectively and quickly pixels are removed:

Opacity sets the maximum opacity of each stroke, from 0% to 100%; opacity is analogous to how well a real-world paint covers a surface. (A brush's Hardness setting also contributes to a stroke's opacity near its edges.)

Figure 13.5 Opacity determines the paint's coverage strength; Flow determines the speed of coverage. Here, the words Opacity and flow are repeated, each time using a lower Opacity or Flow setting, respectively.

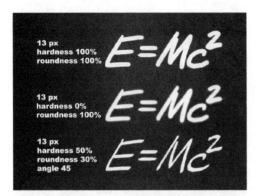

Figure 13.6 This figure shows strokes created by various brush tips.

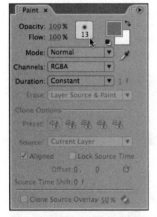

Figure 13.7 In the Paint panel, click the arrow next to the current brush tip icon to reveal the Brush Tips Selector.

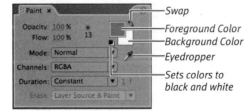

Swap
Foreground Color
Background Color
Eyedropper
Sets colors to black and white

Figure 13.8 In the Paint panel, the upper-left swatch sets the foreground color; the lower-right swatch sets the background, or secondary color.

Flow determines how quickly paint is applied with each stroke, from 0% to 100%. Lower Flow settings apply less of the paint color in a stroke, making the paint appear more transparent; low Flow values also result in greater spaces between brush tip marks when the brush's Spacing option is active (see "Customizing Brush Tips," later in this chapter).

Brush tip

As you'd expect, the brush tip simulates the camel hair on the end of a brush (or the point of a pen, or the spray pattern of an airbrush). Brush tip settings define the character of strokes. The Paint panel displays the currently selected brush tip as an icon that represents its roundness, angle, and hardness settings; a number indicates the brush's size, in pixels (**Figure 13.6**). Clicking the current brush tip icon activates (or if necessary, opens) the Brush Tip panel, from which you can select a preset brush tip or create your own (see "Using Brush Tips," later in this chapter) (**Figure 13.7**).

Color

Like a real panel of paint, the Paint panel lets you choose the color you want to use. The upper-left swatch sets the *foreground color*, which specifies the paint applied by the brush; the lower-right swatch sets the *background color*, or secondary color. Clicking a swatch lets you choose a color from a color picker, or you can sample a color from the screen using a standard Eyedropper tool. Click the smaller icon to reset the foreground and background colors to black and white, respectively; click the Swap icon to switch the colors (**Figure 13.8**).

Mode

The Mode pull-down menu lets you specify how each stroke interacts with underlying pixels (**Figure 13.9**). The menu's blending mode options are explained in Chapter 14, "More Layer Techniques." However, the stroke blending mode menu doesn't include the Dissolve or Dancing Dissolve blending modes. Note that each stroke can use a blending mode, and the layer containing the paint effect (and all its strokes) can use a blending mode also.

Channels

The Channels pull-down menu specifies which of the layer's channels are affected by a stroke. You can affect the visible red, green, and blue channels (RGB), the alpha channel (which defines transparency), or all channels (RGBA). Painting on a layer's RGB channels creates visible strokes, whereas painting on its alpha channel affects its transparent areas. For example, you can animate strokes applied to a layer's alpha channel to reveal portions of the layer's image (**Figure 13.10**).

Duration

The Duration pull-down menu specifies how strokes are displayed over time. Duration options facilitate animating strokes the way you want—or if you prefer, keeping them static:

Constant displays all strokes from the current time to the end of the layer containing the stroke.

Figure 13.9 You can set how brushes interact with lower strokes or the underlying image with blending modes. Here, a soft, transparent brush uses a Dodge mode to lighten shadows in this photo.

Figure 13.10 In this example, strokes are painted on the layer's alpha channel to reveal the parts of the layer's image (a tangerine) just as a mask or matte would do. Note that the Paint effect's Paint on Transparent option is on.

Figure 13.11 Strokes always start at the current time, but you can set how long they appear by setting a duration option. Here, the Write On option makes the strokes appear over time, to simulate handwriting.

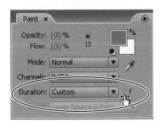

Figure 13.12 When you choose a Custom duration, specify the number of frames you want the stroke to appear.

Write On reveals the stroke over time, from beginning to end, depending on the speed at which you paint it. You can change the speed of the effect by adjusting each stroke's End property; you can reverse or create a write off effect by adjusting the strokes' Start property (**Figure 13.11**).

Single Frame displays the stroke at the current frame only.

Custom displays the stroke for the number of frames you specify. Set the duration by adjusting the value that appears next to the Duration pull-down menu (**Figure 13.12**).

These options set each stroke's initial duration—and, in the case of Write On, the stroke's initial End property's keyframes. After a stroke is created, you can't change the Duration setting in the property outline, per se; instead, you control when strokes are displayed by manipulating their duration bars and by keyframing properties such as Start and End.

✔ Tips

- Remember, paint doesn't always have to act like paint. For example, by applying certain modes, you can subtly retouch an image. Use a lightening mode (like Dodge) to brighten unwanted shadows. If necessary, animate the layer to follow the area you want to affect.

- By painting on the layer's alpha channel, you can use the advantages of various brush tips and duration options to affect the layer's transparency in ways that might be more difficult to do using masks or other methods.

Painting with the Brush Tool

Generally speaking, painting in After Effects is as easy as grabbing a brush and painting on the layer. But at the same time, this straightforward task includes numerous options. Not only can you change the characteristics of the brush, but you can also specify which channels the strokes modify and how long they appear on screen. (See the previous section, "Specifying Paint Stroke Options," for detailed descriptions of each menu option.)

To paint on a layer:

1. Open the layer you want to paint on in a Layer panel.

2. In the Tools panel, select the Brush tool ▧ (**Figure 13.13**).

    If the Auto Open Panels option is selected, the Paint and Brush Tips panels open.

3. In the Brush Tips panel, specify a brush (**Figure 13.14**).

    The selected brush becomes the current brush in the Paint panel.

Figure 13.13 Select the Brush tool.

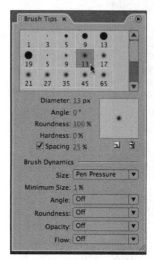

Figure 13.14 To change the current brush tip, choose a brush in the Brush Tips panel.

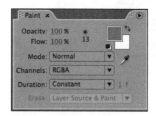

Figure 13.15 In the Paint panel, specify the brush's Opacity, Flow, and Color.

Figure 13.16 Choose a blending mode from the Mode pull-down menu.

4. In the Paint panel, specify options for the brush attributes (**Figure 13.15**):

   Opacity sets the relative opacity of pixels in a stroke.

   Flow sets the speed, or relative number of pixels applied with each stroke.

   Foreground Color sets the brush's color.

   Background Color sets a secondary color.

   When you're using the Eraser tool, Opacity sets the strength of the eraser, and Foreground Color has no effect.

5. To specify how brush strokes in the layer interact with the underlying image, choose a blending mode from the Mode pull-down menu (**Figure 13.16**).

6. To specify the layer channels affected by the strokes, choose an option from the Channels pull-down menu (**Figure 13.17**).

7. To specify how strokes appear over time, choose an option from the Duration pull-down menu (**Figure 13.18**).

   continues on next page

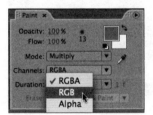

Figure 13.17 Specify the channels you want to paint on in the Channels pull-down menu. In this example, strokes are applied to the layer's RGB channels.

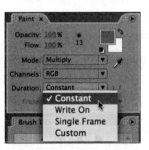

Figure 13.18 Choose how long you want the stroke to appear in the Duration pull-down menu. In this example, the strokes are set to appear from the current frame onward.

8. Set the current time to the frame where you want the first stroke to begin.

9. Using the Brush tool, drag in the Layer panel to paint strokes on the layer (**Figure 13.19**).

The mouse pointer appears as a circle that corresponds with the brush's size, angle, and roundness. Strokes use the options you specified. In the layer's property outline, the Paint effect appears. Expanding the Paint effect reveals that each stroke is listed separately and has a corresponding layer bar under the time ruler (**Figure 13.20**).

To make the painted layer transparent:

1. Select the layer containing the Paint effect.

2. In the layer's expanded property outline, expand the layer's Paint effect property heading.

or

Open the Effect Controls window to view the layer's Paint effect.

3. Under the Paint effect's property heading, set the Paint on Transparent option to On (**Figure 13.21**).

The selected layer becomes transparent, leaving only the Paint effect visible.

✔ Tip

■ The Paint effect discussed in this chapter must be applied to a layer in its Layer panel. After Effects Professional also includes a Vector Paint effect that you can use to paint in the Comp panel. However, it uses a different toolset and procedures.

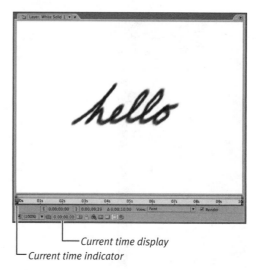

Current time display
Current time indicator

Figure 13.19 Drag the Brush in the Layer panel to create a stroke that starts at the current time. You can't paint in the Comp panel, but you can open a separate Comp panel to see the results.

Figure 13.20 In the Timeline panel, each stroke appears as an individual item.

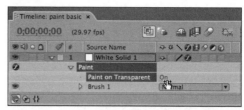

Figure 13.21 Under the Paint effect's property heading, set the Paint on Transparent option to On.

PAINTING WITH THE BRUSH TOOL

Figure 13.22 Select the Eraser tool.

Figure 13.23 In the Paint panel, set the Opacity and Flow. These options help determine how completely pixels are removed with each stroke.

Erasing Strokes

In practice, the Eraser tool does just what you'd expect: It removes pixels from a layer. You can specify whether it affects the target layer's pixels and paint strokes, paint only, or just the most recent paint stroke.

It might be more accurate to say that the Eraser *negates* pixels rather than removes them. A look in the Paint effect's property outline reveals that Eraser strokes appear in the stacking order along with Brush strokes. Like the other paint options, Eraser strokes are nondestructive; they don't permanently affect either the layer or paint strokes. Turn off an Eraser stroke's video (by clicking its Eye icon 👁 in the timeline), and its effects disappear.

In most respects, the Eraser works like a Brush—except it's an "anti-brush." The Eraser tool uses the same brush tips as the Brush tool, but you can't apply a color to an Eraser. And whereas a brush's Opacity and Flow settings control the strength of the brush—how thick you lay on the painted pixels—the same settings control how thoroughly the Eraser removes pixels. Otherwise, the Eraser's settings are analogous to those of the Brush tool.

To use the Eraser tool:

1. In the Tools panel, select the Eraser tool (**Figure 13.22**).

2. In the Paint panel, specify values for Opacity and Flow (**Figure 13.23**).

   When you're using the Eraser tool, Opacity and Flow refer to the Eraser's strength.

continues on next page

3. To specify the layer channels affected by the strokes, choose an option from the Channels pull-down menu (**Figure 13.24**).

RGB—Erases pixels in the layer's red, green, and blue channels; alpha is unaffected.

RGBA—Erases pixels in the layer's red, green, blue, and alpha channels.

Alpha—Erases pixels in the layer's alpha channel (transparency information).

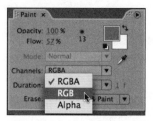

Figure 13.24 Choose which of the layer's channels are affected by the Eraser strokes in the Channels pull-down menu.

4. To specify how strokes appear over time, choose an option from the Duration pull-down menu (**Figure 13.25**):

Constant displays all strokes from the current time to the end of the layer containing the stroke.

Write On reveals the stroke over time, from beginning to end, depending on the speed at which you paint it.

Single Frame displays the stroke at the current frame only.

Custom displays the stroke for the number of frames you specify.

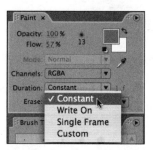

Figure 13.25 Choose how long pixels remain erased in the Duration pull-down menu.

5. To specify the pixels affected by the Eraser, choose an option from the Erase pull-down menu (**Figure 13.26**):

Layer Source & Paint erases pixels in the source layer and any paint strokes at the same time.

Paint Only erases pixels created by paint strokes.

Last Stroke Only erases pixels created by the most recently painted paint stroke.

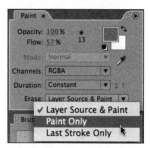

Figure 13.26 Specify the pixels affected by the Eraser by choosing an option in the Erase pull-down menu.

Figure 13.27 Drag the Eraser in the Layer panel to remove pixels.

6. Using the Eraser tool, drag in the Layer panel to remove pixels from the layer (**Figure 13.27**).

Pixels are erased according to the options you specified. Expanding the Paint effect in the layer's property outline reveals that each eraser stroke is listed separately and has a corresponding layer bar under the time ruler (**Figure 13.28**).

Figure 13.28 Like paint strokes, eraser strokes appear as individual items (including a layer bar) in the Paint effect's property outline.

Using Brush Tips

The brush tip you use determines the character of the strokes you paint with any of the paint tools (Brush, Eraser, or Clone Stamp). You can select from a number of preset brush tips that appear in the Brush Tips panel. If the preset brushes aren't to your liking, you can create a brush tip that uses specific characteristics (such as size, roundness, angle, and hardness). The following tasks explain how to choose, save, remove, and restore preset brush tips. The section "Customizing Brush Tips," later in this chapter, covers each brush tip characteristic in detail.

Toggling the Brush Tips panel from the Paint panel:

1. In the Paint panel, click the current brush tip icon (**Figure 13.29**).

   If it's not part of the current workspace, the Brush Tips panel appears. If it's visible, it becomes the active panel.

2. In the Brush Tips panel, click the preset brush you want to use (**Figure 13.30**).

✔ Tip

■ If the presets don't include a brush with the attributes you want, you can create one, as explained in the task "To create a brush tip," later in this chapter.

Figure 13.29 In the Paint panel, click the current brush tip icon...

Figure 13.30 ...to activate or open the Brush Tips panel, where you can specify a different preset brush, modify the current brush, or save a custom brush.

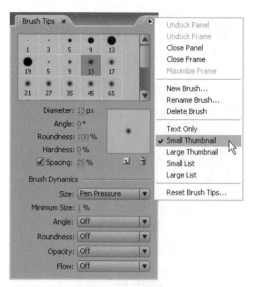

Figure 13.31 In the Brush Tips Selector's pull-down menu, choose a display option.

Figure 13.32 Choosing Text Only makes the brush tips appear in a list without icons.

To customize the Brush Tips panel:

1. In the Brush Tips panel's pull-down menu, *choose one of the following options* (**Figure 13.31**):

   Text Only lists brush descriptions without icons (**Figure 13.32**).

   Small Thumbnail displays brushes in a grid of small icons with their diameter settings.

continues on next page

Large Thumbnail displays brushes in a grid of large icons with their diameter settings (**Figure 13.33**).

Small List displays brushes in a vertical list including a small icon, diameter, and description.

Large List displays brushes in a vertical list, including a large icon, diameter, and description (**Figure 13.34**).

The Brush Tips Selector displays brushes according to your choice.

2. Click the Paint panel to close the Brush Tips Selector.

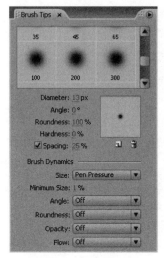

Figure 13.33 Choosing Large Thumbnail makes each brush tip appear as an icon that reflects its settings.

Figure 13.34 Choosing Large List makes each brush tip appear in a list with large icons.

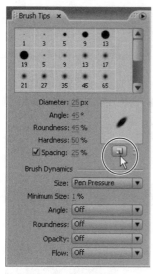

Figure 13.35 In the Brush Tips panel, set the brush's attributes and click the Save icon.

Figure 13.36 Name the new brush tip in the Choose Name dialog box.

Figure 13.37 Your custom brush tip appears in the preset brush tips area (shown here) and in Brush Tips Selector of the Paint panel.

To create a brush tip:

1. In the Brush Tips panel, specify the brush's attributes, including Diameter, Angle, Roundness, and so on.

   In the preview area of the Brush Tips panel, the brush's icon reflects your choices.

   See the section "Customizing Brush Tips," later in this chapter, for a detailed explanation of brush tip options.

2. Click the Save icon ▣ (**Figure 13.35**).

   A Choose Name dialog box appears with a descriptive name for the brush already entered.

3. Leave the suggested name or enter a custom name for the new brush, and click OK (**Figure 13.36**).

   The brush tip appears selected among the other preset brush tips (**Figure 13.37**). The new brush tip uses the attributes of the brush that was selected most recently. How presets appear in the panel depends on the option you choose in the Brush Tips panel's pull-down menu.

USING BRUSH TIPS

To rename a preset brush tip:

1. In the Brush Tips panel, double-click the brush tip you want to rename (**Figure 13.38**).

   A Choose Name dialog box appears.

2. In the Choose Name dialog box, type a new name for the brush tip, and click OK (**Figure 13.39**).

To remove a preset brush tip:

1. In the Brush Tips panel, click the preset brush tip you want to remove, and click the Delete icon 🗑 (**Figure 13.40**).

   After Effects prompts you to confirm your choice (**Figure 13.41**).

2. In the warning dialog box, click OK.

   The brush you selected is removed from the list of presets (**Figure 13.42**).

Figure 13.38 Double-click the brush tip you want to rename in the Brush Tips panel.

Figure 13.39 Enter a new name in the Choose Name dialog box, and click OK.

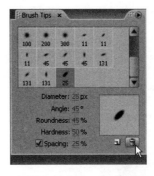

Figure 13.40 In the Brush Tips panel, click the brush tip you want to remove, and click the Delete (trash) icon.

Figure 13.42 The selected brush is removed from the panel.

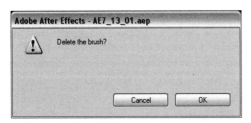

Figure 13.41 Confirm your choice by clicking OK.

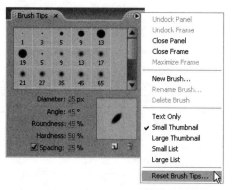

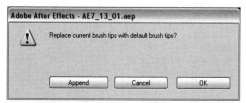

Figure 13.43 In the Brush Tips panel's pull-down menu, choose Reset Brush Tips.

Figure 13.44 In the dialog box that appears, specify whether you want to append the default brush tips to the current set. Otherwise, click OK to replace the current set with the default set.

To restore default brush tip presets:

1. In the Brush Tips panel's pull-down menu, choose Reset Brush Tips (**Figure 13.43**).

   A dialog box appears, prompting you to replace or append the current set of preset brushes with the default set.

2. In the dialog box, *do either of the following* (**Figure 13.44**):

   ▲ To add the default brushes to the current set of presets, click Append.

   ▲ To replace the current set of preset brushes with the default set (removing any custom presets), click OK.

   The default set of brushes either replaces or adds to the current set of presets, depending on your choice.

✔ Tip

■ In older versions of After Effects, clicking the current brush icon in the Paint panel opened a Brush Selector. Because the frame-based interface accommodates both the Paint and Brush Tips panels more easily, the Brush Selector is unnecessary and has been eliminated.

Customizing Brush Tips

Even though the Brush Tips panel includes a useful assortment of preset brush tips, chances are you'll want to create your own brush tips to suit a particular task. As you learned in the previous section, "Using Brush Tips," you can save each of your special brush tips as a preset that appears in the Brush Tips panel. Controlling a brush's attributes gives you a great deal of control over the character of the strokes it produces. This section covers the brush tip options; the next section, "Using Brush Dynamics," explains how to vary these qualities with a pen and tablet.

In the Brush Tips panel, you can specify the following attributes for each brush (**Figure 13.45**):

Diameter determines the size, measured in pixels, across the diameter of the brush's widest axis (for elliptical brushes) (**Figure 13.46**).

Angle specifies the amount, measured in degrees, from which the widest axis of an elliptical brush deviates from the horizontal.

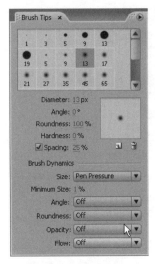

Figure 13.45 The Brush Tips panel includes several options that let you create custom brushes.

Figure 13.46 The strokes in this figure use different diameters.

Figure 13.47 The stroke on top was created using a perfectly round brush; lower strokes used smaller Roundness settings and an Angle of 45 degrees. Otherwise, the strokes are identical.

Figure 13.48 These strokes are identical, except for their hardness settings.

Figure 13.49 The three words, spacing, are identical, except for their spacing values.

Roundness refers to the width of a brush's shortest diameter, expressed as a percentage of its widest diameter (determined by the Diameter value): 100% creates a circular brush; 0% creates a linear brush; intermediate values create an elliptical brush (**Figure 13.47**).

Hardness sets the relative opacity of the brush's stroke from its center to the edges, analogous to feathering the edge of the brush. At 100%, the brush is opaque from its center to its edges (although the edge is antialiased); at 0%, the brush's edge has the maximum feather (although its center is opaque). Don't confuse hardness with the brush's overall Opacity, which you can set in the Paint panel (**Figure 13.48**).

Spacing indicates the distance between brush marks within a stroke, expressed as a percentage of the brush's diameter. Setting the spacing to a relatively low value allows the brush to create continuous stroke marks; setting Spacing to a higher value causes the brush tip to make contact with the layer intermittently, creating a stroke with gaps between brush marks. The speed with which you paint the stroke also affects the spacing. Moving the brush more quickly as you paint results in greater spacing between marks (**Figure 13.49**). You can set the Spacing to values over 100%.

Using Brush Dynamics

You don't have to be a traditionalist to know that painting with a computer program isn't as tactile as using actual brushes and canvas. But swapping your mouse for a tablet and stylus (such as those available from the computer peripheral manufacturer Wacom) can make you feel a lot more like a painter. Just as important, using a stylus makes your strokes look more painterly. That's because you can set the attributes of each stroke— its size, angle, roundness, opacity, and flow—to vary with the pressure you apply to the tablet or the tilt of the pen. If your *stylus* (sometimes referred to as a *pen*) has a wheel control, you can also use it to vary the brush.

To set Brush Dynamics options:

1. In the Brush Tips panel, make sure the Brush Dynamics options are visible (**Figure 13.50**).

   If necessary, resize the bottom of the panel to reveal the options.

Figure 13.50 You may need to resize the Brush Tips panel so that the Brush Dynamics options are visible.

Figure 13.51 Specify which of the pen's characteristics affect each of the brush's attributes in the corresponding pull-down menu.

Figure 13.52 If you enabled Size, specify a Minimum Size.

2. For each of the attributes listed in the Brush Dynamics area, choose an option from the pull-down menu (**Figure 13.51**).

   Off disables the dynamic option and uses the static setting you specified elsewhere in the Brush Tips and Paint panels.

   Pen Pressure varies the attribute according to the pressure of the pen on the tablet; pressing harder increases the value.

   Pen Tilt varies the attribute according to the angle of the pen in relation to the tablet. For example, tilting the pen away from the angle perpendicular to the tablet can decrease the brush's Roundness.

   Stylus Wheel varies the attribute when you scroll the pen's wheel control (a small roller on the side of the pen).

3. If you enabled Size, specify a Minimum Size (**Figure 13.52**).

   The brush's smallest possible diameter is limited by the value (1%–100%) you specify.

USING BRUSH DYNAMICS

497

Adjusting Strokes

As you learned in the chapter's introduction, Paint is an effect. It appears in the layer's property outline under its Effects category. But in contrast to other effects, the Effect Controls window provides almost no controls for Paint. And whereas most effects include a single set of properties (however extensive they may be), the Paint effect lists each stroke individually, and each stroke contains its own set of properties.

Strokes are really layers within the layer containing the effect. Each stroke has its own duration bar, its own video switch, and its own set of properties that can be keyframed (**Figure 13.53**). You can precisely control when each stroke appears and for how long. In the case of animated strokes, this paradigm lets you specify how quickly a stroke draws onto the screen.

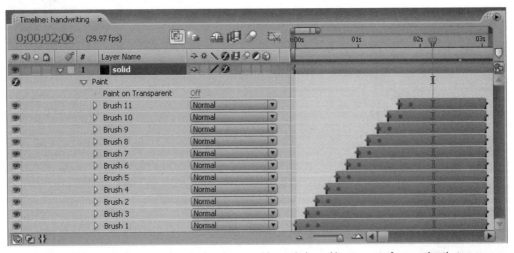

Figure 13.53 Each stroke has its own duration bar, its own video switch, and its own set of properties that you can animate with keyframes.

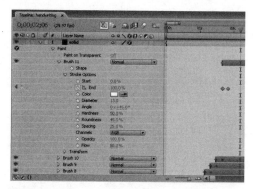

Figure 13.54 Each stroke includes Stroke Options and Transform properties.

Figure 13.55 When a stroke is selected, it appears with a line through its center (assuming the paint is visible). An anchor point icon also appears at the beginning of each selected stroke.

Strokes in the timeline

Setting the current frame determines a stroke's initial In point. Its duration depends on the Duration option you specified in the Paint panel: Constant, Write On, Single Frame, or Custom (see the section "Specifying Paint Stroke Options" earlier in this chapter). As with layers, the strokes' stacking order in the property outline determines the order in which strokes are applied, and their blending mode determines how they interact with strokes lower in the stack.

In general, you can manipulate strokes just as you would adjust layers: switch them on and off; change their stacking order; set their In and Out points and duration; and view, adjust, and keyframe their properties. However, the keyboard shortcuts you use with layers (cuing to or setting In and Out points, for example) don't work with strokes' duration bars.

In addition to all the properties that are unique to strokes, each stroke also includes its own set of Transform properties. You can use these to set each stroke's anchor point, position, scale, and rotation. Remember, for strokes, Opacity is listed in the other Stroke Options property category (**Figure 13.54**).

Selecting strokes

Selecting a stroke in the layer's property outline makes it visible in the Layer panel. A stroke appears as a thin line running through the center of the painted line, much like a selected mask path is visible in the center of a stroked path. An anchor point icon appears at the beginning of the stroke (**Figure 13.55**). When a stroke is selected, you can use the Selection tool ▸ to drag it to a new position within the layer. (You can always move the layer within the comp, but doing so moves the entire layer—its image, its paint, and any other effects it contains.)

However, strokes appear in a Layer panel only when the Paint effect is selected in the Layer panel's View pull-down menu. This occurs automatically when you apply paint, but it can get confusing if you work on other tasks and return to the Layer panel to find the Paint effect is no longer selected—and no longer visible. The same holds true if the layer contains more than one Paint effect; make sure the Layer panel's View pull-down menu is set to the Paint effect you want.

Multiple Paint effects

Painting multiple strokes adds to the current Paint effect, and a single layer can contain more than one Paint effect. This can be useful when you want to treat sets of strokes as separate groups. For example, you can disable all of one Paint effect's strokes by clicking its effect icon. However, the Layer panel can only show the Paint effect you specify in the View pull-down menu. The strokes of any Paint effects higher in the stacking order are *visible*, but you can't tell whether they're selected; Paint effects lower in the stacking order than the selected effect aren't visible in the Layer panel (**Figures 13.56** and **13.57**). You must choose a Paint effect in the View pull-down menu in order to view and drag its selected strokes in the Layer panel.

You can duplicate or add a Paint effect as you would any other effect. When you add strokes to a Paint effect, be sure to select the effect you want to modify in the layer's View pull-down menu.

✔ Tip

■ It can be useful to view the layer you're painting in a Layer panel and the composition that contains the layer in a separate Comp panel.

Figure 13.56 To see and manipulate strokes in the Layer panel, choose the Paint effect in the Layer panel's View pull-down menu.

Figure 13.57 When the Layer contains more than one Paint effect, choose the one you want. Strokes of Paint effects higher in the stacking order are visible, but you can only manipulate strokes in the selected effect.

Figure 13.58 Paint tools include the Brush, Clone, or Eraser. In this example, the Brush tool is selected.

Figure 13.59 Choose Write On from the Paint panel's Duration pull-down menu.

Animating Strokes

The following tasks apply what you learned in this chapter to achieve a few common Paint effects. The first employs the Duration option, Write On, to simulate natural writing. The next task explains how to adjust the timing of the strokes in the Timeline panel. The last task shows how to animate a stroke by keyframing its Shape property, making it appear as though one stroke is transforming into another.

These tasks focus on employing different animation techniques and don't cover other options (such as brush tips, channels, and modes) in any detail. To find out about those options, refer back to the appropriate sections earlier in the chapter.

To animate strokes using the Write On option:

1. In the Tools panel, select a paint tool (**Figure 13.58**).

2. In the Paint panel, specify paint options, including Opacity, Flow, Color, Mode, and Channels.

   For a detailed explanation, see "Specifying Paint Stroke Options," earlier in this chapter.

3. In the Paint panel's Duration pull-down menu, choose Write On (**Figure 13.59**).

4. Set the current time to the frame where you want the first stroke to begin (**Figure 13.60**).

continues on next page

Figure 13.60 Set the current time to the frame where you want the first stroke to begin.

ANIMATING STROKES

5. Using the Brush tool, drag in the Layer panel to paint strokes on the layer (**Figure 13.61**).

The speed at which you paint determines the duration and speed of the stroke animation. Lifting the mouse or pen to start a new stroke creates a separate brush layer in the Paint effect's property outline (**Figure 13.62**).

6. Preview the stroke animation in the Layer or Comp panel.

Strokes appear gradually, as you painted them (**Figure 13.63**).

Figure 13.61 Drag in the layer's Layer panel to draw or write in the layer. Lifting the mouse or pen ends the stroke, and, because Write On is selected, the stroke disappears.

Figure 13.63 When you preview the animation, strokes appear in the same manner in which they were painted.

Figure 13.62 Each stroke appears in the layer's property outline, under its Paint effect. The Write On option animates the stroke's End property automatically.

To adjust the speed of an animated stroke:

1. Animate a stroke using the Write On option, as described in the previous task.

2. Expand the property outline for the layer containing the stroke animation.

3. Expand the Stroke Options property heading to reveal the End property (**Figure 13.64**).

4. In the time ruler, move the End property's keyframes to adjust the speed of the Write On effect (**Figure 13.65**).

5. Change the keyframe's interpolation option to adjust the rate of change between keyframes.

   See Chapter 7, "Properties and Keyframes," and Chapter 9, "Keyframe Interpolation," for more information.

✔ Tips

■ Essentially, the Write On option animates the End property automatically. You can animate any stroke to create the same effect manually by animating the End property and duration of any stroke.

■ The Write On option works effortlessly when animating a single stroke. However, lifting the mouse or pen creates multiple strokes that all begin at the current time. Therefore, multiple strokes will animate simultaneously, which doesn't simulate natural handwriting. To make each stroke animate sequentially, you must change the In points (and, possibly, the durations).

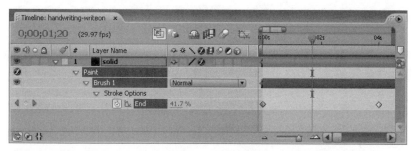

Figure 13.64 Expand a layer's property outline to reveal its Paint effect's End property.

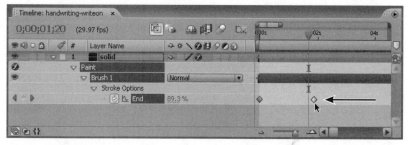

Figure 13.65 Move the End property's keyframes to change the speed of the Write On effect. Here, the last keyframe is moved closer to the first keyframe to make the writing appear more quickly.

To animate a stroke by keyframing its shape:

1. Set the time you want the stroke to begin, and, using a paint tool and the techniques described earlier in this chapter, create a stroke in a layer (**Figure 13.66**).

2. In the Timeline panel, expand the layer's property outline to reveal the stroke you want to animate.

3. Set the current time to the frame where you want the stroke's shape to begin changing, and select the Shape property's Stopwatch icon.

   A Shape keyframe appears at the current time for the stroke (**Figure 13.67**).

4. Set the current time to the frame where you want to paint a new stroke.

Figure 13.66 Set the current time and paint the stroke's initial shape.

Figure 13.67 In the layer's property outline, expand the Paint effect and click the Shape property's Stopwatch icon to set the initial keyframe.

Figure 13.68 With the previous stroke selected, set the current time to the frame where you want the stroke to assume a new shape, and paint that shape.

5. With the first stroke selected, paint a new stroke (**Figure 13.68**).

Instead of creating a new stroke layer, a new Shape keyframe appears in the selected stroke's property outline (**Figure 13.69**).

6. Repeat step 5, as needed.

continues on next page

Figure 13.69 Instead of creating a new stroke, the same stroke gets a new Shape keyframe at the current time.

7. Preview the stroke animation.

The stroke transforms from the shape defined by one keyframe to the shape defined by the next keyframe (**Figure 13.70**).

✔ Tip

■ You can keyframe any stroke or paint option that includes a Stopwatch icon in the Paint effect's property outline or Effect Controls panel.

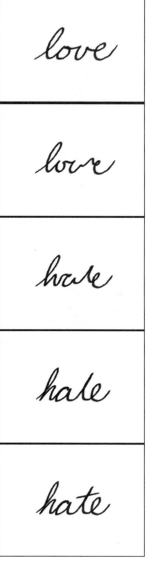

Figure 13.70 When you preview the animation, the stroke transforms from one shape into another. In this example, the line that crosses the t was created as a separate stroke using the Write On option.

Cloning

Like the Brush tool, the Clone Stamp tool adds pixels to a layer, using the paint brush options you specify (Duration, Brush Tip, and the like). But as the name implies, the Clone Stamp doesn't add pixels according to a specified color; instead, it copies, or *clones*, pixels from a layer's image. Photoshop veterans will instantly recognize the Clone Stamp tool and appreciate its value in retouching an image. They'll also have a big head start on using the tool; it works nearly the same in After Effects—except nondestructively, and over time.

As when you use the other paint tools, you must first specify brush options for the Clone Stamp tool. But instead of specifying a color, you specify the layer, frame, and location of the pixels you want to copy to the target layer. Once you've set these options, you paint pixels from the source to the target.

For the sake of clarity, the following sections break the cloning process into smaller tasks: setting the sample point, and then cloning. After that, you'll learn how to make cloning easier by superimposing the source image over the target image and saving clone options as convenient presets.

Setting the sample point for cloning

When cloning, pixels are copied, or *sampled*, from a particular layer, frame, and physical location in a source image. You can specify these three aspects of the clone source by using the Paint panel or by sampling manually. You can change the sample point at any time using either method, as needed.

You also need to understand the difference between setting a fixed sample point and one that maintains a consistent relationship with strokes in the target layer. In terms of space, you specify your choice with the Paint panel's Aligned option; in terms of time, you specify your choice with the Lock Source Time option.

The Aligned option

The starting point for a clone stroke in the target layer always corresponds to the sample point you set in the source image. The Paint panel displays the distance between the stroke's starting point in the target and the sample point in the source as the Offset value. (When the target and source are different images, the distance is the difference in the corresponding points in each image's own coordinate system.)

However, the Aligned option determines which pixels are copied in subsequent strokes (**Figure 13.71**). By default, the Aligned option is selected, and pixels are always copied from a point in the source that is a consistent distance (the Offset value) from the corresponding location of the Clone Stamp in the target image (**Figure 13.72**). In contrast, unchecking Aligned copies pixels using the initial sample as a fixed starting point (**Figure 13.73**).

Figure 13.71 The Aligned option determines whether pixels are copied from a fixed point or offset from a corresponding location of the Clone Stamp.

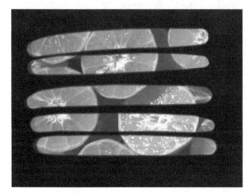

Figure 13.72 With Aligned checked, pixels are copied from a consistent distance from the corresponding location of the Clone Stamp.

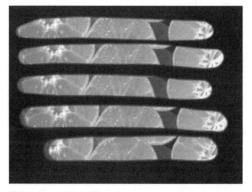

Figure 13.73 With Aligned unchecked, all strokes copy pixels from a fixed sample point in the source.

Figure 13.74
Checking Lock Source Time lets you specify a Source Time—a fixed frame from which to copy pixels.

Figure 13.75
Unchecking Lock Source Time lets you specify a Source Time Shift—a consistent time difference between the target layer frame and source layer frame.

Figure 13.76 Select the Clone Stamp tool.

Figure 13.77 From the Paint panel's Source pull-down menu, specify the layer from which you want to clone.

The Lock Source Time option

The Lock Source Time option sets whether the Clone Stamp tool copies pixels from a fixed frame or maintains a time difference between the target frame and source frame (**Figure 13.74**). When Lock Source Time is selected, pixels are copied from a fixed frame that the Paint panel displays as the Source Time. If you change the target frame, the Source Time remains the same (unless you change it manually or sample from a different source frame). When Lock Source Time is unchecked, the Paint panel displays a Source Time Shift value. This way, After Effects maintains a time difference between the target frame and source frame (**Figure 13.75**).

To set a clone source in the Paint panel:

1. If necessary, arrange the source and target layers in a composition.

2. Select the Clone Stamp tool (**Figure 13.76**). Clone Stamp options appear in the Paint panel.

3. In the Paint panel's Source pull-down menu, select the source layer from which the Clone Stamp tool will sample pixels (**Figure 13.77**).

continues on next page

CLONING

4. *Do either of the following:*

▲ To clone from a point offset from the corresponding point in the target layer, check Aligned (**Figure 13.78**):

▲ To clone from the same starting point in the source layer with each new stroke, uncheck Aligned.

5. Specify the difference, or *offset*, between the starting point of the sample (in the source layer) and the stroke (in the target layer) by setting X and Y values for the Offset value.

Offset values are expressed as the distance from the sample point to the stroke point in pixels, measured along the X and Y axes (**Figure 13.79**).

6. *Do either of the following:*

▲ To specify a specific source frame from which to sample, check Lock Source Time and specify a value for Source Time (**Figure 13.80**).

▲ To specify a consistent time difference between the target frame and source frame, uncheck Lock Source Time and specify a value for Source Time Shift (**Figure 13.81**).

Checking or unchecking Lock Source Time makes the corresponding time value appear in the Paint panel.

Figure 13.78 In the Paint panel, check Aligned if you want the sample point in the source to maintain a consistent relationship with each stroke in the target; uncheck Aligned to sample from the same point in the source layer with each stroke.

Figure 13.79 To specify an offset between the sample point in the source layer and the beginning of the stroke in the target layer, set X and Y values for Offset.

Figure 13.80 To sample from the same source frame regardless of the target frame, check Lock Source Time.

Figure 13.81 To maintain a consistent time difference between the source frame and the target frame, leave Lock Source Time unchecked and specify a value for Source Time Shift.

To set a clone source by clicking:

1. Follow steps 1–2 in the previous task, "To set a clone source in the Paint panel."

2. Specify options for the Aligned and Lock Source Time check boxes, as described in the previous task.

3. Set the current time to the frame from which you want to sample in the source layer, and Option-click (Mac) or Alt-click (Windows) the sample point in the source layer's Layer panel (**Figure 13.82**).

   In the Paint panel, the source layer's name appears in the Source pull-down menu, and values appear for Offset. Values also appear for Source Time or Source Time Shift, depending on the options you chose earlier.

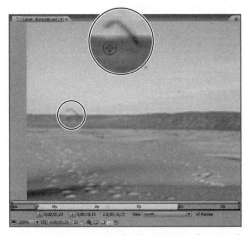

Figure 13.82 Option-click (Mac) or Alt-click (Windows) to set the sample point in the source image. Here, the sample is taken from a future frame in order to eliminate an obtrusive string of dust on the lens.

Using the Clone Stamp Tool

Now that you understand how setting a sample point works, you can integrate that knowledge into the overall cloning process. Once you master this task, turn to later sections to learn about additional features, including overlaying the clone source's image over the target and saving Clone Stamp settings.

To clone pixels:

1. Arrange the clone source and target layers in a Comp panel, and open the target layer in a separate Layer panel (**Figure 13.83**).

   The Comp panel must be selected for the source layer to appear in the pull-down menu in step 4.

2. In the Tools panel, choose the Clone Stamp tool 🔲 (**Figure 13.84**).

3. In the Paint and Brush Tips panels, specify a brush tip and paint options, such as Opacity, Flow, Mode, and Duration (**Figure 13.85**).

   See the "Specifying Paint Options" and "Using Brush Tips" sections, earlier in this chapter.

Figure 13.83 This example uses the same layer for the target and source.

Figure 13.84 Choose the Clone Stamp tool.

Figure 13.85 Specify paint options, such as Opacity, Flow, Mode, and Duration.

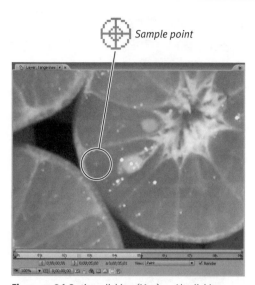

Sample point

Figure 13.86 Option-clicking (Mac) or Alt-clicking (Windows) changes the cursor into a crosshairs icon and sets the sample point (the layer, frame, and location of the source pixels).

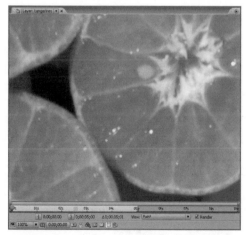

Figure 13.87 Click or drag in the target layer with the Clone Stamp tool to copy pixels from the source layer. Here, cloning eliminates a distracting seed from the tangerine image.

4. Specify the sample source by *doing either of the following*:

   ▲ Using the Clone Stamp tool, Option-click (Mac) or Alt-click (Windows) in the source Layer panel at the frame and location you want to sample (**Figure 13.86**).

   ▲ In the Paint panel, specify the settings you want for the Source, Aligned, Lock Source Time (including the Source Time or Source Time Shift), and Offset options. (See the section "Setting the sample point for cloning," earlier in this chapter.)

5. Set the current time to the frame from which you want to clone pixels onto the target layer.

6. Click or drag in the target layer's Layer panel.

   Pixels from the source layer are painted onto the target layer according to the options you specified (**Figure 13.87**). In the target layer's property outline, the Paint effect appears and includes each clone stroke you make (**Figure 13.88**).

✔ Tip

■ You can create a perfectly straight cloned stroke by clicking the stroke's starting point and Shift-clicking its ending point. This technique is great for cloning out linear elements such as wires or power lines.

Figure 13.88 In the target layer's property outline, the Paint effect appears and includes each clone stroke you make.

Overlaying the Clone Source

Although cloning can be painstaking, the most recent version of After Effects makes the process easier by letting you superimpose the source image over the target layer as you clone.

To superimpose the source over the target layer as you clone:

1. Prepare layers for cloning and set options for the Clone Stamp tool, as explained in the previous task, "To clone pixels."

2. In the Paint panel, check Clone Source Overlay and specify the source layer's opacity (**Figure 13.89**).

   The overlay appears when the Clone Stamp tool is positioned over the target layer's image (**Figure 13.90**).

3. To apply the Difference blending mode to the superimposed source layer image, click the Difference Mode button ![icon] (**Figure 13.91**).

   The Difference blending mode can help you identify differences between similar source and target frames. See Chapter 14 for more about blending modes.

✔ Tip

- You can also toggle the overlay by pressing Option-Shift (Mac) or Alt-Shift (Windows) as you use the Clone Stamp tool.

Figure 13.89 In the Paint panel, check Clone Source Overlay and specify the source layer's opacity.

Figure 13.90 The overlay appears when the Clone Stamp tool is positioned over the target layer's image.

Figure 13.91 To see differences in the source and target layers more easily, click the Difference Mode button in the Paint panel.

Figure 13.92 Select the Clone Stamp tool.

Figure 13.93 In the Paint panel, click a Clone Stamp Preset button and specify the settings you want associated with the button.

Saving Clone Stamp Settings

Meticulous retouching can require that you switch Clone Stamp tool settings often. Luckily, the Paint panel includes five Clone Stamp Preset buttons that you can use to store and quickly recall settings.

To save Clone Stamp settings:

1. In the Tools panel, select the Clone Stamp tool 🖩 (**Figure 13.92**).

   The Clone Options become available.

2. In the Clone Options area of the Paint Panel, click a Clone Stamp Preset button 🖩.

3. Specify the options you want (as described in the previous sections) to associate with the selected preset button (**Figure 13.93**).

   The options you specify are associated with the selected preset button.

To use a Clone Stamp preset:

1. In the Tools panel, select the Clone Stamp tool 🖩.

2. In the Clone Options area of the Paint panel, *do either of the following:*

   ▲ Click the Clone Stamp Preset button that corresponds to the preset you want to use.

   ▲ Press the number keyboard shortcut that corresponds to the preset you want: 3=first preset; 4=second preset; 5=third preset; 6=fourth preset; 7=fifth preset.

3. Use the Clone Stamp tool as explained in the previous tasks.

MORE LAYER TECHNIQUES

This chapter tackles a handful of techniques. First, you'll learn about a pair of layer switches—Frame Blending and Motion Blur—that influence how After Effects deals with motion between frames. Then, you'll play with the comp's frame rate using time remapping. Armed with that knowledge, you'll be ready to take a closer look at the Modes panel. In the Modes panel, you'll discover a long list of ways to blend a layer with underlying layers, and you'll expand your repertoire of compositing tools. You'll also find out what the mysterious T option stands for and, more important, how to use it. Finally, you'll complete your tour of the Modes panel by learning about yet another compositing option, Track Mattes.

Using Frame Blending

When the frame rate of motion footage is lower than that of the composition, movement within the frame can appear jerky—either because the footage's native frame rate is lower than that of the composition, or because you time-stretched the footage. Whatever the case, After Effects reconciles this difference by repeating frames of the source footage. For example, each frame of a 15-fps movie is displayed twice in a composition with a frame rate of 30 fps. However, because there aren't enough unique frames to represent full motion, the result can sometimes resemble a crude flip-book animation.

In these instances, you can smooth the motion by activating the Frame Blending switch. When frame blending is on, After Effects interpolates between original frames, blending them rather than simply repeating them (**Figures 14.1** and **14.2**). Motion footage that has been sped up can also benefit from frame blending.

You can specify either of two types of frame blending: Frame Mix and Pixel Motion. Comparing the two methods, Frame Mix renders faster but is lower quality; hence, the layer's Frame Blending switch resembles a jagged backslash (which looks like the draft quality switch) . Pixel Motion renders more slowly but can produce better results; it's indicated by a smooth slash (similar to the full quality switch) .

Figure 14.1 Ordinarily, After Effects interpolates frames by repeating the original frames. Because this simple animation is interpreted as 15 frames per second, frames are repeated to compensate for a 30-fps composition.

Figure 14.2 When frame blending is applied and enabled, it blends the original frames to create interpolated frames.

To apply or remove frame blending in a layer:

1. If necessary, click the Timeline panel's Switches button to make the layer switches appear.

2. For a layer created from motion footage, click the Frame Blending switch to toggle its icon to the option you want:

   No Icon—no frame blending applied

   Frame Mix ◪—blends frames using a faster but lower-quality method

   Pixel Motion ▟—blends frames using a slower but higher quality method

   The layer uses the frame blending method associated with the icon you specify (**Figure 14.3**). Frame blending must be enabled for its effect to be rendered in the Comp panel (see the next task).

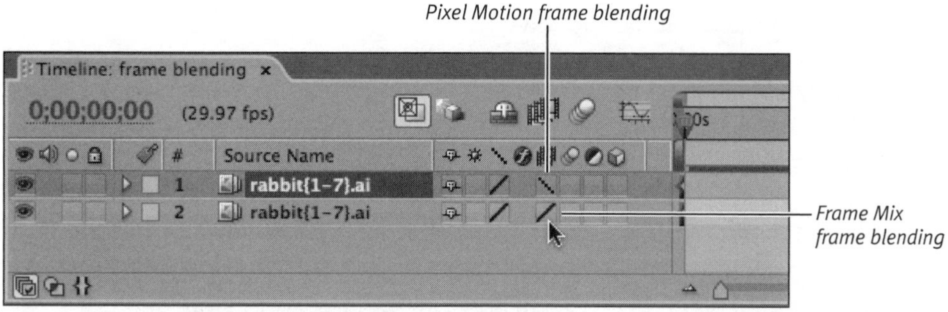

Pixel Motion frame blending

Frame Mix frame blending

Figure 14.3 Clicking a motion footage layer's Frame Blending switch repeatedly changes its state from no frame blending to frame mix to pixel motion.

To enable or disable frame blending for all layers in a composition:

Do either of the following:

◆ Click the Enable Frame Blending button 🔳 at the top of the Timeline panel (**Figure 14.4**).

◆ Select Enable Frame Blending in the Timeline panel's pull-down menu.

When the Enable Frame Blending button is clicked, frame blending is enabled for all layers with frame blending applied.

✔ Tips

■ Previous versions of After Effects used a slightly different icon for the Frame Blending option. Before After Effects 7, frame blending could be on or off only; you couldn't specify whether to use Frame Mix or Pixel Motion.

■ Because frame blending can significantly slow previewing and rendering, you may want to apply it to layers but refrain from enabling it until you're ready to render the final animation.

USING FRAME BLENDING

Figure 14.4 Click the Enable Frame Blending button at the top of the Timeline panel.

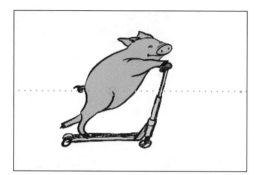

Figure 14.5 Ordinarily, an animated layer appears sharp and distinct as it moves through the frame of the composition.

Figure 14.6 To simulate a more natural-looking, blurred motion, activate the Motion Blur switch for an animated layer.

Using Motion Blur

Ordinarily, an animated layer appears sharp and distinct as it moves through the frame of a composition (**Figure 14.5**). This can appear unnatural, however, because you're accustomed to seeing objects blur as they move. In the time it takes to perceive the object at a single position (or, in the case of a camera, to record it to a frame), that object has occupied a continuous range of positions, causing it to appear blurred.

To simulate this effect, you can activate the Motion Blur switch for an animated layer (**Figure 14.6**). To reduce the time it takes to preview your animation, you may want to apply motion blur to layers but wait to enable it until you're ready to render.

Because motion blur simulates the blur captured by a camera, it uses similar controls. As with a film camera, a Shutter Angle control works with the frame rate to simulate exposure time and thus the amount of blur. For example, using a 180-degree shutter angle with a 30-fps composition simulates a one-fifteenth-second exposure (180 degrees = 50% × 360 degrees; 50% × 30 fps = 1/15 sec). Increasing the shutter angle increases the amount of blur.

To apply or remove motion blur:

1. If necessary, click the Timeline panel's Switches button to make the layer switches appear.

2. Select the Motion Blur switch for a layer with animated motion (**Figure 14.7**).

   When the Motion Blur switch is selected, motion blur is applied to the layer. The Motion Blur button determines whether motion blur is enabled (see the next task for details).

To enable or disable motion blur for all layers in a composition:

Do either of the following:

◆ Click the Enable Motion Blur button at the top of the Timeline panel (**Figure 14.8**).

◆ Select Enable Motion Blur in the Timeline panel's pull-down menu.

   When the Enable Motion Blur button is clicked or the Enable Motion Blur item is selected, motion blur is enabled for all layers with motion blur applied.

Figure 14.7 Select the Motion Blur switch for a layer with animated motion to apply motion blur.

Figure 14.8 Click the Enable Motion Blur button at the top of the Timeline panel to enable motion blur for the layers with motion blur applied to them.

USING MOTION BLUR

Figure 14.9 Choose Composition > Composition Settings.

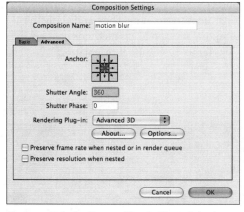

Figure 14.10 In the Composition Settings dialog box, enter a value for the shutter angle, in degrees.

To set the shutter angle for motion blur for previews:

1. Choose Composition > Composition Settings (**Figure 14.9**).

   The Composition Settings dialog box appears.

2. In the Advanced panel of the Composition Settings dialog box, enter a value for the shutter angle, in degrees (**Figure 14.10**).

   You may enter a value between 0 and 360 degrees. The higher the value, the greater the amount of blur. The value you set is applied to playback and preview.

3. Click OK to close the Composition Settings dialog box.

✔ Tips

- After Effects 7's icon for Motion Blur looks different from the icon used in previous versions.

- When you render the final output, you can choose whether to enable motion blur and frame blending in the Render Queue panel. This way, you don't have to return to your composition to check the setting. See Chapter 17, "Output."

- The Render Queue panel also lets you reset the shutter angle for motion blur before you render a movie.

- You can apply motion blur to a mask by selecting the mask, choosing Layer > Mask > Motion Blur, and choosing an option in the submenu.

USING MOTION BLUR

Understanding Time Remapping

Back in Chapter 6, "Layer Editing," you learned how to change the speed of a layer using the Time Stretch command (or by changing the layer's Stretch value in the In/Out panel in the Timeline panel). Although it's useful, the Time Stretch command is limited to changing the layer's overall playback speed. To make the playback speed up, slow down, reverse, or come to a halt (or *freeze frame*), you need to use *time remapping*.

In a normal layer, a direct relationship exists between the layer's time and the frame you see and hear. In a time-remapped layer, the normal time controls show the layer's elapsed time but no longer dictate which frame is displayed (or heard) at that time. Instead, the Time Remap values determine the visible (or audible) frame at that time.

For example, when you first apply time remapping, keyframes appear at the layer's In and Out points, and the Time Remap values at those keyframes match the layer's original time values. Initially, there's no change in the layer's playback (**Figure 14.11**). However, changing the Time Remap value of the keyframe at the end of the clip (say, at 4 seconds) to a frame in the middle of the clip (2 seconds) redistributes, or *remaps*, the first 2 seconds of the layer over 4 seconds—slowing down the frame rate between keyframes (**Figure 14.12**).

This example achieves a result similar to that of the Time Stretch command. But consider that you can set additional time-remapped keyframes in the same layer and apply the temporal interpolation methods covered in Chapter 9, "Keyframe Interpolation."

Figure 14.11 Here, the Time Remap property values match the layer's original time values. The layer time is the top number; the remapped time is the lower number.

Figure 14.12 Here, the last Time Remap keyframe is still positioned at 04;00 into the clip, but its value has been changed to the frame at 02;00. The layer's frame rate slows between the keyframes.

Using the same layer as in the previous example, suppose you set a time-remap keyframe at 2 seconds into the clip and leave its value set to 2 seconds. The layer plays normally between the first and second keyframes (the first 2 seconds). But if you change the Time Remap value of the last keyframe—positioned 4 seconds into the clip—to 0 seconds (not the keyframe's position in time, just its value), then playback reverses between the second and third keyframes (**Figure 14.13**).

Although time remapping can sound confusing, it works just like keyframing other properties. But whereas most keyframes define a visible characteristic (like position) at a given frame, a time-remap keyframe specifies the *frame* you see (or hear) at a given point in the layer's time.

Figure 14.13 Here, the layer plays back normally between the first keyframe and a second keyframe, set halfway through the layer's duration. The Time Remap value of the last keyframe—positioned at 04;00—has been changed to 00;00, which reverses the playback.

Controlling Time Remap Values in the Layer Panel

When you enable time remapping on a layer, the Layer panel displays additional controls for changing the frame rate. In addition to the layer's ordinary time ruler, current time indicator (CTI), and current time display, a corresponding remap-time ruler, marker, and display also appear (**Figure 14.14**). The lower CTI shows the (normal) time; the upper CTI shows the frame you specify to play at that time.

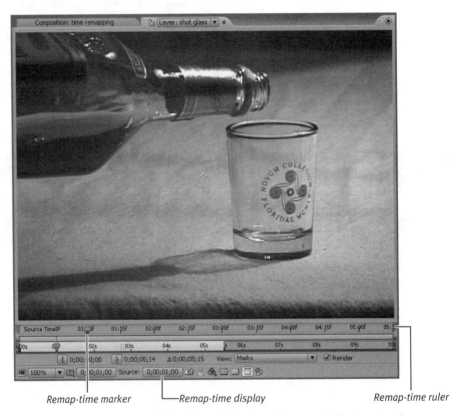

Remap-time marker   *Remap-time display*   *Remap-time ruler*

Figure 14.14 Enabling time remapping makes additional controls appear in the Layer panel.

As is the case for any property value, you can set keyframes for the Time Remap property using controls in the Timeline panel (**Figure 14.15**). As usual, use the Add/Remove Keyframe button in the property's keyframe navigator to set keyframes that use previously interpolated values. You can also view the property's value graph in the Graph Editor and drag control points on the graph to change the value of the corresponding keyframe. This technique lets you accelerate, decelerate, or reverse playback speed (see the task "To change playback speed over time," later in this chapter). For more about viewing and using a value graph and using interpolation methods (how After Effects calculates property values between keyframes), see Chapter 9.

Value graph

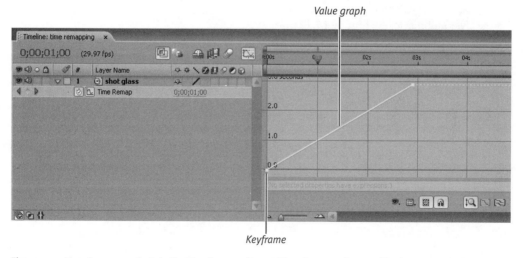

Keyframe

Figure 14.15 You also use controls in the Timeline panel to set Time Remap values and keyframes. Here, the time remapping values are seen in the graph editor view.

Using Time Remapping

The tasks in this section explain how to enable time remapping for a layer and how to set keyframes to pause, reverse, or change the speed of playback. Once you get the hang of these techniques, you can explore other ways to control playback using time remapping. Turn to Chapter 9 for more about keyframe interpolation and how you can specify the way After Effects calculates property changes from one keyframe to the next.

To enable time remapping:

1. Select a layer, and choose Layer > Time > Enable Time Remapping (**Figure 14.16**).

   In the Timeline panel, the Time Remap property appears in the layer outline for the selected layer. After Effects creates keyframes at the beginning and end of the layer automatically (**Figure 14.17**).

Figure 14.16 Select a layer, and choose Layer > Time > Enable Time Remapping.

Figure 14.17 After Effects sets a time-remap keyframe at the layer's In and Out points automatically. However, the values match the layer's original values, and the layer's frame rate remains unchanged.

Figure 14.18 Double-click the layer in the Timeline panel to view it in a Layer panel and use the time-remapping controls.

Figure 14.19 Set the current time to the frame where you want playback to stop. There's no need to change the remap time; it should match the current time.

2. In the Timeline panel, double-click the layer to view it in a Layer panel.

In addition to the standard controls, the Layer panel includes time-remapping controls (**Figure 14.18**).

To create a freeze frame with time remapping:

1. Select a layer, and enable time remapping as explained in the previous task, "To enable time remapping."

After Effects sets beginning and ending keyframes automatically.

2. Set the current time to the frame where you want the layer's playback to stop (**Figure 14.19**).

3. In the Timeline panel, select the keyframe navigator's Add/Remove Keyframe button ◆ for the layer's Time Remap property.

A keyframe appears at the current time, using the previously interpolated value. In this case, the Time Remap value matches the frame's original value (**Figure 14.20**).

continues on next page

USING TIME REMAPPING

Figure 14.20 In the Timeline panel, click the diamond icon in the Time Remap property's keyframe navigator to create a keyframe at the current frame.

4. With the new keyframe selected, choose Animation > Toggle Hold Keyframe (**Figure 14.21**).

The new keyframe uses Hold interpolation, evidenced by its Hold keyframe icon (**Figure 14.22**). This holds the Time Remap value until the next keyframe is reached.

5. Select the last keyframe, and press Delete (Mac) or Backspace (Windows).

The last keyframe is removed (**Figure 14.23**). The layer's frames play back at normal speed; then, the layer freezes when it reaches the Hold keyframe.

6. View the remapped layer in the Layer or Comp panel by dragging the CTI.

You can't use RAM previews to see the layer play back using the remapped frame rate.

Animation	View	Window	Help	
Save Animation Preset...				
Apply Animation Preset...				
Recent Animation Presets				▶
Browse Presets...				
Add Keyframe				
Toggle Hold Keyframe			Ctrl+Alt+H	
Keyframe Interpolation...			Ctrl+Alt+K	
Keyframe Velocity...			Ctrl+Shift+K	
Keyframe Assistant				▶
Animate Text				▶
Add Text Selector				▶
Remove All Text Animators				
Add Expression			Alt+Shift+=	
Track Motion				
Stabilize Motion				
Track this Property				
Reveal Animating Properties			U	
Reveal Modified Properties				

Figure 14.21 With the new keyframe selected, choose Animation > Toggle Hold Keyframe.

✔ Tip

■ The Layer > Time > Freeze Frame command applies Time Remap and sets a hold keyframe so that the current frame plays for the layer's entire duration.

Figure 14.22 The keyframe icon changes to a Hold keyframe icon, indicating that the property value will remain at that value until the next keyframe is reached.

Figure 14.23 Select the last keyframe, and press Delete (Mac) or Backspace (Windows). The layer's playback now freezes at the Hold keyframe you created in steps 3 and 4.

To reverse playback:

1. Select a layer, and enable time remapping as explained in the task "To enable time remapping" earlier in this section.

2. Set the current time to the frame where you want the layer's playback direction to reverse, and select the Add/Remove Keyframe button ◆ in the Time Remap property's keyframe navigator.

   A keyframe appears at the current time, using the previously interpolated value. In this case, the keyframe's value matches the frame's original value (**Figure 14.24**).

3. Set the current frame later in time, to the point where you want the reversed playback to end (**Figure 14.25**).

continues on next page

Figure 14.24 Set the current time to the point where you want the layer's playback to reverse, and click the box in the Time Remap property's keyframe navigator to set a keyframe.

Figure 14.25 Set the current time to the point where you want the reversed playback to end. Here, the current time is set to the Out point (which changes the keyframe value that was set automatically when remapping was applied).

USING TIME REMAPPING

4. In the Layer panel, drag the remap-time indicator to an earlier frame (**Figure 14.26**).

The layer's original frame value is mapped to the frame you specified with the remap-time indicator.

5. View the time-remapped layer in the Layer or Comp panel by dragging the CTI.

You can't use RAM previews to see the layer play back using the remapped frame rate. The layer's frames play back normally until the keyframe you set in step 2; the layer then plays in reverse until the keyframe you set in step 3. The remap frame you set in step 4 determines the actual frame played by the time the last keyframe is reached (**Figure 14.27**).

Figure 14.26 In the Layer panel, drag the remap-time marker to a time earlier than the one you chose in step 3.

Figure 14.27 The layer plays forward between the first and second keyframes and then plays in reverse between the second and last keyframes.

Figure 14.28 In the Timeline panel, expand the layer's Time Remap property to reveal its value graph.

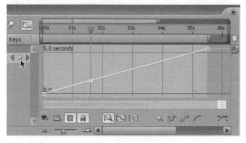

Figure 14.29 Set the current time when you want the speed to change to begin, and click the diamond icon in the keyframe navigator. (For illustration purposes, the Keys column—containing the keyframe navigator—is set to appear near the Graph Editor.)

To change playback speed over time:

1. Select a layer, and enable time remapping as explained in the task "To enable time remapping" earlier in this section.

2. In the Timeline panel, *do either of the following:*

   ▲ Expand the selected layer's Time Remap property to reveal its key-frames in standard view.

   ▲ Enable the Graph Editor, and set the layer's Time Remap property to appear as a value graph (**Figure 14.28**).

   See Chapter 9 for more about using the Graph Editor.

3. Set the current time to the frame where you want the speed change to begin, and click the Add/Remove Keyframe button ◆ in the Time Remap property's keyframe navigator (**Figure 14.29**).

   A keyframe appears at the current time; its value matches the frame's original time value.

   continues on next page

USING TIME REMAPPING

4. In the Time Remap property's value graph, drag the control point that corresponds to the keyframe you set in step 3 *in either of the following ways:*

   ▲ To slow playback speed, drag the control point down (**Figure 14.30**).

   ▲ To increase playback speed, drag the control point up (**Figure 14.31**).

   When the value is higher than the previous keyframe's value, the layer plays forward; when the value is lower, the layer plays in reverse. If the layer is already playing in reverse, drag the value graph's control point in the opposite direction.

5. Repeat steps 3 and 4 as needed.

   The layer's playback speed and direction change according to your choices.

6. View the remapped layer in the Layer or Comp panel by dragging the CTI.

   You can't use RAM previews to see the layer play back using the remapped frame rate.

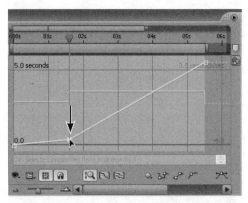

Figure 14.30 In the value graph, drag the control point corresponding to the keyframe. Decreasing the slope decreases speed; here, motion slows between the first and second keyframes. (In this figure, a reference speed graph is visible to better illustrate the result of the change.)

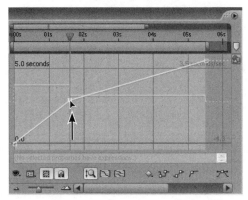

Figure 14.31 Increasing the slope of the line increases speed; here, motion between the first and second keyframe speeds up.

Figure 14.32 When you select a blending mode from the Mode pull-down menu, the Video switch displays a darkened Eye icon.

Using Blending Modes

In previous chapters, you learned that higher layers in the stacking order are superimposed on lower layers according to their alpha channel (which can also be modified with masks) or their Opacity property value. If you want to combine layers in more varied and subtle ways, you can use a variety of blending modes. By default, the blending mode is set to Normal. You can change the mode by selecting an option from the Mode menu in (you guessed it) the Modes panel of the Timeline panel. When you do, the Video switch for the layer displays a darkened Eye icon ■ (**Figure 14.32**).

A blending mode changes the value of a layer's pixels according to the values of the corresponding pixels in the underlying image. Depending on how the values interact, the result often appears as a blend of the two. You may recognize most of the blending modes from Photoshop; you'll find they work the same way here.

Although most layer modes only blend color values (RGB channels), some—such as the Stencil and Silhouette modes—affect transparency (alpha channel) information.

To apply a layer mode:

1. If necessary, click the Switches/Modes button to make the Modes menu appear (**Figure 14.33**).

2. Choose a mode from a layer's Modes menu (**Figure 14.34**).

   The Video switch for the layer becomes a darkened eye ◉. The mode you select affects how the layer combines with underlying layers. See the following section, "Blending Mode Types."

✔ Tips

- You can view the Switches and Modes panels simultaneously. Ctrl-click (Mac) or right-click (Windows) a panel to choose the Modes panel from the contextual menu.

- As you apply blending modes, bear in mind that After Effects renders the bottommost layer first and works its way up the stacking order. Because a blending mode determines how a layer interacts with the image beneath it, the resulting image becomes the underlying image for layer modes applied to the next higher layer in the stacking order, and so on. For more about render order, see Chapter 16, "Complex Projects."

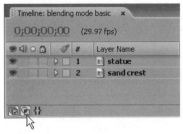

Figure 14.33 If necessary, click the Switches/Modes button to make the Modes menu appear.

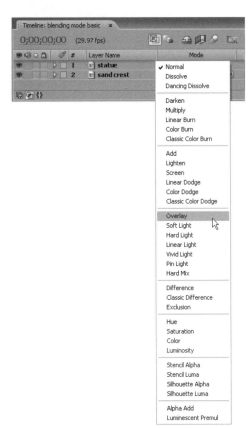

Figure 14.34 Choose a mode from a layer's Modes menu.

Blending Mode Types

This section describes blending modes in the order they appear in the Modes pull-down menu. On the menu, they're grouped by category. However, you may also find it useful to contrast images that use opposite blending modes; for example, contrast Darken to Lighten, Multiply with Screen, or a Burn mode to a Dodge mode.

The effect of any layer mode depends on various aspects of the image to which it's applied and of the underlying image. Certain types of modes are better suited to certain types of images, and vice versa. Note that most modes are based on the pixel values of visible channels, not on transparency information. However, Dissolve and Dancing Dissolve depend on a layer's transparency property. Transparency, Stencil and Silhouette, and Alpha Manipulation categories also affect alpha channels.

The following figures illustrate each blending mode using three images. The upper-left image shows the layer before the blending mode is applied; the upper-right image shows the underlying image; and the larger lower figure depicts the result of applying the blending mode to the top layer (the upper-left image). Because black-and-white figures can't fully represent the way modes affect the resulting color, some modes aren't illustrated here. You can always see the full-color results for yourself.

Transparency modes

Transparency modes alter the alpha channel of the layer to combine it with the underlying image.

Normal is the default layer mode. The layer combines with underlying layers according to its Opacity setting.

Dissolve replaces pixels of the layer with underlying pixels, based on the layer's Opacity value. In contrast to Normal mode, pixels are either completely transparent or completely opaque. Thus, this mode ignores partial transparency, including feathered masks. At 100 percent opacity, this mode has no effect; a lower Opacity value makes more of the pixels transparent. This mode was designed to emulate the Dissolve transition found in programs like Macromedia Director (**Figure 14.35**).

Dancing Dissolve works like the Dissolve mode except that the position of transparent pixels varies over time—even if the layer's opacity value remains the same.

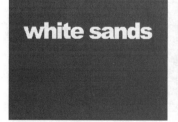

Figure 14.35 Here, the text layer is set to Dissolve mode, and its opacity is set to 50 percent.

Brightness-reducing modes

These modes result in a darker overall image. In the following examples, a nested composition consisting of four images (**Figure 14.36**) is combined with an underlying image (**Figure 14.37**) using various blending modes.

Darken compares the color values of each channel of the layer with those of the underlying image and takes the darker of the two. Because the values of individual channels are compared, colors can shift drastically (**Figure 14.38**).

Multiply multiplies the color values of the layer with the color values of the underlying image and then divides the result by 255. The resulting value is darker than the two and never brighter than the original. When applied to a high-contrast black-and-white image, Multiply preserves the black areas and allows the underlying image to show through the white areas of the layer. Remember, though, that the alpha is not affected (**Figure 14.39**).

Figure 14.36 Different blending modes are applied to this nested comp. Images include white sand dunes (top left); a mountain and blue sky (top right); a red, white, and blue flag with a soft drop shadow; and a grayscale spanning from white to black in 10 steps.

Figure 14.37 This image of bright orange tangerines serves as the underlying image.

Figure 14.38 Darken.

Figure 14.39 Multiply.

Linear Burn darkens the layer by decreasing the brightness according to the color values of the underlying image. White areas in the layer remain unchanged (**Figure 14.40**).

Color Burn darkens the layer by increasing its contrast according to the color values of the underlying image. White areas in the layer remain unchanged (**Figure 14.41**). Color Burn is identical to the Color Burn mode in Adobe Photoshop.

Classic Color Burn is the Color Burn mode in After Effects 5.0 and earlier. It uses the color values of the layer to darken the underlying image, which dominates the resulting image. White areas of the layer allow the underlying image to show through unaffected, whereas dark areas darken the underlying image.

Brightness-enhancing modes

The following modes increase the brightness of the resulting image.

Add combines the brightness values of a layer with the underlying image to produce a brighter image overall. Pure-black areas in the layer reveal the underlying image unchanged; pure-white areas in the underlying image show through unchanged (**Figure 14.42**).

Lighten compares the color values of each channel of the layer with those of the underlying image and takes the lighter of the two. Because the values of individual channels are compared, colors can shift drastically (**Figure 14.43**).

Figure 14.40 Linear Burn.

Figure 14.41 Color Burn.

Figure 14.42 Add.

Figure 14.43 Lighten.

Screen mode, the opposite of Multiply mode, multiplies the inverse brightness values of the layer and underlying image and then divides the result by 255. The resulting value is brighter than the two and never darker than the original. This mode is particularly useful for compositing an image on a black background with the underlying image (**Figure 14.44**).

Linear Dodge lightens the layer by increasing the brightness according to the color values of the underlying image. Black areas in the layer remain unchanged (**Figure 14.45**). This mode is the opposite of Linear Burn.

Color Dodge is identical to the Color Burn mode in Adobe Photoshop. It lightens the layer by decreasing its contrast according to the color values of the underlying image. Black areas in the layer remain unchanged (**Figure 14.46**). This mode is the opposite of Color Burn.

Classic Color Dodge is identical to the Color Dodge mode in After Effects 5.0 and earlier. It uses a layer's color values—not just its brightness—to brighten the underlying image, which ends up dominating the resulting image. Black areas of the layer allow the underlying image to show through unaffected; white areas brighten the underlying image.

Figure 14.44 Screen.

Figure 14.45 Linear Dodge.

Figure 14.46 Color Dodge.

Dodge and Burn Modes

Dodge and *burn* are photography terms that Photoshop uses as well. *Dodging* refers to the technique of blocking light from a photographic print so that the white paper is protected from exposure, allowing the area to remain lighter. *Burning* refers to the technique of lengthening a photographic print's exposure to light in order to darken areas of the image.

Figure 14.47 Overlay.

Figure 14.48 Soft Light.

Figure 14.49 Hard Light.

Combination modes

The modes in this section apply different calculations (such as multiply and screen) depending on whether the underlying image's pixels are above or below a certain threshold value (such as 50 percent gray).

Overlay multiplies areas that are darker than 50 percent gray and screens areas that are brighter than 50 percent gray. This means that dark areas become darker, and bright areas become brighter. Colors mix with the underlying colors, increasing saturation. Middle grays allow underlying pixels to show through unaffected. As a result, the underlying layer tends to be more visible (**Figure 14.47**). A favorite mode for creating attractive blends, Overlay can also be useful when applied to a solid color.

Soft Light lightens the layer when the underlying image is lighter than 50 percent gray and darkens the layer when the underlying image is darker than 50 percent gray. However, black pixels in the layer never result in pure black, and white pixels never result in pure white. The underlying image dominates the resulting image and has diminished contrast (**Figure 14.48**).

Hard Light multiplies the layer when the underlying pixels are darker than 50 percent gray and screens the layer when the underlying pixels are lighter than 50 percent gray. As the name implies, the result is a harsher version of Soft Light, which means the layer comes through more strongly than the underlying image (**Figure 14.49**).

BLENDING MODE TYPES

Linear Light applies a Linear Burn to the layer in areas where the underlying pixels are lighter than 50 percent gray; it applies a Linear Dodge to the layer in areas where the underlying pixels are darker than 50 percent gray (**Figure 14.50**). (Previous sections cover the Linear Burn and Linear Dodge modes.)

Vivid Light applies a Color Burn in areas where the underlying image is lighter than 50 percent gray; it applies a Color Dodge in areas where the underlying image is darker than 50 percent gray (**Figure 14.51**). (Previous sections cover the Color Burn and Color Dodge modes.)

Pin Light replaces colors in the layer with those of the underlying image, depending on the brightness of colors in the underlying image. Pixels in the layer are replaced where the underlying image is lighter than 50 percent gray and the pixels in the layer are darker than the corresponding pixels in the underlying image. Pixels are also replaced where the underlying image is darker than 50 percent gray and the pixels in the layer are lighter than the corresponding pixels in the underlying image (**Figure 14.52**).

Hard Mix replaces colors in the same manner as the Pin Light mode but also reduces the number of tonal levels in the result (as in a Posterize effect) (**Figure 14.53**).

Figure 14.50 Linear Light.

Figure 14.51 Vivid Light.

Figure 14.52 Pin Light.

Figure 14.53 Hard Mix.

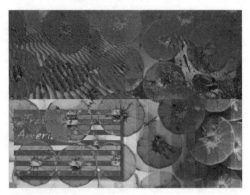

Figure 14.54 Difference.

Figure 14.55 It's easier to see the Difference mode here; wherever the white areas overlap, the pixels are replaced by black.

Figure 14.56 Exclusion.

Difference and exclusion modes

These blending modes are particularly useful in identifying similarities and differences between the pixel values of the layer and the underlying image.

Difference is identical to the Difference mode in Adobe Photoshop. It subtracts the layer's individual channel values from those of the underlying image and displays the absolute value. (In math, the *difference* is the result of subtraction; an *absolute value* is the number without regard to whether it's negative or positive.) Because the values of individual channels are compared, colors can shift drastically. White in the layer inverts the underlying color; black leaves the underlying color unchanged. When colors in the layer and underlying image match, the result is black (**Figures 14.54** and **14.55**). You can use Difference mode to create a *difference matte*. When a scene with a subject is combined with a clean scene (without the subject), only the difference appears in the resulting image.

Classic Difference is identical to the Difference mode in After Effects 5.0 and earlier. It subtracts the layer's channel values from those of the underlying image and displays the absolute value.

Exclusion combines layers in a fashion similar to Difference mode—except the result is lower in contrast. Therefore, similar values result in gray rather than black (**Figure 14.56**).

Chrominance-based modes

Color, or *chrominance*, consists of *hue* (which defines the color) and *saturation* (which describes its intensity). *Luminance*, or brightness, describes an image's grayscale values only. The following modes replace certain calculated color values of the layer with values from the underlying image. The name refers to the value that's preserved in the layer to which you apply the mode.

Hue uses the hue of the layer and the saturation and luminance of the underlying image to create the resulting image (**Figure 14.57**). This blending mode keeps the intensity (saturation) of the underlying image's color but changes the color itself (the hue). It also leaves its luminance (its grayscale tonal range) unaffected. If the underlying image doesn't have vivid (saturated) colors, the new colors also appear muted.

Saturation uses the saturation of the layer and the hue and luminance of the underlying image to create the resulting image. You can use this blending mode to increase or decrease the intensity (saturation) of the colors in the underlying image. For example, applying the Saturation mode to a solid layer that uses a fully saturated color increases the intensity of colors in the underlying image. However, the color (hue) of the solid doesn't appear in the final image. Because a change in saturation alone can't be seen in a grayscale image, no figure is provided here.

Color uses the hue and saturation of the layer and the luminance of the underlying image to create the resulting image (**Figure 14.58**).

Luminosity uses the luminance of the layer and the hue and saturation of the underlying image to create the resulting image (**Figure 14.59**).

Figure 14.57 Hue. (The hues of the image remain, but the saturation and luminance are defined by the underlying image—and thus are nearly impossible to see here in a black-and-white figure.)

Figure 14.58 Color. (The image retains both its hue and saturation—the components of color. In this case, the color is more vivid than in the previous figure, but it's still hard to see in black and white.)

Figure 14.59 Luminosity. (Here, the image uses only the colors of the underlying image—in this case, that of the oranges.)

Figure 14.60 This image contains an alpha channel that isolates the statue.

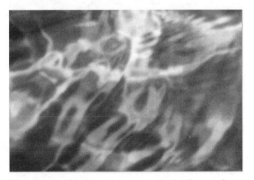

Figure 14.61 This image serves as the background.

Stencil and silhouette modes

Stencil and silhouette modes use a layer's alpha or luminance values to alter the alpha channel of the underlying image, cutting a hole through some areas while leaving other areas black. As you might guess from their names, Stencil and Silhouette are inverse versions of one another. Unlike a matte (see "Track Mattes," later in the chapter), the Stencil and Silhouette modes cut a hole through all the lower layers in the stacking order, not just the next layer down.

In these examples, the image in **Figure 14.60** contains an alpha channel that cuts out the statue, and **Figure 14.61** serves as the underlying image.

Stencil Alpha uses the layer's alpha channel to cut a hole through the layer to reveal the layers beneath it. The area outside the stenciled area becomes transparent (**Figure 14.62**).

Stencil Luma uses the layer's luminance channel to cut a hole through the layer. Lighter areas are more opaque, and darker areas are more transparent, revealing lower layers. The area outside the stencil becomes transparent (**Figure 14.63**).

Figure 14.62 Stencil Alpha.

Figure 14.63 Stencil Luma.

BLENDING MODE TYPES

Silhouette Alpha is the inverse of Stencil Alpha. The alpha channel defines the black portion of the image (the shadow of the silhouette), and everything outside this area reveals the layers below (**Figure 14.64**).

Silhouette Luma is the inverse of Stencil Luma. The luminance of the layer defines the black portion of the image: Darker areas of the layer are more opaque, and lighter areas are more transparent (**Figure 14.65**).

Alpha-manipulation modes

The following modes also alter the alpha channel of the layer and underlying images. As you'll see, their uses are rather specialized.

Alpha Add combines alpha channels to create a seamless, transparent area. When the edges of alpha channels are aligned but either inverted or antialiased, Alpha Add can remove the visible seam between them (**Figures 14.66** and **14.67**).

Figure 14.64 Silhouette Alpha.

Figure 14.65 Silhouette Luma.

Figure 14.66 When the edges of alpha channels are aligned but inverted or antialiased, you can see a seam between the two halves of this broken heart.

Figure 14.67 Alpha Add can heal the broken heart (by removing the visible seam).

BLENDING MODE TYPES

Figure 14.68 The lens flare layer contains a premultiplied alpha that's brighter than the RGB channels.

Figure 14.69 Changing the interpretation to Straight and applying the Luminescent Premul mode prevents clipping in the alpha and reveals the detail of this lighting effect. Note the circular reflections in the "lens" of the Lens Flare effect.

Luminescent Premul prevents the edges of elements that use a premultiplied alpha channel from clipping when composited with other layers. In other words, compositing a layer that's premultiplied with color results in an image that looks bright around the edges. In this event, try changing the interpretation to Straight and applying the Luminescent Premul mode (**Figures 14.68** and **14.69**).

Preserving Underlying Transparency

To the right of the Mode menu is a layer switch in a column marked *T*. This innocuous-looking T switch performs an important function: It preserves the underlying transparency. When you select this option, the opaque areas of a layer display only where they overlap with opaque areas in the underlying image (**Figures 14.70** and **14.71**).

The Preserve Underlying Transparency option is commonly used to make it appear as though light is being reflected from the surface of the underlying solid. You can use Preserve Underlying Transparency in conjunction with any layer mode or track matte. When you activate it, the Video switch becomes a darkened Eye icon 👁.

To preserve underlying transparency:

1. If necessary, click the Switches/Modes button in the Timeline panel to display the Modes panel.

2. For a layer you want to composite with the underlying image, click the box under the T heading (**Figure 14.72**).

   A transparency grid icon ▦ indicates that Preserve Underlying Transparency is active; no icon indicates that it's inactive. When you activate the option, the Video switch becomes a darkened Eye icon 👁.

Figure 14.70 When composited without Preserve Underlying Transparency selected, the entire highlight is superimposed over the underlying image.

Figure 14.71 When Preserve Underlying Transparency is selected, the opaque areas of the highlight layer appear only in the opaque areas of the underlying image.

Figure 14.72 Click the box under the T heading to select Preserve Underlying Transparency.

Figure 14.73 Arrange the matte, the fill, and the background layers in the timeline. Note the settings in the A/V panel and the Modes panel.

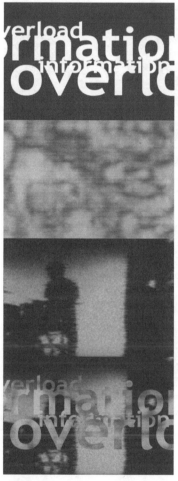

Figure 14.74 The matte, the fill, the background, and the final composite.

Track Mattes

Thus far, you've learned to define transparent areas in a layer by using the Opacity property, alpha channels, masks, and certain layer modes and effects—all options that are part of the layer. Sometimes, however, you won't want to use the transparency provided by the image, or you may find that creating a mask is impractical. This is especially true if you want to use a moving image or one that lacks an alpha channel to define transparency. Whatever the case, you may want to use a separate image to define transparency. Any image used to define transparency in another image is called a *matte*. Because mattes use alpha-channel or luminance information to create transparency, they're usually grayscale images (or images converted into grayscale).

In After Effects, *track matte* refers to a method of defining transparency using an image layer, called the *fill*, and a separate matte layer. In the Timeline panel, the matte must be directly above the fill in the stacking order. Because the matte is included only to define transparency, not to appear in the output, its Video switch is turned off. The track matte is assigned to the fill layer using the Track Matte pull-down menu in the Switches panel. Transparent areas reveal the underlying image, which consists of lower layers in the stacking order (**Figures 14.73** and **14.74**).

Traveling Mattes

The term *track matte* often refers to a matte that's in motion, although in After Effects a track matte doesn't have to move. Animated mattes are also called *traveling mattes*, a term used when the same techniques were accomplished with film.

Types of track mattes

The Track Matte pull-down menu lists several track matte options (**Figure 14.75**). Each option specifies whether the matte's alpha or luminance information is used to define transparency in the fill layer. Ordinarily, white defines opaque areas, and black defines transparent areas. Inverted options reverse the opaque and transparent areas.

In the following example, a grayscale image of the moon serves as the matte layer (**Figure 14.76**). It also contains a corresponding circular alpha channel (**Figure 14.77**). A water image serves as the fill (**Figure 14.78**), and the background image is black.

No Track Matte, the default, specifies no track matte.

Figure 14.75 The Track Matte pull-down menu lists several track matte options.

Figure 14.76 In the following example, the matte layer is an image of the moon...

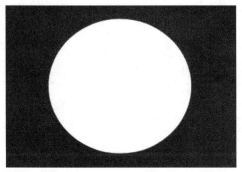

Figure 14.77 ...which also contains an alpha channel.

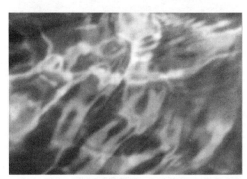

Figure 14.78 The water image serves as the fill layer, and black serves as the background.

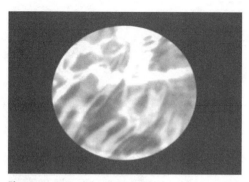

Figure 14.79 An alpha matte.

Alpha Matte specifies the alpha channel of the matte and defines the transparency in the fill. White defines opaque areas; black defines transparent areas. Grays are semi-transparent (**Figure 14.79**).

Alpha Inverted Matte specifies the inverted alpha channel of the matte and defines the transparency in the fill. Black defines opaque areas; white defines transparent areas. Grays are semitransparent (**Figure 14.80**).

Luma Matte specifies the luminance values of the matte and defines transparency in the fill. White defines opaque areas; black defines transparent areas. Grays are semitransparent (**Figure 14.81**).

Luma Inverted Matte specifies the inverted luminance values of the matte and defines transparency in the fill. Black defines opaque areas; white defines transparent areas. Grays are semitransparent (**Figure 14.82**).

Figure 14.80 An alpha inverted matte.

Figure 14.81 A luma matte.

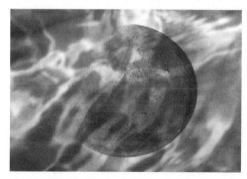

Figure 14.82 A luma inverted matte.

TRACK MATTES

To create a track matte:

1. If necessary, click the Switches/Modes button in the Timeline panel to display the Modes panel.

2. Arrange two layers in the Timeline panel so that the matte layer is directly above the fill layer in the stacking order (**Figure 14.83**).

3. In the Modes panel for the fill layer, *choose one of the following* options from the Track Matte pull-down menu (**Figure 14.84**):

   ▲ No Track Matte

   ▲ Alpha Matte

   ▲ Alpha Inverted Matte

   ▲ Luma Matte

   ▲ Luma Inverted Matte

   The layer directly above the fill layer in the stacking order becomes the track matte, and its Video switch is turned off automatically. In the Timeline panel, the thin border that usually appears between layers no longer appears between the fill and the matte layers (**Figure 14.85**).

4. If you want, place a layer lower in the stacking order to serve as the background.

✔ Tip

■ Any grayscale image—still or moving—can make a good matte layer. Use techniques you've learned throughout this book to create grayscale images, or treat images to convert them into usable mattes. For example, use effects such as Text, Waveform, Block Dissolve, and Fractal Noise to create animated mattes. Or use the Hue/Saturation and Levels effects to turn a movie layer into a high-contrast matte layer.

Figure 14.83 Arrange the fill and matte in the Timeline panel.

Figure 14.84 Choose an option in the Track Matte pull-down menu.

Figure 14.85 The layer directly above the fill layer in the stacking order becomes the track matte, and its Video switch is turned off automatically.

TRACK MATTES

3D LAYERS

Up to now, you've dealt strictly with layers in two dimensions: horizontal and vertical, as measured on the X and Y axes. However, After Effects includes depth as well, measured along the Z axis. As in other 3D programs, you can create one or more cameras from which to view and render your 3D composition. You can also create lights to illuminate 3D layers that cast realistic shadows and have adjustable reflective properties. And despite their unique properties, you can adjust and animate 3D layers, cameras, and lights just as you would any 2D layer.

Although detractors might argue that After Effects' new 3D layers are just 2D panels in 3D space and that the program doesn't incorporate any of the modeling tools or other features you're likely to find in a dedicated 3D application, bringing the program into the 3D space *does* open a new frontier of creative exploration. For example, the sole ability to view the composition from custom camera views fundamentally alters how you would have approached a similar animation in the past. Similarly, 3D lighting features let you manipulate light and shadows in ways that were once difficult or impossible to achieve.

Using 3D

With the exception of adjustment layers, any layer can be designated as a 3D layer. When a layer becomes three-dimensional, it acquires additional transform properties as well as "material" properties exclusive to 3D layers (**Figure 15.1**). (See "Using 3D Orientation and Rotation," "Using 3D Position," and "Using 3D Material Options," later in this chapter.) By default, 3D layers are positioned at a *Z* coordinate of 0.

With After Effects, you can use 2D and 3D layers in the same compositions, although doing so can add complexity to the rendering order. (See "Combining 2D and 3D," later in this chapter for more about rendering order.) Note that cameras and lights are inherently 3D objects and can't be transformed to 2D objects.

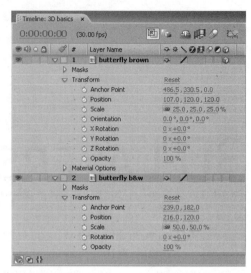

Figure 15.1 When you make a layer three-dimensional, it acquires new transform properties that take Z-depth and rotation into account. 3D layers also have a Material Options property category.

To designate a layer as 3D:

◆ On the Switches panel of the Timeline panel, click the 3D switch that corresponds to the layer you want to designate (**Figure 15.2**).

The Cube icon appears 📦. The layer becomes a 3D layer and acquires 3D transform and material properties.

To convert a 3D layer back to 2D:

◆ On the Switches panel of the Timeline panel, click the Cube icon 📦 to make it disappear and convert the layer back into a 2D layer.

The layer becomes a 2D layer and loses its 3D transform and material properties.

✔ Tip

■ Most effects that simulate three-dimensional distortions (like the Bulge effect) are really 2D effects. Thus, when you make a layer 3D, these effects remain 2D and won't distort the layer along the *Z* axis.

Figure 15.2 In the Switches panel of the Timeline panel, click the 3D switch for a layer to make a Cube icon appear.

Figure 15.3 Orthogonal views (Front, Left, Right, Back, Top, and Bottom) accurately represent lengths and distances at the expense of perspective. (Compare this Front view with Figure 15.5.)

Figure 15.4 By default, Custom View 1 shows the composition from above and to the left. Although Custom views aren't associated with an actual camera layer, you can adjust them using Camera tools.

Figure 15.5 Select a camera's name in the 3D View pull-down menu to see the composition through the lens of that camera.

Viewing 3D Layers in the Comp Panel

The presence of 3D objects in a composition activates additional viewing options in a 3D View pull-down menu in the Composition panel. By selecting different views, you can see and manipulate 3D layers, cameras, and lights from different angles. The views in this list fall into three categories: Orthogonal views, Custom views, and Camera views.

Orthogonal views show the composition from the six sides of its 3D space: front, left, right, back, top, and bottom. In an Orthogonal view, lengths and distances are displayed accurately at the expense of perspective (**Figure 15.3**).

Custom views show the composition from three predefined viewpoints, which you can adjust by using Camera tools (see "Adjusting Views with Camera Tools," later in this chapter). However, these views aren't associated with an actual camera layer in the composition (**Figure 15.4**).

Camera views show the composition from a camera layer you create or—if there's no camera—from a default Camera view (**Figure 15.5**).

Unlike Orthogonal views, both Custom views and Camera views represent the composition from a three-dimensional perspective. Distant objects look smaller; closer objects appear larger. Objects viewed at an angle are foreshortened so that right angles appear acute or obtuse, and lengths and distances appear compressed. The type of lens emulated by a camera also affects perspective. (See "Using Cameras," later in this chapter.)

VIEWING 3D LAYERS IN THE COMP PANEL

To specify a 3D view:

◆ In the Composition panel, select a view from the pull-down menu (**Figure 15.6**):

Active Camera—Activates the Camera view listed at the top of the Timeline panel's layer outline. If no cameras are present, Active Camera uses a default view.

Front—Shows the composition from the front, without perspective.

Left—Shows the composition from the left side, without perspective.

Top—Shows the composition from above, without perspective.

Back—Shows the composition from behind, without perspective.

Right—Shows the composition from the right side, without perspective.

Bottom—Shows the composition from below, without perspective.

Custom View 1–3—Show the composition from a point of view you can adjust using the Camera tools. These views aren't associated with a camera layer.

[Custom Camera Name]—Shows the composition from the view of the camera you create. Camera views appear in the 3D View pull-down menu when you create a camera layer.

The Composition panel shows the composition from the perspective of the selected view.

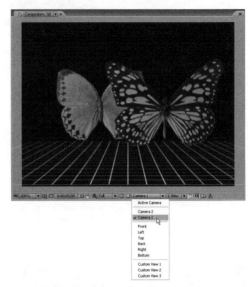

Figure 15.6 In the Composition panel, select a view from the pull-down menu.

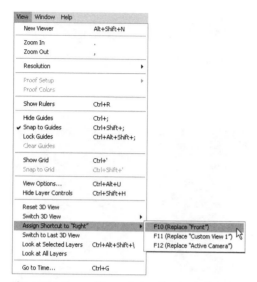

Figure 15.7 Choose View > Assign Shortcut to [3D View Name], and select the view you want to replace for the F10, F11, or F12 shortcut.

To set or replace 3D-view shortcuts:

1. In the 3D View pull-down menu of the Composition panel, select the view to which you want to assign a shortcut.

2. *Do either of the following:*
   - ▲ Choose View > Assign Shortcut to [3D View Name], and select the view you want to replace for the F10, F11, or F12 shortcut (**Figure 15.7**).
   - ▲ Press Shift-F10, Shift-F11, or Shift-F12.

   The view shortcut you selected is replaced by the current 3D view. Pressing the shortcut button selects the corresponding view.

To toggle among 3D views:

- ◆ Press F10, F11, or F12.

   The 3D view saved for the corresponding shortcut is selected in the Composition panel.

✔ Tip

- As you progress through this chapter, view your 3D layers from different angles. After you grow accustomed to adjusting 3D layer properties, you'll learn how to adjust the views themselves using Camera tools. Finally, you'll create your own cameras and move them around the 3D composition. In other words, take it one step at a time.

Adjusting Views with Camera Tools

Camera tools move the perspective of a 3D view much as you would move a real camera left, right, toward, or around a subject. When the 3D view is set to a Custom view, a camera tool changes its perspective for viewing purposes. When the 3D view is set to a camera layer you create, a camera tool moves the camera's position.

In this section, you'll use Camera tools to change the perspective of a 3D view, particularly a Custom view. By definition, the Orthogonal views prohibit camera angles other than their namesake (Front, Back, Left, Right, Top, or Bottom) and thereby prevent the use of the Orbit Camera tool. Orthogonal views do permit the Track XY and Track Z Camera tools, however.

Once you learn how to create and use camera layers, you can use Camera tools to move the camera (see the section "Moving Cameras with Camera Tools" later in this chapter).

To adjust a camera or view using Camera tools:

1. In the 3D View pull-down menu of the Composition panel, select a Custom or Orthogonal view.

   Note that you can't use the Orbit Camera tool in an Orthogonal view (Front, Back, Left, Right, Top, or Bottom).

2. In the Tools panel, select a Camera tool (**Figure 15.8**):

   Orbit Camera —Dragging the tool in a 3D view rotates the perspective around its center in any direction (**Figures 15.9** and **15.10**). This tool can't be used in an orthogonal view.

Figure 15.8 Select a Camera tool.

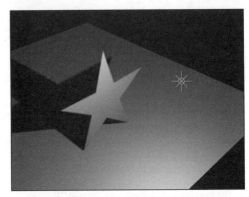

Figure 15.9 Dragging with the Orbit Camera tool...

Figure 15.10 ...rotates the view.

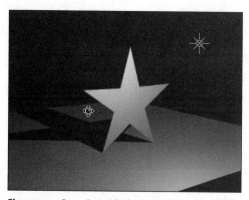

Figure 15.11 Dragging with the Track XY Camera tool lets you move the view or camera along its X and Y axes. Here, the camera has tracked left (from its position in Figure 15.10).

Track XY Camera ✛—Dragging the tool in a 3D view shifts the perspective along the view's X or Y axis (side-to-side or up and down) (**Figure 15.11**).

Track Z Camera ✛—Dragging the tool in a 3D view moves the perspective along the view's Z axis (similar to a camera dollying in or out) (**Figure 15.12**).

In an Orthogonal view, the 3D layers limit how far you can track in along the Z axis.

3. In the Composition panel, drag the selected Camera tool.

The camera position or view changes according to the Camera tool you use.

To focus a 3D view on selected layers:

1. Set the Comp panel to the 3D view you want to adjust.

2. In a Comp panel or Timeline panel, select one or more 3D layers (**Figure 15.13**).

continues on next page

Figure 15.12 Dragging with the Track Z Camera tool lets you move the view or camera along its Z axis. Here, the view has dollied back from its position in Figure 15.11.

Figure 15.13 Select the 3D view you want to adjust, and select one or more 3D layers.

3. Choose View > Look at Selected Layers (**Figure 15.14**).

The 3D view adjusts so that the selected layers appear large and centered in the 3D view (**Figure 15.15**).

To reset a 3D view:

1. Set the Comp panel to the 3D view you want to reset.

2. Choose View > Reset 3D View (**Figure 15.16**).

The view's perspective adjusts to its default setting.

Figure 15.14 Choosing View > Look at Selected Layers...

Figure 15.15 ...adjusts the view to frame-up that layer automatically.

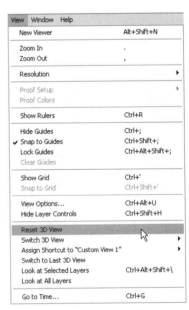

Figure 15.16 Choosing View > Reset 3D View resets the current view to its default state.

Figure 15.17 Although you can change a single 3D view...

Figure 15.18 ...it's better to set the Comp panel's view layout to show several views at once.

Using Comp Panel Layouts

As you've seen, it would be practically impossible to work in 3D without being able to view layers from various perspectives. But the usefulness of 3D views would be severely limited if you could see only one at a time; having to switch from one view to another would make your progress awkward and slow (**Figure 15.17**). Fortunately, you can show several views in a single Comp panel by selecting a Comp panel layout (**Figure 15.18**).

You can make changes in the view best suited to the task. And by seeing the changes you make from different perspectives at once, it's easier to get them right the first time.

You can specify whether the views share Comp View Options and other settings (such as grids and guides, channels, and so on) or use individual settings. However, all views use the same Resolution setting. You can set each view's magnification setting and 3D view (Orthogonal, Custom, or Camera view) individually, and at any time.

To specify a view layout in the Comp panel:

1. In the Comp panel's View Layout pull-down menu (located next to the 3D View pull-down menu), choose an option (**Figure 15.19**):

   1 View

   2 Views – Horizontal

   2 Views – Vertical

   4 Views

   4 Views – Left

   4 Views – Right

   4 Views – Top

   4 Views – Bottom

   The Comp panel reflects your choice.

2. To make all views use the same view options, select Share View Options in the View Layout pull-down menu (**Figure 15.20**).

   Options include those in the View Options dialog box (accessed via the Comp panel's pull-down menu) and other Comp view settings, except for Magnification and Resolution.

Figure 15.19 Choose a layout in the Comp panel's View Format pull-down menu.

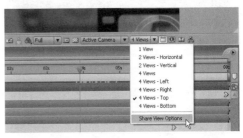

Figure 15.20 Specify whether you want the multiple views to share the same view options.

Figure 15.21 Clicking a view activates it, as evidenced by highlights in the view's corners. Comp panel buttons affect the active view.

To specify the active view:

◆ In the Comp panel, click the view you want to use.

Triangular highlights appear in the corners of the active view (**Figure 15.21**). Comp panel buttons affect the active view.

✔ Tip

■ If your mouse has a scroll wheel, you can hover the mouse over the view and use the scroll wheel to change the view's magnification setting, even if it's not the active view.

Using Axis Modes

In the layer outline, the spatial transform properties (Position and Rotation) are expressed in terms of *X, Y,* and *Z* axes, which intersect at the center of your composition's 3D "world." When you transform a layer by dragging in the Composition panel, however, you won't always want changes to occur according to these world axes.

Axis modes let you specify whether transformations you make in the Comp panel are expressed in terms of the 3D object (Local Axis mode), the 3D world (World Axis mode), or the current view (View Axis mode). Choosing how the axes are aligned makes moving and rotating 3D objects in the Comp panel a more flexible and intuitive process. The axis mode you employ doesn't affect transformations you make using the property controls in the layer outline; instead, these are expressed in terms of the world axis coordinate system.

To change axis modes:

1. Select a 3D layer, camera, or light.

2. In the Tools panel, select an axis mode (**Figure 15.22**):

   Local Axis mode 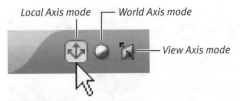—Aligns the axes used for transformations to the selected 3D object (**Figure 15.23**)

Figure 15.22 In the Tools panel, select an axis mode.

Figure 15.23 Here, the Local Axis mode aligns the axes to the selected object (a light). X is red, Y is green, and Z is blue. In Figures 15.22–15.24, the axes are highlighted and labeled to make them identifiable in a black-and-white image.

Figure 15.24 World Axis mode aligns the axes to the 3D world of the composition.

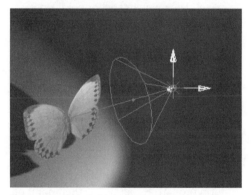

Figure 15.25 View Axis mode aligns the axes to the current 3D view.

World Axis mode ⊙—Aligns the axes used for transformations to the 3D space of the composition **(Figure 15.24)**

View Axis mode 🔲—Aligns the axes used for transformations to the current view **(Figure 15.25)**

The set of axes you select appears in the Composition panel.

3. Transform the selected object in the Composition panel by dragging it or by altering its transform properties in the layer outline.

Transformations occur according to the axes you selected. However, the transformation property values in the layer outline continue to be expressed in absolute terms, according to the world axis coordinate system.

Using 3D Position

For 3D layers, position is expressed as a three-dimensional property with values for *X, Y,* and *Z* coordinates along the world axes. As with 2D position, 3D position corresponds to a layer's anchor point.

To move a 3D layer in the Comp panel:

1. In the 3D View pull-down menu, select a view.

2. In Tools, select an axis mode.

3. Select a 3D layer, camera, or light.

   The selected layer's axes appear. The *X* axis is red; the *Y* axis is green; the *Z* axis is blue. The axes align according to the axis mode you specified.

4. In the Composition panel, position the Selection tool over the axis along which you want to move the layer (**Figure 15.26**).

   The Selection tool icon includes the letter corresponding to the axis: ⬉x to move the layer along the *X* axis, ⬉Y to move the layer along the *Y* axis, or ⬉z to move the layer along the *Z* axis.

5. Drag the layer along the selected axis (**Figure 15.27**).

   In the layer outline of the Timeline panel, the layer's Position property reflects the changes in terms of the world axis coordinate system.

✔ Tips

- You can change the anchor point of a 3D layer just as you would a 2D layer—except that the anchor point for 3D layers includes a value for its *Z*-axis coordinate. You will only be able to adjust the *X* and *Y* values of an anchor point in a Layer panel. To adjust an anchor point's position along the *Z* axis, use the property controls in the layer outline, or drag the anchor point in the Composition panel using the Pan Behind tool ⬛. As you'll recall from Chapter 7, "Properties and Keyframes," the Pan Behind tool recalculates position as it transforms the anchor point, leaving the layer's relative position in the composition undisturbed.

- Lights and cameras can also have transform properties that define their point of interest. See "Using the Point of Interest," later in this chapter.

Figure 15.26 In the Composition panel, position the Selection tool over the axis along which you want to move the layer. The Selection tool icon should include the axis letter.

Figure 15.27 Drag the layer along the selected axis.

Figure 15.28 Three-dimensional layers, cameras, and lights can be rotated using a single Orientation property, or X, Y, and Z Rotation properties.

Figure 15.29 In the Tools panel, select the Rotation tool.

Figure 15.30 In the pull-down menu, choose Orientation.

Using 3D Orientation and Rotation

Making a layer three-dimensional adds a Z-axis dimension not only to its Position property but also to its Rotation property. However, the properties that control the way a layer rotates along its axes fall into two categories: Orientation and Rotation (**Figure 15.28**). The property you choose to adjust depends on the task at hand.

The Orientation property is expressed as a three-dimensional value: *x, y,* and *z* angles. In the Comp panel, you adjust orientation with the standard Rotation tool.

You adjust rotation using three separate property values: X Rotation, Y Rotation, and Z Rotation. Unlike orientation, Rotation properties allow you to adjust the number of rotations in addition to the angle along each axis. You can adjust Rotation values in the Composition panel by using a Rotation tool option.

To adjust the orientation in the Comp panel:

1. In the 3D View pull-down menu, select a view.

2. In the Tools panel, select an axis mode.

3. Select a 3D layer, camera, or light.

   The selected layer's axes appear. The *X* axis is red; the *Y* axis is green; the *Z* axis is blue. The axes align according to the axis mode you specified.

4. In the Tools panel, select the Rotation tool ☉ (**Figure 15.29**).

   A pull-down menu containing rotation options appears in the Tools panel.

5. In the pull-down menu, choose Orientation (**Figure 15.30**).

continues on next page

USING 3D ORIENTATION AND ROTATION

6. In the Composition panel, *do one of the following:*

▲ To adjust the orientation along all axes, drag the Rotation tool in any direction (**Figures 15.31** and **15.32**).

▲ To adjust the orientation along a single axis, position the Rotation tool over the axis you want to adjust so that the Rotation icon displays the letter corresponding to the axis, and then drag (**Figures 15.33** and **15.34**).

If the Orientation property's Stopwatch icon isn't activated, this will remain the Orientation value of the layer for the layer's duration. If the Stopwatch is activated, an orientation keyframe is created at this frame.

Figure 15.31 Drag the Rotation tool in any direction...

Figure 15.32 ...to adjust the orientation along all axes.

Figure 15.33 Position the Rotation tool over the axis you want to adjust so that the Rotation tool icon displays the axis letter...

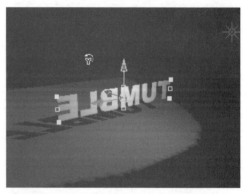

Figure 15.34 ...and drag to rotate the object around that axis.

Figure 15.35 In the Tools panel, select the Rotation tool.

Figure 15.36 In the pull-down menu, choose Rotation.

Figure 15.37 Position the 3D Rotation tool over the axis around which you want to rotate the 3D object, and then drag.

Figure 15.38 Dragging with the 3D Rotation tool adjusts the layer's 3D Rotation properties, not its Orientation properties.

To adjust 3D rotation in the Composition panel:

1. In the 3D View pull-down menu, select a view.

2. In the Tools panel, select an axis mode.

3. Select a 3D layer, camera, or light.

   The selected layer's axes appear. The X axis is red; the Y axis is green; the Z axis is blue. The axes align according to the axis mode you specified.

4. In the Tools panel, select the Rotation tool ⟳ (**Figure 15.35**).

   A pull-down menu containing rotation options appears in the Tools panel.

5. In the pull-down menu, choose Rotation (**Figure 15.36**).

6. In the Composition panel, position the 3D Rotation tool over the axis around which you want to rotate the 3D object (**Figure 15.37**).

   The 3D Rotation tool displays the letter corresponding to the axis.

7. Drag to rotate the 3D layer, camera, or light around the selected axis.

   If the Stopwatch icons for the Rotation properties aren't activated, the Rotation values are set for the layer's duration (**Figure 15.38**). If the Stopwatch icons are activated, rotation keyframes are created at this frame.

✔ Tip

- As usual, don't forget to switch back to the Selection tool after you've finished using the Rotation tool (or any other tool). Otherwise, you could easily make accidental changes to layers.

Auto-Orienting 3D Layers

Using the Auto-Orientation command, you can make a 3D layer automatically rotate along its motion path or toward the top camera layer (see "Using Cameras," later in this chapter)—which saves you the trouble of keyframing the Orientation property manually. Alternatively, you can leave Auto-Orientation off and adjust the layer's rotation independently of other factors.

To specify an Auto-Orientation setting:

1. Select a 3D layer.

2. Choose Layer > Transform > Auto-Orient, or press Command-Option-O (Mac) or Ctrl-Alt-O (Windows) (**Figure 15.39**).

Figure 15.39 Choose Layer > Transform > Auto-Orient.

Orientation vs. Rotation

When you're animating a layer's rotation in 3D, the Orientation property and the Rotation properties offer unique advantages and disadvantages. Choose the method best suited for the task at hand—and to avoid confusion, try not to use both methods simultaneously.

You may find that it's easier to achieve predictable results by animating the Orientation property rather than the Rotation properties, because interpolated Orientation values take the shortest path between one keyframe and the next. You can also smooth orientation using Bézier curves (just as you'd smooth a motion path for position). However, Orientation

doesn't allow for multiple rotations along an axis. And although Orientation's speed graph allows you to ease motion, it doesn't display rates of change in rotations per second. Because of these limitations, some animators prefer to use Orientation to set rotational position—its angle or tilt in 3D space—and animate using the Rotation property.

Separate Rotation property values permit more keyframing options than Orientation does, but the results can be more difficult to control. Each Rotation property permits multiple rotations and can display a velocity graph that accurately measures the rotations per second at any frame.

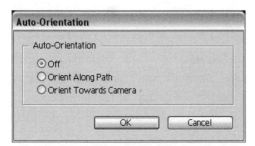

Figure 15.40 The Auto-Orientation dialog box appears.

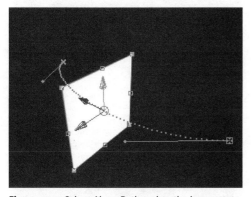

Figure 15.41 Orient Along Path makes the layer rotate so that its local Z axis points in the direction of the layer's motion.

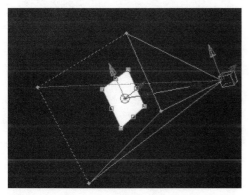

Figure 15.42 Orient Towards Camera makes the layer rotate so that its local Z axis points in the direction of the active camera.

The Auto-Orientation dialog box appears (**Figure 15.40**).

3. *Select one of the following* options:

   Off—Turns off Auto-Orient and adjusts rotation independently

   Orient Along Path—Makes the layer rotate so that its local Z axis points in the direction of the layer's motion path (**Figure 15.41**)

   Orient Towards Camera—Makes the layer rotate so that its local Z axis points in the direction of the top camera layer (**Figure 15.42**)

   For more information, see "Using Cameras," later in this chapter.

4. Click OK to close the dialog box.

✔ Tip

■ You can also apply special Auto-Orientation options to cameras and lights. See "Using the Point of Interest," later in this chapter.

Using 3D Material Options

Three-dimensional layers add a property category called Material Options that defines how 3D layers respond to lights in a comp. For more about lights, see "Using Lights," later in this chapter.

To set a 3D layer's Material Options:

1. Select a 3D layer.

2. Expand the layer outline to reveal the Material Options properties, or press AA (**Figure 15.43**).

   The layer's Material Options properties are revealed in the layer outline.

3. Set each Material Options property:

   Casts Shadows—Turn on this option to enable the layer to cast shadows on other layers within the range of the shadow. This property can't be keyframed.

   Light Transmission—Adjust this value to set the percentage of light that shines through a layer. A value of zero causes the layer to act as an opaque object and cast a black shadow. Increasing the value allows light to pass through the object and cast a colored shadow, much like a transparency or stained glass does.

   Accepts Shadows—Turn on this option to enable shadows cast from other layers to appear on the layer. This property can't be keyframed.

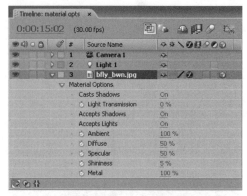

Figure 15.43 Expand the layer outline to reveal the Material Options properties, or press AA.

Figure 15.44 In this example, both 3D layers use the default material options, with Casts Shadows turned on.

Figure 15.45 Here, the Casts Shadows and Accepts Shadows settings are off on the left layer, and the Diffuse property on the right layer has been increased from 50 percent to 100 percent.

Accepts Lights—Turn on this option to enable the layer to be illuminated by lights in the composition. This property can't be keyframed.

Ambient—Adjust this value to set the amount of *ambient*, or nondirectional, reflectivity of the layer.

Diffuse—Adjust this value to set the amount of *diffuse*, or omnidirectional, reflectivity of the layer.

Specular—Adjust this value to set the amount of *specular*, or directional, reflectivity of the layer.

Shininess—Adjust this value to set the size of the layer's *specular highlight*, or shininess. This property is available only when the Specular property value is greater than 0 percent.

Metal—Adjust this value to specify the color of the specular highlight (as defined by the Specular and Shininess values). A value of 100 percent sets the color to match the layer, whereas a value of 0 percent sets the color to match the light source.

The layer in the Composition panel reflects your choices (**Figures 15.44 and 15.45**).

Using Cameras

You can view a composition from any angle by creating one or more 3D cameras. Cameras emulate the optical characteristics of real cameras. However, unlike real cameras, you can move these cameras through space unrestrained by tripods, gravity, or even union rules. This task summarizes how to create a new camera; the following sections explain each camera setting in detail.

To create a camera:

1. *Do either of the following:*

   ▲ Choose Layer > New > Camera (**Figure 15.46**).

   ▲ Press Shift-Option-Command-C (Mac) or Shift-Alt-Ctrl-C (Windows).

   A Camera Settings dialog box appears (**Figure 15.47**).

2. *Do one of the following:*

   ▲ Select a preset camera from the Preset pull-down menu (**Figure 15.48**).

   Presets are designed to emulate a 35mm camera of the specified focal length. Although presets are named for particular focal lengths, they set various camera settings automatically.

   ▲ Choose the custom camera options you want.

   See the next section, "Choosing Camera Settings," for a detailed description of each camera setting option.

3. To give the camera a custom name, enter one in the Name field of the Camera Settings dialog box.

   If you don't enter a name, After Effects uses the default naming scheme.

Figure 15.46 Choose Layer > New > Camera.

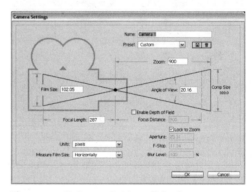

Figure 15.47 A Camera Settings dialog box appears.

USING CAMERAS

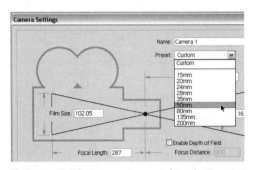

Figure 15.48 Select a preset camera from the Preset pull-down menu.

Figure 15.49 The new camera appears as the top layer in the composition, starting at the current time and using the default duration for still footage.

Figure 15.50 Changing the 3D view allows you to see the camera as a selectable object in the Composition panel.

4. Click OK to close the Camera Settings dialog box.

The new camera appears as the top layer in the composition, starting at the current time and using the default duration for still footage (**Figure 15.49**). The camera's default position depends on the camera settings you chose. Its default point of interest is at the center of the composition (see "Using the Point of Interest," later in this chapter). You can also switch the 3D view to see the camera's positioning in the Composition panel (**Figure 15.50**). (See "Viewing 3D Layers in the Comp Panel," earlier in this chapter.)

✔ Tips

■ If you don't name cameras, After Effects applies default names—Camera 1, Camera 2, and so on. When you delete a camera, After Effects assigns the lowest available number to the next camera you create. To avoid confusion, always give your cameras custom names. Note that always naming cameras will help you avoid problems when using expressions.

■ To revisit a camera's settings, double-click the camera's name in the Timeline panel's layer outline.

Choosing Camera Settings

When you create a camera, the Camera Settings dialog box prompts you to set various attributes for it—such as focal length and film size—that emulate physical cameras.

You can choose from a list of presets, designed to mimic a number of typical real-world cameras. Or, if you prefer, you can customize the settings. The dialog box provides a helpful illustration of the camera attributes (although it's not to scale, of course).

The following tasks divide an explanation of camera settings into two parts. The first explains the basic settings, which govern film size and most of the camera's optical attributes. The next task explains the Depth of Field settings, which can be activated to mimic the limited focus range of real-world cameras.

To choose basic camera settings:

1. *Do one of the following:*
   ▲ To create a new camera, press Shift-Option-Command-C (Mac) or Shift-Alt-Ctrl-C (Windows).
   ▲ To modify a camera in the composition, double-click the name of the camera you want to modify in the layer outline of the Timeline panel.

   The Camera Settings dialog box appears (**Figure 15.51**).

2. Enter a name in the Name field.

   If you don't enter a name, After Effects will use the default naming scheme in which the first camera is called Camera 1 and additional cameras are numbered in ascending order. If you delete a camera that uses this naming scheme, however, new cameras are named using the lowest available number.

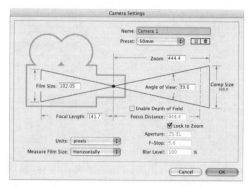

Figure 15.51 Customize the attributes of the camera in the Camera Settings dialog box.

3. If you want to use predefined camera settings, select a preset from the Preset pull-down menu.

Presets are designed to emulate a 35mm camera of the specified focal length. Although Presets are named for particular focal lengths, they set various camera settings automatically. You can also create a Custom camera by modifying individual settings manually.

4. In the same dialog box, choose the units by which measurements are expressed:

Units—Sets whether the variables in the Camera Settings dialog box are expressed in pixels, inches, or millimeters (**Figure 15.52**)

Measure Film Size—Measures film size horizontally, vertically, or diagonally (**Figure 15.53**)

Typically, film size is measured horizontally. In other words, 35mm motion picture film measures 35mm across the image area. Measured vertically, the image is about 26.25mm.

5. Enter the following variables:

Zoom—Sets the distance between the camera's focal point and the image plane.

Angle of View—Sets the width of the scene included in the image. Angle of View is directly related to Focal Length, Film Size, and Zoom. Adjusting this setting changes those variables, and vice versa.

Film Size—Controls the size of the exposed area of the film being simulated. When you change Film Size, Zoom and Angle are adjusted automatically to maintain the width of the scene in the camera's view.

Focal Length—Controls the distance between the focal point and the film plane of the camera. When you change Focal Length, the Zoom value changes automatically to maintain the scene's width in the camera's view.

6. Click OK to close the Camera Settings dialog box.

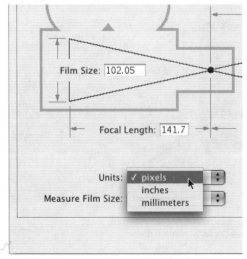

Figure 15.52 Select a unit of measure for the Camera Settings dialog box in the Units pull-down menu.

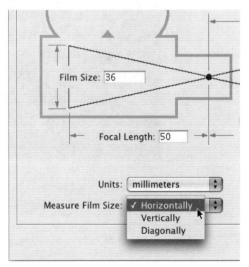

Figure 15.53 Select a unit of measure from the Measure Film Size pull-down menu.

To select Depth of Field options:

1. In the Camera Settings dialog box, select Enable Depth of Field (**Figure 15.54**).

   Selecting this option activates variables that affect the range of distance when the image is in focus, including Focus Distance, Aperture, F-Stop, and Blur Level.

2. To keep Focus Distance and Zoom the same, select Lock to Zoom.

   Deselect this option to allow Focus Distance and Zoom to be adjusted independently.

3. In the same dialog box, set the following options:

   Focus Distance—Sets the distance from the camera's focal point to the focal plane (the plane of space that is in perfect focus) (**Figure 15.55**).

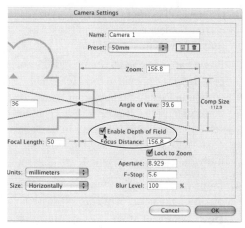

Figure 15.54 In the Camera Settings dialog box, select Enable Depth of Field.

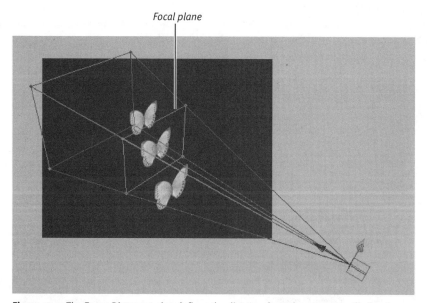

Figure 15.55 The Focus Distance value defines the distance from the camera to the focal plane. When Lock to Zoom isn't selected, you can see the focal plane represented in a selected camera's icon.

Figure 15.56 Here, the focal plane intersects the center butterfly, and objects outside the depth of field appear blurry.

If Lock to Zoom is selected, adjusting Focus Distance also adjusts Zoom.

Aperture—Sets the size of the lens opening. Because the Aperture and F-Stop settings measure the same thing in different ways, adjusting one results in a corresponding change in the other. Aperture (or F-Stop) is directly related to depth of field (see the sidebar "Depth of Field—In Depth").

F-Stop—Sets the aperture in terms of *f/stop*, a measurement system commonly used in photography. An f/stop is expressed as the ratio of the focal length to the aperture. On a real camera, increasing the f/stop by one full stop decreases the aperture to allow half the amount of light to expose the film; decreasing it by one stop doubles the amount of light. The term *stopping down* the lens refers to reducing aperture size.

Blur Level—Controls the amount of blur that results when a layer is outside the camera's depth of field. A value of 100 percent creates the amount of blur appropriate to the other camera settings. Lower values reduce the blur.

4. Click OK to close the Camera Settings dialog box.

   When viewed through the camera, objects outside the depth of field appear blurred (**Figure 15.56**).

✔ Tips

■ After Effects uses the term *position,* which is synonymous with the camera's Position property. In the physical world, the camera's position is synonymous with its focal point. In a real camera, the focal point defines where the light in the lens converges into a single point before it goes on to expose the film at the film plane (**Figure 15.57**). Distances associated with a camera are measured from its focal point.

■ The Camera Settings dialog box includes buttons to save and delete camera presets. They look like the buttons you use to save and delete composition presets.

■ Photographers may wonder why the cameras in After Effects seem to have controls for everything but shutter speed and shutter angle. You'll find these controls in the Advanced panel of the Composition Settings dialog box. See Chapter 4, "Compositions," for more information.

■ You can switch focus from one object in the scene to another, a technique cinematographers call *rack focus* or *pulling focus.* Make sure the Lock to Zoom camera setting is deselected, and animate the Focus Distance property.

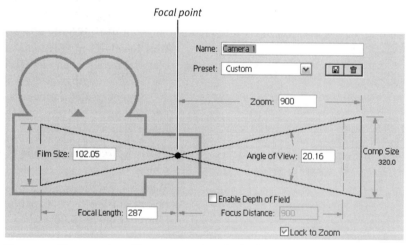

Figure 15.57 The camera's position corresponds to the focal point, which is illustrated in the Camera Settings dialog box but not labeled.

Choosing a Lens

For 35mm film, a 50mm focal length produces an image that closely resembles human sight. Assuming film size remains constant, other focal lengths introduce distortions in perspective and apparent distances. Lenses with shorter focal lengths are called *wide angle*, and lenses with longer focal lengths are referred to as *telephoto*. The differences between the image you capture using wide and telephoto lenses can be summarized as follows:

◆ A wide-angle lens captures a wider area of the scene than a longer lens placed at the same distance from the subject (**Figure 15.58**).

◆ A wide-angle lens makes the subject look smaller than when viewed through a telephoto lens placed at the same distance from the subject.

◆ A wide-angle lens exaggerates depth, so that the movement along the axis seems greater; a telephoto lens compresses depth, so that the same movement along the *Z* axis seems less (**Figure 15.59**).

◆ A change in angle through a wide-angle lens seems less pronounced than the same change in angle through a telephoto lens, when the subject appears at the same apparent size in the frame.

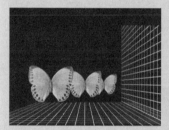 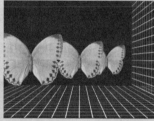 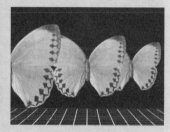

Figure 15.58 A wide-angle lens captures a wider area of the scene than a longer lens placed at the same distance from the subject. In each successive image, the focal length increases, but the distance from the subject is fixed.

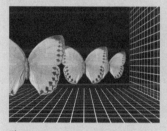 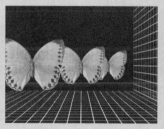 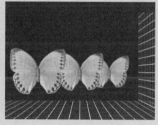

Figure 15.59 A wide-angle lens exaggerates depth, and a telephoto lens compresses depth. These three images show three cameras of different focal lengths. The camera's distance from the subject has been adjusted to maintain the subject's size in the frame.

Depth of Field—In Depth

If you're planning to use Depth of Field options in the Camera Settings dialog box, you should probably know something about how depth of field works in real camera optics:

◆ Depth of field decreases as you increase focal length and increases as you decrease focal length (**Figures 15.60** and **15.61**).

◆ Depth of field increases as you close the aperture (**Figures 15.62** and **15.63**).

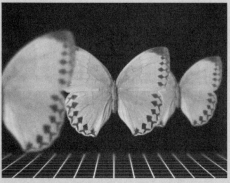

Figure 15.60 Depth of field decreases as you increase focal length...

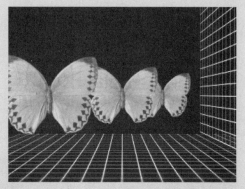

Figure 15.61 ...and increases as you decrease focal length.

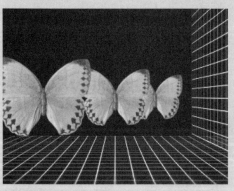

Figure 15.62 Depth of field increases as you close the aperture...

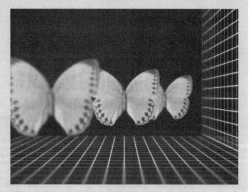

Figure 15.63 ...and decreases as you open the aperture.

Depth of Field—In Depth *(continued)*

◆ Depth of field increases as the distance to the subject increases; depth of field decreases as the distance to the subject decreases (**Figures 15.64** and **15.65**).

◆ There's less depth of field in front of the plane of focus than behind it (**Figure 15.66**).

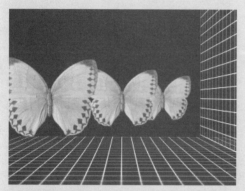

Figure 15.64 Depth of field increases as the distance from the subject increases.

Figure 15.65 Depth of field decreases as the distance from the subject decreases.

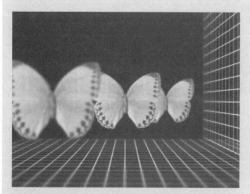

Figure 15.66 There's less depth of field in front of the plane of focus than behind it. In this example, the nearest and farthest butterflies are positioned the same distance from the focal plane, but the near one is much blurrier.

Using Lights

You can create any number of lights to illuminate a 3D scene, and you can select and control these lights much as you would in the real world. In After Effects, however, lights are evident only when they illuminate 3D layers that are set to accept lights. You can select a light to place it in the scene and then point it at a subject, but you'll never see a lighting instrument in the scene. Pointing a light into a camera won't cause a lens flare or overexposed image—you won't see anything at all. And you'll never blow a lamp or overload a circuit breaker.

As in the "Using Cameras" section, this section contains two tasks: The first summarizes how to create a light; the second describes light settings in more detail.

To create a light:

1. *Do either of the following:*
   - ▲ Choose Layer > New > Light (**Figure 15.67**).
   - ▲ Press Shift-Option-Command-L (Mac) or Shift-Alt-Ctrl-L (Windows).

   A Light Settings dialog box appears (**Figure 15.68**).

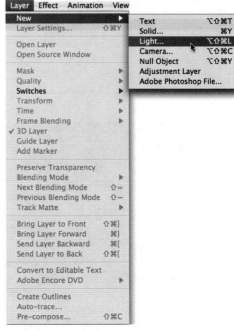

Figure 15.67 Choose Layer > New > Light.

Figure 15.68 A Light Settings dialog box appears.

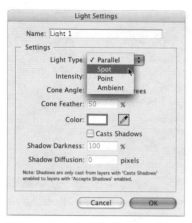

Figure 15.69 In the Light Settings dialog box, select the type of light you want from the pull-down menu.

2. Enter a name for the light in the Name field.

   If you don't enter a name, After Effects uses the default naming scheme.

3. In the same dialog box, select the type of light you want from the pull-down menu (**Figure 15.69**):

   Parallel—Radiates directional light from an infinite distance. In this respect, a parallel light simulates sunlight (**Figure 15.70**).

   Spot—Radiates from a source positioned within an opaque cone, allowing the light to emit only through its open end. Adjusting the cone's angle changes the spread of the light. This type of light emulates those commonly used in film and stage productions (**Figure 15.71**).

continues on next page

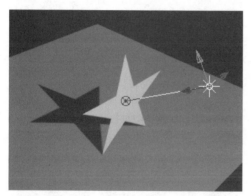

Figure 15.70 A parallel light radiates directional light from a source infinitely far away, much like sunlight.

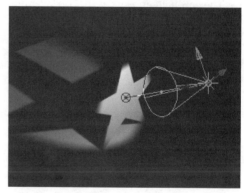

Figure 15.71 A spot light is constrained by a cone and appears much like the lights used in film and stage productions.

USING LIGHTS

Point—Emits omnidirectional light from its point of origin, comparable to a bare bulb or an unflickering signal flare (**Figure 15.72**).

Ambient—Doesn't emanate from a specific source but rather contributes to the overall illumination of the scene. Ambient light settings only include those for intensity and color (**Figure 15.73**).

The type of light you select determines which options are available in the Light Settings dialog box.

4. Specify the light settings available for the type of light you selected.

   See the next section, "Choosing Light Settings," for more information.

5. Click OK to close the Light Settings dialog box.

   The new light appears as the top layer in the composition, starting at the current time and using the default duration for still footage (**Figure 15.74**). The light's default position depends on the type of light you select.

✔ Tips

- You can revisit the Light Settings dialog box at any time by double-clicking the name of a light in the layer outline of the Timeline panel.

- If you need a lens flare or visible light beams, try an effect. After Effects includes a lens flare, and many third-party plug-in packages create light beams and other lighting effects.

Figure 15.72 A point light emits an omnidirectional light, much like a bare bulb.

Figure 15.73 An ambient light contributes to the overall illumination of the 3D space. Here, an ambient light is set to 30 percent intensity.

Figure 15.74 The new light appears as the top layer in the composition, starting at the current time and using the default duration for still footage.

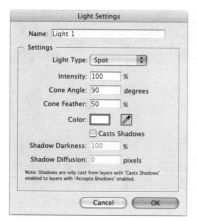

Figure 15.75 In the Light Settings dialog box, specify the settings available for the type of light you're using.

Figure 15.76 Both spot lights are the same intensity and distance from the layer. The light on the left uses a 45-degree cone angle; the light on the right uses a 90-degree cone angle.

Choosing Light Settings

The options available in the Light Settings dialog box depend on the type of light you're using. They control the character of the light and the shadows it casts.

To select light settings:

1. *Do one of the following:*

   ▲ To create a new light, press Shift-Option-Command-L (Mac) or Shift-Alt-Ctrl-L (Windows).

   ▲ To modify a light in the composition, double-click the name of the light you want to modify in the layer outline of the Timeline panel.

   The Light Settings dialog box appears (**Figure 15.75**).

2. In the Light Settings dialog box, specify the following options:

   Intensity—Sets the brightness of light. Negative values create *nonlight*—they subtract color from an already illuminated layer, in effect shining darkness onto a layer.

   Cone Angle—Sets the angle of the cone used to restrict a spot type of light. Wider cone angles emit a broader span of light; smaller angles restrict the light to a narrower area (**Figure 15.76**).

   continues on next page

continues on next page

Cone Feather—Sets the softness of the edges of a spot type of light. Larger values create a softer light edge (**Figure 15.77**).

Color—Selects the light's color; comparable to placing a colored gel over a light. You can use the color swatch or eyedropper control.

Casts Shadows—When selected, makes the light cast shadows onto layers with the Accepts Shadows property selected. See "Using 3D Material Options," earlier in this chapter, for more information.

Shadow Darkness—Sets the darkness level of shadows cast by the light. This option is available only when the light's Casts Shadows option is enabled.

Shadow Diffusion—Sets the softness of shadows, based on the apparent distance between the light and the layers casting shadows made by the light. Larger values create softer shadows. This option is available only when the light's Casts Shadows option is enabled.

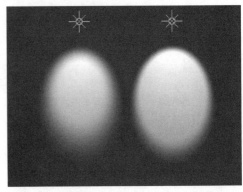

Figure 15.77 Both spot lights here are identical, except the light on the right uses a Cone Feather setting of 25 whereas the light on the left uses a Cone Feather setting of 50.

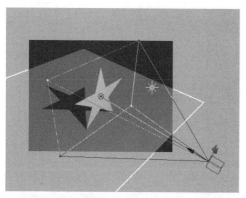

Figure 15.78 In the Composition panel, the point of interest appears as a crosshair at the end of a line extending from a camera or light.

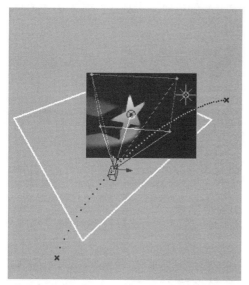

Figure 15.79 You can set a camera or light to automatically orient toward its point of interest as it moves.

Using the Point of Interest

Point of Interest is a transform property unique to cameras and lights. It defines the point in space at which the camera or light is pointed. By default, a new camera's or light's point of interest is at the center of the composition (at the coordinates (0,0,0) in terms of the world axes). In the Composition panel, the point of interest appears as a crosshair at the end of a line extending from a camera or light (**Figure 15.78**).

As you can see, a camera's or light's Point of Interest value is closely related to its other transform property values: A change in position or rotation can affect the point of interest, and vice versa.

Because of its relationship to other transform properties, the Point of Interest property is available only when you activate a 3D object's Auto-Orient option. When you animate the position of a light or camera, auto-orienting a layer saves you the effort of setting rotation keyframes manually.

By default, cameras and lights are set to orient toward the point of interest automatically. That is, moving a camera or light causes it to rotate so that it always points toward its point of interest. When applied to a camera, this setting may create a point of view similar to that of careless drivers who turn their head to see an accident as they drive by (**Figure 15.79**).

You can also set each light or camera to auto-orient along its motion path. When applied to a camera, this setting may mimic the view from a roller coaster, automatically rotating the camera to point in a 3D tangent to the motion path (**Figure 15.80**).

Finally, you can turn off the Auto-Orient setting so that the light's or camera's orientation isn't automatically adjusted to maintain a relationship with its motion path or point of interest. When you set Auto-Orient to off, the light or camera loses its Point of Interest property.

To choose the Auto-Orient setting for cameras and lights:

1. Select the camera or light you want to adjust.

2. Choose Layer > Transform > Auto-Orient (**Figure 15.81**).

   An Auto-Orientation dialog box appears (**Figure 15.82**).

3. *Choose an option:*

   Off—Turns off Auto-Orient, so that the camera or light rotates independently of its motion path or point of interest. Selecting this option eliminates the camera's or light's Point of Interest property.

   Orient Along Path—Makes the camera or light rotate automatically so that it remains oriented to its motion path.

   Orient Towards Point of Interest—Makes the camera or light rotate automatically as you move it so that it remains oriented toward the point of interest.

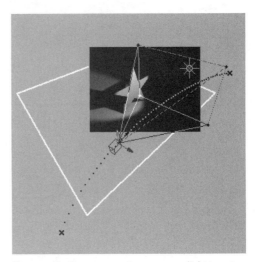

Figure 15.80 Or you can set a camera or light to automatically orient along its motion path.

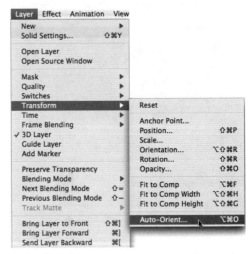

Figure 15.81 Choose Layer > Transform > Auto-Orient.

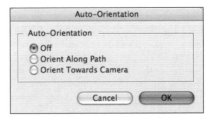

Figure 15.82 An Auto-Orientation dialog box appears.

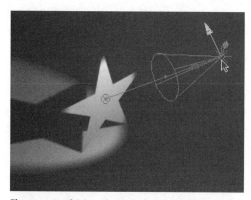

Figure 15.83 If Orient Towards Point of Interest is active...

Figure 15.84 ...dragging the camera or light orients it automatically.

To move a light or camera without changing the point of interest:

1. Select a camera or light.

2. In the 3D View pull-down menu, select a view.

You may also want to choose a different magnification setting in the Composition pull-down menu so that you can see the light or camera in the Composition panel.

3. In the Tools panel, select an axis mode.

The selected layer's axes appear. The X axis is red; the Y axis is green; the Z axis is blue. The axes align according to the axis mode you specified.

4. If necessary, make sure Auto-Orient is set to Orient Towards Point of Interest.

This is the default setting.

5. *Do any of the following:*

▲ In the Composition panel, drag the camera or light (**Figure 15.83**).

Make sure the Selection tool icon doesn't include an axis letter. If it does, you'll move the camera or light by an axis, and the point of interest will move in tandem with the camera or light.

▲ In the Composition panel, position the Selection tool over an axis (so that the cursor displays the letter corresponding to the axis), and Command-drag (Mac) or Ctrl-drag (Windows) (**Figure 15.84**).

▲ In the layer outline, adjust the light's or camera's Position property.

The selected camera's or light's position changes, but the camera rotates so that its point of interest remains stationary.

To move a camera or light and the point of interest:

1. Select a camera or light.

2. In the 3D View pull-down menu, select a view.

   You may also want to choose a different magnification setting in the Composition pull-down menu so that you can see the light or camera in the Composition panel.

3. In the Tools panel, select an axis mode.

   The selected layer's axes appear. The X axis is red; the Y axis is green; the Z axis is blue. The axes align according to the axis mode you specified.

4. If necessary, make sure Auto-Orient is set to Orient Towards Point of Interest.

   This is the default setting.

5. In the Composition panel, position the Selection tool over a camera's or light's axes.

   The Selection tool icon appears with a letter that corresponds to the axis (**Figure 15.85**).

6. Drag the camera or light along the selected axis (**Figure 15.86**).

   As you move the camera or light, its point of interest moves accordingly.

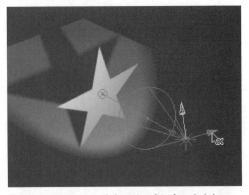

Figure 15.85 Command-dragging (Mac) or Ctrl-dragging (Windows) the camera or light by one of its axes also activates the Orient Towards Point of Interest command...

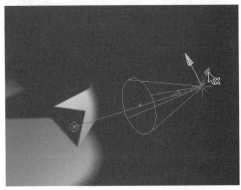

Figure 15.86 ...but dragging the camera or light by one of its axes doesn't allow it to auto-orient. Here, moving the light also moves its point of interest away from the star layer.

Moving Cameras with Camera Tools

Camera tools provide you with another way to easily adjust Camera views. In contrast to dragging the camera from a separate Camera view, Camera tools let you change a camera's Position property while viewing the composition from the camera's point of view. Although it's harder to see the camera's motion path, you get to see the movement from the camera's perspective. You can also use Camera tools to adjust one of the Custom 3D views (see "Viewing 3D Layers in the Comp Panel," earlier in this chapter). By definition, the Orthogonal views (Front, Back, Left, Right, Top, and Bottom) prohibit other camera angles and, hence, the Orbit Camera tool. Orthogonal views do permit the Track XY and Track Z Camera tools.

To adjust a camera using Camera tools:

1. In the Composition panel's 3D View pull-down menu, select a Camera view.

   Selecting another 3D view adjusts that view, not a camera layer's position property. See "Adjusting Views with Camera Tools," earlier in this chapter.

2. If necessary, set the camera's Auto-Orient option to determine how the Orbit Camera tool functions.

   See the next step to learn how Auto-Orient options affect the Orbit Camera tool.

   continues on next page

3. In the Tools panel, select a Camera tool (**Figure 15.87**):

Orbit Camera 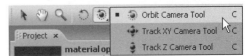—Rotates the camera around its point of interest when Auto-Orient is set to Orient Towards Point of Interest. Otherwise, the camera rotates around its position (much like a camera panning on a tripod) (**Figures 15.88, 15.89,** and **15.90**).

Figure 15.87 Select the Camera tool you want to use.

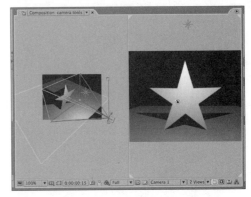

Figure 15.88 When Auto-Orient is set to Orient Towards Point of Interest, dragging with the Orbit Camera tool...

Figure 15.89 ...rotates the camera around its point of interest.

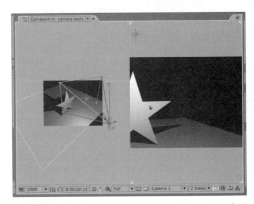

Figure 15.90 Otherwise, the camera rotates around its position.

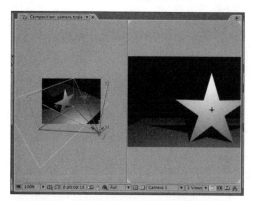

Figure 15.91 Dragging with the Track XY Camera tool lets you move the camera along its X and Y axes. Here, the camera is tracking left (from its position in Figure 15.90).

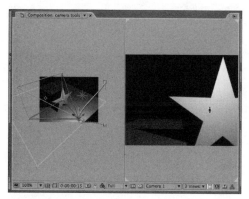

Figure 15.92 Dragging with the Track Z Camera tool lets you move the camera along its Z axis. Here, the camera is dollying back from its position in Figure 15.91.

Track XY Camera ⬢—Moves the camera along its *X* and *Y* axes (similar to a real-world camera tracking right or left, or craning up or down). Regardless of the Auto-Orient setting, the camera's rotation is unaffected (**Figure 15.91**).

Track Z Camera ⬥—Moves the camera along its *Z* axis (similar to a camera dollying in or out). Regardless of the Auto-Orient setting, the camera's rotation remains unaffected (**Figure 15.92**).

4. In the Composition panel, drag the selected Camera tool.

The camera position or view changes according to the Camera tool you use.

Camera Moves

In film and video production, camera movement is described by the following terms:

Pan—To rotate the camera (typically, on a tripod) on its horizontal axis without moving its position. This causes the scene to scroll through the frame left or right, but the camera's view spans an arc, not a line.

Tilt—To rotate the camera on its vertical axis without moving its position. This causes the scene to scroll through the frame up or down, but the camera's view spans an arc, not a line.

Zoom—To change a camera's focal length (using a zoom lens rather than a fixed lens) without moving the camera position. This causes the subject to appear larger (when zooming in) or smaller (when zooming out). Because zooming doesn't give the viewer a sense of moving through space, most filmmakers strongly favor a dolly shot.

Track—To move the camera's position left or right (perpendicular to the direction it's pointing). When tracking to keep a subject in the frame, the camera move is often called a *follow shot*.

Dolly—To move the camera closer to the subject (*dolly in*) or farther away from the subject (*dolly out*).

Crane—To move the camera up (*crane up*) or down (*crane down*), often with the assistance of a crane or a device with a hinged arm, called a *jib*.

Figure 15.93 In the Timeline panel, click the Draft 3D mode button.

Figure 15.94 When Draft 3D mode is off, the Composition panel displays lights, shadows, and depth-of-field blur.

Figure 15.95 With Draft 3D mode on, the Composition panel doesn't preview lights, shadows, or depth-of-field blur.

Previewing 3D

Draft 3D disables lights and shadows as well as blur caused by camera Depth of Field settings. As you've made your way through this book, you've encountered several ways of reducing a composition's preview quality so that you can increase rendering speed. The increased processing demands of 3D compositing will make you appreciate this trade-off even more.

To enable or disable Draft 3D mode:

◆ In the Timeline panel, click the Draft 3D mode button ▣ (**Figure 15.93**).

The image in the Composition panel no longer previews 3D lights, shadows, or depth-of-field blur. Click the button again to deselect it and turn off Draft 3D (**Figures 15.94** and **15.95**).

Understanding 3D Layer Order

As you learned in Chapter 5, "Layer Basics," layers listed higher in the Timeline panel's layer outline appear in front of other layers in the Composition panel. After Effects always renders 2D layers in order, from the bottom of the layer stacking order to the top. (See "Rendering Order" in Chapter 16, "Complex Projects.")

However, the simple 2D stacking order becomes irrelevant in 3D compositing, where object layering is determined by objects' relative positions in 3D space according to the current 3D view.

For 3D layers, After Effects renders from the most distant layer (with the highest Z-coordinate value) to the closest (with the lowest Z-coordinate value).

Combining 2D and 3D

When a composition contains both 2D and 3D layers, the rendering order becomes even more complex, combining aspects of both 2D and 3D rendering. Once again, layers are rendered from the bottom of the stacking order to the top. However, 3D layers are rendered in independent sets, separated by 2D layers.

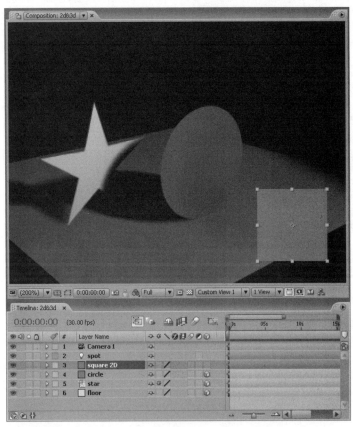

Figure 15.96 In this example, the stacking order prevents the 2D layer from splitting the 3D layers into separately rendered worlds.

In other words, placing a 2D layer so that it doesn't separate the 3D layers in the Timeline's stacking order allows the 3D layers to interact geometrically. 3D layers appear in front of one another and interact with lights and shadows according to their position in 3D space (as well as according to light settings and material options). The 2D layers neither share the same space as 3D layers nor interact with lights or cameras (**Figure 15.96**).

In contrast, positioning a 2D layer between 3D layers in the stacking order splits the 3D layers into separate groups. Although the 3D layers share the same lights and cameras, they exist in identical but separate 3D "worlds" and are rendered independently of one another (**Figure 15.97**).

✔ Tip

- For more on working effectively with the rendering order, see "Rendering Order" in Chapter 16.

Figure 15.97 In this example, the 2D layer's position in the stacking order causes the 3D layers to be rendered separately. Notice how the circle no longer casts shadows.

COMPLEX PROJECTS

As your projects become more ambitious, their structures will grow increasingly complex as well. A typical project contains not only layers created from individual footage items but also layers created from other compositions—called *nested compositions*. In this chapter, you'll find out how to employ nesting to group layers into a single element as well as to manipulate a project's hierarchy to create effects you couldn't otherwise achieve.

After Effects includes several other features that help you create complex projects without resorting to complicated procedures. The Parenting feature, for example, makes it possible to create a hierarchical relationship between a parent layer and any number of child layers, thus allowing you to link or group layers so that they behave as a single system.

Using another powerful feature—Expressions—you can create relationships between layer properties (in the same layer, in different layers, even in layers contained within different compositions). Rather than keyframing multiple properties independently, you can link one property's values to another property's values using a JavaScript-based instruction, or *expression*. (Don't worry: This chapter also provides the JavaScript basics you'll need to feel confident about working with expressions.)

Finally, this chapter provides the lowdown on *render order*, After Effects' hierarchical scheme for rendering frames. You'll learn how render order influences your results as well as how *you* can influence render order. You'll also find out how to inspect your work using the Flowchart view, as well as how to reduce render and preview time via a process called *prerendering*.

Nesting

In Chapter 4, "Compositions," you learned that a composition used as a layer in another composition is called a *nested composition*. Such compositions can serve various interconnected purposes.

Nesting enables you to treat several layers as a group (in much the same way that you group elements in other graphics programs, such as Illustrator). When you're working with a nested composition, you can manipulate several layers as a unit rather than keyframe each individually (**Figures 16.1** and **16.2**).

Similarly, you can use a nested composition as often as you would any single layer—which means you need build a multilayered animation only once to use it several times in a composition. As you can see, nesting can spare you a lot of tedious copying and pasting as well as an unwieldy number of redundant layers (**Figure 16.3**).

Whether a nested composition is used multiple times in one composition or several, you can revise every instance in a single step; each nested composition reflects any changes you make to its source. To speed the revision process, it makes sense to use nested compositions for components you plan to reuse.

Figure 16.1 Doing something as simple as adjusting the rotation can be difficult if you need to apply it to a number of separate layers.

Figure 16.2 Nesting the composition containing those layers lets you treat them as a single element.

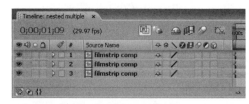

Figure 16.3 It's easier to repeat a sequence of layers as a nested composition. You can revise multiple copies in a single step by altering layers in the source composition.

NESTING

Figure 16.4 By using a nested composition, you can change render order and create effects you couldn't otherwise achieve—for example, compound effects like this one bypass transform adjustments like scale and position.

Figure 16.5 However, you can use a nested composition as the effect source. This way, transform properties are calculated in the nested composition before they're used as an effect source.

Nested compositions can also help you circumvent After Effects' default rendering order. The sequence in which properties are rendered often makes it difficult or impossible to achieve the desired effect. Although you can't break the rules, you can use nesting to work the system (**Figures 16.4** and **16.5**). To learn more about rendering order, move on to the next section, "Rendering Order." To see how rendering order and nesting apply to compound effects (like the one shown in Figure 16.5), see the section "Understanding Compound Effects," in Chapter 11.

To nest a composition:

1. Display the Composition panel or Timeline panel of the composition that will contain the nested composition.

2. Drag a composition you want to nest from the Project panel *to any of the following* (**Figure 16.6**):

▲ Composition panel of the target composition

▲ Timeline panel of the target composition

▲ Name or icon of the target composition in the Project panel

The composition becomes a layer in the target composition, beginning at the current time and having the same duration as the original composition.

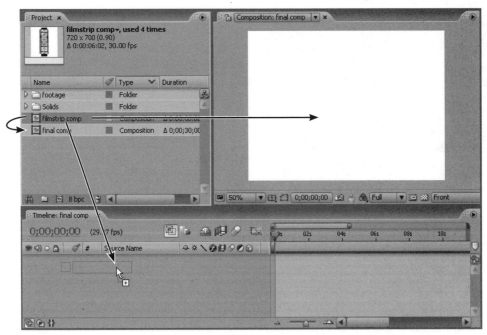

Figure 16.6 Drag a composition you want to nest from the Project panel to the Composition panel, the Timeline panel, or the icon of the target composition.

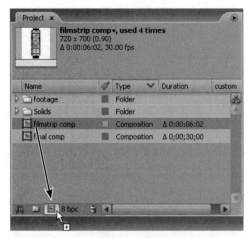

Figure 16.7 Dragging a composition to the Composition icon nests the composition in another composition that has the same settings.

To nest one composition in a new composition with the same settings:

◆ Drag a composition in the Project panel to the Composition icon at the bottom of the Project panel (**Figure 16.7**).

The composition becomes a layer in a new composition that uses the same composition settings as the nested one.

✔ Tips

■ Nesting will help you get around some of the compound-effect restrictions that you learned about in Chapter 11, "Effects Fundamentals."

■ To find out how to turn selected layers into a nested composition retroactively, see "Precomposing," later in this chapter.

■ Like nesting, the Parenting feature can also link layers as a group or system. See "Parenting Layers" later in this chapter.

■ By creating relationships between layer properties, the Expressions feature provides another method of working around After Effects' rendering order.

Rendering Order

When After Effects renders frames for play-back or output, it calculates each attribute in a particular sequence referred to as the *rendering order*.

Having interpreted the source footage according to your specifications, After Effects processes each frame layer by layer. Starting with a composition's bottom layer, After Effects renders layer properties in the order they're listed in the layer outline: masks, effects, and transform. Then, the program processes layer modes and track mattes before combining the layer with the underlying layers. Rendering proceeds in this fashion for successively higher layers in the stacking order until the frame is complete (**Figures 16.8**, **16.9**, **16.10**, **16.11**, and **16.12**).

Figure 16.8 Starting with the bottom layer...

Figure 16.9 ...After Effects renders the masks first...

Figure 16.10 ...then applies effects in the order they appear in the Effect Controls panel...

Figure 16.11 ...then calculates transform properties...

Figure 16.12 ...and finally calculates track mattes and modes before combining the layer with the underlying image.

For audio layers, rendering proceeds in the same sequence: effects followed by levels. If you were to change the audio speed, time remapping would be calculated first and time stretch would be calculated last.

When compositing 3D layers, rendering order is determined by each layer's relative *Z*-coordinate value as well as by whether the composition contains a mix of 2D and 3D layers. See "Understanding 3D Layer Order" in Chapter 15, "3D Layers," for more information.

To identify most problems you're likely to encounter with an animation, you need to understand its render order and how to circumvent it.

Subverting the Render Order

If you were to strictly adhere to the render order, certain effects would be impossible to achieve. For example, you might want to use the Motion Tile effect to replicate a rotating object. However, rendering order dictates that the Motion Tile effect be rendered before the rotation, a transform property. Unfortunately, this causes the layer to rotate after tiling—*not* the effect you desire (**Figure 16.13**). To solve the problem, you must defy the rendering order so that the effects are calculated after transformations (**Figure 16.14**).

Although you can't alter the rendering order directly, you can do so indirectly. For example, you can subvert render order by using the Transform effect or an adjustment layer, or by nesting or precomposing. In some cases, you can use an expression to make continual adjustments to a property automatically, effectively defeating limitations imposed by the rendering order.

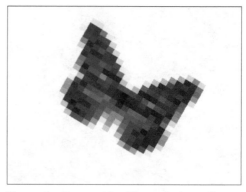

Figure 16.13 Because After Effects calculates effects before transform properties, a mosaic effect is applied to the butterfly image before it's rotated. The squares produced by the mosaic are tilted so they become diamonds—which, in this case, isn't the result we want.

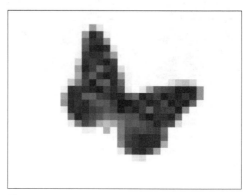

Figure 16.14 To create the desired effect, the effect must be calculated before the rotation. Note how the mosaic squares remain level, parallel to the sides of the comp.

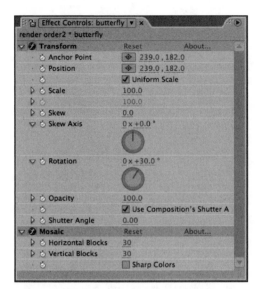

Figure 16.15 The Transform effect emulates the transform properties. To render it before other effects, you can place it higher in the list in the Effect Controls panel.

Transform effect

In many instances, you'll need a transform property to render before an effect property. Fortunately, all the transform properties (as well as the Skew and Shutter Angle properties) are also available as Transform effects. By placing the Transform effect higher on the list in the Effect Controls panel, you can render it before subsequent effects on the list (**Figure 16.15**).

Adjustment layer

Because the render order proceeds from the bottom of the layer stack, you can postpone rendering an effect by placing it in an adjustment layer. After Effects then calculates the properties in the lower layers before the adjustment layer affects them (**Figure 16.16**).

As you'll recall from Chapter 11, the effects contained in an adjustment layer are applied to all the underlying layers. To limit an adjustment layer's effects to just some of those lower layers, you must nest or precompose them with the adjustment layer.

Nesting or precomposing

Another way to effectively change the rendering order is to place layers in a nested composition. (*Precomposing* refers to another method of creating a nested composition—you might think of it as nesting retroactively—so it works the same way.)

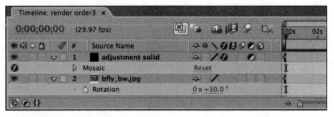

Figure 16.16 You can postpone the rendering of an effect by placing it in an adjustment layer higher in the layer stack.

SUBVERTING THE RENDER ORDER

As you'll recall, *nesting* describes the process of using a composition as a layer in another composition. Before After Effects can render the nested composition as a layer, however, it must complete the rendering sequence within the nested composition. In other words, the properties of the layers contained by the nested composition are calculated first. Then, the nested composition is treated like the other layers, and its properties are processed according to the render order (**Figure 16.17**).

Expressions

In some cases, an expression can compensate for the unwanted effects of the rendering order. For example, an expression can link an effect property to a transform property, so that the effect adjusts dynamically to compensate for the fact that it's calculated before the transformations (**Figures 16.18** and **16.19**). (In contrast to putting the effect in an adjustment layer, this approach also lets you scale or reposition the layer and maintain the effect.)

Figure 16.17 You can also use a nested composition to effectively change the render order. Before After Effects renders the nested composition as a layer, it must complete the rendering sequence within the nested composition.

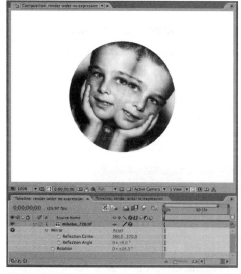

Figure 16.18 Here, the Mirror effect is applied to a rotating layer to achieve a kind of kaleidoscopic effect. Because the effect is calculated first, the angle of reflection rotates with the layer.

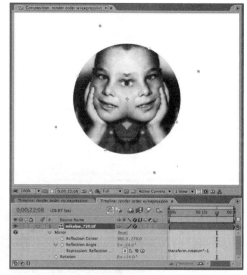

Figure 16.19 Using an expression, the angle of reflection changes opposite of the layer's rotation. The angle of reflection remains vertical even as the image is rotated.

Synchronizing Time

As you've no doubt noticed, panels related to the same composition display the same time. Naturally, panels related to different compositions aren't synchronized in this way. What happens when a composition is nested?

You can set a preference that determines whether the times displayed in windows of nested composition are synchronized with related panels (**Figures 16.20** and **16.21**).

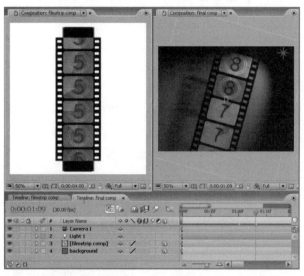

Figure 16.20 Here, the time of the filmstrip comp is independent of the comp in which it's nested.

Figure 16.21 Here, the time in related comps is synchronized.

To synchronize times of related items:

1. Choose Edit > Preferences > General (**Figure 16.22**).

   The General panel of the Preferences dialog box appears.

2. Select Synchronize Time of All Related Items, and then click OK (**Figure 16.23**).

Figure 16.22 Choose Edit > Preferences > General.

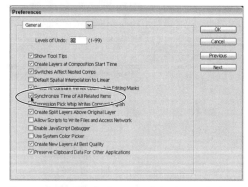

Figure 16.23 In the Preferences dialog box, select Synchronize Time of All Related Items.

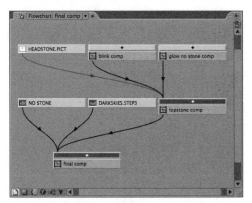

Figure 16.24 The Flowchart view displays the structure of a project or composition as a flowchart.

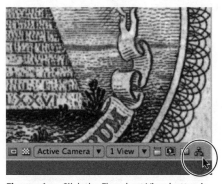

Figure 16.25 Click the Flowchart View button in the Composition panel to view a flowchart of the composition...

Figure 16.26 ...or click the Flowchart View button in the Project panel to view a flowchart of the entire project.

Using the Flowchart View

The Flowchart view enables you to see the structure and hierarchy of the current composition or the entire project. In the Flowchart view, you can see the relationship between project and/or composition elements in flowchart fashion (**Figure 16.24**). This view so can be particularly useful for evaluating your final composition, which typically contains nested compositions. It also provides a good way to familiarize yourself with an old project or one that someone else produced.

You can customize the layout and level of detail of the flowchart. You can even open a composition directly from the Flowchart view. However, you can't use the Flowchart view to change the way your project is organized.

To display the Flowchart view:

Do one of the following:

◆ To view a flowchart for the current composition, click the Flowchart View button ▓ in the Composition panel (**Figure 16.25**).

◆ To view a flowchart for the entire project, click the Flowchart View button ▓ in the Project panel (**Figure 16.26**).

A Flowchart window appears.

To customize the Flowchart view:

Do any of the following:

◆ To expand or collapse a composition in the flowchart, click the plus sign at the top of a composition item in the flowchart (**Figures 16.27** and **16.28**).

◆ To move items in the flowchart, drag them to a new position (**Figure 16.29**).

◆ To show or hide footage items in the flowchart, click the Footage button 🗓.

◆ To show or hide solids in the flowchart, click the Solids button ■.

◆ To show or hide layers in the flowchart, click the Layer button 🗓 (**Figure 16.30**).

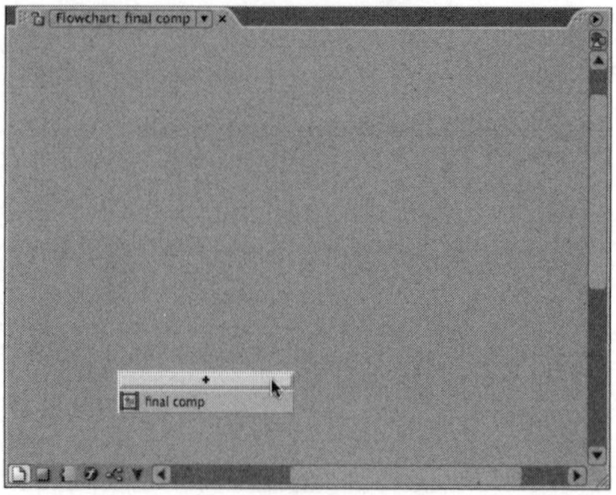

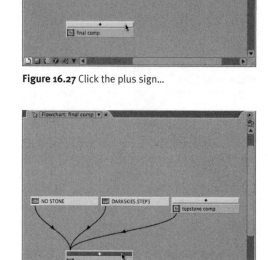

Figure 16.27 Click the plus sign...

Figure 16.28 ...to expand a composition's flowchart. Click again to collapse it.

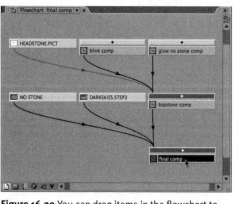

Figure 16.29 You can drag items in the flowchart to arrange them; however, you can't use the flowchart to change the relationships between items in the comp.

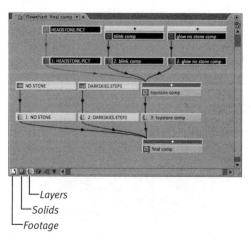

Layers
Solids
Footage

Figure 16.30 Select the buttons that correspond to the type of items you want to show in the flowchart.

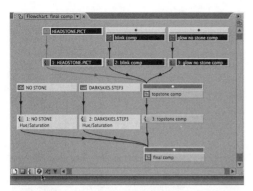

Figure 16.31 Click the Effects button to show or hide effect names with the layers.

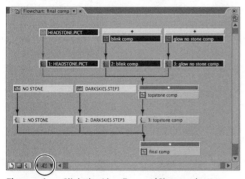

Figure 16.32 Click the Line Format/Cleanup button to toggle between straight and angled lines in the flowchart.

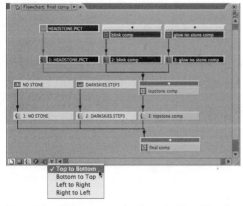

Figure 16.33 Choose an option from the Flow Direction pull-down menu.

◆ To show or hide effects for layers, click the Effects button 🗲 (**Figure 16.31**).

◆ To toggle between straight and curvy lines in the flowchart, click the Line Format/ Cleanup button 🔲 (**Figure 16.32**).

◆ To clean up the flowchart, Option-click (Mac) or Alt-click (Windows) the Line Format/Cleanup button.

◆ To change the arrangement of the flowchart, choose an option from the Flow Direction pull-down menu (**Figure 16.33**):

▲ **Top to Bottom**

▲ **Bottom to Top**

▲ **Left to Right**

▲ **Right to Left**

The direction of the flowchart changes according to your choice (**Figure 16.34**).

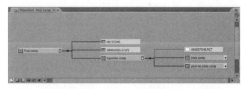

Figure 16.34 The direction of the flowchart changes according to your choice.

Precomposing

As you've no doubt figured out by now, it can take a fair amount of planning to nest compositions and create hierarchies of elements. However, you can't always anticipate the need to nest. Often, you realize that layers should be contained in a nested composition only after they're part of the current composition. Fortunately, you can repackage layers of an existing composition into a nested composition by using a method called *precomposing*.

The Pre-compose command places one or more selected layers in a nested composition (or, if you prefer, a *precomp*), thus accomplishing in a single step what could otherwise be a tedious reorganization process (**Figures 16.35** and **16.36**).

When you precompose more than one layer, the layers' properties (masks, effects, transform) and associated keyframes are retained and moved into the nested composition. When you precompose a single layer, on the other hand, you may choose whether its properties and keyframes move with it or remain in the current composition (becoming properties of the nested composition). After Effects prompts you with a dialog box that lists your choices (**Figure 16.37**):

Leave all attributes in [current composition] moves a single layer into a nested composition. The nested composition has the size and duration of the layer, and it acquires the layer's properties and keyframes.

Move all attributes into the new composition moves one or more layers into a nested composition, which has the size and duration of the current composition. All properties and keyframes are retained by the layers and move with them into the nested composition.

Figure 16.35 Precomposing allows you to select one or more layers...

Figure 16.36 ...and place them into a nested composition.

Figure 16.37 When you precompose one or more layers, After Effects prompts you with a dialog box of options.

Figure 16.38 Select one or more layers in the Timeline panel.

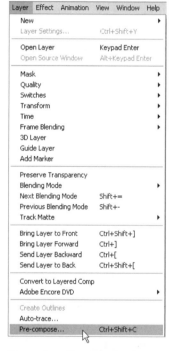

Figure 16.39 Choose Layer > Pre-compose.

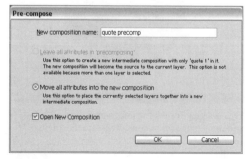

Figure 16.40 In the Pre-compose dialog box, select an option.

Open New Composition opens the newly created nested composition automatically. Leaving this option unselected creates a nested composition but leaves the current composition open.

To precompose one or more layers:

1. Select one or more layers in the Timeline panel (**Figure 16.38**).

2. *Do either of the following*:
   ▲ Choose Layer > Pre-compose (**Figure 16.39**).
   ▲ Press Shift-Command-C (Mac) or Shift-Ctrl-C (Windows).
   A Pre-compose dialog box appears (**Figure 16.40**).

3. *Select an option:*
   ▲ **Leave all attributes in [current composition]**
   ▲ **Move all attributes into the new composition**
   If you're precomposing more than one layer, only the second option is available.

4. To have After Effects open the nested composition automatically, select Open New Composition.

5. Click OK to close the Pre-compose dialog box.
   The selected layers are moved into another composition, which is nested in the current composition (**Figure 16.41**). The nested composition is also listed in the Project panel.

Figure 16.41 The selected layers are moved into another composition, which replaces them in the current composition.

PRECOMPOSING

617

Collapsing Transformations

Sometimes the render order in nested compositions can cause image resolution to degrade. This happens because transform properties, such as Scale, are calculated at every tier in the project hierarchy: first in the most deeply nested composition, then in the next, and so on. At each level, the image is *rasterized*—its resolution is defined and then redefined in successive compositions.

Scaling down an image in a nested composition rasterizes the image at the smaller size and, consequently, at a lower resolution (**Figures 16.42** and **16.43**). Because the smaller image becomes the source for successive compositions, scaling it up again makes the reduced resolution more apparent (**Figure 16.44**).

This rescaling process is sometimes unavoidable, especially when a boss or client dictates revisions. In such circumstances, you can maintain image quality by *collapsing transformations.*

Figure 16.42 When an image at one resolution...

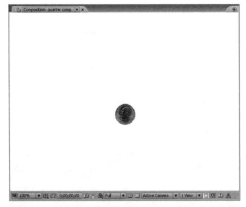

Figure 16.43 ...is scaled down, it's rasterized at the new size.

Figure 16.44 Scaling the image up again in a subsequent composition doesn't restore the original resolution.

Figure 16.45 By collapsing transformations, you can postpone rasterization until rendering reaches the nested composition in which the switch is selected.

Figure 16.46 Click the Collapse Transformations switch for a nested composition.

✔ Tips

- When applied to a layer created from a path-based illustration (such as an Illustrator file), the Collapse Transformations switch functions as the Continuously Rasterize switch. See Chapter 2, "Importing Footage into a Project," for more information.

- Naturally, scaling a bitmapped image beyond 100 percent makes its pixels visible, regardless of the Collapse Transformations setting.

By collapsing transformations, you prevent After Effects from rasterizing the image in every successive composition, instead forcing it to calculate all the transform property changes and rasterize the image only once—in the composition with the Collapse Transformations switch selected. This way, the composition uses the resolution of the source image rather than that of intermediate versions (**Figure 16.45**).

One surprising result of the Collapse Transformations setting is that it ignores the frame size of nested compositions. This means layers that were cropped by the border of a nested composition will appear uncropped in the collapsed composition. You can add a stencil mode or mask to a layer in a nested composition to reestablish the frame edge.

You should also realize that the Opacity settings for the nested compositions are retained and combine with the opacity of the layer that uses collapsed transformations.

To collapse transformations:

1. If necessary, click the Switches/Modes button in the Timeline panel to display the Switches panel.

2. For a nested composition, select the Collapse Transformations switch 🔳 (**Figure 16.46**).

   The same switch is used to continuously rasterize a layer created from path-based artwork.

Setting Recursive Switches

By default, controls for nested compositions operate *recursively*. That is, setting a switch for a nested composition also sets the switch for the layers nested within it. These switches include Collapse Transformations, Continuously Rasterize, and Quality. The composition's Resolution, Enable Motion Blur, and Enable Frame Blending settings also operate recursively.

In general, recursive switches can save you time and effort. Sometimes, however, recursive switches can produce undesired results. In a complex project, for example, you might enable Collapse Transformations for a nested composition. If the nested composition contained yet another composition, its Collapse Transformations switch would be enabled as well. As a result, you might unintentionally reveal parts of layers that had been cropped by the nested comp's frame edges. Similarly, recursive switches could prevent you from enabling Motion Blur selectively in a series of nested compositions. As a rule, use recursive switches. If using a switch has unintended consequences, disable recursive switches.

To enable or disable recursive switches:

1. Choose After Effects > Preferences > General (Mac) or Edit > Preferences > General (Windows) (**Figure 16.47**).

   The General panel of the Preferences dialog box appears.

2. In the Preferences dialog box, select Switches Affect Nested Comps (**Figure 16.48**).

   Select the check box to set recursive switches as the default; deselect it to set switches for nested compositions individually.

✔ Tip

- Previous versions of After Effects used the term *recursive switches*, but the current version avoids jargon and instead uses the phrase *Switches Affect Nested Comps*.

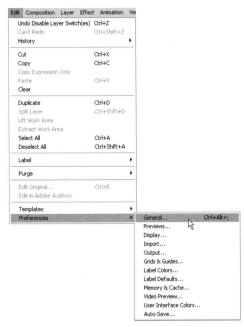

Figure 16.47 Choose After Effects > Preferences > General (Mac) or Edit > Preferences > General (Windows).

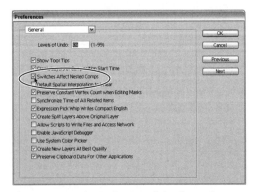

Figure 16.48 In the Preferences dialog box, select Switches Affect Nested Comps.

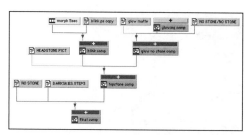

Figure 16.49 By prerendering, you avoid rendering every element of a nested composition...

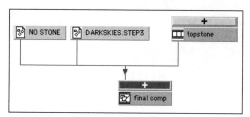

Figure 16.50 ...and replace the nested comp with a rendered version. (This flowchart illustrates the process; the actual Flowchart view continues to show the nested composition.)

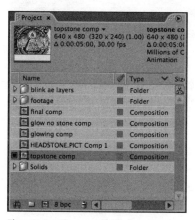

Figure 16.51 Because the prerendered movie is a proxy, you can always switch back to the nested composition.

Prerendering

It seems that if you're not occupied with making the project better, you're preoccupied with making it render faster. A process known as *prerendering* is one strategy you can use to reduce rendering times.

Typically, you'll complete work on nested compositions long before the final composition is ready—which makes it all the more frustrating to wait for the nested comps to render (not to mention unnecessary).

With prerendering, you can render nested compositions and use the movie file as a proxy. Thereafter, render times are reduced because After Effects refers to the movie instead of calculating every element in the nested composition (**Figures 16.49** and **16.50**). If you decide you need to make changes, you can stop using the proxy and switch back to the source composition (**Figure 16.51**). Prerender the composition again to save the changes in the proxy. As you'll learn in Chapter 17, "Output," you can set a post-render action to prerender a comp and set the rendered file as a proxy in a single step.

To reduce render times for the final output, make sure that the Pre-render settings are compatible with the settings of your final file and that you've set the Render settings to Use Proxies.

To use prerendering, consult Chapter 17 as well as the "Proxies and Placeholders" section of Chapter 3, "Managing Footage."

Parenting Layers

Often, you need layers to act as a group or an integrated system. For example, you may want to connect the parts of a machine or simulate the orbits of a planetary system. You can do either of these things by establishing a relationship between one layer's transformation properties and the transformation properties of one or more other layers—a technique fittingly known as *parenting* (**Figures 16.52** and **16.53**).

Figure 16.52 Parenting establishes a relationship between one layer's transformation properties and those of one or more other layers. Using parenting, all the layers that make up the panels of this aperture move in unison.

Figure 16.53 In this example, the logo and book cover are separate layers, but parenting links them so they move as one.

Figure 16.54 Although the child layer's (the rabbit logo's) and parent layer's (the book cover's) transform properties are linked...

Changing a parent layer's transformation properties (with the exception of its Opacity property) provokes a corresponding change in its related child layers. For example, if you were to change a parent layer's position, the child layers' positions would change accordingly. Although you can animate child layers independently, the transformations occurs relative to the parent, not the composition. In the layer outline of the timeline, note that child layers' property values don't reflect the layer's actual appearance, which is a product of the parent's property values. For example, scaling the parent layer also scales the child layer—even though the child layer's Scale property continues to display the same value (**Figures 16.54** and **16.55**).

Figure 16.55 ...changing the parent's property value isn't reflected in the child layer's property value display.

Jumping

When you assign (or remove) a parent-child relationship, you can specify whether the child layer *jumps*—changes its transform properties relative to its parent layer. Ordinarily, assigning a parent-child relationship leaves the child layer's transform properties unchanged until you make subsequent alterations to either the parent or child layers (**Figure 16.56**). In contrast, when you set the child layer to jump, its transformation properties are immediately altered relative to the parent layer (**Figure 16.57**). Conversely, you can make a child layer jump when you remove the parent-child relationship, so that its transform properties immediately shift relative to the composition.

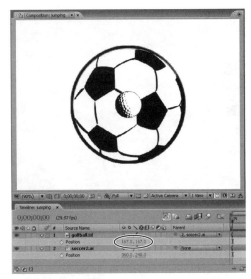

Figure 16.56 Ordinarily, assigning a parent-child relationship leaves the child layer's relative transform properties unchanged in the Comp panel, by changing its values.

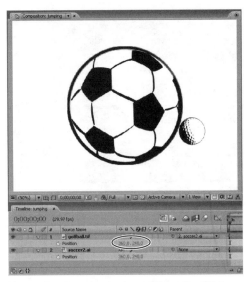

Figure 16.57 In contrast, when you have the child layer jump, its transformation properties are altered relative to the parent layer immediately.

Figure 16.58 Choose the layer you want to assign as the parent in the Parent pull-down menu...

Figure 16.59 ...or drag the Pickwhip to anywhere in the parent layer's horizontal track in the Timeline panel.

Figure 16.60 In the Parent pull-down menu for the child layer, choose None to cut the apron strings.

To assign a parent-child relationship:

1. If necessary, reveal the Parenting panel in the Timeline panel by choosing Panels > Parent in the Timeline pull-down menu.

2. For the child layer, *do either of the following:*

▲ Choose the layer you want to assign as the parent in the Parent pull-down menu (**Figure 16.58**).

▲ Drag the Pickwhip ⊙ to the layer you want to designate as the parent (**Figure 16.59**).

You can drag the Pickwhip anywhere in the layer's horizontal track in the layer outline to select it. The name of the parent layer appears in the Parenting pull-down menu for the child layer.

To remove a parent from a layer:

◆ In the Parent pull-down menu for the child layer, choose None (**Figure 16.60**).

The parent-child relationship is removed, and you can now transform the layer.

To make a child jump when assigning or removing a parent:

◆ Press Option (Mac) or Alt (Windows) when you select a layer name in the Parent pull-down menu, or select a layer with the Parent Pickwhip ⊙.

Using Null Objects

You can add invisible layers, called *null objects,* to a composition to create sophisticated animations that don't rely on the movement of visible layers. For example, a null object can serve as a parent layer, exerting an invisible influence over several child layers. Because these layers aren't visible in previews or output, you can't apply effects to them. When selected, a null object appears in the Composition panel as a framed outline. A null object's anchor point is positioned in its upper-left corner (**Figure 16.61**). Otherwise, null objects behave like other layers.

To create a null object:

◆ Choose Layer > New > Null Object (**Figure 16.62**).

A Null Object layer appears as the top layer in the Timeline, beginning at the current time and using the specified default duration for still images (**Figure 16.63**).

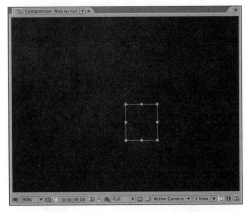

Figure 16.61 When selected, a null object appears in the Composition panel as a framed outline. A null object's anchor point is positioned in its upper-left corner.

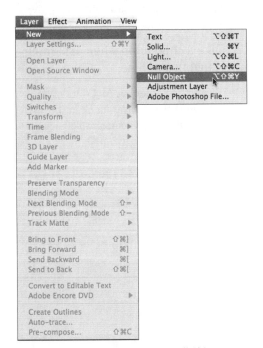

Figure 16.62 Choose Layer > New > Null Object.

Figure 16.63 A Null Object layer appears as the top layer, beginning at the current time and using the specified default duration for still images. Here, the null layer has been assigned as the parent to other layers.

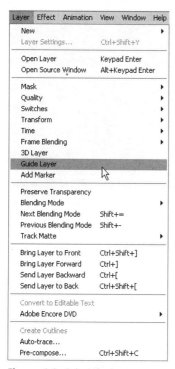

Figure 16.64 Select the layer you want to use as a guide layer, and choose Layer > Guide Layer.

Figure 16.65 The layer appears with a Guide Layer icon; its visibility can be suppressed in the Render Settings dialog box when you output the composition.

Specifying Guide Layers

You can assign any layer to serve as a *guide layer*. As the name suggests, guide layers can help you align other objects in a composition as you work on it. When it's time to export the comp, specifying the appropriate option in the Render Settings lets you easily exclude the guide layers from appearing in the exported file. This way, you can exclude all guide layers at once instead of locating them individually and turning off their video switch. See Chapter 17 for more about exporting a comp and render settings.

To specify a layer as a guide layer:

◆ Select the layer you want to specify as a guide layer, and select Layer > Guide Layer (**Figure 16.64**).

In the Timeline panel's layer outline, the layer name appears with a Guide Layer icon ▦ (**Figure 16.65**). You can suppress the visibility of guide layers when you export the composition (see Chapter 17 for more information).

✔ Tip

■ You can designate a layer containing a useful text note as a guide layer. This way, the information can be included as you work and easily excluded from the final output.

Using Expressions

Expressions define relationships between layer properties (in the same layer, in different layers, or even in layers that reside in different compositions). Rather than keyframe properties independently, you can link the values of one property to another using a JavaScript-based instruction, or *expression*. Expressions allow you to create sophisticated relationships between properties that you could otherwise produce only via painstaking keyframing. Expressions can also use a mathematical formula to arrive at a property's values.

Expressions are especially useful for depicting the parts of a machine: wheels turning as a car moves, a small gear turning in response to a larger gear, or a meter increasing in height as a dial is turned (**Figure 16.66**). Because you can link all kinds of properties using simple or complex formulas, expressions afford endless possibilities. And because you can change the timing of the whole system by modifying a single element, you save time and effort as well.

Because expressions are based on JavaScript, experience with that language or a similar scripting language gives you a definite head start. However, even with no knowledge of JavaScript and only basic math skills, you can create useful expressions. Using the Pickwhip tool, you can generate a basic expression automatically. You can then modify your basic expression by appending a little arithmetic. When you're ready to write your own scripts, After Effects supplies the terms you need in a convenient pull-down menu.

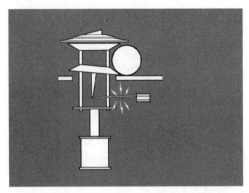

Figure 16.66 Expressions are especially useful in depicting the parts of a machine. Here, the position of the pinball can trigger the movement of parts of the bumper.

Figure 16.67 Expand the layer outline to reveal the properties you want to link using an expression.

Figure 16.68 Choose Animation > Add Expression, or press Shift-Option-Equal sign (Mac) or Shift-Alt-Equal sign (Windows).

To create an expression using the Expression Pickwhip:

1. Expand the layer outline to reveal the properties you want to link via an expression (**Figure 16.67**).

2. With the property selected, *do either of the following:*
   ▲ Choose Animation > Add Expression (**Figure 16.68**).
   ▲ Press Shift-Option-Equal sign (Mac) or Shift-Alt-Equal sign (Windows).
   An Equal Sign icon ▤ appears next to the property to indicate an expression is enabled. The property also expands to reveal buttons in the Switches panel of the timeline. Under the time ruler, the expression script appears selected (**Figure 16.69**).

3. In the Switches panel, click the Expression Pickwhip button ◉, and drag the Pickwhip to the name of the property value to which you want to link the expression (**Figure 16.70**).

continues on next page

Figure 16.69 An Equal Sign icon appears next to the property, and the property expands to reveal buttons in the Switches panel. In the time ruler area, the expression script appears selected.

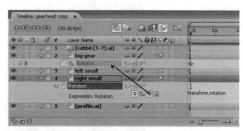

Figure 16.70 In the Switches panel, drag the Expression Pickwhip to the name of the property value to which you want to link the expression.

USING EXPRESSIONS

629

The property's name becomes highlighted when the Pickwhip touches it. When you release the mouse, the expression script is entered in the script area under the time ruler (**Figure 16.71**).

4. Modify the script by doing *either of the following* (**Figure 16.72**):

   ▲ Enter changes or additions to the script using standard JavaScript syntax.

   ▲ Use the Expressions pull-down menu to select from a list of common scripting terms.

If you make a mistake, After Effects prompts you with a warning dialog box and advises you to correct the script.

5. Keyframe the linked property (the one without the expression) using the methods you learned in Chapter 7, "Properties and Keyframes."

The property using the expression changes automatically according to the relationship defined by the expression (**Figure 16.73**).

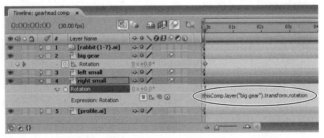

Figure 16.71 When you release the mouse, the expression script is entered in the script area under the time ruler.

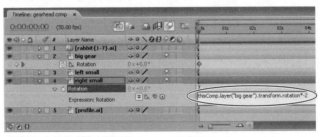

Figure 16.72 If necessary, modify the script manually. Here, *-2 is added to the script to multiply the rotation value by negative two.

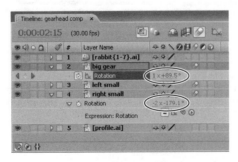

Figure 16.73 The property using the expression changes automatically, according to the relationship defined by the expression.

Expression disabled

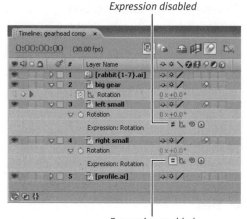

Expression enabled

Figure 16.74 An Equal Sign icon indicates that the expression is enabled; a crossed-out equal sign indicates that the expression is temporarily disabled.

To disable and enable expressions:

◆ In the layer outline, click the Expression icon next to the property containing the expression to toggle it on and off.

   An Equal Sign icon ▤ indicates the expression is enabled; a crossed-out equal sign ▤ indicates the expression has been temporarily disabled (**Figure 16.74**).

✔ Tips

■ Despite their similar names, JavaScript isn't related to Java.

■ Although expressions usually define relationships between layer properties, you can modify a property using an expression alone—without linking it to another property. An expression used to create random values is one such example.

■ You can save an expression by copying and pasting it into a text-editing program such as Simple Text (Mac) or Notepad (Windows). However, because expressions refer to layers and properties specific to the project, you may want to add comments to the expression to help you apply it to future projects. You may even want to save a version of the current project (and the necessary source files) to use for future reference.

■ After Effects includes a project template called Expression Sampler. See Chapter 2 for more about importing project templates.

Viewing Expressions

Although expressions don't create keyframes, you can still see how an expression modifies the property in a property graph.

In contrast to the Graph Editor Set button, which appears to the left of a property, the button that reveals how an expression affects a property appears to the right of the property in the Switches panel's column. Otherwise, the button looks and works just like the Graph Editor Set button. (See Chapter 9, "Keyframe Interpolation," for more about reading property graphs.) This book always refers to the icon as a Graph Editor Set button, even though a tool tip identifies the one next to an expression as the Show Post-Expression Graph button.

To view an expression graph:

1. Expand the layer outline to reveal the layer property containing the expression.

2. In the Switches panel, click the Graph Editor Set icon (**Figure 16.75**).

3. In the Timeline panel, select the Show Graph Editor button.

   In the Graph Editor, a graph shows the property's value or speed/velocity after the expression has been applied (**Figure 16.76**).

✔ Tips

- To view expressions for all layers in the composition, select the layers and press EE.

- You can convert property values calculated by an expression into keyframed values by choosing Animation > Keyframe Assistant > Convert Expression to Keyframes.

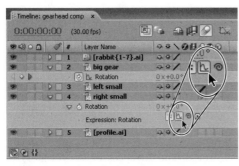

Figure 16.75 In the Switches panel, click the Expression's Graph Editor Set icon...

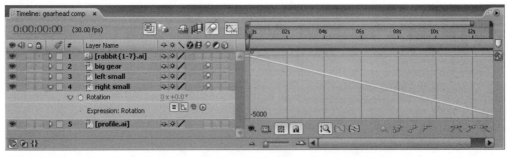

Figure 16.76 ...and then click the Timeline panel's Show Graph Editor button to view how the expression affects the property.

Using the Expression Language Menu

When you start writing your own expressions, you'll discover that the language's vocabulary is extensive. Fortunately, you can plug in most of the terms you'll need automatically by selecting them from a categorized list contained in a convenient pull-down menu.

To use the Expression pull-down menu:

1. Expand the layer outline to reveal the property you want to adjust with an expression.

2. With the property selected, *do either of the following:*

   ▲ Choose Animation > Add Expression.

   ▲ Press Shift-Option-Equal sign (Mac) or Shift-Alt-Equal sign (Windows).

   An Equal Sign icon ▀ appears next to the property, and a default expression appears under the time ruler. The default expression won't modify the property values. The property also expands to reveal buttons in the Switches panel of the timeline.

3. In the Switches panel of the timeline, click the Expressions pull-down menu.

   A categorized menu of expression-language terms appears (**Figure 16.77**).

continues on next page

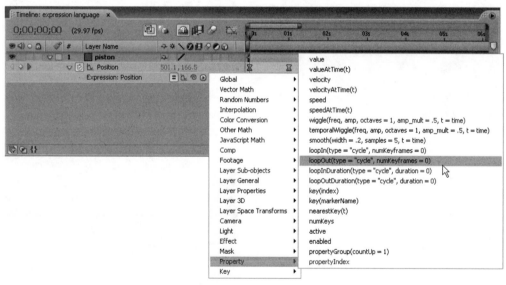

Figure 16.77 In the Switches panel of the timeline, click the Expressions pull-down menu to make a categorized menu of expression-language terms appear.

4. In the pull-down menu, select the term you need.

In the time ruler area of the timeline, the term appears in the expression text. A cursor appears at the end of the text, indicating the insertion point for additional expression terms (**Figure 16.78**).

5. If necessary, enter expression language manually (**Figure 16.79**).

6. Repeat steps 3–5 as needed.

7. Click anywhere outside the expression text field to get out of edit mode.

Figure 16.78 The term appears in the expression text. A cursor appears at the end of the text, indicating the insertion point for additional expression terms.

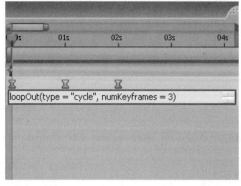

Figure 16.79 If necessary, enter expression language manually.

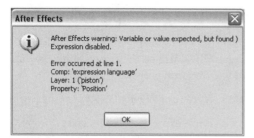

Figure 16.80 If you exit editing mode before the expression is complete or if the expression uses incorrect syntax, an error dialog box appears.

✔ Tip

■ If you exit expression-editing mode before the expression is complete, or if the expression uses incorrect syntax, an error dialog box appears containing a description of the problem (**Figure 16.80**). When you close the dialog box, a Warning icon appears in the Switches panel, and the expression is disabled automatically (**Figure 16.81**). You must correct the expression language to enable it. Click the Warning icon to reopen the warning dialog box.

Figure 16.81 When you close the dialog box, a Warning icon appears in the Switches panel, and the expression is disabled automatically. Click the Warning icon to reopen the Warning dialog box.

Writing Expressions

Once you've created a few simple expressions with the Pickwhip, you'll probably want to try writing some of your own—a process that can appear daunting if you don't have experience with JavaScript or scripting in general (especially because After Effects discourages your early attempts with warning dialog boxes about syntax errors, bad arguments, and the like).

Once you understand a few basic concepts, however, you should feel confident enough to experiment a bit. You'll also find it easier to decipher Adobe's Expressions guide (or an entire book on the subject of JavaScript) and to analyze other expressions.

Expression lexicon

As is the case with any language, an expression must follow rules if it is to make sense. Only certain terms are part of the scripting language's lexicon, and each statement must be constructed using a particular syntax.

Translating a simple expression

Consider the following example, which was created by dragging the Expression Pickwhip to a Rotation property:

```
this_comp.layer("panel1").rotation
```

This simple expression links a layer's property (in this case, Rotation) to the Rotation property of a layer called panel1. A plain-English translation would read something like the following: "To set Rotation values for this property, look in this composition, find the layer called panel1, and take its Rotation value." Adjusting panel1's Rotation property results in a corresponding change in the layer containing the expression.

Typically, you would modify the expression:

```
this_comp.layer("panel1").rotation+60
```

The +60 adds 60 to the rotational value, which is measured in degrees. Setting panel1's Rotation value to 30 degrees would cause the layer containing the expression to rotate 90 degrees (30+60=90).

✔ Tip

- You may be familiar with JavaScript as it applies to Web design. Expressions are based on the same core JavaScript language but not particular JavaScript interpreters, which are browser-specific.

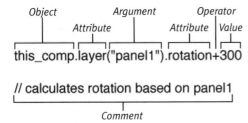

// calculates rotation based on panel1

Comment

Figure 16.82 Familiarize yourself with some of the terms used to describe an expression. Here's a sample of a simple statement that uses the proper dot syntax.

Variables   Indexes the Y-coordinate

```
y = position[1] / this_comp.height;
squash = y * 50;
[100 + squash, 100 - squash]
```

Array (in this case, for a 2-dimensional scale property)

Figure 16.83 Here's another expression applied to a Scale property of a layer depicting a bouncing ball. It makes the ball squash, or compress, according to its position. Note how the expression uses variables to define the layer's scale in terms of its Y-coordinate position.

Expression syntax

By familiarizing yourself with a few basic terms, you'll be better able to decipher Adobe's Expressions reference or a JavaScript guide. Match the following terms with **Figures 16.82** and **16.83** to familiarize yourself with basic Expression/JavaScript terminology and syntax:

Statement denotes a complete thought or command in JavaScript (as it does in any other language).

Dot syntax describes how each statement is constructed. Each part of the statement is separated by a dot, or period. Statements in the same expression are separated by semicolons (;).

Comments are included in scripts for your reference only; the program ignores them. Comments must appear between double slashes (//) and the end of the line: // this is a comment.

Objects are any named data and are comparable to nouns in other languages. After Effects' expression language includes objects unique to the program, such as comps and layers.

Attributes are the named values of an object and can apply to more than one object. For example, width is an attribute in the following statement: this_comp.width. Attributes can also return, or result in, other objects. For example, the statement fragment layer ("panel1") retrieves the layer by name.

Methods are similar to attributes, but rather than retrieve data—such as layer names— they specify data. Methods are followed by parentheses, which (depending on the method) contain certain variables or values. For example, the method random(100) used in an expression for a layer's Opacity value makes the layer's opacity randomly fluctuate between 0 and 100 percent.

Values denote quantitative data, such as numbers. However, a value can also be a string (alphanumeric data) or an array.

Array denotes a collection of data values referred to by a number. Arrays are said to have *dimensions*, which usually correspond to the aspects of a property value. For example, a Position property (in 2D space) has two dimensions: *X* and *Y* coordinate values. A Scale property in 2D space can have one or two dimensions: an overall scale value or separate width and height values. In the Expressions guide, an array's dimension appears within brackets: [ ].

Index denotes the numbering scheme used to refer to values in arrays or objects. Arrays are indexed starting from 0. For example, `position[0]` retrieves the position's *X* coordinate, and `position[1]` retrieves the position's *Y* coordinate. Objects like layers, masks, and effect parameters are indexed starting from 1. For example, `layer(1)` refers to the top layer in the comp. However, it's better to refer to such objects by name than by index, in case changes (like altering the stacking order) invalidate the indexed reference.

Variables are names associated with values. A variable is said to *store* the value. For example, your expression can contain the statement `radius = 20` to assign the variable `radius` the value of 20. Later in the expression, you can use the variable as part of another statement. Variables and attributes are essentially the same, except that you can invent the name of a variable.

Operators are symbols used to perform a calculation, many of which you're familiar with from basic arithmetic. Operators that assign values, such as `x=y`, are known as *assignments*. Operators can also compare values, such as `x<y` (if x is less than y). Such operators are called *comparisons* and result in a value of true or false, or 1 and 0, respectively.

Arguments describe the type of data—such as a number, array, or string—required to specify an object. For example, the object `Comp(name)` requires a string, or alphanumeric data, in place of `name`. Therefore, the argument is a string. In this case, the actual name of the comp should be placed in the parentheses and—because it's a so-called literal string value—within quotes: `Comp("final comp")`. In contrast, the object `this_comp` doesn't require an argument. This type of global object is complete in and of itself; you don't need to specify additional data.

Returns can be thought of as another way of saying, "results in this type of data." For example, the statement `this_comp.layer("panel1").rotation` returns a number—specifically, the Rotation property value of the layer called panel1.

✔ Tips

- Throughout this book, you've been advised to give your layers and comps descriptive names (rather than use the default names) and to refrain from changing them. The former habit helps you make clear expressions; the latter keeps your expressions from losing their links and becoming disabled.

- Although the term *property* is used in JavaScript, After Effects' Expressions reference substitutes the term *attribute* to avoid confusion with layer properties (which can be attributes in an expression).

JavaScript Rules

You'll notice that expressions use JavaScript objects (see the section "Expression syntax") that are unique to After Effects (and thus aren't applicable to scripting for the Web). Other than this difference in vocabulary, JavaScript syntax works the same. Expressions' mother tongue, JavaScript, follows several rules that you should know from the start:

◆ JavaScript is case sensitive, which means words must use capitalization consistently if they are to be interpreted correctly. For example, an object called `tony` is different than one called `Tony`.

◆ JavaScript ignores spaces, tabs, and line breaks, except in certain circumstances. For example, the object `comp("final comp")` uses a space in the string "final comp" that you need to include whenever you refer to that comp. Such spaces are part of the literal string: in this case, the name of the comp, which is in quotes. Also, the accidental placement of spaces in a number or string (alphanumeric) value will cause syntax errors. Otherwise, feel free to use spaces, tabs, or line breaks to make your scripts easier to read.

◆ JavaScript includes a number of reserved words (such as "boolean" and "goto"), which you aren't allowed to use as part of a script. For a full list of these reserved words, consult a JavaScript manual.

OUTPUT

Finally.

The beginning of this book likened your project and compositions to a musical score. Now that you've written and rehearsed that score, it's time to put on the show!

In your case, that show is a movie file or image sequence of a rendered composition. You can create movies for computer presentation (via CD-ROM or the Web). Or—with the aid of additional equipment or a service bureau—you can transfer your animation to broadcast-video format, or even to film. On the other hand, your movie may serve as a prerendered element of a larger composition. Whatever the case, the rendering-process variables are the same.

Your particular output goals (and, unfortunately, your equipment's limitations) will help determine a wide range of output settings; this chapter will guide you through those myriad options. You'll also get a chance to apply what you've learned thus far about your output goals. (You have been reading those sidebars, haven't you?) Although this chapter can't cover every output specification, it can provide you with enough information so that you know which questions to ask to derive your own answers.

The Render Queue Panel

You control the rendering process from the Render Queue panel, listing the items you want to render and assigning their rendering settings (**Figure 17.1**). This section provides an overview of the Render Queue panel; following sections explain each feature in more detail.

Rendering progress

The top of the window contains buttons to start, stop, or pause the render. It also displays information about rendering progress. Clicking the triangle next to Current Render Details reveals detailed information about the current render (**Figure 17.2**). This information not only indicates the remaining rendering time and disk space, but it also helps you identify the areas of the composition that render more slowly than others.

Rendering settings

The lower portion of the Render Queue panel is the "queue" portion of the panel: This is where you list items in the order you want to render them. You can assign rendering settings to each item as well as render the same item with different settings.

By default, the triangle next to each item's name is set to reveal four types of information (**Figure 17.3**).

On the left side, the settings you assign each item in the queue are grouped into two categories: Render Settings and Output Module. The first step, Render Settings, calculates each frame for output. Once the attributes of the frames have been rendered, the Output Module determines how they're saved to disk. Clicking the triangle next to each setting category reveals a summary of the setting (**Figure 17.4**). These settings are explained in detail later in this chapter.

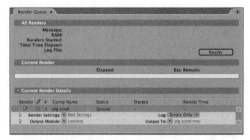

Figure 17.1 You control and monitor the rendering process from the Render Queue panel.

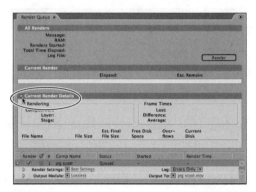

Figure 17.2 Clicking the triangle next to Current Render Details reveals detailed information about the current render.

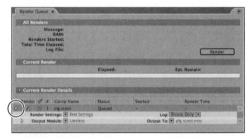

Figure 17.3 By default, the triangle next to the name of each item points down to reveal four categories of information.

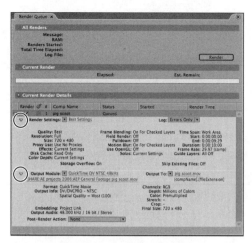

Figure 17.4 Clicking the arrow next to the Render Settings and Output Module options reveals a summary of each group of settings.

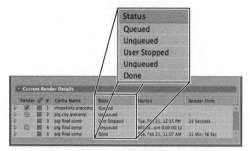

Figure 17.5 When the view of the items in the queue is collapsed, it's easier to see customizable columns of information, including the Render Status.

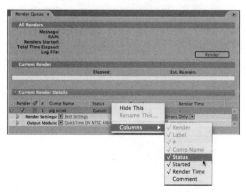

Figure 17.6 Ctrl-click (Mac) or right-click (Windows) to use a contextual menu to customize the panel headings.

On the right side, you can specify the type of record After Effects generates in the Log pull-down menu; you can also specify a name and destination for Output To.

Panel headings and Render Status

Clicking the triangle next to each item collapses the queue information, making several columns of information more apparent (**Figure 17.5**). Although most panel headings are self-explanatory, Render Status merits special attention because it indicates the current state of each item in the queue:

Queued indicates that the item is ready to be rendered.

Unqueued indicates that the item is listed but not ready for rendering, meaning you need to assign a name and destination to it, or you need to check the Render option.

Failed indicates that the render was unsuccessful. Check the render log generated by After Effects to determine the error.

User Stopped indicates that you stopped the rendering process.

Done indicates that the item has been rendered successfully.

After an item is rendered or stopped, it remains in the Render Queue panel until you remove it. Although you can't change the status of rendered items, you can duplicate them as other items in the queue. You can then assign new settings to the new item and render it.

✔ Tip

■ You can customize the panel headings of the Render Queue panel just as you would the Project panel headings. Ctrl-click (Mac) or right-click (Windows) to invoke a contextual menu (**Figure 17.6**).

Making a Movie

This section explains how to add a composition to the Render Queue panel using the Make Movie command. Later sections focus on the Render Queue panel and choosing specific settings.

To make a movie from a composition:

1. Be sure to save your project.

2. Select a composition.

   Projects frequently contain several compositions; make sure you select the one you want to output.

3. Choose Composition > Make Movie, or press Command-M (Mac) or Ctrl-M (Windows) (**Figure 17.7**).

   An Output Movie To dialog box appears (**Figure 17.8**).

4. Specify a name and destination for the final movie.

   If you want to save the movie as a single file, make sure your chosen destination has sufficient storage space to contain it.

5. Click Save to close the Output Movie To dialog box.

   The composition appears as an item in the Render Queue panel (**Figure 17.9**).

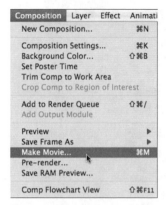

Figure 17.7 Choose Composition > Make Movie.

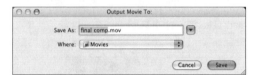

Figure 17.8 An Output Movie To dialog box appears. Specify the name and destination for the rendered composition.

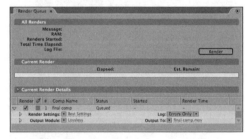

Figure 17.9 The composition appears as an item in the Render Queue panel.

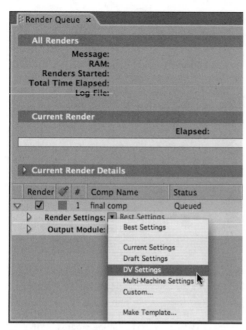

Figure 17.10 Choose a template from the Render Settings pull-down menu, or click the underlined name of the current settings to open a dialog box.

6. In the Render Queue panel, choose render settings by doing *one of the following:*

   ▲ Choose a template from the Render Settings pull-down menu (**Figure 17.10**).

   ▲ Click the name of the current render settings to open the Render Settings dialog box.

7. In the Render Queue panel, choose output options by doing *one of the following:*

   ▲ Choose a template from the Output Module pull-down menu (**Figure 17.11**).

   ▲ Click the name of the current output options to open the Output Options dialog box.

8. In the Render Queue panel, choose an option from the Log pull-down menu (**Figure 17.12**):

   ▲ **Errors Only**

   ▲ **Plus Settings**

   ▲ **Plus Per Frame Info**

continues on next page

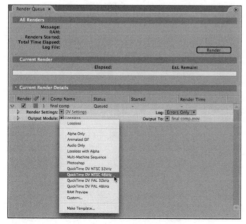

Figure 17.11 Choose a template from the Output Module pull-down menu, or click the underlined name of the current settings to open a dialog box.

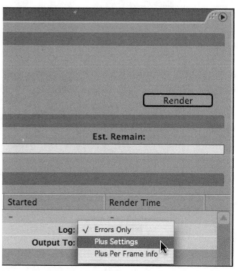

Figure 17.12 Select the type of log After Effects will generate in the Log pull-down menu.

MAKING A MOVIE

645

9. Click the Render button near the top of the Render Queue panel (**Figure 17.13**).

After Effects begins to render the composition. A progress bar and rendering-time data indicate the elapsed render time as well as the estimated time remaining in the rendering process (**Figure 17.14**). After Effects sounds a chime when rendering is complete.

✔ **Tips**

■ To reopen the Output Movie To dialog box so that you can change the name or destination of the saved movie, click the name of the movie next to Output To (**Figure 17.15**).

■ To speed up rendering, close or collapse the Composition panel *before* you begin rendering. This way, After Effects doesn't need to update the Composition panel as rendering progresses.

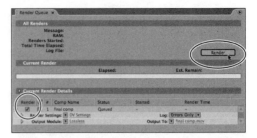

Figure 17.13 Make sure the Render column is checked for the item, and click Render.

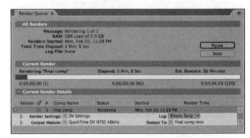

Figure 17.14 Monitor the rendering progress at the top of the Render Queue panel.

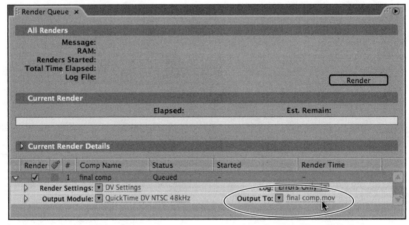

Figure 17.15 To change the name or destination of the saved movie, click the name of the movie next to Output To.

Figure 17.16 To add a composition to the queue, drag a Composition icon from the Project panel to the Render Queue panel.

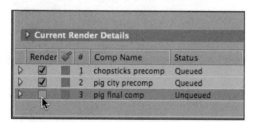

Figure 17.17 To change the order of the compositions in the queue, drag an item up or down.

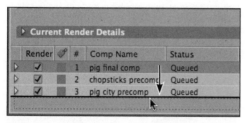

Figure 17.18 To unqueue a composition, click the Render option box to unselect it.

Using the Render Queue Panel

Among other things, the Render Queue panel is just that: a queue, or line, of compositions waiting to be rendered.

To manage items in the render queue:

◆ In the Render Queue panel, *do any of the following:*

▲ To add a composition to the queue, drag a Composition icon from the Project panel to the Render Queue panel (**Figure 17.16**).

▲ To remove a composition from the queue, select a composition in the queue and press Delete.

▲ To change the order of the compositions in the queue, drag a composition up or down (**Figure 17.17**).

A dark horizontal line indicates where the composition's new position in the queue will be when you release the mouse.

▲ To prevent a composition in the queue from rendering, click the Render option box to unselect it (**Figure 17.18**).

The composition remains in the list, but its status changes to Unqueued; it won't render until you select the Render option box.

Pausing and Stopping Rendering

After you click the Render button, Pause and Stop buttons appear in its place. Pausing a render comes in handy if you need to access other programs, or if you didn't plan ahead and find you need to clear some drive space for the render. Stopping a render won't adversely affect a frame sequence—you can pick up where you left off—but it will disturb the integrity of a movie file, creating two movies instead of one.

To pause rendering:

1. After the composition has begun to render, click the Pause button in the Render Queue panel (**Figure 17.19**).

   During the pause in rendering, you can use other applications or manage files on the desktop. However, you can't do anything in After Effects (not even close a window) except restart the render.

2. To resume rendering, click Continue.

   After Effects continues to render to the same file from where it left off.

To stop rendering:

◆ After the composition has begun rendering, click the Stop button in the Render Queue panel (**Figure 17.20**).

   When rendering stops, the composition's status changes to User Stopped. A new item—with an Unqueued status—is added to the queue. If you render this item, it will render a new movie, starting with the next unrendered frame of the interrupted movie (**Figure 17.21**).

✔ Tip

■ Pausing allows you to use other programs or the desktop but not After Effects. If you want to collapse the Composition panel, do so before you start rendering.

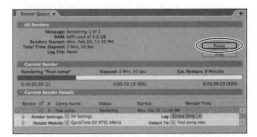

Figure 17.19 Click the Pause button in the Render Queue panel to pause rendering and use the desktop or other programs.

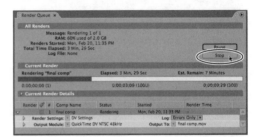

Figure 17.20 Click Stop to halt rendering completely.

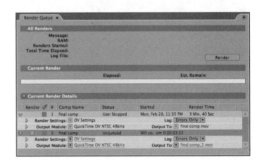

Figure 17.21 When you stop the rendering, the item's status changes to User Stopped, and a new item is added with the status Unqueued. This item will start rendering at the next unrendered frame.

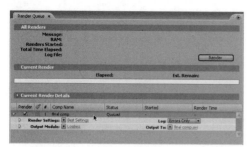

Figure 17.22 Select an item in the Render Queue panel.

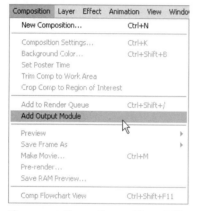

Figure 17.23 Choose Composition > Add Output Module.

Assigning Multiple Output Modules

You can assign more than one output module to a single item in the queue—a capability that allows you to easily create multiple versions of the same composition.

To assign additional output modules:

1. Select an item in the Render Queue panel (**Figure 17.22**).

2. Choose Composition > Add Output Module (**Figure 17.23**).

   Another output module appears for the item in the queue (**Figure 17.24**).

3. Specify settings or a template for the output module, and render the items in the queue (as explained earlier in this chapter in the section "Making a Movie").

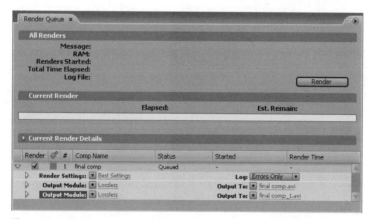

Figure 17.24 Another output module appears for the item in the queue.

Choosing Render Settings

Determining render settings is the first step in the rendering process. These settings dictate how each frame of a composition is calculated for the final output, in much the same way that composition settings calculate frames for playback in the Composition panel.

Initially, the render settings are set to match the composition's current settings. Although in some cases these settings may meet your output goals, it's best to take a more active role in choosing render settings. By selecting each render setting (or by using a template of settings), you can ensure that each layer of your composition (including those in nested compositions) uses the settings you want before it's saved to disk.

To choose render settings manually:

1. In the render queue, click the underlined name of the render settings (**Figure 17.25**).

   A Render Settings dialog box appears (**Figure 17.26**).

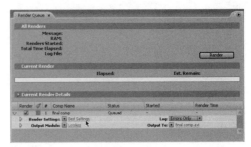

Figure 17.25 In the render queue, click the underlined name of the render settings.

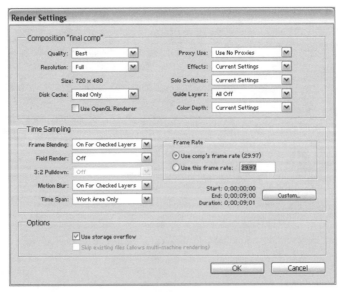

Figure 17.26 In the Render Settings dialog box, specify various settings for rendering the frames of the composition.

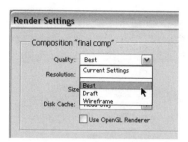

Figure 17.27 Set the Quality setting for all layers from the Quality pull-down menu.

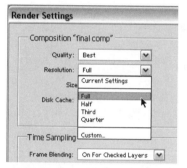

Figure 17.28 Set the resolution for all layers in the composition in the Resolution pull-down menu.

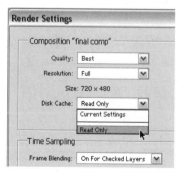

Figure 17.29 Specify an option for Disk Cache.

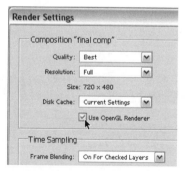

Figure 17.30 To employ OpenGL hardware, select Use OpenGL Renderer.

2. Make a selection *for each of the following options:*

> **Quality** sets the quality for all layers (**Figure 17.27**). (See "Quality Setting Switches" in Chapter 5, "Layer Basics.")
>
> **Resolution** sets the resolution for all layers in a composition. (See "Resolution" in Chapter 4, "Compositions.") Setting the resolution to Half, for example, renders every other pixel, resulting in an image with half the dimensions of the full-sized composition (**Figure 17.28**).
>
> **Disk Cache** specifies whether After Effects uses the current cache settings— the ones you specified in the Memory & Cache panel of the Preferences dialog box. Setting this option to Read Only specifies that no new frames are written to the cache during rendering (**Figure 17.29**).
>
> **Use OpenGL Renderer**, when selected, utilizes an OpenGL graphics card to render (see "Using Open GL" in Chapter 8, "Playback, Previews, and RAM," for more information) (**Figure 17.30**).

continues on next page

CHOOSING RENDER SETTINGS

Proxy Use specifies whether proxies or source footage are used for output (**Figure 17.31**). (See "Proxies and Placeholders" in Chapter 3, "Managing Footage.")

Effects specifies whether effects appear in the output. (See "Disabling Effects Temporarily" in Chapter 11, "Effects Fundamentals.") Set Effects to All On to enable all effects, including ones you had disabled temporarily; set it to Current Settings to exclude effects you disabled deliberately (**Figure 17.32**).

Solo Switches specifies whether After Effects renders only layers with their Solo switch on (see "Switching Video and Audio On and Off" in Chapter 5) or turns off all Solo switches and renders all the layers in the comp (**Figure 17.33**).

Guide Layers specifies whether After Effects renders guide layers or deactivates all guide layers (**Figure 17.34**).

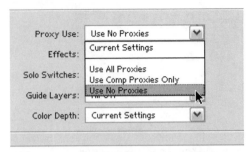

Figure 17.31 Specify whether proxies or source footage are used for output in the Proxy Use pull-down menu.

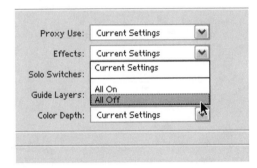

Figure 17.32 In the Effects menu, specify whether effects appear in the output.

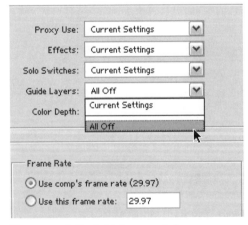

Figure 17.34 In the Guide Layers pull-down menu, specify whether to render guide layers or to turn off guide layers.

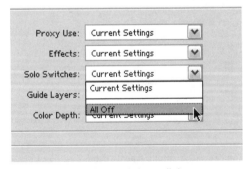

Figure 17.33 In the Solo Switches pull-down menu, specify whether to render layers with the Solo switch activated or to render layers without regard to their Solo switch.

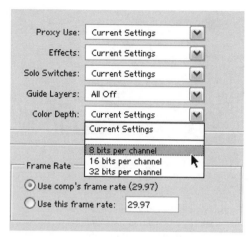

Figure 17.35 In the Color Depth pull-down menu, specify the color depth of the exported file.

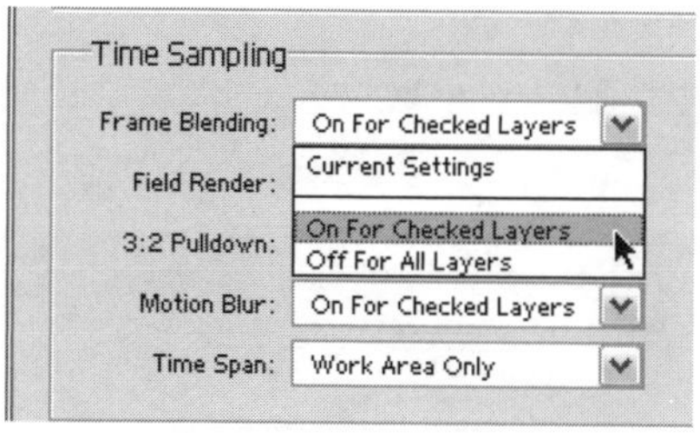

Figure 17.36 In the Frame Blending pull-down menu, specify whether frame blending is applied to layers with the Frame Blending switch enabled.

Color Depth specifies color bit depth, if you're using After Effects Pro, which supports 16bpc and 32bpc processing (see the sidebar "Choosing the Color Bit-Depth Mode" in Chapter 2, "Importing Footage into a Project," for more information) (**Figure 17.35**).

Frame Blending specifies whether frame blending is applied to layers with the Frame Blending switch enabled (regardless of a composition's Frame Blending setting) (**Figure 17.36**). (See "Using Frame Blending" in Chapter 14, "More Layer Techniques.")

Field Render specifies whether to field-render the output movie and, if so, which field is dominant. (See the sidebar "Working the Fields: Interlaced Video" in Chapter 2.") Set this option to Off unless the output is destined for video (**Figure 17.37**).

3:2 Pulldown specifies whether to reintroduce pulldown to the footage and determines the phase of the pulldown. (See the sidebar "The Lowdown on Pulldown" in Chapter 2.) You need to set the proper phase only if the movie will be cut back into the original footage (**Figure 17.38**).

continues on next page

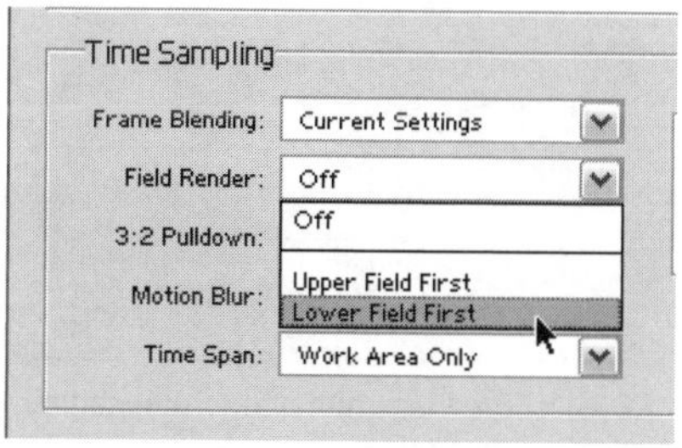

Figure 17.37 In the Field Render pull-down menu, choose whether to field-render the output.

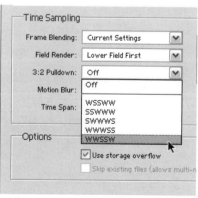

Figure 17.38 To reintroduce pulldown to the footage, choose an option from the 3:2 Pulldown menu.

CHOOSING RENDER SETTINGS

Motion Blur specifies whether motion blur is applied to layers with the Motion Blur switch enabled, regardless of a composition's Motion Blur setting. Or, you can set this option to respect the composition's current Motion Blur setting. When you enable motion blur, it uses the settings you specified in the Composition settings (see "Using Motion Blur," in Chapter 14). Alternatively, you can select "Override shutter angle" and enter the shutter angle to be used instead. A setting of 360 degrees results in the maximum motion blur (**Figure 17.39**).

Time Span defines the part of the composition for output (**Figure 17.40**). Choosing Custom from the Time Span pull-down menu or clicking the Set button opens a Custom Time Span dialog box. (See "Setting the Work Area" in Chapter 8, "Playback, Previews, and RAM.")

Frame Rate sets the frame rate used to render the composition. You may select the composition's frame rate or enter a custom frame rate. (See "Frame Rate," in Chapter 4.) As you'll recall from Chapter 4, the Frame Rate setting doesn't affect playback speed, just smoothness (**Figure 17.41**).

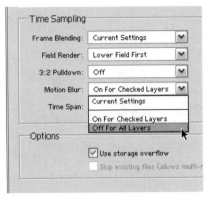

Figure 17.39 In the Motion Blur pull-down menu, specify whether motion blur is applied to layers with the Motion Blur switch enabled.

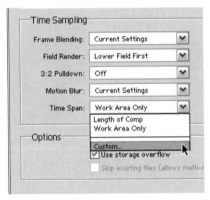

Figure 17.40 Define the part of the composition for output in the Time Span pull-down menu. Choosing Custom lets you specify a custom time span in a dialog box.

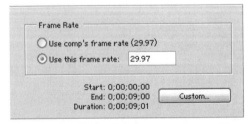

Figure 17.41 Select the frame rate of the composition, or enter a custom frame rate.

Figure 17.42 Select "Use storage overflow" to ensure that rendering continues to an overflow volume when the output file exceeds the capacity of the first storage volume.

Figure 17.43 Select "Skip existing files" to enable After Effects to render or rerender frames of an existing frame sequence.

Use storage overflow determines whether rendering continues to an overflow volume when the output file exceeds the capacity of the first storage volume (**Figure 17.42**). (See "Setting Overflow Volumes," later in this chapter.)

Skip existing files enables After Effects to render or rerender frames of an existing frame sequence. This option also allows multiple computers to render parts of the same image sequence to a Watch folder (**Figure 17.43**). (Consult your After Effects documentation for more about network rendering features.)

3. Click OK to close the Render Settings dialog box and return to the Render Queue panel.

Choosing Output-Module Settings

Choosing output-module settings is the second step in the movie-making process. These settings determine how processed frames are saved.

To choose an output module manually:

1. In the render queue, click the underlined name of the output module (**Figure 17.44**). An Output Module Settings dialog box appears (**Figure 17.45**).

2. Make a selection *for each of the following options:*

   Format determines the output's file format and includes a variety of movie and still-image-sequence formats (**Figure 17.46**). Although your particular project and/or equipment will dictate your choice, QuickTime Movie and Video For Windows are common choices for motion files, and TIFF Sequence and PICT Sequence are common choices for still-image formats.

   Embed determines whether After Effects embeds a project link into the output movie. When opening the output file in a program that supports project links—such as Adobe Premiere Pro—you can use the Edit Original command to reopen the source project and make any necessary changes to it. Select Project Link from the pull-down menu to create a link between the output file and the source project. Select Project Link and Copy to embed both a link to the original project and a copy of the project into the output file. If the original project isn't available when you use the Edit Original command, After Effects will allow you to open the embedded copy of the project (**Figure 17.47**).

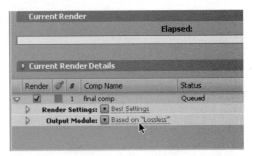

Figure 17.44 In the render queue, click the underlined name of the output module.

Figure 17.45 An Output Module Settings dialog box appears.

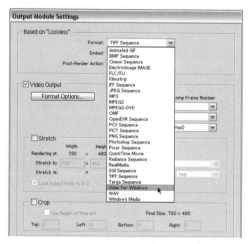

Figure 17.46 Choose the format of the saved file in the Format pull-down menu.

Figure 17.47 Embed determines whether After Effects embeds a project link into the output movie.

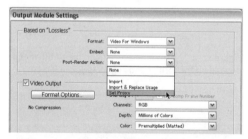

Figure 17.48 In the Post-Render Action pull-down menu, choose whether you want to use the rendered movie in the project. You can import the rendered movie, use it in place of its source footage, or set it as a proxy for its source footage.

Post-Render Action specifies whether After Effects utilizes the rendered movie in the project. You can instruct After Effects to import the movie, replace the source composition (including its nested instances) with the movie, or use the movie as a proxy in place of its source (**Figure 17.48**). This way, you can replace complex, processing-intensive elements with a single, easy-to-render footage item—thereby reducing render times. Using a post-render action is part of a strategy called *prerendering*; see "Prerendering" in Chapter 16, "Complex Projects."

Format Options opens a dialog box that includes options associated with particular formats (**Figure 17.49**). For example, if you choose QuickTime Movie as the format, the Format Options button opens a Compression Settings dialog box for QuickTime movies. (See "Movie Files and Compression," later in this chapter.)

continues on next page

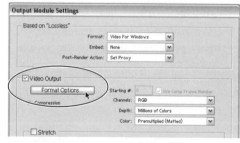

Figure 17.49 Click Format Options to open a dialog box containing format-specific settings.

CHOOSING OUTPUT-MODULE SETTINGS

Starting # lets you specify the starting frame number in the filenames when you're exporting an image sequence. Alternatively, you can select Use Comp Frame Number to match exported frame numbers to the frame numbering in the comp (the option is checked by default) (**Figure 17.50**).

Channels specifies the channels present in the output (**Figure 17.51**). Depending on the format, you can choose to export the RGB channels, the alpha channel, or RGB + Alpha. (See the sidebar "Alpha Bits" in Chapter 2, "Importing Footage into a Project.")

Depth specifies the color depth of the output. The available options depend on the format and channels you selected (**Figure 17.52**).

Color specifies how color channels factor in the alpha channel (if one is present), determining whether the output uses a straight alpha or is premultiplied with black (**Figure 17.53**). (See the sidebar "Alpha Bits" in Chapter 2.)

Stretch lets you specify the frame size of your output. By selecting this option, you can choose common frame sizes from a pull-down menu or enter custom dimensions.

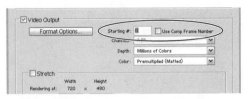

Figure 17.50 When you're exporting a still image sequence, specify the starting number, or select Use Comp Frame Number.

Figure 17.51 Specify the channels present in the output in the Channels pull-down menu.

Figure 17.52 The options available in the Depth menu depend on the format and channels you selected.

Figure 17.53 If you chose to output an alpha channel, use the Color pull-down menu to choose between straight alpha or premultiplied with black.

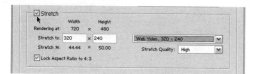

Figure 17.54 Select Stretch options to resize the image after it's been rendered. Several common options are available in a Preset pull-down menu.

Figure 17.55 Select Crop options to add pixels to or remove pixels from the edges of the frame.

Figure 17.56 Specify the sample rate, the bit depth, and whether the audio track is stereo or mono.

You may also choose between a low- and high-quality resizing method in the Stretch Quality pull-down menu. Stretch resizes the image after it's been rendered (**Figure 17.54**).

Crop lets you add pixels to or, more likely, remove pixels from the edges of the image frame (**Figure 17.55**). Cropping is useful for removing black edges from video footage.

Audio Output specifies the audio-track attributes (if any) of your output. Settings include sample rate, bit depth, and format (mono or stereo). (For more about audio, see the sidebars in Chapter 8.) Note that the Format Options button remains grayed out and doesn't permit you to apply audio compression (**Figure 17.56**). To compress the audio, you can use an option available under the Export command, or you can compress the final movie using a program such as QuickTime Pro or Media Cleaner Pro.

3. Click OK to close the Output Module dialog box and return to the Render Queue panel.

Creating Templates

You should save your most commonly used settings as templates so that you can apply them by selecting templates in the Render Settings and Output Module pull-down menus in the Render Queue panel. You can also make your most useful render settings and output-module templates your default settings. You can even save templates as stand-alone files that you can then move to other systems or share with other users.

To create a template:

1. *Do one of the following*:

   ▲ To create a render settings template, choose Make Template in the Render Settings pull-down menu (**Figure 17.57**).

   ▲ To create an output-module template, choose Make Template in the Output Module pull-down menu.

   Depending on your choice, a Render Settings Templates or Output Module Templates dialog box appears. An untitled template appears in the Settings Name field.

2. Click Edit in the Render Settings Templates or Output Module Templates dialog box (**Figure 17.58**).

   Depending on the type of template you're creating, the Render Settings dialog box or the Output Module dialog box appears (**Figure 17.59**).

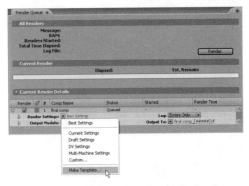

Figure 17.57 Choose Make Template in the Render Settings pull-down menu.

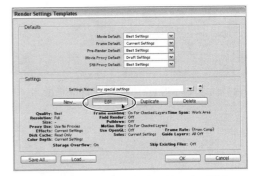

Figure 17.58 In the Render Settings Template dialog box, click Edit to specify settings for the untitled template.

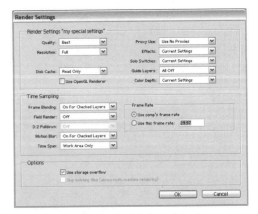

Figure 17.59 In the Render Settings dialog box, choose the options you want to save as a template, and click OK to return to the Render Settings Templates dialog box.

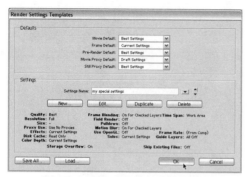

Figure 17.60 In the Render Settings Templates dialog box, enter a name for the new template, and click OK to close the dialog box.

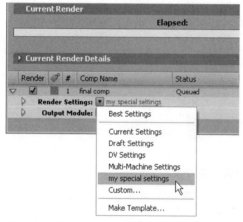

Figure 17.61 From now on, the template will appear in the Render Settings Templates pull-down menu in the Render Queue panel.

3. Choose the render-settings or output-module options you want to save as a template.

4. When you've finished selecting settings, click OK to close the Render Settings or Output Module dialog box and return to the Render Settings Templates or Output Module Templates dialog box.

5. In the Render Settings Templates or Output Module Templates dialog box, enter a settings name for the new template (**Figure 17.60**).

6. Click OK to close the dialog box and save the template.

From now on, the template will appear in the appropriate pull-down menu in the Render Queue panel (**Figure 17.61**).

CREATING TEMPLATES

To set a default template:

1. *Do one of the following*:

   ▲ To set the default render settings template, choose Make Template in the Render Settings pull-down menu.

   ▲ To set the default output module template, choose Make Template in the Output Module pull-down menu (**Figure 17.62**).

   Depending on your choice, the Output Module Templates dialog box or the Render Settings Templates dialog box appears (**Figure 17.63**).

2. To set the default template for output movies, choose a template from the Movie Default pull-down menu (**Figure 17.64**).

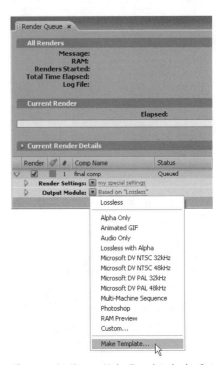

Figure 17.62 Choose Make Template in the Output Module pull-down menu.

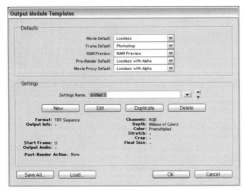

Figure 17.63 The Output Module Templates dialog box appears.

Figure 17.64 To set the default template for output movies, choose a template from the Movie Default pull-down menu.

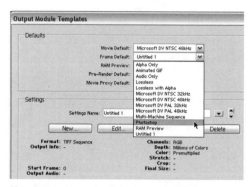

Figure 17.65 To set the default template for output still frames, choose a template from the Frame Default pull-down menu. Repeat the process for RAM previews, Pre-Render, and Movie Proxy.

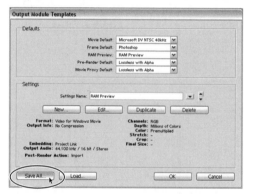

Figure 17.66 In the Render Settings Templates or Output Module Templates dialog box, click Save All.

Figure 17.67 In the Save As dialog box, specify a name and destination for the saved template file.

3. To set the default template for output still frames, choose a template from the Frame Default pull-down menu (**Figure 17.65**).

4. To set the default template for RAM Previews, as well as the default template for Pre-Renders and Movie Proxies, choose options from the appropriate pull-down menus.

Pre-Render and Movie Proxy defaults affect movies created using Post-Render actions, explained in "Choosing Output-Module Settings," earlier in this chapter.

5. Click OK to close the dialog box.

The selected templates become the default templates for the corresponding output types.

To save templates as files:

1. In the Render Settings Templates or Output Module Templates dialog box, click Save All (**Figure 17.66**).

A Save As dialog box appears.

2. Specify a name and destination for the saved template file.

The render settings template files use the `.ars` file extension. Output module template files use the `.aom` file extension (**Figure 17.67**).

3. Click Save to close the dialog box and save the file.

To load saved templates:

1. In the Render Settings Templates or Output Module Templates dialog box, click Load.

   An Open dialog box appears.

2. Locate a render-settings or output-module template file.

   The render-settings files use the `.ars` file extension; output-module template files use the `.aom` file extension.

3. Click OK to close the dialog box and load the settings.

   Depending on the type of file you loaded, the render-settings or output-module templates appear in their respective pull-down menus.

Figure 17.68 Set the current time of the composition to the frame you want to export.

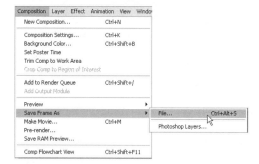

Figure 17.69 Choose Composition > Save Frame As > File.

Saving Single Frames of a Composition

Frequently, you'll want to render a single frame of a composition. For example, when an animation halts its motion, substituting a single still image for multiple static layers can lighten the rendering load. Or you may need a still for a storyboard or client review. After Effects lets you save a single frame using the default frame settings or as a layered Photoshop file.

To save a composition frame as a still-image file:

1. Set the current time of the composition to the frame you want to export (**Figure 17.68**).

2. Choose Composition > Save Frame As > File (**Figure 17.69**).

   The composition appears selected in the Render Queue panel (**Figure 17.70**).

3. To change the destination of the saved image, click the name of the file next to Output To.

   An Output Frame To dialog box opens.

continues on next page

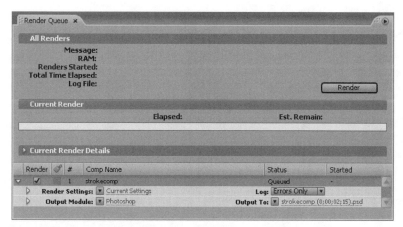

Figure 17.70 The item appears selected in the Render Queue panel.

4. Specify the destination and name of the saved frame (**Figure 17.71**).

5. Click Save to close the Output Frame To dialog box.

6. To change the default settings for frames, select render settings and output module settings, or choose templates.

The previous sections explain how to select settings and save templates.

7. In the Render Queue panel, click Render.

✔ Tips

■ If you want to use the still frame in the project, be sure to specify a post-render action in the output module settings. See "Choosing Output-Module Settings," earlier in this chapter, and "Prerendering" in Chapter 16.

■ You can export the current frame as a layered Photoshop file in a similar manner by choosing Composition > Save Frame As > Photoshop Layers.

Figure 17.71 To change the destination of the saved file, click its name next to Output To; in the Output Frame To dialog box, specify the destination and name of the saved frame.

Exporting to SWF Format

Using After Effects' Export command, you can output your composition to a number of audio and video formats. This section, however, focuses on Macromedia's SWF format—a format that will be of particular interest to users creating animations for the Web.

For the uninitiated, SWF (often pronounced *swif*) stands for Shockwave Flash, the popular Flash Player format. Designed to deliver dynamic content over the Web's limited bandwidths, Flash animations include predominately vector-based graphics. Although they can include bitmapped images, such graphics significantly increase file size, thus limiting delivery speed.

The following tasks take you through the basic exporting process and provide a brief discussion of several export options for SWF files. However, some options require an understanding of the SWF format, HTML, or Web authoring—subjects that can't be addressed fully here.

For example, knowledge of HTML will help you determine whether you want to use the Include Object Names option to make names of objects in the composition appear in the exported file's source code. You'll also need to determine whether to include elements such as bitmapped images and motion blur, which can't be translated directly into SWF's native vector-based format. And only your familiarity with Internet bandwidth restrictions will help you design a composition appropriate for Web delivery. Consult your After Effects documentation to learn more about which features are supported for SWF export and other format-specific options.

To export a composition to the SWF format:

1. Select the composition you want to export.

2. Choose File > Export > Macromedia Flash (SWF) (**Figure 17.72**).

   A Save File As dialog box appears.

3. Specify the name and destination of the exported file, and click OK (Mac) or Save (Windows) (**Figure 17.73**).

   A SWF Settings dialog box appears (**Figure 17.74**).

4. Specify JPEG image quality by *doing any of the following*:

   ▲ Choose a quality setting from the JPEG Quality pull-down menu.

   ▲ Enter a number from 0 to 10 in the JPEG Quality field, where 0 is the lowest possible quality.

   ▲ Drag the JPEG Quality slider.

Figure 17.72 Choose File > Export > Macromedia Flash (SWF).

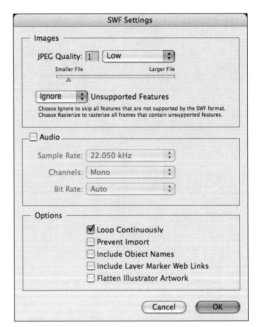

Figure 17.74 In the SWF Settings dialog box, specify JPEG Quality.

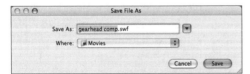

Figure 17.73 In the Save File As dialog box, specify the name and destination of the exported file, and click OK (Mac) or Save (Windows).

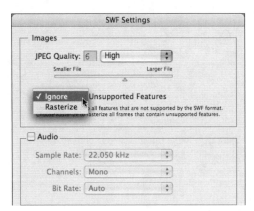

Figure 17.75 In the Unsupported Features pull-down menu, choose an option.

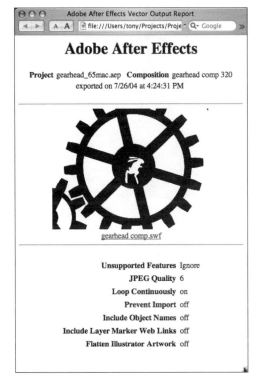

Figure 17.76 You can open the report file in a Web browser to preview the SWF file.

5. In the Unsupported Features pull-down menu, *choose either of the following options* (**Figure 17.75**):

Ignore skips all features that aren't supported by the SWF format.

Rasterize rasterizes all frames that contain unsupported features.

6. To export audio, click Audio, and *specify the following options:*

Sample Rate—Use this pull-down menu to choose from various sample rates. Higher sample rates produce better-quality sound but larger files.

Channels—Use this pull-down menu to choose between exporting stereophonic and monophonic audio.

Bit Rate—Use this pull-down menu to choose from various audio bit depths. Higher bit depths produce better-quality sound but larger files.

See Chapter 8 for an explanation of audio sample rate, channels, and bit rates.

7. In the Options section of the SWF Settings dialog box, select the options you want.

Specific options are explained in the following task.

8. Click OK to close the SWF dialog box and export the composition as a SWF file.

A SWF file and a report file appear in the location you specified. The report file uses the naming convention `filenameR.htm`. You can open the report file in a Web browser to preview the SWF file and to view a report of the elements not supported by the SWF format (**Figure 17.76**).

To specify SWF options:

◆ In the SWF Settings dialog box, *select any of the following options* (**Figure 17.77**):

Loop Continuously makes the SWF file loop continuously during playback.

Prevent Import prevents the SWF file from being imported into editing programs.

Include Object Names gives the SWF file's layers, masks, and effects the same names they have in After Effects. See your After Effects documentation for more about including object names in a SWF file.

Include Layer Marker Web Links allows the Web links you specified in layer markers to be included in the SWF file. See your After Effects documentation for more about using Web links in layer markers and in SWF files.

Flatten Illustrator Artwork flattens multilayer Illustrator artwork when exporting it to a SWF file.

Figure 17.77 In the Options section of the SWF Settings dialog box, check the options you want.

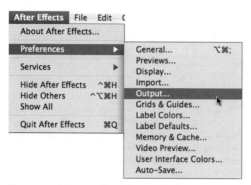

Figure 17.78 Choose After Effects > Preferences > Output (Mac) or Edit > Preferences > Output (Windows).

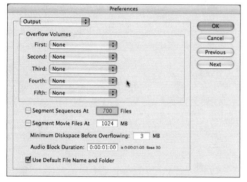

Figure 17.79 The Output panel of the Preferences dialog box opens.

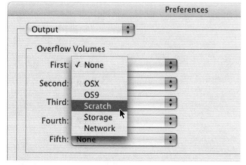

Figure 17.80 To specify overflow volumes, choose a storage volume from the Volume pull-down menus.

Setting Overflow Volumes

As you're already well aware, movie files can consume enormous amounts of storage space. It's not unusual for a file or sequence to exceed either the file size limit imposed by the computer's operating system or the size of the storage volume. Fortunately, you can control overflow and thus avert errors and failed renders. When the rendered file or sequence reaches the limits you specify, it continues to render into a folder on the root level of an overflow volume.

To specify overflow volumes:

1. Choose After Effects > Preferences > Output (Mac) or Edit > Preferences > Output (Windows) (**Figure 17.78**).

   The Output panel of the Preferences dialog box opens (**Figure 17.79**).

2. To specify overflow volumes, choose a storage volume from the Volume pull-down menus in the Overflow Volumes section of the Preferences dialog box (**Figure 17.80**).

   A rendered file or sequence overflows into the first volume, then the second, and so on.

continues on next page

3. To set the maximum number of files that can be rendered to a single folder, click Segment Sequences At, and enter a maximum number (**Figure 17.81**).

4. To set the maximum size of a single rendered file, check Segment Movie Files At, and enter a maximum file size (in MB).

   Your operating system may have its own file size limit.

5. For Minimum Diskspace Before Overflowing, enter the minimum amount of storage space that must remain on the drive before rendering resumes on the next overflow volume.

6. Click OK to close the dialog box.

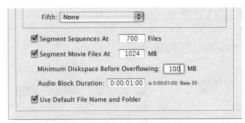

Figure 17.81 Specify the maximum number of files in Segment Sequences At; the maximum size of a file in Segment Movie Files At; and the Minimum Diskspace Before Overflowing.

Compression in a Nutshell

Compression refers to techniques used to store large amounts of data in smaller packages. Without compression, digital video files are too large for most drives and processors to play back smoothly. In other words, an uncompressed file's *data rate*—the amount of data that must be processed in a given amount of time—is too high for most systems to deliver. To reduce the file size and data rates of digital video and audio, developers have devised various compression schemes, or *codecs*.

Compression schemes that reduce file size without discarding data are known as *lossless*. Storing data using lossless compression can be compared to writing a message in shorthand. When it's time to read the message, the data is decoded back into "longhand." Lossless compression reduces file size most when the image contains a lot of redundancy, such as large areas of a single color. Even then, the file sizes are relatively large because no data has been thrown out.

Lossy compression schemes discard data to reduce file size. Although such compression schemes are designed to discard data you're least likely to miss, the loss of quality is almost always noticeable. Usually, you can set the amount of compression to control the reduction in file size and quality.

Movie Files and Compression

When you select QuickTime Movie or Video for Windows as the format, clicking the Format Options button opens a dialog box for choosing compression settings. To choose the settings most appropriate for your output goals, you need to know something about video compression in general as well as particular compression schemes, or *codecs*.

Generally speaking, your playback equipment, image-quality goals, and data-rate limitations will dictate your compression choices. For example, if your movie file is destined for use with a non-linear editing system, such as Premiere Pro or Avid, you'll render it using the codec that matches your source footage or another codec compatible with the editing system. On the other hand, if you want to maintain the highest image quality, you can output an uncompressed file for delivery to a postproduction facility that can transfer it to tape or film (assuming your own hardware isn't able to play back such a large file in real time). Alternatively, you may need to present your movie on the Web—in which case choosing settings that produce a small file with a low data rate will be your top priority.

The following sections offer essential background information and guidance for choosing video compression settings in After Effects.

To set QuickTime compression settings:

1. In the Render Queue panel, click the underlined name of the output module (**Figure 17.82**).

   The Output Module Settings dialog box opens.

2. In the Format pull-down menu, choose QuickTime Movie (**Figure 17.83**).

3. Click Format Options (**Figure 17.84**).

   A Compression Settings dialog box appears (**Figure 17.85**).

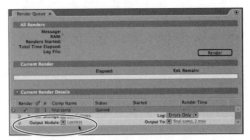

Figure 17.82 In the Render Queue panel, click the underlined name of the output module.

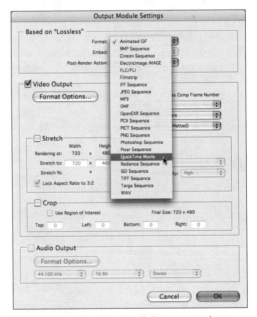

Figure 17.83 In the Format pull-down menu, choose QuickTime Movie.

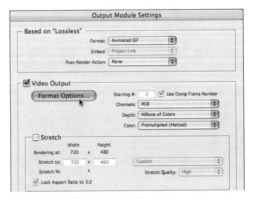

Figure 17.84 Click Format Options.

MOVIE FILES AND COMPRESSION

Data Rates

A clip's file size relates directly to its *data rate*—the amount of information the computer must process in a given amount of time to play back the clip smoothly. Most of the video and audio settings you choose influence the data rate of movies. In addition, many video codecs let you specify the maximum data rate for a movie file. You set a data rate according to the limitations of the target playback device and the specifications of the codec. In the Compression Settings dialog box, data rates are expressed in kilobytes/sec. Be aware that other programs may express data rates as kilobytes/frame or kilobits/sec.

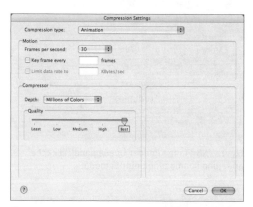

Figure 17.85 A Compression Settings dialog box appears.

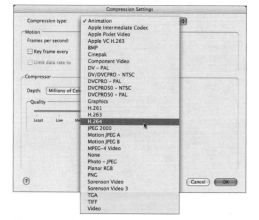

Figure 17.86 Choose a codec from the pull-down menu.

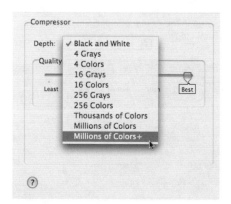

Figure 17.87 Choose a bit depth from the Depth pull-down menu.

4. Choose a codec from the "Compression type" pull-down menu (**Figure 17.86**).

   The codec you specify determines the options available in the Compression Settings dialog box. Choosing certain codecs may open a separate dialog box of codec-specific settings.

5. *If the option is available, do any of the following:*

   ▲ Choose a bit depth from the Depth pull-down menu (**Figure 17.87**).

   ▲ Adjust the Quality slider to set the amount of compression (**Figure 17.88**).

   ▲ Ignore the "Frames per second" option. (The frame rate you set in the Output Module settings overrides this setting.)

   ▲ Specify whether to use keyframes, and, if so, set their frequency.

   ▲ Specify whether to limit the maximum data rate, and, if so, enter the data rate in kilobytes/sec.

   The available options depend on the selected codec.

6. Click OK to close the dialog box.

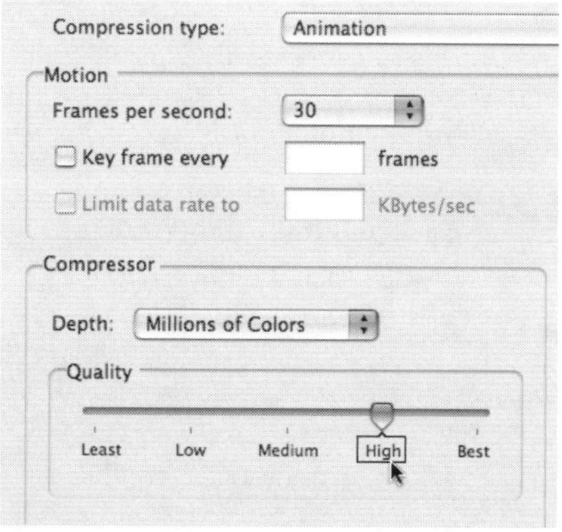

MOVIE FILES AND COMPRESSION

Figure 17.88 Adjust the Quality slider to set the amount of compression. If you want, specify the frequency of keyframes and limit the data rate.

To set Video for Windows compression settings:

1. In the Render Queue panel, click the underlined name of the output module (**Figure 17.89**).

   The Output Module Settings dialog box opens.

2. In the Format pull-down menu, choose Video For Windows (**Figure 17.90**).

3. Click the Format Options button (**Figure 17.91**).

   A Video Compression dialog box appears (**Figure 17.92**).

Figure 17.89 In the Render Queue panel, click the underlined name of the output module.

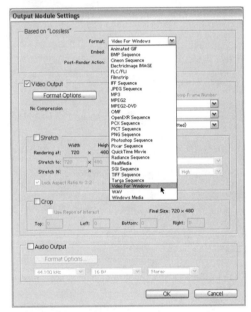

Figure 17.90 In the Format pull-down menu, choose Video For Windows.

Figure 17.91 In the Render Queue panel, click the Format Options button.

Figure 17.92 A Video Compression dialog box appears.

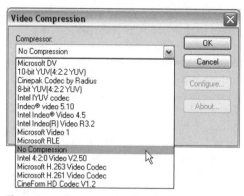

Figure 17.93 Choose a codec from the Compressor pull-down menu.

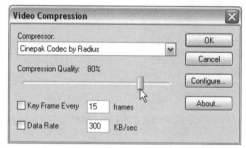

Figure 17.94 Adjust the Quality slider to set the amount of compression.

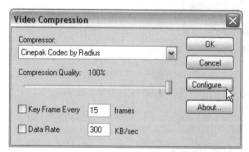

Figure 17.95 To access codec-specific options, click Configure.

4. In the Compression Settings dialog box, *do the following:*

▲ Choose a codec from the Compressor pull-down menu (**Figure 17.93**).

▲ Adjust the Quality slider to set the amount of compression (**Figure 17.94**).

▲ Specify whether to use keyframes, and, if so, set their frequency.

▲ Specify whether to limit the maximum data rate, and, if so, enter the data rate in kilobytes/sec.

5. To access codec-specific options, click Configure (**Figure 17.95**).

A codec-specific dialog box appears, in which you can select settings particular to the codec (**Figure 17.96**).

6. Click OK to close the Video Compression dialog box.

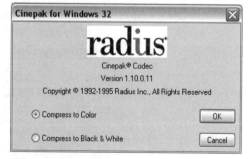

Figure 17.96 When the Cinepak codec is selected, clicking the Configure button opens settings specific to Cinepak. Specifically, you can specify whether to compress to color or black and white.

MOVIE FILES AND COMPRESSION

Using the Adobe Media Encoder

In addition to the Video for Windows format, After Effects for Windows includes several format options not found in After Effects for Macintosh: MPEG2, MPEG2-DVD, RealMedia, and Windows Media. Each of these formats includes numerous settings that merit a specialized export dialog box, generally referred to as the *Adobe Media Encoder*.

Strictly speaking, *Adobe Media Encoder* refers to the output mechanism, not the name of the dialog box. In After Effects, the dialog box bears the name of the specified format and contains options particular to that format. Premiere Pro and Encore DVD also employ the Adobe Media Encoder, although the corresponding dialog boxes differ in appearance and in the way you access them. But in spite of the differences, you can still think of these export settings dialog boxes as incarnations of the Adobe Media Encoder and as consistent in most ways.

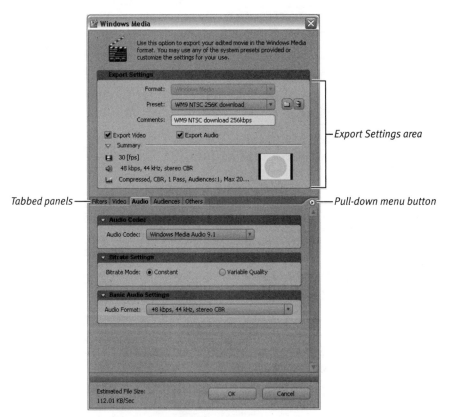

Figure 17.97 Choosing MPEG2, MPEG2-DVD, RealMedia, or Windows Media as the export format invokes a specialized export dialog box automatically. This figure shows the dialog box for Windows Media.

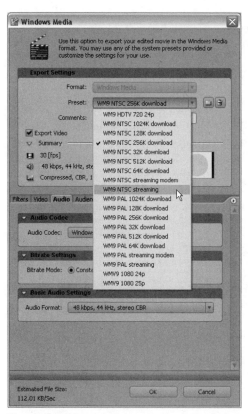

Figure 17.98 A Preset pull-down menu automatically optimizes extensive settings for a particular goal.

In After Effects for Windows, choosing MPEG2, MPEG2-DVD, RealMedia, or Windows Media invokes the appropriate variation of the Adobe Media Encoder automatically. General settings appear in the upper part of the dialog box; the lower part of the dialog box consists of tabbed panels that organize settings by category (**Figure 17.97**).

Settings for these formats are extensive and can require an in-depth understanding of file compression. Fortunately, you can select from a list of presets designed for particular delivery media (**Figure 17.98**). (You can also save custom presets or delete ones you don't need.) For a detailed explanation of each setting, consult the After Effects User Guide/ Help and the documentation provided by the format's developer.

USING THE ADOBE MEDIA ENCODER

Keyframes

Many codecs—especially those designed for low data rates—use *keyframes* to optimize compression while maintaining the highest possible image quality. Keyframes are essential to the compression technique called *frame differencing*.

In *frame differencing*, keyframes act as reference frames against which subsequent frames are compared. Rather than describe each frame completely, frame differencing achieves more efficient compression by describing only the changes between keyframes.

Keyframes are most effective when the image differs greatly from the preceding frame. Some codecs let you set the frequency of keyframes, or they may insert keyframes automatically when the image changes significantly. A greater number of keyframes tends to make for better image quality but bigger files. Fewer keyframes usually results in smaller files but lower image quality.

Codecs

Codec stands for *compression/decompression*. *Compression* refers to encoding a file and is synonymous with capture and rendering. *Decompression* refers to decoding a file and is associated with playback. *Codec* denotes a particular *compression scheme*—a method of compressing and decompressing a file.

There are software- and hardware-based codecs. QuickTime and Video for Windows include several software-based codecs; others are available as software plug-ins.

For most high-quality video capture and playback, however, you need a hardware-assisted codec. If your hardware capture card and its software are installed properly, the codec designed for the card appears in the Compressor menu in the Compression Settings dialog box.

Most capture cards also offer a software-only version of the codec. Although the software codec usually can't enable you to play back the clip smoothly, it does let you open and process the file on computers that don't have the necessary hardware.

Within each codec, you can generally control how much compression is applied by using a Quality slider, or you can define an upper limit for the data rate (see the sidebar "Data Rates," earlier in this chapter).

INDEX

Numbers

3:2 pulldown, 69, 70, 71, 127, 653
3D Channel effects, 374
3D layers, 208, 553–599
  auto-orienting, 570–571, 589
  axis modes, 564–565
  cameras, 574–583, 593
  combining with 2D layers, 598–599
  converting to 2D layers, 554
  designating, 554
  Draft mode, 597
  focusing on selected, 559–560
  lights, 584–588
  Material Options, 572–573
  orienting, 567–568
  Point of Interest, 589–592
  positioning, 566
  previewing, 597
  rendering, 135, 598–599, 607
  rotating, 567, 569
  stacking order of, 598–599
  viewing, 555–563, 593
3D rendering plug-in, 135
3D views, 555–563
  adjusting, 558–560
  Camera tools and, 593
  categories of, 555
  Comp panel and, 555–557, 561–563
  focusing on layers, 559–560
  resetting, 560
  shortcuts for, 557
  specifying, 556
  toggling among, 557

8 bpc images, 35
16 bpc images, 35
16mm film standard, 32
24Pa pulldown, 69, 70, 72–73
32-bit images, 46
35mm film standard, 32
60-fps animation sequences, 67

A

acceleration
  hardware, 4
  speed and, 305–306
action-safe zones, 107
adaptive resolution, 247, 257, 258–259
Add Vertex tool, 318, 342, 350
Adjust Tension icon, 355
adjustment layers, 151–152
  applying effects to, 151, 399
  converting layers to, 400
  creating, 152
  render order and, 609
Adobe Bridge, 5, 59–61
Adobe Illustrator. *See* Illustrator
Adobe Media Encoder, 5, 678–679
Adobe Photoshop. *See* Photoshop
Adobe Premiere Pro. *See* Premiere Pro
Adobe Video Bundle, 2
Advanced 3D rendering plug-in, 135
advanced pulldown, 73
After Effects, 7
  general description, 1
  integration with other Adobe programs, 2, 5
  interface overview, 9–14

O

P

INDEX